LINTHEAD STOMP

Hunter H. George
12534 Honeywood Trail
Houston, Texas 77077

LINTHEAD

THE CREATION
OF COUNTRY MUSIC
IN THE PIEDMONT
SOUTH

PATRICK HUBER

STOMP

THE UNIVERSITY OF NORTH CAROLINA PRESS Chapel Hill

This book was published with the assistance of the Fred W. Morrison Fund for Southern Studies of the University of North Carolina Press.

Manufactured in the United States of America
Designed by Richard Hendel
Set in Arnhem, Quadraat and Smokler types
by Tseng Information Systems, Inc.

Title page illustration courtesy of the Southern Folklife Collection, Wilson Library, University of North Carolina at Chapel Hill.

Lyrics from the following songs are quoted in the text by special permission from the publishers: "Cotton Mill Colic," words and music by David McCarn, copyright © 1930 Southern Music Publishing Co., Inc., copyright renewed 1957 by David McCarn, transferred to Coal Creek Music, all rights administered by Tradition Music Co./Bug Music, all rights reserved, used by permission; "Wreck on the Highway," words and music by Dorsey M. Dixon, copyright © 1946 Sony/ATV Music Publishing LLC, all rights administered by Sony/ATV Music Publishing LLC, 8 Music Square West, Nashville, TN 37203, all rights reserved, used by permission.

The paper in this book meets the guidelines for permanence and durability of the Committee on Production Guidelines for Book Longevity of the Council on Library Resources.

The University of North Carolina Press has been a member of the Green Press Initiative since 2003.

Library of Congress Cataloging-in-Publication Data
Huber, Patrick.
Linthead stomp : the creation of country music in the Piedmont South / Patrick Huber.
p. cm.
Includes bibliographical references, discography, and index.
ISBN 978-0-8078-3225-7 (cloth : alk. paper)
1. Country music—Piedmont (U.S. : Region)—History and criticism. 2. Country music—Southern States—History and criticism. 3. Country musicians—Piedmont (U.S. : Region) 4. Textile workers—Piedmont (U.S. : Region) I. Title.
ML3524.H82 2008
781.6420975—dc22   2008013451

A Caravan book. For more information, visit www.caravanbooks.org.

12 11 10 09 08   5 4 3 2 1

University of North Carolina Press books may be purchased at a discount for educational, business, or sales promotional use. For information, please visit www.uncpress.unc.edu or write to UNC Press, attention: Sales Department, 116 South Boundary Street, Chapel Hill, NC 27514-3808.

For Katie, Genevieve, and William,
whose love and many sacrifices made
this book possible

Lint-head. U.S. dial., a worker in a cotton mill;
(in contemptuous use) a person of whom one
disapproves.

Stomp, n. Chiefly *Jazz*. A lively dance, usu. involving
heavy stamping; also, a tune or song suitable for such
a dance; stomping rhythm.

—*Oxford English Dictionary*, 2nd ed. (1989)

CONTENTS

ILLUSTRATIONS

PREFACE

The textile mills not only produced an important body of folksongs;
they also spawned a high percentage of commercial country singers
(a phenomenon that needs to be explored).
—Bill C. Malone, *Country Music, U.S.A.*, rev. ed. (1985)

"Many of the present generation, having moved to mill towns
and coal camps, are being cut off from their inheritance of traditional
music. But they are beginning to make 'ballets' of their own," wrote
Bruce Crawford in the *New Republic* in 1933, after visiting the celebrated White Top Folk Festival in the mountains of southwestern Virginia. "Textile workers have songs to express sorrow and revolt. Coal
miners are beginning to sing 'blues' of their making. . . . Most songs
of the industrial sections express abject hopelessness and are howled
in tones more woe-begone than the wails of Negro blues. They have,
in fact, little in common with the older folk-songs sung in the hollows
which coal mines and textile mills haven't yet invaded."[1] Crawford's
observations provide an excellent starting point for understanding
the southern industrial and working-class origins of hillbilly music,
an American popular music that was commercially broadcast and recorded between 1922 and 1942 and that eventually evolved into modern country music and the regional genres of western swing, honky-
tonk, and bluegrass.[2]

Beginning with Archie Green's seminal article, "Hillbilly Music:
Source and Symbol," in the *Journal of American Folklore* (1965), and
running through Tony Russell's *Country Music Originals: The Legends
and the Lost* (2007), academic studies of pre–World War II country
music over the past four decades have reached far beyond the music
itself to tell us much about working-class white southerners and
their culture in twentieth-century America.[3] This impressive body of
scholarship has fundamentally reshaped our understanding of this
music, yet relatively little attention has so far been paid to the tremendous impact that large-scale industrialization and urban growth
had on the development of hillbilly music before World War II. Nor
has the significant role of southern textile workers in the evolution

of this genre of America popular music received its rightful consideration.[4]

Examining the significant role that Piedmont textile workers played in the creation of hillbilly music offers new understandings of this music. Writers have long portrayed hillbilly musicians as tradition-bound rural southerners who came of age in the countryside and mountain hollows, often isolated from or little influenced by the main currents of modern urban life and mass culture.[5] To be sure, Bill C. Malone and others have identified the mass migration of rural and working-class white southerners to midwestern and West Coast cities during World War II as one of the central themes in the nationalization of country music during the 1940s and 1950s. But scholars have paid far less attention to the equally significant forces of industrial development, urban growth, and southern migration in the half century before World War II that just as profoundly shaped this commercial musical tradition.[6] Focusing on the hillbilly music that sprang forth from Piedmont textile mill villages helps us to recognize that early country music is, in fact, as thoroughly modern in its origins and evolution as its quintessentially modern counterpart, jazz.

Examining Piedmont millhands and the hillbilly music they created also illuminates their responses to the emerging modern South. By the mid-1920s, Piedmont millhands, like southern industrial workers in general, were members of a modern industrial working class and eager participants in America's mass culture and consumer society. And although sociologists and historians have tended to characterize them as fairly homogeneous, southern millhands actually constituted a comparatively diverse group, one that was often sharply divided by occupational skill and experience, gender, ethnicity, political views, religious beliefs, personal ethics, and career aspirations.[7] Similarities clearly existed among them, but, as this book demonstrates, differences played a critical role in shaping both their lives and the ways in which they understood their world. Piedmont textile workers, for instance, responded in starkly different ways to modern twentieth-century life. Certain new cultural trends and behaviors associated with the rise of the automobile, to take one example, deeply disturbed devout fundamentalist Christians such as North Carolina singer, songwriter, and guitarist Dorsey Dixon, who wrote "I Didn't Hear Anybody Pray" and then, along with his brother Howard, recorded it for RCA-Victor at a January 25, 1938, session in Charlotte. His song, better known as "Wreck on the Highway," is a grisly account of a drunk-driving accident that occurred near his hometown of East Rockingham. In the song, Dixon laments what he saw as modern society's abandonment of Protestant Christianity and its bedrock religious tenets. "Whiskey and glass all together / Was mixing with blood where they lay," Dixon sings on one of the verses. "Death played her hand in destruction, / But I didn't hear nobody pray."[8]

Other millhands, in contrast, celebrated the liberating pleasures and freedoms of modern life. For instance, the Three Tobacco Tags, a Gastonia, North Carolina, stringband that regularly performed on the same *Crazy Barn Dance* radio program as the Dixon Brothers, offered a far different reaction to automobiles in "How Can I Keep My Mind on Driving?" The Three Tobacco Tags recorded their song on the very same day, at the very same RCA-Victor recording session in Charlotte, at which the Dixon Brothers cut "I Didn't Hear Anybody Pray." On their record, the Three Tobacco Tags present a light-hearted, risqué treatment of the changing sexual mores introduced with the mass marketing of automobiles:

How can I keep shifting my gears,
When my gal keeps pecking my ears?
How can I keep throwing my clutch
When my gal keeps clutching so much?
I keep yelling, I keep telling,
T'ain't no time to neck;
She don't listen, just keeps kissing,
That's why I'm a wreck.
How can I keep my mind on driving
When my gal is driving me mad?[9]

Despite their obvious differences, both of these songs, one a stern jeremiad and the other a comical novelty number, are cautionary tales about the dangers of driving, and each of them reveals the widespread recognition that automobiles (and modern life in general) had ushered in some significant changes in Carolina Piedmont textile towns. These changes may be enjoyable and entertaining—such as juggling the pleasures of cruising in a car and fooling around with a woman at the same time—or, as in the Dixon Brothers' song, they may be deeply troubling—such as the perceived loss of fundamental

Christian values. Listening to the Dixon Brothers' "I Didn't Hear Anybody Pray" alongside the Three Tobacco Tags' "How Can I Keep My Mind on Driving?" reveals the wide range of attitudes held by southern textile workers and, equally important, exposes some of the cultural struggles that engulfed Piedmont textile communities during the interwar years.

Performing and listening to hillbilly music helped workers to cope with the challenges of an uncertain and sometimes bewildering modern life. Millhands constructed new social identities for themselves in part around their production and consumption of this commercial music, and some uprooted rural migrants may have turned to hillbilly music to help them acclimate to their new working-class lives and to assuage those anxieties spawned by social dislocation, industrial expansion, and shifting social attitudes and morals. This music also nurtured a strong sense of community and regional identity among Piedmont millhands, anchoring them in what must have seemed to be a turbulent new world. The hillbilly music they heard on radio barn dances and phonograph records, some of it performed by local musicians who were their friends and neighbors, "put millhands across the region in touch with each other" and "bolstered a sense of unique, regionwide identity," writes Jacquelyn Dowd Hall and her coauthors in *Like a Family: The Making of a Southern Cotton Mill World* (1987). Few transcriptions of 1920s and 1930s hillbilly radio shows survive, but 78-rpm hillbilly records, a more permanent cultural artifact, offer historians a means of understanding how southern white workers experienced, negotiated, and responded to the far-reaching economic and social revolutions that had transformed the Piedmont from a region of small farms and market towns into the world's greatest textile-manufacturing district in less than two generations.[10]

Hillbilly records present compelling narratives and images of the modern South from the perspective of those who felt the effects of industrial development most strongly, but who also left few written documents detailing their experiences. But as a commercial product, these records cannot be considered the pure, unmediated expression of white working-class southerners, for, as cultural historian George Lipsitz reminds us, among other examples of production control, recording companies "censored lyrics" and "insisted that performers imitate previous commercial successes rather than giving free rein to their own creativity." These records do, however, offer glimpses of how Piedmont millhands-turned-musicians grappled with modernity in their daily lives. Drawing upon these recordings, *Linthead Stomp* deepens our understanding of the creation of the modern South by contributing these long-absent working-class voices to the larger public dialogue about modernity that engaged Henry Ford, F. Scott Fitzgerald, H. L. Mencken, the Vanderbilt Agrarians, Edmund Wilson, and other elite and middle-class social critics during the Jazz Age and the Great Depression.[11]

Linthead Stomp also complements the growing collection of richly textured histories of textile workers in the twentieth-century South. Most of these regional and community studies have, by necessity, focused on southern textile workers collectively, as members of a social class and of larger communities. As a result, these studies present what I call "collective portraits" of millhands in which the specific details and longer arcs of individual lives are often sacrificed for the good of the larger, more sweeping narrative.[12] In contrast, *Linthead Stomp* departs from this approach in order to focus on individual biographies, an organizational strategy that allows readers to understand the social world and culture of Piedmont textile communities within the context of specific millhands' entire lives and range of experiences. *Linthead Stomp* also differs from conventional studies of southern textile workers by locating leisure, recreation, and musical traditions at the center of the narrative. Much of the existing literature about southern millhands focuses on their experiences on the factory floor, on the picket line, and in the voting booth. With the exceptions of Jacquelyn Dowd Hall and her coauthors' *Like a Family* and Vincent J. Roscigno and William F. Danaher's *The Voice of Southern Labor: Radio, Music, and Textile Strikes, 1929–1934* (2004), few studies consider, in any substantive way, what workers did on their front porches, in YMCA community centers, dance halls, and roadhouses, and at minstrel shows, Fourth of July picnics, and church revivals.[13] *Linthead Stomp* deliberately examines Piedmont textile workers as both active producers and consumers in the meaningful arenas of American popular music and mass entertainment.

This study takes up two questions that lie at the intersection of American popular music and Piedmont textile mill culture before World War II. First, how and to what extent did the Piedmont's urban-industrial society and culture influence the hillbilly music created by millhands? Second, how did these working-class singers, musicians, and songwriters contribute to the development of the hillbilly music industry? To answer these questions, this book considers the lives and careers of five hillbilly radio and recording artists who worked for at least a decade in Piedmont textile mills. *Linthead Stomp* situates the commercial origins and development of hillbilly music within the modern Piedmont South and then explores the impact of urban life, industrial labor, new technologies, and mass culture on these working-class musicians. Collectively, the biographies recounted in *Linthead Stomp* reveal the historical development of hillbilly music within this region chiefly between 1922 and 1942 and, in doing so, help us appreciate the complexity and contradictions of the southern white working-class culture that gave birth to one of America's great popular sounds.

The book contains an introduction and four biographical chapters that each focus on the life history and one or more well-known songs of a particular artist as points of entry for exploring the changing configurations of southern white working-class life and Piedmont textile culture during the 1920s and 1930s. Although this book makes no claim that the five central musicians discussed herein are in any way "typical" southern textile workers, it does argue that their biographies are representative of other millhands' lives and experiences. Furthermore, each of the principal musicians' biographies illuminates certain aspects of the Piedmont textile world they inhabited and the mill culture in which they participated. Chapter 1 looks at Atlanta's Fiddlin' John Carson (1874–1949) and his 1923 debut recording of "The Little Old Log Cabin in the Lane," a Reconstruction-era minstrel song about an elderly ex-slave who nostalgically yearns for the uncomplicated days of the Old South. Although not the first of its kind, it was the modest but surprising sales of this recording, more than any other, that alerted talking-machine company executives to the commercial possibilities of what became the hillbilly recording industry and launched it as an ongoing, lucrative enterprise. Carson stands out as one of the pioneer hillbilly radio and recording stars, and the chapter reveals how he, in conjunction with radio stations and talking-machine companies, contributed to the construction of a distinct, marketable image for this new commercial music during the formative period between 1923 and 1925. Among other themes, Carson's experiences also reflect Piedmont millworkers' political participation and civic activism.

Chapter 2 examines Spray, North Carolina, singer and banjoist Charlie Poole (1892–1931) and his band, the North Carolina Ramblers, and focuses on their famous arrangements of "Ramblin' Blues" and "He Rambled," a pair of early twentieth-century Tin Pan Alley standards that celebrate the rough and rowdy life of social misfits and rounders. Poole epitomizes the hard-drinking, work-shy rambler who turned to a career as a professional musician in a desperate attempt to escape working in the cotton mills he hated. On their recordings, Poole and the North Carolina Ramblers forged a distinctive, tightly knit stringband sound that was widely imitated by other Piedmont textile bands, while his three-finger banjo roll, which he modeled on the "classic" banjo style of popular recording artists, influenced a galaxy of bluegrass banjo stars, including DeWitt "Snuffy" Jenkins, Earl Scruggs, and Don Reno.

Chapter 3 considers singer, guitarist, and harmonica player Dave McCarn (1905–64), of Gastonia, North Carolina, and his satirical "Cotton Mill Colic" and its two sequels—"Poor Man, Rich Man (Cotton Mill Colic No. 2)" and "Serves 'Em Fine (Cotton Mill Colic No. 3)." McCarn wrote this trio of occupational complaint songs based upon his own specific struggles and grievances as a Piedmont millhand. The most famous of these, "Cotton Mill Colic," ranks as one of the earliest hillbilly songs to criticize the human costs of southern industrialism, particularly the failure of mill owners to pay their workers a decent wage. McCarn's other, less-studied recordings, most of them bawdy novelty numbers, reflect the impact of Jazz Age mass culture on Piedmont mill communities.

Chapter 4 explores the Dixon Brothers—guitarist Dorsey (1897–1968) and steel guitarist Howard (1903–61)—of East Rockingham, North Carolina, and discusses the elder Dixon's composition "I Didn't Hear Anybody Pray." Dorsey Dixon composed or arranged more than 130 songs, including at least seven about Piedmont textile life, and the few folklorists and historians who have written about him have focused chiefly on these pieces, especially "Weaver's Life," "Weave Room Blues," and "Spinning Room Blues." But the Dixon Brothers actually specialized in sacred selections and tragic ballads, many of them written by Dorsey, and these recordings reveal the strong evangelical Christianity that underpinned Piedmont textile culture and millhands' responses to the modern world. The book concludes with an epilogue that briefly addresses the serious decline of Piedmont textile culture and the diminishing influence of its singers and musicians in American popular music after World War II. Two appendixes, designed to make this study more useful to readers and to music fans, are also included. Appendix A consists of a directory of southern textile workers or former textile workers who recorded hillbilly music between 1923 and 1942. Appendix B contains a selected discography of their commercial recordings that have been reissued on compact discs.

One final note about this book and my reasons for writing it deserves mention. *Linthead Stomp* takes its title from a 1946 bluegrass instrumental on the Essex label, "Lint Head Stomp," recorded by the obscure mandolin virtuoso Phebel Wright. "Linthead"—along with "factory trash," "cotton mill trash," and the more obscure "ignorant factory set"—has long been used as a derogatory term for textile workers.[14] Nonetheless, I have respectfully borrowed Wright's colorful title, adopted here in modified spelling, to serve as the title for this study because it evokes the sense of condescension and disdain with which hillbilly music was once regarded (both in mainstream America and in academe) and at the same time captures the textile mill origins and cultural dynamism of this music. Despite their significant contributions to hillbilly music, and, in some cases, to folk and bluegrass music as well, none of the five major Piedmont textile musicians discussed in this book is as well known or as celebrated as Jimmie Rodgers or the Carter Family, the two most famous hillbilly recording acts of the prewar era. Nor have any of them been inducted into Nashville's Country Music Hall of Fame, though clearly Charlie Poole and perhaps Fiddlin' John Carson deserve to be. My greatest hope for this book is that it will spark a revived interest in these five often-neglected Piedmont textile musicians and that it will advance the rehabilitation of hillbilly music, which D. K. Wilgus, Archie Green, Bill C. Malone, and other scholars began in earnest in the early to mid-1960s, as a valuable and worthwhile subject of academic inquiry.[15] Now widely reissued on compact discs and available on MP3 internet downloads, the early hillbilly recordings of Piedmont mill-hands reach millions more listeners today than they ever did during the 1920s and 1930s. Someday, perhaps, the names of Fiddlin' John Carson, Charlie Poole, Dave McCarn, and the Dixon Brothers may be almost as familiar to southern historians as are those of Henry W.

Grady, Booker T. Washington, Huey Long, and George Wallace. *Lint-head Stomp*, I hope, will contribute to this renaissance.

Much of this book revolves around song lyrics from pre–World War II 78-rpm commercial recordings and quotations from tape-recorded interviews of several of the profiled artists or their children. Unless otherwise indicated, all of the song lyrics quoted in this book as well as all of the quotations from tape-recorded interviews are based upon my own careful transcriptions, copies of which remain in my possession. Within the transcribed interviews of Dave McCarn, Dorsey Dixon, and several others, I have silently eliminated the false starts and digressions that make up a regular part of everyday conversation and have sometimes rearranged phrases and passages—occasionally from two or more interviews, in the case of Dorsey Dixon—in order to make the transcriptions more readable. But the words themselves remain those of the informants. Furthermore, quotations from Dorsey Dixon's unpublished autobiographical accounts are rendered in Chapter 4 in their original form, including his creative spelling, punctuation (he used periods for commas), and grammar, and in this chapter and throughout the book, the intrusive use of "[*sic*]," which is usually employed to indicate mistakes, has been omitted in most cases.

LINTHEAD STOMP

INTRODUCTION

The mill workers, isolated geographically and socially into separate villages, have developed culture traits peculiar to themselves—traits often despised by farmers and uptown residents alike. Instead of country clubs and garden clubs, they join fraternal lodges with low dues, such as the Patriotic Order of the Sons of America, the Red Men, and the Woodmen of the World. Instead of tea and cocktails, they drink Coca-Cola. Leisure-time activities—since reduction in long hours of work has allowed leisure—include a mixture of rural and urban amusements; such rural sports as hunting, fishing, "blackberryin'," and talking in desultory fashion alternate with attendance at baseball games and, most popular of all, the movies. The Bible, religious papers, pulp magazines, and an occasional rural weekly provide reading matter. "Hillbilly" music is very popular—and, indeed, is still secretly preferred to opera by most uptown citizens. Most mill homes now have a radio and an automobile of one vintage or another.—Liston Pope, *Millhands and Preachers: A Study of Gastonia* (1942)

On August 9, 1927, the *Charlotte Observer* boasted of the Victor Talking Machine Company's upcoming field-recording session in a front-page story headlined "Records Made in Charlotte to Perpetuate Mountain Ballads." "Mountaineer musicians of western North Carolina who know little of cities except by legend and who play by native instinct will come to Charlotte today to perpetuate their art for an invisible audience of hundreds of thousands of people," the newspaper reported. "They will make records for the Victor Talking Machine company for distribution in a dozen nations, it was declared yesterday by Ralph S. Peer, scout for the company. Folk-lore songs and banjo selections by artists of the soil who have never read a note but through whose music runs the passion of river torrents and mountain feuds and the melody of valley meadows are to be recorded." The next day, the headline of a follow-up article echoed this same rustic theme: "Musicians Trek from Mountains to City to Record Old Ballads of Hill Country."[1]

Victor's mobile crew traveled to Charlotte that August as part of a three-city field-recording excursion to the Southeast, and this recording session was to be the first ever held in this important southern commercial and industrial hub. Charlotte sits at the center of the Southern Piedmont, a crescent-shaped region of rolling hills between the Appalachian Mountains and the Atlantic coastal plain that extends southward from Richmond, Virginia, through the central Carolinas and northern Georgia, to Birmingham, Alabama. By 1927, when Victor's field-recording crew arrived in Charlotte, this region, the most urban and heavily industrialized area of the American South, reigned as the world's leading textile-manufacturing center.[2] With almost six hundred mills within a hundred-mile radius, Charlotte and its environs had attracted tens of thousands of white migrants from the surrounding Piedmont and mountain counties in the late nineteenth and early twentieth centuries. As a result of the dense clustering of working-class communities, the city and nearby textile towns flourished as hotbeds of musical activity, energized by a steady stream of newcomers who sought work in the area's cotton mills, factories, railroad yards, and building trades. By 1930, Charlotte ranked as the largest city in the Carolinas, with a population of 82,675 residents that eclipsed even that of the old coastal port of Charleston.[3]

Around August 8, Victor's A & R (artist and repertoire) man, Ralph S. Peer, and his crew of two engineers set up their portable recording equipment in a temporary studio in the auditorium of the newly constructed Charlotte Observer Building, located at the corner of South Tryon and West Stonewall Streets in downtown Charlotte. There, over the course of six days, twelve different musical acts made a total of forty-six recordings, chiefly of what was then called hillbilly music. Since the mid-1920s, Victor and other major record companies had marketed such records in their advertisements and catalogs as the authentic folk music of the rural mountain South. "These old tunes rarely get into the cities," explained Victor's 1924 *Olde Time Fiddlin' Tunes* catalog, "but mountain folk have sung and danced to them for generations. . . . Writers of books and plays, of late years, have gone into the mountains and studied the life of the people there, but this is almost the first of their music that has come into public notice." In order to market these records more effectively to rural and working-class white southern consumers, all of the major talking-machine companies except for Gennett released hillbilly records between

East Trade Street in downtown Charlotte, mid-1920s.
Courtesy of the Levine Museum of the New South.

the mid-1920s and the mid-1930s in specially designated numerical series, and the associated marketing labels, including OKeh's "Old Time Tunes," Vocalion's "Old Southern Melodies," and Paramount's "Olde Time Tunes—Southern Series," underscored the regional and particularly the old-fashioned, folk character of this music. Prior to settling on the name "Native American Melodies" for its hillbilly record series in 1929, Victor sometimes described such recordings in its promotional literature as "Hill Billy Songs," "Popular Ballads and Mountaineer Tunes," or "Mountain Songs and Jigs." Such marketing labels, as well as the quaint pastoral images of the barn dances, log cabins, and stands of mountain pines that often graced the covers of hillbilly record catalogs and promotional brochures, all seemed to hearken back to an idyllic rural South that was deeply embedded in the American popular imagination.[4]

Perhaps due in part to these persuasive advertisements, coupled with their own nostalgia for this music, historians and folklorists have long viewed hillbilly music chiefly as a traditional rural folk music that originated in southern farming communities and mountain hollows. But within the Southern Piedmont, hillbilly music actually emerged in a rapidly modernizing society of cities and towns, railroads, two-lane highways, hydroelectric plants, and textile mills, and much of the music recorded at the 1927 Charlotte session was clearly the product of this modern, urban-industrial world. In fact, contrary to the colorful newspaper publicity surrounding the event, few "mountaineer musicians" or "artists of the soil" recorded at this session. Of the members of the twelve different acts to make recordings in Charlotte that August, most resided in the North Carolina and Virginia Piedmont, and at least three hillbilly stringbands (the Carolina Tar Heels, Kelly Harrell and the Virginia String Band, and Red Patterson's Piedmont Log Rollers) contained members who worked in the region's textile mills. To be sure, some of these millhand singers and musicians, such as harmonica virtuoso Gwin S. Foster and balladeer Kelly Harrell, had been born and raised near the foothills of the Blue Ridge Mountains, but by 1927, most of them had been living and working in Piedmont textile towns for a decade or more. Furthermore, roughly two-thirds of the selections recorded in Charlotte consisted of songs written by Tin Pan Alley tunesmiths within the previous two decades, including sentimental parlor ballads, "coon songs," ragtime numbers, and blues instrumentals. One of the bands, a Charlotte-area

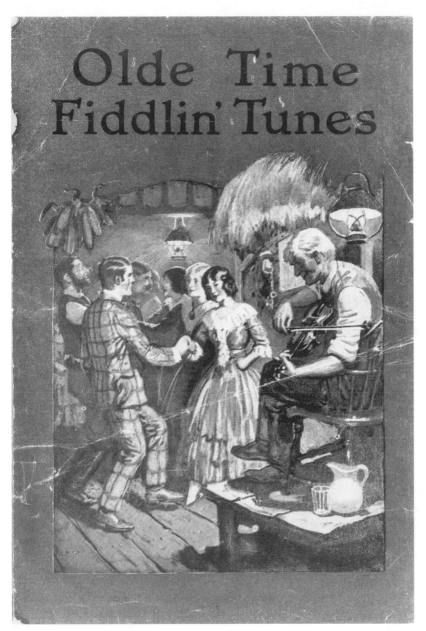

Cover of Victor's *Olde Time Fiddlin' Tunes* brochure, 1924.
Courtesy of the Southern Folklife Collection, Wilson Library,
University of North Carolina at Chapel Hill.

trio billed as Price-Prosser-Teasley, even cut a Hawaiian-guitar duet, with ukulele accompaniment, of Ishman Jones and His Orchestra's million-selling 1922 hit record "Wabash Blues."[5] The evocative and appealing images of mountain fiddlers and rural culture employed in Victor's and other firms' promotional literature, however, effectively obscured much of the modern, urban-industrial origins of hillbilly music. Even to this day, historians and folklorists tend to view early country music as the product of the traditional rural South and have overlooked the importance of modern influences, especially urban and industrial ones, on this commercial music.[6]

"The traveler through some parts of North Carolina is seldom out of sight or hearing of a cotton mill," observed Holland Thompson in 1906. "The tall chimneys rise beside the railway in nearly every town. Side tracks from the main line lead to the low brick mills and the clustering tenements, set down in fields where crops grow almost to the doors, or in the forest where a clearing has been made." Holland's brief description reveals just how dramatically industrialization had transformed North Carolina's landscape in the decades following the end of Reconstruction. In 1860, on the eve of the Civil War, North Carolina contained only 39 textile mills. By 1906, when Thompson published his study, however, that figure had soared to 304 textile mills—almost one-fourth of all those in the United States.[7] Postwar southern industrialization, fueled by the building of railroads and the spread of commercial cotton farming, had taken root in central North Carolina and throughout the Piedmont, and with the rapid construction of textile mills and the gathering of displaced white farm families to tend their whirring spindles and beating looms, a new world of cities and towns, roaring factories, and crowded mill villages rapidly emerged. Amid this modern world, with its factory whistles, industrial discipline, clattering machines, and low-wage labor, Piedmont textile workers created a vibrant regional working-class culture out of which was born a new commercial sound—hillbilly music—one of the most popular American musical genres of the 1920s and 1930s. Within Piedmont textile mill villages and elsewhere across the South, this new music flourished, evolved, and then, with the mass migrations of southerners and greater radio and jukebox exposure during World War II, became a nationwide sensation. And from its humble origins in the 1920s, this new commercial sound eventually developed into the enormously profitable international industry we recognize today as country music.

Within the Southern Piedmont, hillbilly music emerged from the new urban-industrial culture created chiefly by the rapid expansion of a massive, regionwide textile industry. Beginning in the 1880s, businessmen and town boosters in the region embraced industrial capitalism as the engine that would bring progress and economic development to a New South still recovering from the devastation of the Civil War. "The cotton mill is destined to be the most powerful factor of southern progress in [the] future," predicted the editor of the *Atlanta Constitution* in 1894. "When we manufacture our leading staple and sell the product of our mills to home and foreign markets this will be the richest region on the globe." As a result of their aggressive "cotton mill building campaign," textile mills sprouted up all across the Piedmont South, first along the region's swift-running rivers and then, increasingly after 1900, with James B. Duke's Southern Power Company's harnessing of the hydroelectric power of these same rivers, in the region's fast-growing cities and towns. Before the turn of the twentieth century, other industries also contributed to the area's surging economy, including cigarette and tobacco manufacturers in Richmond and Durham, textile equipment manufacturers in Charlotte and Gastonia, furniture factories in High Point and Hickory, and, at the southern tip of the Piedmont, coal mining and iron and steel foundries in Birmingham. But none of these dominated the region, which sociologist Rupert Vance called "The Piedmont Crescent of Industry," more than textile production. "The Piedmont region is one of the great cotton manufacturing districts of the world," crowed the Southern Railway's 1909 *Textile Directory*, "and has such prominence in this industry that the territory of the Southern railway between Danville, Va., and Atlanta, Ga., a distance of 400 miles, has been referred to as one long cotton mill village."[8]

North Carolina spearheaded this industrial expansion, with the greatest mill-building boom occurring in the first two decades of the twentieth century. In 1880, the state contained 49 mills employing slightly more than 3,300 workers. By the mid-1920s, however, it boasted 556 textile mills, including those manufacturing cotton, silk, rayon, and woolen goods, which employed more than 97,500 of the state's workers. By 1929, the Piedmont states of Virginia, North Carolina, South Carolina, Georgia, and Alabama contained almost 1,400

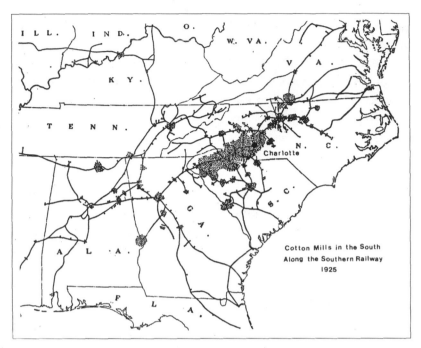

The Piedmont textile region, showing the cotton mills clustered
along the Southern Railway, 1925. Map adapted from Marjorie Potwin's
Cotton Mill People of the Piedmont: A Study in Social Change (1927).

textile mills, three-fourths of them clustered in the Carolinas, and employed more than a quarter-million workers, most of whom were either rural migrants from economically collapsing upcountry and mountain farms or only a generation removed from rural life. With this surge of industrial growth, the Southern Piedmont officially surpassed long-dominant New England in 1927 to become the world's greatest center of textile manufacturing, producing approximately two-thirds of the cotton cloth manufactured in the United States. "A traveller who follows the main line of the Southern Railroad from Lynchburg, Virginia, to Atlanta, Georgia, is hardly out of sight of one cotton mill until he is in sight of another," remarked sociologist Lois MacDonald in 1928, echoing Holland Thompson's observations of two decades earlier. "Some of them are on the outskirts of cities, but many are built in the open field, often within a stone's throw of a cotton field. The mills with few exceptions are modern structures and are equipped with modern machinery. The region," she added, "gives every appearance of being alive with industrial activity."[9]

As a result of its rapid post-Reconstruction industrialization, the Southern Piedmont underwent spectacular urban growth between 1890 and 1940 that was virtually unrivaled by any other region in the United States. Before the Civil War, the Atlantic coastal cities of Wilmington, Charleston, and Savannah had dominated the social and economic life of their respective states, but the most significant postwar shifts in population occurred in the industrializing Piedmont. The population of Greensboro, North Carolina, for example, skyrocketed from 3,317 in 1890 to 19,861 in 1920 and then more than doubled to 53,569 by 1930. By then, the city contained more than 120 industrial plants, including the Cone brothers' Proximity Manufacturing Company, a chain of four local textile mills, one of which ranked as the nation's largest denim-producing factory. Between 3,000 and 4,000 employees worked at the Cones' mills, and the company's mill villages housed an estimated 15,000 residents. A 1921 University of North Carolina *News Letter* article titled "Our Rapidly Growing Cities" reported that several other Carolina Piedmont manufacturing centers, including Gastonia, Winston-Salem, and Durham, had experienced similar population explosions. The significant post–Civil War demographic changes that accompanied industrialization meant that the thriving manufacturing centers of the industrializing Piedmont, rather than the older port cities of the Atlantic coastal plain,

Sparta Cotton Mill, Spartanburg, South Carolina, ca. 1909.
Author's collection.

would henceforth set the pace for social and economic development in the southeastern United States.[10]

Although the Piedmont, like the South as a whole, remained predominantly rural until after World War II, the region experienced a rate of urban growth significantly higher than that of the rest of the United States in the first decades of the twentieth century. In 1900, for example, fewer than one in ten North Carolinians lived in towns of 2,500 or more residents, but by 1930, more than one out of every four did. Urban ratios were even higher for the Piedmont counties of North Carolina, where, according to sociologist Rupert B. Vance, more than half of the population lived in cities and towns in 1932. Since the end of Reconstruction, a mounting assortment of agricultural hardships, including new fence laws, slumping cotton prices, rising costs of fertilizer and equipment, increasing rates of tenancy, and spreading boll weevil infestations, all combined to uproot farm families from the land and send them streaming into the Piedmont's cities and towns. "Thousands of white tenants, who used to live [on farms] in piedmont North Carolina, are now laboring in the cotton mills, the foundries, the machine shops and for building contractors in towns," reported the *Charlotte Observer* in 1906. "The short crop this year will drive thousands more of them to the cities, towns and villages." The large-scale migration of rural white families swelled the population of Piedmont cities and towns and created new working-class communities within them. Sitting at the center of an extensive network of railroads and hard-surface highways that connected them to the rest of the nation, Atlanta, Charlotte, Danville, Gastonia, Greensboro, and Spartanburg emerged as major textile-manufacturing centers, and the number of towns with 2,500 or more inhabitants in the five Piedmont states more than doubled, from 108 in 1890 to 234 in 1920. "Southern Piedmont textile towns cluster along the Southern Railway System like beads on a string," noted sociologist Ben F. Lemert in 1933, "and enjoy not only good railroad transportation, but are connected by many smooth interstate highways over which automobile trucking companies function in addition to the railroads and to the steamship traffic along the coasts."[11]

Another defining feature of the Piedmont's expanding textile-manufacturing industry was its almost complete exclusion of African American workers. Since the industry's antebellum origins, southern cotton mills had been racially segregated occupational enclaves for white workers. After the Civil War, the new mills that dotted the Piedmont's rolling landscape remained rigidly segregated, in large part because white millhands refused to work alongside African Americans for fear of being reduced to their social level or of being compared to them. White wage workers in the industrializing New South demanded that all production line jobs in cotton mills be reserved for them alone and that black workers be restricted to the menial jobs of pickers, firemen, scrubbers, and roustabouts. A 1907 survey of 152 southern textile mills, for example, found that none employed black men on the production line and that only a handful employed them to work outdoors. Piedmont millhands sometimes went on strike to preserve their social and economic status in a segregated workplace. In August 1897, in one of the most spectacular of these incidents, more than 1,400 white workers walked off their jobs at the Fulton Bag and Cotton Mills in Atlanta to protest the hiring of 25 black women in the folding department. The spontaneous strike ended five days later when the strikers, assisted by the Textile Workers Protective Union and the Atlanta Federation of Trades, succeeded in forcing management to dismiss the newly hired black folders. Throughout the late nineteenth century and well into the twentieth century, all but a tiny percentage of those workers employed in the region's mills were native-born white workers. In 1915, the South Carolina state legislature actually passed a law prohibiting textile-manufacturing firms from employing African Americans to work in the same room as white workers or allowing them to use the same entrances, pay ticket windows, restrooms, or other facilities at the same time as white employees. Before the 1960s, African Americans typically made up approximately 2 percent of the labor force in southern mills, with their numbers peaking at slightly more than 8 percent in 1920. "Practically all mill help in the Piedmont section of the Carolinas," boasted a 1926 article in the *Gastonia Daily Gazette*'s special "Industrial Edition," "is native white labor, with the pure American blood in their veins. There is no babel and confusion of tongues heard," the article added, in reference to the foreign-born immigrants who dominated the ranks of the workforce in New England textile mills and who led a series of dramatic strikes there in the first decades of the twentieth century that temporary crippled the region's industry. "There is no great inter-mixture of races that breeds contempt and race hatred. Consequently, there is no trouble arising from labor disputes, misunderstanding of orders or friction between classes."[12]

Located adjacent to textile-manufacturing complexes, hundreds of textile mill villages dotted the Southern Piedmont by 1900, and within these villages, displaced white farm people learned to become industrial workers. Entire families, including children as young as six or seven (before the passage of effective child labor laws during the Progressive Era), worked in the region's textile mills. And most southern millhands, approximately 70 percent in 1929, resided in mill village houses, which textile firms constructed and then rented to their employees. Prior to 1900, most of these Piedmont mill villages were located in the rural countryside near the rivers used to power the mills. But after the turn of the century, with the southern textile industry's increasing reliance on electrical power, mill villages were often constructed on the outskirts of cities and towns, and depending on the size of the workforce needed to run the mills, these villages might contain anywhere from a few dozen houses laid out along a central dirt road to several hundred closely spaced cottages neatly arranged in rows along paved streets. The houses themselves were usually small, uniform, three- to six-room wooden or brick structures, and, depending on the number of rooms, rented for around three dollars to five dollars a week during the mid-1920s. Where electricity and running water were available, textile mills often provided these services to mill villagers for free or for a nominal charge. The worst mill villages, usually smaller, unincorporated rural ones located in the countryside, observed a *New York Times* reporter in 1930, consisted of "huddles of sad shacks on ravaged hillsides," while "the best are suburban developments in the modern manner: prim cottages set behind hedges on curving roads, paved and landscaped." Besides the company-owned housing, most Piedmont mill villages typically contained a few churches, stores, and fraternal lodges and a school and recreation center, most of which the textile firms constructed and financially supported.[13]

Textile workers who resided in even the most modern and well-appointed mill villages came under the close surveillance of the textile mill superintendents and their hired staff of ministers, teachers, nurses, social workers, and recreation directors. Nonetheless, these workers enjoyed an array of significant cultural advantages that would have been virtually unavailable to them in the rural countryside. In 1926, the Loray Mill's village, a suburb of Gastonia, North Carolina, that housed some 4,500 residents in approximately 600 homes, included, among other modern facilities, a business district of "sixteen grocery and general merchandise stores, a bank, a furniture store, and a moving picture theatre, besides several cafés, filling stations, garages, and other small business establishments." In addition, three churches, a school, a number of fraternal lodges, a baseball park, and a cafeteria and community center belonging to the company were located within the village. But even in small, unincorporated textile towns of only several hundred residents, workers could enjoy some of the most modern urban amenities. In Spray, North Carolina, the hometown of the renowned banjoist Charlie Poole, the Central YMCA recreation center contained a reading room, billiard tables, bowling alley, gymnasium, swimming pool, and motion picture theater, which on Monday and Saturday evenings screened "some of the best productions on the market" during the mid-1920s.[14]

Although life in these mill communities was often marked by hardship, disease, and poverty, mill villages did offer opportunities to participate in America's expansive consumer culture, and perhaps no force transformed the lives and culture of Piedmont textile workers more than did their increasing consumerism. As wage earners, millhands entered into a commercial market economy and, according to sociologist Harriet L. Herring, "saw more cash in a month than [they] had in a year on the farm." As early as the 1890s, millhands were already tentatively becoming consumers of new commercial products and mass amusements. These trends accelerated during the first decades of the twentieth century, particularly during the 1920s. Mill wages, however meager, offered textile workers access to a wide assortment of consumer goods and modern technologies, which, despite general stores, mail-order catalogs, and rural free delivery, were far less common in the southern rural countryside. Writing in 1934, Herring described the suddenness and intensity with which Piedmont millhands immersed themselves in the nation's consumer economy and the cornucopia of tantalizing goods it offered:

> Installment sellers convinced the workers that they wanted their houses fitted up with phonographs, parlor suites, and player pianos and presently with radios. They needed such conveniences

as electric irons and electric fans, run by cheap current from the company, a new intense-heating oil stove, a new refrigerator, and some bottles of pop to go in it. Gradually everybody went on wheels and so even the worker who lived a few minutes' walk from his work bought a car the more to enjoy his half day and Sunday off and to look for a better job. . . . His wife had canned goods and baker's bread for the table, his daughters had the silk stockings, the ready-made clothes, and the cosmetics to make them fairly faithful copies of the daughters from the exclusive suburb. All the family had frequent movie tickets and a nickel or a dime to spend for a dope [Coca-Cola] or a hot dog.[15]

Although buying durable goods on easy credit sometimes proved perilous for working-class families, Herring's account reveals the ways in which a broad array of consumer products, purchased from mill village stores, local merchants, and mail-order firms, reoriented the daily lives of textile millhands and other southern industrial workers. Consumer goods, she concluded, were "more than mere silk stockings and automobiles and movies. They were more than a new way of living. They were physical proof of a new life."[16]

The nation's expanding commercial entertainment, particularly vaudeville shows and motion pictures, also provided Piedmont millhands with diversions from workplace pressures and religious observances. By the turn of the twentieth century, cities such as Atlanta, Charlotte, and Richmond represented important emerging regional centers of commercial entertainment and amusements such as vaudeville shows, musical concerts, theatrical productions, nickelodeons, dance halls, and dime museums, and during the first decades of the century, as these cities' populations expanded, the number of such mass entertainments also multiplied. Smaller textile towns like Burlington, North Carolina, with fewer than 10,000 residents, likewise offered a smorgasbord of cultural diversions and amusements in the mid- to late 1920s. As Jacquelyn Dowd Hall and the coauthors of *Like a Family* have observed of the town's rich and varied cultural life:

The Mack Theater in Burlington regularly hosted vaudeville productions throughout the 1920s, shows like Don Davis's Dancing Dollies and the Land of Laughter Company, which featured comedians in blackface, harmony singers, and a crystal ball reader—all for a mere twenty cents. Workers could also take in a movie at the Rose Theaters, such as *The Town That Forgot God*, with the special added attraction of the Galvin Duo steel guitar pickers. Throughout the 1920s Hollywood vied with minstrel shows and local stringband and gospel programs for audience dimes and loyalty. In one week in February 1927 Rudolph Valentino in *The Son of the Sheik* played opposite a fifty-character minstrel show at the Municipal Theater. In 1929 films like Buster Keaton's *Spite Marriage*, Mary Pickford's *Coquette*, and Clara Bow's *Dangerous Curves* ran in town at the same time that the East Burlington Presbyterian Church had an ice cream supper with stringband music and two congregations hosted a special gospel evening with Mr. and Mrs. George Dibble. Mr. Dibble, who had performed with Billy Sunday, was billed as the "Caruso of Gospel Singing"; Mrs. Dibble spoke the gospel.[17]

But controversies quickly erupted about the moral value of movies and other forms of mass entertainment, and the new recreational diversions and behaviors of the 1920s sowed generational and cultural conflict within Piedmont mill communities. Many older and religiously devout members of these mill villages opposed and often publicly condemned the commercial amusements of movies, Charleston dancing, and jazz music, and controversy swirled around these leisure-time diversions. During the 1920s, Piedmont newspapers regularly published articles with such titles as "Erotic Music Befuddles Girls" and "Highway Petting Too Popular in Alamance" that cautioned against moonlight drives, prohibition gin, and jazz music, all of which, notes historian Pamela Grundy, "were blamed for phenomena ranging from fallen women to wayward children to a decline in the quality of college football." "Times are changing," remarked the editor of the *Burlington Daily Times* in an editorial that wondered "Are We Jazz Crazy?" "The young folks can't have a big time any longer unless they are in an automobile with a pint of 'stuff' to give them a kick and a little jazz to liven the thing up a bit. Go to any gathering of the younger set and see what you find. They cannot sit down in the parlor with their best girl and spend a quiet evening. They have to be going places, doing things. Yes, times are changing and people change, their habits change and what would amuse ten years ago fails utterly today. It is probably good that things do change and we are glad that we live in a changing age," he admitted. "But we are not proud of the fact that we live in the jazz age."[18]

Despite the scorn and condemnation heaped on the era's modern amusements and the new behaviors they bred, many textile workers, particularly those in their late teens and twenties, enthusiastically participated in this vibrant, fast-changing mass culture. "Since 1920 life in the mill village has shared in the general twentieth-century change," Spartanburg social worker Marjorie Potwin observed in *Cotton Mill People of the Piedmont: A Study in Social Change* (1927). "We have the auto and the movies and the radio, the lipstick and the boyish bob. We have an almost overwhelming complexity of old customs and old standards with new ways and new ideas. . . . Granny wears a sunbonnet and came to the mill in a farm wagon, the young'uns wear georgette and silk hose and own a Ford car, Grandpaw chaws terbacker and fiddles, Grandson smokes cigarettes and takes home jazz records for the Victrola." Collectively, the new forms of commercial entertainment and consumer goods that became available during the 1920s to Piedmont millhands significantly redefined mill village culture and enabled these workers to create new identities for themselves and express new kinds of behavior that, as Pamela Grundy has noted, "took them well beyond their appointed places in the industrial order."[19]

The momentous social and economic changes that remade the Southern Piedmont in the half century following Reconstruction, particularly the integration of millhands into the nation's commercial mass culture and consumer economy, played a significant role in shaping the regional development of hillbilly music. The music that millworkers performed on radio and records during the 1920s and 1930s emerged out of this modern world and out of the often wrenching working-class experiences of social dislocation, mass migration, class formation, urban life, industrial work, race relations, and labor strife. When hard-pressed white farm families moved to find work in the Piedmont's cities and textile towns, they brought with them their fiddles, banjos, mandolins, guitars, and musical traditions, and although many of them were already accomplished singers and musicians when they arrived, their exposure to a wide range of musical influences and their access to factory-made instruments, radios, phonographs, sheet music, songbooks, and musical instructional booklets led to a flourishing musical culture within

Piedmont mill villages. Atlanta, Charlotte, Greensboro, Gastonia, Spartanburg, and other textile centers across the Southern Piedmont formed the cultural crucibles in which these working-class singers and musicians blended older musical traditions (themselves already a cross-fertilized hybrid of sounds) with Tin Pan Alley songs, ragtime numbers, and African American blues, among others, to create a commercial "hillbilly sound." Residing in mill village suburbs of larger industrial cities and towns, textile workers enjoyed easy access to modern urban amusements and consumer goods, as well as extensive contact and communication with the broader world beyond the Piedmont. This active participation in the nation's mass culture profoundly influenced the hillbilly music that southern millhands created and performed, a music that has been described as "the most playful and democratic of mill workers' contributions to the popular culture of the nation and the world." As Jacquelyn Dowd Hall and her coauthors assert, "Textile mills built the New South," and these same textile mills also gave birth to hillbilly music in the Piedmont South.[20]

Hillbilly music, or old-time music, as it was also sometimes called, was essentially a commercial American popular music broadcast and recorded between 1922 and 1942 chiefly by ordinary white southern singers and musicians, particularly those from the southeastern United States.[21] In 1923, a former Atlanta textile worker nicknamed "Fiddlin' John" Carson recorded two such songs at his debut session for OKeh, "The Little Old Log Cabin in the Lane" and "The Old Hen Cackled and the Rooster's Going to Crow." Although not the first artist to make commercial recordings of minstrel songs and traditional fiddle tunes, the surprising commercial success of Carson's 78-rpm record alerted executives of the General Phonograph Corporation, the manufacturer of OKeh records, to a promising new market for what would soon be called "hillbilly music," a generic industry classification, reportedly coined in 1925 by OKeh executive Ralph S. Peer, that was intended to capture the music's racial, rural, and regional origins. "Many rural dwellers, including a number of musicians, considered ['hillbilly'] 'a fighting word' because of its negative connotations," observes historian Pamela Grundy. "But it was an ideal marketing tool, and its meaning was ambiguous enough for most players and consumers to accept."[22]

Within two years of Carson's debut recording, Columbia, Victor, Vocalion, and other largely New York–based record labels began to release similar old-time records nationwide, and the Southeast, particularly the Piedmont, with its many fledgling radio stations, deep reservoir of musical talent, and dynamic musical culture, became the principal wellspring for this new genre of commercial music. Originally, in the mid- to late 1920s, most of the singers and musicians who appeared on hillbilly records were self-taught amateurs or semiprofessionals who earned a living by working regular jobs, and the overwhelming majority of them recorded only a couple of sides at a single session and then never recorded again. But by the end of the decade, the expansion of the nation's commercial entertainment industry made it possible for more and more hillbilly musicians to cobble together enough radio spots, recording sessions, and concert dates to earn a living as full-time professional entertainers.[23]

Then, the Great Depression struck the nation's talking-machine industry with a punishing force, and the commercial recording of hillbilly music, like almost all other genres, drastically declined. Annual sales of phonograph records plummeted from a peak of 104 million in 1927 to only six million in 1932. During this same period, annual sales of phonographs fell from almost one million to just 40,000. Collapsing sales bankrupted several record companies, and other struggling firms were acquired, in buyouts or in mergers, by more solvent radio and film corporations. The Great Depression devastated the talking-machine industry, and although popular hillbilly stars of the late 1920s, such as Jimmie Rodgers and the Carter Family, continued to make recordings, perform on the radio, and book show dates, the careers of most other hillbilly recording artists of the 1920s succumbed to the ravages of the nation's worst economic catastrophe.[24]

During the years of the Great Depression, hillbilly music underwent several significant transformations. New, more jazz- and pop-oriented styles of music began to eclipse the older stringband music heard on early hillbilly records. Most fans of the 1930s preferred the warm, intricate harmonies of the Delmore Brothers and the Blue Sky Boys or the sophisticated swing- and jazz-inflected sounds of Clayton McMichen's Georgia Wildcats and Hank Penny and His Radio Cowboys to the older, often more raucous fiddle and stringband music of the previous decade. Meanwhile, as the recording industry struggled through hard times, commercial radio soared to unprecedented levels of popularity with American listeners, by broadcasting a wide range of appealing music that was not only free of charge but also more intimate and vibrant than the "canned music" of phonograph records. By 1932, with the collapse of the phonograph record industry, radio emerged as the single most important vehicle for disseminating and popularizing hillbilly music. Although the once-flourishing careers of many of early hillbilly music's biggest stars, including Fiddlin' John Carson, Vernon Dalhart, and Ernest V. Stoneman, declined during the Great Depression, a new generation of artists, such as Roy Acuff, Gene Autry, and Bob Wills, saw their fortunes, boosted by the tremendous popularity of radio, Hollywood westerns, and jukeboxes, rise to even greater heights of commercial success.[25]

By 1935, after the worst years of the economic catastrophe had passed, the hillbilly recording industry began to rebound with the founding of budget-priced labels such as Decca and RCA-Victor's Bluebird. By the late 1930s, virtually all of the artists heard on hillbilly records, budget-priced or otherwise, were radio performers and, increasingly, full-time professional musicians. Coming to a close was the era of amateur singers, fiddlers, banjo players, and guitarists who pursued part-time careers in commercial music while continuing their regular industrial occupations. By the middle of World War II, hillbilly music had broken through to national audiences chiefly as a result of increased radio and jukebox play and large-scale population shifts of southerners to military bases and defense plants in Midwest and West Coast cities. It had also begun to evolve into the more professionalized and conventional sound, complete with electric guitars and pedal steel guitars, which we would today recognize as country music, and the regional styles of western swing, honky-tonk, and bluegrass were either already established or about to be established.[26]

Arguably, southern white working people made their single greatest contribution to American popular music in the form of hillbilly music and its musical descendants—country music, western swing, honky-tonk, and bluegrass. From Fiddlin' John Carson's first scratchy 78-rpm recordings in 1923, country music has mushroomed into an international phenomenon. Today, the combined profits from CD sales, radio airplay, concert tours, celebrity endorsements, television specials, cable television networks, theme parks, and museums have transformed country music into a multibillion-dollar global industry and one of America's greatest cultural exports. It is so popular around the world, in fact, that, as Bill C. Malone points out, it is not uncommon to find Japanese bluegrass bands and German rockabillies, among others, performing music that originally sprang from the fiddles, guitars, and banjos of the white working people of the early to mid-twentieth-century American South. Indeed, the commercial broadcasting and recording of hillbilly music between 1922 and 1942 marked the first time that the southern white working class played a central role in shaping American popular music and mass culture, and no other group of southern industrial workers did more to create this commercial music than Piedmont textile millhands. To be sure, dozens of hillbilly musicians earned their regular livings as farmers and sharecroppers, coal miners, railroaders, and building trades craftsmen, or even as doctors, lawyers, and merchants. But Piedmont textile workers made up the single largest occupational group to sing and play in front of radio and recording studio microphones before World War II. "The southeastern cotton mill industry," observed Bill C. Malone, "has contributed an exceptionally large number of musicians to country entertainment. Performers who previously worked in cotton mills, such as David McCarn and Howard and Dorsey Dixon, or who grew up in mill families, have in fact constituted the single largest body of occupational-derived performers in country music." Although they worked ten- or eleven-hour shifts, tending spinning frames or weaving looms in stiflingly hot, lint-choked textile mills for some of the lowest industrial wages in the nation, and despite their political disfranchisement, lack of formal education, and inferior social status, Piedmont "lintheads" helped to create one of the great American popular sounds of the twentieth century.[27]

Between 1923 and 1942, singers and musicians from Piedmont textile villages played on, conservatively, more than 1,500, or 6 percent, of the approximately 23,000 hillbilly records released in the United States.[28] Although the precise occupational details of many hillbilly musicians' biographies are obscure or now lost to scholars, we know that at least eighty-eight different singers and musicians who worked, at one time or another, in Piedmont textile mills made commercial hillbilly recordings before World War II (see Appendix A).[29] Dozens of others never commercially recorded their music but performed on daily fifteen-minute radio programs and stage shows within and beyond the Southern Piedmont. Several of those fortunate enough to make records enjoyed relatively long, successful careers in the commercial music industry, including Fiddlin' John Carson and Hoke Rice of Georgia; Kelly Harrell of Virginia; Charlie Poole, Homer "Pappy" Sherrill, and J. E. and Wade Mainer of North Carolina; and Claude Casey and Arthur "Guitar Boogie" Smith of South Carolina. A few of them, including Dorsey Dixon and Jimmie Tarlton, even lived long enough to launch second careers in the 1960s and 1970s through folk festival circuits, college concert tours, and long-playing vinyl records. Others had shorter, if no less influential, musical careers. For example, Roy Hall and His Blue Ridge Entertainers, who performed on radio station WAIR in Winston-Salem and then on WDBJ in Roanoke between 1938 and 1942, ranked as one of the most popular stringbands of the Carolina and Virginia Piedmont before Hall's untimely death in 1943, at the age of thirty-six, in an automobile accident. The group's fast-paced, pulsing stringband sound prefigured bluegrass and, like the earlier recordings of another Tar Heel textile stringband, Charlie Poole and the North Carolina Ramblers, helped to lay the foundations for the emergence of this new musical genre immediately following World War II.[30]

Besides cutting records and performing on radio and stage shows, Piedmont textile workers made other significant contributions to hillbilly music, specifically, and to American popular music, generally. Some millhands, for example, forged new singing and instrumental styles that continued to reverberate in country music decades after their deaths. One of these innovative performers, the legendary Joe Lee, a weaver and loom fixer at Pepperell Mills in Lindale, Georgia, helped to transform the north Georgia fiddling heard on hundreds of prewar commercial recordings. Lee fiddled in a smooth long-bow style, and, according to Lowe Stokes, who often visited him at his home, "he could just set and play pretty all day and all night and never play the same tune—play all them ol' hornpipes, and he could really play 'em, too." Lee was, Stokes recalled in a 1981 interview, "the best old-time fiddler I ever heard." Although he never recorded commercially, Lee taught his fiddling style to the teenaged Stokes, later a member of Columbia's best-selling stringband, Gid Tanner and the Skillet Lickers. Stokes, in turn, taught Lee's sophisticated style and several of his tunes to his close friend and bandmate, Clayton Mc-Michen, lead fiddler of the Skillet Lickers and later the leader of the

Georgia Wildcats. McMichen became one of the most influential fiddlers on old-time records, inspiring three generations of musicians to imitate his style, and his dynamic, progressive fiddling won him the National Fiddling Championship an astonishing eighteen times.[31]

Other Piedmont millhands wrote or popularized songs that eventually became part of the American folk song and country music canons. For example, within weeks of the 1903 wreck of the Southern Railway's fast mail train, which killed nine railroad employees on the outskirts of Danville, Virginia, two local cotton millhands named Fred J. Lewey and Charles W. Noell, awestruck by the wreckage they gazed upon at the accident scene, composed the lyrics to the classic train wreck ballad, "The Wreck of the Old 97," one of the most well-known and widely recorded songs in the history of country music. In December 1923, Henry Whitter, an aspiring guitarist and harmonica player who had learned the song some twelve years earlier from a co-worker in a Fries, Virginia, cotton mill, made the first of dozens of commercial recordings of the ballad. Eight months later, in August 1924, Vernon Dalhart recorded the song for the Victor Talking Machine Company, copying the lyrics directly from Whitter's original OKeh disc. Dalhart's recording of "The Wreck of the Old 97," coupled with "The Prisoner's Song," became the first hillbilly record to sell more than one million copies and helped introduce this new field of commercial music to a national audience.[32] Georgia guitarist and singer Paul Rice, who had in his youth worked with his brother Hoke in the mills south of Atlanta, claimed to have written the familiar song "You Are My Sunshine" in 1937 and then sold it for thirty-five dollars to Jimmie Davis, a popular Decca recording artist and future two-term governor of Louisiana. Rice's inspiration for the song, he later explained, had been an enthusiastic letter he received from a South Carolina female fan.[33] Arthur "Guitar Boogie" Smith, a Kershaw, South Carolina, textile worker who made his first recordings in 1938, wrote the 1955 novelty instrumental "Feuding Banjos," which later became famous as "Dueling Banjos" in Warner Brothers' 1972 film *Deliverance*. Other millhands, most notably Dave McCarn and Dorsey Dixon, composed occupational songs based upon their own firsthand knowledge of the miseries of work and life in southern textile mills. Several of these songs, including "Babies in the Mill," "Cotton Mill Colic," and "Weave Room Blues," emerged after World War II as classics within the urban folk music revival and the American labor movement. And the list of

Sheet music cover of "The Wreck of the Old 97,"
by Henry Whitter, Charles W. Noell, and Fred J. Lewey, 1939.
Courtesy of Norm Cohen.

Piedmont millhands' musical accomplishments and contributions goes on.[34]

Several factors account for Piedmont textile workers' dominance within the hillbilly music industry before World War II. One of the primary reasons is that talking-machine companies concentrated their search for new talent and their field-recording sessions in the Piedmont South, where hundreds of thousands of textile workers lived. Certainly, rich traditions of fiddling and stringband music flourished throughout the United States during the 1920s and 1930s, but the overwhelming majority of artists who were recruited to make hillbilly records resided in the South and made at least some of their recordings there as well. Before Nashville's emergence in the mid-1950s as the nation's undisputed capital of the country music industry, talking-machine firms expanded their hillbilly catalogs with new recordings cut either in the North in their permanent studios or in the South in temporary studios. Most of the very earliest hillbilly recordings were made in New York City. But, during the mid-1920s, firms increasingly began to use mobile recording crews and portable equipment to record southern artists on location in what were called "field-recording sessions." Recording crews usually visited several southern cities on these two- to three-month musical excursions. Typically, field-recording sessions ranged from a few days to several weeks at each location, during which time a team of usually two engineers made dozens and sometimes hundreds of wax masters in makeshift studios set up in hotel suites, concert halls, radio studios, vacant warehouses, and other available spaces. An A & R man who traveled with the recording team was responsible for locating and auditioning talent, selecting the material to be recorded, scheduling recording times, and generally supervising the recording of the wax masters from which phonograph records would be pressed. Once a session in a particular location concluded, the A & R man and the engineers crated up and shipped the recorded wax masters to the firm's factory, loaded up their portable recording equipment, and headed to the next designated city. These "remote recordings" or "location recordings," which were usually cheaper to produce than those made at firms' major studios, accounted for perhaps as much as three-fourths of all hillbilly records released between 1927 and 1930.[35]

Between 1923 and 1932, the major talking-machine companies

made regular field-recording excursions to Dallas, New Orleans, Memphis, San Antonio, and other southern cities in their efforts to record new selections for their hillbilly catalogs. But because of its rail accessibility to the New York–area talking-machine companies, its concentration of closely spaced, densely populated cities, and the scores of talented musicians these cities attracted, the Southern Piedmont emerged as the chief field-recording center in the South before World War II. Of the approximately one hundred field sessions at which hillbilly music was recorded between 1923 and 1932, a total of forty-three took place in the Piedmont cities of Richmond, Charlotte, Winston-Salem, Atlanta, and Birmingham. Indeed, firms sponsored almost twice as many field sessions in the Piedmont as they did in Mississippi River counties (twenty-two); more than twice as many as in Texas (twenty-one); and more than five times as many as in the Southern Appalachian Mountains (eight), long mistakenly considered the wellspring of commercial hillbilly music. Once field-recording sessions resumed in 1934 after a two-year hiatus during the worst years of the Great Depression, Piedmont cities remained the principal destination for these musical ventures prior to World War II.[36]

During the 1920s and 1930s, Atlanta ranked as the most important southern field-recording center for hillbilly music. With more than 370,000 residents in its greater metropolitan area in 1930 and two major radio stations that featured local hillbilly music programs, Atlanta boasted such a deep pool of musical talent that major record companies held no fewer than forty-two different field-recording sessions there between 1923 and 1942. Dozens of Atlanta-area old-time musicians, including Fiddlin' John Carson, Smith's Sacred Singers, and Gid Tanner and the Skillet Lickers, made hillbilly recordings in the city, as did national celebrities such as Jimmie Rodgers, the Carter Family, and Bill Monroe. For a brief period, RCA-Victor and Columbia even maintained permanent studios on Atlanta's Peachtree Street. Before World War II, Charles K. Wolfe has observed, Atlanta reigned as "the Nashville of the day."[37]

Charlotte, the largest city in the Carolinas, ranked a close second and, during the late 1930s, even rivaled Atlanta as the premier recording center in the South. During the mid-1930s, Charlotte's powerful 50,000-watt station WBT broadcast a Saturday-night hillbilly show called the *Crazy Barn Dance* and a series of daily fifteen-minute shows featuring artists such as J. E. Mainer and His Crazy Mountaineers, the Blue Sky Boys, and the Monroe Brothers. The city was also the headquarters for the Southern Radio Corporation, RCA-Victor's distributor in the Carolinas. Between 1936 and 1939, RCA-Victor staged six recording sessions in Charlotte, while Decca staged two (one in 1938 and another the following year). According to historian Thomas Hanchett, RCA-Victor and Decca field crews recorded more than 1,500 sides of hillbilly, blues, and gospel music in Charlotte at these sessions, and the records produced there helped these two firms maintain their dominant positions in the hillbilly recording industry during the late 1930s. Although singers and musicians from outside the region, including such nationally known stars as Uncle Dave Macon, Jimmie Rodgers, and the Carter Family, sometimes traveled hundreds of miles to attend a field-recording session in Atlanta or Charlotte, most musicians who recorded at these sessions resided within the urban-industrial corridor of the Piedmont South stretching between Danville, Virginia, and Atlanta, Georgia. And since textile workers accounted for approximately one-third to two-fifths of all manufacturing workers in Virginia, the Carolinas, Georgia, and Alabama during much of the interwar period, it stands to reason that they would constitute a significant proportion of the working-class singers and musicians who made hillbilly recordings at these Piedmont field sessions.[38]

Besides their close proximity to the major field-recording centers of Atlanta and Charlotte, several other factors help account for the overrepresentation of Piedmont millhands on hillbilly recordings. Between the 1890s and World War II, music formed an integral part of textile mill community life, particularly within "porch culture," in which small groups of friends and neighbors gathered on a family's porch in the evenings to visit, gossip, tell stories, sing and play music, and generally enjoy one another's company. Furthermore, southern textile workers, particularly women and girls, sang to themselves under the roar of the machinery as they worked at their spinning frames and weaving looms. Co-workers also sang together during lunch and restroom breaks. Before the mid-1910s, when widespread use of more reliable electrical power ended such occurrences, equipment breakdowns and drought-induced work stoppages at water-powered mills offered additional opportunities for music making. "There was a crowd of 'em that picked guitar and banjo and different string instruments," remembered Ethel Faucette, who worked at a Glencoe, North Carolina, cotton mill. "Well, this gang of boys would get their instruments and get out there in front of the mill, and they would sing and pick the guitar and the banjo, and different kinds of string music. Get out in front of the mill under two big trees, get out there in the shade and sing."[39]

Piedmont mill villages boasted a remarkable concentration of stringbands, brass bands, vocal quartets, and other musical ensembles. Out in the rural countryside, fiddlers and banjo pickers had long furnished the music for square dances, corn shuckings, barn raisings, school closings, and other social affairs in Piedmont farming communities. But the gathering of hundreds and sometimes thousands of workers in a crowded mill village offered millhands greater opportunities to form musical groups and to perform for appreciative audiences. Stringbands "multiplied in the mill villages," write the authors of *Like A Family*, "where musicians lived closer and had more occasions to play." In fact, although hillbilly music is usually characterized as a rural or rural-derived musical expression, the formation of stringbands, with actual names and regular members, was chiefly an urban phenomenon, particularly in the Piedmont South. "Everybody tried to make the old-time music at the cotton mills," recalled guitarist and singer Roy "Whitey" Grant, who worked at Gastonia's Firestone Cotton Mills. "A lot of the boys that we knew, or heard of, after we came in formed bands. They would get together in the cotton mills and the first thing you know they would form bands. On Saturday or Sunday, when the mill wasn't running, they had a little band stand up there and would draw a big crowd." Although millhands generally worked fifty-five to sixty hours a week prior to the 1933 enactment of the New Deal's National Industrial Recovery Act, their leisure time and close proximity to other musicians afforded them the chance to practice their music more regularly and to become proficient, accomplished entertainers. "They'd have a fiddlers' convention down in a mill village," explained fiddler Homer "Pappy" Sherrill, who fronted a Hickory, North Carolina, radio stringband during the mid-1930s, "and man, you'd get a little more classy type of bands, because they lived closer together, and they could practice and they were better bands. If you had an old country band, they played once a month, and sat on the porch and played all night long. But they didn't practice as much as they did in the mill village. So that made the difference."[40]

In addition to regular rehearsals, Piedmont textile musicians and bands also enjoyed frequent occasions to perform their music publicly for neighbors and co-workers. Within their own mill communities and in surrounding cities and towns, millhand musicians and stringbands supplied the entertainment for Fourth of July picnics, Memorial Day parades, county fairs, house parties, square dances, barbecues, ice cream suppers, political rallies, religious revivals, strike meetings, and even civic club meetings. "We've played in trucks out on the street, at an auction," recalled guitarist Rosa Lee Carson, who performed with her father, Fiddlin' John Carson, a fixture in Atlanta's working-class music scene. "They would be auctioning off the land in Lawrenceville and right out from Atlanta at other places, and they'd have a big old truck for Dad and myself to sit in to make music while they were auctioning off the land." Even in smaller textile towns, fraternal lodges, American Legion posts, Boy Scout troops, churches, and Bible study classes often engaged textile bands to play for fund-raisers in exchange for a percentage of the gate receipts. Playing at these functions allowed millhand musicians to earn much-needed extra cash and to hone their musical skills. Moreover, these performances enhanced their musical reputations within their communities, opening the way to recording contracts, radio shows, and additional paid performances. For many millhands, a career as a professional musician was far more attractive and financially rewarding than industrial work, and the monotonous routine, long hours, and low wages of textile work inspired hundreds of ambitious singers, fiddlers, and guitarists to try to escape their dead-end mill jobs through music making.[41]

During the first decades of the twentieth century, the annual fiddlers' conventions that flourished in Piedmont cities and towns attracted talented fiddlers, as well as banjo pickers, guitarists, and stringbands, from the neighboring mill districts by offering the chance to compete for cash prizes. "Seventy-five of North Carolina's most famous fiddlers gathered from far and near," reported a *Washington Post* correspondent about a 1908 Charlotte contest, "and the old familiar quickstep and break-down tunes that arose upon the air kept packed houses stamping and yelling for two nights in Charlotte's newly built auditorium. . . . Charlotte is a good deal of a 'citified' town," he concluded. "It gets most of the best theatrical attractions, the best singers and the best musicians, but it has enjoyed no musical attraction like it did the fiddlers' convention." Other public events, including church services, Sacred Harp conventions, religious revivals, and singing festivals, also nourished the grassroots musical culture of Piedmont millhands. In 1938, for example, approximately 10,000 participants converged on Textile Hall in Greenville for the fifth annual South Carolina Singing Convention. For two sweltering days in mid-August, reported the *New York Times*, the assembled crowds "perspired, fanned themselves with palmetto fans, ate box lunches, and sang sorrowful paeans of a world filled with trouble and disappointment and hardship, an earthly world that is to be followed by heavenly happiness and rest." Most of the singers, the article noted, were "tenant farmers, loom fixers from the mills, second hands, spinners, and weavers." Another *New York Times* article claimed that more than sixty such all-day singing festivals had been scheduled in the South Carolina Piedmont for the month of August 1939 alone. "The songs are all religious," it observed, "and what gratifies the ministers of many country and cotton-mill churches is that the young people have taken up this singing."[42]

In addition to these singing conventions, some Piedmont millhand musicians developed a high degree of musical expertise as a result of the "industrial welfare" programs sponsored by the region's larger, more progressive textile mills. Between the 1890s and the mid-1920s, dozens of firms hired music directors to give violin, guitar, mandolin, and singing lessons to their employees and their families. As a result, thousands of millhands learned to play musical instruments and to read standard musical notation. These corporate-sponsored music programs nurtured the grassroots musical culture that existed in Piedmont mill villages in other ways as well. Often, as part of these welfare programs, textile firms sponsored community brass bands and orchestras and occasionally even minstrel troupes, all of which were made up exclusively of their own employees. The fifteen-piece Glenn-Lowery YMCA brass band of Whitmire, South Carolina, "helps 'mightily' to make life gay when the dances, picnics and speakings are on," remarked the *Mill News* in 1920. In nearby Spartanburg, the Saxon Mills' Woodmen of the World Band, formed in 1920, gave semiweekly concerts at a local park, often furnished the music for the Spartanburg County Fair and the South Carolina State Fair in Columbia, and occasionally entertained the Southern Methodists at their summer assembly in Lake Junaluska, North Carolina.

The band's repertoire was as varied as its performance venues—ragtime numbers, marches, operas, and sacred songs. "It gives one a peculiar tug at the heartstrings," remarked Saxon Mills' social worker Marjorie Potwin, "to attend a band practice, where some twenty men in their working clothes, often covered with lint or grease from the mill, render with genuine depth of feeling 'Trovatore,' 'Poet and Peasant,' Sousa's Marches, or the beautiful old Christmas Carols." Although most of these bands performed chiefly at company functions and other local events, a few of them actually managed to cut some commercial phonographs records. For example, the Tubize Royal Hawaiian Orchestra, sponsored by the Tubize Artificial Silk Company of Hopewell, Virginia, a subsidiary of a Belgian-based corporation, recorded six issued sides for OKeh in 1929—two of which, "Whispering Hope" and "Sweetheart of Mandalay," appeared in the label's "Old Time Tunes" series.[43]

If textile firms, through their corporate sponsorship of music classes and community bands, stimulated the musical development of southern mill culture, so too did trade unions, particularly during periods of labor conflict and unrest. In fact, the unprecedented wave of textile strikes that swept the Piedmont South between 1929 and 1934 had the surprising side effect of further invigorating the musical culture of the region's textile mill communities. Music played a central role in these labor conflicts, not only because of southern millhands' penchant for singing but also because of union organizers' encouragement of singing as an effective means to foster solidarity among striking workers and to sustain their morale as a strike dragged on. To accomplish these goals, labor organizers often taught striking workers union songs to sing on the picket lines and at strike rallies. During the Gastonia Textile Strike of 1929, for example, Fred E. Beal and his staff of organizers for the northern-based Communist union, the National Textile Workers Union, actually distributed to strikers mimeographed typed copies of such labor anthems as "Solidarity Forever," "Casey Jones—The Union Scab," and "The Preacher and the Slave." The result of these interactions between northern labor organizers and southern millhands was an outpouring of musical creativity in the form of new worker-composed songs. Striking Gastonia workers, to cite one example, composed several dozen strike ballads that expressed their grievances and chronicled the major events of the conflict. Women and children displayed a particular gift for com-

Publicity photograph of the Tubize Royal Hawaiian Orchestra,
WRVA-Richmond radio stars and OKeh recording artists, ca. 1929.
Courtesy of the Archive Room, Appomattox Regional Library, Hopewell, Virginia.

posing such songs. "The children of the Gastonia strikers have put their words to tunes," the Communist newspaper, the *Daily Worker*, reported four months into the strike, "and any evening in the tent colony you can hear them singing in the typical 'blues' melody of the South." In creating these new strike songs, balladeers such as Ella May Wiggins, Daisy McDonald, and Odell Corley wrote new lyrics and fitted them to familiar melodies that could be sung by their fellow strikers along with hymns and gospel songs on picket lines and at union meetings. Stringbands also performed at these gatherings, and, in fact, one much-reproduced photograph from the General Textile Strike of 1934 depicts the Gastonia-based stringband, the Tobacco Tags, performing for dancing picketers outside the gates of the Clark Thread Mill near Austell, Georgia.[44]

Even the nature of industrial labor and the organization of the southern textile industry encouraged the blossoming of a vibrant musical culture in Piedmont mill communities. Tending weaving looms and spinning frames required dexterity and nimble fingers, and although some musicians had their musical careers abruptly ended by amputated fingertips, crushed hands, or other occupational accidents, the physical demands of textile work developed many of the fine motor skills used in playing the guitar, fiddle, and banjo. Moreover, before the implementation of scientific managerial practices and new labor-saving equipment in the mid-1920s eliminated the labor shortage that plagued the southern textile industry, labor turnover, especially among single men, remained high in the region's textile mills. This perpetual movement of dissatisfied workers from one mill to the next meant that the dynamic musical culture of almost every Piedmont mill village was continually being reenergized and transformed through the constant introduction of new singers and musicians, who brought with them new songs and tunes, new instrumental techniques, and new musical ideas.[45] And the comparatively cosmopolitan character of Piedmont mill villages, which gathered together workers from all across the region and Southern Appalachia, as well as from outside of the South—all with their own favorite songs and diverse musical skills—also contributed to the rich musical ferment that helped to spawn commercial hillbilly music.[46]

Despite the entrenched racism and segregation of the Jim Crow South and despite the racially exclusionary hiring practices of southern textile mills, perhaps the single most important musical influ-

Strikers dancing to the music of the Tobacco Tags at the Clark Thread
Mill near Austell, Georgia, during the General Textile Strike of 1934.
Courtesy of the Walter P. Reuther Library, Wayne State University.

ence on white millhands came from African Americans. On the outskirts of most Piedmont mill villages sat a black settlement, often disparagingly referred to as "Nigger Town," and within these communities resided the handful of African American men, who were employed in the mills' picker rooms and boiler rooms, and their wives and daughters, who sometimes worked as cooks and maids for white millworkers' families. Textile mill labor and village life brought white millhands and their families into daily contact with African Americans and thereby multiplied the cross-racial cultural exchanges that occurred between musicians of both races. African American fiddlers, guitarists, and gospel quartets, in fact, sometimes performed for audiences of white textile workers at company-sponsored picnics and other mill community gatherings. By introducing elements of Piedmont blues and gospel music into local white musical traditions, African Americans played a significant role, either in face-to-face encounters or indirectly through phonograph records, in the historical development of hillbilly music in the Southern Piedmont.[47]

Other factors also help to account for the explosion of musical creativity that occurred in Piedmont textile mill villages. Mill wages provided at least some millhands with enough disposable income to purchase relatively inexpensive, mass-produced musical instruments, radios, songbooks, sheet music, and the latest phonograph records, all of which exposed them to a broad spectrum of musical influences. During World War I, textile wages had soared to unprecedented levels, and the booming wartime economy allowed Piedmont millhands to take part in the nation's consumer culture more fully and more intensely than during any prior period. Although their wages hovered near the bottom for the nation's industrial workforce throughout the 1920s and 1930s, southern textile workers' active participation in the nation's consumer economy gave them access to a host of musical instruments and products. A 1926–27 study of 500 Gaston County, North Carolina, textile families, for example, reported that almost 40 percent (197) of them owned phonographs, radios, or musical instruments. Only two of these families had a radio in their homes, but over the next decade this tantalizing medium caught on quickly in Piedmont mill communities. By 1935, sociologist Frances Hampton found that of the 122 millhands she surveyed in the adjoining textile villages of Leaksville, Spray, and Draper, North Carolina, 87 of them owned radios, and almost half of these (40) also owned a phonograph. Listening to music on the radio ranked highest on the list of millhands' leisure-time activities, and, according to her informants, their favorite radio programs consisted of those featuring hillbilly stringbands and jazz orchestras.[48]

Although it often looked nostalgically to the past, hillbilly music stood firmly rooted in the new social realities of the twentieth-century South. By the mid-1920s, automobiles, radios, Victrolas, movies, and other modern technologies were transforming the musical sounds heard in mill villages across the Piedmont, and all these new commodities drew southern textile workers into a national mass culture that would profoundly influence the hillbilly music created in the region. Millhand singers and musicians certainly continued to learn new songs in face-to-face musical exchanges with friends, neighbors, and co-workers in Piedmont textile villages. But they also augmented their evolving repertoires with songs and tunes learned directly from phonograph records and radio broadcasts. Greater exposure to new songs and musical genres accelerated musical interchanges and spawned rapid stylistic innovations in which musicians recombined the contemporary sounds of the nation's commercial music industry with local fiddling and stringband traditions. A circa 1928 handbill, for example, announced that the Original Carolina Tar Heels "will entertain you with Hawaiian music on the Banjo [and] Old Time Southern Songs mingled with the latest Broadway Hits."[49]

Then, as now, the epithet "hillbilly" carried a multitude of negative connotations, and some textile stringbands, such as Fiddlin' John Carson and His Virginia Reelers and J. E. Mainer's Mountaineers, deliberately traded in common hillbilly stereotypes by dressing like hayseeds and dashing off raucous square-dance tunes.[50] But "hillbillies" is exactly what these talented and sophisticated entertainers were not. At the heart of hillbilly music stood a generation of white working-class musicians in their twenties to mid-thirties who had grown up in the industrial cities and textile towns of the Piedmont South. Although many of these young musicians often retained close ties to the surrounding rural countryside and sometimes even earned a living by combining industrial work with farming, the far-reaching effects of modernity profoundly touched their lives and music. Indeed, millhand musicians were undoubtedly children of the modern age, for they were among the first generation of southerners to be deeply influenced by automobiles, movies, radios, phonograph

Look Who's Coming!

The Original
CAROLINA TAR HEELS

VICTOR AND COLUMBIA RECORDING ARTISTS
— RADIO ARTISTS —

DOC. WALSH
The Banjo King of The Carolinas
— WITH —
GARLEY FOSTER
The Human Bird

ARTISTS IN THE RENDITION OF POPULAR NUMBERS THAT TOUCH THE HEART, MAKE YOU LAUGH OR PUT A TICKLE IN YOUR FEET

GARLEY FOSTER

DOC. WALSH

HONEST-TO-GOODNESS STRING MUSIC OF THE HILLS

You'll Be Pleased

Mr. Foster will really entertain you with his mockery of many, many birds, including Red Bird, Canary Bird, Mocking Bird, Wren, Pewee, Owls, Hawks, etc. Also imitation of a saw mill in operation. You'll marvel at the unusual talent Foster will display in this program of music with his guitar and harmonica. Nothing used in these imitations except the voice, well trained. An exceptional program. If in doubt come and hear him!

THE HUMAN BIRD

Southern Songs

Doc. Walsh will entertain you with Hawaiian music on the Banjo. Old time Southern Songs mingled with the latest Broadway Hits will be sung as only Doc. and Foster can sing them. A program of music and songs played and sung by Foster and Doc. that will please everyone. Don't miss this unusual program of high class entertainment.

It's Your Time For A Good Time!

PLACE

TIME

ADMISSION

Adults: _____   Children: _____

Handbill for the Original Carolina Tar Heels, ca. 1930.
Courtesy of Norm Cohen.

recordings, and mass-circulation newspapers and magazines. All of these staples of modern life offered textile workers glimpses of a world far beyond the tenant farms, mountain hollows, and rural hamlets that had circumscribed their parents' and grandparents' lives. A few lucky millhand musicians even managed to become full-fledged professional musicians who earned their livings by combining radio and recording work with regular performances in small-town theaters, schoolhouses, and auditoriums across the Southeast.

Those millhands who actually achieved professional or semi-professional status did so in large part thanks to the nation's expanding entertainment industry and mass media. The birth of the hillbilly recording industry in the 1920s and the emergence of Piedmont cities such as Atlanta and Charlotte as important regional recording centers increased the professional music-making opportunities for singers and musicians from Piedmont textile towns and mill villages. Radio also helped to accelerate the commercialization of hillbilly music. On March 15, 1922, WSB became one of the first commercial radio stations in the South when it began broadcasting with a 100-watt transmitter located on the top floor of the Atlanta Journal Building in downtown Atlanta. Within three months, several other Piedmont cities, including Richmond, Charlotte, and Birmingham, also claimed new radio stations. In their wake came a surge of radio-station construction throughout the region, as civic leaders and boosters vied to secure a wireless broadcasting station for their own city or town. Local companies, merchants, and newspapers launched most of these radio stations—the Larus and Brother Company of Richmond, the manufacturer of Edgeworth tobacco, established WRVA; a Charlotte Buick dealer owned WBT; and the Durham Life Insurance Company operated WPTF in Raleigh. By 1936, more than three dozen radio stations were concentrated in the industrial cities of the Southern Piedmont, ranging in size from powerful, 50,000-watt stations like WBT-Charlotte and WSB-Atlanta to small 100-watt stations like WBTM-Danville and WJBY-Gadsden.[51]

The expansion of radio stations across the Piedmont, particularly before the advent of national radio networks in the late 1920s, increased the demand for talented singers and musicians who could perform on live radio broadcasts. Atlanta, Charlotte, Richmond, and Birmingham, all of which boasted multiple stations, soon became important regional broadcasting centers that attracted hundreds of aspiring fiddlers, banjo pickers, and guitarists who wanted a chance to play over the airwaves. By the mid-1930s, Piedmont radio stations were regularly broadcasting a variety of hillbilly music programs, including WRVA-Richmond's *Corn Cob Pipe Club* and WSB-Atlanta's *Cross Road Follies*. Even more famous was WBT-Charlotte's *Crazy Barn Dance*, a Saturday-night hillbilly music show sponsored by the Crazy Water Crystals Company of the Carolinas and Georgia, the manufacturer of a best-selling laxative. Such programs offered great opportunities for the region's textile musicians and stringbands to bring their music to a far broader audience and, at the same time, to use their musical talents to escape the mills. During the 1920s, few musicians were paid to perform on the radio. Even after companies began to sponsor hillbilly radio programs, those musicians who performed regularly on these shows seldom received a salary. What money they earned came chiefly from parlaying their radio fame into stage show bookings in cities and towns across the Piedmont, where the textile mills and other industries had gathered tens of thousands of working-class families into concentrated pockets of music fans. The wages those industries paid allowed radio musicians and stringbands to find audiences with spending money in their pockets virtually every night of the week within a hundred-mile radius.[52]

By the mid-1920s, as a result of intensive road-building campaigns, thousands of miles of two-lane, hard-surfaced roads crisscrossed the Southern Piedmont, making it possible for musicians and stringbands to travel to far-flung recording sessions, radio dates, and concert performances. Stretching through the heart of Virginia, the Carolinas, and Georgia, U.S. Route 29—the Piedmont's central thoroughfare— "tied the principal towns and secondary roads together" in the region, notes historian Allen Tullos, and "paved the way for some of the first hillbilly bands to earn their livings performing at a Spartanburg high school auditorium one night, at a Gastonia mill recreation center the next evening, and on a Charlotte radio station the following morning." By the mid-1930s, dozens of radio stringbands, with names like J. E. Mainer's Crazy Mountaineers, the Briarhoppers, the Honolulu Strollers, Dr. Bennett's Smoky Mountain Boomers, the Crazy Cut-Ups, and Raymond Lindsey's Combinators, were barnstorming throughout Virginia, the Carolinas, and north Georgia, and sometimes as far away as Tennessee, Kentucky, and West Virginia, staging one-night shows for audiences of appreciative textile millhands, tobacco workers, auto mechanics, and farmers. One such 1935 *Crazy Barn Dance* package show in Belmont, North Carolina, sponsored by a local fraternal order, featured five stringbands and musical acts, blackface comedians, trick fiddling, yodeling, and two hours of "fun and frolic." Although it usually paid double or triple a weaver's wages, the life of a touring musician on the "kerosene circuit" was difficult. Fiddler Pappy Sherrill explained:

> Back in those days, you just rode and rode and played and played. It didn't matter how small the buildings were, you played 'em anyway, and just put on the full show. And you got up there and picked your heart out—with no p.a. system, sweat running off your elbows, you couldn't hardly feel the strings on the fiddle. Man, that was rough days then. We played many a place that had no electricity. They'd have an old gas lantern, setting on each side of the stage; that's all the light you had. The windows would be setting full of people, and you just had 'em around the walls. You couldn't even get your breath hardly. You'd just almost suffocate, that's how hot it was. We'd put on two shows sometimes, and it'd be midnight before we even got away from there.[53]

Piedmont textile workers not only avidly participated in the nation's expansive mass culture but also inscribed their working-class culture upon this same mass culture. As inhabitants of an emergent modern South transitioning between the old and the new, mill-hand singers and musicians wrote and performed songs that bore the stamp of both the older rural, largely agricultural world of many of their parents and grandparents and the newer urban-industrial world that they themselves occupied. These musicians lived at the precise historical moment that allowed them to combine the collective memories of the rural countryside with the upheavals of urban-industrial life to create a distinctive American music that spoke to the changing realities of working-class life in the early twentieth-century South. During the 1920s and 1930s, Piedmont textile musicians and stringbands helped create what the authors of *Like a Family* call "a blossoming regional culture," and audiences, both within and outside of the region, responded powerfully to this music. Collectively, commercial hillbilly records sold tens of millions of copies between 1922 and 1942, and powerful radio stations, such as Atlanta's WSB, Charlotte's WBT, and Richmond's WRVA, broadcast live performances of this music not just across the South but throughout the United States. For these two decades, Piedmont textile workers were more intensely involved in America's popular music industry than ever before or since. The following chapters tell the stories of some of these working-class singers, musicians, and songwriters and their enduring contributions to the genre that became American country music.[54]

KING OF THE MOUNTAINEER MUSICIANS FIDDLIN' JOHN CARSON

I'm the best fiddler that ever jerked the hairs of a
horse's tail across the belly of a cat.
—Fiddlin' John Carson, "Who's the Best Fiddler?" (OKeh, 1929)

In 1923, a middle-aged former textile weaver nicknamed "Fiddlin' John" Carson unexpectedly helped to launch a new genre of American popular music at an experimental recording session in downtown Atlanta. There, inside a vacant loft converted into a make-shift recording studio in mid-June, he recorded two selections for the OKeh label—"The Little Old Log Cabin in the Lane" and "The Old Hen Cackled and the Rooster's Going to Crow." The producer of the session, OKeh A & R (artist and repertoire) man Ralph S. Peer, of New York City, was less than thrilled with Carson's performance. Carson's fiddling was competent, if a bit rough and idiosyncratic, but Peer reportedly found his singing to be "plu-perfect awful." As the story goes, Peer refused to release either of Carson's recordings commercially until Polk C. Brockman, OKeh's Atlanta record distributor and talent scout, promised to purchase the entire first pressing of five hundred copies. Carson sounded "so bad," recalled Peer in a 1938 *Collier's* magazine interview, "that we didn't even put a serial number on the records, thinking that when the local dealer got his supply, that would be the end of it." But Peer was mistaken. One month later, he was astounded to learn that Brockman had sold out of his entire stock in a matter of a few days and had wired the company to order additional copies. With Carson's record selling briskly in Atlanta, Peer assigned it a label number in the OKeh catalog and released it on the national market in August 1923. Eventually, the disc sold an estimated several thousand copies. And although neither Peer nor Brockman, nor even Carson himself, realized it at the time, they had just set in motion a commercial music revolution.[1]

Carson's debut record marked the advent of what OKeh would soon designate as a new field of recorded commercial music called "hillbilly music," or, less pejoratively, "old-time music." The modest but surprising sales of this record indicated to Peer and his superiors at the General Phonograph Corporation, the manufacturer of OKeh records, that a promising, previously unrecognized market existed for old-timey grassroots music sung and played by ordinary white southerners. "One of the most popular artists in the OKeh catalog is Fiddlin' John Carson, mountaineer violinist, whose records have met with phenomenal success throughout the country," the *Talking Machine World*, a phonograph dealers' trade journal, reported in April 1925. "When Mr. Carson's first OKeh records were released it was expected that they would be active sellers throughout Southern territory, where this artist is a prime favorite with all music lovers. However, to the keen surprise and gratification of the General Phonograph Corp., the records by Fiddlin' John Carson not only attained exceptional popularity in the South but were received cordially by the public everywhere." Within two years of Carson's debut recording session, Columbia, Victor, Vocalion, and other northern-based phonograph companies were marketing similar old-time discs to record buyers not just in the South but throughout the United States. "The fiddle and guitar craze is sweeping northward!" proclaimed the splashy headline of a June 1924 Columbia ad. "Columbia leads with records of old-fashioned southern songs and dances." By the end of the 1920s, hillbilly records had become big business for the nation's talking-machine companies, and between the peak years of 1927 and 1930, more than one thousand new releases in this genre appeared on the market every year. Clearly, the southern fiddle breakdowns, sentimental ballads, and stringband selections captured on record by OKeh and other labels resonated with music lovers across the nation during the late 1920s.[2]

Although many country music historians credit him with waxing the first commercially successful hillbilly record, Carson was not the first traditional white southern musician to make commercial recordings for a major record label. A. C. "Eck" Robertson of Texas, Henry C. Gilliland of Oklahoma, and (possibly) Henry Whitter of Virginia had all entered recording studios three months to a year before Carson did. Nor did Carson succeed because he was a particularly gifted musician or singer, as Peer himself had quickly recognized. In fact, most of Carson's Atlanta contemporaries, especially younger, more popular music–oriented fiddlers such as Lowe Stokes and Clayton McMichen, regarded him as a mediocre bowman, at best. "He was an awful fine guy," recalled McMichen, "a poor fiddle player, but he sold it good— good showman. And he was a good, good man."[3]

Carson managed to succeed where previous musicians had failed chiefly because of two significant historical transformations that had reshaped early twentieth-century Atlanta. Momentous economic and social changes had swept through the Gate City of the New South in the decades immediately preceding Carson's debut recording session. Between 1900 and 1920, Atlanta's population had skyrocketed (more than doubling, from 89,872 to 200,616), and many of the newcomers, like Carson himself, were rural white migrants who had flooded into the city to work in its booming cotton mills, factories, and railroad yards. Carson's first record found a receptive market among these transplanted working-class Atlantans, who, like industrial workers throughout the modern South, were then an increasingly important but generally overlooked consumer group. Only recently had southern workers' newfound purchasing power thrust them into the vibrant commercial mass culture of Hollywood motion pictures, radios, Victrolas, and Model T Fords, and now their enthusiastic consumption of Carson's records made Peer and other talking-machine company executives take notice. As country music historian Bill C. Malone notes, "Peer had greatly miscalculated the tastes of the Georgia farmers and millworkers who had been hearing Carson at fiddle contests and political rallies for many years, and he apparently failed to realize that there were millions of working-class southerners who yearned to hear music performed by entertainers much like themselves."[4]

Carson also benefited from the publicity he received from Atlanta's powerful mass media, which had made him into something of a local celebrity in the decade before his recording debut. Unlike the tradi-

Fiddlin' John Carson, ca. 1923. Courtesy of the Southern Folklife Collection, Wilson Library, University of North Carolina at Chapel Hill.

tional southern musicians who preceded him on record, Carson aggressively promoted his own career by pandering to Atlanta newspapers and, more important, by performing regularly on the exciting new medium of radio. Since 1913, Carson's much-heralded appearances at Atlanta's annual Georgia Old-Time Fiddlers' Conventions had been attracting extensive newspaper coverage in the city's three major dailies, and, beginning in 1922, he garnered even greater acclaim as one of the earliest stars of Atlanta's fledgling radio station WSB. Over the next few years, his regular broadcasts on WSB, publicized in its parent company's *Atlanta Journal*, increased his popularity across Georgia and the Southeast and, indeed, throughout much of the nation. Like P. T. Barnum, Carson was a clever and relatively sophisticated self-promoter who skillfully manipulated the mass media for his own financial gain. As a consummate opportunist who was prone to recasting the facts of his life to his advantage, Carson claimed as his birthplace the hamlet of Blue Ridge in mountainous Fannin County, Georgia, and he cleverly adopted the identity of a cantankerous, free-wheeling Georgia hillbilly who distilled his own moonshine whiskey and dashed off tunes in a raucous, exuberant fashion. As old-time music historian Charles K. Wolfe has noted, Carson transformed himself into "a darling of the mass media and was written about more than any other [hillbilly recording star] from the 'golden age' of the 1920's."[5]

From that historic first recording, Carson rose to become one of the most popular hillbilly radio and recording stars of the 1920s and one of the most extensively recorded artists in OKeh's "Old Time Tunes" catalog. Billed as the "King of the Mountaineer Musicians," he recorded more than 180 sides for the OKeh and Bluebird labels between 1923 and 1934, consisting of solo selections, duets with his daughter Rosa Lee (known on record as "Moonshine Kate"), numbers with his stringband, the Virginia Reelers, and half a dozen sides with Emmett Miller and other artists as part of "The OKeh Medicine Show." Several of Carson's songs, among them "The Little Old Log Cabin in the Lane," "The Farmer Is the Man That Feeds Them All," and "You Will Never Miss Your Mother Until She Is Gone," are now considered early country music classics. Carson sustained his long, successful radio and recording career through constant innovation and reinvention of himself according to recording executives' demands and consumers' changing musical tastes. He began on record as a solo fiddler and then in 1924 recorded with stringband accompaniment. When they became popular in the late 1920s, Carson waxed nearly twenty "rural drama" skits for OKeh, with musical interludes and thin plots that revolved around the manufacture and consumption of moonshine whiskey in the north Georgia mountains. Meanwhile, throughout much of the 1920s and early 1930s, he continued to perform on Atlanta radio stations and to tour widely throughout Georgia and the Southeast until the Great Depression effectively destroyed his musical career.[6]

Besides his pioneering role as a hillbilly radio and recording star, Carson has attracted considerable attention from country music historians because of his unusual, archaic fiddling and vocal styles.[7] Carson grew up in post–Civil War rural north Georgia, and his music, as Robert Coltman put it, is "discordant, arrhythmic, [and] idiosyncratic." By modern standards of musical taste, he "sounds like a visitor from another world." Carson's biographers have typically portrayed him as coming of age isolated from the main currents of the New South's urban life and mass culture, and his distinctive sound has encouraged country music historians to view him chiefly as a rural folk fiddler who was decidedly out of touch with early twentieth-century popular music. Unlike the overwhelming majority of hillbilly musicians who recorded before World War II, Carson was forty-nine years old, well into middle age, when he cut his first sides. Hence, his biographers believe that much of Carson's musical style and repertoire had coalesced during the late nineteenth century, decades before he ever entered a radio or recording studio. This perception, combined with his primitive fiddling style, has prompted Carson's biographers to treat his recordings as an extraordinary opportunity to hear the premodern folk music, once so popular at barn dances, corn shuckings, and other social gatherings in the rural South, as it was probably performed in the late nineteenth century. In his liner notes to *The Old Hen Cackled and the Rooster's Going to Crow*, for example, Mark Wilson speculates that Carson's recording of the fiddle tune "Sugar in the Gourd" "captures the sound of the country dances of the 1890s" and then asserts that his records "afford a precious glimpse of an older fiddling style native to the deep south . . . which had virtually died out among younger fiddlers." Carson's major biographer, Gene Wiggins, likewise considers him "a representative nineteenth-century folk musician." Carson's recordings are significant, he argues, because they offer music historians the rare privilege of eavesdropping on older, nearly forgotten southern sounds. Musically, Carson "never had changed much since he developed a style back in the 1880s," Wiggins claims, and, thus, listening to his records offers "our best chance at hearing the sort of music many Americans liked in the 1880s."[8]

Certainly, Carson must be considered a historically significant transitional figure in the early development of hillbilly music, for he was undeniably a self-taught grassroots artist who bridged the cultural worlds between the traditional folk music of the 1890s and the commercial popular music of the 1920s. And his musical education did in fact begin in the late nineteenth century. But focusing too much on this aspect of his musical evolution obscures the more decidedly modern, urban influences that shaped Carson's hillbilly music. Even if we concede that he may never have dramatically altered his fiddling and vocal styles after 1900, Carson should not be mistakenly interpreted as an old-fashioned, untutored folk musician. Although he relied heavily upon droning, short-bow fiddling, and ornamented, melismatic singing, which seemed better suited for the country dances and minstrel shows of the late nineteenth-century rural South, his recorded songs were undeniably the product of the early twentieth-century urban South.[9]

Carson's music had its origins in a dynamic rural and small-town southern world that was, already by the end of Reconstruction, deeply enmeshed in the nation's emerging entertainment industry and mass culture. John William Carson was born on March 23, 1874, one of thirteen children, on a Cobb County, Georgia, farm about four miles north of the town of Smyrna. His father, James P. Carson, supported his wife and large family by combining cotton farming with industrial work as a section foreman on a construction crew building the Western and Atlantic Railroad. Around 1884, the Carson family resettled in nearby Marietta, a bustling market town with more than twenty-two hundred residents, some eighteen miles northwest of Atlanta. There, as a boy, John worked briefly—and carelessly—toting pails of water to the black railroad gangs building the Marietta and North Georgia Railroad. "John Carson, a waterboy with the M & NG railroad construction crew at Cox Cut," reported an 1886 newspaper, "tampered with a pistol Monday and accidentally shot himself in the leg."[10]

Apparently, Carson was living in Marietta when he developed a serious interest in music. His life as a musician, he later recalled, began on his tenth birthday, when he received a fiddle—reportedly a Stradivarius reproduction dated 1714—as a gift from his paternal grandfather, Allen W. Carson, the son of Irish immigrants, who, according to his grandson, was "a powerful fiddler too." Carson later claimed that he learned to scrape out his first fiddle tune, "Old Dan Tucker," as he walked home from his grandfather's nearby farm that very same day. "Nobody ever showed me anything about it," he once boasted to an *Atlanta Journal* reporter. "It was just a natural gift from the Lord. I'm proud I didn't take no lessons. They make fiddlers every day now, but I'm just a natural born fiddler." Two years later, according to one of the many legends surrounding him, the twelve-year-old Carson's spirited fiddling at an 1886 political rally in Copperhill, Tennessee, inspired Tennessee gubernatorial candidate Bob Taylor, himself an accomplished fiddler, to give Carson the nickname that would remain with him for the rest of his life: "Fiddlin' John."[11]

Throughout his teens and twenties, Carson mastered a large repertoire of fiddle breakdowns and traditional ballads, most of which he almost certainly learned from family members, neighbors, and other musicians in and around Marietta. But his exposure to traveling medicine shows, circuses, and especially minstrel shows, which staged seasonal appearances in Marietta and nearby north Georgia towns, also fostered his musical development. Wildly popular throughout the nation since at least the 1840s, minstrel shows featured white entertainers in blackface who performed routines of skits, dances, songs, and jokes, usually accompanied by banjo and fiddle music, in crude, exaggerated imitation of African Americans. Carson was especially attracted to the minstrel songs he heard. The first fiddle tune he claimed he ever learned to play, "Old Dan Tucker," was a famous minstrel number written by Dan Emmett in 1843. Carson also favored "Alabama Gal," "Old Uncle Ned," "Gonna Raise a Ruckus," "Turkey in the Straw," "Dixie," and other songs that either originated on the minstrel stage or achieved their greatest acclaim there. He later recorded more than eighteen of these minstrel songs, and although we lack specific evidence, the minstrel troupes he saw in his north Georgia youth may have inspired him to pursue a career as a professional entertainer.[12]

As an aspiring musician, Carson developed his fiddling skills throughout the 1880s and 1890s and earned some modest additional income by entertaining at square dances, political rallies, barbecues, and farm auctions in Marietta and the surrounding farming communities, sometimes accompanied by banjoist Land Norris and fellow fiddler Allen Sisson. At house dances, a host family would clear out the furniture in a room, roll back the rug, and invite their friends and neighbors over to an all-night square dance. A fiddler and sometimes a banjo player furnished the music, and occasionally a straw beater accentuated the rhythm by drumming broom-sedge straws, knitting needles, or wooden sticks ("fiddlesticks") on the fiddler's strings as he bowed them. Homemade whiskey would also be on hand, usually served in a bucket with a dipper, to quench the thirst of the musicians and dancers. Despite a pronounced stutter, Carson learned to call square-dance figures in a gruff, booming voice while he sawed away on the fiddle, which he often held against his shoulder, in the fashion of minstrel show fiddlers, rather than under his chin, in the fashion of classical violinists, so that it would not interfere with his calling. During the summer months, these Saturday night dances usually ended before midnight, but during the winter, when there were fewer farm chores to distract the revelers, such frolics might last as long as three days.[13]

Around 1893, while on his way to such a dance in nearby Roswell, Georgia, Carson met Jenny Nora Scroggins, a Cobb County farmer's daughter who was part Cherokee, and the following year the couple wed. Little else is known about Carson's life before the age of twenty-five, and what few shreds of historical information that do exist are sketchy and obscured by a jumble of half-true tales and legends, many of which Carson himself concocted and popularized in the interviews he later gave to magazine and newspaper reporters. If we believe the colorful journalism that later surrounded him, in his teens and early twenties Carson pieced together a living by working at a variety of jobs, including circus barker, racehorse jockey, cotton farmer, and moonshiner. During the 1890s, he made extra cash peddling wagonloads of apples, vegetables, and perhaps homemade whiskey at the farmers' market in Atlanta. On one such trip in 1899, Carson claimed, revenue agents arrested and incarcerated him in the Fulton County jail for selling moonshine liquor. According to an *Atlanta Journal Magazine* article published almost thirty-five years later, a trusting sheriff, on learning that his prisoner was a fiddler, temporarily freed Carson so he could compete in a local fiddling contest. When Carson won first prize, the legend goes, the sheriff released him from jail with three weeks still left on his sentence. Although this story is undoubtedly apocryphal, such trips to Atlanta would have certainly offered Carson the opportunity to hear the latest Tin Pan Alley ballads, ragtime numbers, and "coon songs" that reverberated throughout the city's vaudeville theaters, dance halls, amusement parks, and saloons. In Marietta, he was probably exposed to the same new music via phonograph cylinders, sheet music arrangements, and traveling entertainment shows. And, like the minstrel numbers he so enjoyed, Carson incorporated several of these new songs into his growing repertoire and later recorded them during the 1920s and early 1930s.[14]

A severe three-year panic rocked the national economy beginning in 1893, and as cotton prices collapsed and hard times besieged southern agriculture, Carson struggled to earn a living as a farmer in north Georgia. So, in January 1900, twenty-five-year-old Carson, his wife, Jenny—then eight months pregnant—and their three children loaded the family's sparse belongings into a wagon and moved to Atlanta to make a better life for themselves. Virtually destroyed by Sherman's army during the Civil War, Atlanta had resurged to become a booming metropolis, the reigning symbol and living embodiment of Henry W. Grady's New South progressivism. By the turn of the century, the city served as the transportation, commercial, and manufacturing hub of the Southeast, with eight major railroads linking it to the rest of the nation. Atlanta's economic expansion, ushered in by Grady and other New South industrial capitalists, sparked spectacular population growth. The number of Atlantans had soared from fewer than 38,000 in 1880 to almost 90,000 by 1900. Many of these new residents, like the Carsons themselves, had fled the hardscrabble farms of the Georgia Piedmont and Southern Appalachia to find jobs in Atlanta's flourishing economy. By 1910, the city's population had climbed to almost 155,000, with rural white migrants making up approximately one-third of its population. The low-wage, manual labor performed by John Carson and others who had fled the countryside fueled Atlanta's manufacturing, transportation, and service industries, making the city, as sociologist Robert E. Park remarked in 1906, "representative of the 'New South,' the South in which the once despised 'poor white' is rapidly becoming a factor. In Atlanta, the 'cracker' has come into his own."[15]

As a result of the steady flood of country migrants, turn-of-the-century Atlanta consisted of a mixture of decidedly rural neighborhoods embedded within a cosmopolitan urban atmosphere. "Back in those days, it was country in Atlanta," recalled Rosa Lee Carson, the youngest of the family's nine children, who was born in 1909 and grew up in one of the city's textile mill districts. "Why, you could even raise a cow out there in your yard, and we did have chickens for a long time. And Mama, she'd have her a big garden out there in the backyard, and we'd raise okra and corn and Irish potatoes, tomatoes, onions." By the early 1910s, as historian Clifford M. Kuhn notes, Atlanta also contained more than a dozen skyscrapers, an excellent streetcar system, swanky, landscaped upper- and middle-class neighborhoods, a bustling entertainment district, and other modern urban amenities. Like New Orleans, the cosmopolitan southern port city that gave birth to jazz around this same time, Atlanta was home to a relatively diverse population that more closely resembled those of New York and Chicago than those of other southern cities. A 1913 *Atlanta Journal Magazine* article, drawing upon then-current ethnic and racial stereotypes, described one of the city's main business districts:

> Decatur Street is the home of humanity as it is, where the negro is found in his element of fried fish and gaudy raiment, and characters which might have walked through the pages of Dickens or O. Henry, have their joys and sorrows, and laugh and cry, make love and die, even as their brothers and sisters of Peachtree Street. Here bearded mountaineers from Rabun County brush shoulders with laborers fresh from the Old Country. Jewish shopkeepers pass the time o' day with the clerk of the Greek ice cream parlor next door. The Yankee spieler cries his wares and the Confederate veteran buys 'em, and through it all negroes, yellow, black and brown, thread their laughing, shiftless way, types of the south which could be seen in no other city in the land in all their native picturesqueness. Decatur is the melting pot of Dixie.[16]

Upon his arrival in Atlanta in 1900, Carson found work at the Exposition Cotton Mills, a textile-manufacturing complex situated along the Western and Atlantic Railroad on the northwestern outskirts of the city. Its main mill was housed in the same building that had been used for the celebrated International Cotton Exposition of 1881, an industrial fair that was intended to showcase Atlanta as an ideal center for cotton textile manufacturing and to attract northern investors. Carson worked there until around 1913, when he took a job at the

Fulton Bag and Cotton Mills in south-central Atlanta, then the city's largest textile plant. Founded in 1889 by a German Jewish immigrant named Jacob Elsas, Fulton Mills was a massive complex consisting of four textile factories, several machine shops and warehouses, and a mill district, originally called the Factory Lot but eventually known as Cabbagetown, which contained dozens of company houses. The firm, which manufactured sheeting and cotton and burlap bags, employed approximately twelve hundred workers, most of them from Georgia Piedmont farms and surrounding textile towns. The Carson family, which by then included nine children, rented a four-room mill house on Carroll Street in the Factory Lot, a working-class neighborhood adjacent to Fulton Mills where most of the firm's workers and their families resided. Carson worked sixty hours a week as a weaver—a relatively high-paying, skilled position—at Mill No. 1 and earned an average of around ten dollars a week by 1914. Unprotected by effective child labor laws, Carson's six older children also eventually went to work there while still in their early teens, as was the custom of the day. Only his three youngest children escaped textile labor entirely.[17]

Carson found greater prospects for industrial employment in Atlanta, and he also seized the new opportunities that the city offered to earn extra money as a street performer. Nearby Decatur Street, located just across the Georgia Railroad tracks from the Fulton Mills complex, formed the center of Atlanta's working-class entertainment district. There, to the increasing alarm of Progressive reformers, different classes of black and white Atlantans mingled and socialized in the restaurants, dance halls, movie theaters, blind tigers, poolrooms, cocaine dens, and brothels that lined this bustling avenue. After his eleven-hour shifts ended, Carson often walked to Decatur Street and played on sidewalk corners and trolley cars for spare nickels and dimes. One of his favorite spots to entertain was Bud Johnson's poolroom, a popular Decatur Street "near-beer" joint, whose clientele of cotton millhands, transient laborers, and rural migrants appreciated Carson's fiddle breakdowns and sentimental songs. On Saturday nights, Carson could often be found fiddling and calling figures for house dances and social gatherings in the Factory Lot neighborhood, accompanied by other musicians with whom he worked at Fulton Mills. As his reputation grew, Carson began to get occasional work as a paid entertainer in greater Atlanta.[18]

WHERE
FULTON BAGS
ARE MADE.

Bird's-eye view of Fulton Bag and Cotton Mills, Atlanta.

Courtesy of Special Collections and Archives, Georgia State University Library.

Fiddling provided Carson with both a sense of male working-class identity and an outlet for public self-expression and creativity usually denied poor, semiliterate men of his social class. It also provided him with a financial hedge against periodic downturns and layoffs in the boom-and-bust cycle of Atlanta's industrial economy, a fact that Carson soon came to appreciate. In 1914, a strike organized by the United Textile Workers erupted at Fulton Mills. On May 20, several hundred millhands, including Carson and his children, walked off their jobs to protest an unfavorable change in the company's labor contract and the firing of more than a hundred union members. Within a week, Oscar Elsas, the president of Fulton Mills, ordered the evictions of more than two hundred striking workers and their families, including the Carsons, from their company-owned houses in the Factory Lot. Interestingly, a photograph of Fiddlin' John Carson's eviction, taken by a local photographer hired by the union, survives. Carson stands on the front steps of his mill house, dressed in a dark, threadbare suit and tie, his trousers hiked up above his midsection, and stares, grim-faced, into the camera. In his left hand, he clutches one of his prized fiddles (he apparently owned several by this time), and, with the other, he pets his coon dog. Behind him, a gaunt-faced company agent relaxes in a chair on the porch and looks on. The inscription reads: "'Fidling' John About to Be Evicted."[19]

Many of the evicted strikers and their families secured temporary lodging in the so-called Textile Hotel, a large boardinghouse leased by the United Textile Workers. But the Carsons relocated to a rented house on nearby Dekalb Avenue, which bordered a predominantly black neighborhood that white millhands called "Niggertown." While on strike, Carson provided for his family by selling hotdogs at Bud Johnson's poolroom and fiddling and passing the hat on Decatur Street sidewalks, on trolley cars, and at the farmers' market near the Georgia state capitol. "For my family things were better than [for] most [strikers'] families," recalled Horace Carson, who went to work sweeping floors in the mill at the age of nine. "We had . . . food from the Union, and money from Dad playing the fiddle and singing." Only days after the walkout began, striking workers erected picket lines around the massive factory complex in an effort to force a settlement. But their efforts failed to cripple production. Elsas stubbornly refused to negotiate a settlement and instead recruited strikebreakers to run the abandoned weaving looms and spinning frames, and hired addi-

Fiddlin' John Carson about to be evicted from his mill house during the Fulton Bag and Cotton Mills strike, 1914. Courtesy of the George Meany Memorial Archives.

tional security guards to police his mill property. Then he simply waited for the starving strikers to concede defeat. On May 15, 1915, nearly a year after it had begun, the bitter strike disintegrated, and Carson and his children returned to their jobs at Fulton Mills.[20]

During the 1914–15 strike at Fulton Mills, Carson managed to keep his family afloat with his music, in part because he had already made a name for himself as a popular public entertainer during the controversial Leo Frank murder case. On April 27, 1913, one year before the Fulton Mills strike began, a night watchman at the National Pencil Factory on Forsyth Street in downtown Atlanta discovered the partially nude body of a thirteen-year-old employee named Mary Phagan, beaten and strangled, on a trash heap in the basement of the factory. Two days later, Atlanta police arrested Leo M. Frank, the twenty-nine-year-old Jewish, Brooklyn-born superintendent of the firm, and charged him with the murder of his employee. Frank's arrest and subsequent trial stirred up a hostile whirlwind of class resentment and anti-Semitism among white working-class Atlantans, who believed that Frank had raped and then murdered the girl.[21]

Carson followed the legal developments in the Frank case with a particularly keen interest, since his in-laws had once been neighbors of the Phagan family in Marietta. Carson himself probably knew Phagan's stepfather, John W. Coleman, when they worked together at Exposition Mills. Convinced of Frank's guilt, Carson used his fiddle music as a political weapon against him. Throughout the trial and the series of court appeals that followed, Carson whipped up popular antagonism against Frank by composing at least three ballads about the murder, including his most famous, "Little Mary Phagan," a maudlin song whose lyrics portrayed Phagan as a sweet, virtuous girl and Frank as a brutal fiend. During the gripping monthlong trial, Carson sang his popular ballad for the huge crowds that gathered outside the Fulton County courthouse, while his children hawked cheaply printed broadsides of the sixteen-stanza song for ten cents apiece.[22]

An overwhelming amount of evidence incriminated Jim Conley, the factory's black janitor, who testified as the prosecution's chief witness. Nonetheless, on August 25, 1913, after a highly sensationalized trial plagued by mob spirit and anti-Semitism, a jury found Frank guilty. The following day, the judge sentenced him to death. As Frank's execution date neared, his case emerged as a cause célèbre, which, according to eminent southern historian C. Vann Woodward, "for a time rivaled the European war as a subject of national attention." National civil rights and Jewish organizations flooded Georgia governor John M. Slaton's office with telegrams and letters pleading for the commutation of Frank's sentence. Then, in June 1915, with only a few days left in office, Governor Slaton, disturbed by the obvious miscarriage of justice at the trial, commuted Frank's sentence to life imprisonment. "Frank belonged to the Jewish aristocracy, and it was determined by the rich Jews that no aristocrat of their race should die for a working class Gentile," thundered Thomas E. Watson, the aged, frustrated newspaper editor and former Populist vice-presidential candidate, in the weekly *Jeffersonian*. "While the Sodomite who took her sweet young life basks in the warmth of Today, the poor child's dainty flesh has fed the worms." Slaton's clemency enraged white rural and working-class Georgians, and when a mob of 5,000 men gathered outside his mansion, the governor declared martial law and mobilized the Georgia National Guard. Ironically, Carson, a guardsman since 1914, may have been in the regiment assigned to protect the very governor he now so despised from the mob that, through his street-corner musical performances during Frank's legal appeals, he had helped to incite. Two months later, on the night of August 16, 1915, twenty-five masked vigilantes calling themselves "the Knights of Mary Phagan" slipped into the Milledgeville Prison Farm, abducted Frank from his cell, and drove him to Marietta. There, near Mary Phagan's birthplace, his self-appointed executioners lynched him.[23]

Carson maintained a high profile throughout the Frank case, and on the day after the lynching he entertained what the *Atlanta Constitution* called "the morbidly curious" throngs of spectators who converged on the Cobb County courthouse in Marietta to gawk at Frank's grisly corpse and to celebrate the triumph of so-called popular justice. "'Fiddlin' John' Carson swayed the crowds," reported the newspaper, fiddling and singing his ballad about Phagan's murder "over and over again," as the "crowd . . . cheer[ed] and applaud[ed] him lustily. . . . 'Fiddling John,' the troubadour of the mountains, basked in 'reflected glory,' and it was not until the courthouse crowds began to tire of his songs and fiddle that he departed, reluctantly." Eventually, Carson's "Little Mary Phagan" emerged as a classic murder ballad, and southern working-class communities continued to sing it for decades afterward.[24]

Just as surely as Carson's class identity as a textile worker shaped his experiences in Atlanta, so too did his racial identity as a white rural migrant. Carson had grown up in Cobb County among ex-slaves and their children and had delivered water to black railroad section gangs in his youth, but his transition to living and working in a crowded, segregated urban environment altered his perceptions of race. By 1900, when Carson arrived in Atlanta, African Americans made up 40 percent of the city's nearly 90,000 residents, and memories of slavery were dissipating as the generations of elderly ex-slaves died and new generations of African Americans, born into freedom, came of age. Despite segregation ordinances and laws, Carson had extensive contact with African Americans in Atlanta. As the foreman of the picker room at Exposition Mills, he supervised the black laborers who unpacked the five- to six-hundred-pound bales of compressed cotton and cleaned the fibers in the hot, sweaty, dusty initial stages of production. Moreover, Carson frequently encountered black Atlantans during his musical excursions to Decatur Street, and, throughout much of his life, Carson and his family resided in working-class neighborhoods that bordered African American neighborhoods, first on Carroll Street in the Fulton Mills district and then on DeKalb Street near "Niggertown." The close proximity of working-class white and black Atlantans and intense feelings of neighborhood territoriality resulted in frequent racial clashes. "Well, after dark a colored man wasn't allowed in Cabbagetown at all," recalled one resident decades later. "We'd rock them out of there, you know. We used to have a time rocking the colored boys back across the railroad track towards Edgewood Avenue and over on Decatur Street."[25]

In Atlanta, Carson inhabited a highly segregated urban world wracked by racial tensions and hostilities, fueled in large measure by entrenched white racist attitudes and by fierce competition for jobs, housing, and public spaces between black and white rural migrants. As historian Clifford M. Kuhn argues, the creation of Atlanta's new urban-industrial order in the decades following Reconstruction also spawned a "new racial order . . . in the region, along with numerous attendant anxieties, fears, and frustrations." Since the 1890s, a rising tide of virulent racism and Jim Crow laws, enacted by anxious white Georgia Progressives, had relegated African Americans to second-class citizenship, "colored only" public facilities, and usually the dirtiest, lowest-paying menial jobs. Occasionally, racial tensions exploded into murderous violence. Carson and his family were living in a mill village near Exposition Mills, which residents called, with no small bit of irony, Happy Hollow, when the devastating Atlanta Race Riot of 1906 erupted. On September 22, the racist rhetoric of a disfranchisement campaign and incendiary newspaper accounts of an "intolerable epidemic of rapes" of white women allegedly committed by "black brutes" sparked five days of sporadic rioting. During the course of the riot, marauding, drunken white mobs destroyed millions of dollars of black-owned property, killed at least twenty-five black Atlantans, and wounded hundreds of others. "The mobs entered barber shops where respectable Negro men were at work shaving white customers, pulled them away from their chairs and beat them," wrote the nationally known muckraking journalist Ray Stannard Baker, who investigated the riot and later wrote a series of exposés for *American Magazine*. "Cars were stopped and inoffensive Negroes were thrown through windows and dragged out and beaten." Although the Carsons did not live near the center of the rioting, Carson nonetheless bought a box of ammunition and, armed with his rifle, kept an all-night vigil at his family's door. Doubtless, the murderous Atlanta Race Riot of 1906, combined perhaps with his anxieties about crumbling racial hierarchies and the "proper place" of African Americans in New South urban centers, later prompted Carson to join the revived Ku Klux Klan, which was founded in Atlanta in 1915.[26]

Although he was already well known among working-class white Atlantans, Fiddlin' John Carson garnered even greater fame as a contestant at the well-publicized Georgia Old-Time Fiddlers' Conventions held annually between 1913 and 1935. Since at least the nineteenth century, fiddlers had furnished the entertainment at county fairs, picnics, square dances, and other social gatherings throughout the nation, and Georgia, like other southern states, claimed a particularly rich old-time fiddling tradition. But fiddlers' contests, at least the larger and more theatrical ones, were a comparatively modern and largely urban phenomenon that did not emerge, for all intents and purposes, until the 1890s.[27] Sponsored by the Georgia Fiddlers' Association (of which Carson was a charter member), sometimes in conjunction with the United Daughters of the Confederacy, the Georgia Old-Time Fiddlers' Conventions were held in Atlanta's Municipal Auditorium, constructed in 1909 and located downtown on the corner of Courtland and Gilmer Streets. Each year between fifty and

61

seventy fiddlers, including a few women, took the stage to compete for cash prizes, ribbons, and sometimes instruments donated by local merchants. Prominent Atlantans such as Judge Richard Russell of the State Court of Appeals and Judge Andy Calhoun of the City Criminal Court often served as contest judges. Thousands of spectators from all classes of Atlanta society and the surrounding towns flocked to this popular event, which usually ran for two to four nights. The first convention, which opened on April 1, 1913, only weeks before the murder of Mary Phagan, drew an estimated audience of more than 8,000 spectators over the course of three evenings. That event, the *Atlanta Constitution* promised in pre-contest advertisements, would include such "old favorites as 'Soldier's Joy,' 'Billy in the Low Grounds,' 'Chickens before Day,' 'Bacon and Collards,' and a score of others your granddaddies used to dance to in the country cabins before they moved to Atlanta and got rich in real estate and turned into grand opera lovers."[28]

With his rousing rendition of "Cacklin' Hen," Carson placed a respectable fourth out of a field of fifty fiddlers at that inaugural 1913 contest. For his efforts, he pocketed twelve dollars in prize money—more than a week's wages at Fulton Mills. Following the contest, Carson "called the figures" as six fiddlers sawed away and Atlanta's society set danced quadrilles and Virginia reels at a re-created mountain hoedown. For more than a decade and a half, Carson remained a featured contestant and crowd favorite at these annual fiddlers' conventions, claiming the state championship three times between 1913 and 1927 and placing at several more contests. Carson was known, however, as much for his droll comedy and superb showmanship at these affairs as he was for his fiddling skills on his prized instrument nicknamed "Sally Gal." In 1914, before an audience of 4,000 spectators, Carson captured the fifty-dollar first prize largely due to his high jinks and amusing stage antics. As one correspondent reported in a colorfully embellished article in the national magazine *Musical America*:

> "Fiddlin'" John Carson started for the Auditorium in the early afternoon of that day, with many a pause to view the sights of the city. His beloved fiddle was tucked under his arm in a pillow slip, and at his heels, tugging at a bit of plow-line, trotted "Trail," the sorriest looking hound that ever bayed at the moon.

Contestants at the annual Georgia Old-Time Fiddlers' Convention outside
Atlanta's Municipal Auditorium, 1920. Courtesy of the Southern Folklife
Collection, Wilson Library, University of North Carolina at Chapel Hill.

"No dogs allowed," said the janitor at the Auditorium, curtly.

"This ain't no common dawg," retorted "Fiddlin'" John, pulling "Trail" closer into view. "That there houn' is the best tribble singer in Gawgy. Ain't you, 'Trail'? Speak up, now."

By this time the custodian of the building, who knew of "Fiddlin'" John's fame, had reached the door. He admitted the "fiddler" and his dog, and that night the mountain Kubelik played while old "Trail" sang. His song was the echo of a fox chase under a Georgia moon, then a memory of the biggest coon ever treed. As he warmed to his work his master's playing became gradually a mere obbligato to his solo.

When he paused "Fiddlin'" John laid down his violin as the audience cheered. The judges withdrew and "Fiddlin'" John sang "Run, Nigger, Run Patterroll'll Ketch You," while they made their decision.

"Fiddlin'" John then was declared the best of Georgia fiddlers, . . . and the convention adjourned.[29]

Carson's performances at the annual Georgia Old-Time Fiddlers' Conventions attracted extensive press coverage in Atlanta's three daily newspapers during the 1910s and 1920s, and some of these stories were picked up by national newswire services and published in newspapers throughout the United States. Some years he performed with a rustic stringband called the Simp Phony Orchestry from Lickskillet. Other years he served as the master of ceremonies. But, always, he was there, clowning with other contestants, hamming it up for newspapermen and photographers, and delighting the large crowds. "We have had fancy fiddlers who played a half-hour at a time and never struck a tune," Carson complained to an *Atlanta Journal* reporter in 1919. "They'd fiddle and fiddle and do all kinds of stunts, and never get nowhere. They may do all right in grand opery, but they don't belong in a fiddling contest for the championship of Georgia. That's flat. Nothing goes but old-fashioned fiddling. Just pure elbow grease and awkwardness and a tune that gets into your feet. I figure that any tune that will let a man keep his feet still ain't worth the playing."[30]

Several of the regular contestants at the Georgia Old-Time Fiddlers' Convention, including Carson, "Uncle Bud" Silvey, and "Red-Neck" Jim Lawson, worked in Atlanta-area cotton mills. Dozens of others hailed from north Georgia market towns and textile villages.

But most of the colorful accounts published by Atlanta newspapers and national magazines depicted Carson and the other contestants as backwoods Georgia hillbillies from remote mountain hollows who were completely divorced from twentieth-century urban life. "The fiddlers," claimed a *Musical America* correspondent in 1919, "know almost nothing of modernity or cities; and their rendition is pure, even antique, often accompanying their fiddle tunes with untrained and old-fashioned but quaintly charming voices." Often abetted by the Georgia Fiddlers' Association's publicists and the fiddlers themselves, Atlanta newsmen perpetuated popular stereotypes of mountain feuds, moonshining, and dangerous gun-totin' hillbillies to attract curious crowds of city dwellers to these circus-like conventions. A 1914 *Atlanta Constitution* headline, for example, assured spectators that "Fiddlers Will Check Weapons before Big Contest Begins."[31]

Newspaper and magazine stories tied the old-time fiddling heard onstage at the Municipal Auditorium to an idyllic rural world that seemed to be rapidly vanishing and whose musical arts, as result, would soon be completely drowned out by the deafening roar of Tin Pan Alley and jazz. A reporter for the *Atlanta Constitution*, for example, emphasized how old-time fiddling conjured up nostalgic longings for a lost agrarian world in his 1918 article, "Days of Old Are Recalled When Georgia Fiddlers Meet." For him and for many other white Atlantans, many of them only a generation removed from farm life, the fiddlers' conventions evoked "the feel of the old red clay hills of Georgia and the little old cabin with the golden corn swaying in the wind. . . . Shut your eyes and you forget you are in Atlanta's big Auditorium. You can see the rafters of the old barn and smell the hay up in the mow and 'most hear the lowing of the cattle and the rustle of the hen who complains about her disturbed nest." Similarly, an *Atlanta Journal* reporter noted, "In these russet festivals, the melodies of the Old South are awakened, and the spirit of folklore comes back to flesh and blood. The life of mountain and meadow, of world-forgotten hamlets, of cabin firesides aglow with hickory logs, the life of a thousand elemental things grows vivid and tuneful." During the 1920s, observers across the nation, including automobile tycoon Henry Ford and Agrarian novelist and essayist Andrew N. Lytle, lamented that old-time fiddling was a musical art that, like the rural America that produced and once sustained it, would soon pass into oblivion. "The old-time fiddler, like the old Confederate soldier, year by year their lines grow thinner and thinner, [and] both will soon be history," mourned a Tennessee newspaper in 1926. "The tunes that filled the frontiersman's log cabin from puncheon floor to rafters . . . will be gone and the rising generation will never know anything of them."[32]

In order to create a compelling, marketable image for himself, Carson cleverly tapped into these and other romantic ideas about rural America, particularly the southern mountains, then swirling about the nation. Beginning in the 1870s, *Scribner's Monthly*, *Harper's Weekly*, *Atlantic Monthly*, and other middle-class magazines that flourished after the Civil War had published scores of travel accounts and local color articles about the strange highlanders of Southern Appalachia. Originally, southern mountaineers were portrayed chiefly as primitive but noble folk of undiluted Anglo-Saxon ancestry, who, living an isolated existence far from modern civilization, maintained the nation's rugged pioneer virtues and folkways. Articles with titles such as "Our Contemporary Ancestors in the Southern Mountains" (1899) and "The Southern Mountaineer: Our Kindred of the Boone and Lincoln Types" (1900) celebrated so-called mountain whites as conservators of these cherished virtues and customs, which seemed to be vanishing in an increasingly modern urban-industrial America. Ironically, the invention of Southern Appalachia as an idyllic, pre-industrial Eden frozen in the eighteenth century actually coincided with sweeping social and economic transformations in the region, as railroads penetrated the mountains and opened the region's abundant natural resources to the exploitation of logging and coal-mining companies. But in a nation undergoing rapid industrial development, urban growth, and technological innovation, Southern Appalachia came to represent, in the words of historian C. Brenden Martin, "a symbolic counterpoint to the progressive thrust of modern urban society," and its mountain whites were seen as noble primitives who, though sorely in need of social and cultural uplift, preserved the nation's pioneer folkways and purest Anglo-Saxon bloodlines.[33]

The prevailing image of the venerable, dignified mountaineer did not last long, however. After the turn of the twentieth century, the image of southern mountaineers as depraved "hillbillies" quickly supplanted earlier portrayals of quaint and dignified "mountain whites." In 1900, for example, in one of the first published definitions of the term, the *New York Journal* described the "Hill-Billie" as "a free and untrammeled white citizen of Alabama, who lives in the hills, has no means to speak of, dresses as he can, talks as he pleases, drinks whiskey when he gets it, and fires off his revolver as the fancy takes him." In the popular imagination, southern mountaineers increasingly came to be perceived as an ignorant, backward people, who, prone to feuding, moonshine drinking, and laziness, seemed ridiculously out of step with modern twentieth-century America. Although earlier local color writers and missionaries had attributed the cultural persistence of pioneer virtues and folkways among "mountain whites" to their prolonged isolation, by the 1920s this same supposed isolation now emerged as the chief explanation for what was increasingly seen as their cultural degeneracy.[34]

Carson seized upon some of these hillbilly themes and images and crafted them into a captivating public persona for himself. For example, in the newspaper and magazine publicity surrounding the fiddlers' contests, Carson usually identified himself—or was identified—as a resident of the remote north Georgia mountain hamlet of Blue Ridge, in Fannin County, despite his birth in Cobb County and long-standing residence in Atlanta. As Bill C. Malone notes, "Fiddlin' John and his publicists . . . surely knew about John Fox, Jr.'s, romantic novels of Appalachia, and about the hit song of 1913, 'Trail of the Lonesome Pine,' which had referred to the 'blue ridge mountains of Virginia.'" Carson or his handlers were also undoubtedly aware of Billie—The Hill Billy (1915), The Feud (1920), Moonshine Valley (1922), and dozens of other nickelodeon films that portrayed stereotypical views of southern mountain life as sometimes idyllic and bucolic, but sometimes degenerate and violent. Carson also promoted his fabricated mountaineer heritage through his outrageous stage antics and the amusing homespun anecdotes with which he regaled magazine and newspaper writers. And he clearly relished his affected role as a whiskey-bent and hell-bound hillbilly fiddler. "The only things I does really well is moonshining and fiddling," he told newsmen in 1914, "and since the 'revenooers' caught me moonshinin' twicet, the old lady 'lows I better quit for good. That leaves me only the old fiddle."[35]

Although he was already an accomplished fiddler when he arrived in Atlanta in 1900, Fiddlin' John Carson matured and developed as an entertainer as a result of his participation in the city's thriving musical culture. During the 1910s, the Fulton Mills district, like Atlanta's other working-class neighborhoods, boasted a lively music scene due to the convergence of dozens of industrial laborers from all across the Georgia Piedmont and the Southeast who sang and played musical instruments. Shortly after moving to the Factory Lot, Carson met several talented musicians who also worked at Fulton Mills, including twelve-string-guitarist Ed Kincaid, who later toured and probably recorded as a member of Carson's stringband, the Virginia Reelers. The wife of another one of Carson's future sidemen, T. M. "Bully" Brewer, was employed as a designer at Fulton Mills. Brewer, a one-legged former railroad brakeman from Knoxville who relocated to Atlanta in 1917, played on more than forty sides with Fiddlin' John Carson and His Virginia Reelers between 1925 and 1929. Guitarist Marion "Peanut" Brown, who moved to Atlanta with his family around 1912 at the age of five and grew up in the Factory Lot, also worked in Fulton Mills alongside his widowed mother and a sister. In 1934, he accompanied Carson on several of his final Bluebird recordings. Carson soon became a mainstay in this vibrant neighborhood music scene, performing with local musicians at house parties and other social affairs in the Fulton Mills district.[36]

With dozens of amateur singers and musicians from across the Georgia Piedmont and parts of Southern Appalachia, the Fulton Mills district functioned as a musical crucible in which Carson and other millhand musicians traded instrumental techniques, musical ideas, and songs and tunes with one another. Likewise, the annual Georgia Old-Time Fiddlers' Conventions also ranked as important forums for musical exchange. When not competing on stage, Carson and the other contestants often gathered in the alleys in back of the Municipal Auditorium, where, according to an *Atlanta Constitution* reporter in 1923, they could be found "holding a reunion, swapping yarns, and picking up new tunes to take home and play at corn shucking and barn dances." Carson also struck up musical friendships with other Atlanta-area musicians whom he met at the Georgia Old-Time Fiddlers' Conventions, including Gid Tanner, Riley Puckett, Clayton McMichen, Lowe Stokes, and Earl Johnson, all of whom went on to make hillbilly records in the wake of Carson's commercial success.[37]

Atlanta's rapid industrial expansion and urban growth also allowed enterprising musicians like Carson to form stringbands and to entertain working-class audiences with spending money in their pockets. After the unsuccessful strike at Fulton Bag and Cotton Mills ended in

May 1915, Carson returned to work for the company. By 1920, however, he had left the textile mills to work as a self-employed housepainter and part-time entertainer. Around that same time, Carson formed the Virginia Reelers, a revolving ensemble of stringband musicians anchored by fellow Atlantans T. M. "Bully" Brewer on guitar and Earl Johnson on second fiddle. The band soon won a large following in the greater metropolitan area as a result of its frequent performances at stage shows, political rallies, store openings, and Confederate veterans' reunions. "FIDDLIN' JOHN CARSON IS COMING!" announced one of his publicity posters. "Fiddlin' John Carson and His World Distinguished Orchestra of Blue Ridge Mountain, Georgia Will Give a Series of Instrumental and Vocal Concerts in the City Auditorium." Circuses and medicine shows that regularly visited Atlanta sometimes hired Carson to attract crowds of ticket buyers. "He'd draw 'em, I guarantee," declared his son Horace Carson. "Every medicine show back then they'd hire my daddy. He'd go down there and play and that field would be full of people every night. And he'd be the only body making music at all." [38]

In addition to the shows he staged in the Atlanta area, Carson and the Virginia Reelers also took their old-time music on tour, following the network of narrow hard-surfaced highways and gravel roads that connected Atlanta to the small cities and textile towns of Georgia and the surrounding states. By 1920, Carson had purchased a second-hand 1913 Model T Ford for $150, so that he and his bandmates could tour more extensively. Later, after he began recording for the OKeh label, he emblazoned the rear of his cars with "FIDDLIN JOHN CARSON Record Artist." On these early road trips, Carson usually took at least three sidemen with him, most of them a generation younger than himself. Besides Brewer and Johnson, among the regulars who toured with Carson were banjo players Bill Badgett and Bill White and twelve-string guitarist Ed Kincaid, with whom Carson had once worked at Fulton Mills. A minstrel comedian, also named Earl Johnson — who was nicknamed "Freckled-Faced Earl" and who played the musical saw and a one-string, cigar-box fiddle — also toured with the Virginia Reelers. Barely in his teens, Carson's son Clyde often chauffeured the band from town to town, so that Carson and his accompanists were free to enjoy their whiskey during the ride. [39]

By 1922, Carson and the Virginia Reelers were barnstorming throughout north Georgia, East Tennessee, and the Carolinas, and sometimes as far away as Kentucky, Virginia, and West Virginia. On their musical excursions, Carson and his bandmates entertained for paying crowds at theaters, auditoriums, and rural schoolhouses. On other occasions, the group gave impromptu performances on courthouse squares and street corners, during which the band members sold twenty-five-cent song sheets and collected tips from the crowds that gathered to listen. Carson's traveling stage show packed small venues across Georgia and the Southeast by combining raucous old-time stringband music, trick fiddling, blackface minstrel routines, and even a few religious numbers and current popular hits. At a June 1924 show at the Charleston, West Virginia, armory, noted a local newspaper review, Carson and the Virginia Reelers performed their version of "You've Got to See Mama Ev'ry Night (Or You Can't See Mama at All)," a 1923 Tin Pan Alley hit that Sophie Tucker had popularized. By all accounts, Carson was a master showman—ripping off a frenzied fiddle breakdown, pausing in mid-measure to deliver droll one-liners or cornpone wisecracks, and then sawing away again. "He'd stand there and pick on that fiddle and stutter and crack jokes so that nobody cared whether he played the thing or not," recalled Peanut Brown, one of Carson's guitarist sidemen in the early to mid-1930s. "He put on a better show than Clayton McMichen did. Clayton could play beautiful fiddle music, but how many people want to hear two hours of beautiful fiddle music? John just sort of had people mesmerized." Carson targeted his stage shows to appeal broadly to ticket buyers, as an advertisement for a 1927 schoolhouse concert in Gwinnett County, Georgia, suggests: "John Carson . . . holds an audience spellbound and uses dexterous skill in handling . . . a fiddle in forty-seven different positions. Some of his selections entertain; some sacred pieces appeal to the finer sensibilities, and in fact, when you come out to the entertainment you will go back home not only feeling that you have been well entertained, but that you have received a full measure of inspiration to urge you onward and upward."[40]

But even more than fiddlers' contests, stage shows, and newspaper features, it was the powerful new mass medium of radio that, as Carson once claimed, allowed him finally to abandon his much-neglected house painting business and become a full-time professional entertainer. "Radio made me," he told a *Radio Digest* correspondent in 1925. "Until I began to play over WSB, more than two years ago, just a few people in and around Atlanta knew me, but now my wife thinks she's a widow most of the time because I stay away from home so much playing around over this part of the country." Carson was one of the first traditional white southern musicians to perform on radio, and he regularly appeared on Atlanta's WSB (whose call letters stood for "Welcome South, Brother"), the self-proclaimed "Voice of the South," throughout most of the 1920s. A subsidiary of the *Atlanta Journal* and originally located on the top floor of the Atlanta Journal Building, WSB became one of the first commercial radio stations in the South when it began broadcasting with a 100-watt transmitter on March 15, 1922, only days before its crosstown rival, the *Atlanta Constitution*'s WGM (later WBBF), went on the air. Three months later, WSB upgraded to a state-of-the-art 500-watt Western Electric transmitter, and in the uncluttered ether of the early 1920s, the station's signal could be heard on clear nights by an estimated two million listeners throughout the United States and as far away as Canada, Mexico, and Central America.[41]

On September 9, 1922, six months after the station went on the air, Carson made his debut on WSB, accompanied by a stringband trio, as part of a Saturday night variety program. That night, a flood of telegrams and telephone calls from appreciative listeners poured into WSB's studio, prompting station manager Lambdin Kay to invite Carson back for an encore performance. The next day, the *Atlanta Journal* published two photographs of Carson, one by himself and the other with his band, under the caption "Georgia Fiddlers Invade Radio World," and reported that "Fiddlin' John Carson, champion southern bowman, fresh from Fannin County . . . , is an institution in himself and his singing of 'The Little Old Log Cabin in the Lane' and the playing of 'Turkey in the Straw,' 'Old Joe Clark,' and 'The Old Hen Cackles,' by Fiddlin' John and his [three] cronies . . . was enough to put any program over with a rush." In fact, Carson proved such a hit with listeners that he made thirteen more appearances on WSB, either solo or with his stringband, in the remaining sixteen weeks of 1922. Like many other radio stations during the experimental period of the early 1920s, WSB broadcast a wide variety of musical entertainers, ranging from opera tenors and glee clubs, to Hawaiian guitarists and jazz ensembles, to whistlers and even clog dancers. But the station built one of its earliest and largest listening audiences around Carson's fiddle music. "No star of WSB's roster has a bigger following than Fiddlin' John," proclaimed the *Atlanta Journal* in a May

71

1923 announcement for one of his band's upcoming broadcasts. "The old fashioned tunes of Dixie seem to grow in favor as the years pass, and no more expressive interpreters exist than the musicians aligned for Friday night's broadcast." Three months earlier, the newspaper had remarked that "there can hardly be a hamlet in the Union where 'The Voice of the South' has not already spread Fiddlin' John's name and fame."[42]

Carson's enthusiastic reception on WSB in late 1922 and early 1923 created new broadcasting opportunities for such legendary Atlanta musicians as blind guitarist and tenor singer Riley Puckett, fiddler Clayton McMichen, blind Holiness preacher, gospel singer, and musician Rev. Andrew Jenkins (who could play harmonica, guitar, whistle, kazoo, trombone, and piano), fiddler Earl Johnson, and, on rarer occasions, Gid Tanner and the Skillet Lickers. On November 29, 1922, for example, WSB hosted an "Old-Fashioned Concert" consisting entirely of old-time music, "in response to many requests, including one from a group of Confederate veterans in Owensboro, Kentucky." Carson and his trio of accompanists performed on that evening's program, as did McMichen, Puckett, and Tanner, the last of whom the newspaper billed as "Dixie's only rival to Fiddlin' John." In fact, during the 1920s, WSB featured more than one hundred different hillbilly acts, including such rustically named stringbands as the Mud Creek Symphony, George Daniell's Hill Billies, and the Fiddlin' Wampus Cats. Following WSB's lead, dozens of radio stations across the South and Midwest broadcast occasional live programs of old-time fiddlers and stringbands. Several of these stations began to feature regular weekly broadcasts of old-time fiddling programs and barn dances, including Chicago's *WLS Barn Dance* (later known as the *National Barn Dance*), which premiered in April 1924, and, even more famously, Nashville's *WSM Barn Dance*, which first aired in November 1925 and became known, in late 1927, as the *Grand Ole Opry*. As country music historian Robert Coltman has noted, "What began with Fiddlin' John Carson in Georgia in 1922 shortly became a musical revolution of explosive force that helped break the bonds of conventionality and create a commercial popular music."[43]

Carson's rising radio stardom helped him to launch his long-lived recording career for OKeh Records. The manufacturer of OKeh records, the General Phonograph Corporation, was founded in 1915 (as the Otto Heineman Phonograph Supply Company), one of more

Georgia Fiddlers Invade Radio World

Journal's Radio Truck

At the places and hours announced below, The Atlanta Journal's radio truck will receive and amplify programs transmitted by WSB, the radiophone broadcasting station of The Atlanta Journal.

Sunday

10:54 a. m., at Piedmont park.
5 to 6 p. m., at city stockade.
8 to 9 p. m., at Grant park.

Monday

7 to 8 p. m., at Riverside.

Tuesday

7 to 8 p. m., at Battle Hill sanatorium.

Wednesday

7 to 8 p. m., at Rock Springs.

Thursday

5 to 6 p. m., at Oglethorpe university.
7 to 8 p. m., at Chamblee, Ga.

Friday

7 to 8 p. m., at corner of Kennedy and Davis streets.

Fiddlin John Carson, famous champion of Georgia, and some of his cronies, who is now spreading his name and fame far and wide with the aid of The Journal radiophone. The Fannin county mountaineer scored heavily on two of WSB's program last week and will be presented again before the picturesque gathering of old-time fiddlers at the auditorium soon.

"Georgia Fiddlers Invade Radio World," *Atlanta Journal*, September 10, 1922. Courtesy of the Southern Folklife Collection, Wilson Library, University of North Carolina at Chapel Hill.

than one hundred talking-machine firms that entered the U.S. market during World War I to take advantage of Americans' growing demand for commercial entertainment. In 1918, the firm introduced its flagship label, OKeh, and within four years it ranked as one of the nation's best-selling independent record labels. By the end of 1922, however, a postwar recession, coupled with a nationwide radio craze, eroded OKeh's and other companies' record sales.[44] Early in June 1923, on one of his regular business trips to New York City, Polk C. Brockman, the enterprising twenty-four-year-old record department manager of James K. Polk, Inc., OKeh's Atlanta wholesale distributor, discussed strategies to boost slumping record sales with Ralph S. Peer, a General Phonograph Corporation executive, at the firm's main office on West Forty-fifth Street. As the A & R director for the firm's OKeh label, the thirty-one-year-old Peer was responsible for auditioning, selecting, and overseeing the recording of artists. Three years earlier, he had assisted Fred W. Hager, the firm's musical director, at the recording session at which Mamie Smith had recorded "Crazy Blues," which had inaugurated OKeh's flourishing new field of "race records." Now, searching for other new artists and material to stimulate sales, Peer proposed to Brockman his idea of recording a selection of musicians at an experimental field-recording session in Atlanta, the first out-of-town excursion of its kind in the South. Brockman liked the idea and agreed to line up a handful of promising new artists to record. Before returning to Atlanta, however, Brockman had a brainstorm. One afternoon he took in a picture show at the Palace Theatre in Manhattan's Times Square, where he watched a newsreel of a Virginia fiddlers' convention. Suddenly, he recalled the annual Georgia Old-Time Fiddlers' Convention, pulled out a memo pad, and jotted himself a note in the darkness of the theater: "Fiddlin' John Carson—local talent—let's record."[45]

The following week, Peer and two engineers set up their portable recording equipment in an empty loft that Brockman had rented on Nassau Street, off Spring Street, in Atlanta. With the assistance of his firm's sales manager, Brockman had recruited an assortment of popular local acts for Peer and his crew to record, including two jazz bands, a black theater pianist, a violinist, a hotel dance orchestra, two female blues singers, the Morehouse College Quartet, and, of course, Fiddlin' John Carson, who cut two of his signature selections, singing and accompanying himself on fiddle, on June 14. His first side, "The

Little Old Log Cabin in the Lane," was an 1871 minstrel song, and the other was a traditional fiddle tune titled "The Old Hen Cackled and the Rooster's Going to Crow." Although Peer expressed serious reservations about releasing them commercially, Brockman, who had a better sense of the Atlanta market, believed Carson's records would sell well locally. Meanwhile, to help promote Carson's record, Brockman cleverly arranged for Carson to sell copies of his disc at the opening night of the annual Georgia Old-Time Fiddlers' Convention, which was being held in the Cable Piano Company Building as part of the entertainment program for the national convention of the Elks Fraternal Order. On July 10, Carson played his record on a large phonograph on the hall's stage and quickly sold dozens of copies. "I'll have to quit makin' moonshine and start makin' records," Carson reportedly quipped.[46]

Peer's initial doubts about the appeal of Carson's music quickly vanished. Delighted by its brisk sales, he released Carson's record for nationwide distribution in August 1923 in OKeh's "Popular Music Series," which included a wide assortment of Broadway tunes, dance orchestra instrumentals, sacred selections, Hawaiian songs, and novelty numbers. Compared to the other selections in this series and to Jazz Age popular music in general, Carson's fiddling and singing sounded primitive and badly outdated. Therein, however, lay much of the charm of his seemingly old-fashioned music. "The OKeh Records by Fiddlin' John Carson, Georgia mountaineer and minstrel, are steadily growing in popularity," the *Talking Machine World* reported in August 1925. "The quaint and little known melodies recorded by this artist have met with the approval of the public, as steadily mounting sales figures show."[47]

Beginning with Carson's recordings, OKeh transformed southern fiddle and stringband music, heard for decades at fiddlers' conventions, square dances, and other social gatherings, into an immensely popular commercial product. But as a largely unknown commodity in American consumer culture, this newly recorded music required definition and explanation before it could be effectively advertised and marketed. Since the 1890s, talking-machine companies had released dozens of recordings of southern folk ballads, banjo instrumentals, fiddle tunes, plantation airs, barn dance medleys, and comic "rube" monologues.[48] But most of these cylinders and discs had been marketed either as novelty records or, as was the case with Carson's debut record, in popular music series. Firms made little distinction in their advertising literature between these recordings and those of standard popular selections. Searching for a marketable image to attach to Carson's record, OKeh's advertising executives seized upon highly romanticized, nostalgic stereotypes of a preindustrial mountain South similar to the ones that Atlanta newsmen had been using to describe the Georgia Old-Time Fiddlers' Conventions since 1913. In September 1923, OKeh Records launched its national advertising campaign for Carson's debut record with a modest description in the *Talking Machine World*. "A picturesque addition to the OKeh record catalog," the press release began, "is the announcement of OKeh records by Fiddlin' John Carson, an old mountaineer from the hills of northern Georgia, who made these records during the recent visit of the special OKeh recording expedition to Atlanta. . . . On his OKeh record Fiddlin' John Carson plays the accompaniment for two famous Southern selections and sings the numbers in his own quaint way."[49]

By 1924, however, the momentum of Carson's record sales encouraged OKeh's advertising agents to promote Carson's recordings, as well as those of fellow southern musician Henry Whitter, a Fries, Virginia, cotton millhand, as a new and discrete genre of American commercial music. On June 15, 1924, in a handsome, full-page ad in the *Talking Machine World*, the General Phonograph Corporation proudly announced that its OKeh label had initiated a promising new field of commercial music called "Hill Country Music." "These two mountaineers were discovered by OKeh!," the ad proclaimed triumphantly. "Seeing the recording possibilities in their quaint style and their 'Old Time Pieces,' OKeh recorded some of their selections and at the same time uncovered a brand new field for record sales." The ad billed Carson as "Seven times Champion Fiddler of Georgia and King of Them All!" and identified Whitter, "another mountain star," as a "most novel entertainer" who accompanies himself on harmonica and guitar "when he sings those quaint 'Old Time Pieces.'" Above the ad copy, pen-and-ink portraits portrayed the two musicians not as stereotypical hillbillies but as sober, respectable working people dressed in their best Sunday clothes. "The craze for this 'Hill Country Music,'" the ad concluded, "has spread to thousands of communities north, east and west as well as in the south and the fame of these artists is ever increasing. And this again gives OKeh Dealers another new field discovered, originated and made possible by the manufacturers of OKeh Records, the Records of Quality."[50]

This June 1924 ad signaled a pivotal shift in the talking-machine industry's promotion of what were soon called hillbilly records, and henceforth firms would aggressively market these numbers, once designated simply as part of novelty or popular record series, as a distinct field of commercially recorded music. To promote this music, advertising agents and copywriters generated a cluster of highly nostalgic marketing images that depicted old-time music as the distant, fading echoes of an imagined preindustrial rural South, particularly a mountain South, that was being rapidly transformed by the modern world. Hillbilly music, what the OKeh ad initially called "Hill Country Music," had arrived.[51]

Meanwhile, in November 1923, at Ralph Peer's invitation, Carson traveled to New York City and recorded a dozen more sides, including the early hits "You Will Never Miss Your Mother Until She Is Gone" and "Be Kind to a Man When He's Down," at the General Phonograph Corporation's main studios on Union Square. During the week he spent in the city, he signed a recording contract as an exclusive OKeh artist. The following month, OKeh published a press release in the *Talking Machine World* that touted Carson's recent recording session and, playing up his hillbilly image, exaggerated his discomfort and unfamiliarity with modern urban America. On Fiddlin' John Carson's first recording trip to New York City, the announcement claimed that he found "too much city and not enough 'country' to suit his taste and he was glad to return to the sunny South." Such a rube-in-the-big-city account, of course, ignored the fact that by the time this release appeared, Carson had been residing in the city of Atlanta for nearly twenty-five years.[52]

Carson's growing national success encouraged Ralph Peer to seek out other southern fiddlers, as well as guitarists, banjo pickers, and Sacred Harp groups, who could play and sing similar old-time numbers for OKeh Records. By the end of 1924, OKeh's "Popular Music Series" contained some forty records by Carson and other traditional southern white musicians, including Henry Whitter, the Jenkins Family, Bascom Lamar Lunsford, A. A. Gray, the Georgia Sacred Harp Quartet, and Chenoweth's Cornfield Symphony Orchestra. In October 1925, OKeh inaugurated a special 45000 "Old Time Tunes" series in which to market its new hillbilly records, which paralleled the label's 8000 race

records series. The first release in OKeh's "Old Time Tunes" series, "Run Along Home with Lindy"/"To Welcome the Travellers Home," recorded in June 1925, featured Fiddlin' John Carson, with his daughter Rosa Lee providing guitar accompaniment. Meanwhile, OKeh's mounting sales encouraged competing talking-machine companies to enter this new market and even to record cover versions of Carson's hits for their own labels. By 1924, Columbia, Vocalion, and Victor were recording similar old-time fiddlers, banjo players, and stringbands in their permanent northern studios and, increasingly after the advent of electrical recording in 1925, at field sessions in southern cities, particularly in Atlanta and other Piedmont textile centers.[53]

By 1924, Carson's phonograph records and radio appearances had made him a celebrity throughout Georgia and much of the South, and he and the Virginia Reelers sought to profit from his fame by touring more extensively than ever. That summer they performed a grueling schedule of one-night engagements at small-town theaters, high school auditoriums, and state fairs. "I'm mighty nigh caught up on this touring business," Carson told WSB listeners in July 1924. "I've seen most of Tennessee, Kentucky, Virginia, West Virginia, Illinois, and other foreign lands since I left, and it only makes me want to come back to Georgia." Carson and the Virginia Reelers scheduled many of these personal appearances in Piedmont textile towns and Appalachian coal centers, where, as a result of industrial development, the appreciative audiences of millhands and miners had enough disposable income to afford his show's comparatively steep fifty-cent, seventy-five-cent, and one-dollar tickets. "The Famous 'Champion Fiddler of the South' and his Virginia Reelers are setting the country wild with their Mountain Tunes and Old-Fashioned 'Folksy' Music," proclaimed a June 1924 advertisement in the *Middlesboro Daily News*. "Their program will contain all the old favorites that everybody has sung and danced to in years gone by." Other newspaper advertisements billed Carson as "the Renowned OKeh Artist" and urged fans, "You've Heard Him on Records and over the Radio—Now Hear Him in Person!"[54]

Neither Carson nor his bandmates received any financial compensation for their WSB performances, but their radio exposure helped them to plug their latest record releases and to book concert dates across the Southeast. Small-town civic organizations, school associations, and theater managers who had heard Carson perform on WSB contacted him in care of the radio station to schedule shows, guaranteeing him a specified amount of money or a percentage of ticket receipts. Carson was so popular, in fact, that in September 1924 an Atlanta theater impresario hired him, reportedly "at stupendous expense," as a country dance fiddler for the Lyric Players' production of *Mrs. Wiggs of the Cabbage Patch*, based on Anne Hegan Rice's best-selling 1901 melodramatic novel about the struggles of an eternally optimistic widow and her large brood of children in a Louisville, Kentucky, shantytown. According to newspaper reviews, Carson "stirred the audience to uproarious applause," and at one point in the performance, the enthusiastic theatergoers "nearly cracked the floor 'patting juba' to his tune." His fourteen-year-old daughter, Rosa Lee, appeared in the production as a hillbilly girl who, according to the *Atlanta Journal*, "demonstrated the approved method of dancing up in the hills." [55]

During the mid-1920s, Rosa Lee Carson often toured with her father as a member of his band. Born in Atlanta on October 10, 1909, she began singing and buck-and-wing dancing as part of her father's musical act when she was only seven years old. "They would send for us when I was just a small tot like this," she recalled. "And I'd sing for my daddy. I'd take his hat off and put it on my head and get on the school stage and sing for him." By the age of fourteen, she was already competent on both the banjo and the guitar, the latter a Christmas gift from her father. When she was fifteen, Rosa Lee accompanied her father for the first time on a recording at a June 1925 session in New York, at which she played guitar on five numbers; at the same session she also recorded two solo sides, the ballads "Little Mary Phagan" and "The Lone Child," accompanying herself on guitar. Thus, she became one of the first women to record old-time music, following the duets and solos of North Carolina fiddler Eva Davis and banjoist Samantha Bumgarner on Columbia in April 1924 and the solos of fourteen-year-old Georgia guitarist Roba Stanley on OKeh four months later. Shortly after she graduated from high school, Rosa Lee became a permanent member of her father's recording and touring bands, and by August 1928 she was being billed on records as "Moonshine Kate," a nickname that OKeh talent scout Polk Brockman gave her to enhance her hillbilly image and one that she embraced for the rest of her life.[56]

Amid his busy schedule of radio broadcasts, concert tours, and the occasional theater production, Carson remained in great demand as

Fiddlin' John Carson and his daughter, Rosa Lee Carson, later known on record as Moonshine Kate. *Talking Machine World*, August 15, 1925. Courtesy of the Southern Folklife Collection, Wilson Library, University of North Carolina at Chapel Hill.

a recording artist, and he recorded at least once and sometimes as many as five times a year for OKeh, producing more than 160 sides for the label, between 1923 and 1931. Almost half of these recordings consisted of traditional southern fiddle tunes and secular folk songs, notably "Soldier's Joy," "Hell Broke Loose in Georgia," "John Henry Blues," and "Sugar in the Gourd," on which Carson and His Virginia Reelers captured the high-spirited dance music of the South. Carson also recorded a smattering of comical novelty songs, among them misogynistic numbers about the pleasures of bachelor life ("The Batchelors' Hall") or the miseries of marriage to nagging wives ("I'm Going to Take the Train to Charlotte" and "I'm Glad My Wife's in Europe"), and some half-dozen numbers that featured drinking as a central theme ("Old Aunt Peggy, Won't You Set 'Em Up Again?," "If You Can't Get the Stopper Out Break Off the Neck," and "The Drunkard's Hiccups"). A devout Baptist and regular churchgoer who refused to fiddle or drink on Sundays and who, in 1919, performed at the popular evangelist Rev. Billy Sunday's revival in Chattanooga, Carson also recorded eight gospel songs, some of them well-known Protestant hymns, including "At the Cross," "Bear Me Away on Your Snowy White Wings," "I Intend to Make Heaven My Home," and "The Old Ship Is Sailing for the Promised Land," but these recordings have been far overshadowed by his more well-known fiddle tunes and ballads.[57]

Carson also displayed his showmanship and comedic talents on a series of "rural dramas" that he and Rosa Lee recorded for OKeh between 1928 and 1930. Apparently, he ventured into this new field of comedy records in response to Gid Tanner and the Skillet Lickers' best-selling rural drama skit for Columbia, "A Corn Licker Still in Georgia," the first installment of which sold more than a quarter of a million copies. Tanner and the band's ongoing skit, which eventually ran to fourteen parts between 1927 and 1930, revolved around a group of moonshiner musicians in the north Georgia mountains. Perhaps at the encouragement of OKeh executives, who sought a competing series of such recordings for their label, Carson cobbled together a few skits of his own, which combined corny comedy routines with brief musical interludes. He and his daughter recorded their first skits, "Moonshine Kate," "John's Trip to Boston," and "John Makes Good Licker," at an August 1928 field session in Atlanta. Over the next two years, they waxed an additional fifteen skits, among them such intriguing titles as "You Can't Get Milk from a Cow Named Ben,"

"She's More Like Her Mother Every Day," "Corn Licker and Barbecue, Parts 1 and 2," and "Who Bit the Wart Off Grandma's Nose?" On most of these numbers, Carson played a wily moonshiner in the north Georgia mountains who spends his days tending his still, lounging around his cabin, bickering with his sharp-tongued daughter, and evading revenue agents.[58]

Although Carson recorded only one song that referred specifically to his adopted hometown ("Fulton County Jail"), Atlanta's cosmopolitan atmosphere played a critical role in shaping his repertoire. The commercial entertainment industry and public amusements that emerged in the Gate City during the early twentieth century introduced Carson to a broad spectrum of American popular music, from Broadway show tunes and vaudeville novelty songs to swinging jazz dance numbers and African American blues. Although often overlooked by country music historians, approximately one-third of Carson's recorded output consisted of sentimental popular songs from the 1890s to the 1910s that had been composed by urban songwriters associated with the Manhattan songwriting and sheet-music-publishing district commonly known as Tin Pan Alley. Carson especially favored sentimental parlor ballads crowded with saintly mothers, orphaned children, wayward sons, and heartbroken lovers; many of these maudlin songs mourned the loss — either through death or circumstances — of family and loved ones. Fiddlin' John Carson, remarked a 1925 OKeh flyer, "has caught all the yearning pathos of the lad who has lost his Mother when he sings 'The Letter Edged in Black.' And the story of that dear little boy on 'The Lightning Express,' penniless and hastening to the bedside of his dying Mother, brings tears to the eyes of the listener, as with anxiety he hears the song to the end, fearing the boy will be put off the train." These and other Victorian tearjerkers, such as "After the Ball" (1892; Charles K. Harris) and "The Baggage Coach Ahead" (1896; Gussie L. Davis), may well have resonated deeply with Carson's working-class record buyers, many of whom had experienced similar wrenching social dislocations and losses when they migrated from the rural countryside to Atlanta and other Piedmont textile centers. Although most of these popular songs dated to the last decade of the nineteenth century, Carson's recordings of "Casey Jones" (1909; T. Lawrence Seibert and Eddie Newton), "Steamboat Bill" (1910; Ren Shields and Leighton Brothers), "Long Way to Tipperary" (1912; Jack Judge and Harry H. Williams), "It Takes a Little Rain with the Sunshine" (1913; Ballard McDonald and Harry Carroll), "I'm Glad My Wife's in Europe" (1914; Howell Johnson, Coleman Goetz, and Archie Goettler), "Darktown Strutters Ball" (1915; Shelton Brooks), and "Dixie Division" (1917; A. C. Mitchell) reflect his debt to more recent Tin Pan Alley hits that he learned after moving to Atlanta.[59]

Popular Tin Pan Alley music strongly influenced Carson's repertoire, and so too did African American musical traditions. Despite the pervasive segregation and racism of Jim Crow Atlanta, Carson and his white working-class contemporaries enjoyed extensive exposure to African American music. As a railroad water boy, Carson grew up in Cobb County hearing black construction crews singing work songs and ballads. After moving to Atlanta, he found himself in even closer contact with African American musicians and music, both in the workplace and in the larger metropolis itself. In the picker room at Exposition Mills, as historian Scott Reynolds Nelson points out, Carson "would have heard the field hollers of black draymen as they arrived with cotton bales" and "the work songs of black cotton pickers as they unloaded cotton." Later, after he took a job at Fulton Bag and Cotton Mills and moved to the Factory Lot district, Carson would have heard black songsters and bluesmen performing for tips on nearby Decatur Street. "On the outskirts of a city like Atlanta," recalled Columbia A & R man Frank B. Walker, who supervised both the firm's hillbilly and its race record series, "you had your colored section, and then you had your white—I'm sorry to use the word—you had what they used to call 'white trash.' But they were right close to each other. They passed each other every day, and a little of the spiritualistic type of singing of the colored people worked over into the white hillbilly, and a little of the white hillbilly worked over into what the colored people did." Likewise, despite his apparently racist views and his membership in the Ku Klux Klan, many of Carson's recordings reflect a considerable African American influence. Not only did he record such traditional black folk songs as "John Henry Blues," "Peter Went Fishing," and "It Ain't Gonna Rain No Mo'," but he also borrowed liberally from popular songs by black composers, including "The Baggage Coach Ahead" (1896; Gussie L. Davis), "You Gonna Get Something You Don't Expect" (1910; Bert Williams and Vincent Bryan), and "The Hesitating Blues" (1915; W. C. Handy). Even Carson's distinctive short-bow fiddling was probably indebted to African American fiddle styles, claims biographer Mark Wilson, either directly through face-to-face encounters or indirectly through minstrel and medicine shows. As a 1914 *Atlanta Journal Magazine* article remarked, Carson's fiddling at the Georgia Old-Time Fiddlers' Convention evoked "the screech of the old negro fiddle."[60]

Carson was certainly not alone among southern white musicians in his adaptation and incorporation of African American songs and musical elements into his own music. Rather, he stands in the company of such hillbilly music contemporaries as Jimmie Rodgers, Jimmie Tarlton, Frank Hutchison, Dock Boggs, and Austin and Lee Allen, to name only a handful, all of whom were deeply influenced by the musical expressions of African Americans. But Carson's appropriation of African American songs, as well as perhaps his fiddling style, highlights an important paradox in the history of hillbilly music and of working-class white southerners. White southerners shared a centuries-old tradition of musical and broader cultural exchange with their black counterparts, but, at the same time, these white southerners maintained virulently racist attitudes and strong support for racial segregation in the social and political arenas. Carson, in this sense, was typical of southern white workers of his generation, and his borrowings of African American musical forms enriched the old-time sound he forged in Atlanta.[61]

Carson should not be singled out for possessing what we today would condemn as racist attitudes. In fact, in the absence of any direct statements on his part, it is difficult to say exactly what he thought about African Americans. Carson's biographers tell us little about his racial views or his response to the murderous attacks on black Atlantans during the 1906 race riot, but they have informed us of his Klan membership and his ardent support for such race-baiting Georgia populists as Thomas E. Watson and Eugene Talmadge. In all likelihood, Carson held the same contemptuous views of African Americans that most working-class white southerners of his generation shared. Carson's racism merits discussion here principally because it helps us to understand him better as a historical figure, and, equally important, it underscores the conflicted and complicated tensions he embodied as a working-class white southerner in the modern, urban-industrial South.

Despite his hillbilly fool persona, Carson was an intensely political, civic-minded man who was deeply immersed in the turbulent world of early twentieth-century Georgia woolhat politics, in which candidates courted rural voters with their populist appeals for pro-agricultural legislation, hard-line segregation, and old-time religion. In Carson's one-party Democratic South, white voters still turned out to the election polls in large numbers, believing that the outcome of grassroots political contests significantly affected their daily lives. Political elections then often resembled three-ring circuses, and as a veteran campaign fiddler and comedian, Carson provided both entertainment and political instruction to the crowds for which he performed at Georgia political meetings and rallies over the course of more than thirty years. Fiddling and music making had deep roots in southern political campaigns, and Carson regularly employed his music to promote his own populist and seemingly racist political agendas, as well as those of his Democratic patrons. He composed highly propagandistic ballads about high-profile crimes, wrote catchy campaign songs for Ku Klux Klan candidates and race-baiting Georgia demagogues, and recorded a handful of populist anthems to elicit sympathy for hard-pressed southern farmers. His politics, as well as those of his political patrons Thomas E. Watson and Eugene Talmadge, can best be described as what historian Nancy MacLean calls "reactionary populism," that is, a position in which "the anti-elitism characteristic of populism coexists with, actually garners mass support for, a political agenda that enforces the subordination of whole groups of people," especially African Americans and Jews. In fact, Carson's musical career reflects the various ways in which reactionary populism, labor conflict, and racial strife profoundly shaped white working-class people in the twentieth-century urban South.[62]

With selections ranging from traditional fiddle tunes and minstrel songs to Tin Pan Alley hits and folk blues, Carson's recordings reflected the tremendous musical diversity of his cosmopolitan environment. It remains difficult, however, to sort out the direct sources of his complete repertoire. Certainly, Carson learned many of the popular ballads and songs he recorded from face-to-face musical exchanges with his friends and neighbors in the Fulton Mills district and from his musical contemporaries in greater Atlanta, especially Bully Brewer's wife, an employee of Fulton Bag and Cotton Mills, who knew dozens of turn-of-the-century Tin Pan Alley numbers. But Carson also clearly borrowed from current phonograph records, radio broadcasts, and even printed sources. He claimed, for example, that his composition of "Be Kind to a Man When He's Down" was based on an article he had read in *True Story*, one of the best-selling pulp magazines of the 1920s. He found the lyrics to "The Little Old Log Cabin in the Lane," he once explained, in an old tattered copy of *Greer's Almanac*. According to biographer Gene Wiggins, Carson probably modeled his 1934 rendition of "Since She Took My Licker from Me" on a Carolina Twins' 1929 Victor recording of "Gal of Mine Took My Licker from Me." The 1914 Tin Pan Alley song "I'm Glad My Wife's in Europe," which Al Jolson had introduced in the Broadway revue *Dancing Around*, came to Carson via either a phonograph record or a vaudeville show. And he almost surely gleaned a few numbers from the traveling circuses, medicine shows, and vaudeville acts that regularly visited Atlanta during the 1910s and 1920s. All of these examples reflect the ways in which the expansion of the nation's commercial entertainment industry and mass media influenced Carson's old-time sound and his evolving repertoire.[63]

Not only did Carson absorb many of the new sounds of early twentieth-century Atlanta, but several of his most enduring songs commented on the contemporary social and political issues of the modern South. His rollicking drinking songs, for example, indirectly criticized National Prohibition and Georgia's own "dry law," passed in 1908. Moreover, Carson also recorded several topical songs about local and national events, including "Dixie Boll Weevil" (about the 1920s pest infestation of Georgia cotton fields), "The Death of Floyd Collins" (a ballad written by fellow Atlantan, Rev. Andrew Jenkins, about a trapped spelunker who perished in a Kentucky cave in 1925), and "The Storm That Struck Miami" (about a devastating 1926 hurricane that killed 1,000 people). Carson's 1925 recording of "There's a Hard Time Coming" satirizes "old maids," who, in their attempts to keep up with the Jazz Age fashions of far younger flappers, "bob off their hair" and "powder up their face." Carson likewise used his humorous rural drama skits to make overtly political statements about modern southern society. Many of these skits slyly mocked a legal system that afforded little justice to ordinary southerners who were arrested and prosecuted for perpetuating the centuries-old tradition of distilling their own whiskey. Carson's moonshining skits, in fact, often highlighted the political corruption, hypocrisy, and arbitrariness of those judges and law enforcement officials charged with enforcing unpopular prohibition laws. On "John Makes Good Licker, Part 4," for example, Rosa Lee Carson's character exposes the judge presiding over her father's moonshining trial as a drunkard and an adulterer. And the revenue agents and sheriff's deputies who sometimes managed to arrest Carson on these hokey skit records are likewise revealed to be corrupt—they can usually be bribed to release him for nothing more than a jar of liquor and a fiddle tune.[64]

More pointed examples of Carson's social commentary can be found on his recordings of two late nineteenth-century populist anthems, "The Farmer Is the Man That Feeds Them All" and "The Honest Farmer," both of which complain about an unjust credit system, money-grubbing merchants, and the plight of farmers in the agriculturally depressed South. "The farmer is the man, the farmer is the man, / Buys on credit till the Fall," Carson sings in the former song. "Then they take him by the hand, and they lead him through the land, / But the merchant, he's the man that gets it all." Once a farmer himself in Cobb County, Carson later refashioned the song into "Taxes on the Farmer Feeds Them All," for a 1934 RCA-Victor session, in order to decry what he saw as the disproportionately high tax burden that farmers bore during the Great Depression. Carson inserted a ringing endorsement of President Franklin D. Roosevelt and his federal New Deal programs into one of the stanzas of "The Honest Farmer," which was recorded in February 1934, one year before Carson's political patron, Georgia governor Eugene Talmadge, emerged as one of the state's most outspoken public critics of the New Deal. Collectively, Carson's agrarian-oriented recordings expressed his strong populist sympathies with the beleaguered small farmers and rural refugees of the Georgia Piedmont against the exploitation of merchants and the government.[65]

Carson's alarm at the decline of agrarianism and rural communities is perhaps best showcased in his most famous song, "The Little Old Log Cabin in the Lane." Written in 1871 by the Louisville, Kentucky, newspaper editor and best-selling songwriter Will S. Hays and originally titled "The Little Old Cabin in the Lane," this minstrel song belongs to a vast and popular musical genre of nostalgic paeans to the passing of the Old South that flourished in the decades following the Civil War. Such songs, perhaps the best known of which is the African American song composer James A. Bland's "Carry Me Back to Old Virginny," published in 1878, featured romanticized, idyllic images of antebellum plantation life peopled with benevolent masters and contented, loyal slaves. Often narrated from the perspective of former slaves, these songs bemoaned the arrival of emancipation and yearned for the days of old. In the half century following the Civil War, these mass-marketed songs espousing this plantation mythology racked up tremendous sales in the form of sheet music and, later, phonograph recordings. Prior to Carson's 1923 recording, for example, more than a dozen different versions of "The Little Old Cabin in the Lane" had appeared on phonograph cylinders and discs, including those by such classical or popular artists as Alma Gluck, Carroll C. Clark, and the Edison Male Quartet. However, Len Spencer's circa 1901 Victor rendition, sung in pseudo–African American dialect to the famed banjoist Vess L. Ossman's accompaniment, remained the most popular recording of the song before World War I and may have been how Carson himself actually learned it.[66]

Regardless of his original source, "The Little Old Cabin in the Lane" ranked as one of Carson's favorite songs. It was the first song he ever recorded and, according to legend, the first song he ever performed on radio. He actually recorded it three times over the course of his career, once each under the various titles "The Little Old Log Cabin in the Lane" (1923), "The Little Old Log Cabin by the Stream" (1927), and "I'm Old and Feeble" (1934).[67] Ostensibly narrated by an elderly, unnamed ex-slave, "The Little Log Cabin in the Lane" laments the disintegration of a once-thriving southern plantation after the Civil War. The pathos-laden lyrics of Carson's 1923 OKeh recording are as follows:

Now I'm getting old and feeble and I cannot work no more,
That rusty-bladed hoe I've laid to rest;
Old Massa and old Missus, they are sleeping side by side,
Their spirits now are roaming with the blessed.
Things have changed about the place now, and the darkies, they
    have gone;
You'll never hear them singing in the cane;
But the only friend that's left here is that good old dog of mine,
And the little old log cabin in the lane.

Chorus:
The chimney's falling down and the roof's all caved in,
Lets in the sunshine and the rain;
But the angels watches over me when I lay down to sleep
In my little old log cabin in the lane.

Sheet music cover of "The Little Old Log Cabin in the Lane," by Will S. Hays, 1913.
Courtesy of the Rare Book, Manuscript, and Special Collections Library, Duke University.

Now this footpath has growed up that led us 'round the hill;
The fences all gone to decay;
The pond, it's done dried up where we once did go to mill;
Things have turned its course another way.
Well, I ain't got long to stay here, what little time I've got,
I'll try and rest contented while I remain
Until Death shall call this dog and me to find a better home
Than a little old log cabin in the lane.

Chorus

Carson recognized that, even more than a half century after it was written, "The Little Old Log Cabin in the Lane" remained relevant to his Jazz Age and, later, his Depression-era audiences because of its depiction of a crumbling rural world in an era of sweeping social change. In fact, "The Little Old Log Cabin in the Lane" resonated for Carson in the 1920s precisely because it suggested a nostalgic rural alternative to the troubling and often alienating modern urban world of Atlanta. His white audiences, largely composed of hard-pressed white farmers and rural migrants like himself who had left the countryside for southern cities and textile towns, could likewise identify with the song's sentiments. In Carson's rendition, "The Little Old Log Cabin in the Lane" became a metaphor for the disintegration of rural southern communities and, by extension, the erosion of bed-rock traditional values in the modern South. Indeed, since Carson's original 1923 recording of the song, a deep-rooted nostalgia for a by-gone world that seems far better than the present one has formed a central theme of American country music.[68]

"The Little Old Log Cabin in the Lane" may also have appealed to Carson because it fit so well with his own racial attitudes and anxieties. In 1915, a modern version of the Reconstruction-era Ku Klux Klan was revived in Atlanta, and, although Indiana would later claim a larger state membership, Georgia would remain the center of Klan activism during the first half of the 1920s, with Atlanta serving as the national headquarters and the national convention site of the Invisible Empire until 1925. With an estimated 40,000 members in Atlanta alone in 1921, the Klan emerged as a powerful force in municipal and state politics. Indeed, several of Atlanta's high-ranking city officials and much of its police department belonged to the organization. Carson himself joined the revived Ku Klux Klan, probably sometime in the early 1920s, but his biographer Gene Wiggins downplays the fiddler's involvement in this terrorist organization by asserting that Carson was "probably not an ardent" Klansman. In fact, there is little surviving evidence concerning his participation in the night-riding and vigilantism of the Klan, which, as Clifford M. Kuhn writes, targeted "radicals, Jews, aliens, Roman Catholics, labor organizers, and suspected violators of Victorian moral standards, as well as members of the black community." It is possible that Carson viewed his membership simply as an opportunity to make important political connections that could boost his musical career. But what few insights we have into his racial views suggest that the Klan's agenda conformed to his own racist politics. Regardless of why he joined the secret fraternal organization, Carson frequently performed at Klan functions in the Atlanta area and, occasionally, at those in surrounding states. On May 8, 1925, for example, he competed in a Klan-sponsored fiddlers' convention in Mountain City, Tennessee. One much-reproduced photograph from the contest shows Carson and five other distinguished old-time musicians, all of them dressed in dark suits and ties and holding their banjos and fiddles, assembled in front of a local bank. To their far right, a Klan handbill in the bank's window advertises the contest. In addition, Carson worked as a paid campaign fiddler for Georgia gubernatorial candidate and Klansman Clifford Walker and probably for other Klan candidates during the Invisible Empire's sweep of the 1922 state elections.[69]

It remains difficult to determine exactly where Carson the opportunist ended and where Carson the racist began. Indeed, our image of Klansman Carson is complicated by the fact that, in May 1933, assisted by Rosa Lee and one of his sons, Carson performed as the opening act at a racially integrated benefit rally for the imprisoned African American communist organizer Angelo Herndon at Atlanta's Royal Theater, located "in the heart of the Negro district." Four months earlier, an all-white jury had found Herndon, who had organized an interracial hunger march and demonstration of unemployed workers at the Atlanta courthouse, guilty of "attempting to incite insurrection against the state of Georgia," and he was sentenced to eighteen to twenty years on a chain gang. His case, like Leo Frank's frame-up two decades earlier, soon became a national cause célèbre. Sponsored by the International Labor Defense, the left-wing legal organization whose attorneys had defended Herndon in court, the 1933

Fiddlin' John Carson, far right, with five other contestants at the May 8, 1925, Mountain City, Tennessee, fiddlers' convention, sponsored by the Ku Klux Klan. Courtesy of the Southern Folklife Collection, Wilson Library, University of North Carolina at Chapel Hill

rally at which Carson performed attracted "more than 800 black and white workers and intellectuals," according to the *Daily Worker*, the newspaper of the Communist Party U.S.A. The newspaper identi-fied Carson as "a famous white Georgia mountain fiddler" and fur-ther noted that "one of his numbers 'Can't Live on Corn Bread and Peas' tells the story of the chain gang diet of the oppressed southern workers." Carson's performance at the Herndon defense rally, which also featured music "by several Negro worker-artists," suggests that he was not above playing for almost any engagement, so long as it paid, especially during the depths of the Great Depression. Then again, it is also possible that Carson performed at this rally because he sympathized with Herndon's campaign on behalf of unemployed working-class Atlantans. But wherever Carson's actual political sym-pathies lay, it seems clear that he profited from his Klan membership. It may have even garnered him some of the relatively high-paying musical engagements for Atlanta policemen's balls, at which he often performed during the 1920s.[70]

Surprisingly, especially given his Klan membership, none of Carson's biographers have commented on the explicit racial themes of "The Little Old Log Cabin in the Lane." But the important issue of race is critical to understanding Carson and why he may have treasured this old minstrel song. Living alone with only his faithful dog as a companion, the devoted, elderly "darky" in the song seems peculiarly uninterested in his freedom and, in fact, seems to lan-guish under emancipation. He apparently longs for the bygone days of slavery and, unable to recapture them, hopes only for a quick and merciful death. Far removed from the Red Summer of 1919 and the racial strife of the post–World War I South, the song fondly evokes an idealized pre–Civil War Old South where the existence of slavery sim-plified, at least for white southerners, the complex issues of race and racial subordination. But unlike most previous recordings of the song, Carson sings "The Little Old Log Cabin in the Lane" in a straightfor-ward, serious manner without resorting to minstrel-style racial par-ody. As a result, his earnest rendition lends a sadness and gravity to the song that most prior recordings of it lacked. Nonetheless, through his recordings and performances of "The Little Old Log Cabin in the Lane," Carson promoted a strain of racism and white supremacy that helped to assuage his white working-class audiences' anxieties about the social and economic progress of African Americans and the erosion of traditional racial hierarchies. Likewise, Carson's incorporation of blackface minstrelsy routines into his road show concerts, often with "Freckled-Faced Earl" Johnson playing the part of a stereotypically shiftless, slow-witted "darky" to Carson's interlocutor "straight" man, served a similar purpose in reassuring his white audiences of their supposed racial superiority and dominance. Thus, Carson's recordings of "The Little Old Log Cabin in the Lane" combined both populist and racial commentary to help alleviate white fears of industrial expansion, urban growth, and black progress and thereby to promote Carson's own brand of reactionary populism.[71]

The Great Depression decimated hillbilly record sales, and though Fiddlin' John Carson continued to make records, perform on the radio, and entertain at show dates, his fortunes substantially declined as the 1930s wore on. In 1927, WSB had joined the recently organized NBC network. Thereafter, the station increasingly relied on the network's regular national programs and on corporate-sponsored hillbilly music shows to fill its broadcast schedule, and Carson and other Atlanta pioneer old-time musicians made fewer and fewer appearances on the station. Although WSB made a tradition of inviting Carson to perform over the airwaves on his birthday each year, after 1927 he no longer appeared regularly on the station. By the mid-1930s, more polished, urban styles of hillbilly music had eclipsed Carson's own in popularity. Most Atlanta radio listeners now preferred the sweet, close harmonies of the Blue Sky Boys or the sophisticated swing- and jazz-inflected music of the Rice Brothers Gang to Carson's old-time fiddling.[72]

As the Great Depression intensified, Carson also saw his recording opportunities shrink as phonograph record sales plummeted in 1932 to less than 6 percent of their 1920s peak and most of the nation's once-flourishing record labels either went bankrupt or were acquired in mergers. Carson's record label, OKeh, a subsidiary of the Columbia Phonograph Company since 1926, limped along until 1934, when it discontinued its "Old Time Tunes" series, thereby ending the fiddler's long-standing relationship with the label. No longer under contract, Carson approached the RCA-Victor Company, Inc., formed in a 1929 merger between the Victor Talking Machine Company and the Radio Corporation of America. The firm, one of the few major talking-machine companies to survive the Wall Street crash and its aftermath, ranked as one of the nation's leading manufacturers of radios, phonographs, and records. In 1934, Carson traveled to RCA-Victor's main studios in Camden, New Jersey, to cut what were to be the last commercial recordings of his career. On February 27 and 28, he made two dozen recordings for the company's budget-priced Blue-bird label, accompanied by his guitarist daughter Rosa Lee, guitarist Peanut Brown, and banjo player Bill Willard. Most of the sides from this session consisted of slightly revised versions of Carson's previous OKeh hits, and apparently none of them made much of an impact on the still-depressed record market. Almost eleven years after he had made his first recordings, Fiddlin' John Carson now found himself edged out of the very hillbilly recording industry that he had helped both to pioneer and to popularize.[73]

After his recording career ended, Carson continued to play stage shows with a skeleton road band wherever he could get the bookings, and during the 1930s he and his daughter performed widely across the nation and even in other countries, playing as far away as Canada, Cuba, and Mexico. To help make ends meet, though, Carson ran a fishing camp on the Chattahoochee River, renting boats and fishing tackle to sportsmen. He also managed to parlay his musical popu-larity among rural and working-class Georgians into a successful side-line occupation as a political campaign entertainer. As early as 1914, he and Rosa Lee, who was then only four, had worked as campaign entertainers for Nathaniel E. Harris, a prominent Macon judge and Confederate veteran, in his successful Georgia gubernatorial cam-paign. Throughout the rest of the 1910s and 1920s, Carson's political interests led him to campaign for several of Georgia's most celebrated Democratic politicians, notably Thomas E. Watson and Ed Rivers.[74]

But Carson's longest political association emerged in the mid-1920s with Eugene Talmadge, a Forsyth, Georgia, native and arch-segregationist who liked to remind the state's hard-pressed farmers that they had only three friends—"God, Sears Roebuck, and Gene Talmadge." Although he wore horn-rimmed glasses and held a law degree from the University of Georgia, Talmadge passed himself off as a "just plain-folks" Georgia "cracker." One of his 1926 campaign posters for his bid for state commissioner of agriculture, for example, proudly identified him as "a Real Dirt Farmer." On the campaign stump, Talmadge gestured wildly and pounded his fist as he delivered his speeches, dressed in his trademark red suspenders and rolled-up shirtsleeves. His staunch rural Georgia supporters referred to him endearingly as "the Wild Man from Sugar Creek." Apparently, Carson first met Talmadge, then a student at the University of Georgia, when Carson was touring in Athens. Two decades later, in 1926, when Talmadge was running for state commissioner of agriculture, he employed Carson to play the fiddle, crack a few jokes, and entertain his political supporters and voters. "I played for him in every campaign after that," Carson recalled. "Every place he spoke, I was there entertaining the crowd an hour before he got there."[75]

In 1932, while running for governor, Talmadge hired Carson and his stringband to entertain crowds at outdoor political rallies across Georgia. "We'd go from town to town," Rosa Lee Carson recalled, "and he would have a big truck for us to get up there and make some music. We'd sing and I'd buck-and-wing dance, and Pa would tell a few jokes in the courthouse square." During the campaign, Talmadge promised to lower the high tax burden on rural Georgians, beginning with a reduction in the cost of automobile license plates to a flat three-dollar fee. Carson, in turn, mobilized support for Talmadge's proposal by composing a light-hearted ditty titled "Georgia's Three-Dollar Tag." "Farmer in the cornfield hollering 'Whoa, gee haw,'" Carson sang time and again from speakers' platforms and the backs of flatbed trucks at political rallies that year. "Cain't put no thirty-dollar tag on a three-dollar car." Rural Georgians swept Talmadge into office, and when he was inaugurated governor in January 1933 he promptly appointed Carson to the position of elevator operator in the Georgia State Capitol, a political patronage position the elderly fiddler would hold throughout Talmadge's three terms as governor. The gregarious Carson soon became a popular figure in the marble halls of the capitol. Early in 1935, the Georgia House of Representatives elected Carson assistant doorkeeper and, at the end of one of its legislative sessions, designated him "the Official Fiddler of the House of Representatives of the 1935 session." After Talmadge died in 1946, Carson worked as a campaign entertainer for his son, Herman Talmadge, during his successful 1948 bid for the governorship of Georgia, and the younger Talmadge likewise rewarded Carson with the position of elevator operator in the capitol.[76]

Meanwhile, although his recording career had ended and his radio appearances had declined to only occasional broadcasts, Carson continued to perform at public gatherings and events in the greater Atlanta area during much of the 1930s and 1940s. Around 1934, after the repeal of National Prohibition, the manufacturers of True Blue Beer hired Carson and Rosa Lee to entertain their company executives and salesmen, and Carson even wrote a commercial jingle for the brewery. Occasionally, he and his musician friends staged old-time medicine shows in the city and the surrounding towns. Carson also regularly fiddled for the few surviving Confederate veterans who resided at the Old Soldiers' Home in Atlanta, and, in 1941, he and banjo player John Patterson performed for them at an old-fashioned cotillion sponsored by the United Daughters of the Confederacy. But Carson also continued to make appearances outside of Georgia. In July 1939, for example, he was profiled on CBS's *We the People*, a nationally syndicated human-interest radio program, on which he was billed as "America's Number One Hillbilly." Despite his regular state job, Carson also remained on the lookout for show business opportunities, and, in September 1935, he even traveled to Hollywood with the hope of landing a starring role in a motion picture comedy. According to his sideman, Peanut Brown, motion picture executives at an unidentified studio were considering Carson as a possible replacement for the late Will Rogers, the plainspoken Oklahoma humorist who had died in an airplane crash earlier that year. Unfortunately for Carson, however, his Hollywood scouting failed to pay off.[77]

By 1946, now in his seventies, Fiddlin' John Carson reigned as the aged patriarch of his neighborhood, now known as Cabbagetown, and presided over a large extended family that included sixteen grandchildren and seventeen great-grandchildren. In their old age, he and his wife remained relatively secure financially, thanks to his political connections to the Talmadge family. After his wife passed away from cancer on November 27, 1948, Carson spent his final months living with his daughter Maggie Collins and her family. In March 1949, as was customary on his birthday, Carson played his fiddle and sang on WSB, but his health was rapidly deteriorating. "I remember the last thing my daddy did," recalled Horace Carson. "His fiddle was up on a chifforobe, and he'd point at it. Me and my brother-in-law, we couldn't understand what he wanted. And finally, my brother-in-law picked up his fiddle, and he nodded his head 'yes.' We brought it down to him, and there was a string off, and he wanted it put back on. We put it back on, and he didn't live but a few hours after that. But he knew a string was off the fiddle." Carson died of cancer on December 11, 1949, at the age of seventy-five. His funeral services were held two days later at Atlanta's East Side Baptist Church, and his body was interred in Sylvester Cemetery. Honorary pallbearers included his political patron and longtime friend, Governor Herman Talmadge.[78]

Carson himself would probably like to be remembered as a pioneer hillbilly fiddler and entertainer who helped to preserve and popularize old-time southern music. As he (or more likely his ghostwriter) claimed in the introduction to his 1932 WSB song folio, *Fiddlin' John Carson: Dixie's Champion of Champions*: "If I have helped to keep the old songs alive and if I have been partly responsible for making a place for them in the hearts and homes of young and old today in competition with jazz music and other music that will pass away and be forgotten, I feel that I have done some good in the world." Carson's prediction about jazz proved to be dead wrong, but he considered the fiddle music and the old ballads he performed to be a much-needed alternative to the influential jazz music of the 1920s and 1930s, whose enormously popular sounds reflected the expanding African American influence on mainstream popular music. He also perceived his old-time music as distinct from—and, in fact, far superior to—what he took to be the watered-down, effeminate hillbilly music that had eclipsed his own in popularity in the 1930s and 1940s. "Those fellows on the radio don't know nothing about old-time fiddling," scoffed Carson in an *Atlanta Journal* interview six months before his death. "They don't know none of the old-time songs, and they couldn't play 'em anyway. Sometimes when I hear 'em, I just wish I could show 'em how it's done." Carson may have helped launch hillbilly music, but near the end of his life the evolving music trends he heard on radio and records surely disappointed him. "He was a hillbilly," Rosa Lee Carson explained. "When I was a little girl and my daddy was making music, it was really hillbilly music, mountain music. Good old mountain music. You don't hear that kind of music now days. We used to sit and laugh at them. He said, 'It sounds so silly for those boys to get up there and play and call themselves hillbillies when they wasn't.' Said, 'There's so much difference in the music.'" Despite a sustained campaign by one of his grandsons, Fiddlin' John Carson has failed to win induction into the Country Music Hall of Fame in Nashville, but, considering his scorn for the country music of the 1930s and 1940s, perhaps he would be pleased by his exclusion.[79]

Although Carson traded on his persona of a Georgia mountaineer fiddler and moonshiner from the tiny hamlet of Blue Ridge, it was actually his cosmopolitan life in Atlanta that played the most significant role in defining his professional career and his recorded music. Much of his success resulted from his ready access to major metropolitan newspapers, mass-circulation magazines, commercial radio, and phonograph records, all of which he used to promote his music, expand his repertoire, and build a broad fan following. Carson did spend much of his first twenty-five years on north Georgia farms and certainly absorbed traditional rural folkways. But his music transcended his rural origins to become a complex mixture of southern old-time fiddling and modern American popular music. At the same time, Carson's music often specifically addressed the new realities of southern working-class life in early twentieth-century Atlanta. A sizable percentage of his recordings, including his populist anthems, his rural drama skits, and particularly his minstrel number "The Little Old Log Cabin in the Lane," directly addressed the socioeconomic transformations of the modern South, especially the plight of hardpressed farmers and the disintegration of rural southern communities. Carson's music embodied the tensions between traditionalism and modernism, between the grassroots southern folk music of the 1890s and the commercial popular music of the 1920s. Yet his biographers have largely failed to devote the same amount of attention to his modern influences as they have to his more traditional influences. And their failure to do so has created a distorted understanding of Carson's music that suggests it was far more old-fashioned and anachronistic than was actually the case.[80]

Biographers' failure to recognize the modern, urban-industrial influences on Carson's music has also led to his being mischaracterized as culturally isolated and even backward. Too often, country music historians have conflated Fiddlin' John, the hillbilly character, with Carson, the clever showman. Even Gene Wiggins, his principal biographer, who clearly admires and respects his subject, portrays Carson as an out-of-touch country fiddler in Jazz Age Atlanta. "It makes little difference to [Carson's] qualifications as a nineteenth-century folk musician that some of his recordings were based on twentieth-century popular songs," Wiggins notes. "His alterations in words, music, and style jerked them back into an earlier day." Despite the considerable evidence that Carson was highly attuned to early twentieth-century mass culture, Wiggins insists on interpreting him almost solely as a traditional artist of the late nineteenth-century, though he lived for nearly a half century in the heart of one of the largest and most cosmopolitan cities in the American South.[81]

Carson, of course, was far more worldly and sophisticated than he pretended to be on stage or in the studio, or than scholars have generally given him credit for. His skillful and aggressive self-promotion, especially his manipulation of modern mass media to create an appealing public persona for himself, places him squarely within the tradition of early twentieth-century show business. But sorting out to what degree he manipulated his own highly embellished mountaineer moonshiner image and to what degree others in the media manipulated it amounts to a difficult, if not impossible, historical challenge. What we can say with absolute certainty is that Carson deliberately promoted and traded on his Georgia hillbilly persona, as his many personal appearances, newspaper and magazine interviews, radio broadcasts, and phonograph records attest. Except for Uncle Dave Macon, the wise-cracking banjo player and early star of WSM's *Grand Ole Opry*, no other hillbilly musician of the 1920s created a more dynamic, colorful persona for himself on radio and records than did Carson. Far from the simple, naïve folk musician he claimed to be, Carson was in fact an enterprising, profit-driven entertainer. In his quest for financial gain, he composed a commercial jingle for True Blue Beer, peddled twenty-five-cent broadsides to the crowds that attended his stage shows, hawked his *Fiddlin' John Carson: Dixie's Champion of Champions* song folios to WSB listeners, scouted for Hollywood movie roles for himself, performed concerts for Klansmen and Communists alike, and regularly worked as a political campaign fiddler for some of Georgia's most distinguished politicians. In fact, Carson would likely have recorded only a handful of sides for OKeh and then been largely forgotten by country music historians if not for his talent as a master showman and hillbilly image-maker.[82]

To view Carson's old-time music as simply a commercialized rural southern folk music is to diminish and distort the important contributions that he and other southern white working-class musicians made to American popular music. Atlanta's commercial entertainment industry undeniably shaped Carson's old-time music and his musical career, just as he and his music helped to shape this evolving commercial entertainment industry. Perhaps more than any other single artist, Carson helped to inaugurate the hillbilly recording boom of the 1920s and to make Atlanta the most important recording center of old-time music in the South before World War II. His music comforted working-class white southerners, many of them less than a generation removed from the farm, as they coped with the wrenching changes of urban growth, industrial expansion, racial tensions, and shifting social mores that came to define the turbulent early twentieth-century South. Taken together, Carson's career and music reveal the modern urban origins of old-time music and, in doing so, expose the complexities of the southern white working-class culture out of which American country music arose.

ROUGH AND ROWDY WAYS
CHARLIE POOLE AND THE
NORTH CAROLINA RAMBLERS

You've often heard his records, played on your phonograph,
Some of them would make you cry, and some would make you laugh;
He was just a rambler, he rambled east and west,
But his rambling days are over, they've laid him down to rest.
—Walter "Kid" Smith, "The Life and Death of Charlie Poole" (1931)

As early as 1924, even before he appeared on radio or records, the hard-drinking textile millhand Charlie Poole was already broadcasting his high-spirited, percussive dance music throughout the mountains of southwestern Virginia. Besides performing for paying audiences at formal stage shows, the renowned five-string banjoist and his brother-in-law, fiddler Posey Rorer, often entertained in private homes for parties and dances around Franklin County, Virginia, where Rorer had been born and raised. Sometimes the duo "broadcast" using their host's hand-crank telephone, thereby sharing their music, via the telephone party line, with avid listeners in the community. During the mid- to late 1920s, even after he became one of Columbia's best-selling recording stars, Poole and his revolving ensemble of stringband musicians, the North Carolina Ramblers, regularly spent weeks playing the towns and villages of southwestern Virginia and southern West Virginia, sometimes for paying audiences but most often just for the sheer pleasure of making music. One Christmas, the band brightened the holiday season in the Blue Ridge Mountain community of Ferrum, Virginia, entertaining a few nights at one home and then moving on to another. In return for their music making, appreciative hosts supplied the North Carolina Ramblers with a place to stay, country suppers, and moonshine whiskey. "The people always hated to see us leave," recalled fiddler Lonnie Austin, who often accompanied Poole on these excursions, "because they knew we took the music with us."[1]

More than seventy-five years after his death, Charlie Poole remains a legendary figure among the elderly residents of south-central Virginia and north-central North Carolina, where he worked off and on as a textile millhand for more than twenty-five years. According to biographer Kinney Rorrer, Poole had a "forceful personality" and "wherever [he] rambled he seemed to leave in his wake a lot of colorful stories about his escapades and exploits." One of his nieces remembered Poole as "a real individual, one of a kind." Her Uncle Charlie, she fondly recalled, "talked ninety miles an hour and patted his foot the whole time he was talking. Why he would even sing you the answer to a question some times." Throughout much of his adult life, Poole seemed to alternate between stone-cold sobriety and alcoholic benders, and his behavior, like that of many alcoholics, vacillated wildly. When he was not drinking, he was a charming, generous man capable of small but meaningful acts of kindness such as, as Rorrer notes, "taking time to play music for a little blind girl or flipping a silver dollar to a small street urchin so he could go to the circus." But when he was on the bottle, Poole could be a mean, selfish, antisocial drunk who got into roadhouse fistfights and scrapes with the law and who often left his wife and friends for up to six weeks at a time to ramble around the country. After one 1930 recording session in New York, he even pawned a treasured Gibson banjo he had borrowed from a friend in order to finance a drunken spree. And more than one of his sidemen in the North Carolina Ramblers accused him of squandering their share of the earnings from recording sessions on bootleg whiskey. Considering how well known he was within parts of the Southern Piedmont and, more broadly, within the hillbilly recording field during his lifetime, we know surprisingly little about Charlie Poole, since he, like so many other working-class southerners of his generation, left few surviving personal documents and no firsthand testimonies of his life. Unlike Fiddlin' John Carson, who so successfully promoted himself in Atlanta newspapers and, occasionally, national magazines, Poole gave no known published interviews during his lifetime, and, barely literate, he wrote few letters and postcards. So, despite the legendary stories that still circulate about him in parts of the North Carolina and Virginia Piedmont, and, despite the remarkable research Kinney Rorrer did in piecing together his great-uncle's biography in *Rambling Blues: The Life and Songs of Charlie Poole* (1982), Charlie Poole, in the end, remains an enigma.[2]

We catch some of our best glimpses of Poole in his extensive body of commercial recordings. Between 1925 and 1930, he and the North Carolina Ramblers recorded a total of eighty-three sides for Columbia, Paramount, and Brunswick, including such classics as "Don't Let Your Deal Go Down Blues," "White House Blues," and "If the River Was Whiskey." Their bluesy fiddle breakdowns and sentimental ballads, performed in a highly disciplined ragtime style, made them one of the most celebrated hillbilly stringbands during the last half of the 1920s. The North Carolina Ramblers' first two releases, recorded in July 1925, together sold more than 165,000 copies, in an age when old-time record sales of more than 20,000 would be considered a minor hit. Within two years, the band had racked up sales of nearly a half-million records. "Last Saturday our first shipment of Charlie's Records were sold out almost before they were unpacked," announced a 1927 newspaper advertisement for a Burlington, North Carolina, music store, "but we have just received another 100 of this number and will have plenty on hand from now on." "Out of North Carolina, probably the biggest thing for the dance field was Charlie Poole and the North Carolina Ramblers," recalled Columbia A & R (artist and repertoire) man Frank B. Walker, who supervised most of the band's recording sessions. Walker claimed that the North Carolina Ramblers ranked as "the biggest record seller everywhere," and he attributed much of their commercial success to Poole's compelling vocals. "He was just the best singer that they had up there in that area," Walker recalled, "and he seemed to blossom out as he got to be known a little bit. He seemed to take on a know-it-all attitude, which showed up in the music, and it was really good. He was the North Carolina big boy, I'll tell you."[3]

Clearly, much of Poole's success as a hillbilly musician can be credited to his commanding vocals, instrumental virtuosity, selection of excellent sidemen, and clever arrangements of once-popular Tin Pan

Charlie Poole, left, and the North Carolina Ramblers
(Posey Rorer, center, and Roy Harvey, right), 1927.
Courtesy of Kinney Rorer.

Alley songs of the 1890s and 1900s, many of which he learned from his guitarist, Roy Harvey, who worked as a clerk in a Beckley, West Virginia, music store. Although the North Carolina Ramblers did record traditional southern fiddle tunes and ballads, the majority of the band's recorded output consisted of arrangements of turn-of-the-century "coon songs," vaudeville numbers, and sentimental parlor pieces, such as "Leaving Home," "There'll Come a Time," and "He Rambled," which the band rendered as spirited dance music. Despite the occasional inclusion of cornpone dialogue on their records (they even made a four-part comedy skit for the Brunswick label, titled "A Trip to New York," about the misadventures of a rube stringband out of place in the big city), the North Carolina Ramblers presented themselves as serious professional musicians, dressing in formal suits and ties and polished shoes. Their meticulous, tightly knit stringband music, which bore the deep imprint of Tin Pan Alley sheet music, phonograph recordings, and Hollywood films, was a product of Piedmont millhands' increasing contact with American popular music and mass culture during the 1910s and 1920s. An avid fan of contemporary popular and even classical music, Poole experimented with five-piece ensembles, incorporated solo instrumental breaks into his selections, and emulated the records of well-known popular singers Arthur Collins, Billy Murray, Eddie Morton, and Al Jolson, even imitating their vocal phrasings and nuances on some of his recordings. Accompanied by only a piano, Poole also covered several showcase banjo medleys and instrumentals originally recorded by the classic banjo virtuoso Fred Van Eps, Poole's role model and perhaps his most important musical influence.[4]

After 1927, Poole increasingly perceived himself not simply as an old-time musician but, like Van Eps, as a technically gifted, popular banjoist with the potential to achieve broader national appeal. Not wishing to tinker with a successful commercial formula, Columbia's A & R man, Frank B. Walker, repeatedly resisted Poole's attempts to transform himself into a popular music star. Throughout this artistic tug-of-war, however, Poole and the North Carolina Ramblers remained one of the biggest-selling hillbilly acts of the late 1920s. Columbia's 1929 *Old Familiar Tunes* catalog featured a photograph of Poole on its cover and inside, in a brief sketch, noted that he "is the leading banjo picker and singer in the Carolinas. But the other two Ramblers, with their fiddle and guitar, are good, too, and all three ramble 'way outside Carolina to supply the pep for many an all-night dance." By 1930, however, the Great Depression had wrecked Poole and the North Carolina Ramblers' once-flourishing recording career, and his legendary rambling and uncontrolled alcoholism had ruined his health, foreshadowing the lives of several postwar country music stars, most notably Hank Williams. Although his music was profoundly shaped by a modern twentieth-century world, Poole refused to accommodate himself to its industrial demands of wage labor, time clocks, and assembly lines. In fact, several of his best-known songs, including "Don't Let Your Deal Go Down Blues," "Ramblin' Blues," "He Rambled," and "If the River Was Whiskey," celebrate shiftless, whiskey-soaked rogues and ne'er-do-wells who embraced a wandering, hand-to-mouth existence free from the responsibilities of married life and steady employment.[5]

Poole and the North Carolina Ramblers produced a highly disciplined and tightly interwoven sound, at the center of which was Poole's distinctive three-finger banjo style, which he clearly refined as a result of, and perhaps even originally adapted from, the phonograph recordings he heard of classic banjoists. In an age when most traditional southern banjo players played their instruments in a percussive "frailing" or "clawhammer" style, which featured a two-fingered downward stroke, similar to the style heard on the minstrel stage of antebellum America, Poole used his thumb and fingers to pick the banjo in a technique modeled on the parlor and concert banjoists of the day. This three-finger "up-picking" style enabled him to perform more intricate melodies on the banjo and, in turn, to elevate the five-string banjo from being merely a rhythmic backup instrument in southern stringband music to, on occasion, a highly effective lead instrument in its own right. And, in doing so, Poole and the North Carolina Ramblers created an enormously influential musical sound that dozens of other Piedmont stringbands from north-central North Carolina and south-central Virginia attempted to imitate. Although his contributions to hillbilly music and country music generally have long been overshadowed by the accomplishments of such canonized stars of the Nashville establishment as Jimmie Rodgers, the Carter Family, and Uncle Dave Macon, Poole's banjo style on his prewar commercial recordings provided the instrumental foundations for modern bluegrass banjo and thus dramatically altered the historical trajectory of postwar country music.[6]

Cover of Columbia's *Old Familiar Tunes* catalog,
featuring Charlie Poole in the inset, 1929.
Courtesy of Kinney Rorrer.

Charlie Poole and the North Carolina Ramblers' ragtime-inflected music emerged from a southern cotton mill culture that, already by the time of his birth, was engulfed in swift social and cultural transformation. Charles Cleveland Poole was born into a white working-class family, one of thirteen children, on March 22, 1892, in Randolph County, North Carolina, probably in the textile village of Millboro. His paternal grandfather, an Irish immigrant, had arrived in the United States sometime in the 1840s as part of the massive exodus escaping Ireland's catastrophic potato famine. According to the census, Charlie's father, John Phillip Poole, was born in March 1850 in North Carolina. By 1875, John and his wife, Bettie Ellen (Johnson) Poole, were living in Iredell County, in the western Piedmont of North Carolina, when the first of their thirteen children was born.[7] Sometime before 1879, the Poole family relocated to Randolph County, one of the state's rapidly industrializing Piedmont counties. When Charlie Poole lived there as a child, Millboro was a small textile village with no more than a few hundred residents, one of more than a half-dozen area textile mill communities that had sprung up on the banks of the Deep River and its tributaries before 1900. Both of Poole's parents worked in local cotton mills, and with few other opportunities to earn a living available to them, tending looms and spindles emerged as a way of life for the Poole family. Five of the eight surviving children spent much of their adult working lives as textile millhands, including Charlie. Of those who managed to escape the mills, one son, Ralph, became a Holiness preacher, and another, Henry, who shared his brother Charlie's wanderlust, worked as a circus roustabout.[8]

Shortly after 1900, the Poole family moved to Haw River, seven miles east of Greensboro, in Alamance County. There, John Poole and his older children found work in Granite Mill, originally built in 1844 and later purchased and expanded by Thomas M. Holt, a former governor of North Carolina and scion of one of the state's textile dynasties. By the turn of the twentieth century, Holt descendants owned twenty-five textile mills in Alamance County, including the Thomas M. Holt Manufacturing Company in Haw River, where a bitter labor strike erupted just prior to the Poole family's arrival. In September 1900, dissatisfied weavers staged a work stoppage at the Holt Mill to protest what they considered the unfair firing of a weaver. The workers, many of whom were members of the National Union of Textile Workers, demanded only that the mill superintendent dismiss the abusive overseer who had unreasonably fired the weaver. The Holt owners, however, refused to concede to workers' demands, and on September 28, the workers at the Holt Mill, as well as those at the nearby Holt-controlled Cora Mill and Granite Mill, went on strike. The Holt family promptly closed all three mills. Then, in collusion with other mill owners, the Holts posted notices explaining that Alamance County textile mills would not employ union labor and demanded that strikers either renounce their union membership and return to work or resign from their jobs and move out of the company-owned mill village when the mills reopened on October 15. When the mills resumed operations, approximately 3,000 millhands refused to return to work and instead remained on strike. By November, the ranks of the strikers had swelled to approximately 5,000. The deadlocked labor dispute dragged on until the third week of November, when the mill owners began evicting the strikers and their families from their company-owned houses. Some of the striking millhands renounced the National Union of Textile Workers and returned to their looms and spindles, but, according to the *Alamance Gleaner*, "a large number, the great majority, remain[ed] firm" and continued the strike. Others, estimated to number around three hundred, began "moving away—to Georgia, South Carolina, and Virginia." When the Pooles arrived in Haw River, only a short time after the strike had been broken, they apparently took jobs recently vacated by these union strikers, making the Pooles, in a word, "scabs."[9]

Around 1904, at the age of twelve, Charlie Poole began working as a doffer at Granite Mill to help support his large family. Doffing, one of the entry-level jobs in the mills usually reserved for young boys, required a set of fast, dexterous hands to snatch the filled bobbins of thread from the spindles and replace them with empty ones. Doffers typically worked only twenty to forty minutes of every hour, but when they did, it was at a furious clip. Though just a boy, Poole worked a man's schedule: five eleven-hour shifts, plus a half day on Saturdays, for around three dollars a week. Charlie Poole and his family would remain in Haw River for the next thirteen or so years.[10]

Even before he began to work in the mills, young Charlie Poole was already immersing himself in music making. He fashioned his first banjo out of a dried gourd when he was nine years old, inspired, no doubt, by his father and his older brother Leroy, both of whom played the five-string banjo and probably taught him the rudiments of the instrument. A few years later, with some of his hard-earned wages from Granite Mill, he replaced his crude homemade instrument with a factory-made five-string banjo that cost $1.50, perhaps purchased from the Sears, Roebuck mail-order catalog, and set himself to mastering the instrument. An accident resulting from a drunken wager assisted him in this endeavor. On a bet, an intoxicated teenaged Poole tried to "catch a baseball without a glove," explains biographer Hank Sapoznik, "no matter how hard it was thrown. He lost the bet." The ball broke several fingers on his right hand, and the bones failed to set properly. As a result, his fingers permanently curled in toward his palm. Amazingly, according to Kinney Rorrer, Poole's accident improved his banjo playing, because the permanently arched fingers on his right hand "formed a natural picking position."[11]

Poole began playing the five-string banjo at a time when the instrument was undergoing swift changes in American culture. First introduced into the British North American colonies by West African slaves in the seventeenth century, the banjo originally was a simple, fretless, four-string instrument often fashioned out of long-necked gourds, like Poole's first handmade one. By 1800, with the addition of a fifth or "drone" string, these instruments had evolved into the five-string banjo, but it remained chiefly an African American instrument until white entertainers made the banjo the central instrument of the minstrel show in the mid-1840s. Before the Civil War, the five-string banjo achieved its greatest popularity on the minstrel stage, where its adoption by blackfaced white northern entertainers, in enthusiastic parody of southern black slaves, caused the instrument to become closely associated with antebellum plantation life. By the mid-1840s, white musicians in the Carolina Piedmont had also adopted the five-string banjo, and, in fact, the first documented white banjo player in the region, Manly Reece, was born and raised, like Charlie Poole, in Randolph County. According to his biographer, Andy Cahan, Reece probably learned to play the instrument from local slaves or from traveling minstrel entertainers, who frequently toured central North Carolina before the Civil War.[12]

Early minstrel banjoists and southern white banjoists both played mainly in a percussive downstroking style now called "clawhammer." (This style is also often called "frailing," though some banjoists distinguish between the two, since frailing involves "downstroking with chords" and clawhammer, or "brushless frailing," is without chords.)

The clawhammer style was apparently adapted from African American traditions, in which the musician struck the melody strings of the instrument with the fingernail of the index or middle finger in a downward motion followed by the thumb plucking the fifth or "drone" string. After the Civil War, however, a new style of "classic" banjo eclipsed this older downstroking style. Classic banjoists performed in a more modern, three-finger, up-picking style, in which they plucked the strings of the banjo using the index and middle fingers and the thumb of the playing hand in a technique modeled on the then-popular parlor and concert guitarists of the day. This method of playing expanded the instrument's musical possibilities, allowing banjoists to perform more complex arrangements in more technically sophisticated styles. This classic or "guitar" style quickly spread throughout the transatlantic banjo-playing world, originally through such influential instruction booklets as *New and Complete Method for the Banjo, with or without Masters* (1865) and then, during the 1890s, chiefly through cylinder recordings and vaudeville shows. Meanwhile, as a result of America's post–Civil War industrial surge, mass-produced five-string banjos, with steel-reinforced fretted necks, machined steel rims, and steel strings, became widely available throughout the United States, including in small textile towns in the Carolina Piedmont. By 1908, for example, the Sears, Roebuck catalog offered nine different five-string banjo models, ranging in price from $2.25 to $18.95. As a result of its greater accessibility, the instrument increasingly became one of the principal instruments in rural and working-class southern musical culture in the early decades of the twentieth century.[13]

Just as the banjo was becoming more technologically sophisticated and expanding in popularity in the southern white folk tradition, the instrument experienced a marked redefinition in American culture. During the 1870s and 1880s, banjo manufacturers, music teachers, and professional musicians launched an intensive campaign to "elevate" the banjo, to borrow their phrase, from its déclassé minstrel stage origins to the refined, respectable concert stage and parlor of middle-class America. "The banjo is becoming a recognized musical instrument and gradually finding its proper place in first class concerts as well as in the parlor and drawing room," remarked S. S. Stewart, in 1877, in the pages of his company magazine, *S. S. Stewart's Banjo and Guitar Journal*. "The coming banjoist will be a musician; an artist; and will not have to 'black up' to make his salary. He will find his way to the concert stage and will be heard at musical entertainments where comic songs, gags and big shoes are not considered an attraction." As a result of this campaign to dignify the banjo, notes Hank Sapoznik, "the once-popular image of a banjo-playing white man in blackface was superseded by that of a banjo-playing white man in black tie and tails."[14]

By the 1890s, refined middle-class American culture had fully embraced the five-string banjo as an instrument of serious and popular music. Banjo clubs were common in northeastern cities and on college campuses across the nation, and soloists and ensembles achieved great popularity on the vaudeville stage and on cylinder recordings with their banjo renditions of marches, rags, cakewalks, and sometimes even classical pieces. Between 1890 and 1920, musically literate classic banjo virtuosos such as Vess L. Ossman, Alfred A. Farland, Fred Van Eps, and Fred Bacon rose to national acclaim, and through their recordings and concerts they popularized the classic three-finger picking style that Poole came to embrace. Although the national banjo fad had waned by the outbreak of World War I, the five-string banjo continued to increase in popularity in the southern United States, where rural and small-town white residents played the instrument, either in combination with the fiddle or as part of larger stringbands, at dances, parties, and other social affairs. Likewise, although most of the region's white banjoists, particularly those in Southern Appalachia, played in the older, more traditional clawhammer or frailing style, the classic banjo style, which had filtered down from the concert stage and phonograph recordings, exerted a particularly strong musical influence on the Carolina Piedmont's banjoists well into the 1920s and beyond. "At the beginning of the nineteenth century, the banjo was essentially a black folk instrument," banjo historian Robert B. Winans has noted, but "by the early years of the twentieth century the five-string banjo was largely a mountain white folk instrument." And within southern white folk tradition, few banjo players would do more to push the instrument in exciting new directions than Charlie Poole.[15]

As a boy, Poole probably first learned to pick the banjo in this three-finger classic style from his older brother Leroy, who reportedly played in this fashion, but his early musical influences almost certainly extended far beyond his immediate family. Poole may also

Fred Van Eps. Courtesy of the Library of Congress.

have been taught to play in this style by the legendary North Carolina banjo picker Daner Johnson, a Randolph County textile worker who was twelve years his senior and his second cousin. Johnson worked as a boiler operator in the cotton mills in Randleman, not far from where Poole was born and spent his early childhood. According to other musicians who heard him perform, Johnson picked the five-string banjo in a classic-derived three-finger style, perhaps adapted from the banjo players he heard in touring vaudeville and medicine shows and on phonograph cylinders and discs; his style closely resembled the one that Poole himself eventually mastered. According to family legend, Johnson won the first prize of a gold-plated Stewart banjo in a banjo contest at the 1904 St. Louis World's Fair, edging out even the renowned classic banjoist and recording artist Fred Van Eps. Later in life, Johnson reportedly performed in both England and California and, though probably an apocryphal story, entertained at Gloria Vanderbilt's 1923 wedding in New York City. Johnson seems to have been an outstanding banjo picker and to have led a colorful life, but his exact musical impact on his second cousin is now lost to history. What is clear, however, is that by the turn of the twentieth century, when Charlie Poole took up the banjo, several vigorous banjo traditions, including clawhammer, frailing, double-thumbing, and two- and three-finger picking styles, were flourishing among white and black musicians in central North Carolina. The dynamic interaction between the popular classic banjo approaches heard on the concert stage and phonograph recordings and the traditional down-stroking styles originally derived from African American slaves and traveling minstrel shows reflected the complex borrowings and adaptations that were transforming the white working-class musical culture of the Piedmont.[16]

By his mid-teens, Charlie Poole had gained a local reputation in Haw River for being both a fine banjo picker and a neighborhood rowdy. He and his younger brother Henry sometimes drank heavily and got into fistfights with other local toughs in nearby Gibsonville, and on several occasions Poole was arrested for public drunkenness and disturbing the peace. In 1913, Poole and several of his brothers hijacked an electric trolley car in Haw River, ousted the conductor and passengers, and went joy-riding up the line toward Burlington. Over the next decade and a half, Poole would have several serious encounters with the law, including an episode during which he was shot in the mouth while resisting arrest, and would be arrested on at least a half-dozen occasions.[17]

On February 25, 1912, at the age of nineteen, Poole married a seventeen-year-old Haw River textile worker named Maude Gibson, and the newlyweds moved in with Maude's parents. Poole attempted to reform his rowdy bachelor ways and settle down to a steady married life. But he soon began backsliding into his old habits, skipping work on a regular basis in order to pick his banjo on the streets of Haw River. Soon the lure of the open road beckoned, and he began rambling away from home for weeks on end; on one occasion he hopped a freight train and rode as far west as Missoula, Montana. Poole was hoboing in Canada when his only child, James Clay Poole, was born on December 2, 1912. "Ramble!" scoffed his still-embittered ex-wife, Maude, years later. "He couldn't be still! He loved to go. You couldn't have a conversation with him. He was gone! Bet he never stayed over a month in any town in his life." Early in 1913, Maude Poole thought she had convinced her irresponsible husband to settle down and accompany her and her parents to Danville, Virginia, where they might find better-paying textile jobs. But on the day of their departure, Poole failed to show up at the Greensboro train depot. Annoyed, she searched for him, only to find that he had been arrested for public drunkenness and was sleeping off his bender in a Greensboro jail cell. Poole's rambling became too much for his neglected wife to bear, and they divorced after only a year of marriage. "Mama, after they separated, she was so mad she didn't even want to hear his records," recalled James Poole. "I think [they] brought back a few memories."[18]

After his divorce, Poole spent the next six years working sporadically in mills around Greensboro and rambling through Virginia, West Virginia, Maryland, and Pennsylvania, carousing, drinking, and playing music until his money ran out. Often, he busked for spare nickels and dimes at general stores and on courthouse squares, passing the hat among the townspeople and farmers who gathered to listen. "Mister, would you lend a poor dime a cripple?" he would sing in one of his favorite comical crowd-pleasers. "I'm a thousand dollars away from home, / Ain't got no mile in my pocket, / No head to poke my hole through, / No back to lay my bed upon, / Don't known where I'm gonna die when I go to."[19]

In 1918, during his wanderings, Poole met a crippled fiddler named

Posey Rorer, who was then working in the coal mines near Sophia, West Virginia, five miles southwest of Beckley. Born on September 22, 1891, in Franklin County, Virginia, Posey Wilson Rorer was the youngest of six children and the only son of Wilson Taylor "Wit" and Lucy (Moore) Rorer. The Rorers lived in a two-room log cabin and scratched out a living on a thirty-eight-acre mountain farm near the village of Ferrum. Wit Rorer added to the family's income by cutting crossties for the railroad and working at the nearby Bailey Distillery, one of the county's nearly one hundred government-licensed whiskey distilleries in 1900. Born with two clubfeet, Posey walked with great difficulty. Unable to participate in the rough-and-tumble activities of mountain boys his age, he occupied those hours not spent on farm chores and small-game hunting with music. A banjo player himself, Wit Rorer taught his son to play, and soon Posey fashioned his own banjo out of a lard bucket. Around the age of twelve, he took up the fiddle—his first was a homemade cigar-box instrument—and while still in his teens he began furnishing the music for local dances. Rorer left the family farm in 1917 at the age of twenty-five to find work in the coal mines near Sophia, West Virginia, where he was told he could earn some "real money." But his physical disability prevented him from landing a better-paying mining job deep underground, so he took a job as a trapper at the Pemberton Coal Company in Big Stick, a poor-paying, entry-level position usually occupied by teenage boys. Rorer supplemented his meager wages by entertaining with his now store-bought fiddle at square dances and house parties in the coal camps with a banjo-playing childhood friend, Harvey Stone, and another miner, Jim McMillan, also originally from Franklin County, who played the guitar.[20]

It was probably at one such coal-miners' dance, in early 1918, that Poole and Rorer first met. The two young musicians soon became close friends and began teaming up as a banjo-and-fiddle duo to entertain in the coal camps and railroad towns in Raleigh County, West Virginia. In the fall of 1918, Poole accompanied Rorer on a visit to Franklin County and, with no real home of his own, temporarily moved in with the Rorer family. Occasionally, Poole and Rorer furnished the music for dances in the surrounding farming communities and villages. Unwilling to work as farm laborers, the two men found an easier, more lucrative way to earn a living in rural Franklin County, where, as a result of Virginia's adoption of statewide prohibition in 1914 and the closing of its licensed distilleries, the local economy remained depressed. Poole and Rorer went into business with one of the Rorer family's neighbors making a batch of illegal moonshine whiskey, and while they tended the moonshine still in the woods they passed the hours playing music together. When the operation folded, Poole and Rorer netted a profit of $1,100 each. Rorer saved his earnings for an operation on his severely twisted feet, and, seven years later, in 1925, he underwent corrective surgery (which required the doctors to break both of his legs) at the Johns Hopkins University Hospital in Baltimore. Throughout the remainder of his life, however, he still hobbled around with great difficulty, often with the aid of a walking stick. Poole, on the other hand, felt no compulsion to save his money. He immediately bought himself a top-of-the-line Orpheum No. 3 Special banjo for $132, which he later used on all of his early recordings.[21]

Around 1919, Poole moved to the textile village of Spray (later incorporated, in 1967, as part of Eden), North Carolina, some ten miles south of the Virginia border, in Rockingham County. Poole may have settled there because he had an older married sister, Sarah Weaver, who had been working as a spinner in Spray for more than five years. Poole took a job at the Leaksville Cotton Mill as a speeder hand, tending the machines that drew out and twisted several strands of thread-like roving into a single strand of yarn and wound it onto bobbins. Initially, he probably resided with his sister's family in Carolina Heights, a textile village suburb of Spray. In 1920, Poole's friends, the Rorer family, sold their small farm in Franklin County and moved to Spray, where one of their daughters, Lou Emma Rorer, had been living and working as a spinner since 1910. Posey Rorer and his father went to work at the Nantucket Mill. Around this time, Poole began courting Lou Emma, who was almost ten years his senior. The couple was married in nearby Reidsville on December 11, 1920, and moved into a house on Flynn Street in Spray. Although he traveled extensively over the next decade, Poole would reside in Spray until his death in 1931.[22]

By the time Charlie Poole arrived there shortly after the end of World War I, Spray and the adjoining villages of Leaksville and Draper formed a sprawling textile-manufacturing center containing fourteen mills. "The cotton and woolen mills of Leaksville, Spray and Draper may not be so imposing as some of the other large manufacturing

Charlie Poole in Spray, North Carolina, 1925. Courtesy of Kinney Rorrer.

establishments that have all of their equipment centralized in a smaller space," remarked the *Danville Bee* in 1924, "but, taking everything into consideration, this is one of the most enterprising and progressive groups of textile plants to be found anywhere." Between 1896 and 1905, businessman B. Frank Mebane, the son-in-law of textile magnate and former U.S. congressman James Turner Morehead, constructed seven textile plants in Spray and one in Draper. In 1911, however, in the aftermath of an economic recession, Marshall Field and Company of Chicago acquired several of the Morehead family's bankrupt mills and consolidated them as the Carolina Cotton and Woolen Mills Company. By 1920, the firm controlled a chain of ten textile plants in Leaksville, Spray, and Draper. Several thousand people resided in the three villages, and, unlike Poole, a second-generation Piedmont millhand, many of them were recent arrivals from the Blue Ridge Mountains of western North Carolina and southwestern Virginia. Enticed by labor recruiters, they had flocked to Spray, Leaksville, and Draper to work in the area's bustling textile mills.[23]

Upon settling in Spray, Poole was delighted to discover a thriving musical culture in the three textile villages, stimulated in large part by the Carolina Cotton and Woolen Mills Company's extensive "industrial welfare" programs. Such programs, which often included a musical element, were common among larger, more progressive southern textile firms before World War I and were designed to promote employee loyalty to the company, help rural migrants assimilate to mill village life, and provide recreational outlets for employees and their families. Since 1898, one of the local Spray mills had sponsored brass bands and stringbands, as well as mandolin, guitar, and violin classes, under the direction of R. L. Martin, a graduate of the Peabody Institute in Baltimore, Maryland. One of the firm's brass bands, the Leaksville-Spray Band, won a prize at a musical competition in Charlotte, North Carolina, in 1908. Once it acquired control of the mills, the Carolina Cotton and Woolen Mills Company expanded the existing musical programs for the three textile villages and hired a succession of full-time musical directors, including Paul Manker and Otto A. Kircheis, to provide the workers and their children with violin, guitar, mandolin, and singing lessons. "No Mill Company Lays More Stress upon the Musical Feature Than the Carolina Cotton & Woolen Mills," proclaimed a 1920 *Mill News* profile of the firm. The article went on to explain:

The musical clubs and various pursuits of study in this branch comprise one of the big things in the life of the people of these towns. A musical director is employed at the expense of the Carolina Cotton and Woolen Mills Co. Classes are conducted in practically any line of music desired. He has in his employ several assistants. The lessons are not confined to the employees of the Carolina Cotton and Woolen Mills exclusively, but anyone in the town or the other mills may attend the classes and receive instruction. This branch of work is now about two years old and has made rapid strides in growth of membership. Here are some of the things taught in this branch: Band music, violin (65 members now), Hawaiian guitar clubs, mandolin clubs, guitar clubs for girls, glee clubs, three male quartets (and splendid ones).

There are 1,000 people taking voice, in class or group singing. The children are taught in community "sings" of from 500 to 800. Group singing is one of the features upon which stress is particularly laid. The people are urged to come and sing. And they are taught simple old time songs, classical selections, religious songs, and jazz tunes of the day. The same methods are taught in group singing as are used in public schools. In the violin classes the same methods are used as are taught in the New York city public schools.[24]

The Carolina Cotton and Woolen Mills Company's music programs nurtured the further development of local stringband traditions in Spray, Leaksville, and Draper. The firm's sponsorship of bands and formal musical instruction not only introduced hundreds of mill-hands and their children to a wide range of classical and popular music but also fostered among them an advanced level of musicianship and a high rate of musical literacy that on their own they probably could have neither afforded nor achieved. In fact, Poole himself may well have enhanced his own instrumental skills by enrolling in such music classes.[25]

With the encouragement of the Carolina Cotton and Woolen Mills Company's musical directors, fiddlers' conventions made up a regular feature of the public entertainment in north-central North Carolina and south-central Virginia textile towns throughout the 1920s. Often judged by the firm's music director, Otto A. Kircheis, these contests offered cash prizes for the best fiddlers, as well as for the best

Carolina Cotton & Woolen Mills Co.

Spray, N. C.　　　　　Draper, N. C.　　　　　Leaksville, N. C.

A great deal of work is being done by the Carolina Cotton and Woolen Mills in the villages of Draper, Leaksville, North Spray and Spray, where there are a number of mills owned and operated by it.

There are ten mills in the chain comprising the Carolina Cotton Mills. Their names and the products made at each mill are as follows:

The Mills and the Products.

Draper, N. C.: Draper-American Mills, cotton blankets; Wearwell Sheeting Mill, fine sheetings.

Spray, N. C.: Spray Woolen Mills, wool blankets; Rhode Island Mill, cotton blankets; Lily Mill, fine gingham; Nantucket Mill, ginghams and outing; Spray Bleachery, bleaches and finishes sheetings and narrow goods, and also makes up pillow cases, sheets, etc; American Warehouse finishes blankets, outings, ginghams, etc., and does the shipping for all the cotton mills.

Leaksville, N. C.: Athena Mills, ladies' and children's un-derwear; Wearwell Bedspread Mill, satin and crochet bedspreads.

Carolina Heights.

Carolina Heights comprise a suburb for the employes of the mills, of which any city might be proud. The entrance is through a grove, which is being developed into a park. The streets are graded, and cement sidewalks made. Stone pavement will be placed upon the streets through the village. The village consists of a number of splendid bungalows. Now these homes are "real" bungalows. They are the kind that the bette rclass in the large towns build as homes for themselves. They are modernly equipped and very attractive. Flowers and shrubs will be planted when all the work of grading and street work has been completed. It is the intention of the company to make one of the prettiest cotton mill residential sections in the state, and some of the other mills will have to make a big jump to head them in the race.

Road building committees of the various towns and coun-

No Mill Company Lays More Stress Upon the Musical Feature Than the Carolina Cotton & Woolen Mills. A Few of the Many Musical Clubs Organized in the Musical Department and Not Confined to the Employes of the Mills Alone.

"No Mill Company Lays More Stress upon the Musical Feature Than the Carolina Cotton & Woolen Mills." Carolina Cotton and Woolen Mills Company profile, *Mill News* (Charlotte, North Carolina), October 14, 1920. Courtesy of the North Carolina Collection, Wilson Library, University of North Carolina at Chapel Hill.

cloggers and Charleston dancers and the best musicians on a number of other stringed instruments, including guitar, banjo, and mandolin. Like the corporate-sponsored textile bands and formal music classes, these competitions not only served as important forums for the cross-pollination of regional musical repertoires and styles but also encouraged millhand musicians to sharpen their instrumental skills and showmanship before live audiences. Poole and other area musicians avidly competed in these contests, which were held in Spray and Leaksville and the surrounding towns of Madison and Mayodan, North Carolina, and Fieldale, Virginia. In fact, in April 1926, at a contest held in the Leaksville Graded School, Poole won the first place prize of $7.50 in the banjo competition.[26]

With their large population of millhands and the encouragement of corporate-sponsored music programs, the textile villages of Spray, Leaksville, and Draper emerged as an important center of string-band music after World War I. Among the most talented musicians to emerge from this environment was a Leaksville loom fixer named Will J. Heffinger, a highly accomplished fiddler whose smooth long-bow style was emulated by younger local fiddlers, such as Lonnie Austin and Odell Smith, both of whom later recorded with the North Carolina Ramblers. Already a gifted breakdown fiddler, Heffinger had further refined his skills by taking private violin lessons from Paul Manker, a Norwegian who served as one of the Carolina Cotton and Woolen Mills Company's musical directors. During the early 1920s, Heffinger fronted a loose-knit, twin-fiddle stringband consisting of himself and several future North Carolina Ramblers, including guitarist Will Woodlieff, banjo player Gabe Nowlin, and tenor banjo player Hamon Newman. Called the Leaksville String Band, the group often entertained crowds at square dances, house parties, Brunswick stews, and school closings with their dance numbers such as "Flyin' Clouds," "Golden Slippers," "Flop-Eared Mule," and Heffinger's personal favorite, "Richmond."[27]

But Spray, Leaksville, and Draper formed only part of a much larger regional network of stringband activity that flourished in north-central North Carolina and south-central Virginia. Thirty-five miles to the northeast sat the textile center of Danville, Virginia, a city of more than 21,000 residents, some 6,000 of whom were employed at the Riverside and Dan River Cotton Mills, Inc., one of the largest textile firms in the South. Perhaps the most renowned millhand active in that local music scene was fiddler Charley LaPrade, who fronted a stringband trio called the Blue Ridge Highballers. Originally from Franklin County, Virginia, LaPrade settled in Spray around 1900, where he worked in a cotton mill, before moving in 1918 to Schoolfield, a textile village suburb of Danville. There, he worked as a weaver and a machinist in local cotton mills. Already a sophisticated fiddler who played in a smooth long-bow style, he enhanced his music skills by taking private violin lessons from a Swedish-born music teacher at Averett College in nearby Danville. Other noted musicians who worked in Danville-area textile mills included the guitarist Lewis C. McDaniel, who recorded in 1930 for Columbia with Posey Rorer and two other local musicians as the Carolina Buddies, and the Bigger brothers, fiddler Richard and guitarist Elvin, who together with two other local millhands formed the Four Virginians in the mid-1920s.[28]

Thirty miles north of Spray, the textile town of Fieldale formed another important center of stringband music. Established in 1917 as a company town, Fieldale revolved around Fieldcrest Mills, owned and operated by Marshall Field and Company. In the mid-1920s, Kelly Harrell, a ballad singer originally from Wythe County, Virginia, settled in Fieldale, where he worked as a loom fixer at the Fieldcrest Mills. Later, in 1927, Harrell recruited first Posey Rorer and then Lonnie Austin to provide the fiddling for his recordings with his studio band, the Virginia String Band, whose regular members consisted of two local millhands, banjo player Raymond D. Hundley and guitarist Alfred Steagall. As a result of the concentration of working-class communities and the stimulation of corporate-sponsored musical programs, a rich stringband tradition emerged in the textile centers of Danville and Fieldale, and many of the musicians active in Spray and Leaksville, including Charlie Poole and other members of the North Carolina Ramblers, performed and sometimes even recorded with their colleagues from these neighboring Virginia textile mill communities. This vibrant musical cross-pollination among millhands made this geographical region, bounded by Rockingham County, North Carolina, and Henry County and Pittsylvania County in Virginia, one of the richest centers of old-time stringband music during the 1920s.[29]

During the early 1920s, Charlie Poole met several of the musicians active in these textile mill towns and soon immersed himself in the local Spray music scene, sitting in as a banjo player and singer with established stringbands and swapping songs and tunes with other millhand musicians. Not only an accomplished five-string banjoist but also a talented singer who apparently had a sizable repertoire of traditional ballads and sentimental parlor songs, Poole was a particularly welcome addition to the local stringband scene. Working at the Leaksville Mill, he soon struck up friendships with several local millhand musicians, including banjoist John Fletcher "Red" Patterson, who was born in 1900 on a tobacco farm outside Leaksville. Patterson worked as a weaver in a Leaksville cotton mill and, as a self-taught musician, picked the banjo in a three-finger style that closely resembled Poole's own. Together, he and Poole entertained for house parties and country dances in Rockingham County until around 1925, when Patterson moved to Fieldale, Virginia, and formed his own stringband called the Piedmont Log Rollers. Another young textile millhand, guitarist Will Woodlieff, a regular member of Will Heffinger's Leaksville String Band, sometimes joined Patterson and Poole in their music making.[30]

Around 1920, Poole formed the North Carolina Ramblers with fiddler Posey Rorer and guitarist Will Woodlieff, and soon the band attracted a large following in its hometown and in surrounding textile towns and farming communities. On Saturday afternoons, after their half-day shift at the mill, the musicians busked outside the Spray post office for the crowds of millhands and farm families shopping in the nearby business district. Often accompanied by Red Patterson, Hamon Newman, and other local musicians, the trio also entertained at house parties, square dances, corn huskings, watermelon slicings, and other social gatherings, which played a prominent role in the social life of the textile towns and farming communities of the Carolina Piedmont. When Woodlieff got married and dropped out of the band around 1923, his younger brother Norman, also a textile millhand, replaced him as the regular guitarist in the North Carolina Ramblers. Born in Rural Hall, North Carolina, around 1900, Norman Woodlieff had moved to Spray with his family in 1910, and, at the age of fourteen, he followed his father and older siblings into the textile mills, working sixty hours a week for $5.50. Shortly afterward, he became interested in music, and his brother Will taught him a few guitar chords and how to play a number of simple songs. By the age of seventeen, Norman Woodlieff was entertaining at house parties and country dances around Spray. In 1919, however, he enlisted in the navy and left town. After his military discharge in 1921, Woodlieff returned to Spray and began to sit in occasionally with the North Carolina Ramblers at local venues, before he became the band's regular guitarist. Another guitarist who sometimes played with the band was Clarence Foust, one of Poole's childhood friends from Alamance County.[31]

Besides playing locally, Poole and the North Carolina Ramblers further enhanced their musical skills and their regional reputation by entertaining on the road, following the rail lines and highways through the small towns and coalfields of the Upper South. By 1924, the band was performing throughout southwestern Virginia and southern West Virginia and sometimes as far away as Kentucky, Tennessee, and Ohio. One of the members, usually Woodlieff or Foust, traveled ahead of the other Ramblers to schedule shows and paste up handbills about the band's upcoming performances in a particular railroad town or coal camp. On their musical excursions, Poole and his bandmates sometimes played in schoolhouses, theaters, and roadhouses for appreciative crowds of paying audiences. Mostly, though, they played for country dances and house parties for little more than food, lodging, and whiskey, winning a large following among the residents of Southern Appalachia.[32]

In early 1925, on one of their musical tours, Poole and the other two North Carolina Ramblers, Posey Rorer and Clarence Foust, fell in with a shady Baptist minister, Rev. Rufus E. Holder, who hired the musicians as part of a musical troupe to perform at a series of fiddlers' contests he was promoting in East Tennessee and southwestern Virginia. The group entertained at fiddlers' contests in Bristol in February and, the following month, in Kingsport, Tennessee, where the local *Kingsport Times* reported, "This six piece fiddling [troupe] is fast gaining a reputation in this section of the country." At least some of Rev. Holder's musical shows featured individual fiddle and banjo competitions, stringband entertainment, and clog dancing. Poole and his bandmates competed against local musicians for prizes in the musical contests and also performed together as a featured trio. The *Kingsport Times* identified them as hailing from the rustically named mountain hamlet of Gobbler's Knob, North Carolina. At the Kingsport event held on March 4 at a local high school, Poole won first prize in the banjo contest, and Rorer took second in the fiddlers' contest.[33]

Rev. Holder claimed that the proceeds from these contests would go to support an orphanage in Bluefield, West Virginia. But, according to Poole's biographer, Kinney Rorrer, the itinerant evangelist, whom he identifies in *Rambling Blues* as "Reverend Holner"—surely one and the same person—was something of a flimflam artist. Rorrer alleges that at least some of the fiddle contests that Rev. Holder staged were rigged and that Poole and his bandmates willingly participated in this con game. According to Rorrer, their scheme required Holder to travel ahead of the band to promote his fiddlers' contests in a community, enlisting local businesses to sponsor the event and to donate cash prizes. Then, on the day of the event, the North Carolina Ramblers would stroll into town and casually enter the contest. As superior musicians, they would be almost guaranteed to win the first place cash prize, which they would then split with the minister. For several weeks, Rorrer reports, Rev. Holder and the North Carolina Ramblers barnstormed from town to town across Southern Appalachia in an open-topped jalopy, bilking local merchants and musicians and amassing a sizable amount of cash. Then, one night in Tazewell, Virginia, Rev. Holder skipped out on his trusting partners-in-crime, absconding with the entire ill-gotten bankroll and leaving them to nurse their bruised egos.[34]

Although Charlie Poole and the North Carolina Ramblers had established a considerable musical reputation for themselves in the Virginia and Carolina Piedmont and Southern Appalachia, when their musical tour ended in the spring of 1925, they returned to work in Spray's textile mills. They did not remain there for long, however. Poole had long been dissatisfied with the time-clock discipline, enforced sobriety, and settled existence of factory work. Awakened now to the possibility of turning his music into a full-time profession, Poole struck upon the idea of making commercial phonograph recordings of what within the year would be called "hillbilly music." According to Kinney Rorrer, Poole's friend Kelly Harrell, a Fieldale, Virginia, textile loom fixer and ballad singer with whom he sometimes played, may have inspired him. Harrell had made his recording debut in January 1925 when he sang four songs, accompanied by studio musicians, for the Victor Talking Machine Company in New York City. Or Poole's motivation may have come from Ernest V. Stoneman, a Bluefield, West Virginia, singer and harmonica and autoharp player with whom Poole had briefly toured sometime in the fall of 1924 or the spring of 1925.

Stoneman had waxed his first recordings, "The Face That Never Returned" and "The Titanic," for the OKeh label in September 1924.[35]

Whatever the source of his inspiration, Poole and the other two regular members of the North Carolina Ramblers quit their factory jobs and took the train to Passaic, New Jersey, in late June 1925. There, while awaiting a recording audition, they boarded with one of Posey Rorer's boyhood friends and secured temporary jobs to support themselves. Poole and Norman Woodlieff worked in a railroad car manufacturing plant, while Rorer hired on at a textile mill. Meanwhile, Poole managed to finagle an audition for the band with Frank B. Walker, the Columbia Phonograph Company's A & R man in charge of the firm's hillbilly records series, which was variously called "Old Familiar Tunes" or "Familiar Tunes—Old and New." Although the firm had only entered the hillbilly record market in March 1924, it had quickly risen to become the nation's leader in this field of commercial popular music. Columbia's national marketing and distribution networks, combined with its aggressive advertising campaign in the *Talking Machine World*, propelled the firm's meteoric rise to prominence in the hillbilly recording industry. So too did Frank B. Walker's progressive leadership and skillful selection of recording artists. In November 1924, Walker had inaugurated the innovative practice, soon adopted almost industry-wide, of releasing Columbia's old-time records in a discrete, special numerical series, its famous 15000-D "Old Familiar Tunes" series, as a counterpart to the firm's 14000-D race records series, inaugurated in 1923, and its nearly three dozen foreign-language records series. By the middle of 1925, Columbia's "Old Familiar Tunes" series contained some 30 records, and, eventually, 782 records were released in this series, more than in any other label's old-time music series, before its demise in 1932.[36]

In creating a marketable image for its old-time music and in distinguishing it from other genres of commercial popular music, Columbia, like the other major talking-machine firms, linked old-time records to highly romanticized images of a preindustrial mountain South out of touch with modern Jazz Age America. Columbia's first old-time records catalog, *Familiar Tunes on Fiddle, Guitar, Banjo, Harmonica and Accordion*, issued in November 1924, claimed to feature musical selections by "popular rustic talent . . . whose names are best known where the square dance has not been supplanted by the fox-trot." To embellish these textual descriptions, Columbia's illustrators

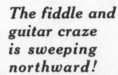

"The fiddle and guitar craze is sweeping northward! Columbia leads with records of old-fashioned southern songs and dances." Columbia Records advertisement, *Talking Machine World*, June 15, 1924. Courtesy of the Southern Folklife Collection, Wilson Library, University of North Carolina at Chapel Hill.

and designers created iconic visual images of old-time music, which they hoped would make these records highly appealing and instantly recognizable to American consumers. For example, Columbia often illustrated the front covers of its *Old Familiar Tunes* catalogs with sentimental scenes of log cabins nestled in stands of tall pines, rustic fiddlers coaxing a tune from their instruments, and snow-capped mountains. Inside, the catalogs presented "the old, familiar melodies, the songs and dances that outlive the years," and promised that the artists interpreted these selections "in a manner that brings the memories crowding back." In a jazz-mad nation, Columbia's old-time ballads and banjo tunes of southern mountaineers could not have seemed more anachronistic, but for hundreds of thousands of Americans, only a generation or two removed from their rural roots, these records offered comforting reassurance that authentic traditional music and joyous preindustrial pastimes could survive in a modern, urban-industrial America.[37]

On July 27, 1925, Poole and the North Carolina Ramblers auditioned for Walker at Columbia's main studio in the Gotham National Bank Building in downtown Manhattan. Their spirited stringband music impressed the A & R man, and later that afternoon the group recorded its first four sides. Columbia assigned the North Carolina Ramblers' records to its newly inaugurated 15000-D "Old Familiar Tunes" series and, less than two months later, released the trio's first record. It proved an instant sensation. The North Carolina Ramblers' debut coupling, "Don't Let Your Deal Go Down Blues"/"Can I Sleep in Your Barn Tonight Mister," sold an astonishing 102,000 copies at a time when Columbia's hillbilly releases averaged sales of around 12,000 copies, and it remained one of the best-selling records in the company's hillbilly catalog before 1933. Sales of their second release, "The Girl I Left in Sunny Tennessee"/"I'm the Man That Rode the Mule 'Round the World," issued a few weeks later, sold more than 65,000 copies. Altogether, Columbia made an estimated $40,000 profit on the band's first two records. The musicians, however, received only a one-time payment of $75, which, according to their agreement, they were to split three ways. But Woodlieff later claimed that neither he nor Rorer ever saw a dime of this money. Poole pocketed the entire sum.[38]

After the spectacular sales of the band's first two releases, Walker wired Poole to invite the North Carolina Ramblers to record some additional selections, but Poole simply ignored him. Perhaps he felt that, in light of their tremendous record sales, Walker had swindled him and his bandmates. Eager to cash in on the band's current popularity, Walker nonetheless persisted, and over the next year he sent Poole a succession of telegrams and letters imploring the North Carolina Ramblers to record again. Instead of returning to Columbia's studios, the North Carolina Ramblers launched an extended musical tour across the coalfields of southwestern Virginia and southern West Virginia, where their best-selling records brought the band even greater acclaim. The band gravitated to coal towns and railroad centers, where, as a result of sustained industrial development, populations were densely concentrated and workers had enough money to splurge on tickets to the band's shows. But Woodlieff, who suffered from tuberculosis and aspired to become a professional cartoonist, soon tired of the road. When his fragile health began to deteriorate seriously in 1926, he left the North Carolina Ramblers.[39]

After Woodlieff's departure, Poole replaced him with a more talented West Virginia musician named Roy Harvey, who would remain the band's regular guitarist for the next four years. Roy Cecil Harvey was born on March 24, 1892 (two days after Charlie Poole), in Monroe County, West Virginia. His father moved the family to Princeton, West Virginia, when Roy was a boy, and there, at the age of eighteen, Harvey took a job with the Virginian Railroad, first as a fireman and then, five years later, as a railroad engineer. Harvey loved railroading, but as a loyal member of the Brotherhood of Locomotive Engineers, he walked off his job with his fellow railroaders during the Virginian Strike of 1923. He was deeply disappointed when the protracted strike, which dragged on for six years, forced him into another line of work. In 1925, Harvey moved his family to Beckley, West Virginia, where he worked as a streetcar conductor and occasionally as a clerk in his brother-in-law E. D. Terry's Beckley Music Store, which sold musical instruments, sheet music, radio sets, and Columbia and Edison phonographs and records. By then, Harvey had been playing the guitar for at least a decade, and it was during this period in his life that he began composing songs, many of them railroad ballads such as "The Railroad Blues," "The Wreck of the Virginian No. 3," and "The Virginian Strike of '23," the last of which remains one of only a few songs about southern labor struggles to appear on commercial hillbilly records before World War II.[40]

Poole had first met Harvey in 1925 during one of the North Carolina Ramblers' musical excursions to West Virginia. Harvey, then running a trolley car between Bluefield and Princeton, noticed three passengers board his car carrying instrument cases. At one of his stops, he asked the strangers to play him a song, and when they finished, Harvey borrowed Woodlieff's guitar and played a tune that demonstrated his own talent on the instrument. Poole was impressed with Harvey's smooth, polished guitar work, and, after Woodlieff's departure, he immediately recruited Harvey to become the band's regular guitarist, recognizing that he would provide a near-perfect complement to the North Carolina Ramblers' distinctive sound. Harvey's membership in the band also provided an additional bonus; as the most educated and certainly the most responsible member of the group, Harvey willingly shouldered the responsibility of managing the band, arranging travel schedules, securing transportation, booking shows, and eventually scheduling recording sessions. Although Harvey served as the band's manager, Poole, it seems, insisted on handling the money.[41]

Shortly after Harvey joined the band, Frank B. Walker finally managed to entice Poole and the North Carolina Ramblers back into the studio by agreeing to pay them $150 per side plus royalties. In September 1926, almost fourteen months after their debut session, Poole and Rorer, accompanied by Harvey, returned to Columbia's studios in New York City, where, over the course of five days, they recorded eighteen sides, ranging from traditional fiddle tunes ("Flyin' Clouds" and "Ragtime Annie") and blues ballads ("White House Blues") to vaudeville numbers ("Hungry Hash House" and "Monkey on a String") and old Tin Pan Alley chestnuts ("Leaving Home," "There'll Come a Time," and "Budded Rose"). The band even recorded a railroad disaster ballad, "The Brave Engineer," a version of "The Wreck on the C & O," with Roy Harvey singing the lead. During these sessions, in order to relax the musicians and perhaps to calm their jittery nerves, Walker or one of his assistants supplied the band members with alcohol, an illegal but common practice at hillbilly recording sessions during the 1920s. As a result, Poole likely recorded drunk on a number of sides. His rendition of "White House Blues," waxed on September 20, seems particularly marred by intoxication; though usually a commanding vocalist, at a couple of moments during the recording Poole forgets the lyrics and just mumbles along until he recalls them.[42]

While in New York, Poole also signed a contract to record exclu-

Charlie Poole, center, flanked by the North Carolina Ramblers
(Posey Rorer, left, and Roy Harvey, right), 1927.
Courtesy of Kinney Rorer.

sively for Columbia, under the terms of which, he later claimed, he received several thousand dollars. Sales from the second North Carolina Ramblers' session remained high — "There'll Come a Time"/"Leaving Home" sold more than 81,000 copies; sales of "White House Blues"/"Monkey on a String," despite Poole's botched singing on the former, exceeded 76,000 copies. With the increased earnings from his recording work, coupled with ticket receipts from his musical tours, Poole finally achieved the financial freedom to abandon the textile work he so despised and to earn his living as a full-time professional musician. Over the next four years, he and a revolving combination of musicians in the North Carolina Ramblers would return to Columbia's studios five more times to record fifty-one additional sides, several of which were to emerge as bluegrass standards after World War II. Except for a brief stint working in the Spray mills in 1931, Poole would spend the remainder of his short life as a professional musician.[43]

Poole and the North Carolina Ramblers' mounting string of commercial successes encouraged several other Piedmont textile string-bands across north-central North Carolina and south-central Virginia to try their luck at making phonograph records, including Kelly Harrell and the Virginia String Band, Red Patterson's Piedmont Log Rollers, Charley LaPrade and the Blue Ridge Highballers, the Four Virginians, the Carolina Buddies, and the Floyd County Ramblers. Several of these bands covered the North Carolina Ramblers' hits in a stringband style that closely echoed the original recordings, and some, including the Carolina Buddies and Kelly Harrell and the Virginia String Band, even enlisted Posey Rorer and Lonnie Austin to supply their distinctive fiddle work on these recordings. Between 1926 and 1931, at least fifteen different bands from north-central North Carolina and south-central Virginia (excluding Charlie Poole and the North Carolina Ramblers) recorded nearly two hundred sides for major talking-machine companies. Furthermore, Poole himself, in personal encounters, inspired several musical contemporaries, including Preston Young and Fred Miller (of the Tar Heel Rattlers), to either adopt the banjo as their instrument of choice or to perform in a similar three-fingered picking style.[44]

Arguably, much of Charlie Poole's success as a hillbilly star can be attributed to the fact that he remained, throughout his life, a tremendous fan of a diverse range of American popular music. Although his own phonograph records were confined to Columbia's "Old Familiar Tunes" series, his musical tastes varied widely. Poole owned an extensive record collection, and, according to his family, his favorite record was a 1929 Victor disc titled "Cherokee Rag," by Big Chief Henry's Indian String Band. But Poole also admired the recordings of classical violinist Fritz Kreisler, the "Banjo King" Vess L. Ossman, ragtime blues guitarist Blind Blake, *Grand Ole Opry* banjoist Uncle Dave Macon, hillbilly balladeer Vernon Dalhart, and vaudeville singer and film star Al Jolson. "My father was a hillbilly musician," recalled James Poole, "but he loved good stuff, you know. Like, say, Blind Blake, he had some awful good runs on guitar, you know, with a thumb pick. My father liked anything that a man did in that style that was good in that style. He used to listen to Rudy Vallee when he came out. He liked his stuff. He liked any of it if it was good. You take Fritz Kreisler, he listened to his music a lot. He bought a lot of his records." According to James Poole, he and his father went to see Al Jolson in Warner Brothers' 1928 box-office smash *The Singing Fool* seven times at the Rockingham Theatre in nearby Reidsville. "Yea, he'd go for that 'Sonny Boy,'" James recalled, referring to the million-selling hit song that the film produced. Poole, in fact, so idolized Jolson that he even emulated him on a whistling solo that he incorporated into "Rambling Blues." But Poole's favorite recording artist by far was Fred Van Eps, the most widely recorded classic banjoist of the 1910s and early 1920s. While living in Spray or perhaps even earlier, Poole became fascinated with Van Eps's banjo solos and medleys, and bought many of his available releases to play on his phonograph. Once, in the mid-1920s, Poole even traveled with his son to Chicago to see Van Eps perform and afterward recorded two of his musical idol's showcase medleys and instrumentals, "The Infanta March" and "Dixie Medley," sometimes using piano accompaniment, just like several of Van Eps's original recordings, in order to demonstrate his own technical proficiency on the banjo.[45]

Poole not only copied many of his own numbers from the recordings of Van Eps and his other favorite recording stars, but he also modeled his professional image in part on some of these same musicians. From early in his career, Poole maintained a serious, professional image, and although Columbia sometimes released the North Carolina Ramblers' recordings on its budget-priced Velvet Tone and Clarion labels under such rustic pseudonyms as the Smoky Blue Highballers and Pete Harrison's Bayou Boys, Poole steadfastly refused to play or dress the "hillbilly fool." Always a snappy dresser himself, Poole demanded that his bandmates wear formal suits and ties for all their publicity photographs and stage shows. On one of his later theater tours, Poole and his band even dressed in matching crisp white shirts and pants, with black bow ties and black belts, that made them look more like a dapper vaudeville troupe than a small-town hillbilly stringband. As Hank Sapoznik notes, "Although he had a preference for slicked-down haircuts ending inches above his jug handle ears, accentuating his eager, boyish appearance, Poole never played up the country bumpkin look. No hayseed he. Pictures of the North Carolina Ramblers always show them in dressy dark suits, sporting natty bow ties and looking for all the world like Rotarians with instruments." Although Poole never owned an automobile and seemed to care little for store-bought luxuries, he insisted on using top-of-the-line instruments, and, around 1926, he bought himself a $250 Gibson Mastertone banjo. In fact, he later appeared in a Gibson promotional catalog, testifying as a professional musician to the exquisite craftsmanship and quality of the instrument—a sign in itself of Poole's emerging status as a nationally recognized recording artist.[46]

By all accounts, Poole was a chronic drunk and an unreliable millhand, but he demonstrated an intense professional work ethic when it came to his music. He practiced the banjo diligently, sometimes two or more hours a day, locked in a room by himself, and became so proficient that he could play in three flat keys as well as in the key of C. His occasional intoxicated performances on recordings notwithstanding, Poole demanded the same high level of musical competency from his band members, and the North Carolina Ramblers' recordings attest to his rigorous standards of precise timing, flawless execution, and instrumental virtuosity. Moreover, at least by 1927, if not earlier, Poole had stopped identifying himself as a textile millhand and instead listed his occupation in the Spray city directory as "professional musician and recording artist." Apparently, his musical contemporaries also acknowledged his professional status, for they barred him from competing in amateur music competitions. The *Leaksville News*, for example, reported that at a 1927 Fourth of July fiddlers' convention in Spray Park, "a combination prize of $10 was won by Mr. Charlie Poole of Spray, a professional musician, [who] did not enter the contest, but did his bit by playing to entertain the crowd." In fact, Poole's local celebrity status prompted Leaksville tex-

137

tile magnate B. Frank Mebane, himself a fan of fiddle and stringband music, to hire the North Carolina Ramblers to perform for several high-society soirees at his mansion. According to sideman Lonnie Austin, though, the whiskey-drinking Poole was disappointed to discover that at these high-class affairs only fine wines were served.[47]

Despite such locally prestigious engagements, Poole remained largely outside of more respectable working-class society. In fact, he seems to have wholeheartedly embraced the roughest elements of working-class culture in the textile towns and mining camps he wandered through. Neither a churchgoer nor a homebody, he largely ignored his family responsibilities to his wife, Lou Emma, and his son, James, in order to carouse with his hard-drinking buddies and to play music and ramble through the mountains of Southern Appalachia. Always attracted to the seamier sites, Poole performed in roadhouses, at moonshiners' stills, and even in brothels, all venues at which he could satisfy his thirst for corn whiskey. For two solid weeks in 1930, for example, Poole and a piano player entertained for tips at Black Annie's, a mixed-race whorehouse in "Cinder Bottom," the infamous red-light district of the coal-mining town of Keystone, West Virginia.[48]

Between 1926 and 1930, Poole and the North Carolina Ramblers maintained a hectic schedule of recording sessions, stage shows, and, occasionally, radio broadcasts that kept them away from home for weeks and sometimes months at a time. Poole's drinking and long absences away from home had already destroyed his first marriage to Maude Gibson, and doubtless his life on the so-called kerosene circuit also severely strained his relationship with his second wife, Lou Emma, and his son, James, who spent several weeks each summer in Spray. His father, James recalled, "just toured all the time. That's why they called them Ramblers. I think that the reason my mother and him separated to start with was because he was always gone." Poole's excessive drinking led, on several occasions, to his arrest for public drunkenness and brawling, and he spent a number of nights "drying out" in jail cells. Around 1925, in a particularly close brush with the law, Poole was nearly killed when police raided a roadhouse in which he and Posey Rorer were performing just across the North Carolina border in Leaksville Junction, Virginia. Refusing to submit peacefully, Poole clobbered a police officer over the head with his banjo. Then, while wrestling with a second policeman over his service revolver,

Poole was shot in the mouth. Fortunately for him, he was not seriously wounded, and he even managed to beat several officers with Rorer's walking stick before he and Rorer escaped in an automobile. A wanted man, Poole at first hid out in the mountains, but eventually he surrendered to Spray police. His escapade cost him bloodied lips, a few chipped front teeth, and a one-hundred-dollar fine, which his wife paid. No evidence survives to indicate what Lou Emma Poole thought of her husband's rough and rowdy ways, but backup guitarist Roy Harvey, a teetotaler and nonsmoker, condemned Poole's heavy drinking and for a long time tried in vain to get him to give up the bottle. But drinking, after all, was an integral part of Poole's occupational culture as a traveling professional musician who spent weeks on the road and is perhaps one significant reason why this life so appealed to him.[49]

Originally, in the mid-1920s, Poole had traveled primarily with just Rorer and Harvey, but he began to experiment with larger orchestras in his stage shows, and eventually he expanded his road band to include as many as six or even seven musicians, at times adding a second fiddle, tenor banjo, piano, and ukulele accompaniment to augment the band's regular guitar-fiddle-banjo combination. Among the more regular members of the larger ensemble were fiddlers Lonnie Austin and Odell Smith, tenor banjoist Hamon Newman, yodeler and ukulele player Earl Shirkey, and pianist Lucy Terry, Roy Harvey's sister, who played piano accompaniment for silent films at a Beckley movie theater. During their musical tours, the North Carolina Ramblers proved exceptionally popular in the small towns and farming communities of the Piedmont and Southern Appalachia, and, despite Poole's reputation as a hard-drinking scoundrel, textile millhands, coal miners, and farmers often brought their wives and children to the shows. Poole toned down his act for these more family-oriented shows, skipping racier musical numbers such as "Take Your Leg Off Mine" and discreetly concealing his whiskey on stage in a Coca-Cola bottle.[50]

Typically, the North Carolina Ramblers opened their stage shows with the gospel number "Beautiful Crown" and closed with another, "The Great Reaping Day," in order to present a wholesome facade meant to assure the religiously devout among their audiences of the band's moral rectitude and respectability. In between, Poole and his sidemen performed a crowd-pleasing combination of fiddle break-

The North Carolina Ramblers road band of 1930. *Left to right, standing*: Charlie Poole, Odell Smith, Gilmer Nowlin; *seated*: Hamon Newman, James Poole, Earl Shirkey. Courtesy of Kinney Rorrer.

downs, classic banjo selections, comic novelties, and sentimental popular ballads to thunderous applause. Besides performing his Columbia hits, Poole often incorporated his new arrangements of older, turn-of-the-century Tin Pan Alley songs into the road band's repertoire. These performances gave him and the North Carolina Ramblers an opportunity to refine these new numbers and to determine which ones elicited the most enthusiastic responses before heading into the recording studio. With his colorful, charismatic personality, Poole made an engaging master of ceremonies at these shows, entertaining the crowd between musical sets by cracking jokes, clogging and dancing the buck-and-wing, and spinning yarns about a fictional rube character named "Uncle Billy Arnt." Apparently, even when drunk, Poole was an exceptionally well-coordinated, athletic man, and onstage he performed acrobatics—turning cartwheels, flipping somersaults over chairs, and dancing on his palms while doing a handstand. According to his son, Poole "knew an audience, and he knew how to work to it. And he knew what people would go for In fact, if the show was sagging, he'd get back out there and pick it up."[51]

Poole also attempted to transform his expanded road band into a studio recording band. After coming off one of his lengthy musical tours in the spring of 1927, Poole began to assemble a larger, five-piece studio band in order to produce a fuller, more pop-oriented sound at his next recording session. That July, the North Carolina Ramblers returned to New York, accompanied by Lucy Terry and Bob Hoke, a Princeton railroad-worker friend of Harvey's who played the banjo-mandolin. The band's regular lineup of Poole, Rorer, and Harvey recorded eight sides of their characteristically eclectic numbers, including a Spanish-American War number ("If I Lose, I Don't Care"), a 1901 "coon song" ("Coon from Tennessee"), a black blues ballad about cocaine reworked into a drinking song ("Take a Drink on Me"), a World War I song ("On the Battle Fields of Belgium"), a 1909 Broadway show tune ("You Ain't Talkin' to Me"), and two late nineteenth-century Tin Pan Alley numbers ("The Letter That Never Came" and "Falling by the Wayside"). With the addition of Hoke, the band also cut another railroad disaster ballad, "The Wreck of the Virginian No. 3," on which Harvey supplied the lead vocals. But the most unorthodox sides of the sessions were a series of classic banjo solos with piano accompaniment. The piano was seldom heard on hillbilly records before the mid-1930s, but seeking to emulate the popular sound of Fred Van Eps, Poole enlisted Terry to accompany him on four classic banjo-and-piano pieces: "Don't Let Your Deal Go Down Medley," "Sunset March" (Poole's arrangement of Van Eps's 1911 Edison cylinder recording of "The Infanta March"), "Down in Georgia," and "Teasin' Fritz" (probably a mistranslation of the classic banjo standard "Teasin' the Frets"). By the time of this 1927 session, the four-string tenor banjo, which made up part of the rhythm section of jazz and dance bands of the 1920s, had eclipsed the five-string banjo that Poole played. And with the rise of the tenor banjo, which musicians typically played in a strummed-chord style using a single plectrum or pick, Van Eps's style of classic playing had likewise fallen out of popularity. The new stars were now tenor banjoists such as Eddie Peabody, Roy Smeck, and Harry Reser (leader of the Clicquot Club Eskimos, the popular NBC network radio band). Nonetheless, Poole remained enamored with the three-finger classic approach and insisted on making recordings in this style.[52]

Prior to this session, Poole and the North Carolina Ramblers' numbers had corresponded closely to the other recorded selections that made up Columbia's "Old Familiar Tunes" series and to the rustic, old-fashioned, and highly nostalgic marketing image the firm sought to create for its hillbilly records series. But Poole perhaps hoped that Columbia would market these classic banjo-and-piano sides in its 100-D popular music series, rather than in the 15000-D old-time music series in which his discs were usually released. "My father recorded some stuff that was too high class for 'corn music,'" explained James Poole. "He used piano accompaniment on 'Sunset March' and 'Don't Let Your Deal Go Down Medley.' But Frank Walker, the head of the Columbia organization, told my daddy he didn't have him listed for that class of music, see. Said he wouldn't sell." Walker, not willing to risk a change, assigned one of Poole's experimental records to his standard "Old Familiar Tunes" series, the one reserved for southern white fiddlers, banjoists, stringbands, Sacred Harp singers, and similar old-time artists. As a result, the novel sound of Poole's instrumentals not only failed to reach popular music enthusiasts but also failed to impress his loyal hillbilly music fans. "Sunset March"/"Don't Let Your Deal Go Down Medley" sold a discouraging 8,538 copies. Based upon these low sales figures, Walker shelved Poole's other two classic banjo selections rather than releasing them. Over the next three years, he and Poole repeatedly squared off in an artistic battle over the North Carolina Ramblers' evolving musical style. Despite Poole's frustrated attempts to break into the more lucrative popular music field, he and his band remained enormously popular with hillbilly record buyers. "Charlie Poole," proclaimed a Columbia Records' 1927 *Old Familiar Tunes* catalog, "is unquestionably the best known banjo picker and singer in the Carolinas. A dance in North Carolina, Virginia, or Kentucky isn't a dance unless Charlie and the North Carolina Ramblers supply the pep. People everywhere dance all night long when these favorites supply the music."[53]

The year 1928 marked a critical turning point for the North Carolina Ramblers. By that spring, Poole's relationship with fiddler Posey Rorer, his brother-in-law and, during most of the 1920s, his closest friend, had cooled considerably. Early that year, Rorer had angrily confronted Poole, accusing him of withholding some of his recording and royalty proceeds to bankroll an extended drinking binge. Tensions had arisen long before this incident, though. Since at least 1926, Poole and Rorer had often disagreed about the band's musical direction and its evolving style of music. Under the influence of Roy Harvey, Poole increasingly favored a more polished, pop-oriented approach, with a repertoire that featured an ever-larger number of selections drawn from Tin Pan Alley songs of the 1890s and 1900s. In contrast, Rorer, who fiddled in a traditional short-bow shuffle style of his native southwest Virginia, steadfastly adhered to a more conventional old-time stringband sound and to interpreting more traditional selections.[54]

The argument over misspent royalties, coupled with diverging musical approaches, finally convinced Rorer to quit the North Carolina Ramblers sometime in early to mid-1928 and embark on his own separate musical career with other Piedmont stringbands. That September, Rorer teamed up with guitarist C. M. "Matt" Simmons and tenor singer Frank Miller to cut twenty-four sides (two takes each of twelve selections) in New York City for Thomas A. Edison, Inc. The firm, in an obvious attempt to cash in on the widespread fame of Poole's band, released all eight issued numbers from these sessions under the artist billing "Posey Rorer and the North Carolina Ramblers." Over the next three years, Rorer recorded more than forty sides with various local musicians and stringbands from the North

Carolina and Virginia Piedmont, including the Carolina Buddies, the Dixie Ramblers, Walter "Kid" Smith, Norman Woodlieff, and Buster Carter and Preston Young. Until Rorer's acrimonious departure, the North Carolina Ramblers had stood firmly atop the hillbilly recording industry, and although Poole and Rorer each pursued independent recording careers after their 1928 breakup, neither of them ever again approached the level of commercial success they had achieved during their musical partnership. Nor, reportedly, did they ever speak to one another again.[55]

Meanwhile, Poole recruited a gifted twenty-three-year-old Spray fiddler named Lonnie Austin to replace his estranged brother-in-law at two upcoming North Carolina Ramblers recording sessions. Born on March 30, 1905, in Leaksville, Austin was playing the pump organ and the piano by the age of six. Under an uncle's influence, he soon took up the guitar, and on weekends he shined shoes on the streets of Spray and Leaksville in order to earn enough money to buy a new fifteen-dollar guitar. Austin's natural ability so impressed Paul Manker, the Carolina Cotton and Woolen Mills Company's music director, that he assigned the ten-year-old boy the responsibility of tuning the guitars for the community music classes, and a few years later Manker appointed him his assistant in teaching those same classes. By his early teens, Austin was playing the fiddle, a Stainer purchased by his father for twenty-five dollars, and refining his technique in corporate-sponsored violin classes under Manker. Austin also developed friendships with local fiddlers Will Heffinger and Dan Carter, both of whom taught him to play in a smooth, long-bow style. By his late teens, Austin was playing the piano in a local Dixieland jazz band, in addition to the more traditional fiddle and guitar accompaniment he supplied for Spray and Leaksville old-time stringbands. Meanwhile, he also became a much-sought-after session fiddler for the stringbands of the North Carolina and Virginia Piedmont. Only twenty-two years old, Austin made his debut recordings as the lead fiddler for Kelly Harrell's Virginia String Band at its August 1927 session for Victor. Already well on his way to a professional musical career, Austin signed on, in June 1928, as the piano player with H. M. Barnes and His Blue Ridge Ramblers, a nine-member vaudeville troupe whose advertisements described it as "America's Great Old-Time Novelty and Dance Orchestra," and over the two years, he toured with the group on the Loew's circuit on the East Coast. Although still on the road with Barnes's novelty hillbilly orchestra, Austin found time to accompany Poole and Harvey at the North Carolina Ramblers' recording session in New York in July 1928 and again in May 1929.[56]

With the addition of Austin and later Odell Smith, both of whose ragtime fiddling featured smooth long-bow strokes and fancy embellishments, the North Carolina Ramblers began to produce a more sophisticated, bluesy sound modeled in part on the popular music of the Jazz Age. And with Posey Rorer out of the way, the band's musical selections increasingly gravitated toward vaudeville and Tin Pan Alley numbers, among them "I Once Loved a Sailor," "A Husband and Wife Were Angry One Night," and "What Is a Home without Babies." Undaunted by Frank Walker's intransigence, Poole continued his efforts to create a more popular contemporary sound and to escape what he must have felt was the limiting classification of "hillbilly musician." Poole began hatching a plan to mimic the fuller sounds of the large jazz and dance orchestras of the late 1920s for what he hoped would be a breakout recording session that would launch him into the popular music world.[37]

In May 1929, Poole and the North Carolina Ramblers returned to Columbia's New York studios with the intention of recording as a five-piece band. In addition to Austin and Harvey, Poole brought along twenty-year-old Odell Smith on second fiddle and Lucy Terry on piano. To add to the confusion, Harvey had scripted a lengthy "rural drama" comedy skit that he wanted to audition. An obstinate Frank Walker, however, firmly rejected the idea of recording either the larger ensemble or—despite the incredible success that Columbia had so far realized with the initial releases of Gid Tanner and the Skillet Lickers' "A Corn Licker Still in Georgia" series—Harvey's comedy routine. Walker had latched onto a commercially successful formula to sell hillbilly records by the North Carolina Ramblers, and, considering the poor sales of Poole's previous experimental recordings, he refused to meddle with a good thing. Walker, it should be noted, had similarly discouraged Atlanta fiddlers Clayton McMichen and Lowe Stokes of the Skillet Lickers from deviating from their best-selling old-time music formula. Once, at a New York City recording session, the two fiddlers had raised the possibility of cutting a few jazz and pop tunes. "If I want violinists I can just stick my head out the window and whistle," Walker told them. "I didn't bring you guys all the way up here from Georgia to play violin music." Ever mindful of record sales,

Walker likewise insisted that Poole and the North Carolina Ramblers imitate their previous hits and forget about dabbling in larger ensembles and skit recordings. A disappointed Poole, accompanied only by Harvey and Austin, cut a total of eight sides at their May 6 and 7 sessions, consisting of the minstrel song "Sweet Sunny South," the railroad ballad "Bill Mason," the topical number "Baltimore Fire," the Spanish-American War piece "Good-Bye Mary Dear," and the Tin Pan Alley selections "The Mother's Plea for Her Son," "Leaving Dear Old Ireland," "The Wayward Boy," and "He Rambled."[58]

Although under contract as exclusive Columbia artists, the frustrated North Carolina Ramblers responded to Walker's stubbornness by surreptitiously recording for two competing labels during their New York trip. A day or two after completing their eight sides for Columbia, the band entered rival Paramount's studios to record as a five-piece band the tunes they had initially offered to Walker. Sometime between May 8 and 10, the expanded North Carolina Ramblers cut six sides for Paramount, which, in order to conceal the band's identity and thereby avoid legal complications, released these records under the billing of the Highlanders. Four of their recorded numbers, "Under the Double Eagle," "Richmond Square," "Flop Eared Mule," and "Lynchburg Town," featured not only lightning-fast twin fiddling but also banjo and piano breaks—highly unusual for hillbilly recordings yet commonly found on the classic banjo recordings that Poole so ardently admired. In addition to these sides, the North Carolina Ramblers also accompanied singer Fred Newman, who apparently had made the trip with the band, on two selections that Paramount released under his name. On May 11, at their third recording session of the week, the North Carolina Ramblers cut Roy Harvey's four-part rural comedy script for Brunswick. Titled "A Trip to New York," the hokey skit recounted the humorous misadventures of a rube stringband on their first big-city recording trip. Brunswick released the skit on two records under the artist billing of the Allegheny Highlanders. But, like the illicit extracontractual Paramount sides, they sold poorly. Although these three recording sessions failed to produce any hit songs, or even much money for the band, they nonetheless reveal the evolving musical preferences of the North Carolina Ramblers, and particularly of Poole himself, who was increasingly turning away from a conventional old-time approach to embrace a more mainstream popular sound.[59]

On their recordings, especially their later ones, Charlie Poole and the North Carolina Ramblers brought an unparalleled degree of elegance and sophistication to old-time music. Although he usually sang in a clipped, often garbled nasal baritone, Poole consciously modeled his singing in part on that of Arthur Collins and particularly of Al Jolson, sometimes even imitating some of their distinctive vocal phrasings and flourishes, as his singing on "It's Movin' Day" and "If I Lose, I Don't Care" attests. Poole's approach to the banjo, in turn, represented a dramatic departure from the more traditional clawhammer, or frailing, style of most other hillbilly banjoists. He picked the banjo with three, sometimes four, fingers in a complex, highly percussive, syncopated style, which he adapted from newer classic banjo techniques popularized by such virtuosos as Vess L. Ossman and Fred Van Eps. Poole was by no means the only banjo player to perform in such a style on hillbilly records; Uncle Dave Macon, Frank Jenkins, and Mack Woolbright, among others, all sometimes recorded in this style. But far more than any of these other banjo players, Poole employed the three-fingered roll most consistently, and was arguably its most accomplished exponent, on old-time records.[60]

Especially on his experimental solos with piano accompaniment, Poole elevated the banjo to a featured instrument in the North Carolina Ramblers' distinctive sound and in old-time stringband music generally, and, as a consummate innovator, he employed the instrument in ways then unheard-of in commercial hillbilly music. Occasionally, he performed jazz-inspired breakneck runs and instrumental solos on his recordings, both of which anticipated the development of modern bluegrass. Together, Poole and the North Carolina Ramblers crafted a signature sound of cleanly articulated, tightly knit dance music that, as several country music historians have noted, closely resembled a "chamber music" sound. Under Austin's bluesy fiddle lead, Poole and Harvey constructed a complex, fluid foundation of "arpeggios and chromatic runs," which, according to folk revival musician and old-time music scholar John Cohen, "flowed into each other in such a way that one couldn't tell where the guitar left off and the banjo began." As such, the North Carolina Ramblers created a highly disciplined signature sound that differed markedly from the loose, riotous sound of Gid Tanner and the Skillet Lickers, the only other stringband to rival them in popularity during the late 1920s.[61]

Even though Poole is largely remembered for his distinctive three-finger picking style, his unusual ability to arrange old Tin Pan Alley standards marked another of his musical innovations that contributed to the North Carolina Ramblers' commercial success. Not much of a songwriter, Poole himself composed few, if any, original numbers. But he was an extraordinarily gifted arranger who, with the assistance of his bandmates, reworked sentimental popular ballads and vaudeville numbers of the 1890s and 1900s into lively country dance numbers for stringband accompaniment. Many of the direct sources for the North Carolina Ramblers' eclectic repertoire remain elusive, but Poole, who only learned to read when he was in his twenties, certainly learned many of the popular ballads and songs the band recorded from his older sister and his immediate family, his wives and their families, and his neighbors and musical contemporaries in Spray and Leaksville. Poole picked up other songs from musicians and people he met on his extended musical tours throughout North Carolina, Virginia, and West Virginia, and he also probably gleaned a few numbers from the traveling medicine shows and vaudeville acts that regularly visited his hometown during the 1920s.[62]

With Lou Emma's assistance, Poole appropriated other numbers, especially older minstrel songs and sentimental Victorian ballads, from inexpensive mass-marketed songbooks such as *Good Old-Time Songs* and from the "Song and Verse" columns in *Good Stories*, a "hearth and home" magazine, based in Augusta, Maine, to which his wife subscribed. Furthermore, his Columbia producer Frank Walker may have supplied him with "professional copy" sheet music for older selections he believed would sell well if recorded by the band. Most important, though, Poole acquired new material from his own extensive phonograph record collection and from band members, particularly Roy Harvey and Lucy Terry, whose jobs as clerks in the Beckley Music Store gave them access to a large collection of Tin Pan Alley sheet music. Apparently, popular songs such as "The Letter That Never Came," "Falling by the Wayside," "Leaving Dear Old Ireland," and "The Mother's Plea for Her Son" came from either one or the other of his West Virginia accompanists. "Where Charlie Poole found his songs and tunes will probably never be known with certainty," his biographer Kinney Rorrer concludes. "It is most likely that his sources were oral since he was barely literate but whatever the source, he had a good ear for a good tune."[63]

On their recordings, Charlie Poole and the North Carolina Ramblers interpreted a wide range of American popular music, but approximately half of their recorded output consisted of popular songs of the 1890s and 1900s, especially maudlin sentimental ballads like "Good-Bye Mary Dear," "Mother's Last Farewell Kiss," and "The Girl I Left in Sunny Tennessee," which were deeply informed by a mournful sense of sorrow and loss. "You could hear those darkies singing, / As she bid farewell to me," Poole sings on his recording of the last of these numbers. "Far across the fields of cotton, / My old homestead I could see. / But as the moon rose in the glory, / There I told the saddest story / To that girl I loved in sunny Tennessee." On "Sweet Sunny South," the narrator longs to return to his old community from which he has strayed: "Take me home to the place where I first saw the light, / To the sweet sunny South, take me home, / Where the mockingbirds sing me to sleep every night; / Oh, why was I tempted to roam? / Oh, I think with regret of the dear home I left, / And the warm hearts who cheered me then, / And the wife and the dear ones of whom I'm bereft, / And the sight of the old place again." With their evocation of the old homestead and loved ones left behind, such sentimental songs may have deeply touched Poole's working-class record buyers, many of whom had perhaps experienced similar feelings of loss and regret as a result of their migration to the industrial centers of the Piedmont and the greater South.[64]

The North Carolina Ramblers' recordings of sentimental parlor ballads may have lamented the loss of gray-haired mothers, sweethearts, and cabin homes, but this was far from the only message presented on their Columbia records. A significant portion of the band's recorded numbers, particularly some of its best-known blues and blues ballads, celebrated the pleasures and freedoms available outside of a stable life of marriage and gainful employment. Gritty songs such as "Don't Let Your Deal Go Down Blues," "Take a Drink on Me," and "If I Lose, I Don't Care" romanticized not the home and family but rather the rough, masculine world of gambling, drinking, hoboing, and generally living on the margins of respectable society. These songs are crowded with hoboes, tramps, and rounders who, much like Poole himself, drank hard and would not, or could not, accommodate themselves to the modern industrial order and its ascendant values. "If the river was whiskey, and I was a duck," Poole sings in one of the band's most famous songs, "I'd dive to the bottom and I'd never come up; / Oh, tell me how long have I got to wait? / Oh, can't I get you now, must I hesitate? / If the river was whiskey and the branch was wine, / You could see me in bathing just any old time."[65]

Poole explored similar themes in one of the North Carolina Ramblers' well-known ragtime numbers, "He Rambled." Originally titled "Oh! Didn't He Ramble," this 1902 Tin Pan Alley song, from the pen of African American vaudevillian and "coon song" composer Bob Cole, achieved its earliest popularity through the vaudeville stage performances of the renowned white minstrel singer George H. Primrose. By the time Poole and the North Carolina Ramblers cut the song in May 1929, however, it had already become established as an instrumental standard among New Orleans jazz bands. On Poole's recording of "He Rambled," the narrator recounts the misadventures of Buster, his unfortunate and misunderstood brother, who wanders widely in search of excitement and masculine pleasures:

My mother raised three grown sons, Buster, Bill, and I,
Buster was the black sheep of our little family;
Mother tried to break him of his rough and rowdy ways,
Finally had to get the judge to give him ninety days.

Chorus:
And didn't he ramble, ramble,
He rambled all around,
In and out the town;
And didn't he ramble, ramble,
He rambled till the butchers cut him down.

He rambled in a gambling game, he gambled on the green,
The gamblers there showed him a trick that he had never seen;
He lost his roll and jewelry, he like to lost his life,
He lost the car that carried him there and somebody stole his
    wife.

Chorus

He rambled in a swell hotel, his appetite was stout,
And when he refused to pay the bill, the landlord kicked him out.
He reached a brick to smack him with and when he went to stop,
The landlord kicked him over the fence right in a barrel of slop.

Chorus[66]

The incorrigible Buster routinely suffers punishments and misfortunes as a result of his rambling and gambling, yet he refuses to heed the lessons that his mother, the judge, and the landlord try to teach him about the potentially serious repercussions of his irresponsible behavior. Eventually, of course, he comes to an inevitable bad end, cut down by "the butchers," possibly an epithet for police officers, hired thugs, or underworld hit men, perhaps sent to collect gambling debts. Whatever the reference, the song is a sympathetic portrait of the misguided Buster, and the use of the word "butchers" suggests that he is not completely to blame for his own premature demise. Perhaps Poole found this song attractive for its high opinion of the rounder who refused to settle down and make his mother proud.

Poole extolled the raucous, wild life of society's outcasts even more vigorously on his famous reinterpretation of the great African American composer W. C. Handy's 1917 blues composition, "Beale Street Blues," another widely recorded jazz standard of the 1920s. A longtime resident of Memphis and the self-proclaimed "Father of the Blues," Handy captured in his song a portrait of the notorious black tenderloin district of that city, nationally known for its saloons, cafés, brothels, and blues singers. Apparently, Handy's song was one of Poole's favorites, because he and the North Carolina Ramblers recorded it twice, for Columbia in 1928 under the title "Ramblin' Blues" and the following year for Paramount as "Tennessee Blues." In both cases, the song became, in Poole's hands, a joyful paean to the rough underworld of bootleggers, petty criminals, gamblers, prostitutes, and street musicians, which, despite Progressive municipal reforms and National Prohibition, flourished on Beale Street in the mid-1920s. The following lyrics, taken from the band's better-known 1928 Columbia version, celebrate a litany of chiefly masculine, working-class pleasures available in Memphis:

> I've seen the life of old gay Broadway,
> Old Market Street down by the 'Frisco Bay,
> Saw the Prado, I've gambled all these parts, in Paris, France;
> Now the seven wonders of this world I've seen,
> There's many other different places I have been,
> Take my advice, folks, please see Beale Street once,
> It's in Memphis, Tennessee.

Oh, your Nehi mama browns,
Beautiful gowns,
Make tailor-mades and your hand-me-downs,
You'll meet honest men
And pickpockets, too,
But your business never closes till somebody gets killed.

Oh, your Nehi mama browns,
Chitlin' cafes,
Talk about your whiskey and your bygone days;
Be not offend,
I've got it to spend,
You'll find gold enough along to pave the New Jerusalem.

If Beale Street could talk,
If Beale Street could talk,
Married men would have to pick their beds up and walk.
All except one or two,
Who never drink booze,
And the blind man on the corner who sings the "Memphis Blues."

I'd rather be here than anyplace I know,
I'd rather be here than anyplace I know,
For it's gonna take a sergeant for to make me go.

Now we see the river, baby, by and by,
See the river Mississippi, I'll tell the reason why.
For the river's wet and Beale Street's done gone dry—bone dry.[67]

It remains unclear whether Poole ever actually visited Memphis's famed Beale Street during his travels. But what is certain is that he fully participated in the raucous subculture he depicts in "He Rambled" and "Ramblin' Blues," drinking bootleg whiskey, gambling, getting into fistfights and close scrapes with the law, sobering up in small-town jails, and perhaps even soliciting prostitutes. Far from a homebody himself, Poole may have recorded songs about life's seamy underside because their antisocial ideology so closely corresponded with his own. Both of these selections elevate the selfish pursuit of excitement and pleasure over steady productive labor and responsible citizenship. As such, they promote immediate gratification rather than a New South capitalist ethos of industry, self-discipline, and thriftiness. And unlike the North Carolina Ramblers' sentimental ballads, neither of these songs expresses any regret for or guilt about someone or something left behind or lost. Nor do the colorful characters within them aspire to a respectable working-class life of family, home, steady jobs, and church attendance. These gamblers and rounders clearly prefer instead to live a shiftless, nomadic life on the margins of "decent" southern society. Like Poole, they found their own social and cultural niche outside of the American mainstream.

Several of Poole's biographers have stressed the correlation between what is known about Poole's life and the many rounder songs that he and the North Carolina Ramblers recorded. "If any old-time country music singer ever 'lived' the words he sang," writes Kinney Rorrer, "then surely it was Charlie Poole. One could almost string together a biography of Poole from the words to the seventy songs he recorded between 1925 and his untimely death in 1931." Similarly, Hank Sapoznik has argued that, "like Jimmie Rodgers and Hank Williams, he sang his life, and his fans idolized him for it." Sapoznik does acknowledge that Poole "gravitated to songs that echoed his life or badly contrasted it," and Rorrer, too, admits that Poole "seem[ed] to have a paradoxical attitude toward the type of material he chose to record. He leaned heavily toward the 'home and mother' type song . . . , while at the same time he liked the 'rounder' type song about drinking and rambling." Matching Poole's life to the songs he recorded often results in a strained, uneasy fit. Yet it remains true that his rounder songs mirrored his rough and rowdy life, which, like Buster's in "He Rambled," was rapidly drawing to a tragic conclusion.[68]

On January 23, 1930, Poole and Harvey, accompanied by fiddler Odell Smith, recorded again for Columbia in New York City. Poole had enlisted Smith to replace Lonnie Austin, who, perhaps because of a conflicting engagement with H. M. Barnes and His Blue Ridge Ramblers, could not attend the session. On this day, the trio waxed ten sides, among them "Sweet Sixteen," "If the River Was Whiskey," and "It's Movin' Day." But the most avant-garde selection of the session was "Southern Medley," a banjo-and-guitar duet featuring only Poole and Harvey. The instrumental medley, modeled on Fred Van Eps's 1911 Edison cylinder recording of the classic banjo instrumental "Dixie Medley," incorporated snippets of "Dixie," "My Old Kentucky Home," "Arkansas Traveler," "Swanee River," and "Turkey in the

Straw." This derivative recording reflects Poole's continuing efforts to promote a more popular banjo style on his recordings. Forbidden by Walker from recording with piano accompaniment, as Van Eps often did, Poole perhaps believed that Harvey's guitar might provide a suitable substitute in creating the "uptown" popular sound he sought.[69]

Despite the North Carolina Ramblers' characteristically superb performances, the records from this session sold poorly in the midst of the Great Depression. Nevertheless, Walker invited the trio to record again, eight months later, on September 9, 1930. This session, again heavily oriented toward Tin Pan Alley material, produced six issued sides, including "Good-Bye Sweet Liza Jane," "Milwaukee Blues," and "Just Keep Waiting Till the Good Time Comes." Although Poole did not know it at the time, this was to be his final recording session. As the Great Depression worsened, sales of their records continued to slump. None of the North Carolina Ramblers' releases from this final session sold more than 2,000 copies, and one of them, "Milwaukee Blues"/"One Moonlight Night," released in the summer of 1931, sold a mere 878 copies. Sometime in the fall of 1930, Columbia canceled Poole's recording contract, sending him into a deep depression that he exacerbated by drinking heavily.[70]

Within a month or so, however, Poole dragged himself out of his doldrums and launched a comeback intended to rescue his floundering musical career. He and the North Carolina Ramblers performed a series of live broadcasts on radio stations, first on WDBJ in Roanoke, Virginia, and then on an unidentified one in Henderson, North Carolina. In the winter of 1930, Poole embarked on an extended, thirty-theater tour across West Virginia and Ohio with a much-expanded North Carolina Ramblers, consisting of tenor banjoist Hamon Newman, fiddler Odell Smith, guitarist Gilmer Nowlin, yodeler and ukulele player Earl Shirkey, and Poole's eighteen-year-old son, James, who sometimes sang with the band. Poole even hired a taxicab driver to chauffeur the band over the treacherous, snow-choked mountain roads to their engagements. But the tour flopped. Worse, Poole's health, compromised by years of hard living and even harder drinking, deteriorated, and he suffered several heart seizures while on the road. According to one of his sidemen, "We were afraid he was gonna die on us right there in West Virginia." His serious health problems, combined with poor ticket sales, prompted Poole to cancel the remaining shows partway through the tour in Cincinnati and return to

North Carolina. No longer able to earn a living as a professional musician, he reluctantly returned to shift work in one of Spray's textile mills, where his wife had continued to work throughout the 1920s. Poole's return to the mills, from which he had struggled so hard to escape, appears to have devastated him. Back in his hometown, he alternated between periods of domestic sobriety and drunken binges, lapsing into another funk similar to the one that had consumed him before his ill-fated theater tour. Poole lost all interest in his music and even sold his prized Gibson Mastertone banjo to one of his musician friends.[71]

Poole's bout with depression, severe as it was, was to last only a couple of months. Good news lifted his sagging spirits in mid-February 1931, when a Hollywood motion picture company hired him to bring his band to California to perform in a low-budget western. Poole celebrated his reversal of fortune by assembling a crew of his hard-drinking buddies and embarking on a marathon thirteen-week bender, part of which he spent carousing in southwestern Virginia and playing music when the mood struck him. He ignored his concerned nephew's warnings to sober up before his big trip. "Don't worry," Poole reassured him. "I'll be straightened out when the time comes." On May 21, 1931, less than two weeks before he was to leave for California, Poole collapsed from a heart attack on the front porch of his sister's home in Spray. Attended by a doctor, he lingered for a few hours and then died an hour or so before midnight. He was only thirty-nine years old. His death certificate listed his occupation not as musician or recording artist but as "mill work[er]" and noted that his heart attack was brought on in part by "intoxication 13 weeks." Two days later, on May 23, Poole's widow, son, and hundreds of mourning friends and family members attended his funeral in Spray. He was laid to rest in the North Spray Cemetery, with several of his former musical companions, including Norman Woodlieff, Hamon Newman, Lonnie Austin, and Walter "Kid" Smith, serving as pallbearers. Sadly, Poole died at the height of his artistic powers, a victim of hard living and unchecked alcoholism.[72]

Poole's premature death, like those of Jimmie Rodgers and Hank Williams later, inspired several tribute songs over the next few years from musicians and friends, who appreciated his musical influence and now mourned his passing. In 1931, three months after Poole's death, a West Virginia railroad telegrapher and recording artist named Bernice "Si" Coleman composed a memorial titled "Charlie Poole." That same year, Walter "Kid" Smith, another Spray millhand and a friend of Poole's, wrote and published on broadside "The Life and Death of Charlie Poole." Smith's first public performance of the song was for Poole's widow at her home in Spray. "Accompanied by Norman Woodlieff and Odell Smith, he was to deliver the song before a crowd of neighbors who gathered on the front porch," explains Kinney Rorer. "However, before he could complete the third verse, the neighbors, Mrs. Poole and even the musicians themselves had broken into hysterical weeping. Smith couldn't go on himself by now, and he never completed singing the song for Mrs. Poole." In 1936, Raymond Chaney, a Spray banjoist who often picked with Poole, contributed "Memories of Charlie Poole," which Claude Casey, a former Danville, Virginia, textile worker, recorded the following year for the American Record Corporation. It went unissued, however.[73]

If Poole was a victim of his own self-destructive alcoholism, then the recording careers of most of his close musical associates were casualties of the Great Depression. In June 1931, slightly more than a month after Poole's death, his estranged brother-in-law, Posey Rorer, made the final recordings of his career, for the OKeh label, as the fiddler for the banjo-and-guitar duo Buster Carter and Preston Young. By 1934, Rorer had sold his fiddle and given up music entirely. On June 6, 1936, he suffered a fatal heart attack in Spray Park at the age of forty-four and was buried in the North Spray Cemetery, not far from Poole's unmarked grave.[74] After Poole's death, the other central figure in the North Carolina Ramblers, Roy Harvey, managed to sustain his independent recording career for only five more months. During the mid-1920s, besides his regular sessions with the North Carolina Ramblers, Harvey had launched a separate recording career, teaming up for recording sessions with Posey Rorer for Columbia in 1927 and, as Roy Harvey and the North Carolina Ramblers (sans Poole), with Rorer and banjo-mandolin player Bob Hoke for Gennett and Paramount in 1927 and for Brunswick in 1928. Over the next three-and-a-half years, Harvey recorded more than eighty sides, the most famous of which are a series of well-regarded ragtime guitar duets with Leonard Copeland for Columbia in 1929 and 1930. In late October 1931, Harvey made his final eight recordings, accompanying fiddler Bernice "Si" Coleman and banjoist Ernest Branch, for the OKeh label at an Atlanta field session. After the Great Depression derailed his recording career, Harvey returned to Beckley, West Virginia, where he supported his wife and six children by working variously as a policeman, newspaper circulation manager, and furniture salesman. In 1941, Harvey moved his family to New Smyrna Beach, Florida, where he returned to his beloved railroading, taking a job as a train engineer on the Florida East Coast Railroad. He worked for the railroad until his death from lung cancer on July 11, 1958, at the age of sixty-six. Of the former North Carolina Ramblers, only Norman Woodlieff and Lonnie Austin managed to sustain their recording careers much beyond Poole's death, and in the late 1930s, after the worst period of the talking-machine industry's hard times had subsided, both of them recorded again, with a Spray-area stringband called the Four Pickled Peppers, for RCA-Victor's Bluebird label.[75]

Despite the passing of the core members of the band, Charlie Poole and the North Carolina Ramblers' stringband music was not forgotten. After his father's untimely death, James Poole carried on his father's musical legacy by performing several of the North Carolina Ramblers' original hits with his own bands. In 1931, attempting to capitalize on his late father's popularity, James Poole formed a string band billed as Charlie Poole Jr. and the North Carolina Ramblers, and then, after 1936, as the Swing Billies, a six-man swing orchestra. All of the Swing Billies reportedly could sight-read musical notation and all wore matching tuxedoes at their personal appearances, and, according to Piedmont music historian Bob Carlin, the band combined the old-time numbers of Poole's father with "modern swing and jazz pieces." Between 1936 and 1939, the Swing Billies performed on a daily fifteen-minute noontime program on WPTF in Raleigh, North Carolina, and recorded ten sides for RCA-Victor's budget-priced Bluebird label at an August 1937 Charlotte field session. Among the sides they cut were not only versions of such pop hits as "St. Louis Blues," "Melancholy Baby," and "I Can't Give You Anything but Love" but also swing arrangements of two North Carolina Ramblers' hits, "Leaving Home" and "White House Blues." "See, we was playing 'corn stuff,'" James Poole later explained, "but we were swinging it." Although the group disbanded during World War II, the Swing Billies, in many ways, represent the fulfillment of Charlie Poole's largely unrealized dream of achieving a modern popular sound.[76]

Even though his recording career lasted barely five years, Charlie Poole ranks as one of the most important figures in the history of pre-

Publicity photograph of the Swing Billies, WPTF-Raleigh radio stars, ca. 1938.
Charlie Poole Jr. is standing, second from the left. Courtesy of Kinney Rorrer.

war country music. Not only did he establish a model of success for other Piedmont millhand musicians and bands, but he also exerted a lasting influence on the stringband traditions of north-central North Carolina and south-central Virginia, which is evident in many of the commercial recordings made by these Piedmont stringbands between 1926 and 1931. After World War II, Poole and the North Carolina Ramblers' records influenced generations of American musicians, particularly bluegrass pioneers and folk revival artists. Their recording of "White House Blues," for example, was reissued on Harry Smith's landmark 1952 Folkways collection, *The Anthology of American Folk Music*, which Greil Marcus has hailed as "the founding document of the American folk revival." Literally dozens of musicians, including Bill Monroe and His Blue Grass Boys, Lester Flatt and Earl Scruggs, Sonny Osborne, the Stanley Brothers, Doc Watson, and the New Lost City Ramblers, have covered at least one of the North Carolina Ramblers' old classics. In fact, several of the band's songs emerged in the postwar music scene as country and bluegrass standards, especially "White House Blues," "Budded Rose," and "There'll Come a Time." But perhaps Poole's most enduring contribution to American popular music remains his distinctive three-finger banjo style, which profoundly influenced the instrumental styles of such legendary banjoists as DeWitt "Snuffy" Jenkins, Earl Scruggs, Don Reno, and Ralph Stanley and is today widely regarded as the forerunner of modern bluegrass banjo. "Poole's treatment of three-finger banjo picking," observes biographer Hank Sapoznik, "came to contain the critical DNA for bluegrass, the branch of mountain music he inspired but did not live to see."[77]

For his revolutionary contributions to bluegrass and country music generally, Sapoznik has canonized Poole as "the patron saint of modern country music," but despite his pronounced impact on prewar hillbilly music and postwar bluegrass and country music, Poole has yet to be inducted into Nashville's Country Music Hall of Fame. In 1984, his great-nephew Kinney Rorrer, a history professor at Danville Community College in Virginia, and three other longtime fans launched an eighteen-month campaign to promote Poole's induction into the institution. Together, they collected more than 5,200 signatures on their petition, including those of bluegrass stars Bill Monroe, Jim and Jesse McReynolds, Josh Graves, and Mac Wiseman, but the petition made little impression on the Country Music Association, which oversees the Hall of Fame's election process. Nevertheless, the North Carolina Ramblers' commercial recordings have been extensively reissued on albums, including four volumes, originally released between 1965 and 1975, by Dave Freeman's Virginia-based County Records, which helped to spark a revival of interest in Poole and the North Carolina Ramblers. With the advent of the CD age, an outpouring of digitally remastered compact discs of the band's recordings followed, culminating in the 2005 release of Columbia/Legacy's critically acclaimed three-CD boxed set, titled *"You Ain't Talkin' to Me": Charlie Poole and the Roots of Country Music*, with liner notes by Hank Sapoznik. In addition, Kinney Rorrer published the definitive *Rambling Blues: The Life and Songs of Charlie Poole* (1982), a nuanced, exhaustively researched biography sensitive to both the historical context of Poole's life and the modern influences on his music. Poole's legend has also attracted the attention of cultural tourism promoters in north-central North Carolina. In 1991, the North Carolina Division of Archives and History erected a historical marker in Poole's adopted hometown of what is now Eden, North Carolina, honoring him as a "pioneer country music recording artist," who, along with the North Carolina Ramblers, "popularized old-time music." Since 1995, the town has hosted the annual Charlie Poole Music Festival, held in June, which commemorates his life and enduring musical legacy.[78]

Charlie Poole's music emerged from his experiences navigating a modernizing Carolina Piedmont that was closely attuned to the latest trends in the nation's mass culture. The early twentieth-century world of sheet music, phonograph records, motion pictures, and mass-circulation newspapers and magazines that he inhabited offered him models of professional musicians and high standards of musicianship without which he might have never escaped the drudgery of cotton mill work. These modern influences also allowed him to participate in a world of Jazz Age popular music that stretched far beyond the confines of Spray and the North Carolina Piedmont. Under these influences, Poole generated his own distinctive old-time stringband versions of turn-of-the-century Tin Pan Alley ballads and classic banjo pieces. In doing so, he anticipated many postwar country musicians who attempted to cross the recording industry's genre boundaries, including Dolly Parton, Shania Twain, and, most notably, Garth Brooks, whose daring but ill-fated foray into rock music as the fictional Chris Gaines in 1999 met the same kind of stubborn resistance and commercial failure that Poole's classic banjo instrumentals encountered in the late 1920s. Charlie Poole never enjoyed great commercial success outside of the hillbilly recording field, and, despite the best-selling hits in his considerable body of recorded work, he died an impoverished, alcoholic millhand. But even today, more than seven decades after his death, echoes of Poole's distinctive three-finger banjo roll and stringband music can still be heard on modern bluegrass and country albums, enduring testimony to his far-reaching musical innovations and artistic genius.

CAIN'T MAKE A LIVING AT A COTTON MILL DAVE McCARN

I'm a-gonna starve, ever'body will,
'Cause you cain't make a living at a cotton mill.
—Dave McCarn, "Cotton Mill Colic" (RCA-Victor, 1930)

In May 1930, Dave McCarn found himself in Memphis, Tennessee, six hundred miles from home and nearly flat broke. When the onset of the Great Depression threw him out of work, McCarn, a twenty-five-year-old Gastonia, North Carolina, millhand, and his fourteen-year-old brother, Homer, joined tens of thousands of other unemployed workers wandering across the country in a desperate search for jobs. Hoboing out west, the McCarn brothers hopped freight trains and thumbed rides, slept in city parks, and picked up odd jobs wherever they could find them. But after several weeks, with opportunities for work becoming ever scarcer and their pocket money running low, they decided to return home to North Carolina. En route, in a remarkable twist of fate, McCarn literally stumbled into a recording career. By sheer coincidence, the brothers' arrival in Memphis, then an important regional center of African American blues and jug band music, coincided with a monthlong field-recording session that the RCA-Victor Company, Inc., was conducting in the city.[1]

Unaware of the recording session in progress and down to their last few dollars, the McCarns made the rounds in the Memphis pawnshops hoping to sell the prized Stewart guitar Dave always carried with him on his travels. But three dollars was the most he was offered for the instrument, and he refused to take so little. "So the last hock shop we stopped in," McCarn recalled, "there was a couple of colored boys in there wanting to get strings for their instruments. And the proprietor, he asked the boys, 'Were they going to make some records?' And they said, 'Yeah, if we can get some strings to stay on these instruments.' Well, I perked my ears up then, you know. I said, 'Where?' They told me, 'Right across the street in the auditorium.'"

During the late 1920s, McCarn had played guitar with a South Gastonia jug band called the Yellow Jackets and had even written a handful of original songs that the group sometimes performed. So McCarn decided that, instead of pawning his guitar, he would take a chance and use it to audition for RCA-Victor. "Well, I took my brother and we went up in the auditorium," McCarn continued, "and the room was full of people from Arkansas, Mississippi, Virginia, and all around." But shortly after McCarn and his brother arrived that Friday afternoon, Ralph S. Peer, the firm's innovative A & R (artist and repertoire) man in charge of the field session, closed auditions for the week and invited those remaining in the auditorium to return on Monday morning. "Everybody left," McCarn recalled. "Me and my brother, we sit right on. When everyone got gone, I told Mr. Peer, I said, 'We cain't be here Monday.' I said, 'We're just passing through.' He said, 'Well, come on in this audition room.' I went in there and he put his face down in his hands so he wouldn't embarrass me. He knew I was already nervous. So I played the two tunes, and we got through, and he said, 'Well, we'll give twenty-five dollars a piece for these kinda songs.' I said, 'You mean you gonna buy 'em?' He said, 'Yeah.' Said, 'How much money do you need to be here Monday?' I said, 'I don't know.' So he advanced me ten bucks."

On Monday, May 19, 1930, McCarn recorded two of his original compositions, "Everyday Dirt" and "Cotton Mill Colic," accompanying his nasal tenor vocals with his distinctive raggy guitar picking, in a makeshift recording studio in the Memphis Auditorium.[2] For his efforts, McCarn received a one-time, flat fee payment of twenty-five dollars per side, a windfall that enabled him and his brother to return to North Carolina. "So I made my two records," McCarn continued, "and me and my brother come back to Forest City. We had a sister living in Forest City, North Carolina, up here, kind of the western part of the state. And we come back there 'on our thumb' [hitchhiking], of course. So that's all it was. I forgot about the record, didn't think no more about it."[3]

McCarn's debut record sold well enough for Ralph Peer to invite him to make ten more recordings for RCA-Victor over the course of the next year, including two sequels to "Cotton Mill Colic," one titled "Poor Man, Rich Man (Cotton Mill Colic No. 2)" and the other titled "Serves 'Em Fine (Cotton Mill Colic No. 3)." But McCarn's small recorded output of only a dozen sides and his own casual indifference to them should not diminish his significance in the history of hillbilly music. In the revised edition of his classic study, *Country Music, U.S.A.* (1985), Bill C. Malone praises him as "the greatest of the textile-worker songwriters," an artist who developed both "a flair for writing topical songs" and "one of the 'hottest' guitar styles heard on early country records." Old-time revival musician and historian Mike Paris admires McCarn's "superb talent for revealing, without bitterness, the grim lot that any 'linthead' might expect, and a natural ability to lighten that lot with wry humor."[4] Considering that McCarn recorded so little, the breadth of his influence is astonishing. In 1973, the West German company Folk Variety Records reissued all of his extant commercial recordings on an album titled *Singers of the Piedmont*, and his recordings, especially his cotton mill numbers, have appeared on no fewer than eleven old-time music anthologies.[5] More than a dozen musicians and bands, including Pete Seeger, J. E. Mainer, the Blue Sky Boys, Doc Watson, and the New Lost City Ramblers, have covered his songs. As one of his biographers, Charles K. Wolfe, notes, McCarn is probably better known today, almost eighty years after his hillbilly records were originally released, than he was during his brief recording career.[6]

During the 1920s and 1930s, hundreds of southern white singers and musicians waxed only a few, largely forgettable hillbilly sides apiece and then receded into the obscurity of their working-class lives.[7] But what distinguished McCarn, a self-taught guitar and harmonica player from Gaston County, North Carolina, was his remarkable talent for composing darkly comical social protest songs that have resonated with listeners for decades. Far more than any other hillbilly singer of his generation, McCarn articulated a pronounced sense of working-class alienation in his series of three cotton mill songs that chronicled the daily hardships of mill life. One song in

Dave McCarn with his granddaughter, 1950.
Courtesy of Helen McCarn Wertz.

particular, "Cotton Mill Colic," secured McCarn's legacy in the annals of country music. Unlike most other textile songs that appeared on commercial hillbilly records before 1942, McCarn's song directly criticized the Piedmont textile industry for its refusal to pay millhands a decent wage. And more so than these other textile songs, "Cotton Mill Colic" circulated orally within southern working-class communities during the Great Depression and eventually emerged as a classic protest song in New York City folk music revival circles during the 1950s and 1960s. In fact, Woody Guthrie identified "Cotton Mill Colic" as "one of my favorite songs." "You can tell by the way its wrote up that it aint 'put on'—I mean its the real thing," observed Guthrie in the 1967 folk song anthology, *Hard Hitting Songs for Hard-Hit People*.[8]

McCarn's reputation rests largely on "Cotton Mill Colic" and its two sequels, but the bulk of his recordings consists of high-spirited novelty songs that glorify drinking, rambling, joy-riding, petting, and other pleasures. McCarn was profoundly influenced by the brash, new Jazz Age culture that emerged in the Carolina Piedmont after World War I, and his sophisticated lyrics and instrumental style demonstrate his familiarity with hillbilly and race records, contemporary fashions, and current lingo of that era. Even though he was a lifelong resident of Gaston County textile towns, his personal experiences and extensive travels, combined with his contact with the powerful mass media of commercial radio and phonograph records, enabled him to engage, through his songwriting, in serious cultural conversations about some of the most significant social and economic changes then transforming Carolina working-class life. As one of his biographers, William Henry Koon, notes, "Although McCarn is remembered for his cotton mill material, [his] 'hot' songs certainly are an equal index of the time of the flapper and '[ten-cent] Bay Rum,' neither of which were the sole property of F. Scott Fitzgerald or John Held, Jr."[9] Considering his novelty songs alongside his more well-known textile songs illuminates the chaotic, emotionally tangled life McCarn led and, at the same time, the changing configuration of white working-class culture in the Carolina Piedmont during the 1920s and early 1930s.

Examining McCarn's less-appreciated novelty songs also helps to expose significant but previously unrecognized facets of his textile mill songs. At the heart of McCarn's music lies both a revolt against the starvation wages of factory labor and a celebration of escapist pleasures and uninhibited consumption. If McCarn's trio of "Cotton

Mill Colic" songs expressed his complaints about the economic hardships and frustrations of Piedmont textile life, then his novelty songs celebrated the various ways one could forget, if only temporarily, those same difficulties. Ultimately, his novelty songs represent as much a flight from the class injuries and economic exploitation that defined daily mill village life as they do a rush to the joyous hedonism of casual sex, bootleg alcohol, and footloose rambling—all of which for McCarn represented escape routes, albeit largely self-destructive and apolitical ones, from his industrial plight. "When you cain't get liquor, / And you cain't get no gin, / Don't get disgusted, / For you have a chance to win," McCarn sings on his 1931 recording, "Bay Rum Blues." "Get a long, goose-neck bottle, / And you'll never be sober again." On his textile songs, McCarn expresses a deep frustration with an emerging urban-industrial society that tempted southern millhands with an abundance of new consumer products and seductive credit plans, but at the same time denied workers a living wage with which to purchase these goods. "I'm a-gonna starve, ever'body will," McCarn declares in the chorus of "Cotton Mill Colic." "'Cause you cain't make a living at a cotton mill." McCarn was a strident critic of the modern South's textile industry, but he ended up one of its countless human casualties, a rambling, work-shy alcoholic at odds with the settled existence of married life and, equally important, unable to adjust to the time-clock regimen of factory labor.

McCarn's music emerged from a Piedmont cotton mill world undergoing swift social and economic changes in the first decades of the twentieth century. John David McCarn was born into a white working-class family, the second of eight children, on March 23, 1905, in the textile town of McAdenville, North Carolina. His paternal grandfather, John McCarn, a retired industrial gold miner and Confederate veteran (for whom he was named), had settled in McAdenville with his large extended family sometime before the depression of 1893.[10] Located six miles north of the South Carolina border, McAdenville took its name from Rufus Y. McAden—president of the First National Bank of Charlotte and former speaker of the North Carolina House of Representatives—and developed alongside McAden Mills, two textile-manufacturing plants constructed during the first half of the 1880s. The McAden family and the other principal investors prided themselves on their plants' modern, state-of-the-art equipment, including an Edison electric dynamo and incandescent lights ("light in a bottle," local residents called it, an amazing technological wonder that attracted scores of curious onlookers from the surrounding countryside). By 1900, McAdenville was the second-largest town in Gaston County, with a population exceeding 1,100 residents. "When you visit . . . McAden mills," declared a local textile executive in 1902, ". . . you will find some of the best-paid, best-behaved, most contented, church-going, school-attending people . . . than you can find in any other line of work in the State." The textile workers, he claimed—drawing on current industrial propaganda that masked the long hours, low wages, and hardscrabble poverty that characterized most millhands' lives—"are robust and healthy, happy and contented. They get the money for their work and can buy anything from a pint of peanuts to a circus [ticket]."[11]

When Dave McCarn lived there as a small child, McAdenville was a bustling textile-manufacturing center complete with three cotton mills (a third plant had been constructed in 1906–7), a company-run store and boardinghouse, a few Protestant churches, a school, a company-sponsored baseball team and brass band, and a company-owned mill village containing enough housing to accommodate the mills' 450 employees and their families. His father, Levi L. McCarn, a member of the local Methodist church, worked as a carder at McAden Mill No. 1, a 15,000-spindle spinning mill that manufactured carded yarns. Dave's mother, Sallie Elizabeth (Cousins, also Cozzens) McCarn, was eighteen years younger than her husband and originally from Randolph County, North Carolina. She had once worked as a quiller at the Lowell Cotton Mill in the nearby textile town of Lowell, but after her marriage in 1904, she left the mill to keep house and raise her children. Hard times plagued the McCarns as they struggled to subsist on the meager wages of a cotton mill worker. "There was eight of us young'uns," recalled Dave's sister, Nellie Sansing, "and papa worked in a mill at McAdenville and never brought home more than $6 a week in his whole life. He'd always worked in the mill and raised chickens, hogs, kept a cow and raised a garden to feed us all."[12]

Around 1909, the McCarn family moved to find higher wages and better living conditions in Belmont, a textile town a few miles southeast of McAdenville. Belmont was then an industrial boomtown. As late as 1900, the tiny railroad hamlet claimed only 145 residents, but after 1902, when its first cotton mill, the Chronicle Manufacturing

Company, began operation, the town's population soared, as down-on-their-luck farm families from Gaston County and surrounding Piedmont counties flooded in to find work in the mill. By 1910, shortly after the McCarns arrived, Belmont contained three textile-manufacturing plants and more than 1,150 residents, making it the third-largest town in Gaston County. In Belmont, Levi McCarn found work as a carder at the Chronicle Mill, and the McCarn family, which now included three children, resided in one of the company's mill houses, along with Dave's maternal grandfather and an uncle, who together ran a modest shoe-making shop in the town. The biographical details of McCarn's early life remain sketchy, but he apparently received his first musical instruction in the form of fiddle lessons from his maternal grandfather, who bore the royal biblical name of King David Cousins (and for whom McCarn was also named). Although McCarn's mother sang around the house, no one in his family played a musical instrument except for his grandfather Cousins who, according to his grandson, was an accomplished contest fiddler. "He was what they called a *fiddler's* fiddler back then," McCarn proudly explained. "He never failed, he always won fiddlers' contests. He'd win it every time, real easy. He just had it. He knew how to play it." While still a child, McCarn also briefly attended a shape-note singing school, sponsored by a Belmont church, but his singing teacher's efforts, by McCarn's own admission, proved a dismal failure. "They sent me to music school," he later confessed, "but I couldn't learn it to save my life." [13]

McCarn attended elementary school in Belmont, but, according to his younger sister, Nellie, he hated it and completed only a few grades because, like many working-class children of the day, his labor was needed to help support his family. In 1917, McCarn dropped out of school and took a doffing job that paid $12.24 a week at the Chronicle Mill, where his father and several of his uncles, aunts, and cousins also worked. Only twelve years old, he entered wage work during World War I, when government defense orders for war materials brought tens of thousands of new jobs to Piedmont mills and sent industry wages soaring to unprecedented levels. [14] Before the war ended, however, a series of tragedies destroyed the new life the McCarn family had made for themselves in Belmont. First, one of Dave's younger sisters died of colitis in February 1917. Then, in October 1918, he lost both of his one-year-old twin brothers to the deadly Spanish influenza epidemic. The hardest blow came eight months later when, at the age of fifty-four, Levi McCarn died of pulmonary tuberculosis. "Papa had the flu the year before and it ruint his lungs," Nellie Sansing explained. "I remember Dave was over at Camp Greene in Charlotte the day papa died. I can see him as good as yesterday, coming in the back door late that evening. He had both hands outstretched and was holding a great big magnolia bloom he'd picked somewhere for papa. And we told him papa was dead—and that he died calling for him. Just about broke him up. He never did let himself forget it."[15]

His father's death in June 1919, when McCarn was fourteen, unexpectedly thrust him, as the oldest son, into the adult position of breadwinner for his devastated family. By January 1920, according to the census, he and his older married sister and her husband, both of whom also worked at the Chronicle Mill, were struggling to support the widowed mother and three surviving siblings who were too young to work. To make ends meet, the family was forced to rent one of its rooms to two boarders. Three weeks later, in February, Dave McCarn was again counted in the census. Within this brief period, Sallie McCarn had remarried, to a textile mill sweeper named James T. Harrison, originally from Virginia, and the entire family had relocated to the Arlington Heights neighborhood in Gastonia. Dave McCarn was working as a doffer at the Arlington Cotton Mills, one of the Gray-Separk chain's six local textile mills, along with his new stepfather, his brother-in-law, and his older sister. Then, in July 1920, Sallie Harrison died. Dave and the other McCarn children suddenly found themselves orphans, but Gaston County relatives stepped in to care for them. "Dave went to Bessemer City to live with one of four aunts," recalled his sister Nellie. "But he never stayed nowhere long. He was a wanderer, just had to be moving about."[16]

Shortly after his mother's death, McCarn, then only fifteen years old, hopped freight trains to California in search of both work and excitement, following a series of postwar strikes in Gaston County's cotton mills. His wanderings may have represented a desire not to burden his already economically strapped relatives, or perhaps he was dodging his unwelcomed adult responsibilities as a wage earner. Whatever the cause, McCarn journeyed as far as Los Angeles and then, after a period of time, returned home to Gaston County. His travels on the open road must have opened new, previously unimagined worlds to him, and although most of his personal aspirations remain elusive and uncertain, McCarn's first experiences hoboing across the country established a pattern of extended rambling that would continue for much of the rest of his adult life. "You know, Dave was a roamer, and he done a lot of hoboing in his life," explained his niece, Martha Sipe. "There was a wanderlust in him, seems like. He was looking for something, I guess. But I don't think he ever found it."[17]

Upon his return to the North Carolina Piedmont around 1922, the teenaged McCarn settled in Gastonia, a small industrial city of around 15,000 residents that reigned as the South's leading textile-manufacturing center. Beginning with the "cotton mill building campaign" of the 1880s, Gaston County textile promoters and town boosters, like those elsewhere across the Carolina Piedmont, had trumpeted industrial development as the savior of a New South still recovering from the economic wreckage of the Civil War. Chief among their economic and social benefits, textile mills would, in the words of one South Carolinian, assemble "indigent, unemployed labor in villages, where through the influence of churches, schools, and factories, they could be improved mentally, morally, and physically, [and] many saved from vicious lives." As the mythology of southern industrialism would have it, an altruistic Christian impulse had motivated southern capitalists "not merely to build another mill," as one North Carolina apologist put it, "but to gather about it an orderly community of happy, God-fearing, working people, enjoying all the conveniences and comforts of improved social conditions."[18] As a result of this cotton mill campaign, Gastonia and the surrounding towns had undergone spectacular population growth and industrial development in the late nineteenth and early twentieth centuries. Gastonia's population had soared from 236 in 1880 to 12,871 in 1920. Fueled by a booming wartime economy, more than a dozen mills had been constructed in the city alone between 1915 and 1918. By 1926, Gaston County contained one hundred textile mills, more than any other county in the South and the third most in the nation. Its county seat and largest city, Gastonia, which alone contained forty-two mills, was touted as "The Combed Yarn Center of the South" and "The South's City of Spindles." An estimated 25,000 workers, more than one-third of Gaston County's entire population, made their living tending spindles and looms. Meanwhile, Gastonia's tremendous industrial expansion consolidated the power of a new class of mill owners and businessmen, whose ascendant middle-class values of self-control, industry, sobriety, thriftiness, and respectability came to govern the public life of the Carolina Piedmont in the early decades of the twentieth century.[19]

Gastonia's paternalistic textile owners, like those elsewhere across the Southern Piedmont, attempted to impose modern capitalist values on their employees through an intrusive system of corporate supervision and control. During the 1920s, McCarn inhabited an industrial world in which textile manufacturers not only usually owned the houses, recreation centers, stores, churches, and schools around which mill village life revolved, but they also maintained paid staffs of ministers, teachers, nurses, and social workers to supervise their workers closely. In addition, mill owners sponsored a variety of "industrial welfare" programs, ranging from domestic sciences classes and village beautification campaigns to baseball teams and brass bands. Such programs were specifically designed to consolidate company control of their workforces and to inculcate those middle-class values that, according to textile mill owners and superintendents, would transform their employees into sober, responsible, and productive workers. By the 1920s, most Gaston County mills had established an elaborate set of company rules, which, among other things, required regular church attendance and prohibited drinking. Concerns for the bottom line inspired such regulations. "Eighty-five per cent of our industrial accidents occur on Monday morning," one Gastonia mill superintendent told sociologist Liston Pope in 1939. "People . . . loaf over the week end, instead of going to church Sunday morning and Sunday night, eat too much, get drunk, wear themselves out gadding about, and as a result are not at their best for production until Tuesday morning." Although most Gastonia textile workers made respectable, hard-working lives for themselves and their families, McCarn and hundreds of others refused to abide by such company regulations. Nor did they embrace many of the capitalist values of their employers.[20]

In Gastonia, McCarn began a difficult period of discontent and frustration. Throughout the 1920s, he worked sixty-hour weeks in one of Gastonia's textile-manufacturing plants, usually as a doffer, one of the least skilled and lowest-paying positions in the industry. Doffing required workers to remove full bobbins of thread from the spinning frames and replace them with empty ones, and, although the job offered periodic breaks while waiting for the bobbins to fill,

GASTONIA

"The Combed Yarn Center of the South"

Gastonia, a thriving industrial city of 20,000 inhabitants, invites you, as a prospective home-seeker or manufacturer, to locate here where every opportunity and advantage is open.   Here, you will find the wonderful Piedmont climate, the best of health conditions, good churches and schools---and what counts more than all---the best people on earth

The New Half-Million Dollar High School

Gastonia leads every southern city in the number of cotton mills and producing spindles. There are:

42 COTTON MILLS

—and—

570,775 SPINDLES

In Gastonia
"The South's City of Spindles"

Gastonia Post Office and the First National Bank

What Gastonia Has---

A population of 20,000.

A city manager form of government.

Twenty churches of eight denominations.

A thoroughly modern school system.

Three railroads, 30 passenger trains daily.

Leading fraternal organizations—four civic clubs.

A fine Country Club and Golf Club.

35 miles paved streets.

Four hospitals.

Banking resources $11,381,954.37.

42 cotton mills.

A daily mill payroll of $17,555.00.

A mill capitalization of $16,154,600.00.

Manufactured products $26,476,195.00 annually.

Many industries allied with textile trade.

Largest textile machinery builders in the South.

A thriving Chamber of Commerce with 600 members.

THE GASTONIA CITY HOSPITAL

This city has admirable hospital facilities. The City Hospital, shown above, the Gaston Sanatorium, and the negro hospital are in the city. The Orthopaedic Hospital, owned by the state, is situated a mile from the city. The latter institution, on the governing board of which there are several prominent Gastonians, cares for children from all over North Carolina. It is headed by Dr. O. L. Miller.

What Gastonia Offers—

With all her array of cotton mills, Gastonia still feels the need for smaller industries, other than textile manufacturing plants, which will have a payroll that can add to the city's welfare.

Manufacturing plants for cigars, cigarettes, novelties, clothing, implements, wooden ware, and many other things are needed.

There is every advantage here for the manufacturer. Tax rates are low. Power is plentiful and cheap. Transportation is good and manufactured goods can be carried direct to any part of the country.

Native white labor is easily available, thus insuring the best of intelligent and skilled help, with freedom from misunderstanding of orders and labor disputes.

The Gastonia Chamber of Commerce is ready at all time to assist in any way in dispensing information about Gastonia to those who are interested in the city. Write or call the executive secretary.

The Gastonia Chamber of

Commerce

serves as

A Clearing House

For All Business

Interests

Two Representative Residences in Gastonia

Ladies' Rest Room

Shoppers' Parcel Room

Information Bureau

American Red C.

American Legion Service

For Disabled Soldiers

County Nursing Service

Gastonia Chamber Of Commerce

JOE S. WRAY, Executive Secretary

"Gastonia, 'The Combed Yarn Center of the South.'" Gaston County Industrial Edition, *Gastonia (N.C.) Daily Gazette*, September 10, 1926. Courtesy of the North Carolina Collection, Wilson Library, University of North Carolina at Chapel Hill.

according to Nellie Sansing, her brother chafed under the regimentation and discipline of factory work. As a result, he never established himself in one textile plant for any extended period of time. Rather, McCarn drifted from one mill to the next in search of a job that paid better wages and perhaps offered a sense of personal satisfaction, but textile work brought him only exhaustion, frustration, and disappointment. McCarn's experiences in Gaston County mills left him with precious few illusions about the promised blessings of so-called industrial progress. For McCarn, a member of the first generation of southern children to grow up in mill villages, those gilded promises rang hollow, because the working-class life he had always known was one of body-numbing labor, working poverty, and limited opportunities. Still, he refused to submit to his destiny without a struggle, and he spent much of his adult life searching for escape routes out of the circumscribed working-class life he faced in Gastonia's textile mills.[21]

McCarn found temporary relief from the industrial pressures and boredom of his workaday life in Gastonia's emerging Jazz Age culture. During the 1920s, a youthful social revolution, fueled chiefly by wider access to cheap automobiles and other new, mass-produced commodities and forms of commercial entertainment, rapidly took shape in cities and towns across the Carolina Piedmont and the entire nation. During World War I, many southern textile workers enjoyed more comfortable lifestyles as a result of fatter pay envelopes and better working conditions. Wages soared to all-time highs, in some cases tripling between 1915 and 1920. With those wages, millhands were soon purchasing Model T Fords, furniture suites, radios, phonograph records, and myriad other consumer products, often on the installment plan.[22] Other newfangled amusements also beckoned. On Saturdays, after their half-day shift at the mills, textile workers converged on Gastonia's business district to enjoy their leisure hours. At one of the city's five theaters, millhands could attend a Tom Mix western, a Harold Lloyd comedy, or a Clara Bow melodrama. Cheap restaurants, vaudeville shows, theatrical productions, music shops, and poolrooms also attracted crowds of working-class patrons eager to spend some of their hard-earned wages. Gastonia's three dozen or so department stores and shops offered fashion-conscious young women the latest "Parisian Adaptation" lines of cloche hats, crepe and satin dresses, silk stockings, and cosmetics and beauty supplies.

By the mid-1920s, the newfound purchasing power of Gastonia textile workers had ushered them into the mainstream of America's consumer society and mass culture.[23]

For millhands in their late teens and twenties, Gastonia's working-class amusements and an ever-expanding array of consumer goods opened the door to once unimaginable pleasures. They also offered these young textile workers new opportunities to escape their pre-ordained places, both within their parents' homes and in their closely controlled mill village world, and to form new identities for themselves. Outside of work, many millhands attended church services, gathered on neighbors' porches, or hung out at mill community centers, but many of them also flivvered to riverside picnics, dance halls, and roadhouses, where they drank bootleg whiskey and gin, flirted with members of the opposite sex, and danced the fast-stepping Charleston and the peppy fox-trot. Taking their fashion cues more from Hollywood starlets like Clara Bow and Louise Brooks than from their mothers, Gastonia's daring young working-class women transformed themselves into flappers. Only days after the outbreak of the Gastonia Textile Strike of 1929, for example, Cora Harris of the *Charlotte Observer* noted a crowd of stylish female millhands at a strike rally who were "dressed in their gay Easter frocks and a few with spring coats. I was particularly attracted," she added, "by the popularity of silk stockings." A few months later, Harris commented on another group of young mill women — "flappers," she called them — who "wore brief skirts, colorful blouses, and chokers, bracelets and hats at jaunty angles." Gastonia's working-class women also eagerly embraced other Jazz Age fads and fashions. They cropped their hair in short wavy bobs, wore makeup and lipstick, and smoked cigarettes. And, as McCarn recounted in one of his racier songs, some of these flappers went joy-riding in Ford roadsters and "petted" with their dates on deserted country roads.[24]

This social ferment of the 1920s contributed to the breakdown of traditional gender roles and patterns of family life in Gastonia's working-class communities and, in the process, opened liberating social spaces for discontented young millhands like McCarn. But fast-changing sexual attitudes and behaviors disturbed conservative Gastonians who clung to more traditional standards of morality and propriety. One Gastonia mill neighborhood gained a reputation as "a notorious resort for bootleggers and immoral women," complained a local minister, and the state highway that ran through the village reportedly became "a street for picking up girls at night." During the Gastonia Textile Strike of 1929, working-class flappers flouted community standards of accepted public behavior. "To younger girls of the mill village," observed *Charlotte News* reporter Mary Pressley, "the strike is a thrilling affair. It gives them an excuse to ramble about at leisure, chatting with their friends, and hoping for more excitement. Many of them are wearing knickers or overalls, not at all disconcerted by the contrast of these utilitarian garments with lacy collars or other feminine adornments." But the mannish attire and raucous public behavior of these female strikers shocked older residents of Gastonia's textile mill communities. "It isn't decent for a respectable lady to go on the streets," one appalled millhand wrote to the *Gastonia Daily Gazette*. "I have seen the young girls, I mean the strikers, going up and down the street with old overalls on and men's caps, with the bills turned behind, cursing us, calling the cops all kinds of dirty things and us people who are trying to work, until I'm sick and tired." Another resident complained about young strikers on the streets brazenly "hugging and kissing and smoking." "That went on all day," she snapped. "These people stood right in front of the window and hugged and kissed right before my sister and what company we had one night." She found it "downright disgusting."[25]

McCarn captured his generation's preoccupation with these changing Jazz Age codes of behavior in several of his novelty songs. But unlike many of the more conservative members of his community who condemned such newfangled fads and fashions, his songs suggest that he embraced—and, indeed, reveled in—these new forms of recreation. For instance, on "Take Them for a Ride," which he recorded in 1930, McCarn chronicles, without censure, the new dating rituals and sexual behavior that had become common across the Carolina Piedmont as a result of widespread ownership of, or access to, automobiles:[26]

> I've taken my gal for a ride one night;
> We rode in a Cadillac,
> But I don't think she liked to ride,
> 'Cause she wanted to walk back.
> And then we went again one night;
> Rode in a rattletrap,

Rode all night till the break of daylight,
And then I had to throw her out.

Now, all these Carolina girls,
They're easy on the hook,
But when you take them out to drive,
You'd better watch your pocketbook.
They used to stroll in the daytime
And chew their chewing gum,
But now they ride around at night
And drink ten-cent bay rum.

Now some girls like to drive your car
And some, they like to snooze,
But my girl likes to pet the best
When she's full of booze.
Her daddy loved her mama,
Her mama, she loved men;
Now her mama's in the graveyard,
And her papa's in the pen.

Two girls and I went riding,
Their names were Jack and Jill;
I soon found out they loved to pet
In a new Ford automobile.
Now one of them was wonderful,
She danced and she could sing,
But the other one had a hump on her back
From shaking that doggone thing.

Replete with details that indicate his familiarity with such intimate scenarios, McCarn's risqué song represents a marked departure from the cotton mill protest songs for which he is better known, and in it, as in most of his other novelty numbers, he depicts women as assertive, independent figures who receive as much pleasure as men from sex, booze, and joy-riding. It is also worth noting that McCarn's bold and relatively enlightened view of modern women clashes with the conservatism of hillbilly music found in such selections as George Reneau's "Woman's Suffrage" (1925) and Blind Alfred Reed's "Why Do You Bob Your Hair, Girls" (1927).

Several of McCarn's other songs likewise explore his generation's modern sexual attitudes and behavior, in the fashion of the bluesy, double-entendre records popularized by more famous hillbilly singers such as Jimmie Rodgers and Jimmie Davis. On "Fancy Nancy (Every Day Dirt No. 2)," for example, McCarn portrays the title character as a gorgeous, redheaded femme fatale whose sexuality men find threatening but enthralling. "She sure can shake two wicked hips; / She knows how to kiss with them red lips," he exclaims of this epitome of Flaming Youth. "She looks just like an angel on the level, / But when she gets done, she's the very old devil; / If you see a little girl that looks like a dear, / Just take a tip and don't go near; / She'll fix you so you'll ride in a hearse, / But I'll tell you all of that in the next darned verse." McCarn's best example of a bawdy song, however, is undoubtedly "My Bone's Gonna Rise Again," a parody of "Dese Bones Gwine Rise Again," an African American spiritual based on Ezekiel's Old Testament prophecy of resurrection. McCarn transformed this venerable old spiritual about the biblical promise of bodily resurrection into a risqué number about the promise of sexual arousal, complete with a sexually suggestive title that decades later prompted Tony Russell, editor of *Old Time Music*, to slyly remark, "What a funkily-placed apostrophe Victor let by there!" The slang term "bone," to refer to a penis, especially an erect one, dates at least to World War I in the American vernacular, and McCarn's song is a macho declaration of male sexual virility. "My Bone's Gonna Rise Again" is suffused with raunchy images of a hen and a rooster "a-romping and a-playing all in their lot," and of the narrator's wife accidentally sitting upon a "long black snake," a common phallic symbol in African American country blues, as in Blind Lemon Jefferson's best-selling 1927 hit "Black Snake Moan."[27]

McCarn himself became a living exemplar of this Jazz Age counterculture that he so enthusiastically documented. "He was a man of the world, you know," explained his son, Johnnie E. McCarn. "And that's from the way he was raised, I suppose, and the way he grew up in his early life that may be on the bawdy side occasionally." Dave McCarn spent part of his twenties and thirties hoboing freight trains across the country, and he became a sort of working-class bohemian, whose wanderings carried him to some of America's great cosmopolitan centers: Los Angeles, New York, Philadelphia, Atlanta, and Memphis. He also immersed himself in some of the more popular male-oriented diversions available to him in Gastonia. Strong drink allowed McCarn to blow off steam and forget his worries, providing a welcome break from the industrial pressures and enforced sobriety of factory work. Although the passage of National Prohibition and Gaston County's own "dry laws"—which were enacted in 1903 as a result of evangelical Protestant convictions and, more important, industrialists' desire for a sober, productive workforce—somewhat reduced the availability of alcohol in Gastonia's working-class neighborhoods, thirsty millhands turned to moonshine whiskey and home-brewed beer. More hard-core drunks among them resorted to drinking adulterated concoctions of Jamaica ginger, Sterno, aftershave lotion, and other inexpensive, alcohol-based household products.[28]

McCarn's own drink of choice seems to have been bay rum, a popular hair tonic and aftershave lotion of the day with a high alcohol content, drink-sized bottles of which could be purchased for a dime in most of Gastonia's drugstores and ten-cent chain stores. During Prohibition, bay rum was a particularly popular intoxicant in Carolina Piedmont mill towns. It could be drunk straight or mixed with water or soft drinks, and, according to regular consumers of the beverage, it was both cheaper and "better than the sort of stuff called bootleg whiskey" and packed the "wallop of [a] pile driver." Moreover, unlike bootleg liquor, bay rum was perfectly legal to purchase and possess. "It isn't sold for beverage purposes," noted a 1929 *Burlington Daily Times* article, "and, there, perhaps is the reason that it may be sold and drunk without anybody getting pinched—except the drunks." In 1931, McCarn and Howard Long, his sometime singing partner, recorded a rollicking paean to the tonic's intoxicating properties, titled "Bay Rum Blues." "Now some use bay rum just for a tonic," McCarn advises. "But take it from me it's best for your stomach." Perhaps one reason Gastonia's working-class musical scene so attracted McCarn was because it facilitated his rampant alcoholism. Bootleg liquor flowed freely at the more raucous house parties and dances in Gaston County's textile mill communities, and many of the musicians who furnished the music for these affairs drank heavily. McCarn recalled, for example, that the itinerant banjoist Dock Walsh, whom he occasionally heard perform in Gastonia, always carried a flask of Jake (Jamaica ginger) in his coat pocket.[29]

McCarn's rough and rowdy life repeatedly clashed with the Carolina Piedmont's working-class standards of hard work, respectability, and family responsibility. His freeloading and heavy drinking exasperated family members with whom he boarded during his stints of self-imposed unemployment. "My mom was the one that he and his brother Homer always moved in on when they got out of money," recalled his niece, Martha Sipe. "But my daddy wouldn't tell them they couldn't stay. He'd just quit his job in the mill and move us out." McCarn was also a committed bachelor who enjoyed carousing and drinking with fellow millhands and who, according to his niece, "didn't particularly care about marriage." Beginning around 1930, McCarn did court Maefry Dell Sprinkles, a Gaston County spinner ten years his junior, who was originally from East Tennessee, and, between 1931 and 1935, fathered three children by her. Whether or not they ever legally married remains uncertain, but what is clear is that McCarn refused to be saddled with the demanding roles of sober, reliable husband and father. "I didn't know my old man too much," explained his son, Johnnie McCarn, who was born in 1933 in the Gaston County textile town of Bessemer City. "He was never in the family. He came around whenever he felt like coming around, you know. And when it come time for him to say he wants to get married and settle down, well, he'd pack a bag and he'd be gone." [30]

Occasionally, Dave McCarn vented his frustrations and resentments in more antisocial, violent behavior. In November 1937, while working at the Ranlo Manufacturing Company, five miles east of Gastonia, McCarn was arrested and held on an $1,800 bond in the Gaston County jail for an attempted holdup and assault on a man named Will Brown. Witnesses told a deputy sheriff that, at eleven o'clock on the night of November 24, in the Smyre mill village, McCarn had "attempted to hold Brown up with a toy pistol and struck him with the pistol, inflicting painful injuries, in a struggle that ensued when Brown resisted the holdup attempt." The deputy told the *Gastonia Daily Gazette* that "bystanders ran to Brown's aid and held McCarn until officers arrived." Even before he was arrested for attempted robbery and assault, however, McCarn was already a wanted man in Gaston County. For three weeks prior to his arrest, authorities had been searching for McCarn for assaulting Maefry Sprinkles and for failing to support his children, and he was facing "another similar charge for beating up his wife last night prior to the alleged holdup attempt on Brown," reported the newspaper in a front-page story. On November 29, McCarn was indicted by a Gaston County grand jury for "highway robbery," and his case was consolidated with several other charges against him, including assault on his wife and abandonment and nonsupport. McCarn pled guilty to these charges in Superior Court and was sentenced to six months on the chain gang working the state roads. In February 1939, after several continuances, he was convicted of a second count of "assault on a woman" in Gastonia Municipal Court and sentenced to thirty days on the chain gang.[31]

McCarn's struggles with Maefry Sprinkles, in particular, and gender roles and community expectations, in general, may have prompted him to explore these issues in his music. His recorded songs, like his own behavior, reflect a deep distrust of women and a wariness of marriage, especially of the financial and emotional responsibilities the institution imposes upon men. On "The Bashful Bachelor," for example, McCarn cautions against female deceit and the entrapment of marriage. "Now listen hear, young fellers, / Take my advice and quit," McCarn advises. "Don't fool around with them country girls, / Don't monkey with them a bit." In the ballad, McCarn's suitor comically recounts his harrowing encounters with a marriage-minded farmer's daughter, her shotgun-toting father, and her rolling pin wielding mother. Having escaped unharmed and unwed, he boasts at the song's conclusion, "I've been a bachelor forty years, / And I'll be for forty more." On "Everyday Dirt" and "Take Them for a Ride," McCarn warns of adulterous wives, a taboo subject seldom addressed in the mainstream American popular music of the 1920s and 1930s but one that, in so-called cheatin' songs, eventually emerged as one of the defining themes of post–World War II honky-tonk music. McCarn's compositions also frequently cast women as beguiling gold diggers who use their sexual charms to acquire money. "Now, all these Carolina girls, / They're easy on the hook," McCarn counsels on "Take Them for a Ride." "But when you take them out to drive, / You'd better watch your pocketbook." And of "Fancy Nancy"—a "fast-stepping mama" who "don't wear hosiery to hide her knees" and who's so "red-hot" she "wears asbestos underwear"—he sings: "She'll take you in her room and then call you honey, / And when you come out you won't have no money." Positive depictions of wives, mothers, and girlfriends are noticeably absent from McCarn's lyrics, but there is no shortage of dangerous, deceitful women.

McCarn shrank from the responsibilities and entanglements of a steady industrial job and a stable romantic relationship, instead im-

DAILY GAZETTE
COMBED YARN CENTER OF AMERICA

TEMPERATURE

Low Last Night 31
2 p. m. Today 44
Low Wednesday 33
High 53
November rainfall to date, 1.22 inches; November rainfall quota, 2.57 inches; Amount lacking quota, 1.35 inches.

SDAY AFTERNOON, NOVEMBER 25, 1937.   ASSOCIATED PRESS LEASED WIRE   SINGLE COPIES 5c

STORMING RICE SHOPS

Thanks

Suspect In Holdup And Shooting Is Arrested

TWO MILLION CHINESE SUFFER ACUTE HUNGER

CT FOR TAX ES BRIGHTER

vocating Revision In Business Taxes evelt Will Not Block Action If Vote ched; Solons Take Thanksgiving

, Nov. 25.—(AP)—Congressmen advo- evision of corporate taxes expressed the President Roosevelt would not block a session.

John David McCarn of Ranlo Nabbed Following Alleged Attempted Holdup With Toy Pistol At Smyre Last Night; To Face Wilkerson and Davis For Identification.

John David McCarn, 32, of Ranlo, was held in the county jail without bond today for an attempted toy pistol holdup and assault on Will Brown of Modena extension and as a suspect in the shooting of Scoutmaster Weber Wilkerson, 25, of South Gastonia and the $45 highway robbery of Taxi Driver Robert Davis and three passengers, twin crimes of last Friday night in which city and county officers and Federal agents had unsuccessfully sought clues for the past five days.

Deputy Sheriff Dorie Smith ar- rested McCarn last night. He said he was informed by witnesses McCarn attempted to hold Brown up with a toy pistol and struck him with the pistol, inflicting painful injuries, in a struggle that ensued when Brown resisted his holdup attempt.

Deputy Smith said the attempted holdup occurred last night about 11 o'clock in the Smyre mill sec- tion, East Gastonia. Bystanders ran to Brown's aid and held Mc- Carn until officers arrived. Deputy Smith said.

Sheriff Clyde Robinson said Mc- Carn fitted the description of one of two men sought since last Friday night in the Wilk- erson shooting and taxi robbery. Taxi Driver Davis and three pas- sengers were robbed of a total of $45 by two men who commandeer- ed a Diamond Cab Company taxi, forced the driver to go to Bowling

Fixed Bayonets Guard Large Cargo Of Rice At Shanghai Dock

TRAGIC PICTURE

Many Sleeping In Cold On City Streets

SHANGHAI, Nov. 25.— (AP)—Mobs of hungry, war- stricken Chinese stormed Shanghai rice shops today in a Thanksgiving day effort to buy or beg something to eat.

The Shanghai volunteer corps guarded docks with fix- ed bayonets when a British steamer unloaded a cargo of rice at the Bund. Other guards protected rice-laden trucks from attacks by starv- ing refugees.

With the advent of cold weather 2,000,000 Chinese refugees suffered acutely. They presented a tragic pic- ture—roaming the streets by day and sleeping on pave- ments at night.

International settlement officials said political problems resulting from Japanese occupation of the city were minor compared with the task of furnishing food for Shang- hai's swollen population.

On the war front to the west, Chinese reinforcements rushed for- ward to meet a threatened grand offensive aimed at Nanking, 100 miles away. Although the Japanese big push awaited final preparations, Japanese planes bombed troop con- centrations along the Wusih-Kiang- yin line. Japanese batteries bom- barded scattered Chinese defense po- sitions.

With the coast blockaded by Nip- pon's warships, railroads and canals to the interior damaged by repeat- ed bombardment, and 1,500 square

(Concluded on Page 9)

LAST OF PURPLE GANG WIPED OUT

Gangland Executioners In- vade Cocktail Bar, Kill Harry Millman; Four Others Wounded.

DETROIT, Nov. 25.—(AP)—Gang- land executioners invaded a res- taurant and cocktail bar crowded with Thanksgiving eve merrymak- ers at 1 a. m. today, killed Harry Millman, described by police as "the last of the purple gang lead- ers," and wounded four other men.

Nine pistol shots struck Millman as he reached for a drink at a bar- tender had just poured for him.

Two of the wounded men were identified by police as employes of Millman's horse race handbook. They were: Harry Gross, in criti- cal condition with wounds in the right shoulder, back and abdomen, and Harry Cooper, who was treat- ed for a flesh wound in the neck.

The others, police said, were by- stander. They were: Harry

(Concluded on Page 9)

OPPOSITION TO HOUSE FARM ACT

Scattered But Determined Fight On Compulsory Crop Control Develops.

WASHINGTON, Nov. 25.—(AP)— Scattered but outspoken opposition developed today to the House agri- culture committee's newly-completed draft of a compulsory crop control program.

Leaders scarcely had agreed to start House debate next Monday when protests against the bill arose from these groups:

1. Some members of the corn bloc called for a caucus for tomorrow to consider methods of attaining stricter compulsory control of corn production.

2. Other committee members com- plained that the bill did not carry authorizations for increased appro- priations to finance an expanded soil conservation program. Rep. Cof- fee (D-Neb) said it provided only for additional government "regimen- tation."

3. Dairy members, defeated in the committee, agreed to try on the floor to write in safeguards against use

(Concluded on Page 4)

ABBEY DOWNS CAMPBELL IN GRID CONTEST

Belmont School Gains 43-7 Victory

—BY JOHN J. DERR—
(Gazette Sports Writer)

BELMONT'S MEMORIAL STA- DIUM, Nov. 25.—Belmont Abbey's

SYPHILIS LEADS DISEASES IN N. C.

val Tuesday resent undis- subcommittee aise as much ney proposed

e then, how- ncertainty on ved decision nore detailed

—Ky) of the 'age 9)——

lon Killed

& N.W. ts Tragic Today.

CASTONIANS TAKE

mersing himself in drinking, carousing, and rambling. But he also surrounded himself with music. Around 1926, at the age of twenty-one, McCarn took up and soon mastered the harmonica, one of the cheapest and most readily accessible instruments, and then he taught himself to play the guitar. Unable to read standard musical notation, he learned guitar chords from cheap, mass-produced instruction booklets of guitar tablature, which were popular during the 1920s and 1930s—another example of how modern influences shaped his music. Although he had dabbled with the fiddle as a child, McCarn developed a serious interest in music relatively late in life, compared to other Carolina Piedmont musicians of his generation. But music soon consumed him. In 1962, he told interviewers Archie Green and Ed Kahn that "as a young man he was so eager to play that he used to shake all over till he could get his hands on a guitar."[32]

During the 1920s, with the gathering of large numbers of industrial workers from all across the Carolina Piedmont and Southern Appalachia, a lively musical scene flourished in Gastonia's working-class neighborhoods and in surrounding Gaston County textile towns. Among the most famous musicians in the area was Gwin S. Foster, a superb harmonica and guitar player who worked in a Dallas textile mill. Born in 1903 in Caldwell County, North Carolina, Foster had moved to Dallas with his family around 1909 and a few years later took a job in the local mills. During the mid-1920s, he formed a stringband called the Four Yellow Jackets with two Belmont mill combers—guitarists Dave Fletcher and Floyd Williams—and a drifting banjo player named Dock Walsh, originally from the mountains of Wilkes County, North Carolina. Between 1927 and 1932, Foster and Walsh recorded a total of fourteen duets for the Victor label as the Carolina Tar Heels, including their best-selling hits, "Bring Me a Leaf from the Sea" and "I'm Going to Georgia." Foster recorded an additional sixty-five sides between 1927 and 1939, consisting of solo selections, duets with Clarence "Tom" Ashley (Ashley and Foster) and with Dave Fletcher (the Carolina Twins), and stringband numbers with the Blue Ridge Mountain Entertainers. But he was far more than simply a hillbilly artist. For example, in 1927, when he performed on a special series of musical variety programs on a local radio station, the *Gastonia Daily Gazette* identified Foster and his guitarist partner, Floyd Williams, as "two jazz musicians" and praised their renditions of the Jazz Age popular songs and dance orchestra hits "Wabash Blues,"

"Wang Wang Blues," and "Waikiki," which they rendered, the newspaper noted, "with such feeling and rhythm that the listeners begged for more."[33]

Another well-known Gaston County musician was the Belmont banjo player Wilmer Watts, who worked as a loom fixer at the Climax Mill and performed with several local textile stringbands during the mid- to late 1920s. Originally from Columbus County, North Carolina, where he was born in 1892, Watts had settled in Belmont shortly after World War I. By 1926, he and a Hawaiian guitarist and tenor singer named Percy Alphonso "Frank" Wilson, a Rockingham County, North Carolina, native who worked in the same textile mill, were teaming up to entertain their fellow millhands at Gaston County social gatherings. The following year, the duo recorded eight selections under the billing "Watts and Wilson" for the Paramount label in Chicago. After Wilson left the area around 1928, Watts organized the Gastonia Serenaders, a stringband trio that included two other textile workers, guitarists Palmer Rhyne and Charles Freshour. In October 1929, the band, now renamed the Lonely Eagles (apparently a reference to Charles Lindbergh's famous nickname), waxed sixteen sides for Paramount in New York City, including "Cotton Mill Blues," "Knocking Down Casey Jones," "Been on the Job Too Long," "Charles Guitaw," and "Fightin' in the War with Spain."[34]

During the 1920s, in addition to these and other now long-forgotten musicians, McCarn likely heard a remarkably broad spectrum of popular and traditional music in Gastonia—from old mountain ballads to turn-of-the-century ragtime songs, Piedmont blues to Tin Pan Alley hits, jazz dance numbers to Hawaiian guitar instrumentals. Gastonia's Webb Theater regularly featured vaudeville shows, which included such acts as the Cow Girls Band from the Golden West, an all-female string and brass ensemble, and H. M. Barnes and His Blue Ridge Ramblers, billed as "10 natives of the mountains of North Carolina and Tennessee playing their inimitable brand of music." Meanwhile, Gastonia's 100-watt station WRBU, which was owned and operated by the A. J. Kirby Music Company, broadcast all kinds of local and regional entertainment, as did the more powerful 25,000-watt WBT in nearby Charlotte. "A good program of music, including everything from a jazz orchestra to a negro spiritual choir, will be broadcast over station WRBU tonight," announced one of the station's 1929 newspaper listings. But, on clear nights, McCarn and other Gastonia residents could also tune in to broadcasts of classical and popular musical programs that originated on nearly two dozen powerful radio stations in such faraway cities as New York, Atlanta, Chicago, New Orleans, and Memphis. Although McCarn resided for most of the 1920s in the small textile city of Gastonia, he was neither limited nor isolated in his exposure to a wide range of musical influences.[35]

Around 1926, McCarn met Gwin Foster at the Victory Yarn Mills in South Gastonia, where they worked together as doffers. Victory Mills, like other textile plants across the Carolina Piedmont, formed an important site for musical exchanges among aspiring musicians such as McCarn and Foster. Nicknamed "China" because of his dark complexion and supposedly Asian features, Foster often entertained his fellow millhands with his harmonica during workday breaks. "Gwin Foster," McCarn recalled glowingly, "was the best mouthharp player I've ever heard." According to McCarn, Foster's powerful harmonica blowing "sounded like a pipe organ" and was so ethereally beautiful that it could raise the hair on the back of one's neck. Apparently, Foster taught McCarn how to blow harmonica in a bluesy, ragtime style, and one can readily discern Foster's strong influence on his protégé when listening to McCarn's "Gastonia Gallop," a harmonica-and-guitar rag named for his adopted hometown.[36]

Besides Foster, McCarn also learned from other musicians he encountered in Gastonia, and he soon began experimenting with a raggy finger-picking guitar style he copied from a local guitarist he knew. "Back then I had to fram [strum chords], you know, just a-fram, fram," McCarn recalled in a 1961 interview, "But there's one boy—I don't know his name now—he was really good with his fingers, and I got to watching him some. And being around him, I got to where I could in place of framming so much, I'd use my fingers to pick guitar, you know." But like other southern musicians of his generation, McCarn also developed his guitar style and musical repertoire by listening to radio programs and the latest phonograph records, particularly those of Riley Puckett, a blind Atlanta musician best known as the lead singer and guitarist for Gid Tanner and the Skillet Lickers, one of the best-selling stringbands in Columbia's "Old Familiar Tunes" series. Puckett ranks as one of the two or three most influential guitarists on prewar hillbilly records, and his syncopated finger picking, idiosyncratic bass runs, and clear, strong singing were deeply informed by ragtime, Piedmont blues, and vaudeville vocal styles. "Riley Puckett, he had a good style I liked," explained McCarn. "I think every guitar player there was really liked his style. He'd really get on top of a guitar, all through it. Now he recorded one song they call 'Fuzzy Rag,' ol' Riley did. I copied a little bit of that on one of my songs, 'Take Them For A Ride,' but I wasn't nothing like he was. Boy, he was all over that guitar neck."[37]

Like many of his musical contemporaries, McCarn was an eclectic performer who never confined himself to a single instrumental approach and who, as a result, defies easy categorization. Besides Puckett's stylings, McCarn incorporated into his guitar playing melodies and riffs he learned from the records of Jimmie Rodgers and the Carter Family, the two most commercially successful hillbilly recording artists of the late 1920s and early 1930s, both of whom drew heavily upon the bluesy guitar styles of African Americans musicians. But McCarn also apparently liked Piedmont blues, which he probably heard performed by street corner musicians and race record artists, and he developed a "hot," ragtime-inflected finger-picking style similar to those popularized by the Piedmont blues guitarists Blind Willie McTell and Blind Blake. McCarn may, in fact, have developed his raggy guitar style in part from consciously imitating these bluesmen's commercial recordings.[38]

With its ragtime chord progressions, syncopated rhythms, and slurred blue notes, McCarn's guitar playing reflected the extensive interplay between Piedmont musical traditions at the height of Jim Crow segregation. His eclectic guitar sound, which mingled black and white musical traditions, owed its development chiefly to the expanded commercial recording of American popular music during the first decades of the twentieth century. By the mid-1920s, Piedmont millhands had access to a wide assortment of phonograph records, which brought the sounds of blues, jazz, and hillbilly music into their own homes. Although black and white southerners had participated in face-to-face musical exchanges for three centuries, radios and phonographs disseminated an extraordinary range of popular music to new mass audiences during the 1920s and, as a result, accelerated the recombination of distinctive musical traditions into innovative, thoroughly modern sounds by musicians of both races.[39]

By 1928, besides developing his skills on the guitar and harmonica, McCarn had also begun expressing himself by writing his own songs. He composed a small but diverse array of songs and instrumentals, and his compositions, or "little ditties," as he called them, combined the older traditional music he learned from friends and neighbors with the new, more modern sounds he heard in Gastonia's urban-industrial environment. One of the first songs McCarn recalled writing was "Everyday Dirt," a comic ballad about a faithless wife's adultery and her angry husband's retribution. He based his composition of domestic discord on "Will the Weaver," a traditional Anglo-American ballad about cuckoldry (published on English and Scottish broadsides as early as 1793), which he had learned from Celia Long. During the late 1920s and early 1930s, McCarn sometimes roomed and boarded with Celia Long and her husband, Howard Long, a friend with whom he worked at Winget Yarn Mill in South Gastonia. She often sang "Will the Weaver" to her children, McCarn recalled, in a "real mountain twang." Mrs. Long had learned the song from her father-in-law, Mance Long, a textile worker and banjo player, who, in turn, had learned it as a boy from his mother in the Blue Ridge Mountains of western North Carolina. The Longs and other displaced Southern Appalachian families played an important role in the infusion and mingling of more traditional rural culture with the urban-industrial folkways found in Gastonia and, as a result, also introduced McCarn to songs and ballads like "Will the Weaver," which he added to his repertoire and upon which he based some of his original novelty songs.[40]

McCarn dramatically refashioned this centuries-old ballad to suit his own personal tastes and concerns. In writing "Everyday Dirt," not only did he reconfigure the melody of "Will the Weaver," but he also rewrote most of the ballad's original lyrics. Of particular significance, McCarn revised the ending of "Will the Weaver," in which the adulterous wife beats her cuckolded husband with a stick for beating up her lover. "Well, I didn't exactly like the words of 'Will the Weaver' too much," he explained, "because the woman's husband come out worst at the last, you see. So I changed that, because I thought it ought to come out for the husband a little bit, you know, because he's the one getting two-timed." In McCarn's updated version of the ballad, it is the cuckolded husband, John, who, after returning home unexpectedly and catching his unfaithful wife and her lover (a Mr. Hendley), proceeds to thrash both of them: "John reached up and down he fetched him [from his hiding place inside the chimney], / Like a raccoon dog he catched him, / He blacked his eyes and then did better, /

He kicked him out upon his setter. / His wife, she crawled in under the bed, / He pulled her out by the hair of her head; / 'When I'm gone, remember this,' / And he kicked her where the kicking is best." John is prosecuted for his assault, convicted, and sentenced to serve on "the old chain gang, / For beating his wife, the dear little thing." Following his release, his wife hauls him into court again, this time for nonsupport, and again, he "sock[s] her in the eye" and draws a jail sentence. So, in McCarn's reworking of "Will the Weaver" to create his new "Everyday Dirt," the everyman character of John, though sentenced to hard physical labor for assaulting his wife, at least enjoys a modest measure of revenge. This recasting of "Will the Weaver" oddly foreshadowed McCarn's own future violent assaults on his wife and his resulting stints on the chain gang.[41]

McCarn may have modeled some of his compositions on pre-twentieth-century Anglo-American ballads like "Will the Weaver" and African American spirituals like "Dese Bones Gwine Rise Again," but he also admittedly borrowed melodies and ideas for his songs from current hillbilly records, among them those of Riley Puckett ("Fuzzy Rag"), Frank Luther and Carson Robison ("The Railroad Boomer"), Jimmie Rodgers ("The Brakeman's Blues [Yodeling the Blues Away]"), and (perhaps) Bob Miller ("Eleven Cent Cotton Forty Cent Meat, Parts 1 and 2"). "Oh, everything I recorded, that was my own ideas," McCarn explained. "'Course, I did copy a few melodies, but all the words were exactly mine. I just liked to try to rhyme up songs, and I didn't want to copy somebody else's lyrics. Sometimes I'd pick the melody first and add the words to it, and sometimes I'd have the words and try to locate a tune to match, to get up with that song."[42]

By 1928, McCarn was performing some of his new compositions and playing guitar with a group of millhands in a South Gastonia jug band called the Yellow Jackets. The seven-man band played both old-time numbers and current pop hits and often entertained at house parties and dances in Gastonia's working-class neighborhoods. Occasionally, the group also performed on Gastonia's radio station, WRBU, which regularly broadcast evening concerts of local amateur singers and musicians. "It was mostly free, you know, just to be on the air most of the time," McCarn recalled. "'Course, we didn't try to get radio sponsors because Gastonia was too small a town. But we also used to play for a lot of dances. And we played a lot of times just for the fun of it, you know." Like other working-class musicians,

McCarn played guitar and harmonica and wrote songs, in part as a release from the pressures and boredom of workaday industrial life. But his preoccupation with his music making and songwriting annoyed some members of his extended family, who believed that such pursuits were just another excuse to loaf and waste time. "Dave was different from the rest of us," his sister, Nellie Sansing, recalled. "He was always sitting around writing on pieces of paper. I remember how we used to come home from the mill at night, . . . and Dave would be sitting on the porch, scribbling when I thought he ought to be working."[43]

Although Gaston County remained his major stomping ground, McCarn also took his music on the road, sometimes accompanied by his friend and co-worker Howard Long. Once, around 1931, McCarn recalled, he and Long entertained a crowd of drunken speakeasy customers in Philadelphia. McCarn's rambling allowed him to shed his millhand identity and create for himself a new one as a musician and, equally important, to escape the censure of mill bosses, family members, and neighbors who frowned upon his music making and his more dissolute pastimes.[44] It also opened up opportunities for him to pursue an actual career as a professional musician. Indeed, McCarn's interest in music might have remained merely that of an enthusiastic amateur had it not been for his chronic wanderlust, which brought him in May 1930 to Memphis, where he made his debut recordings of "Cotton Mill Colic" and "Everyday Dirt" for RCA-Victor. A & R man Ralph Peer probably assumed that the topicality of "Cotton Mill Colic," combined with its ironic humor, would appeal to record buyers in the aftermath of the 1929 Piedmont textile strikes and the Wall Street crash. When McCarn's record was released that August in RCA-Victor's "Old Familiar Tunes and Novelties" series, it sold briskly, especially in Gastonia and other Piedmont textile towns, despite the fact that, at seventy-five cents, a single Victor record cost millhands approximately one-third of a day's wages. No reliable sales figures exist for McCarn's debut record, but he later claimed that one Gastonia music store, the S. W. Gardner Music Company, on West Main Avenue, sold as many as a thousand copies. "Nary a one left in town," he recalled.[45]

On the strength of his debut record's sales, McCarn received invitations to make recordings at two additional RCA-Victor field sessions. On November 19, 1930, he waxed four sides at a second

Memphis session, during which he accompanied his singing with guitar and, with the aid of a neck rack, harmonica. These songs included "Hobo Life," a recomposition of "citybilly" composers Frank Luther and Carson Robison's 1929 Victor recording of "The Railroad Boomer"; "The Bashful Bachelor," a reworking of the whimsical traditional courting song "The Stern Old Bachelor"; and "Take Them for a Ride," a "hot" guitar number perhaps inspired by Jimmie Rodgers's blue yodels. The popularity of "Cotton Mill Colic" also prompted McCarn to compose and record a sequel titled "Poor Man, Rich Man (Cotton Mill Colic No. 2)." The following day, McCarn recorded two harmonica-and-guitar ragtime instrumentals, one named for his hometown, "Gastonia Gallop," and the other, which went unissued, titled "Mexican Rag." For these six recordings, McCarn received the standard fee of twenty-five dollars per side, plus a small royalty, which, he recalled, amounted to about fifty dollars a month for a while. Six months later, on May 19, 1931, McCarn and Howard Long recorded four vocal duets at an RCA-Victor session in nearby Charlotte under Peer's direction: "Bay Rum Blues," "My Bone's Gonna Rise Again," "Fancy Nancy (Every Day Dirt No. 2)," and—the swan song of McCarn's recording career—"Serves 'Em Fine (Cotton Mill Colic No. 3)." On these sides, McCarn sang lead and played guitar and, on three of them, harmonica, while Long supplied vocal harmonies and, on "Serves 'Em Fine," a lively, buzzing kazoo. The four recordings, released in July and August 1931 on the Victor label, appeared under the billing "Dave and Howard."[46]

The greatest impact of McCarn's limited recorded output was that he brought songs of social protest about the economic hardships of Piedmont textile life to Depression-era southern audiences. Although at least four textile songs preceded his on commercial hillbilly records, none of them proved as popular or enduring as McCarn's "Cotton Mill Colic." Nor were any of them as incisive or creative.[47] When interviewed in 1961, McCarn claimed that he had written the song around 1926. Old-time music historian Mark Wilson, however, has speculated that McCarn may have modeled it on "citybilly" composers Bob Miller and Emma Dermer's "Eleven Cent Cotton Forty Cent Meat," a popular lament first recorded in August 1928, as a two-part record, by Miller himself, which chronicled the worsening plight of farmers in the agriculturally depressed South. Lending further support to Wilson's conjecture, McCarn also apparently lifted the bluesy guitar introduction to "Cotton Mill Colic" almost note for note from Jimmie Rodgers's "The Brakeman's Blues (Yodeling My Blues Away)," recorded in February 1928. Thus, it seems likely that McCarn did not write "Cotton Mill Colic" until the fall of 1928, at the very earliest.[48]

Although the precise year of the song's composition remains uncertain, what is clear is that McCarn wrote "Cotton Mill Colic" during an unprecedented period of labor strikes and industrial turmoil in the Carolina Piedmont. World War I had ushered in a time of booming prosperity for the region's millhands, but then, in the mid-1920s, a severe depression struck the Piedmont textile industry, throwing tens of thousands of mill workers out of work. In addition to massive layoffs, textile superintendents responded to the economic crisis by slashing wages, installing more efficient machinery, and adopting new scientific managerial practices. Chief among these new managerial practices was the notorious "stretch-out" system, the name workers used to describe the combination of labor-saving machinery and workload redistributions that not only often doubled the amount of work required of spinners and weavers but also often reduced their wages. "Well, if you was lucky enough to have a job," McCarn recalled, "you didn't make too much money. The wages didn't compare with the price of food and things, because food was always higher than the wages, you know. And then, things got worse after that, especially after '29. But it was bad enough before." Throughout much of the late 1920s, textile manufacturers struggled to stay afloat, and by the end of the decade, with many of the Piedmont's textile plants running only sporadically, some millhands' wages sank as low as five dollars a week. Many Gastonia textile workers were now unable to pay off the automobiles, furniture, and radios they had purchased on credit, and additional durable goods were now completely out of reach. The destructive economic downturn, which thwarted their participation in America's consumer culture and their access to desired consumer products, left many millhands feeling angry and betrayed.[49]

Their frustrations soon boiled over in the form of a large-scale labor revolt. During the spring of 1929, a series of textile strikes erupted across the Piedmont South, resulting in bitter standoffs between mill owners and millhands, as well as deep community divisions between strikers and nonunion workers, which disrupted class relations and patterns of everyday industrial life in textile mill communities across the region. Labor conflict first broke out in March 1929 at two

German-owned rayon spinning plants in Elizabethton, Tennessee, and then swept across the cities and mill towns of the Carolina Piedmont. "Textile mill strikes flared up last week like fire in broom straw across the face of the industrial South," *Time* magazine reported in an April 15, 1929, article titled "Southern Stirrings." "Though their causes were not directly related, they were all symptomatic of larger stirrings in that rapidly developing region." That year, eighty-one strikes involving more than 79,000 workers occurred in South Carolina alone. In a particularly appalling episode in October 1929, special sheriff's deputies fired into a crowd of unarmed picketers at the Baldwin Mill in Marion, North Carolina, killing six and wounding twenty-five others.[50]

But the most famous strike that year took place in McCarn's hometown of Gastonia. There, the strike revolved around the Loray Mill, a massive five-story brick factory that manufactured combed yarn and automobile tire cord fabric. With 2,200 workers, the mill, a subsidiary of the Manville-Jenckes Company of Pawtucket, Rhode Island, was the largest textile plant in Gaston County, and had been one of the first mills in the county to introduce the stretch-out system. In 1927, under these new cost-cutting measures, the Loray Mill superintendent had laid off one-third of the plant's 3,500 employees and trimmed a half-million dollars from the annual payroll without sacrificing production. After the layoffs, those millhands still lucky enough to have jobs scrambled even harder to make a living under the new nerve-wracking pressures of sped-up work rhythms and thinner pay envelopes. "We worked 13 hours a day, and we were so stretched out that lots of times we didn't stop for anything," recalled one Loray Mill spinner. "Sometimes we took sandwiches to work, and ate them as we worked. Sometimes we didn't even get to eat them. If we couldn't keep our work up like they [the bosses] wanted us to, they would curse us and threaten to fire us."[51]

Although only one of literally dozens of episodes of labor strife that rocked Piedmont textile communities in 1929, the Gastonia strike captured more national and international media attention than any of the others. The strike in this small southern city made headlines around the world chiefly because of the participation of a New York–based Communist trade union, the recently founded National Textile Workers Union (NTWU), but also because of the sensational murders that punctuated the five-and-a-half-month strike. In the ensuing decades, the Gastonia Textile Strike of 1929 would achieve enduring infamy as one of the most bitter labor conflicts in the history of the union-busting South, an episode of industrial strife whose outbursts of antilabor violence, deep social divisions, and intense red-baiting prompted a *New York Times* reporter to describe it as nothing short of a "class war."[52] The Gastonia strike began on April 1, 1929, when 1,800 Loray Mill workers walked off their jobs in protest of the intolerable shop-floor conditions under the stretch-out. Under the leadership of Fred E. Beal, a thirty-three-year-old Massachusetts Communist who had secretly been organizing a union local in the plant since January, the NTWU promptly called a strike. Among other concessions, the strikers demanded a minimum twenty-dollar weekly wage, a forty-hour work week, union recognition, and an end to the hated stretch-out. Within weeks, hundreds of workers from other Gaston County mills joined the rebellion.[53]

Two days after the strike began, Governor O. Max Gardner, himself the owner of a nearby Cleveland County textile mill, sent five companies of National Guardsmen to the city to protect mill property and to maintain order on the picket line. The pro-business city newspaper, the *Gastonia Daily Gazette*, exacerbated the already-heightened tensions in the community by publishing inflammatory anti-Communist editorials and a series of full-page advertisements paid for by a group calling itself "Citizens of Gaston County." One of these advertisements, captioned "Red Russianism Lifts Its Gory Hands Right Here in Gastonia," declared that the Communist Party "seeks the overthrow of capital, business, and all of the established social order. . . . It has no religion, it has no color line, it believes in free love—it advocates the destruction of all those things which the people of the South and of the United States hold sacred." When the governor withdrew some of the state troops, civic leaders organized a vigilante group called the "Committee of One Hundred" to patrol the strike zone. Shortly after midnight on April 18, using sledgehammers and crowbars, the committee's mob demolished the NTWU's headquarters and relief store. Three weeks later, the Loray Mill evicted striking workers and their families from company-owned housing, and the union erected a tent colony on a vacant lot a few blocks from the mill. "All over our village," one striker remembered, "you could see whole families with their household belongings in the street—sometimes in the pouring down rain, and lots of them with their little children and babies."[54]

Over the next few months, the violence escalated. On the night of June 7, Gastonia police chief Orville F. Aderholt was fatally wounded during a police raid on the evicted strikers' tent colony. Sixteen organizers and strikers, including Fred Beal and Vera Buch, the NTWU's deputy strike leader, were arrested and charged with first-degree murder and conspiracy. On September 9, after the first trial ended in a mistrial, a mob stormed the rebuilt union headquarters and tent colony, kidnapped three organizers, and terrorized strikers and their families. Five days later, in broad daylight, a caravan of gun thugs ambushed a truckload of unarmed strikers en route to a union rally in nearby Bessemer City and shot Ella May Wiggins, a twenty-nine-year-old single mother of five and one of the strike's most prolific balladeers, in the chest. "Lord-a-mercy," she gasped as she slumped against two strikers standing beside her, "they done shot and killed me." Shortly after her murder, the Gastonia strike collapsed.[55]

Aside from the Communist union's involvement and the outbursts of repressive antiunion violence, perhaps the most remarkable feature of the Gastonia Textile Strike of 1929 was the original protest songs that striking workers composed and the central role that these songs played in the conflict. Although songs of social protest had deep roots in the South, the Gastonia strike marked the first labor conflict in the region to produce a large documented repertoire of protest songs written specifically for the occasion. In part, this resulted from the fact that singing constituted a key element of the NTWU's calculated strategy for building a strong, viable union movement in the hostile atmosphere of the American South. Strike leader Fred Beal, a veteran of several New England textile strikes, had encouraged Gastonia strikers to sing from the onset of the conflict. "From experience," he later wrote, "I knew the tremendous value of singing the right songs on a picket line. These workers knew none of the union's strike songs. To overcome this, I typed a number of copies of *Solidarity* and told them to sing it to the tune of *Glory, Glory Hallelujah*." Beal and his staff of chiefly northern and midwestern organizers also taught Gastonia strikers several other labor anthems to sing on the picket lines, including such Industrial Workers of the World standards as "Casey Jones—The Union Scab," "The Preacher and the Slave," and "The Tramp." But singing also complemented the industrial folkways of the striking workers, especially the middle-aged women, who, according to Vera Buch, "knew any number of ballads, most of them rather mournful."[56]

Strikers composed literally dozens of protest songs that described the grim plight of the cotton mill workers, outlined the broader issues of the strike, and chronicled the major events of the conflict. Since such protest songs were designed to be sung by large groups and since it was far easier to compose new lyrics than new melodies, striking workers simply fitted new words to existing favorite tunes. One striker, an eleven-year-old spare hand named Odell Corley, wrote several strike ballads, including "Up in Old Loray," which she set to the tune of the melancholy folk song "On Top of Old Smoky." Corley replaced, as one group of historians has pointed out, "the false-hearted lover [in the original song] with a crooked boss and the betrayed woman with a spirited striker." One particularly poetic stanza warns: "The bosses will starve you, / They'll tell you more lies / Than there's crossties on the railroads, / Or stars in the skies." Another young Loray striker, Kermit Hardin, wrote "Union Boys," which he modeled on Al Jolson's million-selling hit song "Sonny Boy," which was featured in Warner Brothers' 1928 "talkie" motion picture *The Singing Fool*. Several organizers and journalists remarked on the strikers' penchant for composing their own protest songs. "A remarkable feature of these two gatherings," commented the editor of the Communist Party's *Daily Worker* in his coverage of a joint labor conference and defense rally in Bessemer City, "was the singing of union songs composed by the union members themselves and set to the crooning airs of southern folk music. The southern class struggle," he added, "is developing its own battle songs already."[57]

Although men and boys did write a few strike songs, women and teenaged girls were the predominant composers of new protest ballads for the strike. In Gastonia, as elsewhere across the Southern Piedmont that spring and summer, labor conflict opened new public opportunities for women to serve in their union locals, perform strike committee work, recruit union members, administer strike funds, distribute food and relief supplies, walk picket lines, deliver speeches, and, of course, compose strike ballads. Ballad composing accorded women a status and prestige in their communities usually unavailable to them under peaceful conditions. It also offered women the chance to speak out on issues of importance to them, and no issues figured more prominently in their songs than the plight of wage-earning mothers and their children. For example, Daisy Mc-Donald, a Loray spinner who supported her tubercular husband and seven children on $12.90 a week, wrote "The Speakers Didn't Mind," a nine-stanza ballad that chronicled the arrest of the strike leaders, the terrorizing of strikers and their families, and the destruction of the tent colony. Two stanzas recount: "They arrested the men, left the women alone, / To do the best they can; / They tore down the tents, run them out in the woods, / 'If you starve we don't give a damn.' / Our poor little children had no homes, / They were left in the streets to roam; / But the W.I.R. [Workers' International Relief] put up more tents and said, / 'Children, come on back home.'"[58]

By far the most famous grassroots balladeer to emerge out of the Gastonia strike was Ella May Wiggins, a spinner at American Mill No. 2 in nearby Bessemer City, whom the Communist press hailed as "the songstress of working class revolt in the South." Deserted by her ne'er-do-well husband, Wiggins struggled to raise her five surviving children on nine dollars a week. During the strike, she reportedly composed more than twenty songs championing the union's cause, including "All Around the Jailhouse," "The Big Fat Boss and the Workers," "Chief Aderholt," and the now-famous "Mill Mother's Song." And, like the other women balladeers, Ella May Wiggins worked her concerns as a wage-earning mother into her songs. According to Margaret Larkin, a left-wing New York City journalist who covered the conflict, Wiggins modeled her "strike ballets," as she called them, on "old mountain ballads" that she had learned as a girl growing up in the Blue Ridge Mountains of western North Carolina. But, like other Gastonia strike balladeers, she also borrowed melodies from commercial hillbilly records, particularly those containing songs that were deeply marked by sorrow, death, and tragedy. Wiggins modeled "All Around the Jailhouse," for example, on Jimmie Rodgers's best-selling "Waiting for a Train" (Victor, 1928), which was issued less than two months before the Gastonia strike began. Vernon Dalhart's "The Death of Floyd Collins" (Columbia, 1925), a topical ballad about a doomed Kentucky cave explorer, which sold around 300,000 copies, almost certainly provided the tune for her "Chief Aderholt." The other side of Dalhart's disc contained his version of "Little Mary Phagan," a topical ballad written by Fiddlin' John Carson about the 1913 mur-

LABUR DEFENDER

Oct. 1929   10¢

ELLA MAY~
MARTYR FOR AN ORGANIZED SOUTH

Ella May Wiggins, "Martyr for an Organized South." Cover of the
October 1929 issue of the *Labor Defender*. Courtesy of the North Carolina
Collection, Wilson Library, University of North Carolina at Chapel Hill.

der of an Atlanta factory girl. Wiggins used its melody for "The Mill Mother's Song."[59]

Ella May Wiggins often performed her strike songs from the beds of trucks and on speakers' platforms at mass meetings and union rallies throughout Gaston County during the spring and summer of 1929. As Vera Buch recalled, "She would write little ballads about the strike, set them to some well-known ballad tune, and sing them from the platform in a rich alto voice. Her rather gaunt face would light up and soften as she sang; her hazel eyes would shine; she became for the moment beautiful." Fred Beal, in his autobiography, *Proletarian Journey: New England, Gastonia, Moscow* (1937), likewise remembered her as a central figure at the union's nightly meetings. "No evening passed," he later wrote,

> without getting a new song from our Ella May, the minstrel of our strike. She would stand somewhere in a corner, chewing tobacco or snuff and fumbling over notes of a new poem scribbled on the back of a union leaflet. Suddenly some one would call for her to sing and other voices would take up the suggestion. Then in a deep, resonant voice she would give a simple ballad. . . . The crowd would join in with an old refrain and Ella May would add verse after verse to her song. From these the singers would drift into spirituals or hymns and many a "praise-the-Lord" would resound through the quiet night.[60]

Ella May Wiggins proved to be an extraordinary ballad composer because she translated her personal experiences into universal songs that spoke directly to other textile workers, especially mill mothers, and through her songs she inspired support among her fellow mill-hands for the union. "When Ella May sang, 'How it grieves the heart of a mother / You every one must know . . .' every woman in her audience did know, and responded to the common feeling," observed Margaret Larkin. "When she sang, 'We're going to have a union all over the South,' the strike meetings thrilled to the ring of militancy in her voice." Fellow strikers firmly believed that the Loray Mill's gun thugs had targeted her for assassination because of her influential role as a strike balladeer and her unswerving dedication to the union. "The bosses hated Ella May," claimed one striker, "because she made up songs, and was always at the speakings."[61]

Of the more than twenty strike songs Ella May Wiggins composed, the most famous was "The Mill Mother's Song," a beautiful blues ballad that Larkin described as a "classic expression of a working mother's love." The song, sung by a fellow female striker at Wiggins's September 17, 1929, funeral in Bessemer City, is now better known as "Mill Mother's Lament," after folklorist John Greenway retitled it in his 1953 study *American Folksongs of Protest*. The original version of Wiggins's song, published posthumously in the October 1929 issue of the *Labor Defender*, goes as follows:

We leave our home in the morning,
We kiss our children good-bye,
While we slave for the bosses,
Our children scream and cry.

And when we draw our money
Our grocery bills to pay,
Not a cent to spend for clothing,
Not a cent to lay away.

And on that very evening,
Our little son will say:
"I need some shoes, dear mother,
And so does sister May."

How it grieves the heart of a mother,
You every one must know.
But we can't buy for our children,
Our wages are too low.

Now listen to me, workers,
Both women and men,
We are sure to win our union,
If all would enter in.

I hope this will be a warning,
I hope you will understand,
And help us win our victory
And lend us a hand.

It is for our little children
That seems to us so dear,

But for us nor them, dear workers,
The bosses do not care.

But understand, all workers,
Our union they do fear,
Let's stand together, workers,
And have a union here.[62]

Due primarily to the ballad collecting of Margaret Larkin and other sympathetic journalists, no fewer than fourteen Gastonia strike songs, including six of Wiggins, have survived. Collectively, these songs reveal the inner story of that famous labor conflict from the perspective of the strikers themselves. They also suggest the extraordinary effectiveness of singing as a means of mass political mobilization in that protracted struggle. Singing such innovative songs united beleaguered strikers in public displays of union solidarity, expressed the shared grievances of the strikers, and revived flagging spirits as the doomed strike dragged on. Such functions, of course, were crucial in sustaining the Gastonia strike amid the brutally repressive campaign waged by the powerful combined forces of textile mill owners, civic leaders, National Guardsmen, and local law enforcement officers. Although the Gastonia strike songs were ephemeral, chiefly concerned with specific personalities and events that quickly faded from the headlines, a few of the songs, particularly those of Ella May Wiggins, circulated in Piedmont textile mill communities and even outside of the South, although on a far more limited scale than Dave McCarn's "Cotton Mill Colic" eventually would.[63]

McCarn was living in Gastonia during the failed 1929 strike, but his biographers have provided no information about his response to the five-and-a-half-month labor conflict. Nonetheless, the class-conscious textile songs that he later recorded reveal something about his labor politics. As the depression gripping the southern textile industry deepened during the late 1920s, McCarn drew upon his own frustrating experiences to compose his sardonic songs about the daily hardships of textile life. "Well, I composed 'Cotton Mill Colic,'" he told interviewers Archie Green and Ed Kahn in 1961, "due to the conditions of the textile mills in the South at that time and the hard times we was having. But that's mostly the reason I wrote the words for it like that, 'cause things were just about that bad. 'Course, I exaggerated right smart in it, but a lot of it was true. It was mostly to be a humorous song, you know." McCarn also explained how he had come up with the song's curious title. "Well, around the South a lot of people say, 'Well, quit colicking,' you know, be griping about something. Well, I just put it down 'Cotton Mill Colic,' because I was colicking about the hard times and the cotton mills, you know. So that seemed a pretty fit word for the song."[64]

With its bitter satire and quiet defiance, "Cotton Mill Colic" expresses not only the hopelessness felt by millhands trapped in the vicious textile mill economy but also a deep sense of working-class anger and resentment seldom heard on the hillbilly records of the 1920s and 1930s:

When you buy clothes on easy terms,
The collectors treat you like measly worms.
One dollar down, and then, Lord knows,
If you don't make a payment, they'll take your clothes.
When you go to bed, you cain't sleep,
You owe so much at the end of the week.
No use to colic, they're all that way,
Pecking at your door till they get your pay.
I'm a-gonna starve, ever'body will,
'Cause you cain't make a living at a cotton mill.

When you go to work, you work like the devil,
At the end of the week, you're not on the level.
Payday comes, you pay your rent,
When you get through, you've not got a cent,
To buy fatback meat, pinto beans,
Now and then you get turnip greens.
No use to colic, we're all that way,
Cain't get the money to move away.
I'm a-gonna starve, ever'body will,
'Cause you cain't make a living at a cotton mill.

Twelve dollars a week is all we get,
How in the heck can we live on that?
I got a wife and fourteen kids,
We all have to sleep on two bedsteads.
Patches on my britches, holes in my hat,
Ain't had a shave since my wife got fat [became pregnant?].

No use to colic, ever' day at noon,
The kids get to crying in a different tune.
I'm a-gonna starve, ever'body will,
'Cause you cain't make a living at a cotton mill.

They run a few days and then they stand [briefly shut down],
Just to keep down the working man.
We cain't make it, we never will,
As long as we stay at a lousy mill.
The poor're gettin' poorer, the rich're gettin' rich,
If I don't starve, I'm a son of a gun.
No use to colic, no use to rave,
We'll never rest till we're in our grave.
I'm a-gonna starve, nobody will,
'Cause you cain't make a living at a cotton mill.

"Cotton Mill Colic" became McCarn's signature song, and when he recorded the number in May 1930 he became one of the first hillbilly singers to address the economic exploitation and class injuries wrought by southern industrialization.[65] But his record also cost him his job. According to McCarn, after he was laid off at the Victory Yarn Mills in South Gastonia around 1931, the mill superintendent who had heard his song blacklisted him and refused to rehire him. "I heard a few guys say, 'I bet after that song you'll never get another job with a textile mill around this part of the country,'" McCarn recalled. "Which I didn't care whether I did or not anyway, you know. I'd have written anything I'd wanted about the cotton mills. As long as you don't libel yourself, you know. You can't libel fourteen thousand cotton mills at one time, I guess. 'Course, 'Cotton Mill Colic,' it was mostly just fun, you know. I didn't actually mean that's exactly the way the textile mills were, but the conditions they were in give me the idea for the song."[66]

McCarn's "Cotton Mill Colic" fostered, even as it was shaped by, the stirrings of class consciousness that exploded between 1929 and 1931 into one of the greatest labor uprisings in the history of the Piedmont South. Unlike most other textile songs found on prewar hillbilly records, however, it is not specifically about the miseries of factory labor. In fact, the song only refers once to the actual work routine. Instead, "Cotton Mill Colic" concerns itself with working-class consumption—or, rather, the lack of it—and the vicious downward spiral of debt and poverty that ensnared tens of thousands of textile worker families. Millhands occupied an impossible economic position, McCarn suggests, because the longer they worked in the mills, the deeper they sank into debt. Beyond these class resentments, he also uses the song to explore an important gender dilemma that plagued male textile workers. In "Cotton Mill Colic," McCarn complains about the refusal of mill superintendents to pay him a living wage with which he could purchase not only little luxuries, such as a shave at the barbershop, but also the barest necessities, such as food and clothes for himself and his wife and children. The paltry wages millhands received, McCarn asserts, emasculated workingmen by preventing them from fulfilling their traditional masculine roles as family bread-winners. In this sense, the gender dimensions of McCarn's "Cotton Mill Colic" serve as an interesting complement to Gastonia strike balladeer Ella May Wiggins's "The Mill Mother's Song," which she composed a few months before her murder on September 14, 1929. In her song, Wiggins condemns industrial capitalism for essentially making it impossible for working mothers to fulfill their traditional gender responsibilities of homemaking and child rearing. Not only do textile mill owners prevent her from caring for her children during the eleven-hour shifts she is forced to work, she asserts, but they also refuse to pay her a decent wage with which to provide her children with the food and clothing they need.[67]

McCarn includes similarly barbed class commentary in his sequel, "Poor Man, Rich Man (Cotton Mill Colic No. 2)," which he recorded in November 1930. Here, he presents a fuller, more detailed description of the regular mill workday and extends his critique of industrial work by chronicling the hardships with which southern millhands were forced to contend, including abusive foremen, eleven-hour shifts, starvation wages, paycheck deductions, and greedy merchants.

> Let me tell you people something that's true,
> When you work in the mill, I'll tell you what you have to do:
> You get up every morning before daylight,
> You labor all day until it gets night.
> You work a few days, get pale in the face,
> From standing so long in the same darn place.
> Along comes the boss as hard as he can tear,
> He wants you to think he's a grizzly bear.

Ashes to ashes, dust to dust,
Let the poor man live and the rich man bust.

When you go to dinner, you have to run,
Or they'll blow the whistle before you're done.
Payday comes, you won't have a penny,
When you pay your bills, 'cause you got so many.
Sometimes you hear a racket like peckerwoods,
But it's only peddlers trying to sell their goods.
The merchants, they're all just about gray,
From studying how to get the poor man's pay.
Ashes to ashes, dust to dust,
Let the poor man live and the rich man bust.

Now some people run the mill man down,
But the cotton mill people make the world go round.
They take a little drink to have a little fun,
Whenever they manage to rake up the mon'.
Now I left the mountains when I was a strip,
I never will forget that awful trip.
I walked all the way behind a apple wagon,
When I got to town, the seat of my pants was a-dragging.
Ashes to ashes, dust to dust,
Let the poor man live and the rich man bust.

When wintertime comes, there's hell to pay,
When you see the boss, you'll have to say:
"I want a load of wood, a ton of coal.
Take a dollar out a week, or I'll go in the hole."
You have to buy groceries at some chain store,
'Cause you cain't afford to pay any more.
If you don't starve, I'm a son of a gun,
'Cause you can't buy beans without any mon'.
Ashes to ashes, dust to dust,
Let the poor man live and the rich man bust.

In the first stanza of this song, McCarn recounts the exhausting drudgery of the long workday, but in most of the remaining stanzas, he again complains, as he does in "Cotton Mill Colic," about his inability to participate in the nation's consumer economy beyond the barest minimum.

McCarn's final textile mill song, "Serves 'Em Fine (Cotton Mill Colic No. 3)," recorded with Howard Long at his last session in May 1931, chronicles the 1920s economic collapse of the Piedmont textile industry and its effect on wages as the depression intensified. Here, McCarn debunks the mythology of southern industrialism by criticizing textile promoters and civic boosters for duping tens of thousands of southern mountaineers into believing that mill work would provide a more lucrative and comfortable livelihood than farming and other occupations. In "Serves 'Em Fine," McCarn punctures the overblown proclamations of these architects of southern industrialization by providing unflinching descriptions of how the boom-to-bust business cycle of the cotton mills and mounting debt victimized working-class families:

Now, people, in the year nineteen and twenty,
The mills ran good, ever'body had plenty.
Lots of people with a good free will,
Sold their homes and moved to a mill.
"We'll have lots of money," they said,
But everyone got hell instead.
It was fun in the mountains rolling logs,
But now when the whistle blows they run like dogs.
It suits us people, it serves us fine,
For thinking that a mill was a darn gold mine.

Now in the year nineteen and twenty-five,
The mills all stood but we're still alive.
People kept coming when the weather was fine,
Just like they were going to a big gold mine.
As time passed on, their money did too,
Everyone began to look kinda blue.
If we had any sense up in our dome,
We'd still be living in our mountain home.
It suits us people, it serves us fine,
For thinking that a mill was a darn gold mine.

Now in the year nineteen and thirty,
They don't pay nothing and they do us dirty.
When we do manage to get ahead,
It seems like all of the mills go dead.

We're always in the hole, getting deeper every day,
If we ever get even, it'll be Judgment Day.
There's no use to colic, no use to shirk,
For there's more people loafing than there are at work.
It suits us people, it serves us fine,
For thinking that a mill was a darn gold mine.

Now all you mountaineers that's listening to me,
Take off your hats and holler, "Whoopee."
For I'm going back home in the "Land of the Sky,"
Where they all drink moonshine and never do die.
I'll take my dogs while the moon shines bright,
Hunt coon and possum the whole darn night.
If you can't get the money to move away,
It's too bad folks, you'll have to stay.
It suits you people, it serves you fine,
For thinking that a mill was a darn gold mine.

In "Serves 'Em Fine," McCarn extends the blame for the blighted economic circumstances in which Piedmont millhands found themselves, chiding them for their own stupidity and naïveté in exchanging the economic independence and preindustrial freedoms of mountain life for the economic dependence and low wages of textile life, and thus for participating in their own exploitation. McCarn's solution to the miseries of textile work is for dissatisfied millhands to quit their jobs and return to their former lives in Southern Appalachia—an untenable plan for many workers.

Critics have claimed that McCarn's three "Cotton Mill Colic" songs cannot properly be considered social protest songs, because they offer no solutions to the deplorable conditions they describe (his fantasy of returning to the mountains in "Serves 'Em Fine" notwithstanding). To be sure, none of his textile mill songs challenge the basic power structure of labor relations. Nor do any of them propose substantive social reforms to redress industrial exploitation and class injustices. But, contrary to critics' charges, those omissions should be expected and forgiven. After all, as literary scholar William L. Andrews and his co-editors remind us, McCarn's "Cotton Mill Colic" "claims that there was 'no use to colic,' [that it was] literally pointless for workers to bellyache, about their situation." Archie Green agrees. McCarn wrote "Cotton Mill Colic" "to help make his way through a rough work day,"

Green notes, "for to him laughter seemed more effective than complaint." Although he did join the Textile Workers Union of America, one of the new, aggressive CIO industrial unions, in the early 1940s, McCarn seems to have been disappointed by the union's failure to secure higher wages and better shop-floor conditions, and he remained a lukewarm unionist, at best. How and to what degree, he must have wondered, could an exploitative industrial system be reformed, when he had witnessed the violent, state-sponsored crushing of the Gastonia Textile Strike of 1929 and, later, of the General Textile Strike of 1934 as well. The Gastonia conflict had politicized Ella May Wiggins and other Gaston County textile workers, but the tragic defeat for the workers only seemed to confirm McCarn's skepticism about the effectiveness of grassroots labor insurgency. In the end, McCarn did not want to reform the southern textile mill industry so much as he wanted to escape it altogether.[68]

Unfortunately, not even McCarn's music could provide him with the escape he so desperately sought. With the onset of the Great Depression, once-flourishing hillbilly record sales plummeted as financially strapped white southern workers and farmers could no longer afford to purchase much beyond the barest essentials. Except for his first record, none of McCarn's releases apparently sold very well, and little more than a year after he first entered that Memphis studio, his promising recording career ended. After his final RCA-Victor recording session in May 1931, McCarn faded back into his Gastonia textile worker life with the realization that professional music making was not going to rescue him from his dead-end factory job. But his dozen recorded selections, particularly "Cotton Mill Colic," assured that his name would not be lost to history. McCarn's musical influence continued after the end of his active recording career, and he is remembered today primarily for creatively expressing his experiences and observations in songs of pointed social commentary that resonated with his embattled fellow millhands. On his recording of "Cotton Mill Colic," McCarn captured the struggles of tens of thousands of hard-pressed Piedmont mill workers, who, no matter how hard they worked, barely managed to stay one payment ahead of creditors, at best. In *The Literature of the American South* (1998), William L. Andrews and his co-editors write that the song's "tough-minded details, wry humor, complaint against injustice, and refusal to engage in self-pity" made it "particularly meaningful as a mirror of the plight

Strikers participating in a Labor Day parade on the streets of downtown
Gastonia, North Carolina, during the General Textile Strike of 1934.
Courtesy of the Library of Congress.

of exploited and desperate textile mill workers." Folklorists Doug De-Natale and Glenn Hinson argue that McCarn's "exclamation was not a straightforward complaint, but a complicated result of anger transposed through deflecting humor. It was precisely McCarn's skillful blending of the two sentiments that made his 'Cotton Mill Colic' one of the most powerful of the mill songs."[69]

When McCarn recorded "Cotton Mill Colic" in 1930, he was probably not intending to make a serious social statement; he was, as the song's title indicates, merely grousing. Nonetheless, the song carried important meanings for—and struck a chord with—hard-hit Piedmont textile workers. More than any other textile song found on prewar hillbilly discs, "Cotton Mill Colic" entered oral tradition and spread rapidly across the Depression-era South, chiefly through the powerful modern medium of phonograph records. Only five months after its release, Tom Tippett, a labor organizer and activist from Brookwood Labor College in Katonah, New York, heard the song at a January 1931 United Textile Workers union rally during a textile strike in Danville, Virginia. "A small boy, not yet in his teens, sang a solo accompanying himself with a guitar swung from his shoulder," wrote Tippett, in *When Southern Labor Stirs* (1931). "It was called 'Cotton Mill Colic' and accurately portrayed in a comic vein the economics of the textile industry, as well as the tragedy of cotton mill folk." Significantly, Tippett's account reveals how striking Danville workers appropriated hillbilly records to express their class grievances just as, less than two years earlier during the Gastonia Textile Strike of 1929, Ella May Wiggins and other balladeers had modeled their strike songs on melodies borrowed from hillbilly records.[70]

Other musicians embraced McCarn's song for its satirical humor. For example, in the mid-1930s, Bill Bolick learned a version of "Cotton Mill Colic" from a friend in his hometown of Hickory, North Carolina. Bolick, a mandolin player, and his guitarist brother Earl, who performed together on radio and records between 1935 and 1951 as the Blue Sky Boys, later reprised McCarn's song on their 1965 comeback album, *Presenting the Blue Sky Boys*. The two brothers' parents worked in Hickory textile mills, but, unlike the Danville strikers, who incorporated the song into their union meetings, Bill Bolick did not invest it with any overtly political meaning. "I didn't sing 'Cotton Mill Colic' with the idea of protesting," he explained. "I thought it was more of a comedy song."[71]

Not only was McCarn's "Cotton Mill Colic" enormously popular in Piedmont textile towns during the Great Depression, but it also penetrated Southern Appalachian communities. In 1938, Joe Sharp, a mandolinist and guitarist from the Federal Emergency Relief Administration's New Deal resettlement community of Skyline Farms, Alabama, recorded the song for Alan Lomax, the director of the Library of Congress's Archive of American Folk Song in Washington, D.C.[72] Consequently, "Cotton Mill Colic" entered the American folk song canon. But it was Sharp's 1938 Library of Congress field recording—not McCarn's 1930 Victor record—that came to be enshrined as the definitive aural version of the song. In 1941, Lomax and his renowned folk song collector father, John A. Lomax, published a transcription of Sharp's recording in one of their now-classic American folk song anthologies, *Our Singing Country: A Second Volume of American Ballads and Folk Songs* (1941), describing the song as "the story of what happens to the cotton farmer when he becomes a cotton-mill worker, with the 'collection man' as the villain of the piece." Later, the younger Lomax, who considered "Cotton Mill Colic" "the best of all . . . cotton-mill songs," also included it in *The Folk Songs of North America* (1960), as well as in *Hard Hitting Songs for Hard-Hit People* (1967), which he compiled and edited in collaboration with folksingers Woody Guthrie and Pete Seeger. In addition, "Cotton Mill Colic" has also appeared in folklorist Benjamin A. Botkin's *A Treasury of Southern Folklore: Stories, Ballads, Traditions, and Folkways of the People of the South* (1949) and, most recently, in *The Literature of the American South* (1998), edited by William L. Andrews and his colleagues.[73]

Besides its inclusion in prominent folk song and literature anthologies, "Cotton Mill Colic" was extensively recorded on post–World War II albums. A founding member of the folk group the Weavers and one of the towering figures of the American folk music revival, Pete Seeger was the first postwar artist to record the song, on his 1956 Folkways LP, *American Industrial Ballads*. In addition to Seeger and the Blue Sky Boys, other musicians who have covered McCarn's song include J. E. Mainer, Mike Seeger, and the Southern Eagle String Band, to name only a few. Joe Glazer, the self-proclaimed "Labor's Troubadour" and former assistant education director for the Textile Workers Union of America, recorded "Cotton Mill Colic" on his 1970 Collector concept album, *Textile Voices*. Chiefly through Glazer's concerts and albums, "Cotton Mill Colic" became immensely popular within the labor movement. But because most of the commercial recordings and published transcriptions of "Cotton Mill Colic" since the 1940s do not credit him as the song's composer, McCarn largely escaped the notice of ballad collectors, folk revivalists, labor singers, and academic folklorists, despite the song's increased popularity after World War II.[74]

Interest in McCarn's old 78-rpm recordings during the American folk music revival of the 1950s and 1960s did lead to his rediscovery, however. At the height of the revival, the New Lost City Ramblers, a neo-traditionalist stringband based in Washington, D.C., recorded two of McCarn's original compositions for Folkways Records: "Serves 'Em Fine," on their 1959 album, *Songs from the Depression*, and "Everyday Dirt," the following year, on *New Lost City Ramblers, Vol. 2*. One of the band's founding members, Mike Seeger—a New York musician and musicologist, the younger half-brother of banjoist Pete Seeger—was particularly interested in McCarn's songs. In April 1961, based upon the clue from the title of McCarn's 1930 Victor record of "Gastonia Gallop," he located the former hillbilly recording artist in Stanley, North Carolina, a small Gaston County textile town twelve miles north of Gastonia. By the time Seeger met him, McCarn had been retired from the mills for more than a decade and was running a small radio and television repair shop in front of his house, which sat alongside the Seaboard Railroad. His second wife, Ruby, a South Carolina textile worker whom he had married in 1943, worked at United Spinners Inc., in nearby Lowell. McCarn, then fifty-six, was a handsome, well-built man, who, with his lean, weathered face, angular jaw, and shock of wavy gray hair, bore some resemblance to Woody Guthrie. McCarn was friendly, Seeger later recalled, and he was willing to reminisce about his Depression-era recording career, but he seemed "shocked" that anyone still remembered him from the handful of hillbilly records he had made some thirty years earlier.[75]

Four months after Seeger initiated contact with the retired musician, folklorists and hillbilly music scholars Archie Green and Ed Kahn visited McCarn and conducted a lengthy, tape-recorded interview with him, during which he recounted his life story. When his recording career ended in 1931, McCarn told the interviewers, he had reluctantly resumed working in Gaston County's textile mills, but around four years later, in yet another attempt to escape the mills, he enlisted in the Army Signal Corps, where he learned the rudiments of electronics and radio repair. During World War II, McCarn opened a radio repair shop near Gastonia, and over the next decade he provided for himself and his new wife by combining radio repair and textile work. "Well, the way I'd do it," he explained, "I worked in the cotton mill till I got disgusted with it, and didn't want to work there anymore. Till it got monstrous. Then, I'd get into the radio business and stay with it a year or so. When it got monstrous, maybe I'd go back to the cotton mill and vice versa." In 1950, McCarn quit his job at East Gastonia's Rex Mill No. 1 and opened a television repair shop, a far-sighted venture, considering that, at that early date, television broadcasting was an unproven media gamble and that few small-town North Carolina residents then owned television sets. "And since then," McCarn told Green and Kahn, "I haven't been back to the mills."[76]

During the 1930s, even after his recording career had ended, Mc-Carn had continued to play music and to compose what he described as "humorous" songs, including such titles as "Mountain Gal" and "Peg's Wooden Leg." But by the time Green and Kahn interviewed him, he professed to have "lost interest" in music and had forgotten most of the words to "Cotton Mill Colic" and his other songs. He no longer even owned a guitar and had not played one regularly since 1959, when his last guitar had been ruined after a frozen water pipe burst in his repair shop. When Kahn retrieved his own guitar from the trunk of his car and asked McCarn to pick a few tunes, he apologetically declined. "I tried here awhile back," he explained. "Somebody had a nice-looking guitar, and I was gonna go to town, don't you know. And I got in here, and I got my fingers hung up in the strings. I'm just plumb out of practice." McCarn did, however, promise that he would purchase a cheap guitar and rehearse his old songs and sing a few of them for Green and Kahn on their next visit. When they returned for a second visit, in August 1963, McCarn did sing and pick out on the guitar, with some fumbling, "Mountain Gal," a song that he claimed he had written sometime before World War II "while he was plowing with mules" near Mill Springs, North Carolina.[77]

Overall, Green and Kahn's visits with McCarn must have disappointed them. The washed-up hillbilly singer and songwriter was amused but nonetheless perplexed by the scholars' genuine interest in his music, and they in turn seemed dismayed by his lack of interest in music and his inability to perform his old hillbilly songs. McCarn, it seems, dismissed the importance that Green and Kahn accorded to "Cotton Mill Colic" and his other recorded numbers, and he remained "modestly disparaging about his own songs," according to old-time music historian Mark Wilson, "although they in fact stand out as some of the finest of their type." "Anybody was better than I was," McCarn told his visitors. "I couldn't sing. I sound like a frog a-trying to croak." "On this particular afternoon," Kahn wrote of the 1963 visit, "the rain was intermittent and Dave was sitting on his front porch. He was obviously glad to see us, but had been drinking. As a result he was relaxed and somewhere between humorous and cynical about his experiences in the recording business. . . . He generally had forgotten most of his songs and required prodding—usually his own—to get words together. . . . His past was merely a memory which seemed to evoke little emotion thirty years later. He described his early recording activity as calmly as he might have described his agricultural or mill experiences."[78]

Unlike Clarence "Tom" Ashley, Dock Boggs, Dorsey Dixon, and a few dozen other elderly hillbilly artists who staged brief comeback careers on independent record labels and folk festival circuits during the 1960s and 1970s, McCarn could not be coaxed out of his self-imposed musical retirement. In 1961, acting on a recommendation from Green, University of North Carolina folklore professor Arthur Palmer Hudson invited McCarn to perform at the North Carolina Folklore Society meeting in December and again at the North Carolina Folk Festival the following May, but McCarn declined. "He said that he has not touched a guitar or sung in years," Hudson wrote to Green, "and indicated that he is permanently off folksinging. . . . I am sorry, of course, for he must be an interesting man, and his songs seem to be something rare." Despite the avid interest that record collectors, academic folklorists, and folk revival musicians expressed in the songs he had written and recorded, McCarn refused to revive his moribund musical career.[79]

Over the course of his life, McCarn suffered as a result of his choices, as did his two wives and three children, and he ended up another working-class victim of self-destructive alcoholism and grinding poverty. According to several family members, his chronic bouts of heavy drinking grew increasingly severe in later years. "After Dave got his rambling days over if it hadn't been for his drinking I think he would have turned out all right, you know, and been a good man," observed his son, Johnnie McCarn. "And everybody liked him. And he was talented in his radio and TV repair work and then plus mu-

sically, everybody appreciated that." On November 7, 1964, Dave Mc-
Carn died suddenly of aspirated pneumonia, resulting from cirrhosis
of the liver, at the age of fifty-nine. His brief obituary in the *Gastonia
Gazette* failed to mention his music and recording career, identifying
him only as a "radio and TV repairman," who had belonged to the
Ebenezer Methodist Church and who had "lived in this community
all of his life." McCarn, the largely unacknowledged singer and songwriter of cotton mill songs and bawdy novelty numbers, was buried in
Hillcrest Gardens Cemetery in Mount Holly, North Carolina, within
five miles of his birthplace.[80]

McCarn's selfish abandonment of his children caused emotional
wounds that more than sixty years later refused to heal completely.
Johnnie McCarn, who was only two years old when his father deserted
the family and who died in Gastonia in 2004, spent much of his life
struggling to overcome his bitterness at Dave McCarn's departure
and to salvage some meaning from his estranged father's troubled,
chaotic life. He explained in a 1996 interview:

> Dave was just a rambling-type of fellow. He rode the rails, and he
> just bummed around a lot of his life, drinking and having fun. And
> even when he got his recording contract, drinking was the most
> important thing, and that's how he lost everything, you know. I
> think he could have been real famous, and he was fairly intelli-
> gent not having no more education than he did. So I think he just
> missed out on a good opportunity to have a real interesting and
> successful life. And I say that because of the drinking. And it's a
> shame, but that's life, I guess.[81]

As an adult, Johnnie McCarn learned to play and sing his father's
hillbilly classics from a reel-to-reel tape of the original Victor records
that Archie Green had sent to his father in 1963. Doing so in some
ways seemed to bring him closer to his father's memory, but Johnnie
never could reconcile himself to some of his father's life choices. "I
don't hold any grudges, you know," he confessed,

> but I know in my own heart that I couldn't have done what Dave
> did, you know. Being responsible for bringing life into the world
> and just turn my back and escape. I couldn't do that. But not know-
> ing his life and the problems maybe he had that nobody knew, I
> can't judge that part of it, you know. And so realizing that Dave was

a lot more intelligent, a lot smarter, than probably he even knew—that he could've been something—in that regard, I can have a little bit of respect for him, and understand and realize that when I do sing one of his songs that it was something special in his life and something that he experienced. Well, I respect that, you know. So that's my way of living, I guess, as much as it is.

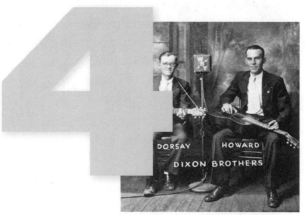

A BLESSING TO PEOPLE
THE DIXON BROTHERS,
HOWARD AND DORSEY

I'm trying to serve the Lord in my weak way and trying to be a
blessing to people, is what I been trying to do. In fact, I've tried to
live right all my life, but, you know, we're not going into the story
about my life because I don't want that mentioned. I don't want
nothing about my life wrote out, because I had it too rough in life.
—Dorsey Dixon, on a 1961 homemade tape recording

Carolina textile singer and songwriter Dorsey Dixon was
never supposed to live. At birth, he was a puny, oxygen-starved baby
weighing only three pounds, what in the vernacular of the day was
called a "blue baby." "I heard [my parents] tell friends and neighbors many times that I was a blue baby. Which I did not understand,"
Dixon later explained in one of his autobiographical writings. "But I
have learned that such babies requared the greatest of care by doctors
and nerses. and was right up next to imposible to keep one of them
from slipping out from the living. But a great unknown Power kept
me. and I made it." Dixon's pious Christian parents interpreted his
near-miraculous survival as a sign that God had spared him for what
they frequently referred to as "a great purpose." Throughout most of
his life, however, gnawing doubts about his success in carrying out
his divinely ordained mission tormented him. "I do not know if I have
full filled the purpose that mother and father said I was left here for

or not," Dixon confessed in a memoir written when he was fifty years old. "But I do know that I have had a real tough time in life."[1]

For more than thirty-five years, Dorsey Dixon struggled to earn a living in the textile mills of the Carolina Piedmont, but by calling he was a guitarist, singer, and songwriter who believed that his special mission in life was to spread the gospel through music. A devout Free Will Baptist and regular churchgoer, Dixon transformed accounts of small-town tragedies and national disasters into songs about the wages of sin, the unknown hour of death, and the promise of eternal salvation. The classic song "Wreck on the Highway," which *Grand Ole Opry* star Roy Acuff turned into a national hit in 1942, ranks as Dixon's most famous composition, but many of his other songs similarly recount tragic events—millpond drownings, train wrecks, schoolhouse fires, ship sinkings, and other calamities. Such misfortunes became, in Dixon's hands, moral parables about God's wrath and the self-destructive sins of human pride and godlessness; furthermore, as jeremiads intended to generate spiritual renewal, his songs of tragedy usually concluded with somber warnings to sinners to repent of their wickedness and to lead righteous Christian lives in anticipation of heavenly rewards. "Look out we may be next, brother, / In a mad raging storm may go down, / It may be too late to start praying, / When a twister is sweeping the ground," he wrote in "The Alabama Storm," a 1932 song inspired by a deadly series of tornados that killed more than three hundred residents of that state. "Get your hearts right now this evening / And then you'll be right when she comes, / Death, Hell, and the furor of a twister / Can't undo what Jesus has done." Perhaps such dreadful incidents resonated with him in part because, as he made clear in his late-life interviews and two unpublished autobiographical writings, hardship and suffering had deeply scarred his own life. But Dixon's religious faith and his belief in his "great purpose" sustained him throughout fragile health, bouts with chronic depression, unstable personal relationships, intense pangs of self-doubt, and—despite modest songwriting success—lifelong poverty. In many ways his ongoing financial and health problems seemed only to strengthen his abiding faith. "And friends," he once wrote, "I know that the Great Power of God help[ed] me to win in every battle that I fought to stay in the world."[2]

Beginning in 1929, Dixon composed or arranged dozens of sacred and secular songs, including textile mill songs about his life as a frustrated weaver and sermonizing evangelical numbers about his beliefs as a fundamentalist Christian. As a southern working-class songwriter, he stands out as one of the few to write and publish songs that chronicled both his occupational and his spiritual life. (He also wrote an apparently unfinished melodramatic novella titled "The Angel Guided Child.") Several of his songs, which he and his younger brother Howard recorded together as a guitar-and-steel-guitar duo called the Dixon Brothers for RCA-Victor between 1936 and 1938, are now considered country and bluegrass standards, including "Weave Room Blues," "Intoxicated Rat," and "Wreck on the Highway" (originally, when published in his local newspaper, titled "I Didn't Hear Nobody Pray"). But Dixon essentially saw himself, especially in the last decades of his life, as a hillbilly evangelist, a modern-day prophet—part long-suffering Job and part damnation-thundering Jeremiah—teaching the gospel with country and sacred songs. As such, Dixon did not concern himself much with trade-union politics or other "worldly" issues, focusing instead on ensuring the redemption of his own soul as well as the souls of as many listeners as he could reach through his radio programs, phonograph recordings, and stage shows.[3]

Despite Dixon's own deliberate focus on the spiritual life, his sermonizing tragic songs have long been overshadowed by his textile mill songs. A perceptive observer of southern working-class life, Dixon either wrote or arranged seven songs about Piedmont textile work (all but one of which he also recorded), more than any other hillbilly songwriter of his generation, and most of his biographers have foregrounded these compositions, especially "Weaver's Life," "Weave Room Blues," and "Spinning Room Blues." Archie Green, an occupational folklorist and hillbilly music scholar who assisted Dixon in his brief early 1960s comeback, considers him "the poet laureate of the cotton mill industry." "Dorsey is distinguished from his peers," Green writes, "precisely because he adds to the normal characterization of the hillbilly musician a deep knowledge [of] and feeling for industrial life. Except for a few dollars earned on the radio and in phonograph recording studios, his fortune has been that of a 'millhand.'" Though Dixon shied away from a sustained critique of southern industrialism, his textile mill songs represent a powerful voice of class consciousness and offer important insights into the working conditions and struggles of Piedmont millhands during the 1930s. Several of

The Dixon Brothers, Dorsey, left, and Howard, right, with an unidentified
radio announcer, ca. 1934. Courtesy of the Southern Folklife Collection,
Wilson Library, University of North Carolina at Chapel Hill.

them, particularly "Weave Room Blues" and "Weaver's Life," achieved a new level of popularity as protest songs among folk music revivalists and trade unionists after World War II. Pete Seeger, the New Lost City Ramblers, and Joe Glazer, among others, have recorded one or both of these songs on long-playing albums, and Dixon's textile songs have also been published in such folk song studies and anthologies as John Greenway's *American Folksongs of Protest* (1953) and Alan Lomax, Woody Guthrie, and Pete Seeger's *Hard Hitting Songs for Hard-Hit People* (1967). Dixon's compositions about the hardships of cotton mill work represent significant cultural documents of Depression-era southern working-class life, but his often overlooked tragic numbers reveal his deepest personal concerns, which, in turn, shed light on many of the under-examined social and cultural tensions endemic in Piedmont textile mill villages during this same period.[4]

Dixon's tragic songs are essentially spiritual and social commentaries that address the transformations of the modern South, especially the erosion of family bonds and religious values, but his songs should not be mistakenly interpreted as primitive or unsophisticated merely because of the conservative spiritual messages that many of them convey. Although his evangelical compositions often relied upon a stark fundamentalist morality, maudlin sentimentality, and rhetorical devices that seem better suited for Victorian audiences, his songs were in fact undeniably modern. Dixon resided for most of his life in small Carolina mill towns, but his exposure to sensational newspaper journalism, radio broadcasts, phonograph records, Hollywood films, and a diverse array of musical influences fostered his serious engagement with contemporary national events and pressing religious issues. And many of the ideas for his songs, especially his tragic ones, stemmed directly from these sources. He also sometimes borrowed melodies for his songs from current hillbilly records, especially those of the Carter Family, Jimmie Rodgers, and Vernon Dalhart. Moreover, Dixon ranks as one of the first songwriters regularly to compose "answer songs" to the hillbilly hits of the Great Depression, including responses to "Maple on the Hill," "I'm Just Here to Get My Baby Out of Jail," and "What Would You Give in Exchange?" Dixon's access to, and participation in, the nation's commercial recording industry and regional radio broadcasting served him in another way as well, because phonograph records and radio enabled his spiritual message to reach tens of thousands of listeners and thereby magnified his impact to a degree that only a generation earlier would not have been possible. Dixon's homiletic songs of sin, death, and destruction provide valuable insights into his sacred mission, and such songs, particularly "Down with the Old Canoe" and "Wreck on the Highway," also suggest the ways in which Dixon believed he could save his fellow Christians from the temptations of an increasingly materialistic and secular modern South.[5]

Dixon's complex musical agenda emerged from a life indelibly marked by poverty, illness, and factory labor. Dorsey Murdock Dixon was born on October 14, 1897, the third of seven children of a white working-class family, in Darlington, South Carolina, the state's largest tobacco market and one of its full-blown industrial centers. His brother, Howard Briten Dixon, with whom he performed on radio and records, was born on June 19, 1903, in the nearby community of Kelley Town. Their father, William McQuiller "Quilley" Dixon, worked at a local cotton mill, the Darlington Manufacturing Company, where he fired the steam engines that powered the plant. "Now, Father worked in the different textile departments some," Dorsey recalled, "but he had bronchitis asthma. And he just couldn't stand the lint in the cotton mill, you know. Them days, they run the mills by steam engines, and he most always ended up operating the engines that run the plant." Dorsey's mother, Mary Margaret "Maggie" (Braddock) Dixon, cared for her children and kept the small, three-room mill village house in which the large family lived.[6]

Like most other poor families in turn-of-the-century South Carolina, the Dixons scrambled to earn a living, and, as a result, they never remained in one place for any extended period of time. Their restless search for a better life took them back and forth across northeastern South Carolina, from sharecropper farms to the market towns of Hartsville, McColls, and Bennettsville. Here and there, Quilley Dixon picked up jobs in cotton mills, sawmills, and machine and woodworking shops. When he fell out with his boss or grew dissatisfied with a job, he rented a farm on shares and raised a crop of cotton. As a young boy, Dorsey quickly learned that even the children were expected to help the family make ends meet. He recalled:

> I just loved moving, you know, because I was a kid, and I didn't have to lift nothing or help load the wagon, you know. That just suited me to move. But when I got out there to the country and

they put me in the field picking cotton, I wasn't a bit happy about it. And I'll never forget it as long as I live, I was picking cotton, and I was lagging back behind. First news I know, Mama was on top of me with a cotton stalk. I guess I needed working on, 'cause I was lazy and I didn't want to work. And when it thundered, it tickled me to death, 'cause I knowed it was going to be too wet to pick cotton. But anyway, as I grew older, I found out that we had to work to live.

Finally, in 1909, the Dixons returned to Darlington. Quilley Dixon found work in one of the town's carpentry shops and sent his two oldest children, sixteen-year-old Nancy and fourteen-year-old Walter, to work at the Darlington Manufacturing Company. Later that year, Dorsey dropped out of the fourth grade and joined them in the mill. Only twelve years old, he initially helped his sister tend her spinning frames, but by the age of thirteen, he was making bobbin bands in the mill's machine shop for fifty cents a day. Dixon's memories of his childhood labor in Darlington, combined with those of his sister Nancy, would later form the basis for his classic "Babies in the Mill."[7]

Because store-bought amusements were a rare luxury for the Dixons, they relied instead on "singings" and other homemade entertainment to lighten their workaday life. Although neither of Dorsey's parents played a musical instrument, they often sang around the house, especially his mother, who knew many old Victorian parlor ballads, like "Be at Home Soon Tonight, My Dear Boy" and "The Ship That Never Return'd." Dorsey's sister, Nancy, taught him folk songs about cotton mill work such as "Factory Girl" and "Hard Times in Here," which she had learned from older spinners in the mill. Friends and neighbors regularly gathered on the Dixon family's front porch for an evening of singing and music making, and one of Dorsey's earliest memories was of his excitement at hearing a banjo-playing millhand named Gaston Hales perform. "He used to come to our house," recalled Dorsey. "Mother and Daddy said I'd almost jump out of their arms when he was picking." By the age of five, Dorsey was singing sacred hymns and sentimental ballads during these sessions. "We'd have company," he recalled, "and it wouldn't be long there before they'd want me to sing a song. And so there must've been something or other about it that they enjoyed, or it might've been cute, a kid that small singing. They tell me," he continued, "that I wore a pair of shoes that was too small for a six-month old baby when I was two years old, and so you can imagine that I must've been mighty small at five years old." (Dixon never would be a physically imposing man. Among his fellow millhands, his slight, wiry stature later earned him the nicknames "Shorty" and "Pipsqueak," both of which remained with him for the rest of his life.)[8]

As he grew older, Dorsey's interest in music deepened, and in 1912, at the age of fourteen, he began taking violin lessons from a Darlington music teacher and orchestra director named Angus Gainey. "There was a visitor in our home one day and he had a fiddle," Dixon recounted. "And I listened at him play it, and I become interested. And he finally laid the fiddle on the bed, and I picked it up, and I played a tune. Well, my mother and father was amazed! There's a man in our town, his name was Mr. Angus Gainey, and he was a music professor and dealer. He was—well, I always thought he was a master of the violin, and, oh, I thought a lot of him. He had a business there in Darlington called the Old Barn. So Dad told me, says, 'Son,' said, 'you go uptown tell Mr. Gainey I said, "Fix you up a fiddle and charge it to me." Impressed by the boy's enthusiasm, Gainey gave Dixon violin lessons and taught him to read musical notation, free of charge, in exchange for Dixon's agreeing to perform in the violin orchestra at Sunday school. "And I played the violin with Mr. Gainey in Sunday school as long as I stayed in Darlington," Dixon recalled. "I never will forget that old man. I loved him."[9]

By the age of fifteen, Dixon had also taught himself to play the guitar, one of the instruments then becoming established, as a result of mass production and mail-order catalogs, in southern working-class culture. "I just banged, just frammed [strummed chords], you know, but I just thought I was 'it' when I learnt that. I was tickled to death. And I started from there. I just kept on banging." Soon he was entertaining neighbors in Darlington's mill village. One of his favorite songs was "Christmas Cake," a comical play-party number about a holiday cake so stale and tough that a hammer, hatchet, and saw were needed to slice it. The song required the singer to insert the names of three listeners, and Dixon used this whimsical piece to amuse neighborhood mill girls. "When I first started off playing the guitar, I'd get out in the summertime on the front porch, playing and singing. And I'd get some of the girls, find out what their names was, you know, and I'd sing that song on them. I've had more fun with that song than a little. Yeah, it'd tickle them girls to death! But some of them, it'd heck them, you know. And I just got a kick out it."[10]

Meanwhile, Dorsey taught his younger brothers, Howard and Tommy, to play the guitar. He explained:

> Well, Howard and my brother Tommy sang together, but they didn't play any instruments. I learnt both of them how to pick the guitar. One would pick a guitar, and they'd sing together. Howard could play a tune on most anything he picked up. In fact, when us boys played together I let Howard do the tuning, because I'm deaf in one ear and blind in one eye. And I always let him do the tuning of the guitars so they'd be right, because I couldn't hear good, and I was afraid I wouldn't tune them right. But my baby brother Tommy, I expect he'd have been better than any of us at music 'cause he could play most anything he could get his hands on. But he died at fifteen, and Howard and I was the only ones left of the family that taken to music. So Howard and I started singing together.[11]

When the Dixon family resided there during the 1910s, Darlington claimed a population of approximately 4,000 residents and contained numerous tobacco warehouses and manufacturing establishments, including tobacco stemmeries and leaf-processing plants, furniture factories, woodworking plants, cotton mills, and two soda-bottling plants. By 1915, the town's largest textile mill, the Darlington Manufacturing Company, where Dorsey and several of his siblings worked, employed more than 500 millhands, and the firm's mill village, which was located adjacent to the plant, was home to more than 1,500 residents. Within the village, boasted the *Darlington News and Press*, the recreational welfare of the workers and their families was served by a park, lighted playground, bandstand, baseball field, and community center, which contained a library, a "thoroughly-equipped gymnasium," and a theater for exhibiting "high-class moving pictures."[12]

Darlington's community life exposed Dorsey Dixon to a wide range of traditional and popular music, and his early repertoire, which consisted of parlor ballads, traditional folk songs, minstrel stage ditties, play-party songs, and sacred hymns, reflected the musical diversity found in small textile towns all across the Carolina Piedmont. Besides the songs his parents and siblings taught him, the teenaged

Dixon also learned "I Saw the Wood," "Burglar Man," and the occasionally vulgar "Three Nights Drunk" from friends and neighbors who sang on the Dixons' front porch or in the mill village. He picked up other songs from listening to a local stringband, composed of textile millhands. "That was about nineteen and nine, I believe, when I first begin to take notice of them boys playing and singing," he recalled. "And they sang them old songs such as 'Hungry Hash House,' 'The Last Mile of the Way,' 'The Wreck of the Old 97'—old-time folk songs, you know. And I used to love to hear them boys sing. They'd come around and play and sing, and I'd listen at them." Dixon also incorporated selections that he learned from commercial phonograph records into his expanding bag of songs. Around 1915, for instance, he heard an Edison cylinder recording of "coon singer" Arthur Collins's comical minstrel number, "The Preacher and the Bear," and, enchanted by it, he later taught himself the song. "I thought that was the prettiest thing I ever listened at," he recalled.[13]

In 1915, Dixon briefly left the mills to work as a signalman on the Columbia and Darlington Division of the Atlantic Coast Line Railroad in the Darlington switchyard. Barely in his teens, Howard also soon secured a signalman's job by concealing his legal age from the switchyard supervisor. During the slow hours of his railroad shift in the signal tower, Dorsey continued to practice and to refine his skills on the guitar. One of his favorite songs was "The Wreck of the Old 97," an account of a dreadful 1903 accident in which the Southern Railway's fast mail train, along with five railroad cars, plunged off a high wooden trestle on the outskirts of Danville, Virginia, killing nine on board, including the engineer and two firemen. This railroad disaster ballad was a new song, composed within weeks of the wreck by a pair of local millhands whose visit to the scene of the horrific accident had inspired them to memorialize the event in verse. In 1909, when Dixon first heard it performed by a Darlington mill stringband, the song was just beginning to circulate in the South Carolina Piedmont, carried there probably by railroad workers or migratory textile millhands. When interviewed in 1962, Dixon clearly recognized the irony of him, a railroad signalman, practicing this ballad while on the job, but as he explained, "I thought 'The Wreck of the Old 97' was mighty thrilling."[14]

Although he appreciated the ample time he had to practice his music during the slow hours of his shift, Dorsey disliked the seven-day-a-week schedule of a signalman. In 1920, he resumed work at the Darlington Manufacturing Company and soon began to learn the weaver's craft, one of the most skilled and highest-paying jobs in the textile industry. "I went in what they called the cloth room," Dorsey Dixon later recalled, "and I run the stitchers, stitching the cloth together, and the folding machine that folded the cloth up. Well, I didn't stay there long before I went into the weave room and taken a day job sweeping, you know, so I could learn how to weave. But, see, in learning to weave, I had a lot to learn. But I learned to weave, and then I wove for about twenty years."[15]

In 1922, at the age of twenty-four, Dorsey Dixon left home and set out to earn a living as a weaver. He moved first to Lancaster and then to Greenville, South Carolina, but by 1924 he had returned to Darlington, where most of his family still lived. He remembered:

> I stayed about five or six weeks in Darlington, I reckon, before me and the boss fell out. I was weaving in a cotton mill there, but I wanted more looms so I could make more money. And my boss got me mad. He wouldn't give me any more looms, you know. So I quit and come up here to Rockingham, North Carolina, in 1924, and I got a job weaving at Entwistle. And I worked there awhile and then I quit, and I got a job weaving over at what they called Roberdel No. 2 then. And I made a good weaver on them types of looms, and my boss didn't want me to leave. But just like a single man will, you know, I rambled hither and yonder. And I left Rockingham and went back to Greenville, South Carolina, and went to work as a weaver for Woodside Mill. Worked there a while, and then I come back to Rockingham and couldn't get a job. So I headed for Durham, North Carolina, and I got on a job up there helping to build a colored schoolhouse. And when we got that completed, they laid me off. And I come back to Rockingham and got a job in the weave room at the Hannah Pickett Mill.[16]

In 1925, Dixon settled in Rockingham, North Carolina, the county seat of Richmond County and a bustling town of more than 2,500 residents. His new place of employment, Hannah Pickett Mill No. 1, was one of eleven textile mills in the area. "I got plenty of weaving work when I come up here to Rockingham, and I guess that's one reason that's caused me to stay," he later explained. "But I also learned a little about these folks in Rockingham. And it just finally become home to me." Later that summer, he convinced Howard, who had married Mellie Barfield in 1920 and started a family, to join him in Rockingham. Dixon remembered:

> I was working as a weaver at the Big Hannah Pickett, but they needed a folding hand in the cloth department, and they were borrowing me from my looms. I'd have to go down there and run the folder and let a spare hand take my looms. Well, a spare hand won't take care of a job like the man that owns the job does. And so I was getting tired of that, and Howard come up here hunting a job, and I told him I had two jobs, and I'd be glad to give him one of them. But I told him I'd have to learn him how to run the folder. I says, "It's a dangerous machine, and it'll fold you up just like it do the cloth." So I taken Howard in there, and in a couple of days I had him running the folder as good as I could. I let him work on, and I got a big transfer truck and went to Darlington and got his wife and two small children and house things and brought them up here to Rockingham. And then, later that year, I moved my Daddy and Mother and my sister Nancy up here, and we all got in a four-room house out there in the mill village. Big house, big rooms. We got along fine, and my family all stayed here in Rockingham as long as they lived.[17]

Upon Howard's arrival in Rockingham, the two brothers formed a violin-and-guitar combination to entertain at house parties and other social gatherings in the Hannah Pickett mill village. "Howard and I begain teaming together," Dorsey later wrote, "and played in homes in the neighbor hood. because we injoyed trying to make people happy and forget their cares and troubles for an hour or so." Occasionally, the duo also furnished the musical accompaniment for silent films at a local theater. "The manager'd give us three dollars a piece to play music while the people was looking at the pictures," Dixon explained. "And it just seemed like our music was inspired to them. We'd see a lot of them close around us wiping their eyes with handkerchiefs, you know. They were showing *Ten Nights in a Bar Room*, I believe, the night we made them bawl and cry so. We just happened to select the right kind of melody that fitted that picture." Besides the music that filled his evenings and days off, Dorsey Dixon also started courting Beatrice Lucele Moody, a textile worker fourteen years his junior from Greenville, South Carolina. On Valentine's Day, 1927, he married the

227

fifteen-year-old Beatrice, and together they would raise four sons. But supporting his growing family on a weaver's meager wages became more and more of a struggle for Dixon.[18]

Dixon always believed his parents' claim that God had chosen him to fulfill a great purpose, but it was not until the age of thirty-one that he discovered that this mission might be accomplished through songwriting. In 1929, he composed his first song, "Cleveland School House Fire," an elegy memorializing seventy-seven people who had died at an end-of-the-semester celebration in a rural schoolhouse fire near Camden, South Carolina, six years earlier. Twenty-nine adults and forty-eight children, including eleven victims named Dixon, had perished in the inferno, which drew front-page newspaper headlines across the nation. Though none of the Dixons were related to him, the horrifying accounts he had read in the Greenville newspapers in 1923 had haunted him ever since. "Well, they said that the little children could be heard screaming in them roaring flames, 'Daddy, come and get your baby,'" Dixon recalled in 1961. "I could hear those little children screaming, and that was ringing in my mind—all the time. And so it worried me and wore on my mind for years until I wrote that song in their memory. And after I wrote that song, why, I got relief. I didn't think about it anymore."[19]

Because of the warm reception his first song received from local audiences, Dixon's passion for songwriting intensified. He regularly began publishing his songs and poems about personal experiences and national events in the local weekly newspaper, the *Rockingham Post-Dispatch*. When the 1932 Lindbergh baby kidnapping dominated national headlines and news broadcasts, for example, Dixon quickly composed a poem about the incident ("The Lindbergh Baby"). Writing in between his shifts at the mill, Dixon produced a remarkable collection of topical pieces that addressed such issues as National Prohibition ("Prohibition or What Have You?"), the 1932 U.S. presidential election ("The Democratic Call to Arms"), natural disasters, ("The Alabama Storm"), high-profile crimes ("An Officer on Duty"), and front-page news stories ("The Shooting of Otto Wood").[20] But what Dixon did best was to craft verses commemorating the victims of local tragedies. When, in the summer of 1932, two East Rockingham girls drowned in the Pee Dee millpond, Dixon promptly penned "Two Little Rosebuds" in their memory. The following year, when a local youth was crushed to death under the wheels of a freight train,

Dorsey M. Dixon and his son, Dorsey Jr., ca. 1934.
Courtesy of the Southern Folklife Collection, Wilson Library,
University of North Carolina at Chapel Hill.

Dixon responded with "Phifer's Last Ride." He prefaced this particular piece with a brief explanation: "I have been told that young Phifer was a good Christian boy and when a good man or woman goes down in life I like to write and tell the world about it in a poem."[21]

The tributes Dixon published in his local newspaper (some three dozen songs and poems between 1932 and 1938) brought him wide recognition as a gifted poet and songwriter in East Rockingham's mill communities. Soon friends and neighbors began asking him to compose memorials to their deceased loved ones, and, in his efforts to comfort the grieving, Dixon obliged them whenever he could. In 1936, for example, when Beatrice Rowland, an Entwistle spinner whom he had known since she was a girl, died suddenly, Dixon composed an elegy, at the request of her friends, that was published in the *Rockingham Post-Dispatch*. "It will be impossible for me to express my regret and sympathy," he remarked in a note preceding his composition. "So I am going to remember Mrs. Rowland in a poem that the many, many friends that she leaves behind may have for a keepsake in memory of her." His 1932 composition "When Little Brother Fell," to cite another example, appeared in the Rockingham newspaper with this note: "A little friend of mine at Pee Dee lost a little five-year old brother three years ago, and requested me to write this one entitled 'When Little Brother Fell.' I am sure you all know of the fate of the little Snead boy that fell out of the boat and was drowned in Pee Dee Mill pond; his brother, Sammie, told me that this is the way it happened."[22]

Dixon's memorials were more than merely descriptive narratives chronicling the unfortunate passing of East Rockingham residents, however. He used their deaths as religious exempla about divine judgment and redemption. In fact, Dixon came to believe that his songs were divinely inspired and channeled the word of God. In "Phifer's Last Ride," for example, Dixon reminds sinners in no uncertain terms of their Christian obligations: "So let us live for Jesus / And work with all our might, / And at the end we'll smile with Jim / In the Glory Land so bright. / Memorize this little poem, / For it may guide you straight; / Don't wait untill your footholt slips / On the last ride you will take." Or, in "Charles and Dannie," an elegy commemorating two young drowning victims, Dixon concludes: "Let us all take warning / While we yet have time left, / For we all know surely / The pay for sin is death. / I'm satisfied, dear brother, / You want that great reward, / The gift of God, Eternal Life, / Through Jesus Christ, Our Lord." Dixon genuinely feared for the souls of his fellow Christians and pleaded with sinners to repent and open themselves to God's saving grace. When pleas proved ineffectual, he sometimes resorted to more ominous warnings. In a 1932 poem written in memory of a twenty-three-year-old millhand who died of heart failure, Dixon cautions: "Happy times you think you have / While on this earth you dwell, / But, Oh, how sad when life is through / To face a flaming hell."[23]

Dixon's songwriting grew directly out of his church's theology. During the 1930s, Dorsey studied the Bible and joined the Free Will Baptist Church, a branch of the Baptist tradition that flourished in Carolina mill villages. Dixon's wing of the Free Will Baptists embraced the doctrines of "holiness," the belief that God frees the most dedicated believers from the capacity for sin, and Pentecostalism, the belief that true holiness enables believers to "speak in tongues" like the early Christians described in the book of Acts 2:1–4. The Pentecostal Holiness movement, which had its origins in a small Topeka, Kansas, Bible college around 1901, was a modern religious phenomenon, and during the first decades of the twentieth century it spread rapidly among poor black and white southerners who sought in their churches a refuge from the materialism and spiritual complacency they saw in mainstream Protestant churches. Holiness Christians shunned the worldly amusements of drinking, dancing, card playing, and gambling, in favor of a religion rooted in Bible study, fervent prayer, evangelism, and personal conversion. Commonly dismissed as "Holy Rollers," Pentecostal denominations featured ecstatic, emotional church services marked by exuberant testifying, shouting, and singing. Despite the ridicule and scorn that more staid, middle-class Protestants heaped upon them, Pentecostal Holiness churches nurtured a strong sense of religious community, badly needed among dispossessed millhands, that anchored them in a troubling and uncertain world.[24]

The Scripture-based morality of the fundamentalist Christianity to which Dixon adhered viewed the world as a battleground between God and Satan and explained that world in stark oppositions. Thus, Dixon's religious faith and moral certainty inspired his responses to his modernizing society and the senseless tragedies that often befell its inhabitants. It also intensified his sense of mission to spread the gospel and convert sinners in preparation for eternal salvation. Free Will Baptists rejected the Calvinist doctrine of predestination and instead emphasized that God offers salvation to everyone who asks for it. And this particular theological belief informed Dixon's songs of death and destruction, in which he entreated sinners to use such tragedies as occasions to repent and seek salvation. Collectively, the stories of human suffering he read about in newspapers and heard about from radio broadcasts and from friends and neighbors deeply impressed him, and he drew upon them time and again when writing songs. Dixon wholeheartedly believed the biblical injunction that, as he put it, "a man's life is a few short days and full of trouble, disappointment, and sorrow. And pains that we got to suffer." Even though he accepted tragedy and suffering as the marrow of daily life, his sensitivity to the anguish of others never diminished. Dixon endeavored to comfort the afflicted and the bereaved through song, and he saw his songwriting as a gift from God, intended, as he often said, to "bless the people." Much of his music's appeal lay in the hopeful alternatives he presented to the ongoing struggles of impoverished working-class life. Their suffering in the present world, Dixon consoled beleaguered listeners, would be richly rewarded in the next. "Our trials on earth are treasures in heaven; / There's wonderful things Jesus has for His own," he wrote in "Planway of Salvation." "If we'll overcome our trials and temptations, / There won't be any more in that heavenly home."[25]

If Dixon's songs of death and tragedy reflected the theological teachings of his own sect of fundamentalist Christianity, on a more popular level they constituted part of a larger subgenre within commercial hillbilly music called "event songs." Modern incarnations of a broadside ballad tradition that dated to Elizabethan England, these topical songs consisted of stark, simple ballads that chronicled and commented on recent tragedies—such as train wrecks, tornados, earthquakes, murders, and other newsworthy events—and usually concluded with a moral tagline intended to impart an important lesson for the social or spiritual benefit of listeners. In 1925, while the hillbilly recording industry was still in its infancy, a nationwide vogue for these event songs led to a boom in phonograph record sales. That year, Vernon Dalhart's Victor recording of "Wreck of the Old 97," coupled with "The Prisoner's Song," became the first national hit of this fledgling industry. Recognizing the windfall profits to be reaped, record companies rushed out more than 150 event song recordings, often within weeks of the tragedy being commemorated, between

1925 and 1927. "Such songs as 'Little Rosewood Casket,' 'The John T. Scopes Trial (The Old Religion's Better After All)' and 'The Death of Floyd Collins' may not make a strong appeal to jazz hounds on Broadway," noted a 1925 *Talking Machine World* article, "but the sales indicate that they are distinctly popular in the so-called 'sticks.'"[26]

Professional hillbilly songwriters such as Carson J. Robison and Bob Miller, often working from newspaper accounts, specialized in dashing off these formulaic ballads so that they could be quickly recorded and released while the headline-making occurrence remained fresh in the American public's consciousness. In some cases, as many as two dozen different record labels issued discs memorializing the same event. Dalhart himself recorded scores of these ballads—often cutting the same song for six or more different record companies— about highly publicized national disasters, tragedies, and current news events, including "The Death of Floyd Collins" (1925), "The John T. Scopes Trial" (1925), "The Santa Barbara Earthquake" (1925), "There's a New Star in Heaven Tonight—Rudolph Valentino" (1926), and "Lindbergh (The Eagle of the U.S.A.)" (1927). As Hugh Leamy, writing in *Collier's*, in 1929, remarked, "Earthquakes, shipwrecks and railroad collisions are useful in other ways than as material for newspaper headlines. Almost before the echoes die away tearful ballads are dashed off, and in short order phonograph records of the catastrophe are on sale. Millions of people find diversion and edification in these rhymed and bemoraled chronicles of doom." In them, Dixon also found models for his own songs of tragedy. Indeed, Dalhart's 1925 recording of "The Sinking of the Titanic," which Dixon heard shortly after moving to East Rockingham, inspired his own 1938 composition about the maritime disaster, "Down with the Old Canoe." But by 1929, when Dixon composed his first tragic number, the national craze for event songs was waning, although such numbers continued to be commercially recorded and remained popular in many localities throughout the Midwest and South during the Great Depression. Unlike professional songwriters such as Robison and Miller, however, Dixon composed such songs chiefly for spiritual reasons rather than financial rewards.[27]

Despite the handicap of only a fourth-grade education, the prolific Dixon composed or arranged more than 130 sacred and secular songs, several of which other country artists later recorded and, in the case of "Wreck on the Highway," turned into national hits. But he was a composer primarily for whom, as hillbilly music scholar Norm Cohen notes, "songwriting was not a commercial venture but an act of personal catharsis. . . . An event that he read about, whether it involved dear ones or strangers, captured his attention and gave him no rest until he was driven to seek release by framing the incident in poetry." Dixon's lifelong struggle with depression and the nagging anxieties that weighed upon his mind indicate that he was an extremely sensitive man who agonized about his own soul and the souls of others and who struggled with doubts about his ability to achieve the "great purpose" that he believed God had intended for him. But he persisted in writing songs based on inspirations that, he was certain, came directly from God. "There was a something that compelled me to set down and write and composed," Dixon wrote in a 1948 memoir. "I realy had no controle over my self. when I was grip[p]ed with an inspirition to write. My first sacred song I composed was 'I'M NOT TURNING BACKWARD' After watching the afect that this had on the people in many different churches that Howard and I went to on special accassions I begain to realize that the song was indeed a great message that God had sent out to His people."[28]

Several of Dixon's most popular compositions of the 1930s criticized what he saw as one of the most profoundly disturbing trends of modern southern life—the erosion of bedrock Christian morals. Alarmed by society's increasing secularism and materialism, he attempted to inspire spiritual renewal and a return to Jesus by composing songs that asserted the ultimate authority of the Bible as God's true word. His sacred songs, such as "Have Courage to Only Say No" and "Where Shall I Be," admonished listeners to live a righteous Christian life and often foretold of the everlasting punishment they would suffer for abandoning religion in favor of worldly pleasures. "Oh, sinners, hear my mournful cry, / Please change your ways before you die," he sings on his 1938 Bluebird recording of "Where Shall I Be." "For after death, it'll be too late / When you're passing by that pearly gate." For him and, he hoped, his audience, fundamentalist Christianity offered a much-needed bulwark against the secularizing forces unleashed by modernity.

At the same time, modern technological innovations, especially automobiles, airplanes, and trains, figured prominently as symbols in Dixon's songs. Dixon may have associated the breakdown of traditional, Bible-based religiosity with the modernizing forces of industrial development and urban growth, but he himself never considered modern conveniences as sinful—in fact, for years he longed to be able to afford his own car.[29] Sin, he believed, arose when people replaced their traditional Christian faith with faith in the mechanical and material trappings of life, using modern machines as vehicles, literally, to stray from God's chosen path. A good Christian could own a car without risk to his soul, Dixon might say, if he used that car to drive to church and to work but not to roadhouses, dance halls, brothels, or other dens of iniquity. Likewise, a devout soul could freely enjoy the latest fashions, movies, or music, if one remained humble and devoted to Christian beliefs. It was the arrogance and impiety that so often attended a materialistic lifestyle that Dixon saw as an affront to God, and he preached through his songs that the pursuit of, and pride in, worldly things could lead only to sorrow and destruction.

Nowhere did Dixon make this point more clearly than in his famous reinterpretation of the 1912 sinking of the luxury liner *Titanic*. This internationally publicized catastrophe, often called "the first major news story of the twentieth century," inspired at least three dozen popular songs from professional songwriters on both sides of the Atlantic, as well as an equal, if not greater, number of traditional American ballads from both black and white folk composers, including Dorsey Dixon. Calling his composition "Down with the Old Canoe," a satiric title that lampoons what cultural historian Steven Biel calls the "technological hubris" of the modern age, Dixon connected what was then the greatest symbol of modern Machine Age technology, the *Titanic*, with the folly of human pride and godlessness. He was particularly appalled by magazine and newspaper accounts he read that claimed "not even God himself could sink the Titanic," and even a quarter-century after this maritime disaster, he still believed that the shipwreck contained an important moral lesson for his Depression-era audience. Dixon explained:

And they wrote a song called "The Titanic," and I heard that old song in nineteen and twenty-five, I believe it was, when I first come to Rockingham. And I got to thinking about that old song, and I wrote me one around 1936, and I called mine "Down with the Old Canoe." In other words, I was making a sacred number out of it. You see, the *Titanic* was a type of Ark. Noah and the Ark, you see. And when she hit that iceberg, slivers of ice flew all over the deck, and—I read the history of it—they said that people made fun, says "Go up there and get us some sherbet to put in our cocktails." Made fun of it, you know, just like they did in the days of Noah, when Noah was building the Ark. And I wanted to make a religious number out of it. And that's the reason I wrote it.[30]

On January 25, 1938, the Dixon Brothers recorded the song in Charlotte, North Carolina, for RCA-Victor's Bluebird label, and two months later Dorsey published its lyrics in the *Rockingham Post-Dispatch*.[31] "Down with the Old Canoe," as it appears on the Dixon Brothers' Bluebird record, goes as follows:

It was twenty-five years ago,
When the wings of death came low
And spread out on the ocean far and wide.
A great ship sailed away
With her passengers so gay,
To never, never reach the other side.

Chorus:
Sailing out to win her fame,
The *Titanic* was her name;
When she had sailed five hundred miles from shore,
Many passengers and her crew
Went down with that old canoe:
They all went down to never ride no more.

This great ship was built by man,
That is why she could not stand;
"She could not sink" was the cry from one and all.
But an iceberg ripped her side
And it cut down all her pride;
They found the Hand of God was in it all.

Chorus

Your *Titanic* sails today,
On life's sea you're far away,
But Jesus Christ can take you safely through.
Just obey His great command,
Over there you'll safely land;
You'll never go down with that old canoe.

Chorus

When you think that you are wise,
Then you need not be surprised
If the Hand of God should stop you on life's sea.
If you go on in your sin,
You will find out in the end
That you are just as foolish as can be.

Chorus

Like the folk composers of many other *Titanic* songs, Dixon recasts the disaster as a religious parable for his listeners, exhorting them to turn to Christ in order to avoid going down with their own "canoe" into everlasting perdition. In the end, according to Dixon, neither wealth nor social station but rather faith in Jesus Christ alone ensures that one will be called to share in God's promise of eternal salvation.

Dixon addressed similar themes in what is his best-known and arguably his greatest composition, "Wreck on the Highway," or, as he originally titled it, "I Didn't Hear Nobody Pray," which is based upon a deadly automobile accident that occurred on the outskirts of East Rockingham, probably in late 1937. Dixon was tending his looms at Entwistle Mill one gray, drizzly winter morning when he heard the news of a fatal collision on nearby U.S. Highway 1. At the end of his shift, Dixon and a co-worker went to view the crumpled Ford sedan in which two local residents had been instantly killed. "So we put out around there where they'd pulled the old wreck in," Dixon later recalled. "And that car was completely demolished; it was tore up. And I was looking in on the floorboard, and I seen bottles—broken bottles—and blood all mixed up there. 'Course, they probably was Co'-Cola bottles. But it was glass, you know, all broken to pieces and mixed up with blood there on the floorboard of that old wrecked car. And the thought came across my mind that many times cars had wrecked and killed people and that whiskey was mixed up with the broken glass and blood. And that's how I was inspired to write 'Wreck on the Highway.'"[32]

A couple of months later, on January 25, 1938, the Dixon Brothers recorded the new song, titled on the record label as "I Didn't Hear Anybody Pray," at an RCA-Victor field session in Charlotte. Then, on March 10, Dorsey published this tragic song in the *Rockingham Post-*

Dispatch, along with a headnote announcing that Bluebird records of this particular selection were available for purchase at local dime stores.[33] The lyrics to the Dixon Brothers' recording of the song follow:

Who did you say it was, brother?
Who was that fell by the way?
When whiskey and blood run together,
Did you hear anyone pray?

Their names I'm not able to tell you,
But here is one thing I can say:
There was whiskey and blood mixed together,
But I didn't hear nobody pray.

Chorus:
I didn't hear nobody pray, dear brother,
I didn't hear nobody pray;
I heard the crash on the highway,
But I didn't hear nobody pray.

Yes, I heard the crash on the highway,
I knew what it was from the start;
I went to the scene of destruction,
This picture was stamped on my heart.

Whiskey and glass altogether
Was mixing with blood where they lay;
Death played her hand in destruction,
But I didn't hear nobody pray.

Chorus

I wish I could change this sad story
That I am now telling to you;
But there is no way I can change it,
For somebody's life is now through.

A soul has been called by the Master,
They died in a crash on their way;
I heard the groans of the dying,
But I didn't hear nobody pray.

Chorus

Please give up the game and stop drinking,
For Jesus is pleading with you;
It cost him a lot in redeeming,
Redeeming the promise for you.

But it'll be too late if tomorrow
In a crash you should fall by the way,
With whiskey and blood all around you,
And you can't hear nobody pray!

Chorus

Dixon's composition is more than just another hillbilly song about a fatal drunk-driving accident. As music historian Billy Altman has noted, "What is even more horrifying [to Dixon] than the violence itself is the reaction of those who run out from their homes to witness the tragedy—namely, their failure to lift even a single voice in prayer for the souls of the dead and the dying." Not only is the drunken driver to blame, but, according to Dixon, equally morally culpable are the curious onlookers who only gawk at the twisted wreckage and bloody bodies instead of beseeching God to receive these souls into his hands. Thus, in the song, Dixon transformed a grisly accident scene on a small southern highway into a compelling indictment of what he saw as an increasingly secular and godless society.[34]

Yet Dixon also recognized the song's relevance and the powerful effect it had on listeners:

Now, a lot of people in and around Rockingham thought that I wrote that song on other wrecks, but I finally got them convinced that the song was universal. It was wrote on every wreck that ever had been and every wreck that ever will be. And I believe it's been a good warning to people, too. I've had boys that tell me they were speeding in their cars, and "Wreck on the Highway" would come on the radio, and said that they would automatically slow the car down. Said there was something about that song that scared them and made them have a feeling they better slow down. And so if it helped that-a-way, it helped some. I believe the song has blessed a lot of people, and I do hope that it's done a lot of good.[35]

By pointing out the disastrous outcome of drunk driving, "Wreck on the Highway" also serves as a cautionary tale that instructs listeners to modify their behavior in order to protect themselves from both bodily and spiritual destruction.

During the 1930s, besides his considerable collection of sacred and tragic songs, Dixon also composed songs about the hardships and frustrations of textile work. But unlike Dave McCarn's trio of satirical "Cotton Mill Colic" songs, Dixon's numbers were less "colicky" and more plaintive. In 1932, while operating sixteen blue chambray looms at Hannah Pickett Mill No. 2, Dixon composed one of his most famous selections, "Weave Room Blues," which was the first song he and his brother cut at their debut recording session in February 1936. In the song, Dixon recounts both his difficulties operating his looms and his struggles raising a family on his weaver's wages. The song's original lyrics, as published in the February 25, 1932, edition of the *Rockingham Post-Dispatch*, are as follows:

Working in a weave room, fighting for my life,
Trying to make a living for my kiddies and my wife,
Some are needing clothing and some are needing shoes,
But I'm getting nothing but the "weave room blues."

Chorus:
I've got the blues so bad till I wish I had
An aeroplane that would fly,
I'd give her the gun and away we'd run,
We'd fly up to the sky,
We would fly so awful high
Till the control I would lose
But when I came back to the ground
I wouldn't have them "weave room blues."

With your looms a-slamming, shuttles bouncing on the floor;
And when you flag your fixer, you can see that he is sore,
I try to make a living but I'm thinking I will lose,
For I am going crazy with them "weave room blues."

Harness eyes a-breaking with the doubles coming through,
The devil's in your alley and he's coming after you;
Our hearts are aching, let us take a little booze,
For we are going crazy with them "weave room blues."

Slam-outs, break-outs, matups by the score,
Cloth all rolled back and piled upon the floor;
Batteries running empty, strings a-hanging to your shoes,
I am simply dying with the "weave room blues."

If you would like to meet me, come to Hannah-Pickett two
Be sure and make it snappy, for I'm feeling mighty blue;
Just a little letter, a word or two will soothe,
Hurry ere I pass out with them "weave room blues."[36]

The original chorus printed above may surprise readers familiar
with "Weave Room Blues," because it is not the same one sung on the
Dixon Brothers' 1938 Bluebird recording of the song. Dixon's surreal-
istic chorus about an airplane ride contrasts dramatically with the
realistic portrayal of textile work found in the song's stanzas, and, by
the time he and Howard recorded the song six years later, Dorsey had
revised this section of the song into a more traditional blues chorus.
On the Dixon Brothers' 1938 Bluebird record, the chorus goes: "I've
got the blues, I've got the blues, / I've got them awful weave room
blues. / I've got the blues, the weave room blues." The reasons for this
change remain unknown. Musically, the altered chorus represents
an improvement, but the new lyrics are far less interesting. There is
simply no escaping the "weave room blues" in the revised version
of the song. In the original version, however, Dixon incorporates an
escape fantasy that takes the form of an airplane flight—perhaps the
only possible method of escape from his workplace aggravations.

The final lines of the chorus can be read at least two different
ways. In one interpretation, the chorus implies that a temporary escape from the mill, in this case in the form of a thrilling airplane
ride, would provide a much-needed respite from the nerve-wracking
job and thus cure his "weave room blues." Another reading, one that
is far bleaker and somewhat more political, proposes that Dixon's
fantasy airplane flight ends in a crash ("We would fly so awful high /
Till the control I would lose, / But when I came back to the ground /
I wouldn't have them 'weave room blues'"). This interpretation suggests that the only escape from his "weave room blues" is death, perhaps by suicide. Regardless of how he actually intended his cryptic
chorus to be read—and the former interpretation conforms more
closely to his overall songwriting style and worldview—Dixon recognized that his song's potentially subversive political meanings

might have drastic implications for his tenure at Hannah Pickett Mill No. 2.

When Dixon first published these lyrics to "Weave Room Blues" in the local newspaper, he prefaced them with the following conciliatory headnote: "This writer wants it understood he is working steady at H.P. No. 2 and that this in no way applies to conditions at that mill; on the contrary, the mill is running full time and smoothly—and there is no 'weave room blues' there." Clearly, Dixon's own experiences had provided the inspiration for "Weave Room Blues," but he also denied that the occupational miseries enumerated in the song in any way reflected conditions at his current place of employment. Although not overtly critical of the economic exploitation of mill workers, Dixon's lament does reveal how difficult and frustrating a weaver's day-to-day work could be. Dixon claimed that he did not intend to offend his employer with his song, but he nonetheless feared losing his job after its publication. He recalled that William B. Cole, the president and owner of the Hannah Pickett Manufacturing Company, had asked Dixon's foreman which of his employees had written "Weave Room Blues," and later Mr. Cole paid a visit to Dixon in the weave room. "So later on," Dixon remembered, "Bill Cole come by my work, you know, looking at me a while. And I stepped out there and introduced myself. He said, 'Yes,' says, 'I know all about it [the song].' I says, 'How'd you like that?' He says, 'I just think that's great!' Says, 'I think that's the greatest piece of work I ever read.' Said, 'So you a poet?' I said, 'Well, I wrote that one,' and laughed. He said, 'We're just glad to have you, Dorsey.' Said, 'We just proud to have a poet like you working for us.' And I thought he was gonna fire me, see," Dixon laughed. "I thought he was gonna fire me."[37]

Dixon's composition of "Weave Room Blues" in 1932 coincided with dramatic labor struggles in East Rockingham's textile mills, suggesting that, contrary to his claims in his apologetic headnote to the song, shop-floor conditions at Hannah Pickett Mill No. 2 were just as miserable as Dixon had described them in "Weave Room Blues." That August, a series of wage cuts, combined with the institution of mandatory periods of unpaid labor and the firing of six men suspected of union organizing, sparked a fifty-eight-day strike in Rockingham, involving the city's three major textile mills and more than 1,200 workers. Although William B. Cole might have appreciated the poetry of employees like Dorsey Dixon, he would not countenance a union challenge to his authority, and he closed his company's two mills for "an indefinite period." "We will be glad to consider starting the plant up again, under the same schedule of wages and conditions that were in force when we closed down," Cole promised in a message posted on his Mill No. 1's gates, "when enough of our loyal operatives advise us either singly or by petition, that they are not in sympathy with this bunch of agitators who are trying to bring about strife and trouble in our plant, and who will promise their loyalty to this Company in the future." Cole and the president of the other textile plant, Entwistle Mill, refused to recognize the strike or to meet with strike leaders. Within the week, Governor O. Max Gardner, himself the owner of a Cleveland County textile mill, dispatched a squad of motorcycle highway patrolmen to the strike zone to maintain peace on the picket lines and to protect mill property. The governor eventually visited Rockingham in an effort to negotiate an end to the strike, and, through his intervention, the bitter dispute ended on October 19, with a favorable settlement for the strikers, who won the restoration of their wages, reinstatement of the fired workers, and recognition of their independent union, the Richmond County Association of Textile Workers.[38]

Both Dorsey and Howard Dixon participated in the strike at Hannah Pickett Mill No. 2 and, according to Dorsey, even entertained at a few of the strike rallies. One of the songs the duo frequently performed was "Weave Room Blues." As a result, Dixon's new song soon achieved great local popularity, and, according to folklorist Douglas DeNatale, Rockingham strikers sang it "with relish." It remains unclear, however, whether or not Dorsey Dixon ever joined the Richmond County Association of Textile Workers, but he was at one time or another a member, though certainly not a diehard one, of at least three other labor unions, including the Textile Workers Union of America. As a peaceable, God-fearing man, he remained wary of grassroots labor insurgency and conflict, as evidenced by his published disclaimer prefacing "Weave Room Blues."[39] Dixon's "Weaver's Life," which dates to about 1930, is also indicative of his labor politics. In this, the first textile mill song he ever wrote, Dixon locates the work-weary weaver's salvation from grinding factory toil not in union organizing or working-class collective action but literally in heavenly salvation: "Soon we'll end this life of weaving, / Soon we'll reach a better shore," Dixon and his brother sing in the chorus, "Where we'll rest from filling batt'ries, / We won't have to weave no more." Nor do any of Dixon's other occupational songs offer constructive solutions to the industrial hardships that Piedmont millhands faced. As William Dixon points out, his father "wasn't a troublemaker or a rabble-rouser. His songs about the hardships of mill life weren't intended as a slap at the mill owners, but simply as expressions of sympathy for people who were in the same shape he was, working hard, trying to scrape together a living and raise a family in the face of all the problems that poor people have—layoffs, illness, plant shutdowns."[40]

Dorsey Dixon's work in East Rockingham textile mills not only inspired the ideas for several of his occupational songs, but the town's mill communities also introduced him to a group of similarly musical millhands with whom he and his brother often performed locally. Like other textile towns across the Carolina Piedmont, East Rockingham brought together a large cohort of millhands who had their own song repertoires, musical abilities, and cultural backgrounds, and, as a result, the Hannah Pickett mill villages, home to some 800 workers and their families, served as an active center of musical exchange among amateur working-class musicians. During the 1930s, Dorsey and Howard Dixon often played informally with fellow millhands such as guitarists Mutt Evans and Frank Gerald and others who participated in the vibrant musical culture that flourished among East Rockingham's textile workers.[41]

One particularly important friendship that Dorsey struck up around this time was with Jimmie Tarlton, an extraordinary blues singer and steel guitarist who became the Dixon Brothers' most important musical influence. In many ways, Tarlton's childhood resembled Dorsey Dixon's own. Born in 1892 near Cheraw, South Carolina (some thirty miles from Dixon's birthplace), Johnnie James Rimbert Tarlton grew up in a transient white family that alternated between sharecropping and industrial work as they drifted back and forth across the Carolinas and Georgia. After learning to play the banjo, harmonica, and accordion, Tarlton took up the guitar at the age of ten, and within two years he was playing in the bottleneck style of local African American bluesmen. In 1909, at the age of seventeen, he left home to earn a living with his guitar. His wanderings took him to Hoboken, New Jersey, and New York City, where he played in cafés and busked on the Bowery, to Arkansas, Oklahoma, and Texas, where he worked in oilfields and textile mills and played in medicine shows and honky-tonks, into Mexico, and then up to California. Along the way, Tarlton absorbed a wide range of songs and musical influences. In 1922, he met the famous Hawaiian guitar virtuoso and recording artist Frank Ferera in a Los Angeles hotel. Ferera, a Hawaiian of Portuguese descent, had, through his extensive vaudeville tours and prolific phonograph recordings, helped fuel the Hawaiian music craze of the 1910s and early 1920s in the continental United States. During this chance encounter, Ferera introduced Tarlton to several new Hawaiian guitar techniques, particularly the use of a steel bar for a slide instead of the knife Tarlton had been using. Thus, the steel guitar style that Tarlton eventually mastered reflected strong influences of both Hawaiian guitarists and Piedmont bluesmen.[42]

More so perhaps than any other recording artist, Tarlton popularized the steel guitar in hillbilly music during the late 1920s. In 1927, after returning to the Piedmont, he formed a duo with Tom Darby, a guitarist and singer of Scots-Irish, German, and Cherokee descent originally from Columbus, Georgia, and they recorded almost eighty sides, either together or solo, for Columbia, Victor, and the American Record Corporation, between 1927 and 1933. "This singing and playing team," remarked Columbia Records' 1929 *Old Familiar Tunes* catalog, "travel all over the South, ready to entertain wherever they may be. A yodeling voice and Hawaiian guitar are Jimmie Tarlton's priceless possessions. Tom Darby is known for his straight singing and guitar playing." The duo's loose, improvisational sound, which featured Darby's beautiful lead singing and blues-inflected guitar and Tarlton's slashing slide guitar work and soulful harmonies, falsettos, and yodels, was deeply informed by African American Piedmont blues. Their repertoire consisted of an eclectic mix of traditional ballads, vaudeville numbers, parlor songs, Tin Pan Alley hits, and gutbucket blues. Their biggest hit, "Birmingham Jail"/"Columbus Stockade Blues," recorded in November 1927 in Atlanta, sold approximately 200,000 copies and became one of the best-selling records in Columbia's hillbilly catalog. However, Darby and Tarlton reaped little financial reward from this enormously popular record, because, unfortunately, they had opted to accept the seventy-five-dollar flat fee for making the two recordings rather than a percentage of the royalties on the record's sales.[43]

Between 1930 and 1932, Tarlton occasionally worked at East Rockingham's Hannah Pickett Mill No. 2, the same plant that em-

Publicity photograph of Tom Darby, right, and Jimmie Tarlton, left, from a
Columbia Records monthly supplement, 1930. Courtesy of the Southern Folklife
Collection, Wilson Library, University of North Carolina at Chapel Hill.

ployed the Dixon brothers. Dorsey remembered him as a hard-drinking rounder. "Jimmie never was too much for work," he recalled. "He stayed around here in East Rockingham a long time, but he didn't work much no where. He rambled mostly. He caught freight trains and hoboed a whole lot. I think he was pretty rough, bad to drink, and so on, but he had the most wonderful singing voice, and he could put a feeling behind it, you know. They tell me just a short while before I come to the Entwistle Mill in 1924 that Jimmie would get his old guitar out in the evening, and he'd sing 'Careless Love.' They said he'd just make all them girls bawl and squall singing that song."[44]

In 1931, Dixon and his brother Howard heard Tarlton entertaining in an East Rockingham home, and, as Dorsey recalled, "we were both carried away with his style of playing." Until then, Dorsey had played guitar by simply "framming," or strumming chords, but he was impressed with how Tarlton plucked the individual strings of his steel guitar with finger picks. And Tarlton inspired Dorsey to develop his own distinctive guitar-picking style, using picks on all four fingers and thumb of his right hand. "I could hear an inspiration of a guitar playing, and I knew it could be done," Dixon explained, "So I got me some picks, and I knew the best way to do it was to get by myself. And I set my clock alarm for three o'clock in the morning, and I'd get up when everybody was sleeping and go in a room and close the door and concentrate on this type of picking. Sit up in a room and study my music. And I'd work on my music till seven when I had to go to mill. So I concentrated on it and went to developing it."[45]

After weeks of practice, Dixon fashioned a new, intricate finger-picking guitar style whose complex, layered sound closely resembled that of many black bluesmen of the Carolina Piedmont and, as is often remarked, created the impression of a mandolin or banjo accompanying his guitar. Meanwhile, unbeknownst to Dorsey, Howard had bought a cheap guitar for three dollars, converted it into a steel guitar, and begun to teach himself to play it in a style modeled on Tarlton's. "Howard later told me this story about it," Dorsey recalled. "He and Jimmie and all of them went out on the river to a fish fry, and he tried to get Jimmie to show him something about the guitar. And I don't know why, but Jimmie wouldn't do it. But Howard caught Jimmie's guitar laid down, and he slipped up to it and picked it up and strummed across the strings. And Howard was a very sensitive person. He listened at those strings as he strummed across them and learnt how to tune the guitar like Jimmie tuned his'n. And that's the way Howard started off. He started off the hard way."[46] Dorsey continued:

> Well, after I developed this five-pick way of picking, nobody didn't know anything about it but me. I was sitting on my front porch one summer evening playing and singing them old mountain songs. And my neighbors must've taken to my new style of playing, 'cause the first news I know, they commenced to congregating in my front yard to listen at it. I had quite a number standing out there listening. And I was in the middle of a song, and I noticed Brother Howard standing out there in the crowd. Howard lived about a block or two away, and he got up and come over. And when I got through singing, he come up on the porch and he said, "Dorsey," says "Where'd you get that style of playing?" And I told him all about what I'd been doing. And he says, "Well, when I left my house over there," he says, "I was dead sure somebody was playing a mandolin or banjo with you." He says, "I was hecked when I walked over here and seen nobody was playing with you." He said, "I ought to know. I ought to heared how it sounded," you know. He says, "I got an old steel guitar at home I been banging on." Said, "I believe I'll go back and get it. See if we can chord in together." So Howard went back and got his guitar, and we just went right to work together.[47]

Their success on Dorsey's front porch that evening in 1932 inspired the brothers to abandon their violin-and-guitar combination and instead begin playing the guitar and steel guitar together as the Dixon Brothers. Soon they became one of the most sought-after musical groups in Richmond County. "We entertained in homes, you know," Dorsey explained, "but we were called to do more work at churches than anywhere else. We were the only duet that I know of that was ever called to play at funerals, and we played and sang at several funerals." Meanwhile, Dorsey also occasionally performed with Jimmie Tarlton around Richmond County. "After I developed that way of playing, why, me and Jimmie put on shows at two or three schoolhouses, you know," Dixon recalled. "Jimmie wanted to team with me, but I couldn't team with him, because Jimmie was kinda rough, and I was afraid of him. He rambled and caught freight trains and that never was in my line, a-catching freight trains. I was always scared of them." A devout evangelical Christian and temperance advocate, Dixon shied away from the rougher side of southern working-class life. Nor did he perform at many weekend dances because of the potential for whiskey-fueled brawls and gunplay at such affairs. Once a Richmond County farmer approached him about furnishing the music for a Saturday night dance, Dixon recalled, but he declined the man's invitation. Later, Dixon learned that a jealous husband had shot two men to death at the dance. "Mighty few dances I ever played for on account of that," he later wrote a friend. "I don't like to play music in places where people are liable to get killed."[48]

Sometime in 1934, Dorsey and Howard Dixon traveled to Charlotte, North Carolina, probably by train, to attend an open audition for musical talent at WBT, the most powerful radio station in the Carolinas. The Crazy Water Crystals Company of the Carolinas and Georgia was searching for talented musical acts and stringbands to perform on its new *Crazy Barn Dance* program, a Saturday evening hillbilly music jamboree that had become immensely popular since its inaugural show in March 1934. The Dixon Brothers impressed the firm's executives and landed a regular spot on the show. "I got Howard and we went up there to WBT one Saturday for an audition," Dorsey told interviewers Archie Green and Eugene Earle in 1962. "Charlotte was seventy-six miles from Rockingham, and that was quite a trip, but WBT was the nearest radio station to us. But Howard and I both had a hard time. It taken all we could do to live, you know. At that time my wife had run off and left me the first time, and I was by myself. So I furnished the expenses up there, and Howard, he had a family, you know, and he didn't have the expenses. But they gave me that expense back, the Crazy Water Crystals Company did, because they fell hard for our music, and I thought they was gonna work us to death."[49]

Sponsored by the Carolinas and Georgia Division of the Crazy Water Crystals Company, the Texas-based manufacturer of a best-selling laxative, the *Crazy Barn Dance* featured a roster of more than twenty musical acts, chiefly from the textile cities and towns of the central and western North Carolina Piedmont. Besides the Dixon Brothers, other regular members of the cast included J. E. Mainer's Crazy Mountaineers of Concord, the Crazy Tobacco Tags of Gastonia, Shell Allen's W.O.W. String Band of Kannapolis, Homer Sherrill's Crazy Hickory Nuts of Hickory, and the Carolina Vagabonds of Belmont. Under the aggressive leadership of J. W. Fincher, the firm's president and general manager, the Crazy Water Crystals Company also

Cover of WBT *Official Radiologue*. Courtesy of the Collection of the Public Library of Charlotte and Mecklenburg County, reproduced by Tom Hanchett.

expanded its radio sponsorship of other hillbilly music shows, and by mid-1934, the firm sponsored 147 weekly broadcasts on fourteen stations across the Carolinas and Georgia. "It has been our constant aim," noted Fincher in the foreword to one of the *Crazy Barn Dance* souvenir programs, "to further promote the native string musical talent in these great states, and to furnish entertainment to our many thousands of loyal friends who genuinely appreciate and cherish the melody of good old fashioned string music." Despite many of the *Crazy Barn Dance* performers' urban, industrial backgrounds, Fincher encouraged his artists to trade their dark suits and ties for the more rustic costumes of stereotypical "hayseeds" when performing before the program's live, paying studio audiences in the Charlotte Observer Building's auditorium. One publicity photograph, for example, shows Dorsey and Howard Dixon and their sometimes-partner Mutt Evans standing in front of a microphone on Raleigh's WPTF—one of the thirteen other stations across the Southeast that carried Crazy Water Crystals Company–sponsored programs—dressed in matching straw hats, checkered work shirts, overalls, and neckerchiefs.[50]

Although the precise details are unclear, it appears that Dorsey and Howard Dixon briefly gave up their positions in the East Rockingham mills in order to pursue their musical careers in Charlotte. While Howard's family remained in East Rockingham, Dorsey sent his wife and children to stay with his mother-in-law in Greenville, South Carolina. The Dixon Brothers threw themselves into their fast-paced new life as professional radio performers, playing not only on the Saturday night *Crazy Barn Dance* but also on a daily fifteen-minute program sponsored by the Crazy Water Crystals Company. Sometimes Dorsey and Howard Dixon performed with fiddler J. E. Mainer's Crazy Mountaineers, a Concord, North Carolina, stringband composed of former textile millhands. Mainer's stringband, which consisted of Mainer, his banjo-playing brother Wade Mainer, and guitarist "Daddy" John Love, were particularly well known for their repertoire of weepy sentimental songs, somber religious numbers, and high-spirited, raucous fiddle tunes. "The Dixon Brothers, Dorsey and Howard" explained a circa 1934 *Crazy Barn Dance* souvenir program, "have been among the most popular groups heard on our Barn Dance Programs. They are now heard every day over WBT, Charlotte, with J. E. Mainer's Crazy Mountaineers, on the Crazy Water Crystals broadcasts. The Dixon Brothers compose most of the songs they sing, some of the most popular of which are 'The Weave Room Blues,' 'Don't Sales Tax the Gals,' and 'Two Little Rose Buds.' We predict a big future for the Dixon Brothers in radio."[51]

With its extraordinary lineup of stringband musicians and performances of wholesome sentimental and religious numbers, the *Crazy Barn Dance* delighted listeners across the Carolina Piedmont. Each week an average of one thousand telegrams, letters, and telephone calls from the show's appreciative fans flooded the Crazy Water Crystal Company's Charlotte offices. Bea Smith, Howard Dixon's daughter, recalled the throngs of East Rockingham millhands who gathered to listen to the Dixon Brothers' *Crazy Barn Dance* broadcasts on the family's radio set. "That was back in the thirties, they'd be on the radio on Saturday nights," she remembered. "And our house would just fill up, people all out in the yard listening to them on the radio. 'Cause everybody didn't have a radio in those days."[52]

As a result of their WBT radio shows, the Dixon Brothers became one of the best-loved hillbilly duos in the Carolina Piedmont during the mid-1930s. But, despite the popularity of their daily radio broadcasts, they could not manage to get on the *Crazy Barn Dance*'s payroll and thus be assured of a steady income. Only the show's biggest headliners drew a regular salary from the Crazy Water Crystals Company. The rest of the performers, including the Dixons, were reimbursed only mileage and expenses. Trading on their radio exposure, the Dixon Brothers, like most of the show's other musical acts, tried to generate much-needed income through personal appearances at ten- and twenty-five-cent admission shows. The brothers combined a hectic schedule of daily radio programs with nightly performances at schoolhouses, movie theaters, churches, and even revivals throughout south-central North Carolina and northeastern South Carolina. "The Dixon Brothers, fresh from Crazy barn dance music over Station WBT, will give a concert at [the] grammar school in Hartsville [South Carolina] Aug. 31st at 8 o'clock," announced one of the duo's 1934 advertisements in the *Rockingham Post-Dispatch*.[53]

The Dixons attracted a large fan following throughout the Carolina Piedmont, but their grueling schedule as professional musicians placed enormous emotional and financial strains on both them and their families. By October 1935, circumstances had forced them to give up their regular WBT radio shows and return to work in East Rockingham's textile mills. While still performing on the *Crazy Barn*

J. E. Mainer's Crazy Mountaineers, with the Dixon Brothers, ca. 1934.
Courtesy of Tom Hanchett.

Cover of the Crazy Water Crystals Company of the Carolinas and Georgia's *Souvenir of the Crazy Barn Dance and the Crazy Bands*, ca. 1934. Courtesy of Tom Hanchett.

Dance, as Dorsey later explained in a 1962 interview, he received word from Greenville, where his wife and children were staying, that his infant son had become gravely ill. He recalled that he had to leave Charlotte "to go home with my sick baby, why, he was so sick, and I never did get away from him. And it tore the group up. They couldn't find nobody to team with Howard. And so Howard had to come home, and we both lost our radio jobs on account of my baby. And we never did get back." Although the Dixon Brothers continued to perform at stage shows across the Carolina Piedmont, the big future predicted for them on WBT's *Crazy Barn Dance* never panned out, and they never again worked steadily on a radio program as a duo.[54]

Nevertheless, on the strength of their popular but short-lived radio shows, the Dixon Brothers did manage to launch a moderately successful recording career with RCA-Victor, one of the nation's leading manufacturers of phonographs and phonograph records during the Great Depression. On February 12, 1936, the duo cut its first six sides in a makeshift studio in RCA-Victor's regional distributor's warehouse, located on South Tryon Street in downtown Charlotte, then an important field recording center for hillbilly, blues, and gospel music. Over the next two-and-a-half years, the duo recorded an additional forty-nine sides, which were released on RCA-Victor's budget-priced Bluebird label, as well as on Montgomery Ward's mail-order label. Altogether, the Dixon Brothers participated in six recording sessions in Charlotte, plus in one final session in September 1938 in nearby Rock Hill, South Carolina. Occasionally, guitarist Mutt Evans joined them to record as a trio. At two of the Charlotte sessions, Dorsey and his sometimes-estranged wife, Beatrice, waxed a total of twelve duets, almost all of them sacred numbers. Howard also recorded two dozen sides with guitarist Frank Gerald, a fellow East Rockingham mill-hand, under the name of the Rambling Duet. "The Dixon Brothers went to Charlotte June 23rd," reported the *Rockingham Post-Dispatch* in 1936, "and again recorded for the R.C.A. Victor Recording Co. eight more songs, five of which were their own compositions. Their buddy, Mr. Mutt Evans, a member of their outfit, recorded four songs with them in a trio. The boys left Charlotte after their recording was completed and motored to Raleigh where they were welcomed by their friends the 'Crazy Mountaineers' who heartily invited them to sing one of their latest songs on their program over W.P.T.F. radio station at 11:45 a.m. The number was 'Answer to Maple on the Hill,' composed by [Dorsey]."[55]

The Dixon Brothers' records covered a broad spectrum of sacred and secular songs, most of which Dorsey himself composed or arranged. Roughly one-third of their recorded output consisted of religious numbers ("Not Turning Back," "Easter Day," and "When Gabriel Blows His Trumpet for Me"), and on these selections, the brothers' strong devotion to fundamentalist Christianity is readily apparent. The Dixons were not dour, somber Bible-thumpers, however. They had a lively sense of humor and playfulness, which they displayed on their comic novelty songs ("Intoxicated Rat," "She Tickled Me," and "Time for Me to Go"). In addition, they recorded social commentaries ("Sales Tax on the Women," "The Old Home Brew," and "How Can a Broke Man Be Happy"), as well as Depression-era portraits of textile mill life ("Weave Room Blues," "Spinning Room Blues," and "Weaver's Life"). Another major component of the Dixon Brothers' recorded repertoire consisted of nineteenth-century parlor ballads ("That Old Vacant Chair" and "After the Ball") and tragic event songs ("Two Little Rosebuds" and "The School House Fire"), which evoked sentimental images of pious mothers, wayward sons, untimely deaths, and a traditional Victorian morality that corresponded with the brothers' deep-seated religious beliefs. Even on many of the secular numbers, particularly "Down with the Old Canoe" and "I Didn't Hear Anybody Pray," the Dixons presented spiritual messages, with an evangelical narrative voice admonishing listeners to renounce their sinfulness and devote themselves to Jesus Christ.

The Dixon Brothers' recordings featured strident, gospel-inspired harmonies in which their mismatched voices mixed uneasily. Dorsey usually sang lead in a grim, gnarled baritone that sounded like it rose straight out of a dark, dank mausoleum. Under his harsh, almost deadpan vocals, he picked his Gibson guitar in a delicate, blues-inflected style. Howard supplied high tenor harmonies and a melancholy Hawaiian guitar accompaniment that featured both his subtle, understated picking and his signature tremolo. Not surprisingly, the Dixon Brothers' discordant sound was a throwback to the late 1920s sound of Tom Darby and Jimmie Tarlton, the latter of whose steel guitar playing directly influenced the instrumental styles of both brothers. The Dixon Brothers performed as a guitar-and-steel-guitar act in an age of guitar-and-mandolin duos, and their music sounded markedly different from the sweet-sounding, close harmonies of the Monroe Brothers, the Blue Sky Boys, and the Delmore Brothers, who dominated hillbilly radio during the Great Depression. Publicity photographs from this period indicate that the Dixon Brothers looked as dissimilar as they sounded. One 1934 WBT studio portrait, for example, shows the bespectacled Dorsey appearing gloomy and uncomfortable, his lips pinched in a pained grimace, his Gibson guitar enormous against his undersized body. Only thirty-seven years old, he could have easily passed for a man almost twice that age. Howard, in contrast, looks athletic and handsome and could be posing for a college yearbook picture. But the Dixon Brothers' earnest, poignant songs, such as "I Won't Accept Anything for My Soul" and "Speak Evil of No Man," resonated deeply with their hard-working, God-fearing Carolina Piedmont audiences.[56]

Although other country and bluegrass stars later recorded and even scored hits with several of Dorsey's original compositions, the Dixon Brothers themselves never achieved great commercial success or lasting fame. Nor did they ever manage to translate their music making into a long-term professional career. According to Dorsey, unscrupulous record producers and recording artists took advantage of him, swindling him out of the copyrights and royalties to several of his most popular songs. Dixon understood perfectly well that his musical compositions had monetary value, but he struggled to understand how best to secure copyrights and protect his work. Eli Oberstein, the notoriously devious RCA-Victor A & R (artist and repertoire) man who produced the Dixon Brothers' sessions, copyrighted several of Dorsey's songs—as well as those of some other artists he recorded, including the Monroe Brothers—in his own name with various New York City music-publishing firms. "Well, the first night we recorded, the contract, it looked all right, what I read, you know," explained Dixon. "And it was laying on a desk, and I just signed it without thinking. But when I put in claim for copyright, why, they sent that paper to me, and I could tell where that part had been folded back. Eli Oberstein tricked me, you know, and he tricked me all the way through, 'cause when I put in claim, why, my copyrights was scattered all over New York City."[57]

But, according to Dixon, it was Wade Mainer, the banjo player for J. E. Mainer's Crazy Mountaineers with whom he sometimes performed on the radio, who deceived him worst of all. Dixon later al-

Publicity photograph of the Dixon Brothers from the Crazy Water Crystals Company of the Carolinas and Georgia's *Souvenir of the Crazy Barn Dance and the Crazy Bands*, ca. 1934. Courtesy of Tom Hanchett.

leged that Mainer had hoodwinked him into copyrighting six of his original compositions, including "I Didn't Hear Anybody Pray," in both of their names. As a result, Mainer collected half of the royalties on these songs. "Wade Mainer, he sweet talked me," Dixon explained. "He acted like he was a friend of mine, you know, and he was gonna help me get my songs copyrighted, and what I come to find out, he was trying to get control of them. And when I seen it, I just got disheartened and quit." Bewildered, Dixon later wrote, "I'll never know what happened, but we finally got pushed back in the woods and the name Dixon brother[s] was forgotten for many years." Shortly after their recording contract expired in 1938, the Dixon Brothers felt so betrayed and discouraged by the ruthlessness of the music industry that they stopped performing together professionally.[58]

After the Dixon Brothers split up, both Howard and Dorsey left East Rockingham. By 1941, Howard Dixon was playing steel guitar with Wade Mainer and the Sons of the Mountaineers on a regular radio spot on WWNC in Asheville, North Carolina. The following year, Howard returned to East Rockingham, where he went to work as a cloth-room fixer at the Entwistle (later the Aleo) Mill and played with several local stringbands, including the Richmond County Ramblers and the Southern Hillbillies.[59] Meanwhile, in 1941, Dorsey took a job as a weaver at the Dunean Mill in Greenville, South Carolina, and occasionally performed on the local radio station, WFBC. In 1942, while living in Greenville, he discovered that the *Grand Ole Opry*'s biggest headliner, Roy Acuff and His Smoky Mountain Boys, had recorded a weepy, pathos-filled version of his composition "I Didn't Hear Anybody Pray," under the title of "Wreck on the Highway." Acuff, a lean, lanky thirty-nine-year-old fiddler from a middle-class Chattanooga family, was then the most popular and highest-paid star in the hillbilly music industry. His income for 1943 alone exceeded $200,000. "When a unit, say, like Roy Acuff and his Smoky Mountain Boys is scheduled to hit a town like Albany, Georgia," the *Saturday Evening Post* reported in 1944, "farmers will pour into Albany from a 200-mile radius, and night after night Acuff will play to audiences of 4,000 in places where Betty Grable or Tommy Dorsey or Bob Hope would only succeed in drawing boll weevils."[60]

Acuff's 1942 Columbia recording of "Wreck on the Highway" became a national best-selling hit on wartime America's jukeboxes and phonographs, and eventually the number became one of his signature songs. But the record listed Acuff, not Dixon, as the song's composer. Acuff later claimed that he had purchased the lyrics of "Wreck on the Highway" from a man in Knoxville and that Fred Rose, his Nashville music-publishing partner at Acuff-Rose Publications, had composed the song's melody. But it appears more probable that Acuff learned the song directly from the Dixon Brothers' 1938 Bluebird record, since the melody on his 1942 Columbia recording so closely resembles Dorsey's original one. Meanwhile, Dixon's sons regularly got into schoolyard scraps with classmates for claiming that their father had written Roy Acuff's hit song. "The other kids didn't believe that our dad, who worked in the mill right along their dads, was a songwriter," recalled William Dixon. Their skepticism is perhaps understandable. After all, one might ask, how could a poor "linthead" with only a fourth-grade education compose what would become an American musical classic? Dixon finally instructed his sons to stop mentioning his authorship of "Wreck on the Highway" at school, but he himself continued to pursue his rightful copyright claim. "No one but God," Dorsey later confided in a letter, "will ever know the heartaches we suffered over that song."[61]

Over the next four years, Dixon wrote letter after letter to Acuff-Rose Publications in Nashville claiming authorship of "Wreck on the Highway," but he received no answer. Finally, in 1946, after a threatened lawsuit, Dixon and Fred Rose reached an out-of-court settlement at the Poinsett Hotel in Greenville. Under the agreement, Dixon received only one-third of the initial $5,000 royalties for "Wreck on the Highway" and an undisclosed percentage of future royalties. But much of Dixon's compensation went to pay his legal fees and to buy out Wade Mainer, who, in 1938, had tricked the trusting songwriter into copyrighting the song in both of their names. After they reached a settlement, Dixon and Rose, along with Dixon's son William, visited Mainer at his home in Concord, North Carolina, and convinced him to sign back complete control of the song for $250. More than thirty years later, Dixon's son's memories of that meeting with Mainer remained bitter. "I'll never forget that musician," William Dixon recalled acidly. "He drove up in a station wagon with 'Jesus Saves' painted on both sides."[62]

Surprisingly, Dorsey Dixon bore no hard feelings toward the Nashville publishing duo for pirating his song. "I'm certain the Lord worked through Acuff and Rose in my favor," he later wrote. "To my dieing day Acuff and Rose will have a warm place in my heart." Dixon also believed that Acuff was completely innocent of any wrongdoing, and that their protracted copyright dispute had been the result of a simple misunderstanding. "Roy picked up the song without the slightest idea of who wrote the song," Dixon maintained. "Little did he dream that in doing so. He would pull the writer out of many dark places in life. . . . I truly believe if there ever was a man or men with God rooted and grounded in their heart Roy Acuff is one of them." Dixon not only later adopted Acuff's title for the song, but after 1946 he sang "Wreck on the Highway" using Acuff's slightly different melody. "I knew that when me and Roy got the 'Wreck on the Highway' cleared up, if I went on using my old tune it might hurt the song," he explained, "so I just went to using Roy's tune." Eventually Dixon's song became a beloved country-and-western classic, and its extensive recording history reflects its immense popularity. Hawkshaw Hawkins, Wilma Lee and Stony Cooper, the Louvin Brothers, Bill Haley and His Comets, the New Lost City Ramblers, Jean Ritchie, George Jones, the Nitty Gritty Dirt Band, and Townes Van Zandt, all have recorded their own versions of Dixon's "Wreck on the Highway."[63]

In 1947, with hope of additional royalty settlements, Dixon moved his family to New York City and, while working the day shift in a Union City, New Jersey, rayon mill, attempted to regain control of all of his song copyrights. But he soon discovered that they were assigned to several different music-publishing firms and that regaining control of those copyrights would be nearly impossible. Defeated, Dixon and his family returned the following year to East Rockingham, where he worked in his last textile mill, the Aleo Manufacturing Company. Almost twenty years of weaving in dimly lit factories had ruined his eyes, and when his vision became too poor to weave, he gave up his longtime trade and took a less-skilled, lower-paying job in the cloth room where his brother Howard worked as a fixer. Dixon worked at the Aleo Mill until 1951, when at the age of fifty-three his deteriorating eyesight finally forced him to retire. Later that year, Dixon and his wife, Beatrice, and their youngest son, William, moved to Baltimore, a popular postwar destination for working-class white migrants from the Carolinas, and there, despite his poor vision, Dorsey worked in a munitions plant. In 1953, Beatrice Dixon left him, after twenty-five years of troubled marriage (although they were not legally divorced until 1966). Devastated, Dixon returned to East Rockingham alone in

1958, a depressed and sick man, who, as he later explained to a local newspaper reporter, "felt that he had failed in everything he tried to achieve."[64]

Separated from his wife and with most of his immediate family dead or scattered, Dixon rented a small, two-room apartment near the Aleo Mill and subsisted on meager Social Security disability payments and occasional royalty checks. Completely blind in one eye and suffering from kidney stones, he sank into a deep depression and lost interest in music. "There was a time," he later explained, "when I was going through a lot of tribulations and heartaches and sorrow, and I didn't have no spirit in me to play." Still, he continued to compose songs, especially sacred numbers such as "When That Beautiful City Comes Down" and "Across the Shining River," the latter of which became the most requested song of the Reaping Harvesters, a gospel quartet that Howard and his friend and co-worker Lloyd "Slim" Harris, an Aleo Mill cloth inspector, had formed around 1950. Before his kidney stones and depression had become so debilitating, Dorsey had sometimes performed with the group, which was based at a little country church outside of nearby Hamlet, the Hamlet Church of God of Prophecy. Since the end of his radio and recording career, Dixon had increasingly concentrated on composing and performing religious songs. But by 1958, he had become too depressed even to continue his special mission of spreading the gospel. "I was down and out. a very sick man. and hope all gone," he later confided in a memoir. "Yet in my mind's eye. I could still see that tiny light shining from 'Wreck On The Highway.' Inspite of the fact. that one time I thought it would be best for me to not live. any more. But when death rubbed up against me again. as usel I fought back at death and won again. . . . Death came very near wining. But the ONE who holds the keys of death and the grave said NO. and through Him I lived on unto this day. Truly my work was'nt finished."[65]

The ever-faithful Dixon credited God with miraculously curing his painful kidney stones and reasoned that his life had once again been spared because he had not yet fulfilled his "great purpose." This conviction, coupled with the fortuitous timing of an enthusiastic fan letter from halfway around the world, inspired the lonely, depressed Dixon to resume his songwriting and music. In the summer of 1960, Dixon received a letter from John Edwards, a twenty-eight-year-old record collector and hillbilly music historian from Sydney, Australia,

whose interest in Dixon's old Bluebird recordings flattered the retired textile weaver. More important, Edwards's letter kindled Dixon's
desire to revive the Dixon Brothers' musical career, and he tried to
convince Howard to join him. "John Edwards told me in one of his letters," Dixon recalled, "that it would be surprising if I could know the
great number of people that would like to hear [the] Dixon Brothers
on recordings again." Dorsey showed the letter to his brother, but
Howard, although impressed that their songs had touched people
so far away, was reluctant to abandon his stable home life and regular job for the financial uncertainties of the music industry. Dorsey
recalled that, after reading Edwards's letter, Howard just shook his
head and said, "It's too late for you and me, Dorsey." But Dorsey refused to accept his brother's answer. He wrote back to John Edwards
and meanwhile stepped up his efforts to persuade Howard to agree
to a comeback.[66]

Dixon and Edwards began corresponding regularly, and through
their letters the pen pals developed an increasingly close friendship.
Their relationship, however, would not survive the year. Dixon remembered.

> Well, we got to corresponding with each other, and John become
> one of my top correspondents. He wrote the most interesting let-
> ters, and I really enjoyed them. They won my heart. And we began
> to build up a correspondence. And one week I was waiting on a
> letter from John. I just looked forward to his letters, they were so
> warm and friendly. And I was a little late in hearing from him, and
> finally I got a letter from his mother. And I opened it and read it.
> Well, I'm telling you what's the truth. It broke my heart. I just can't
> express the feelings that I had that lonesome Saturday evening
> when I received the tragic news that John was instantly killed in
> a car wreck on Christmas Eve morning in 1960. And it really did
> hurt me so bad. It just broke me down. Never had met John, didn't
> know much about him, but his letters had drawed love in between
> me and him so strongly till I wept when I got the news.

Dixon was particularly disturbed to learn that the last record to which
Edwards had listened on his record player on the night of his death
was one of Dixon's own, a copy of his 1936 Bluebird recording of the
sacred number "Not Turning Back," and for weeks afterward Dixon
blamed himself for his friend's death. Eventually, though, Dixon re-

Dorsey Dixon playing his Jumbo Gibson guitar outside his apartment in East Rockingham, North Carolina, 1962. Courtesy of the Southern Folklife Collection, Wilson Library, University of North Carolina at Chapel Hill.

sponded to Edwards's demise, as he had to the deaths of so many friends and neighbors before, by memorializing him in song. Dixon titled his elegy "Our Johnny of Sydney, Australia." "It's just an inspiration of a tune that come to me," Dixon recalled. "I just don't know how to explain it. They say all inspirations comes from God, and I reckon that to make it understandable, the tune for this song must have come from God. And I made a recording of 'Our Johnny of Sydney, Australia,' and sent it to [Edwards's mother] on a tape."[67]

The death of his friend only intensified Dorsey's desire to reunite the Dixon Brothers. "My hearts desire (after a way was made for me to live) was for Howard and me to make a come back," he wrote. "I still wanted to try to continue to be a blessing to people and make them happy." But his reluctant brother refused to have any part of Dorsey's scheme. Since 1942, Howard had been employed at the Aleo Mill in East Rockingham, and with his hard-earned savings, he and his wife had bought a tract of land and built a house on the outskirts of Hamlet, a Seaboard Railroad town about three miles southeast of Rockingham. There, they raised their family of six boys and two girls. Eventually, with Howard's help, five of his children built houses in the area, which locals appropriately called Dixonville. "Howard was very devoted to his family, and he had a nice place out there," Dorsey explained. "And Howard billed his time, eight hours in the mill, and he worked out there helping them children build them homes probably till late at night, probably till bedtime. I begged Howard to take it easy, because I seen that his health was failing. It done come to the point where we couldn't work together playing music; he didn't feel like it. He worked too hard, he didn't feel like working with me anymore, although the last time I seen him alive we sung a song together in church, 'God Loves His Children.'"[68]

Six weeks after receiving the news of Edwards's fatal accident, another tragic blow staggered Dixon. He was out of town performing at a nearby church when, on March 24, 1961, he learned of Howard's sudden death at the age of fifty-seven from a massive heart attack. Dorsey recalled:

> Howard, he worked every day at the Aleo Mill, and the day he died I know that he wasn't able to work, but he did work. He was down at the dope [Coca-Cola] stand, folks said that he was taking a Alka-Seltzer tablet. Said he told them he thought an indigestions were

working on him. And when they told me that, I knew he worked sick all that day. And at 11 o'clock he suffered his first heart attack. Well, his boss and friends tried to get him to go to the doctor then, but he didn't do it. He just swapped jobs with a feller. And at 1:30 p.m. he had a second attack, and then he went and got two of his boys. That was pretty bad. His boys, they rushed him to the Hamlet Hospital, and he got out of the car, walked into the out-patient department, and they put him in a little room there and hooked him up to an oxygen tent. And his boys was checking him in at the desk. And the nurse commenced motioning to them to come quick. And when they got in there, why, the doctor says, "Well, boys, looks like it's all over with." And Howard died of another heart attack within minutes after he got to the hospital.[69]

As he had done numerous times before, the grief-stricken Dorsey again turned to his songwriting to help him cope with his loss:

The evening when we came back from the funeral, from the burying, his youngest daughter asked me, said, "Uncle Dorsey," said, "if you write one about Dad," says, "I want a copy of it." Well, the child knew that I might write about him, but when she asked me that, it just didn't seem like it would be possible for me to write one about my brother. I just thought that would be the most impossiblest thing that I could do, is to write one about him and his death. And I told her, I said, "Honey," I says, "you know how it's done." I says, "I have to wait on an inspiration." And three days after Howard was buried, I caught the first verse of it at four o'clock in the morning, and I was inspired to write that song. That night I handed his daughter a copy of that poem. It was only poem that I remember writing that I didn't have to go back over and change words.

Dixon titled his touching tribute to his brother "Howard." "Howard played the steel guitar / And when he pulled the steel," the opening stanza goes, "His thrilling music made one know / The power of God was real. / But Howard went away one day / And joined a musical band, / Across the shining river / To a rich and better land."[70]

When Howard's death ended Dorsey's dreams of reuniting the Dixon Brothers act, Dorsey shifted his efforts to reviving his own musical career. In May 1961, for example, he sent Wesley Rose, the son of the late Fred Rose and the president of Acuff-Rose Publications, a reel-to-reel tape of himself singing and performing twenty-four original compositions, in the hope that Rose would publish a few of these selections and then place them with Nashville recording artists, but nothing came of it. Dixon did, however, manage to launch a short-lived solo comeback during the American folk music revival. In 1962, with the assistance of hillbilly music scholars and record collectors Archie Green and Eugene Earle, Dixon recorded a nineteen-track album, *Babies in the Mill: Carolina Traditional, Industrial, Sacred Songs*, which appeared three years later on the small Chicago-based blues label, Testament Records (HMG/HighTone Records rereleased it, on compact disc, in 1997).[71]

Dixon had written the title track of *Babies in the Mill* in 1945 while working as an oiler in the weaving department at the Dunean Mill in Greenville, South Carolina. In composing this, his last commercially recorded textile song, he drew upon his and especially his sister Nancy's memories of their childhood industrial experiences. Unprotected by child labor legislation, Nancy had gone to work as a spinner at the Darlington Manufacturing Company in 1901 at the age of eight. She was so small, she recalled, that she had to stand on the dangerous machinery in order to do her job. She earned forty-seven-and-a-half cents a week, and in a 1962 interview with Green and Earle, she marveled that, when she was paid every two weeks, her work brought in the small sum of ninety-five cents. "That didn't even make a paper bill," she laughed. "It was all in change. Wasn't even a dollar of it. But I thought that was something big!" Despite the pride she felt at being able to contribute to her family's income, the mill overseers' brutal treatment of small children frightened her. "When I went to work in the mill," Nancy recalled, "they run the spinning room with children. And the section hands and bosses that was over them treated little children bad, too. They were all right to the near-about grown children, but the little ones they'd push them around and slap them about. Some of them, they'd beat them and jerk them around like little dogs, where their parents would allow it. But our dad wouldn't allow them to treat us mean."[72]

One particularly cruel incident still distressed her after more than sixty years. "One night I was working," she remembered, "and I saw a little orphan boy, and he was a-sweeping. And he would get over his floor, and he'd crawl up in the waste box and go to sleep. And I'd wake him up a heap of times to keep them from getting after him.

Cover of Testament Records' *Babies in the Mill: Carolina Traditional, Industrial, Sacred Songs*, 1965, featuring a 1908 Lewis Hine photograph of a young South Carolina spinner. Courtesy of the Southern Folklife Collection, Wilson Library, University of North Carolina at Chapel Hill.

And one night they taken him down in the basement and whipped him, and when he come up the steps, he was just screaming as hard as he could. And then the next night, they didn't whip him, but they tied him to the waste box. And I told my father about it, and he told me to keep my mouth out of it. Well, I was too little to talk about it, but it hurt my feelings real bad." Her brother Dorsey took such stories and distilled them into the lyrics for "Babies in the Mill," which documents the southern textile industry's shameful abuse and exploitation of child labor as poignantly as any of Lewis Hine's famous photographs. "To their jobs those little ones were strictly forced to go, / Those babies had to be on time through rain and sleet and snow," one of the stanzas goes. "Many times when things went wrong their bosses often frowned; / Many times those little ones was kicked and shoved around." Dixon's haunting song, which has appeared widely in folk song anthologies and documentary films about the South, remains the definitive musical portrayal of child textile labor in America.[73]

Babies in the Mill also featured another historically significant song: Nancy Dixon's a cappella rendition of "Factory Girl," a ballad she had learned from the older girls in the spinning room shortly after she went to work at the Darlington Mill. The song, a variant of the widely collected folk song about Massachusetts textile operatives, "The Lowell Factory Girl," which dates from the mid-1830s, is considered America's oldest surviving industrial ballad. Nancy's recording of "Factory Girl" almost certainly marks the last performance of this generations-old folk song by a singer who had learned it in a genuinely traditional singing community. Because of Nancy's and Dorsey's industrial backgrounds, Green designated *Babies in the Mill* as "the first commercial album to present the voice of any traditional textile folksinger."[74]

When released in 1965, *Babies in the Mill* garnered rave reviews from music critics, including Irwin Silber of *Sing Out!* and Nat Hentoff of *HiFi/Stereo Review*. But album sales proved disappointing. "I only hope that enough records will sell to pay back expences to get it out," Dixon wrote Archie Green. "I believe they will. But not in my life time. I believe there will come a time when the world will [be] hungry for it and really want it, and it will sell. But not yet. . . . When it happens . . . I'm sure I won't be here. But I do have hope of injoying the fruits of my work in a new life free from aflections." Nonetheless, Dixon's 1962 recording session became a catalyst for his return to public performance. The following year, he was invited to appear at the Newport Folk Festival, along with such musical giants as Maybelle Carter, Mississippi John Hurt, Brownie McGhee and Sonny Terry, Joan Baez, Bob Dylan, and Pete Seeger. Three of Dixon's concert performances there appeared on the Vanguard album *Old Time Music at Newport*. Later that same year, in November 1963, Dixon played a two-week engagement in a Washington, D.C., folk music club called Ontario Place, but he drew only sparse crowds and considered the shows "a complete flop." While there, he cut additional tracks for an album with Piedmont Records (but it was never released). He also recorded thirty-eight numbers, including his classic songs "Wreck on the Highway," "Intoxicated Rat," and "Weave Room Blues," for the Library of Congress's Archive of Folk Song (now the Archive of Folk Culture), the nation's premier repository of American traditional music.[75]

After his tour ended in late 1963, Dixon returned to his lonely and spartan existence in his East Rockingham apartment. He spent his days composing sacred songs, playing his cherished Gibson guitar, and listening to the radio. Despite his poor vision, he maintained a steady correspondence with a handful of record collectors and music aficionados from around the world, including Rodney McElrea, Dick Spottswood, Eugene Earle, David Crisp, and Archie Green, and frequently sent them self-recorded reel-to-reel tapes of himself performing some of his latest songs. Two or three days a week, he visited his last surviving sibling, Nancy, in a nearby nursing home. Though in his mid-sixties, Dixon's drive to perform God's work remained as strong as ever, and he often performed his sacred songs at the East Rockingham Free Will Baptist Church and at other evangelical Protestant churches in Richmond County.[76]

Dixon also continued to expand his repertoire, adding to it several popular gospel and sentimental songs by Bill Monroe and His Blue Grass Boys, Red Foley, and Lester Flatt and Earl Scruggs that he heard on the *Grand Ole Opry* and other radio programs. He also persisted in his songwriting. With the aid of a Motorola tape recorder, Dixon recorded the new songs that he wrote and sent them to music publishers, in the hope of producing another hit song like "Wreck on the Highway" that would bring him the financial security that had eluded him. But his musical aspirations were further stymied in October 1964 when a heart attack, coupled with glaucoma-induced blindness in one eye, forced him to suspend his music making.[77] No longer able to care for himself, he moved to Plant City, Florida, to live with his oldest son, Rev. Dorsey Dixon Jr., who was pastor of the Turkey Creek Church of God. There, in March 1965, he suffered yet another heart attack, which required a long stay in the hospital. Dixon regained some of his vision following two cataract surgeries, but he still struggled with what had become a long-standing battle with depression, which he believed stemmed from his tremendous anxiety about his failure to accomplish his life's ordained work. Not long after he recovered from his heart attacks, Dixon was again hospitalized, this time for a nervous breakdown and related stomach ulcers. His doctors attributed his psychological fragility to his painful ulcers, but Dixon claimed that "worrying about things that happen[ed] to me down through my rugged life brought it on. It caused me to be depressed."[78]

Fortunately for Dixon, small royalty checks from "Wreck on the Highway" continued to arrive at regular intervals. Despite the anguish it had caused him during his four-year copyright dispute with Acuff-Rose Publications in the early to mid-1940s, Dixon considered "Wreck on the Highway" both his proudest accomplishment and his greatest blessing:

> You know I believe in God, and I believe He can foresee all things. And I believe He foreseen dark places in life that I was coming to, and He preserved that song that it might pull me out of those dark places. I remember one time in Baltimore, Maryland, I paid my rent that morning, and I lacked about $10 of paying it all. The landlady was so sweet to me. She said, "Mr. Dixon," says, "you a good man." And says, "Don't you worry if you don't pay no rent. You're not gonna be throwed out." Said, "Don't you worry one bit about it." 'Course, her words broke my heart, and I know tears fell down my cheeks. I always tried to live right, but it seemed like I had those hard things to go through with. So I walked down the street to an old address, and there was a [royalty] check for "Wreck on the Highway" for $58. And I paid my rent. And it seemed like those checks come at a time when I was in great need each time.[79]

In return for caring for him during his illness, Dixon bequeathed Dorsey Jr. the copyrights to his songs, including "Wreck on the Highway," his most valuable possession.

On April 18, 1968, at the age of seventy, Dorsey Dixon died of heart failure. His body was returned to his adopted hometown of East

Rockingham, where funeral services were held at the East Rocking-ham Free Will Baptist Church, and he was buried there in the Eastside Cemetery. Only a cheap plastic funeral-home card placard marked the gravesite of the man who, along with harmonica bluesman Sonny Terry, remains one of the city's most famous residents.[80]

Despite the grinding poverty, dead-end mill work, and many hard-ships, disappointments, and health problems he faced, Dorsey Dixon never lost his faith. For much of his life, he adhered to a steady Chris-tian philosophy of living. He saw the fundamentalist faith of the past as a soul-saving alternative to the secularism of the present, and he sought to ease people's suffering by providing spiritual messages that might convince them to shun the selfishness and materialism of modern life. But carrying out his life's great purpose was far from easy for the humble textile worker turned songwriter and musician. "I concentrated in this songwriting work here, and it looks like I lost in it, too," he lamented a few years before his death. "That is, as far as this life's concerned, looks like I've lost. Wonderful songs that I've wrote, seems like I can't get them published, but I can't quit. It's a thing that I can't quit. I got to go on with it. And I hope that this work I'm doing will bless many people's hearts that I may never see." Yet whatever frustration Dixon might have felt with his lack of commer-cial success was eased somewhat by his steadfast conviction that his songs, especially his sacred and tragic numbers, were inspired by God and therefore intended, as he often said, to be "a blessing to people." "The money is not the important thing," he once remarked. "It makes me happy to think about all the people who enjoy my music."[81]

More so than most working-class southern musicians of his gen-eration, Dorsey Dixon was keenly aware of his own place in American music history, and he went to great lengths to document his life ex-periences through his extensive correspondence, his tape-recorded interviews, and, most of all, his autobiographical writings. Despite his claim that he never wanted "nothing about [his] life wrote out, be-cause [he] had it too rough in life," Dixon actually wrote two separate memoirs, which chiefly focus on his musical career and which, when taken together, cover his life up to the age of sixty-four. He pecked out his first one, titled "Early Life of Dorsey M. Dixon, Song Writer and Composer and Author of the Famous Wreck on the Highway and Many Others"—a single-spaced, three-and-a-half-page sketch—on a typewriter in 1948, while he was living in New York City and working at a New Jersey rayon plant. He scribbled his second account, "Dixon Bros. Howard-Dorsey"—a twelve-page narrative—in 1962, a few years after he had returned to East Rockingham. Dixon's unique writing style featured creative spelling, punctuation (he used periods, for example, in place of commas), grammar, and capitalization. And he himself was acutely aware of his tendency, as he put it, to "murder up the English language." But despite the fact that his formal education ended in the fourth grade, his writings are remarkably articulate and conform reasonably well to standard written American English. Reflecting on his rudimentary self-education, Dixon once commented in amazement to one of his pen pals that "a lot of folks call me a great writer. Can you imagine that?" But anyone who has ever heard "Wreck on the Highway" can easily understand such a glowing assessment, for, like his fellow country songwriter Hank Williams, Dixon possessed a rare gift for expressing complicated spiritual and social messages in an ordinary, plainspoken language that is all the more poignant for its simplicity.[82]

Like the songs he composed and recorded, Dixon's memoirs are historical documents significant for what they suggest about the uneasy responses that many southerners had to the onrushing modern South. And his memoirs, along with his songs, interviews, and letters, offer rare glimpses into the life of a Piedmont millhand, evangelical Christian, and hillbilly singer and songwriter. But despite all of this documentation and his eagerness to discuss at length the suffering he endured throughout his professional musical career, Dorsey Dixon successfully concealed many of the painful details of his turbulent private life, especially his marital and family problems. "There are many hard things that I had to go through with. hard ships heartaches and pain," Dixon once wrote cryptically. "I have set at my radio and heard other song writers tell their life's story[.] But their story was nothing to compare with things that I have had to meet in the song writing and composeing. unless they did like I'm doing[,] keeping the most of it in their heart."[83]

EPILOGUE

At the east end of town, at the foot of the hill
Stands a chimney so tall that says "Aragon Mill."
But there's no smoke at all coming out of the stack.
The mill has shut down and it ain't a-coming back.

And the only tune I hear
Is the sound of the wind,
As it blows through the town,
Weave and spin, weave and spin.
—Si Kahn, "Aragon Mill" (1974)

Collectively, oral histories, labor histories, sociological studies, journalistic exposés, photographs, and even phonograph records reveal beyond any reasonable doubt that throughout the late nineteenth century and much of the first half of the twentieth century the lives of ordinary Piedmont textile workers were riddled with poverty, hunger, hardship, disease, and, in some cases, despair. Before the passage of the New Deal's National Industrial Recovery Act in 1933, these workers, disparagingly called "lintheads" or "factory trash" by townspeople and farmers alike, operated clattering weaving looms and spinning frames for ten or eleven hours a day, five days a week, plus a half day on Saturdays, for some of the lowest industrial wages in the United States. They worked in hot, humid conditions. Fine strands of lint and dust choked the air amid the deafening roar of the machinery, and these made eventual hearing loss and brown lung disease strong probabilities. When their shifts ended sometime between 6:00 and 6:30 in the evening, the workers emerged exhausted from the mills, their overalls and dresses stained with sweat and grime and cotton lint clinging to their hair and clothes. "Stretch-outs" and temporary shutdowns were common during the late 1920s, disease and malnutrition ran rampant, educational opportunities were sparse, and the chances of social and economic advancement, especially for the bulk of unskilled laborers, were slim. For many mill families, literally nothing more than a few weeks' wages stood between them and starvation. During much of this period, mill owners and superintendents used every weapon in their formidable arsenal, including labor spies, gun thugs, strikebreakers, repressive violence, and mass evictions, to prevent unions from infiltrating and gaining a foothold in their workforces. Prior to the enactment of child labor laws in the first decades of the twentieth century, exploitative bosses thought nothing of putting children as young as seven or eight years old to work doffing spindles or running spinning frames on dangerous machinery for pennies an hour.[1]

Amid these bleak conditions, though, a dynamic musical culture flourished in Piedmont textile villages between 1890 and 1940, as it did in few other places. Its roots were in the preindustrial traditional music of the southern mountains and rural countryside that had been handed down for generations, but its unique sound, which was deeply informed by modern influences, was forged in cities and towns. There, textile millhands combined older fiddle tunes, traditional ballads, and Civil War–era minstrel songs with the more contemporary sounds of ragtime, vaudeville, Tin Pan Alley, and blues to create a distinctive American music that addressed the changing circumstances of working-class life in the early twentieth-century South. Today, the term "hillbilly" connotes all that is rural, unsophisticated, backward, and disadvantaged; it is seldom used as a compliment.[2] But, at least within Piedmont textile villages in the decades prior to World War II, hillbilly music was urban, modern, and, in its way, tremendously sophisticated. Spread throughout the Southeast and the nation via radio broadcasts, phonograph records, sheet music, motion pictures, and touring musical shows, the hillbilly music created by Piedmont textile musicians and stringbands profoundly influenced the musical sounds of the nation and gave birth to the multibillion-dollar international industry that we now call country music.

World War II, for all intents and purposes, marked the end of hillbilly music. A 1942 nationwide strike by the American Federation of Musicians union, combined with wartime shellac rationing, severely restricted the manufacture of new phonograph records. Studio recording, prohibited during the sixteen-month strike by the so-called Petrillo Ban, resumed in 1943, but the southern stringband music that, along with cowboy songs and western swing, soared to national popularity during World War II, though often still referred to as "hillbilly music," differed markedly from that of the previous two decades. Fading from the scene was the prewar, largely acoustic stringband sound of the original generation of hillbilly musicians. In its place emerged an even more modern music that increasingly featured full-time professional musicians, more carefully orchestrated recordings, songs written by professional songwriters, and electric guitars, basses, and pedal steel guitars. It was this wartime version of hillbilly music that first broke through to national audiences in any kind of sustained way, chiefly as a result of southern working-class migrations to military bases and defense plants in Midwest and West Coast cities. *Time* magazine proclaimed in October 1943:

> The dominant popular music of the U.S. today is hillbilly. By last week the flood of camp-meetin' melody, which had been rising steadily in juke joints and on radio programs for over a year, was swamping Tin Pan Alley. Big names in the drawling art of country and cowboy balladry like Gene Autry, the Carter Family, Roy Acuff and Al Dexter were selling discs like never before. Top-flight songsters like Bing Crosby and Frank Sinatra were making their biggest smashes with hillbilly tunes. . . . Even many of Tin Pan Alley's best-sellers, such tunes as "You'll Never Know," "Comin' in on a Wing and a Prayer," "There's a Star-Spangled Banner Waving Somewhere," were fragrant with hillbilly spirit.

But, despite such claims about hillbilly music's popularity, the truth was that these wartime anthems were a generation removed, stylistically, from the original old-time sounds of the pre-1933 era. The prewar music that had once captivated southern farm and working-class audiences had already evolved into what, by 1949, *Billboard* magazine and much of the music industry were calling "country and western music." And out of hillbilly music also emerged the distinctive regional subgenres of western swing, honky-tonk, and bluegrass, pioneered by innovators such as Bob Wills, Ernest Tubb, and Bill Monroe.[3]

The wartime demise of hillbilly music roughly coincided with the diminished presence of Piedmont textile millworkers in the nation's commercial music industry. Several reasons account for this comparative dearth of postwar textile musicians. The increasing corporate consolidation and professionalization of country music, begun in the mid-1920s, accelerated dramatically after World War II. The founding of hundreds of small, independent record labels during the mid- to late 1940s did create more opportunities for working-class singers and musicians to cut records for local and sometimes regional jukeboxes and radio airplay, but it became increasingly difficult for part-time or semiprofessional singers, musicians, and songwriters to break into the emerging national country music scene. Moreover, the major record labels no longer relied on the prewar field-recording system, which had allowed so many Piedmont textile musicians and stringbands to audition and make records in nearby regional cities such as Atlanta, Charlotte, Richmond, and Rock Hill, South Carolina. Instead, these firms established permanent recording studios in such cities as Chicago, Los Angeles, and particularly Nashville—which, by 1955, with its constellation of major record label offices, song publishers, recording studios, music promoters, and *Grand Ole Opry* radio stars, had emerged as the nation's undisputed country music capital—drastically reducing the recording opportunities that had benefited Piedmont textile workers in the period between 1923 and 1942.[4] In addition, Piedmont millhands, who had enjoyed a number of cultural advantages over southern farmers and other white industrial workers during the 1920s, began to lose much of their edge. By 1930, for example, most textile firms had terminated their sponsorship of employee bands and music classes, which had done so much to nurture and invigorate the musical culture of Piedmont mill villages. Other advantages that millhands once held, such as their ready access to radios, Victrolas, motion pictures, and factory-made instruments, were also lost during the late 1940s and early 1950s as recent southern migrants living in cities and towns, as well as many of those rural southerners who remained in the countryside, benefited from rising incomes and greater access to postwar America's abundance of consumer goods.

Postwar changes in the southern textile industry also contributed to the declining presence of millhand musicians within commercial country music. One of the most revolutionary changes was the dismantling of Piedmont textile villages and the subsequent destruction of much of the distinctive mill culture that had helped to produce hillbilly music. Since the late nineteenth century, textile firms had built mill villages to accommodate their employees, chiefly because most of the earliest mills relied on waterpower and were located along fast-running rivers in rural areas where little adequate housing existed. Even at the beginning of the Great Depression, mill villages remained a common feature of the Piedmont textile industry. A 1929 study of

322 North Carolina mills, for example, estimated that approximately 70 percent of the state's millhands lived in these company-owned villages. As early as the mid-1930s, however, mill owners were finding that mill villages were not worth the expense, especially since the development of good roads, cheap automobiles, and buses and streetcars had made textile millhands less dependent on mill-owned housing. By the outbreak of World War II, Piedmont textile firms had sold off more than seven thousand houses in some eighty villages to mill families and other buyers. After the war, the sales of mill houses accelerated, and the influx of new owners and tenants, not all of whom worked in the local textile mills, transformed and, arguably, diminished the distinctive Piedmont mill village culture that had given rise to hillbilly music less than a generation earlier.[5] Textile communities also weakened as many of the sons and daughters of millhands left the mill villages during and after World War II to pursue military service, college education, or better economic opportunities in other fields of employment. As workers began living in greater numbers outside of mill districts and their children left to make better lives for themselves, the rich social worlds of Piedmont textile mill villages, with their kinship networks, neighborly bonds, and strong sense of community, began to erode. So too did the once-vibrant musical culture of these villages.

A few postwar country music stars, however, did emerge from the textile mills of the Piedmont South, most notably Lester Flatt and Earl Scruggs, two of the pioneering giants of bluegrass music. Born in 1914 and raised on an East Tennessee farm, Lester Flatt worked in a series of textile mills, first in Sparta, Tennessee, then in Johnson City, Tennessee, and finally in Covington, Virginia, before becoming, in 1945, the guitarist for Bill Monroe and His Blue Grass Boys, regulars on WSM's *Grand Ole Opry* in Nashville. There, he met another new band member, a twenty-one-year-old banjo player named Earl Scruggs. Ten years younger than Flatt, Scruggs had grown up on a forty-acre farm in Flint Hill, North Carolina, and then went to work on the third shift at a thread mill in nearby Shelby during World War II, before moving to the up-and-coming country music capital of Nashville to pursue a career in music. Scruggs joined Monroe's band the same year as Flatt, and together they helped to forge musical elements of hillbilly music and blues into a fast-paced, virtuoso-oriented string-band music called bluegrass—"folk music with overdrive," as folklorist Alan Lomax famously described it. In 1948, Flatt and Scruggs left Monroe's Blue Grass Boys and soon formed their own band, the Foggy Mountain Boys, which performed on the *Grand Ole Opry* from 1955 until the group disbanded in 1969. More than any other musical act of their generation, Flatt and Scruggs brought bluegrass to a national audience as a result of their "crossover" appeal during the urban folk music revival. For example, their 1962 recording of "The Ballad of Jed Clampett," which served as the theme song for the long-running CBS television sitcom *The Beverly Hillbillies* (1962–70), and their soundtrack for the Academy Award–winning 1967 film *Bonnie and Clyde* introduced bluegrass music to millions of Americans who had never considered themselves country music fans. With the Blue Grass Boys and later with the Foggy Mountain Boys, Earl Scruggs in particular popularized a highly influential style of three-finger banjo picking that bears his name, a lineal descendant of the "classic" banjo-inflected style that Charlie Poole himself had showcased on commercial hillbilly recordings with the North Carolina Ramblers between 1925 and 1930.[6] Other former Piedmont textile workers (or children of textile workers) who rose to regional and, in some cases, national prominence in the postwar American music industry include Claude Casey, Roy "Whitey" Grant, and Arval Hogan of the Briarhoppers; Arthur "Guitar Boogie" Smith; Jerry Reed; and several members of the Marshall Tucker Band.[7] During the 1940s and 1950s, musicians and stringbands with roots in the textile mills remained at the forefront of the Southern Piedmont's commercial music industry, but these musicians and bands did not dominate country music nationally in the same way their predecessors had twenty or thirty years earlier.

Today, as the Piedmont textile industry continues to decline and its textile towns reel from the devastating effects of deindustrialization, only rarely do former millworkers, such as singer and songwriter Jimmy Wayne of Kings Mountain, North Carolina, emerge onto the Nashville country music scene.[8] As a result of plant closings, automation, and relocations of companies overseas, U.S. textile mills employ fewer workers now than at any other time since the end of World War II, and opportunities for these workers to break into the music industry are far more restricted than they were for those who performed on radio and records during the 1920s and 1930s. "Padlocked gates and knee-high grass surround many of the textile mills that were the lifeblood of this region for much of this last century," remarked the

Charlotte Observer in 2001. "The scars—like the silent brick smoke-stacks—will remain for some time. Few parts of America are suffering as much from the economic slowdown as the textile belt that runs through the western Carolinas and into northern Georgia. Textile job losses are among the worst since the Great Depression." For more than a century, the textile mill industry dominated the Piedmont South's economy, but by the turn of the new millennium, the industry had been suffering a deep decline for more than three decades. Since the 1970s, as a result of stiffer foreign competition and other forces of globalization, hundreds of the region's mills have closed down, at the cost of several hundred thousand jobs, and many of the bustling textile communities they once supported have become, in the words of historian Timothy P. Minchin, virtual "ghost towns." And, along with the shutdown of the textile mills and the disintegration of mill communities, the vibrant occupational culture that gave rise to hillbilly music in the Southern Piedmont some eighty to ninety years ago has largely vanished. The massive brick hulks of scores of textile mills now sit quiet, boarded up and abandoned, and crippled textile towns face uncertain economic futures, but echoes of the distinctive hillbilly music that Piedmont millhands created on radio and records during the 1920s and 1930s continue to reverberate throughout the United States and, indeed, the world.[9]

APPENDIX A

Directory of Southern Textile Workers Who Made Hillbilly
Recordings, 1923–1942

The following directory contains entries for 128 hillbilly recording artists who emerged out of the southern textile mills. The first two sections list those recording artists who worked, at one point or another, in the region's mills and broadly groups these entries into two geographical divisions: the Piedmont and other regions of the American South. In order to provide a sense of the textile musicians who were active in particular musical scenes, the first section is further divided by state and then by city or town, beginning at the northern tip of the Southern Piedmont in Virginia, and moving southward through the Carolinas to Georgia (Alabama has no entries). Those millhand musicians who worked outside of the Piedmont are included in the second section. In cases of artists such as Charlie Poole and Dorsey Dixon, who worked in several different textile towns, I have assigned them to the community in which they worked the longest or with which they are most closely associated. Within each urban subdivision, artist entries are organized alphabetically. The third section includes entries, arranged alphabetically without respect to region or state, for those hillbilly recording artists who were the spouses, children, or immediate family members of millworkers but who themselves are not known to have worked in textile mills. In all three sections, whenever possible, I have provided the years of the artists' births and deaths in parentheses following the entry headings. Only those recording artists identified as textile workers (or, in the third section, as the spouses, children, or immediate family members of textile workers) in the census, other government documents, and secondary sources are included. This directory, like Doug De-Natale and Glenn Hinson's original one upon which it is based, should by no means be considered comprehensive, and, to quote them, "further documentary research would no doubt reveal that many other recording artists came from a mill-worker background."[1] For a comprehensive discography of these musicians' pre-1943 commercial hillbilly recordings, interested readers should consult Tony Russell's monumental *Country Music Records: A Discography, 1921–1942*, with editorial research by Bob Pinson, assisted by the staff of the Country Music Hall of Fame and Museum (New York: Oxford University Press, 2004).

HILLBILLY RECORDING ARTISTS WHO WORKED
IN PIEDMONT TEXTILE MILLS

VIRGINIA
Danville/Schoolfield/Fieldale Area

 Elvin Bigger (1902–68). Born in Pittsylvania County, Virginia; brother of James Bigger; worked as a looper in a Danville, Virginia, knitting mill; lead guitarist and singer for the Four Virginians, which cut six sides for OKch at a 1927

Winston-Salem, North Carolina, field session; recorded an equal number of sides with Troy Martin for the American Record Corporation in New York in 1936.

James Richard Bigger (1908–?). Born in Pittsylvania County, Virginia; brother of Elvin Bigger; worked at the Danville Knitting Mill in Danville, Virginia, sometimes as a timekeeper; fiddler for the Four Virginians, which recorded six sides for OKeh at a 1927 Winston-Salem, North Carolina, field session.

Claude Casey (1912–99). Born in Enoree, South Carolina; while in his early teens moved with his family to Danville, Virginia, where he worked at the nearby Schoolfield Cotton Mills; lead singer, guitarist, and leader of Claude Casey and His Pine Mountain Boys, which recorded a total of thirty-six sides for the American Record Corporation and RCA-Victor between 1937 and 1941.

Alonzo "Lonnie" Griffith. Native of Virginia; worked as a speeder hand in a Schoolfield, Virginia, textile mill; guitarist and singer for the Blue Ridge Highballers, which recorded seventeen sides for Columbia and Paramount between 1926 and 1927; also accompanied Luther B. Clarke on three sides for Columbia in 1926.

Crockett Kelly Harrell (1889–1942). Born near Pulaski, in Wythe County, Virginia; worked in a Fries, Virginia, cotton mill in his youth; in 1926, moved to Fieldale, Virginia, where he worked as a loom fixer at the Fieldcrest Mills until his death on the job from a heart attack in 1942; as a singer, recorded a total of forty-six sides, including some with the Virginia String Band, for Victor and OKeh between 1925 and 1929.

Raymond D. Hundley (1897–?). Worked in a Fieldale, Virginia, textile mill; played banjo on thirteen sides with Kelly Harrell and His Virginia String Band for Victor in 1927.

Leonard Jennings. Worked in various Danville, Virginia, textile mills; played the tiple on six sides with the Four Virginians at a 1927 OKeh field session in Winston-Salem, North Carolina.

Charley Washington LaPrade (1888–1958). Born in Franklin County, Virginia; moved to Spray, North Carolina, in 1900, where he worked in local textile mills; around 1917 settled in Pittsylvania County, Virginia; worked as a weaver and machinist in Danville and Schoolfield textile mills; leader and fiddler of the Blue Ridge Highballers, which recorded seventeen sides for Columbia and Paramount between 1926 and 1927; also accompanied Luther B. Clarke on three sides for Columbia in 1926.

Lewis C. McDaniel (1907–98). Born in Floyd County, Virginia; worked in textile mills in Danville and Schoolfield, Virginia; in 1930, waxed nine solo sides as a guitarist and singer for the American Record Corporation and six duets with Walter "Kid" Smith for Victor; also recorded with several other groups, including the Carolina Buddies, the Dixie Ramblers, the Hawaiian Pals, and possibly Patt Patterson and His Champion Rep Riders, between 1930 and 1931.

Lee Nolen (ca. 1903–?). Originally from Stuart, Virginia; worked in a Fieldale, Virginia, textile mill, along with his brother Dick; guitarist for Red Patterson's Piedmont Log Rollers, which recorded eight sides at a 1927 Victor field session in Charlotte, North Carolina.

Richard T. "Dick" Nolen (ca. 1907–ca. 1982). Originally from Stuart, Virginia; worked in a Fieldale, Virginia, textile mill, along with his brother Lee; tenor banjo player for Red Patterson's Piedmont Log Rollers, which recorded eight sides at a 1927 Victor field session in Charlotte, North Carolina.

John Fletcher "Red" Patterson (ca. 1900–1969). Born near Leaksville, North Carolina; around 1914 moved with his family to Leaksville to work in the textile mills; later, in the mid-1920s, settled in Fieldale, Virginia, where he continued to work as a weaver in the mills; banjo player, singer, and leader of Red Patterson's Piedmont Log Rollers, which recorded eight sides at a 1927 Victor field session in Charlotte, North Carolina.

Fred Richards. Worked in various Danville, Virginia, textile mills; guitarist for the Four Virginians, which cut six sides at a 1927 OKeh field session in Winston-Salem, North Carolina; also recorded a total of nine (largely unissued) solo sides for various labels between 1929 and 1933.

Jesse T. Shelor (1894–1985). Born near Meadows of the Dan, Virginia; worked in his youth, along with his brother Pyrhus, in the textile mills in Danville, Virginia, and Spray, North Carolina; fiddler for the Shelor Family (alternately billed as Dad Blackard's Moonshiners), which recorded five sides at Victor's historic 1927 Bristol, Tennessee, field session.

Pyrhus Davis Shelor (ca. 1888–1933). Born near Meadows of the Dan, Virginia; worked in his youth, along with his brother Jesse, in the textile mills in Danville, Virginia, and Spray, North Carolina; fiddler for the Shelor Family (alternately billed as Dad Blackard's Moonshiners), which recorded five sides at Victor's historic 1927 Bristol, Tennessee, field session.

Alfred Steagall. Worked in a Fieldale, Virginia, textile mill; played guitar on nineteen sides with Kelly Harrell and His Virginia String Band for Victor between 1927 and 1929.

John Thomasson. Worked as a weaver in a Schoolfield, Virginia, textile mill; fiddler for the Blue Ridge Highballers at the band's 1927 Paramount session in New York.

NORTH CAROLINA

Leaksville/Spray/Draper Area

Lonnie William Austin (1905–97). Born in Leaksville, North Carolina; worked in Leaksville-area textile mills and as a youth learned the violin in music classes sponsored by the Carolina Cotton and Woolen Mills Company; served as an assistant to the firm's musical director and, later, as an instructor in these same music classes; appeared on thirty sides between 1928 and 1929 as the fiddler for Charlie Poole and the North Carolina Ramblers; also recorded between 1927 and 1938 as a fiddler and, occasionally, a pianist with several other groups, including Kelly Harrell and His Virginia String Band, the Four Pickled Peppers, the Weaver Brothers, and H. M. Barnes and His Blue Ridge Ramblers, a vaudeville band with which he toured on the Loew's Theater circuit between 1928 and 1930.

Esmond Harris (1907–93). Native of Virginia and son of a textile worker; worked as a weaver in a Leaksville, North Carolina, textile mill; guitarist for the Four Pickled Peppers, which recorded twenty sides for RCA-Victor between 1938 and 1939.

Dallas Hubbard (ca. 1907–?). Native of North Carolina and son of a textile mill foreman; worked as a weaver in a Leaksville, North Carolina, textile mill; singer and bones player for the Four Pickled Peppers, which recorded twenty sides for RCA-Victor between 1938 and 1939.

Hamon Newman (ca. 1882–?). Native of North Carolina; worked in textile mills in Leaksville and Spray, North Carolina; around 1900 played in a mill-sponsored Leaksville community band; tenor banjo player for the Four Pickled Peppers, which recorded twenty sides for RCA-Victor between 1938 and 1939.

Charles Cleveland "Charlie" Poole (1892–1931). Born in Randolph County, North Carolina, where his parents worked in local textile mills; grew up in adjacent Alamance County and went to work as a doffer at the age of twelve at the Granite Mill in Haw River; worked sporadically in textile mills in the Greensboro area before moving to Spray, North Carolina, around 1919; lead singer, banjo player, and leader of Charlie Poole and the North Carolina Ramblers, which recorded eighty-three sides for Columbia, Brunswick, and Paramount between 1925 and 1930.

Posey Rorer (1891–1936). Born in Franklin County, Virginia; around 1920 moved to Spray, North Carolina, where he went to work at the Nantucket Mill and became the fiddler in his brother-in-law Charlie Poole's stringband, the North Carolina Ramblers; performed on twenty-nine sides with Charlie Poole and the North Carolina Ramblers between 1925 and 1927; also recorded more than 120 additional sides between 1926 and 1931 with such acts as Posey Rorer and the North Carolina Ramblers, Roy Harvey, the Carolina Buddies, the Dixie Ramblers, Kelly Harrell, Walter "Kid" Smith, Norman Woodlieff, and Buster Carter and Preston Young.

Francis Odell Smith (1908–59). Born near Germantown, in Stokes County, North Carolina; worked with his father, a loom fixer, and a brother, a weaver, in Spray, North Carolina, textile mills; later worked at various mills in High Point, North Carolina; played the fiddle on twenty-eight sides with Charlie Poole and the North Carolina Ramblers between 1929 and 1930; also recorded with the Carolina Buddies, Kid Smith and His Family, and the Virginia Dandies between 1930 and 1931.

Walter "Kid" Smith (1895–1977). Born in Carroll County, Virginia; worked in Spray, North Carolina, textile mills, before becoming a professional musician in the 1930s; lead singer and leader of Kid Smith and His Family, which waxed fourteen sides for the American Record Corporation between 1931 and 1936; also recorded with Norman Woodlieff, Buster Carter, Lewis McDaniels, the Carolina Buddies, and the Virginia Dandies between 1929 and 1931.

Norman Woodlieff (1901–85). Born near Rural Hall, North Carolina; in 1910 moved with his family to Spray, North Carolina, to work in the textile mills; guitarist for Charlie Poole and the North Carolina Ramblers, with whom he waxed four sides at the band's 1925 debut recording session in New York for Columbia; also later recorded under his own name and with Walter "Kid" Smith, the Carolina Buddies, the Virginia Dandies, and the Four Pickled Peppers between 1929 and 1939.

Durham/Greensboro/Burlington Area

Jay Hugh Hall (1910–74). Raised near Waynesville, in Haywood County, North Carolina; brother of Roy Hall; worked in various textile mills in the central Carolina Piedmont before pursuing a career as a professional musician around 1937; singer and guitarist for the Hall Brothers, a duo that waxed twenty-four sides for RCA-Victor between 1937 and 1938; also recorded a total of more than forty-five sides with Steve Ledford and the Mountaineers, J. E. Mainer's Mountaineers, the Happy-Go-Lucky Boys, and Wade Mainer and the Sons of the Mountaineers between 1938 and 1941.

Roy Davis Hall (1907–43). Raised near Waynesville, in Haywood County, North Carolina; brother of Jay Hall; worked as a weaver in textile mills in Burlington, Marion, and various other towns in the central Carolina Piedmont before embarking on a career as a professional musician around 1937; singer, guitarist, and leader of Roy Hall and His Blue Ridge Entertainers, which made thirty-eight sides for Vocalion and RCA-Victor between 1938 and 1941; also recorded twenty-four sides for RCA-Victor with his millhand brother, Jay Hugh, as the Hall Brothers between 1937 and 1938.

Samuel Lee "Sam" Pridgen (1910–89). Born in Henderson, North Carolina, son of a machinist who worked in textile mills in Henderson and later in Durham; worked in Durham textile mills before becoming a professional musician; recorded nearly forty sides for RCA-Victor as a guitarist, bass player, and singer for the Tobacco Tags and the Swing Billies between 1937 and 1941.

Boonville Area

Earl Rufus Nance (1894–1954). Native of Surry County, North Carolina; lived near Boonville, in Yadkin County, North Carolina; supplemented his income as a shape-note singing teacher and leader of a family singing group by working in local textile mills during the Great Depression; bass singer and leader of the Nance Family/Nance Singers, which recorded forty (mostly unissued) sides, chiefly for the American Record Corporation and Gennett, between 1930 and 1931.

Lexington Area

Robert Dewey Cooper (1899–1951). Son and grandson of textile workers; worked in textile mills in the Lexington, North Carolina, area; fiddler and lead singer for the North Carolina Cooper Boys, which included his cousin Tom Cooper; recorded six sides with this band for OKeh in Winston-Salem, North Carolina, in 1927 and another four sides for Columbia in Atlanta in 1931.

Thomas Franklin "Tom" Cooper (1894–1983). Born in Randolph County, North Carolina, son and grandson of textile workers; worked as a weaver at White

Oak Cotton Mills in Greensboro and later at Winona Cotton Mill in Lexington, North Carolina; guitarist and tenor singer for the North Carolina Cooper Boys, which included his cousin Dewey Cooper; recorded six sides with the band for OKeh at a 1927 Winston-Salem, North Carolina, field session and another four sides for Columbia at a 1931 Atlanta field session.

Hickory Area

Julius Plato "Nish" McClured (1897–1949). Born in Cleveland County, North Carolina; later settled in nearby Catawaba County, North Carolina; was working in a Newton, North Carolina, textile mill when he formed the Hickory Nuts; recorded six sides for OKeh at a 1927 Winston-Salem, North Carolina, field session as the banjo player and singer for the Hickory Nuts.

Horace Propst (ca. 1902–28). Born in Cleveland County, North Carolina; worked in textile mills in Burke County and, later, Catawaba County, North Carolina; guitarist and singer for the Hickory Nuts, which recorded six sides for OKeh at a 1927 Winston-Salem, North Carolina, field session.

Homer Lee "Pappy" Sherrill (1915–2001). Born in Sherrill's Ford, North Carolina, near Hickory; worked for a period in a Hickory hosiery mill between his radio and recording work; fiddler for the Blue Ridge Hill Billies (Homer, Shorty, and Mac), which waxed eight sides for RCA-Victor at a 1936 Charlotte, North Carolina, field session; also recorded thirty-three additional sides for RCA-Victor between 1936 and 1941 as a member of several other Carolina Piedmont stringbands, including Wiley, Zeke, and Homer (The Smilin' Rangers) and Byron Parker and His Mountaineers.

Charlotte/Concord Area

Lester "Pete" Bivins (1903–ca. 1978). Born near Shelby, North Carolina; worked in textile mills in the Charlotte, North Carolina, area for much of his adult life; as a singer and guitarist, cut fourteen solo sides, including "Cotton Mill Blues," for RCA-Victor and Decca at Charlotte field sessions between 1937 and 1938.

"Daddy John Love." Worked in a Concord, North Carolina, textile mill; singer and guitarist who made eighteen sides, either solo or with the Hilliard Brothers, for RCA-Victor between 1935 and 1936, including "Cotton Mill Blues"; also recorded as a member of J. E. Mainer's Mountaineers and the Dixie Reelers during this same period.

Joseph Emmett "J. E." Mainer (1898–1971). Born near Weaverville, in Buncombe County, North Carolina; moved in 1909 with his family to Union, South Carolina, where he went to work as a doffer at a local textile mill; worked in mills in Knoxville, Tennessee, and Glendale, South Carolina, before settling in Concord, North Carolina, in 1922; worked there at the Gibson Cotton Mill before embarking on a career as a professional musician around 1934; fiddler, singer, and leader of J. E. Mainer's Mountaineers, which recorded sixty-one sides for RCA-Victor between 1935 and 1939.

Wade Mainer (1907–). Born near Weaverville, in Buncombe County, North Carolina; worked at the Glendale Cotton Mill in Glendale, South Carolina, before settling in Concord, North Carolina, in 1923; worked in the card room at the local Gibson Cotton Mill before pursuing a career as a professional musician with his brother J. E. Mainer's stringband around 1934; singer, banjo player, and leader of Wade Mainer and the Sons of the Mountaineers and of Wade Mainer and His Little Smilin' Rangers; recorded more than one hundred sides, either with his stringbands or with Zeke Morris, for RCA-Victor between 1936 and 1941; also recorded between 1935 and 1939 with J. E. Mainer's Mountaineers and Steve Ledford and the Mountaineers.

Claude "Zeke" Morris (1916–99). Born in Old Fort, North Carolina, but moved to Concord, North Carolina, in 1933; worked in textile mills in Concord and later in nearby Gastonia; guitarist, mandolin player, harmony singer, and member of the duo, the Morris Brothers (Wiley and Zeke), which waxed thirty-six sides for RCA-Victor between 1938 and 1939; also recorded more than eighty additional sides with other stringbands, including J. E. Mainer's Mountaineers, Wade Mainer and His Little Smilin' Rangers, and Charlie Monroe's Boys, between 1935 and 1939.

Gastonia/Belmont/Shelby Area

Henry Luther "Luke" Baucom (1902–67). Born in McDowell County, North Carolina; worked as a twister in a Gastonia, North Carolina, textile mill; mandolin player and lead singer for the Three Tobacco Tags, with whom he cut more than ninety sides, chiefly for RCA-Victor, between 1931 and 1941.

Harvey L. Ellington (1910–97). Born in Warren County, North Carolina; worked in a Gaston County, North Carolina, textile mill; recorded a total of fifty-two sides for RCA-Victor between 1937 and 1941 as the fiddler for the Swing Billies and the Tobacco Tags.

David O. Fletcher (ca. 1901–?). Worked as a comber in a Belmont, North Carolina, textile mill; recorded twenty-two sides as a guitarist and singer with fellow millhand Gwin S. Foster, under the billing Fletcher and Foster or the Carolina Twins, chiefly for Victor, between 1928 and 1930.

Gwin Stanley Foster (1903–54). Born in Caldwell County, North Carolina; moved around 1909 with his family to Dallas, North Carolina; his father, a section hand, and several of his siblings worked in Gaston County textile mills; worked as a doffer in Gastonia and other Gaston County mills; singer, guitarist, and harmonica player for the Carolina Tar Heels, with whom he made fourteen sides for Victor between 1927 and 1932; also recorded sixty-five sides, either solo or with Clarence Ashley, the Blue Ridge Mountain Entertainers, or the Carolina Twins, between 1928 and 1939.

Charles Freshour (1900–1959). Born in Newport, Tennessee; settled in Gaston County, North Carolina, around 1920 after his military discharge; worked at the Climax Mill in Belmont; guitarist for Wilmer Watts and the Lonely Eagles, which waxed sixteen sides, including "Cotton Mill Blues," for Paramount at a 1929 New York recording session; also recorded with the duo Wilmer Watts and Frank Wilson for Paramount in 1927.

Roy "Whitey" Grant (1916–). Born in Shelby and grew up in Rutherfordton, North Carolina; settled in Gastonia, North Carolina, in 1935; worked at the local Firestone Cotton Mills, where he met his musical partner Arval

Hogan; lead singer and guitarist of the duo Whitey and Hogan, which recorded sixteen sides for Decca in 1939.

Shannon Howard Grayson (1916–93). Born in Cleveland County, North Carolina,
son of a textile worker family; worked as a doffer in a Shelby, North Carolina, textile mill; recorded as a mandolin player and guitarist with several of
the Carlisle brothers' groups at Charlotte field sessions between 1936 and
1940, including Milton and Marion Carlisle, Bill Carlisle's Kentucky Boys,
Cliff Carlisle's Buckle Busters, and the Carlisle Brothers (Cliff and Bill).

Arval Hogan (1911–2003). Born in Robbinsville and raised in Andrews, North
Carolina; moved to Gastonia, North Carolina, around 1935; employed at
the local Firestone Cotton Mills, where he met his musical partner Roy
"Whitey" Grant; mandolin player and tenor singer of the duo Whitey and
Hogan, which recorded sixteen sides for Decca in 1939.

Howard Long (ca. 1906–ca. 1975). Native of western North Carolina; employed
at the Winget Yarn Mill in Gastonia, North Carolina, where he worked with
Dave McCarn; recorded four sides, supplying harmony vocals and, on one,
kazoo, with McCarn, as Dave and Howard, at a 1931 RCA-Victor field session in nearby Charlotte; one of the recordings was McCarn's composition,
"Serves 'Em Fine (Cotton Mill Colic No. 3)."

John David "Dave" McCarn (1905–64). Born in McAdenville, North Carolina, son
of textile worker parents; began working as a doffer at the age of twelve
at the Chronicle Mill in nearby Belmont; later worked at a succession of
textile mills in Gastonia, North Carolina; waxed eight solo sides, accompanying himself on guitar and sometimes harmonica, for RCA-Victor, between 1930 and 1931; also recorded four sides with fellow Gastonia millhand Howard Long, as Dave and Howard, at a 1931 RCA-Victor field session
in Charlotte; his recordings include three original compositions he wrote
about Piedmont textile mill life: "Cotton Mill Colic" and the sequels "Poor
Man, Rich Man (Cotton Mill Colic No. 2)" and "Serves 'Em Fine (Cotton
Mill Colic No. 3)."

Palmer Rhyne (1903–67). Worked in a Gastonia, North Carolina, textile mill;
steel guitarist for Wilmer Watts and the Lonely Eagles, which made sixteen
sides, including "Cotton Mill Blues," for Paramount at a 1929 New York
recording session.

Edgar Reid Summey (1903–?). Born in Gaston County, North Carolina, son of a
textile mill superintendent; worked as a doffer in local mills beginning in
his teens; guitarist, steel guitarist, and tenor singer for the Three Tobacco
Tags, with whom he recorded more than ninety sides, chiefly for RCA-
Victor, between 1931 and 1941.

George Wade (ca. 1905–?). Native of North Carolina; worked in a Gastonia, North
Carolina, textile mill; played the mandolin and sang on more than fifty
sides with the Three Tobacco Tags between 1931 and 1938; also recorded
two vocal duets with Francum Braswell for Columbia in 1929 and ten sides
as the leader of George Wade and the Caro-Ginians for RCA-Victor in 1938.

Wilmer Wesley Watts (1892–1943). Born in Mount Tabor, in Columbus County, North Carolina; settled in Gaston County, North Carolina, around 1919; worked as a loom fixer in textile mills in Belmont, Gastonia, and, later, Bessemer City and Hickory, North Carolina; banjo player and leader of Wilmer Watts and the Lonely Eagles, a textile stringband that made sixteen sides for Paramount at a 1929 New York session, including "Cotton Mill Blues"; also recorded eight duets with fellow Belmont millhand Frank Wilson, under the billing Watts and Wilson, for the same label in 1927.

Percy Alphonso "Frank" Wilson (1900–?). Born in Chinquapin, in Rockingham County, North Carolina; worked in textile mills in Alamance County and several other locations before taking a job at the Climax Mill in Belmont, North Carolina, where he met Wilmer Watts, with whom he made eight duets for Paramount in 1927 under the billing Watts and Wilson; Hawaiian guitarist and leader of Frank Wilson and His Blue Ridge Duo, which cut two sides for Columbia in 1929; also recorded between 1928 and 1929 with H. M. Barnes and His Blue Ridge Ramblers, Charlie Bowman and His Brothers, Al Hopkins and His Buckle Busters, and Jack Reedy and His Walker Mountain String Band.

Rockingham Area

Beatrice Lucele (née Moody) Dixon (ca. 1912–?). Born in South Carolina, where she worked in a Greenville textile mill, before marrying weaver Dorsey M. Dixon in 1927; made twelve duets with her husband for RCA-Victor at Charlotte field sessions in 1937 and 1938; also accompanied her husband and his brother Howard as a vocalist on two of the Dixon Brothers' recordings.

Dorsey Murdock Dixon (1897–1968). Born in Darlington, South Carolina; began working as a spinner at the age of twelve at the local Darlington Manufacturing Company; worked as a weaver in textile mills in Darlington, Lancaster, and Greenville, South Carolina, before settling, in 1925, in East Rockingham, North Carolina, where he worked as a weaver at Hannah Pickett Mill No. 2; later worked at mills in South Carolina and New Jersey, before retiring from the Aleo Mill in East Rockingham in 1953; guitarist and lead singer of the duo, the Dixon Brothers, which recorded fifty-five sides for RCA-Victor between 1936 and 1938; also waxed twelve duets with his wife, Beatrice; he composed or arranged seven songs about his experiences as a textile millhand, the most famous of which are "Babies in the Mill," "Spinning Room Blues," and "Weave Room Blues."

Howard Briten Dixon (1903–61). Born in Kelley Town, Darlington County, South Carolina; worked at the local Darlington Manufacturing Company before settling in East Rockingham, North Carolina, in 1925; worked there as a cloth room hand at the Hannah Pickett Mill No. 2 and then as a cloth room fixer at the Entwistle (later Aleo) Mill for much of his adult life; suffered a heart attack on the job in 1961 and died shortly after reaching the hospital; tenor singer and steel guitarist for the Dixon Brothers, which made fifty-five recordings for RCA-Victor between 1936 and 1938, including "Spinning

Room Blues," "Weave Room Blues," and "Weaver's Life"; also recorded twenty-four sides with fellow East Rockingham millhand Frank Gerald as the Rambling Duet for RCA-Victor during this period.

"Mutt" Evans. Worked in East Rockingham, North Carolina, textile mills, where he met fellow millhands Dorsey and Howard Dixon; occasionally recorded as a singer and guitarist with both the Dixon Brothers and the Rambling Duet between 1936 and 1938.

Frank Gerald. Worked in East Rockingham, North Carolina, textile mills, where he met his musical partner, Howard Dixon; singer and guitarist for the Rambling Duet, which waxed twenty-four sides for RCA-Victor between 1937 and 1938.

Johnnie James Rimbert "Jimmie" Tarlton (1892–1979). Born near Cheraw, in Chesterfield County, South Carolina; worked in textile mills in Texas and the Carolinas, including a stint between 1930 and 1932 at the Hannah Pickett Mill in East Rockingham, North Carolina; steel guitarist and tenor singer for the duo Darby and Tarlton, which waxed sixty-six sides, chiefly for Columbia, between 1927 and 1933; also recorded a total of thirteen solo sides for RCA-Victor and Columbia between 1930 and 1932, including "The Weaver's Blues" (a version of "Weaver's Life"), which he had learned first-hand from its composer, Dorsey Dixon.

SOUTH CAROLINA

Kershaw Area

Arthur "Guitar Boogie" Smith (1921–). Born in Clinton and grew up in Kershaw, South Carolina; son of a weaver and loom fixer at the local Springs Mills plant, who also directed the mill's brass band; began working in the card room at Springs Mills before the age of twelve; fiddler, mandolin player, singer, and leader of Smith's Carolina Crackerjacks, which recorded a total of four sides for RCA-Victor at a 1938 Rock Hill, South Carolina, field session.

Whitmire Area

Carl A. Boling (1912–92). Native of South Carolina; his father worked as a loom fixer in textile mills in Union and Whitmire, South Carolina; worked as a blow-off hand in a Whitmire textile mill in his late teens; tenor guitarist, tenor banjoist, harmonica player, and leader of Carl Boling and His Four Aces, which cut a total of twenty-two sides at RCA-Victor field sessions in Rock Hill, South Carolina, in 1939 and in Atlanta in 1940; also recorded eighteen sides as the tenor guitarist for Claude Casey and His Pine State Playboys for RCA-Victor in 1938.

GEORGIA

Gainesville Area

George Elmo Chumbler (1907–56). Native of Georgia and brother of William Archer Chumbler; worked as a doffer at the New Holland Mill, near Gainesville, Georgia; guitarist for the Lee Brothers Trio (and related Chumbler Family groups), with whom he cut at least ten sides for Columbia and

Brunswick between 1929 and 1930, including "Cotton Mill Blues"; also recorded with Jim King and His Brown Mules for Columbia in 1928.

Irene Chumbler (ca. 1913–?). Native of Georgia and probably the niece of George Elmo and William Archer Chumbler; worked as a spinner at the New Holland Mill, near Gainesville, Georgia; sang on four sides with the Chumbler Family at a 1929 Columbia session in Atlanta.

William Archer Chumbler (1902–37). Born in Clermont, Georgia; worked as a doffer and, later, a machinist at the New Holland Mill, near Gainesville, Georgia, along with his brother George Elmo Chumbler; waxed fourteen sides, including "Cotton Mill Blues," as a singer, autoharp player, and mandolin player for the Lee Brothers Trio (and related Chumbler Family groups) for several labels between 1929 and 1930; also recorded between 1928 and 1930 with Jim King and His Brown Mules, John Dilleshaw, and possibly Hoke Rice and His Southern String Band.

Howard Coker (1898–1959). Native of Georgia and son of a textile worker family; was working as a spinner by the age of twelve at a Gainesville, Georgia, textile mill; later worked as a doffer at the New Holland Mill, near Gainesville; recorded in 1929 as the fiddler for Chumbler's Breakdown Gang and possibly for Hoke Rice and His Southern String Band.

James King (ca. 1895–?). Worked as a loom fixer at a Gainesville, Georgia, textile mill; leader of Jim King and His Brown Mules, which cut two unissued sides at a 1928 Columbia field session in Atlanta.

Lester O. Smallwood (1900–1988). Born in Gainesville, Georgia; began working as a sweeper at the age of fourteen at the local New Holland Mills; recorded four solo sides, accompanying himself on banjo and harmonica, at a 1928 Victor field session in Atlanta; one of them was "Cotton Mill Girl."

Henry Thomas. Worked at the New Holland Mill, near Gainesville, Georgia; fiddler for Jim King and His Brown Mules, which waxed two unissued sides for Columbia at a 1928 Atlanta field session; also possibly recorded three sides for QRS with the Davis Trio in 1929.

Rome Area

Hazel Cole. Native of Fannin County, Georgia; worked in a Rome, Georgia, textile mill, where she met her future husband and singing partner, Grady Cole; also later worked in an Atlanta textile mill; recorded twelve sides as part of the vocal duo Grady and Hazel Cole for RCA-Victor between 1939 and 1940.

Henry W. Grady Cole (1909–81). Born in LaFayette, Georgia; worked in a Rome, Georgia, textile mill, where he met his future wife and singing partner, Hazel; recorded twelve sides as part of the vocal duo Grady and Hazel Cole for RCA-Victor between 1939 and 1940.

Frank Locklear (ca. 1907–?). Native of Georgia; worked as a knitter in a Rome, Georgia, hosiery mill; recorded in 1929 as a mandolin player with Dupree's Rome Boys for OKeh, Uncle Bud Landress for Victor, and Shores Southern Trio for Gennett.

Elias S. Meadows (1886–ca. 1938). Native of Georgia; head of the weaving department at Echota Cotton Mill in Calhoun, Georgia; recorded four sides for Victor at a 1927 Atlanta field session as a tenor singer and guitarist for the Georgia Yellow Hammers.

Atlanta Area

Marion A. "Peanut" Brown (1907–2003). Born in Gwinnett County, Georgia; settled, in 1912, with his widowed mother and siblings in Atlanta in the mill neighborhood now known as Cabbagetown; his mother and a sister worked at the Fulton Bag and Cotton Mills; went to work there while still in his teens and later worked in other Atlanta textile mills; recorded for RCA-Victor as a guitarist with Fiddlin' John Carson in 1934 and with Pink Lindsey and His Bluebirds in 1935.

Fiddlin' John Carson (1874–1949). Born in Cobb County, Georgia; moved to Atlanta in 1900, where he worked for the next two decades as a weaver and at various other jobs in several mills, including the Exposition Cotton Mills and the Fulton Bag and Cotton Mills; recorded more than 180 sides, solo, with his daughter, Rosa Lee, or with his stringband, the Virginia Reelers, for OKeh and RCA-Victor between 1923 and 1934.

Belvie Freeman (ca. 1903–46). Native of Georgia; worked as a doffer at the Scott-dale Mills, near Decatur, Georgia; played banjo-mandolin on two sides for OKeh in 1926 as a member of the Scottdale String Band, which took its name from Scottdale Mills.

Marvin Head (?–1961). Native of Georgia; worked at the Scottdale Mills, near Decatur, Georgia; recorded thirty-three sides for OKeh and Paramount between 1926 and 1932 as a guitarist for the Scottdale String Band, which took its name from Scottdale Mills.

Ed Kincaid (1897–?). Born near Blue Ridge, in Fannin County, Georgia; moved to Atlanta around 1912; worked at Fulton Bag and Cotton Mills, where he struck up a friendship with Fiddlin' John Carson; probably accompanied Carson on twelve-string guitar as a member of the Virginia Reelers at several OKeh sessions between 1924 and 1930, although personnel for the stringband are not listed on most of firm's studio ledger sheets.

Barney L. Pritchard (?–1965). Worked at the Scottdale Mills, near Decatur, Georgia; recorded thirty-three sides for OKeh and Paramount between 1926 and 1932 as the lead singer and guitarist for the Scottdale String Band, which took its name from Scottdale Mills.

LaGrange Area

Dewey Bassett (1905–72). Native of Randolph County, Alabama, and son of a cloth inspector who worked at a LaGrange, Georgia, textile mill; worked as a doffer in a LaGrange textile mill, as did several of his siblings; recorded twenty vocal duets with his wife, under the billing Dewey and Gassie Bassett, for RCA-Victor between 1938 and 1940.

Buster McClendon (1911–78). Native of Alabama (probably born in Randolph County); worked in a LaGrange, Georgia, textile mill, as did his father and several of his siblings; lead guitarist for the McClendon Brothers with Georgia Dell, which recorded a total of nineteen selections at RCA-Victor field sessions in Charlotte, North Carolina, and Rock Hill, South Carolina, between 1936 and 1938.

Ralph Rupert McClendon (1907–76). Native of Alabama (probably born in Randolph County); husband of Adelle Bassett (who performed under the name Georgia Dell); worked as a weaver in a LaGrange, Georgia, textile mill, along with his father and several of his siblings; fiddler and singer for the McClendon Brothers with Georgia Dell, which recorded a total of nineteen selections at RCA-Victor field sessions in Charlotte, North Carolina, and Rock Hill, South Carolina, between 1936 and 1938.

Thomaston/Manchester Area

William Joseph "Bill" Helms (1902–ca. 1985). Born near Thomaston, Georgia; worked as a loom fixer in local textile mills for much of his adult life before his retirement in 1964; fiddler and leader of Bill Helms and His Upson County Band, which made four recordings for Victor in 1928; also recorded with Riley Puckett for Columbia in 1929 and with the Home Town Boys for Columbia in 1931.

John R. Hogan (ca. 1884–?). Native of Georgia; worked as a machinist in an East Thomaston, Georgia, textile mill; banjo player for Bill Helms and His Upson County Band, which recorded four sides for Victor in 1928.

Ty Cobb Hogan (1910–86). Native of Georgia and son of textile machinist John R. Hogan; worked as a doffer in an East Thomaston, Georgia, textile mill; guitarist for Bill Helms and His Upson County Band, which recorded four sides for Victor in 1928.

Hoke Rice (1909–74). Born near Gainesville, Georgia; worked as a teen with his divorced mother and siblings in textile mills around Manchester and Griffin, Georgia; brother of Paul Rice and stepson of Rufus M. "Bud" Silvey, a textile mechanic, fiddler, and fiddling contest promoter; guitarist, vocalist, and co-leader of the Rice Brothers' Gang, which cut nearly sixty sides for Decca between 1938 and 1941; also recorded for several other labels, either solo or as part of various Atlanta-area groups, between 1927 and 1930.

Paul Rice (1919–88). Born near Gainesville, Georgia; worked as a teen with his divorced mother and siblings in textile mills around Manchester and Griffin, Georgia; brother of Hoke Rice and stepson of Rufus M. "Bud" Silvey, a textile mechanic, fiddler, and fiddling contest promoter; guitarist, vocalist, and co-leader of the Rice Brothers' Gang, which recorded nearly sixty sides for Decca between 1938 and 1941.

HILLBILLY RECORDING ARTISTS WHO WORKED IN TEXTILE MILLS OUTSIDE THE SOUTHERN PIEDMONT

TENNESSEE

Knoxville

Millard Whitehead (ca. 1902–ca. 1966). Born at Halls Crossroads, Tennessee, near Knoxville; worked at the American Clothing Company's mill in Knoxville; guitarist and singer for Ridgel's Fountain Citians, with whom he recorded a total of eight sides for Vocalion at Knoxville field sessions in 1929 and 1930.

Rockwood

> *James "Jimmy" McCarroll* (1892–1985). Born in Roane County, Tennessee; worked as a coal miner, tenant farmer, and, according to Bob Fulcher in his liner notes to *Roane County Ramblers: Complete Recordings, 1928–1929*, "mill worker," presumably a textile millhand; fiddler for the Roane County Ramblers, which recorded sixteen sides for Columbia between 1928 and 1929.

VIRGINIA

Hopewell

> *Hudson W. Armistead* (1903–81). Native of Virginia; worked as a mechanic for the Tubize Artificial Silk Company in Hopewell, Virginia; singer for the Tubize Royal Hawaiian Orchestra, a company-sponsored band, which recorded six issued sides for OKeh in 1929.
>
> *Elbert Andrew Coley* (1903–66). Born near Faison, Duplin County, North Carolina; moved to Hopewell, Virginia, in 1924 to work for the Tubize Artificial Silk Company, where his brother Robert Hinton Coley also worked; musical director and Hawaiian steel guitarist for the Tubize Royal Hawaiian Orchestra, a company-sponsored band, which recorded six issued sides for OKeh in 1929.
>
> *Robert Hinton Coley* (ca. 1906–ca. 1990). Employed, along with his brother Elbert Andrew Coley, at the Tubize Artificial Silk Company plant, in Hopewell, Virginia; singer and guitarist for the Tubize Royal Hawaiian Orchestra, a company-sponsored band, which recorded six issued sides for OKeh in 1929.
>
> *Howard N. Webb* (ca. 1908–?). Native of Virginia; worked as a reeler at the Tubize Artificial Silk Company plant, in Hopewell, Virginia; ukulele player for the Tubize Royal Hawaiian Orchestra, a company-sponsored band, which recorded six issued sides for OKeh in 1929.

Roanoke

> *Ray Barger* (1900–1984). Employed at the American Viscose Company rayon mill, near Vinton, Virginia; guitarist for the Roanoke Jug Band, all of whose members except one worked at the plant; recorded four sides with the band at a 1929 OKeh field session in Richmond, Virginia.
>
> *Walter E. Keith* (ca. 1897–ca. 1947). Native of Virginia; worked as a foreman at the American Viscose Company rayon mill, near Vinton, Virginia; banjo player for the Roanoke Jug Band, all of whose members except one worked at the plant; recorded four sides with the band at a 1929 OKeh field session in Richmond, Virginia.
>
> *Richard Mitchell* (1907–ca. 1985). Native of Virginia; employed at the American Viscose Company rayon mill, near Vinton, Virginia, mandolin player for the Roanoke Jug Band, all of whose members except one worked at the plant; recorded four sides with the band at a 1929 OKeh field session in Richmond, Virginia.

Mahlon B. Overstreet (1905–92). Native of Virginia; worked at the American Viscose Company rayon mill, near Vinton, Virginia; guitarist for the Roanoke Jug Band, all of whose members except one worked at the plant; recorded four sides with the band at a 1929 OKeh field session in Richmond, Virginia.

Fries/Galax

Ernest V. Stoneman (1893–1968). Born near Galax, Virginia; worked in a Fries, Virginia, cotton mill with future recording artist Henry Whitter; singer, guitarist, and harmonica and autoharp player; one of the most prolific hillbilly recording artists of the pre-Depression era; recorded more than 230 sides, solo, as part of a duo, or with his stringband, the Dixie Mountaineers (also sometimes billed as the Blue Ridge Corn Shuckers), between 1924 and 1934; also recorded with Frank Jenkins's Pilot Mountaineers, the Sweet Brothers, and Fields Ward and the Grayson County Railsplitters between 1928 and 1929.

Benjamin Wade Ward (1892–1971). Born in Independence, Virginia; worked in Grayson County, Virginia, textile mills; banjo player and leader of the Buck Mountain Band, which waxed four sides for OKeh at a 1929 Richmond, Virginia, field session; also recorded four solo sides (all unissued) for the same label at a 1925 Asheville, North Carolina, field session.

Henry Whitter (1892–1941). Born near Fries, Virginia; after completing sixth grade, took a job as a doffer at Washington Mill in Fries and later worked in other local textile mills before becoming a professional musician in the mid-1920s; as a singer, guitarist, and harmonica player, recorded nearly 140 sides, chiefly for OKeh and Victor, between 1923 and 1930, including a series of acclaimed sides with the blind fiddler G. B. Grayson.

HILLBILLY RECORDING ARTISTS WHOSE IMMEDIATE FAMILY MEMBERS WORKED IN SOUTHERN TEXTILE MILLS

Gassie Y. (née Whitley) Bassett (1908–89). Native of Randolph County, Alabama, and wife of Dewey Bassett, who worked as a doffer in a LaGrange, Georgia, textile mill; recorded twenty vocal duets with her husband, under the billing Dewey and Gassie Bassett, for RCA-Victor between 1938 and 1940.

Jesse R. Bassett (1919–92). Native of Alabama and son of a cloth inspector who worked in a LaGrange, Georgia, textile mill; several of Jesse's siblings, including his older brother, Dewey, worked as doffers and spinners in LaGrange textile mills, and, although it appears likely that he did as well, this has not been confirmed; played lead guitar on several sides with his brother and sister-in-law, who recorded as the husband-and-wife team Dewey and Gassie Bassett for RCA-Victor between 1938 and 1940; also probably appeared as a guitarist and singer on several sides with his brother-in-law and sister in the group called the McClendon Brothers with Georgia Dell, which recorded nineteen selections for RCA-Victor between 1936 and 1938.

Earl A. Bolick (1919–98). Born in Hickory, North Carolina, son of textile worker parents; lead vocalist and guitarist for the brother duo, the Blue Sky Boys, which recorded ninety sides for RCA-Victor between 1936 and 1940.

William A. "Bill" Bolick (1917–2008). Born in Hickory, North Carolina, son of textile worker parents; tenor vocalist and mandolin player for the brother duo, the Blue Sky Boys, which recorded ninety sides for RCA-Victor between 1936 and 1940.

Ernest Boling (1916–?). Native of South Carolina; his father and brother Carl, with whom he recorded, worked at a Whitmire, South Carolina, textile mill, and although no conclusive evidence has surfaced, he also probably worked there; sang on a total of six sides with Carl Boling and His Four Aces at two RCA-Victor field sessions, the first in Rock Hill, South Carolina, in 1939, and the second in Atlanta, in 1940.

Lawrence Boling (1910–86). Native of South Carolina; his father and brother Carl, with whom he recorded, worked in a Whitmire, South Carolina, textile mill, and although no conclusive evidence has surfaced, he also probably worked there; guitarist for Carl Boling and His Four Aces, with whom he cut twelve sides at an RCA-Victor field session in Atlanta in 1940; also recorded eighteen sides as the guitarist for Claude Casey and His Pine State Playboys for RCA-Victor in 1938.

T. M. "Bully" Brewer (1885–?). Born in Knoxville, Tennessee; in 1917, moved to Atlanta, where his wife worked as a designer at Fulton Bag and Cotton Mills; guitarist, banjo player, and second fiddler for Fiddlin' John Carson and His Virginia Reelers, with whom he recorded at least forty-two sides for OKeh between 1925 and 1929.

Rosa Lee "Moonshine Kate" Carson (1909–92). Born in Atlanta, the youngest child of Fiddlin' John Carson, who worked in several local textile mills before 1920; waxed sixteen sides as a singer, guitarist, and banjo player, under her own name (or billed as Moonshine Kate), for OKeh between 1925 and 1931; also appeared on more than one hundred sides with her father and his band, the Virginia Reelers, for OKeh and RCA-Victor between 1925 and 1934.

Sarah E. Casey (1916–90). Sister of Claude Casey, who worked in Danville, Virginia, textile mills; recorded one unissued vocal duet with her brother, under the billing Claude and Sara [*sic*] Casey, for the American Record Corporation at a 1937 New York session.

Laura (née Sosbee) Chumbler (1903–88). Wife of textile doffer George Elmo Chumbler, who worked at the New Holland Mill, near Gainesville, Georgia; sang on five sides with the Chumbler Family at a 1929 Columbia field session in Atlanta.

Julia "Princess" (née Brown) Mainer. Wife of Wade Mainer, who worked in textile mills in Glendale, South Carolina, and Concord, North Carolina; before her marriage, performed as a radio singer on WSJS in Winston-Salem, North Carolina, under the name Hillbilly Lilly; recorded two sides as a vocalist with Wade Mainer and the Sons of the Mountaineers for RCA-Victor at a 1938 Charlotte, North Carolina, field session.

Adelle (née Bassett) McClendon (1909–2001). Wife of Rupert McClendon and sister of Dewey and Jesse Bassett; native of Alabama (probably born in Randolph County) and daughter of a cloth inspector who worked in a LaGrange, Georgia, textile mill; her husband and several of her siblings worked as doffers and spinners in LaGrange textile mills, and, although it appears likely that she did as well, this has not been confirmed; singer for the McClendon Brothers with Georgia Dell (her recording name), which recorded a total of nineteen selections at RCA-Victor field sessions in Charlotte, North Carolina, and Rock Hill, South Carolina, between 1936 and 1938.

Charles E. Nabell (1887–1970). Native of Atlanta and son of a German immigrant father, who sometimes worked in local textile mills; Nabell's blindness prevented him from working in Atlanta cotton mills, but at least four of his siblings were at one time employed as weavers, carders, or sweepers; as a singer and guitarist, recorded eighteen issued sides for OKeh at St. Louis field sessions between 1924 and 1925.

Helen Nance (ca. 1915–?). Daughter of Earl R. Nance, a shape-note singing teacher and leader of a family singing group, who supplemented his income during the 1930s by working in textile mills around Yadkin County, North Carolina; alto singer for the Nance Family/Nance Singers, which recorded forty (mostly unissued) sides, chiefly for the American Record Corporation and Gennett, between 1930 and 1931.

Maddie Nance (ca. 1889–?). Wife of Earl R. Nance, a shape-note singing teacher and leader of a family singing group, who supplemented his income during the 1930s by working in textile mills around Yadkin County, North Carolina; soprano singer for the Nance Family/Nance Singers, which recorded forty (mostly unissued) sides, chiefly for the American Record Corporation and Gennett, between 1930 and 1931.

James Clay "Charlie Poole Jr." Poole (1912–68). Native of North Carolina and son of textile worker parents; his father, the hillbilly recording artist Charlie Poole, worked in textile mills in Haw River, Greensboro, and Spray, North Carolina; lead vocalist and leader of the WPTF-Raleigh radio band, the Swing Billies, which recorded ten sides for RCA-Victor at a 1937 Charlotte, North Carolina, field session.

Dorothy Smith. Daughter of Walter "Kid" Smith, who worked in Spray, North Carolina, textile mills; sang and played the ukulele on a total of fourteen sides with Kid Smith and His Family, which recorded for RCA-Victor in 1931 and for the American Record Corporation in 1936.

Ralph Smith (ca. 1923–?). Brother of Arthur Smith, with whom he recorded, and son of a weaver and loom fixer at Springs Mills in Kershaw, South Carolina, who directed the mill's brass band; banjo player and singer for Smith's Carolina Crackerjacks, which recorded a total of four sides for RCA-Victor at a Rock Hill, South Carolina, field session in 1938.

Sonny Smith. Brother of Arthur Smith, with whom he recorded, and son of a weaver and loom fixer at Springs Mills in Kershaw, South Carolina, who directed the mill's brass band; guitarist and singer for Smith's Carolina

Crackerjacks, which recorded a total of four sides for RCA-Victor at a Rock Hill, South Carolina, field session in 1938.

Thelma Smith. Daughter of Walter "Kid" Smith, who worked in Spray, North Carolina, textile mills; sang and played the guitar on fourteen sides with Kid Smith and His Family, which recorded for RCA-Victor in 1931 and for the American Record Corporation in 1936.

Eddie Stoneman (1920–?). Son of Ernest V. Stoneman, who once worked in a Fries, Virginia, textile mill; as a banjo player and singer, recorded eighteen duets with his father for the American Record Corporation in 1934.

Hattie (née Frost) Stoneman (1900–1976). Wife of Ernest V. Stoneman, who once worked in a Fries, Virginia, textile mill; singer, fiddler, banjoist, and mandolin player; recorded more than eighty sides with her husband, including duets and selections with his stringband, the Dixie Mountaineers, chiefly for Victor and Edison, between 1926 and 1928; also waxed a total of six duets with Uncle Eck Dunford for Victor between 1927 and 1928.

Walter Titterington (ca. 1891–?). Native of Lancaster, England, who immigrated to the United States and settled, around 1923, in Hopewell, Virginia, where his wife worked as a spinner at the Tubize Artificial Silk Company plant; tenor singer for the Tubize Royal Hawaiian Orchestra, a company-sponsored band, which recorded six issued sides for OKeh in 1929.

Davy Crockett Ward (1873–1964). Born in Grayson County, Virginia; his daughter Verna Mae, who lived in his home, worked as a hemmer in a local knitting mill; recorded six sides for OKeh at a 1927 Winston-Salem, North Carolina, field session as the fiddler and leader of Crockett Ward and His Boys.

Fields M. Ward (1911–87). Born in Grayson County, Virginia; his sister Verna Mae worked as a hemmer in a local knitting mill; guitarist and lead singer for Crockett Ward and His Boys, which cut six sides for OKeh at a 1927 Winston-Salem, North Carolina, field session; also recorded as the guitarist, singer, and leader of Fields Ward and the Grayson County Railsplitters, which made fifteen recordings (all rejected) for Gennett in 1929.

Sampson Ward (1899–1966). Born in Grayson County, Virginia; his sister Verna Mae worked as a hemmer in a local knitting mill; banjo player for Crockett Ward and His Boys, which made six sides for OKeh at a 1927 Winston-Salem, North Carolina, field session; also recorded as the banjo player for Fields Ward and the Grayson County Railsplitters, which cut fifteen sides (all rejected) for Gennett in 1929.

Vernon Ward. Born in Grayson County, Virginia; his sister Verna Mae worked as a hemmer in a local knitting mill; autoharp player for Crockett Ward and His Boys, which recorded six sides for OKeh at a 1927 Winston-Salem, North Carolina, field session.

APPENDIX B

Discography of Southern Textile Workers' Commercial Recordings, 1923–1942, Reissued on CD

The following discography lists CDs that contain some of the reissued prewar hillbilly recordings performed by the southern textile musicians and stringbands discussed in *Linthead Stomp*. For each of the principal artists profiled in this book, I have included the definitive compilations of their recorded works. In the case of Dave McCarn, who currently has no CD devoted exclusively to his music, I have listed several anthologies that, collectively, contain half of his issued 1930–31 recordings. Whenever possible, I have listed CDs that are readily available to American consumers, but in some cases the absence of domestic reissues has led me to include harder-to-acquire British and other European imports. Several of the CDs listed below are now out of print, but copies can usually be obtained at reasonable prices from internet merchants and online auction houses. For a comprehensive discography of these musicians' pre-1943 commercial hillbilly recordings, readers should consult Tony Russell's *Country Music Records: A Discography, 1921–1942*, with editorial research by Bob Pinson, assisted by the staff of the Country Music Hall of Fame and Museum (New York: Oxford University Press, 2004).

Principal Textile Mill Musicians and Stringbands

FIDDLIN' JOHN CARSON
Fiddlin' John Carson: Complete Recorded Works in Chronological Order, Vols. 1–7 (1923–1934). Document DOCD-8014–DOCD-8020.

THE DIXON BROTHERS
The Dixon Brothers: Complete Recorded Works in Chronological Order, Vols. 1–4 (1936–1938). Document DOCD-8046–DOCD-8049.
The Dixon Brothers: How Can a Broke Man Be Happy? Acrobat 4022.
The Dixon Brothers: Spinning Room Blues. Old Homestead OHCD-4164.
The Dixon Brothers: Weave Room Blues. Old Homestead OHCD-4151.

DAVE MCCARN
Black and White Hillbilly Music: Early Harmonica Recordings from the 1920s and 30s. Trikont US-0226.
Drunk and Nutty Blues: Hillbillies Foolin' with the Blues. Indigo IGODCD 2520.
Hard Times Come Again No More: Early American Rural Songs of Hard Times and Hardships, Vols. 1–2. Yazoo 2036/2037.
Hard Times in the Country: Down and Out in the Rural South: Songs and Tunes from 1927–1938. County CO-CD-3527.
Harmonica Masters: Classic Recordings from the 1920's and 30's. Yazoo 2019.
Hillbilly Honeymoon: Manhaters, Misogynists, and Marital Mayhem. Acrobat 4015.
Jake Leg Blues. Jass J-CD-642.

The Road to Nashville: A History of Country Music, 1926–1953. Indigo IGOTCD 2559.

CHARLIE POOLE AND THE NORTH CAROLINA RAMBLERS

Charlie Poole and the North Carolina Ramblers: Old Time Songs Recorded from 1925 to 1930. County CO-3501.

Charlie Poole and the North Carolina Ramblers: Old Time Songs Recorded from 1925 to 1930, Vol. 2. County CO-3508.

Charlie Poole with the North Carolina Rumblers and the Highlanders. 4-CD boxed set. JSP JSP7734.

The Legend of Charlie Poole: Original Recordings, 1925–1930, Vol. 3. County CO-3516.

"You Ain't Talkin' to Me": Charlie Poole and the Roots of Country Music. 3-CD boxed set. Columbia/Legacy C3K-92780.

Selected Secondary Textile Mill Musicians and Stringbands

H. M. BARNES'S BLUE RIDGE RAMBLERS

It's Hotter in Hawaii: Early Hits From a Unique Musical Style. 4-CD boxed set. JSP JSP7738.

BLUE RIDGE HIGHBALLERS

The Cornshucker's Frolic: Downhome Music and Entertainment from the American Countryside, Vol. 2. Yazoo 2046.

Cotton Mills and Fiddles. Flyin' Cloud FC-014.

Paramount Old Time Recordings. 4-CD boxed set. JSP JSP7774.

Rural String Bands of Virginia. County CO-CD-3502.

Worried Blues: The Complete Commercial Output of Frank Hutchison and Kelly Harrell. 4-CD boxed set. JSP JSP7743.

CAROLINA BUDDIES

Mountain Blues: Blues, Ballads, and String Bands, 1927–1938. 4-CD boxed set. JSP JSP7740.

My Rough and Rowdy Ways: Badman Ballads and Hellraising Songs, Vol. 2. Yazoo 2040.

The Story That the Crow Told Me: Early American Rural Children's Songs, Vol. 1. Yazoo 2051.

CAROLINA TAR HEELS

The Carolina Tar Heels. Old Homestead OHCD-4113.

CAROLINA TWINS/FLETCHER AND FOSTER

Old-Time Mountain Guitar: Vintage Recordings, 1926–1931. County CO-CD-3512.

The Victor Label: Classic Old Time Music. British Archive of Country Music BACM CD C 129.

GRADY AND HAZEL COLE

Something Got a Hold of Me: A Treasury of Sacred Music. RCA 2100-2-R.

DARBY AND TARLTON

Darby and Tarlton: Complete Recordings. 3-CD boxed set. Bear Family BCD-15764.
Darby and Tarlton: On the Banks of a Lonely River. County CO-3503.
Darby and Tarlton: Ooze It Up to Me. Acrobat ACMCD 4016.

DIXIE REELERS

The Dixon Brothers: Complete Recorded Works in Chronological Order, Vol. 4 (1938).
    Document DOCD-8049.

GWIN S. FOSTER

The Carolina Tar Heels. Old Homestead OHCD-4113.
Drunk and Nutty Blues: Hillbillies Foolin' with the Blues. Indigo IGODCD 2520.
Good for What Ails You: Music of the Medicine Shows, 1926–1937. 2-CD set. Old Hat
    CD-1005.
*Hard Times in the Country: Down and Out in the Rural South: Songs and Tunes from
    1927–1938*. County CO-CD-3527.
Harmonica Masters: Classic Recordings from the 1920's and 30's. Yazoo 2019.
Hillbilly Blues: 25 Country Classics, 1929–1947. Living Era CD AJA 5361.
Mountain Blues: Blues, Ballads, and String Bands, 1927–1938. 4-CD boxed set. JSP
    JSP7740.
Old-Time Mountain Blues: Rural Classics, 1927–1939. County CO-CD-3528.
The Victor Label: Classic Old Time Music. British Archive of Country Music BACM
    CD C 129.

FOUR PICKLED PEPPERS

Cotton Mills and Fiddles. Flyin' Cloud FC-014.

FOUR VIRGINIANS

Cotton Mills and Fiddles. Flyin' Cloud FC-014.
The OKeh Label: Classic Old Time Music. British Archive of Country Music BACM
    CD C 050.

GEORGIA YELLOW HAMMERS

Georgia Yellow Hammers: Johnson's Old Grey Mule. British Archive of Country
    Music BACM CD D 073.

GRAYSON AND WHITTER

G. B. Grayson and Henry Whitter: Early Classics, Vols. 1–2. Old Homestead OHCD-
    157/165.
*Grayson and Whitter: Complete Recorded Works in Chronological Order, Vols. 1–2
    (1927–1929)*. Document DOCD-8054/8055.
Grayson and Whitter: Recordings, 1928–1930. County CO-3517.

ROY HALL AND HIS BLUE RIDGE ENTERTAINERS

Can't You Hear Me Callin'—Bluegrass: 80 Years of American Music. 4-CD boxed set.
    Columbia/Legacy C4K 90628.

KELLY HARRELL AND HIS VIRGINIA STRING BAND

Kelly Harrell: Complete Recorded Works in Chronological Order, Vols. 1–2 (1925–
1929). Document DOCD-8026/8027.

Worried Blues: The Complete Commercial Output of Frank Hutchison and Kelly
Harrell. 4-CD boxed set. JSP JSP7743.

BILL HELMS AND HIS UPSON COUNTY BAND

The Victor Label: Classic Old Time Music. British Archive of Country Music BACM
CD C 129.

HICKORY NUTS

Man of Constant Sorrow and Other Timeless Mountain Ballads: Classic Recordings of
the 1920's and 30's. Yazoo 3001.

My Rough and Rowdy Ways: Badman Ballads and Hellraising Songs, Vol. 2. Yazoo
2040.

Old Time Mountain Ballads. County CO-CD-3504.

Outside the Law: Gangsters, Racketeers, and the Feds: Vintage Songs, 1922–1947.
Buzzola 012.

LEE BROTHERS TRIO/CHUMBLER FAMILY

Hard Times in the Country: Down and Out in the Rural South: Songs and Tunes from
1927–1938. County CO-CD-3527.

Mountain Gospel: The Sacred Roots of Country Music. 4-CD boxed set. JSP JSP7755.

DADDY JOHN LOVE

Sounds Like Jimmie Rodgers: Stars That Followed the Master. 4-CD boxed set. JSP
JSP7751.

J. E. MAINER'S MOUNTAINEERS

The Golden Age of J. E. Mainer's Mountaineers. Cattle CCD 238.

J. E. Mainer's Mountaineers, 1935–1939. British Archive of Country Music BACM
CD D 122.

WADE MAINER AND THE SONS OF THE MOUNTAINEERS

Wade Mainer's Mountaineers, Vol. 1 (1935–1936). Old Homestead OHCD-4043.

MORRIS BROTHERS (WILEY AND ZEKE)

Mountain Gospel: The Sacred Roots of Country Music. 4-CD boxed set. JSP JSP7755.

NORTH CAROLINA COOPER BOYS

Goodbye, Babylon. 6-CD boxed set. Dust-to-Digital DTD-01.

The OKeh Label: Classic Old Time Music. British Archive of Country Music BACM
CD C 050.

RED PATTERSON'S PIEDMONT LOG ROLLERS

Cotton Mills and Fiddles. Flyin' Cloud FC-014.

Rural String Bands of Virginia. County CO-CD-3502.

The Victor Label: Classic Old Time Music. British Archive of Country Music BACM
CD C 129.

RAMBLING DUET

The Dixon Brothers: Complete Recorded Works in Chronological Order, Vols. 3–4 (1937–1938). Document DOCD-8048/8049.

RICE BROTHERS' GANG

The Decca 5000 Series: Classic Old Time Music. British Archive of Country Music BACM CD C 077.

King Cotton Stomp. British Archive of Country Music BACM CD C 117.

RIDGEL'S FOUNTAIN CITIANS

Goodbye, Babylon. 6-CD boxed set. Dust-to-Digital DTD-01.

Rural String Bands of Tennessee. County CO-CD-3511.

The Vocalion Label: Classic Old Time Music. British Archive of Country Music BACM CD D 140.

ROANE COUNTY RAMBLERS

Roane County Ramblers: Complete Recordings, 1928–1929. County CO-CD-3530.

ROANOKE JUG BAND

Mountain Blues: Blues, Ballads, and String Bands, 1927–1938. 4-CD boxed set. JSP JSP7740.

Rural String Bands of Virginia. County CO-CD-3502.

Virginia Roots: The 1929 Richmond Sessions. 2-CD set. Outhouse Records 1001.

SCOTTDALE STRING BAND

The OKeh Label: Classic Old Time Music. British Archive of Country Music BACM CD C 050.

Rags, Breakdowns, Stomps and Blues: Vintage Mandolin Music, 1927–1946. Document DOCD-32-20-3.

SHELOR FAMILY/DAD BLACKARD'S MOONSHINERS

The Bristol Sessions: Historic Recordings from Bristol, Tennessee. 2-CD set. Country Music Foundation CMF-011-D.

Rural String Bands of Virginia. County CO-CD-3502.

Times Ain't Like They Used to Be: Early American Rural Music, Vols. 2 and 8. Yazoo 2029 and 2068.

WALTER "KID" SMITH

Walter Smith and Friends: Complete Recorded Works in Chronological Order, Vols. 1–3 (1929–1936). Document DOCD-8062–DOCD-8064.

ERNEST V. STONEMAN

Ernest V. Stoneman: Edison Recordings, 1928. County CO-CD-3510.

Ernest V. Stoneman: With Family and Friends, Vols. 1–2. Old Homestead OHCD-4172/4173.

TOBACCO TAGS/THREE TOBACCO TAGS

The Tobacco Tags: Get Your Head in Here. British Archive of Country Music BACM CD D 131.

Songs of the Tobacco Tags. Old Homestead OH-4156-CD.

TUBIZE ROYAL HAWAIIAN ORCHESTRA
Hawaiian Steel Guitar Classics, 1927–1938. Arhoolie 7027.
Virginia Roots: The 1929 Richmond Sessions. 2-CD set. Outhouse Records 1001.

VIRGINIA DANDIES
Goodbye, Babylon. 6-CD boxed set. Dust-to-Digital DTD-01.
Mountain Gospel: The Sacred Roots of Country Music. 4-CD boxed set. JSP JSP7755.

WATTS AND WILSON
My Rough and Rowdy Ways: Badman Ballads and Hellraising Songs, Vol. 1. Yazoo
      2039.

WILMER WATTS AND THE LONELY EAGLES
The Iron Horse: Vintage Railroad Songs, 1926–1952. Buzzola 008.
The North Carolina Banjo Collection. 2-CD set. Rounder 0439/0440.
Paramount Old Time Recordings. 4-CD boxed set. JSP JSP7774.
The Stuff That Dreams Are Made Of: Super Rarities and Gems of the 1920s and '30s.
      2-CD set. Yazoo 2202.
Times Ain't Like They Used to Be: Early American Rural Music, Vols. 1–3 and 5. Yazoo
      2028, 2029, 2047, 2063.

NORMAN WOODLIEFF
Cotton Mills and Fiddles. Flyin' Cloud FC-014.

NOTES

Abbreviations

AFC   Archive of Folk Culture, American Folklife Center,
Library of Congress, Washington, D.C.

ALUA   Archives of Labor and Urban Affairs, Walter P. Reuther Library,
Wayne State University, Detroit, Michigan

NCC   North Carolina Collection, Louis Round Wilson Library,
University of North Carolina at Chapel Hill

NCDAH   North Carolina Department of Archives and History,
Raleigh, North Carolina

SFC   Southern Folklife Collection, Louis Round Wilson Library,
University of North Carolina at Chapel Hill

Preface

1. Bruce Crawford, "Folk Music at White Top," *New Republic* 76 (August 30, 1933): 75. On the White Top Folk Festival, see David E. Whisnant, *All That Is Native and Fine: The Politics of Culture in an American Region* (Chapel Hill: University of North Carolina Press, 1983), 183–252.

2. The best and most comprehensive historical overview of country music remains Bill C. Malone's *Country Music, U.S.A.*, rev. ed. (Austin: University of Texas Press, 1985 [1968]). On the history and development of these regional subgenres, see, for example, Charles R. Townsend, *San Antonio Rose: The Life and Music of Bob Wills* (Urbana: University of Illinois Press, 1976); Cary Ginell, with special assistance from Roy Lee Brown, *Milton Brown and the Founding of Western Swing* (Urbana: University of Illinois Press, 1994); Ronnie Pugh, *Ernest Tubb: The Texas Troubadour* (Durham: Duke University Press, 1996); Robert Cantwell, *Bluegrass Breakdown: The Making of the Old Southern Sound* (New York: Da Capo Press, 1992 [1984]); and Richard D. Smith, *Can't You Hear Me Callin'. The Life of Bill Monroe, Father of Bluegrass* (Boston: Little, Brown, 2000).

3. Archie Green, "Hillbilly Music: Source and Symbol," *Journal of American Folklore* 78 (July–September 1965): 204–28; Tony Russell, *Country Music Originals: The Legends and the Lost* (New York: Oxford University Press, 2007). For some of the more illuminating studies of prewar country music, see, for example, Tony Russell, *Blacks, Whites and Blues* (New York: Stein and Day, 1970); Robert Coltman, "Across the Chasm: How the Depression Changed Country Music," *Old Time Music* 23 (Winter 1976–77): 6–12; Bill C. Malone, *Singing Cowboys and Musical Mountaineers: Southern Culture and the Roots of Country Music* (Athens: University of Georgia Press, 1993); George Lipsitz, *Rainbow at Midnight: Labor and Culture in the 1940s* (Urbana: University of Illinois Press, 1994), 303–33; Pamela Grundy, "'We Always Tried to Be Good People': Respectability, Crazy Water Crystals, and Hillbilly Music on the Air, 1933–1935," *Journal of American History* 81 (March 1995): 1591–1620;

Richard A. Peterson, *Creating Country Music: Fabricating Authenticity* (Chicago: University of Chicago Press, 1997); Charles K. Wolfe, *A Good-Natured Riot: The Birth of the Grand Ole Opry* (Nashville, Tenn.: Country Music Foundation Press/Vanderbilt University Press, 1999); William Howland Kenney, *Recorded Music in American Life: The Phonograph and Popular Memory, 1890–1945* (Oxford: Oxford University Press, 1999), 135–57; Louis M. Kyriakoudes, *The Social Origins of the Urban South: Race, Gender, and Migration in Nashville and Middle Tennessee, 1890–1930* (Chapel Hill: University of North Carolina Press, 2003), 7–18; J. M. Mancini, "'Messin' with the Furniture Man': Early Country Music, Regional Culture, and the Search for an Anthological Modernism," *American Literary History* 16 (Summer 2004): 208–37; and Charles K. Wolfe and Ted Olson, eds., *The Bristol Sessions: Writings about the Big Bang of Country Music*, Contributions to Southern Appalachian Studies no. 12 (Jefferson, N.C.: McFarland, 2005).

4. Scholars have written at least three book-length biographies and a few dozen articles about southern textile mill musicians and stringbands and occasionally have commented on the significant number of performers who emerged from this occupational culture. For a sampling of these biographies and articles, see Kinney Rorrer, *Rambling Blues: The Life and Songs of Charlie Poole* (Danville, Va.: McCain Printing Company, 1992 [1982]); Gene Wiggins, *Fiddlin' Georgia Crazy: Fiddlin' John Carson, His Real World, and the World of His Songs* (Urbana: University of Illinois Press, 1987); Ivan M. Tribe, *The Stonemans: An Appalachian Family and the Music That Shaped Their Lives* (Urbana: University of Illinois Press, 1993); Rodney McElrea, "A Portrait of the Life and Phonograph Recordings of the Dixon Brothers— Howard and Dorsey," *Country News and Views* 1 (July 1963): 6–12; Chris A. Strachwitz, "Mainer's Mountaineers," *American Folk Music Occasional* 1 (1964): 49–55; Archie Green, "Dorsey Dixon: Minstrel of the Mills," *Sing Out!* 16 (July 1966): 10–12; Norm Cohen and Anne Cohen, "The Legendary Jimmie Tarlton," *Sing Out!* 16 (September 1966): 16–19; Malcolm V. Blackard, "Wilmer Watts and the Lonely Eagles," *John Edwards Memorial Foundation Quarterly* 5 (Winter 1969): 126–40; Bill Rattray, "Scottdale Boys," *Old Time Music* 1 (Summer 1971): 22; Tony Russell, "Kelly Harrell and the Virginia Ramblers: An OTM Report," *Old Time Music* 2 (Autumn 1971): 8–11; Kinney Rorrer, "The Bunch of Nuts from Hickory," *Old Time Music* 2 (Autumn 1971): 19; Donald Lee Nelson, "'Walk Right in Belmont': The Wilmer Watts Story," *John Edwards Memorial Foundation Quarterly* 9 (Autumn 1973): 91–96; Mike Paris, "The Dixons of South Carolina," *Old Time Music* 10 (Autumn 1973): 13–16; Kinney Rorrer, "The Four Virginians," *Old Time Music* 14 (Autumn 1974): 18; Norm Cohen, "'Fiddlin' John Carson: An Appreciation and a Discography," *John Edwards Memorial Foundation Quarterly* 10 (Winter 1974): 138–56; Norm Cohen, "Henry Whitter: His Life and Music," *John Edwards Memorial Foundation Quarterly* 11 (Summer 1975): 57–66; Janet Kerr, "Lonnie Austin/Norman Woodlieff," *Old Time Music* 17 (Summer 1975). 7–8; Tony Russell, "Alias Walter Smith," *Old Time Music* 17 (Summer 1975): 12–17; Ivan M. Tribe and John W. Morris, "J. E. and Wade Mainer," *Bluegrass Unlimited* 10 (November 1975): 12–21; William Henry Koon, "Dave McCarn," *John Edwards Memorial Foundation Quarterly* 11 (Winter 1975): 167–76; Tom Carter, "The Blackard-Shelor Story: Biography of a Hillbilly Stringband," *Old Time Music*

24 (Spring 1977): 4–7, 31; Charles K. Wolfe, "Lester Smallwood and His Cotton Mill Song," *Old Time Music* 25 (Summer 1977): 22–23; Kinney Rorrer, "Red Patterson and the Piedmont Log Rollers," *Old Time Music* 34 (Summer/Autumn 1980): 5–6; Kip Lornell, "'The Jug Didn't Mean a Thing': The Roanoke Jug Band," *Old Time Music* 41 (Spring 1985): 15–16; Doug DeNatale and Glenn Hinson, "The Southern Textile Song Tradition Reconsidered," in *Songs about Work: Essays in Occupational Culture for Richard A. Reuss*, ed. Archie Green, Special Publications of the Folklore Institute no. 3 (Bloomington: Folklore Institute, Indiana University, 1993), 77–107; Patrick Huber and Kathleen Drowne, "'I Don't Want Nothin' 'Bout My Life Wrote Out, Because I Had It Too Rough in Life': Dorsey Dixon's Autobiographical Writings," *Southern Cultures* 6 (Summer 2000): 94–100; Patrick Huber, "'Cain't Make a Living at a Cotton Mill': The Life and Hillbilly Songs of Dave McCarn," *North Carolina Historical Review* 80 (July 2003): 297–333; Gregg D. Kimball and Ron T. Curry, "On the Beach of Waikiki: Hopewell's Tubize Royal Hawaiian Orchestra," *Virginia Cavalcade* 51 (Summer 2002): 112–23; Patrick Huber, "A Hillbilly Barnum: Fiddlin' John Carson and the Modern Origins of His Old-Time Music in Atlanta," *Atlanta History* 46 (2004): 24–53; Patrick Huber, "'A Blessing to People': Dorsey Dixon and His Sacred Mission of Song," *Southern Cultures* 12 (Winter 2006): 111–31; and Kinney Rorrer, "Posey Rorer of Franklin County, Virginia," *Old-Time Herald* 11 (December 2007–January 2008): 31–35.

5. Even the foremost scholar of country music, Bill C. Malone, in his desire to characterize hillbilly music as an expression of the traditional rural South, perpetuates this myth in one of his latest books, *Don't Get Above Your Raisin': Country Music and the Southern Working Class* (Urbana: University of Illinois Press, 2002). Although he is more sensitive to the ways in which urban growth and industrial development influenced this music before World War II here than he is in most of his previous books, he still insists on casting hillbilly music as a chiefly rural phenomenon. When, for instance, Malone argues in the book that "virtually all of the early hillbilly entertainers, beginning with Eck Robertson, Henry Gilliland, Henry Whitter, and Fiddlin' John Carson . . . , lived in rural settings" and then refers to Carson as a "southern rural musician," he mischaracterizes Carson and many of his urban contemporaries. Although he grew up on a farm outside of Marietta, Georgia, by June 1923, when he made his first recordings, Carson had been living in Atlanta for almost a quarter century. It is not clear what Malone means when he describes Carson and these other hillbilly pioneers as "rural" musicians. Nor does he explain what the broader historical implications of this designation are for hillbilly music. See ibid., 36, 54.

6. On the development of country music during the 1940s and 1950s, see Malone, *Country Music, U.S.A.*, 177–97; and Jeffrey J. Lange, *Smile When You Call Me a Hillbilly: Country Music's Struggle for Respectability, 1939–1954* (Athens: University of Georgia Press, 2004), 67–88. See Malone's brief discussion of the mass media and industrial influences on hillbilly music in *Don't Get Above Your Raisin'*, 31–36.

7. Southern millhands have been consistently characterized as a homogeneous group, and this is especially true in the sociological and economic studies of the

southern textile industry published during the 1920s and 1930s. Writing in 1928, for example, economist Lois MacDonald described Piedmont textile workers as a "uniform" population—"native born, Southern, and rural"—and spoke of "the mind of the workers," as if their attitudes and thoughts formed a monolithic consensus. See Lois MacDonald, *Southern Mill Hills: A Study of Social and Economic Forces in Certain Textile Mill Villages* (New York: Alex L. Hillman, 1928), 69, 104, 135, 146.

8. On Dixon's now-classic song, see Tony Hilfer, "'Wreck on the Highway': Rhetoric and Religion in a Country Song," *John Edwards Memorial Foundation Quarterly* 21 (Fall/Winter 1985): 116–19.

9. Ivan M. Tribe, liner notes to Tobacco Tags, *Songs of the Tobacco Tags, Vol. 1* (Old Homestead OHCS 156). For a larger discussion of southerners' conflicted responses to the automobile, see Blaine A. Brownell, "A Symbol of Modernity: Attitudes toward the Automobile in Southern Cities in the 1920s," *American Quarterly* 24 (March 1972): 20–44.

10. Jacquelyn Dowd Hall, James Leloudis, Robert Korstad, Mary Murphy, Lu Ann Jones, and Christopher B. Daly, *Like a Family: The Making of a Southern Cotton Mill World*, with a new afterword by the authors (Chapel Hill: University of North Carolina Press, 2000 [1987]), 261, 262; Grundy, "'We Always Tried to Be Good People,'" 1592.

11. James C. Cobb, "From Rocky Top to Detroit City: Country Music and the Economic Transformation of the South," in *You Wrote My Life: Lyrical Themes in Country Music*, ed. Melton A. McLaurin and Richard A. Peterson, Cultural Perspectives on the American South, vol. 6 (Philadelphia: Gordon and Breach, 1992), 64. Within the broader historical literature on this period, *Linthead Stomp* most directly complements Daniel J. Singal's fascinating study of southern intellectuals, *The War Within: From Victorian to Modernist Thought in the South, 1919–1945* (Chapel Hill: University of North Carolina Press, 1982). Like Singal's book, *Linthead Stomp* traces a select group of southerners over the course of their entire lives within the specific contexts of their social and cultural worlds in order to reveal their experiences in and shifting responses to a modernizing American South.

12. Over the past three and a half decades, historians have produced an impressive collection of studies of Piedmont textile life and culture, a significant number of which rely heavily on oral histories in reconstructing their "collective portraits" of southern millhands. For some of the best of these studies, see, for example, Hall et al., *Like a Family*; I. A. Newby, *Plain Folk in the New South: Social Change and Cultural Persistence, 1880–1915* (Baton Rogue: Louisiana State University Press, 1989); Allen Tullos, *Habits of Industry: White Culture and the Transformation of the Carolina Piedmont* (Chapel Hill: University of North Carolina Press, 1989); Douglas Flamming, *Creating the Modern South: Millhands and Managers in Dalton, Georgia, 1884–1984* (Chapel Hill: University of North Carolina Press, 1992); Gary M. Fink, *The Fulton Bag and Cotton Mills Strike of 1914–1915: Espionage, Labor Conflict, and New South Industrial Relations* (Ithaca, N.Y.: ILR Press, 1993); Bryant Simon, *A Fabric of Defeat: The Politics of South Carolina Millhands, 1910–1948* (Chapel Hill: University of North Carolina Press, 1998); Janet Irons, *Testing the*

New Deal: The General Strike of 1934 in the American South (Urbana: University of Illinois Press, 2000); G. C. Waldrep III, *Southern Workers and the Search for Community: Spartanburg County, South Carolina* (Urbana: University of Illinois Press, 2000); and Clifford M. Kuhn, *Contesting the New South Order: The 1914–1915 Strike at Atlanta's Fulton Mills* (Chapel Hill: University of North Carolina Press, 2001). For an overview of this historical literature, see Robert H. Zieger, "Textile Workers and Historians," in *Organized Labor in the Twentieth-Century South*, ed. Robert H. Zieger (Knoxville: University of Tennessee Press, 1991), 35–59.

13. See Hall et al., *Like a Family*, especially 135–37, 237, 249–55, 257–62; and Vincent J. Roscigno and William F. Danaher, *The Voice of Southern Labor: Radio, Music, and Textile Strikes, 1929–1934*, Social Movements, Protest, and Contention, vol. 19 (Minneapolis: University of Minnesota Press, 2004), especially 26–27, 29–30, 46–70.

14. Eugene Chadbourne, "Phebel Wright," *All Music Guide*, MusicMatch Guide, <http://www.mmguide.musicmatch.com/artist/artist.cgi?ARTISTID=1225 343&TMPL=LONG#bio> (September 2, 2006). On the epithet "linthead," see J. A. Simpson and E. S. C. Weiner, eds., *The Oxford English Dictionary*, 2nd ed., 20 vols. (Oxford: Clarendon Press, 1989). I first heard Phebel Wright's "Lint Head Stomp" in 1995 on a cassette tape sent to me by the late Bob Pinson, then the longtime director of record acquisitions at the Country Music Foundation Library and Media Center of the Country Music Hall of Fame and Museum in Nashville, and I wish to acknowledge his generosity in sharing that recording of the song with me.

15. For a sampling of the early published academic writings on country music, see, for example, John Greenway, "Jimmie Rodgers: A Folksong Catalyst," *Journal of American Folklore* 70 (July–September 1957): 231–35; D. K. Wilgus, "An Introduction to the Study of Hillbilly Music," *Journal of American Folklore* 78 (July–September 1965): 195–203; Green, "Hillbilly Music," 204–28; Norm Cohen, "The Skillet Lickers: A Study of a Hillbilly String Band and Its Repertoire," *Journal of American Folklore* 78 (July–September 1965): 229–44; Ed Kahn, "Hillbilly Music: Source and Resource," *Journal of American Folklore* 78 (July–September 1965): 257–66; and Bill C. Malone, *Country Music, U.S.A.: A Fifty-Year History* (Austin: University of Texas Press, 1968).

Introduction

1. *Charlotte Observer*, August 9 and 10, 1927.

2. On the Piedmont South and its industrialization during the late nineteenth and early twentieth centuries, see, for example, Holland Thompson, *From the Cotton Field to the Cotton Mill: A Study of the Industrial Transition in North Carolina* (New York: Macmillan, 1906); Broadus Mitchell and George Sinclair Mitchell, *The Industrial Revolution in the South* (Baltimore: Johns Hopkins University Press, 1930); Rupert B. Vance, *Human Geography of the South: A Study in Regional Resources and Human Adequacy* (Chapel Hill: University of North Carolina Press, 1932), 275–315; Ben F. Lemert, *The Cotton Textile Industry of the Southern Appalachian Piedmont* (Chapel Hill: University of North Carolina Press, 1933); Rupert B. Vance, *All These People: The Nation's Human Resources in the South* (Chapel Hill: University of North

Carolina Press, 1945), 279–317; David L. Carlton, *Mill and Town in South Carolina, 1880–1920* (Baton Rouge: Louisiana State University Press, 1982); Jacquelyn Dowd Hall, James Leloudis, Robert Korstad, Mary Murphy, Lu Ann Jones, and Christopher B. Daly, *Like a Family: The Making of a Southern Cotton Mill World*, with a new afterword by the authors (Chapel Hill: University of North Carolina Press, 2000 [1987]); and Allen Tullos, *Habits of Industry: White Culture and the Transformation of the Carolina Piedmont* (Chapel Hill: University of North Carolina Press, 1989).

3. *Gastonia (N.C.) Daily Gazette*, January 29, 1927; Tom Hanchett, "Recording in Charlotte, 1927–1945," in *The Charlotte Country Music Story*, ed. George Holt (Charlotte: North Carolina Arts Council, 1985), 12–14; Thomas W. Hanchett, *Sorting Out the New South City: Race, Class, and Urban Development in Charlotte, 1875–1975* (Chapel Hill: University of North Carolina Press, 1998), 2, 90–96.

4. Hanchett, "Recording in Charlotte," 12–16; Brian Rust, comp., *The Victor Master Book, Vol. 2 (1925–1936)* (Pinner, Middlesex, England: privately published, 1969), 146–48; Victor Talking Machine Company, *Olde Time Fiddlin' Tunes* (New York: Victor Talking Machine Company, 1924), n.p.; Archie Green, "Commercial Music Graphics: Four," *John Edwards Memorial Foundation Newsletter* 4 (March 1968): 8–13; Tony Russell, *Country Music Records: A Discography, 1921–1942*, with editorial research by Bob Pinson, assisted by the staff of the Country Music Hall of Fame and Museum (New York: Oxford University Press, 2004), 25. For Victor's use of such marketing labels, see, for example, *Uniontown (Pa.) Morning Herald*, July 23, 1927; and *Uniontown (Pa.) Daily News Standard*, May 18 and July 28, 1927.

5. Rust, *The Victor Master Book, Vol. 2*, 146–48; Mike Paris, liner notes to Dave McCarn and Gwin S. Foster, *Singers of the Piedmont* (Folk Variety FV 12505); Tony Russell, "Kelly Harrell and the Virginia Ramblers: An OTM Report," *Old Time Music* 2 (Autumn 1971): 8–11; Kinney Rorrer, "Red Patterson and the Piedmont Log Rollers," *Old Time Music* 34 (Summer/Autumn 1980): 5–6.

6. Tom Hanchett, review of various artists, *Cotton Mills and Fiddles* (Flyin' Cloud FC-014), in *Old-Time Herald* 3 (Winter 1991/1992): 51.

7. Thompson, *From the Cotton Field to the Cotton Mill*, 50, 74.

8. *Atlanta Constitution*, May 30, 1894, June 15, 1909; Lemert, *The Cotton Textile Industry of the Southern Appalachian Piedmont*, 137–38; Vance, *Human Geography of the South*, 275, 301–15.

9. Harriet L. Herring, *Welfare Work in Mill Villages: The Story of Extra-Mill Activities in North Carolina* (Chapel Hill: University of North Carolina Press, 1929), 17, 25, 43; Vance, *Human Geography of the South*, 301; Lemert, *The Cotton Textile Industry of the Southern Appalachian Piedmont*, 3; Lois MacDonald, *Southern Mill Hills: A Study of Social and Economic Forces in Certain Textile Mill Villages* (New York: Alex L. Hillman, 1928), 5.

10. Hall et al., *Like a Family*, 25; Gerald L. Ingalls, "Urbanization," in *The North Carolina Atlas: Portrait of a New Century*, ed. Douglas M. Orr Jr. and Alfred W. Stuart (Chapel Hill: University of North Carolina Press, 2000), 105, *Twelfth Census of the United States, 1900*, vol. 1, *Population* (Washington, D.C.: U.S. Census Office, 1901), 466; *Fourteenth Census of the United States, 1920*, vol. 1, *Population* (Washington,

D.C.: Government Printing Office, 1921), 267; *Fifteenth Census of the United States, 1930*, vol. 1, *Population* (Washington, D.C.: Government Printing Office, 1931), 780; Tom Tippett, *When Southern Labor Stirs* (New York: Jonathan Cape and Harrison Smith, 1931), 196–97; Bruce Bastin, *Red River Blues: The Blues Tradition in the Southeast* (Urbana: University of Illinois Press, 1995), 27–28.

11. Ingalls, "Urbanization," 105; Vance, *Human Geography of the South*, 32–33; Hanchett, *Sorting Out the New South City*, 95; *Fourteenth Census of the United States, 1920*, 1:55; Vance, *Human Geography of the South*, 32–33; Lemert, *The Cotton Textile Industry of the Southern Appalachian Piedmont*, 36–7.

12. Hall et al., *Like a Family*, 66–67; I. A. Newby, *Plain Folk in the New South: Social Change and Cultural Persistence, 1880–1915* (Baton Rogue: Louisiana State University Press, 1989), 462–66, 474–81; Herbert J. Lahne, *The Cotton Mill Worker* (New York: Farrar and Rinehart, 1944), 81–82; *Gastonia (N.C.) Daily Gazette*, September 10, 1926.

13. On southern mill villages, see Hall et al., *Like a Family*, 114–20, 126–27; Newby, *Plain Folk in the New South*, 244–53; and *New York Times*, June 15, 1930.

14. Hall et al., *Like a Family*, 131–39; *Danville (Va.) Bee*, August 23, 1924.

15. Harriet L. Herring, "The Industrial Worker," in *Culture in the South*, ed. W. T. Couch (Chapel Hill: University of North Carolina Press, 1934), 353, 354–55.

16. Ibid., 355.

17. Hall et al., *Like a Family*, 252–54, 258. On the growth of commercial entertainment in Atlanta, Charlotte, and Richmond, see, for example, Steve Goodson, *Highbrows, Hillbillies, and Hellfire: Public Entertainment in Atlanta, 1880–1930* (Athens: University of Georgia Press, 2002); Gavin James Campbell, *Music and the Making of a New South* (Chapel Hill: University of North Carolina Press, 2004); Hanchett, *Sorting Out the New South City*, 185, 191; Pamela Grundy, "From *Il Trovatore* to the Crazy Mountaineers: The Rise and Fall of Elevated Culture on WBT-Charlotte, 1922–1930," *Southern Cultures* 1 (Fall 1994): 51–73; and Michael Ayers Trotti, "When Coney Island Arrived in Richmond: Leisure in the Capital at the Turn of the Century," *Virginia Cavalcade* 51 (Autumn 2002): 168–79.

18. Jennings J. Rhyne, *Some Southern Cotton Mill Workers and Their Villages* (Chapel Hill: University of North Carolina Press, 1930), 199; Grundy, "From *Il Trovatore* to the Crazy Mountaineers," 58, 70n18; *Charlotte News*, January 12, 1922; *Burlington (N.C.) Daily Times*, April 16, 1928.

19. Marjorie Potwin, *Cotton Mill People of the Piedmont: A Study in Social Change* (New York: Columbia University Press, 1927), 34, 64; Pamela Grundy, "'We Always Tried to Be Good People': Respectability, Crazy Water Crystals, and Hillbilly Music on the Air, 1933–1935," *Journal of American History* 81 (March 1995): 1594.

20. Hall et al., *Like a Family*, xvii, 377.

21. For other definitions of this commercial musical genre, see, for example, D. K. Wilgus, "An Introduction to the Study of Hillbilly Music," *Journal of American Folklore* 78 (July–September 1965): 195–203; D. K. Wilgus, "The Hillbilly Movement," in *Our Living Traditions: An Introduction to American Folklore*, ed. Tristram Potter Coffin (New York: Basic Books, Inc., 1968), 263–71; and Bill C. Malone and

Ronnie Pugh, "Hillbilly Music," in *The New Grove Dictionary of American Music*, ed. H. Wiley Hitchcock and Stanley Sadie, 4 vols. (London: Macmillan, 1986), 1:387.

22. Archie Green, "Hillbilly Music: Source and Symbol," *Journal of American Folklore* 78 (July–September 1965): 204–7, 213–14; Anthony Harkins, *Hillbilly: A Cultural History of an American Icon* (Oxford: Oxford University Press, 2004), 71–101; Grundy, "'We Always Tried to Be Good People,'" 1600.

23. Charles K. Wolfe, "Columbia Records and Old-Time Music," *John Edwards Memorial Foundation Quarterly* 14 (Autumn 1978): 120; Bill C. Malone, *Country Music, U.S.A.*, rev. ed. (Austin: University of Texas Press, 1985 [1968]), 28–29; Bill C. Malone, *Don't Get Above Your Raisin': Country Music and the Southern Working Class* (Urbana: University of Illinois Press, 2002), 32–37. On the birth and formative period of the hillbilly recording industry, see Green, "Hillbilly Music: Source and Symbol," 204–28; Norm Cohen, "Early Pioneers," in *Stars of Country Music: Uncle Dave Macon to Johnny Rodriguez*, ed. Bill C. Malone and Judith McCulloh (Urbana: University of Illinois Press, 1975), 3–39; Charles K. Wolfe, "The Birth of an Industry," in *The Illustrated History of Country Music*, ed. Patrick Carr (New York: Random House/Time Books, 1995 [1980]), 33–75; and Malone, *Country Music, U.S.A.*, 31–75.

24. Roland Gelatt, *The Fabulous Phonograph, 1877–1977*, 2nd rev. ed. (New York: Collier Books, 1977 [1955]), 255; Andre Millard, *America on Record: A History of Recorded Sound* (Cambridge: Cambridge University Press, 1995), 164–66; Malone, *Country Music, U.S.A.*, 93–135.

25. Malone, *Country Music, U.S.A.*, 93–135; Robert Coltman, "Across the Chasm: How the Depression Changed Country Music," *Old Time Music* 23 (Winter 1976–77): 6–12.

26. Coltman, "Across the Chasm," 6–12; Malone, *Country Music, U.S.A.*, 177–97.

27. Malone, *Don't Get Above Your Raisin'*, 14–15, 34–35.

28. Patrick Huber, comp., "Southern Textile Workers on Hillbilly Records, 1923–1942," unpublished list, compiled in 2006 (a copy of which remains in the author's possession). The total number of approximately 23,000 domestic hillbilly releases is based upon two samplings that I conducted of the discographical information found in Russell, *Country Music Records*. Records released in foreign markets such as Canada, England, Ireland, Australia, and India are not included in this total. See also Norm Cohen, *Long Steel Rail: The Railroad in American Folksong* (Urbana: University of Illinois Press, 1981), 31–32. Admittedly, 6 percent may seem a modest figure, but it becomes more impressive when one considers that professional, New York–based freelance singers and musicians (including Arthur Fields, Frank Luther, Frankie Marvin, Carson Robison, and Vernon Dalhart, the latter of whom alone cut more than 1,200 old-time sides between 1924 and 1934), Cajun performers, singing cowboys, and southwestern swing bands collectively recorded perhaps as much as half of the total number of domestic hillbilly releases during this period. Thus, when adjusted to account for this huge block of recordings, Piedmont textile workers participated in the making of approximately

13 percent of all remaining 11,500 hillbilly records issued in the United States before 1943.

29. These include only musicians who have been identified as textile workers or former textile workers in the census, in other government documents, or in secondary sources, but no doubt represents an undercount of the total figure. The lack of detailed record company studio logs and files listing the personnel who recorded at particular sessions before 1943 makes it difficult, if not impossible, to ever arrive at an exact total. Presumably, at least one, if not all, of the band members of the Cotton Mill Weavers, who recorded two unissued sides for Columbia at an Atlanta field session on April 18, 1928, worked in Piedmont textile mills, but none of their names were recorded in Columbia's company files. Other textile millhands were no doubt among the Sacred Harp groups, gospel quartets, and church choirs that made hillbilly records, but here again few lists of the personnel of these groups exist. With further research, the total number of recorded singers and musicians who worked in Piedmont textile mills might include perhaps as many as a few dozen more names. See Russell, *Country Music Records*, 223.

30. *Roanoke (Va.) Times & World-News*, November 24, 1978; Ivan M. Tribe, "Roy Hall," in *Definitive Country: The Ultimate Encyclopedia of Country Music and Its Performers*, ed. Barry McCloud (New York: Perigree Books, 1995), 361–62.

31. Charles Wolfe, "Five Years with the Best: Bill Shores and North Georgia Fiddling," *Old Time Music* 25 (Summer 1977): 5, Charles Wolfe, "Joe Lee: A Further Note," *Old Time Music* 26 (Autumn 1977): 4; Joe LaRose, "An Interview with Lowe Stokes," *Old Time Music* 39 (Spring 1984): 7; Joyce H. Cauthen, *With Fiddle and Well-Rosined Bow: Old-Time Fiddling in Alabama* (Tuscaloosa: University of Alabama Press, 1989), 119–24; Norm Cohen, "Clayton McMichen: His Life and Music," *John Edwards Memorial Foundation Quarterly* 11 (Autumn 1975): 117–24; Charles K. Wolfe, "Clayton McMichen," in *Definitive Country*, 537–38.

32. Shirley Lewey-Payne, "Daughters in Search of Their Father," ezFolk.com, <http://www.ezfolk.com/bgbanjo/bgb-tabs/wreck97/wreckbio/wreckbio.html> (June 18, 2006); Jack Palmer, *Vernon Dalhart: First Star of Country Music* (Denver, Colo.: Mainspring Press, 2005), 113–30; Norm Cohen, "Henry Whitter: His Life and Music," *John Edwards Memorial Foundation Quarterly* 11 (Summer 1975): 57; Norm Cohen, "Robert W. Gordon and the Second Wreck of the 'Old 97,'" *Journal of American Folklore* 87 (January 1974): 20–21. Victor sales figures for "Wreck of the Old 97"/"The Prisoner's Song" combine Dalhart's original August 1924 acoustical record and his March 1926 electric record of these same songs on the firm's flagship and subsidiary labels. Once Dalhart had rerecorded these numbers using the new electric recording process, Victor removed the older acoustical version from its catalog and replaced it with the higher fidelity electric version, assigning the same label number as the original (Victor 19427). See Palmer, *Vernon Dalhart*, 123, 126, 128–29.

33. Paul Rice is by no means the only person to have claimed authorship of "You Are My Sunshine." On the song's murky origins, see Wayne W. Daniel, *Pickin' on Peachtree: A History of Country Music in Atlanta, Georgia* (Urbana: University of

Illinois Press, 1990), 149–51; and Wayne W. Daniel, "The Rice Brothers: Hillbillies with Uptown Ambitions," HillbillyMusic.com, <http://www.hillbilly-music.com/groups/story/printgroup.php?groupid=11764> (July 16, 2006).

34. See Dave Samuelson, "Arthur 'Guitar Boogie' Smith," in *The Encyclopedia of Country Music: The Ultimate Guide to the Music*, ed. Paul Kingsbury (New York: Oxford University Press, 1998), 489. For a relatively complete list of southern textile songs composed and recorded before World War II, see Appendix A, in Doug DeNatale and Glenn Hinson, "The Southern Textile Song Tradition Reconsidered," in *Songs about Work: Essays in Occupational Culture for Richard A. Reuss*, ed. Archie Green, Special Publications of the Folklore Institute no. 3 (Bloomington: Folklore Institute, Indiana University, 1993), 102–4.

35. The best overviews of talking-machine companies' practice of staging field-recording sessions in the South are Charles K. Wolfe, "The Bristol Syndrome: Field Recordings of Early Country Music," in *Country Music Annual 2002*, ed. Charles K. Wolfe and James E. Akenson (Lexington: University Press of Kentucky, 2002), 202–21; and Tony Russell, "Country Music on Location: 'Field Recording' before Bristol," *Popular Music* 26 (January 2007): 23–31. But see also Charles K. Wolfe, "Ralph Peer at Work: The Victor 1927 Bristol Sessions," *Old Time Music* 5 (Summer 1972): 10–15; Charles Wolfe, "Early Country Music in Knoxville: The Brunswick Sessions and the End of an Era," *Old Time Music* 12 (Spring 1974): 19–31; Charles K. Wolfe and Tony Russell, "The Asheville Session," *Old Time Music* 31 (Winter 1978/1979): 5–12; Kip Lornell and Ted Mealor, "A & R Men and the Geography of Piedmont Blues Recordings from 1924–1941," *ARSC Journal* 26 (Spring 1995): 1–22; Christopher Lornell, "Spatial Perspectives on the Field Recording of Traditional American Music: A Case Study from Tennessee in 1928," *Tennessee Folklore Society Bulletin* 47 (1981): 153–59, reprinted in *The Sounds of People and Places: A Geography of American Folk and Popular Music*, ed. George O. Carney (Lanham, Md.: Rowman and Littlefield, 1994), 77–84; Charles K. Wolfe, "The Legend That Peer Built: Reappraising the Bristol Sessions," in *The Bristol Sessions: Writings about the Big Bang of Country Music*, ed. Charles K. Wolfe and Ted Olson (Jefferson, N.C.: McFarland, 2005), 17–39; and Charles K. Wolfe, "The Rest of the Story: Other Early Recordings Sessions in the Tri-Cities Area," in ibid., 235–56.

36. Patrick Huber, comp., "Southern Field-Recording Sessions of Hillbilly Music, 1923–1932," unpublished list, compiled in 2006 (a copy of which remains in the author's possession); the figures on this list are based upon my tabulations from Russell, *Country Music Records*. For accounts of some of these Piedmont sessions, see, for example, Bob Carlin, *String Bands in the North Carolina Piedmont* (Jefferson, N.C.: McFarland, 2004) 151–53; "Recording and Radio: WRVA and the 1929 Richmond OKeh Sessions," *Virginia Cavalcade* 51 (Summer 2002): 136–42; Hanchett, "Recording in Charlotte," 12–16; and Daniel, *Pickin' on Peachtree*, 67–86.

37. This figure is based upon my tabulation of Atlanta field sessions in Russell, *Country Music Records*. On Atlanta as a major field-recording center, see Daniel, *Pickin' on Peachtree*, 67–86; Clifford M. Kuhn, Harlon E. Joye, and E. Bernard West, *Living Atlanta: An Oral History of the City, 1914–1948* (Atlanta and Athens: Atlanta

Historical Society/University of Georgia Press, 1990), 278; Goodson, *Highbrows, Hillbillies, and Hellfire*, 175–76; Charles K. Wolfe, *Tennessee Strings: The Story of Country Music in Tennessee* (Knoxville: University of Tennessee Press, 1977), 43.

38. On Charlotte as a field-recording center, see Hanchett, "Recording in Charlotte," 12–16; and Rust, *The Victor Master Book, Vol. 2*, 146–48, 406–8, 571, 583–85, 599–604. On the percentage of textile workers in the Piedmont states' industrial workforces, see Vance, *Human Geography of the South*, 281, 297, 298. In 1932, sociologist Rupert B. Vance reported that "two thirds of the industrial workers in South Carolina, one half in North Carolina, and 35 per cent in Georgia are in textiles." See ibid., 297.

39. Hall et al., *Like a Family*, 87, 88, 174.

40. Ibid., 174; *New York Times*, August 6, 1939; Vincent J. Roscigno and William F. Danaher, *The Voice of Southern Labor: Radio, Music, and Textile Strikes, 1929–1934*, Social Movements, Protest, and Contention, vol. 19 (Minneapolis: University of Minnesota Press, 2004), 48; DeNatale and Hinson, "The Southern Textile Song Tradition Reconsidered," 96. In 1936, Grant began appearing with a mandolin-playing co-worker named Arval Hogan in a duo called the Spindle City Boys, and the pair performed chiefly at church services before breaking into radio in 1938 and then commercial recording the following year. Their professional musical partnership would continue for the next sixty-eight years—until Hogan's death in 2003 at the age of ninety-two. See *Charlotte Observer*, September 13, 2003.

41. Kuhn et al., *Living Atlanta*, 276. See, for example, *Gastonia (N.C.) Daily Gazette*, September 12, 1928, for a report of Gwin Foster and Dave Fletcher performing "a splendid musical number" at the semimonthly luncheon meeting of the Civitan Club of Mount Holly, North Carolina.

42. *Washington Post*, January 26, 1908; *New York Times*, August 21, 1938, August 6, 1939. On early twentieth-century fiddlers' conventions in the Piedmont, see Daniel, *Pickin' on Peachtree*, 15–44; Cauthen, *With Fiddle and Well-Rosined Bow*, 164–66, 184–96; and Campbell, *Music and the Making of a New South*, 100–142.

43. Herring, *Welfare Work in Mill Villages*, 112–13, 141–44; *Mill News* (Charlotte, N.C.), October 14, 1920, 37; Potwin, *Cotton Mill People of the Piedmont*, 126–27; Gregg D. Kimball and Ron T. Curry, "On the Beach of Waikiki: Hopewell's Tubize Royal Hawaiian Orchestra," *Virginia Cavalcade* 51 (Summer 2002): 112–23.

44. Fred E. Beal, *Proletarian Journey: New England, Gastonia, Moscow* (New York: Hillman-Curl, 1937), 132; folder "Textiles—Gastonia Strike Songs," Mary Heaton Vorse Papers, ALUA; *Daily Worker* (New York, N.Y.), July 26, 1929; Vincent J. Roscigno and William F. Danaher, "Media and Mobilization: The Case of Radio and Southern Textile Insurgency, 1929 to 1934," *American Sociological Review* 66 (February 2001): 39, 40. On the Gastonia strike songs, see Margaret Larkin, "Ella May's Songs," *Nation* 129 (October 9, 1929): 382–83; John Greenway, *American Folksongs of Protest* (Philadelphia: University of Pennsylvania Press, 1953), 133–39, 244–52; Stephen R. Wiley, "Songs of the Gastonia Textile Strike of 1929: Models of and for Southern Working-Class Women's Militancy," *North Carolina Folklore Journal* 30 (Fall–Winter 1982): 87–98; Patrick Huber, "'Battle Songs of the Southern Class Struggle': Songs of the Gastonia Textile Strike of 1929," *Southern Cultures* 4 (Sum-

mer 1998): 109–22; and Timothy P. Lynch, *Strike Songs of the Depression* (Jackson: University Press of Mississippi, 2001), 12–48.

45. Rhyne, *Some Southern Cotton Mill Workers and Their Villages*, 18, 105–21; Hall et al., *Like a Family*, 107–9. A 1926 investigation by the Women's Bureau of the Department of Labor indicated that the annual labor turnover rate in southern textile mills ran as high as 190 percent. See Paul Blanshard, *Labor in Southern Cotton Mills* (New York: New Republic, 1927), 60.

46. A 1926–27 study of five hundred Gaston County textile families, for example, found that almost three-fourths of them were natives of North Carolina. Of these, one-fifth hailed from the Blue Ridge Mountains in the western part of the state. A significant proportion of the others, some 18 percent, came from South Carolina. Although these findings were not surprising, the survey also indicated that among the five hundred families were a few each from Texas, Louisiana, Oklahoma, Pennsylvania, Arizona, Ohio, and Indiana, and even one immigrant from Italy. See Rhyne, *Some Southern Cotton Mill Workers and Their Villages*, 46–48, 54–55, 68–70.

47. Blanshard, *Labor in Southern Cotton Mills*, 67; Potwin, *Cotton Mill People of the Piedmont*, 60; Hall et al., *Like a Family*, 66–67. For accounts of African American singers and musicians performing for audiences of white Piedmont millhands, see, for example, Potwin, *Cotton Mill People of the Piedmont*, 60; and *Gastonia (N.C.) Daily Gazette*, July 2, 1936.

48. Rhyne, *Some Southern Cotton Mill Workers and Their Villages*, 137–38; Frances Hampton, "New Leisure: How Is It Spent? A Study of What One Hundred Twenty-Two Textile Workers of Leaksville, Spray, and Draper Are Doing with the New Leisure Created by the N.R.A., as Applied to Certain Types of Activities" (master's thesis, University of North Carolina, 1935), 60–63. On Piedmont textile workers' increased participation in the nation's consumer culture during and after World War I, see Hall et al., *Like a Family*, 183–85, 252–55.

49. Carol J. Oja, "The USA, 1918–45," in *Modern Times: From World War I to the Present*, ed. Robert P. Morgan (Englewood Cliffs, N.J.: Prentice Hall, 1993), 208; George Lipsitz, *Rainbow at Midnight: Labor and Culture in the 1940s* (Urbana: University of Illinois Press, 1994), 310; Archie Green and Eugene Earle, liner notes to Carolina Tar Heels, *The Carolina Tar Heels* (Folk-Legacy FSA-24). The "original" Carolina Tar Heels actually consisted of banjoist Dock Walsh and harmonica player and guitarist Gwin S. Foster, the latter of whom worked in several Gaston County, North Carolina, textile mills. This handbill, however, featured a Carolina Tar Heels lineup of Dock Walsh and Garley Foster (no relation to Gwin), neither of whom was ever known to have worked in Piedmont textile mills.

50. On the epithet "hillbilly" and the adoption of this stereotype by hillbilly musicians, see Harkins, *Hillbilly*, especially 71–101.

51. On the rise of Piedmont radio stations, see, for example, Grundy, "'We Always Tried to Be Good People'"; "Recording and Radio," 136–42; Daniel, *Pickin' on Peachtree*, 45–66, 109–26, 127–51; Roscigno and Danaher, *The Voice of Southern Labor*, 21–23; and Carlin, *String Bands in the North Carolina Piedmont*, 172–96.

52. John W. Rumble, "Charlotte Country: A Sixty Year Tradition," in *The Char-*

lotte Country Music Story, 4–5; Grundy, "'We Always Tried to Be Good People,'" 1591–1620; "Recording and Radio," 136–42; Daniel, *Pickin' on Peachtree*, 109–26, 127–51; Carlin, *String Bands in the North Carolina Piedmont*, 172–96.

53. Tullos, *Habits of Industry*, 2; *Gastonia (N.C.) Daily Gazette*, April 27, 1935; Della Coulter, "The Piedmont Tradition," in *The Charlotte Country Music Story*, 10.

54. Hall et al., *Like a Family*, 237, 261–62. Old-time music historian Charles K. Wolfe estimates that Columbia's 15000-D "Familiar Tunes—Old and New" series alone sold some eleven million records between 1925 and 1932. See Wolfe, "Columbia Records and Old-Time Music," 119.

Chapter One

1. The definitive account of Carson's first recording session, upon which much of this paragraph is based, is Archie Green, "Hillbilly Music: Source and Symbol," *Journal of American Folklore* 78 (July–September 1965): 207–10. But see also Kyle Crichton, "Thar's Gold in Them Hillbillies," *Collier's* 101 (April 30, 1938), 24–27, reprinted in Linnell Gentry, *A History and Encyclopedia of Country, Western, and Gospel Music* (Nashville, Tenn.: McQuiddy Press, 1961), 39–45; Bill C. Malone, *Southern Music, American Music* (Lexington: University of Kentucky Press, 1979), 62; and especially Nolan Porterfield, *Jimmie Rodgers: The Life and Times of America's Blue Yodeler* (Urbana: University of Illinois Press, 1992 [1979]), 92–94. Peer's often-quoted account of Carson's debut session forms what Archie Green has called the "semi-official baptismal narrative" of hillbilly music, and it first appeared in Kyle Crichton's 1938 *Collier's* magazine article "Thar's Gold in Them Hillbillies," published nearly fifteen years after the event it describes. Perhaps as a result of a combination of the passage of time, the imperfections of memory, and the addition of dramatic embellishments, it is probably historically inaccurate on at least two crucial points. As country music historian Richard A. Peterson points out, Peer's pronouncement of Carson's recordings as "plu-perfect awful"—if he indeed did make such a statement—may have been in reference not to the quality of Carson's singing but rather to the poor audio quality of the acoustical recordings themselves. Peer's recollection of initially releasing Carson's record as a custom, uncataloged selection for Atlanta distribution only has also been disputed. See Green, "Hillbilly Music," 206; and Richard A. Peterson, *Creating Country Music: Fabricating Authenticity* (Chicago: University of Chicago Press, 1997), 241n15.

2. "Fiddlin' John Carson OKeh Records Popular in Trade," *Talking Machine World* 21 (April 15, 1925): 56; Columbia Records ad, *Talking Machine World* 20 (June 15, 1924): 17, reprinted in Archie Green, "Commercial Music Graphics: Three," *John Edwards Memorial Foundation Newsletter* 3 (December 1967): 45; Bill C. Malone, *Country Music, U.S.A.*, rev. ed. (Austin: University of Texas Press, 1985 [1968]), 38–42; Norm Cohen, *Long Steel Rail: The Railroad in American Folksong* (Urbana: University of Illinois Press, 1981), 32.

3. On Robertson, Gilliland, and Whitter, see Green, "Hillbilly Music," 210, 217; and Norm Cohen, "Early Pioneers," in *Stars of Country Music: Uncle Dave Macon to Johnnie Rodriguez*, ed. Bill C. Malone and Judith McCulloh (Urbana: University of

Illinois Press, 1975), 11–16. For contemporaries' assessments of Carson's fiddling, see Joe LaRose, "An Interview with Lowe Stokes," *Old Time Music* 39 (Spring 1984): 7; and Fred Hoeptner and Bob Pinson, "Clayton McMichen Talking," *Old Time Music* 1 (Summer 1971): 10. Whitter, a self-taught guitarist and harmonica player who worked in a Fries, Virginia, cotton mill, claimed that he had made some test recordings of ballads and instrumentals for OKeh at its New York studios around March 1, 1923, three and a half months before Carson. These test recordings were supposedly shelved and never released, but none of them have ever surfaced, nor do OKeh's studio ledgers indicate that Whitter recorded at that time. Fred W. Hager, OKeh's musical director, confirmed Whitter's account, however. Whitter's first documented recording session, for OKeh on December 10, 1923, resulted in the release of nine sides, including the famous "Wreck on the Southern Old 97" and "Lonesome Road Blues." See Green, "Hillbilly Music," 210; Norm Cohen, "Henry Whitter: His Life and Music," *John Edwards Memorial Foundation Quarterly* 11 (Summer 1975): 58; and Tony Russell, *Country Music Records: A Discography, 1921–1942,* with editorial research by Bob Pinson, assisted by the staff of the Country Music Hall of Fame and Museum (New York: Oxford University Press, 2004), 954.

4. Jacquelyn Dowd Hall, "Private Eyes, Public Women: Images of Class and Sex in the Urban South, Atlanta, Georgia, 1913–1915," in *Work Engendered: Toward a New History of American Labor,* ed. Ava Baron (Ithaca, N.Y.: Cornell University Press, 1991), 260–61; Jacquelyn Dowd Hall, James Leloudis, Robert Korstad, Mary Murphy, Lu Ann Jones, and Christopher B. Daly, *Like a Family: The Making of a Southern Cotton Mill World,* with a new afterword by the authors (Chapel Hill: University of North Carolina Press, 2000 [1987]), 237, 252–55, 257–62; Malone, *Southern Music, American Music,* 62.

5. Gene Wiggins, "Fiddlin' John Carson," in *The Encyclopedia of Country Music: The Ultimate Guide to the Music,* ed. Paul Kingsbury (New York: Oxford University Press, 1998), 81; Charles K. Wolfe, "Fiddling John Carson," in *Definitive Country: The Ultimate Encyclopedia of Country Music and Its Performers,* ed. Barry McCloud (New York: Perigree Books, 1995), 135–36.

6. See OKeh Records ad, *Talking Machine World* 20 (September 15, 1924): between pp. 58 and 59; Russell, *Country Music Records,* 175–79, 667–68; Wolfe, "Fiddling John Carson," 135–36; and Wiggins, "Fiddlin' John Carson," 81.

7. For biographical studies of Carson, see, in addition to those cited above, Chris Comber, "Fiddlin' John Carson," *Country Music People* (March 1972): 26–27, clipping in "Artists Files," SFC; Mark Wilson, liner notes to Fiddlin' John Carson, *The Old Hen Cackled and the Rooster's Going to Crow* (Rounder 1003), 1–7; Bob Coltman, "Look Out! Here He Comes . . . Fiddlin' John Carson, One of a Kind and Twice as Feisty," *Old Time Music* 9 (Summer 1973): 16–21; Norm Cohen, "'Fiddlin' John Carson: An Appreciation and a Discography," *John Edwards Memorial Foundation Quarterly* 10 (Winter 1974): 138–56; Wayne W. Daniel, "Fiddlin' John Carson: The World's First Commercial Country Artist," *Bluegrass Unlimited* (July 1985): 40–43; Phil Hardy and Dave Laing, "Fiddlin' John Carson," in *The Da Capo Companion to 20th-Century Popular Music* (New York: Da Capo Press, 1995), 151;

and Patrick Huber, "A Hillbilly Barnum: Fiddlin' John Carson and the Modern Origins of His Old-Time Music in Atlanta," *Atlanta History* 46 (2004): 24–53. Despite his groundbreaking career, few reissues of Carson's original recordings were available to record buyers until 1973, when Rounder Records released an entire album of his music, *The Old Hen Cackled and the Rooster's Going to Crow*. In 1987, the University of Illinois Press marketed a cassette tape of his songs and tunes in conjunction with the publication of Gene Wiggins's full-length biography, *Fiddlin' Georgia Crazy: Fiddlin' John Carson, His Real World, and the World of His Songs* (Urbana: University of Illinois Press, 1987), upon which much of this chapter is based. And, recently, Austria-based Document Records released its landmark series of seven compact discs of Carson's complete recordings, making his entire body of work easily accessible for the first time: Fiddlin' John Carson, *Fiddlin' John Carson: Complete Recorded Works in Chronological Order, Vols. 1–7 (1923–1934)* (Document DOCD-8014–DOCD-8020).

8. Coltman, "Look Out! Here He Comes . . . Fiddlin' John Carson," 16; Norm Cohen, "Folk Music Discography," *Western Folklore* 30 (July 1971): 235–37; Wilson, liner notes to Carson, *The Old Hen Cackled and the Rooster's Going to Crow*, 3; Wiggins, *Fiddlin' Georgia Crazy*, xii, xv.

9. On Carson's fiddle and vocal styles, see Wilson, liner notes to Carson, *The Old Hen Cackled and the Rooster's Going to Crow*, 3; Coltman, "Look Out! Here He Comes . . . Fiddlin' John Carson," 17–18; Cohen, "'Fiddlin' John Carson," 141.

10. Tenth Census of the United States, 1880: Cobb County, Georgia, Population Schedule, 190B (microfilm); *Atlanta Journal*, June 5, 1949, reprinted as "Fiddlin' John Carson: The Last Interview?" *Old Time Music* 1 (Summer 1971): 20; George Gordon Ward, *The Annals of Upper Georgia Centered in Gilmer County* (Carrollton, Ga.: Thomasson Print and Office Equipment Company, 1965), 661; Wiggins, *Fiddlin' Georgia Crazy*, 3–5, 7. Despite the long-standing academic interest in him as a pioneering hillbilly musician, the exact date and place of Carson's birth remain uncertain, with his birth date traditionally recorded as March 23, 1868, almost a year and a half before his parents married. According to his major biographer, Gene Wiggins, however, the best historical evidence suggests that Carson was probably born on March 23, 1874, in Cobb County, Georgia. The 1880 Census, which lists John's age as six in June of that year, corroborates Wiggins's claim for the later birth year. So, too, does the 1900 Census, which lists Carson's "date of birth" as March 1874. See Wiggins, *Fiddlin' Georgia Crazy*, 3–5; Tenth Census of the United States, 1880: Cobb County, Georgia, Population Schedule, 190B (microfilm); and Twelfth Census of the United States, 1900: Fulton County, Georgia, Population Schedule, 8A (microfilm).

11. Tenth Census of the United States, 1880: Cobb County, Georgia, Population Schedule, 190B (microfilm); *Atlanta Journal Magazine*, April 12, 1933, March 18, 1934; *Atlanta Journal*, June 5, 1949; Wiggins, *Fiddlin' Georgia Crazy*, 5–6.

12. Norm Cohen, liner notes to various artists, *Minstrels and Tunesmiths: The Commercial Roots of Early Country Music* (JEMF LP-109), 2, 3; Bill C. Malone, *Singing Cowboys and Musical Mountaineers: Southern Culture and the Roots of Country Music* (Athens: University of Georgia Press, 1993), especially 50–56; Edward L.

Ayers, *The Promise of the New South: Life after Reconstruction* (New York: Oxford University Press, 1992), 373–78, 393–96; Wiggins, *Fiddlin' Georgia Crazy*, 156–58.

13. Wiggins, *Fiddlin' Georgia Crazy*, 7–9, 10–11.

14. Ibid., 6, 10, 14–15, 19–20; Wilson, liner notes to Carson, *The Old Hen Cackled and the Rooster's Going to Crow*, 2; *Atlanta Journal Magazine*, April 12, 1933, March 18, 1934; Rosa Lee (Carson) Johnson interview by Archie Green and Ed Kahn, Decatur, Georgia, August 27, 1963, SFC.

15. Twelfth Census of the United States, 1900: Fulton County, Georgia, Population Schedule, 8A (microfilm); Wiggins, *Fiddlin' Georgia Crazy*, 19–20; Ronald H. Bayor, *Race and the Shaping of Twentieth-Century Atlanta* (Chapel Hill: University of North Carolina Press, 1996), 7; Clifford M. Kuhn, *Contesting the New South Order: The 1914–1915 Strike at Atlanta's Fulton Mills* (Chapel Hill: University of North Carolina Press, 2001), 33–34, 40; Robert E. Park, "The National Negro Business League," *Colored American Magazine* 11 (October 1906): 222.

16. Kuhn, *Contesting the New South Order*, 33, 36–37, 47–48. For another lengthy, turn-of-the-century newspaper description of Decatur Street, see *Atlanta Constitution*, October 15, 1893.

17. Twelfth Census of the United States, 1900: Fulton County, Georgia, Population Schedule, 8A (microfilm); *Atlanta Constitution*, April 10, 1913; Horace Carson, *Time and Changes in a City Called Atlanta: The Story of a Man, His Family and a City* (Atlanta: privately published, 1979), 7, 9, 11; Stephen W. Grable, "The Other Side of the Tracks: Cabbagetown—A Working-Class Neighborhood in Transition during the Early Twentieth Century," *Atlanta Historical Journal* 26 (Summer–Fall 1982): 52, 55–57; Kuhn, *Contesting the New South Order*, 56–59, 75, 139; Wiggins, *Fiddlin' Georgia Crazy*, 20, 22. Carson's father and brother Bud also began working at Exposition Mills around 1900, and, eventually, according to Gene Wiggins, all but one of Carson's twelve siblings worked in Piedmont textile mills. See ibid., 20.

18. Kuhn, *Contesting the New South Order*, 48; Wiggins, *Fiddlin' Georgia Crazy*, 22. On the Decatur Street entertainment district, see Steve Goodson, *Highbrows, Hillbillies, and Hellfire: Public Entertainment in Atlanta, 1880–1930* (Athens: University of Georgia Press, 2002), 167–68; Harvey K. Newman, "Decatur Street: Atlanta's African American Paradise Lost," *Atlanta History* 44 (Summer 2000): 5–20; and Tera W. Hunter, *To 'Joy My Freedom: Southern Black Women's Lives and Labor after the Civil War* (Cambridge, Mass.: Harvard University Press, 1997), 145–86. In 1914, for example, Carson performed at a St. Patrick's Day celebration at Atlanta's Railroad YMCA. "Irish songs and Irish recitations, abounding with Irish wit," noted a brief announcement in the *Atlanta Constitution*, March 17, 1914, "will be in vogue."

19. Carson, *Time and Changes in a City Called Atlanta*, 15; Wiggins, *Fiddlin' Georgia Crazy*, 23. The following account of the Fulton Bag and Cotton Mills strike is based chiefly upon Gary M. Fink, *The Fulton Bag and Cotton Mills Strike of 1914–1915: Espionage, Labor Conflict, and New South Industrial Relations* (Ithaca, N.Y.: ILR Press, 1993); Kuhn, *Contesting the New South Order*; and Hall, "Private Eyes, Public Women," 243–72.

20. Carson, *Time and Changes in a City Called Atlanta*, 15; Wiggins, *Fiddlin' Georgia Crazy*, 23, 25.

21. The following account of the Leo Frank case draws upon Leonard Dinnerstein, *The Leo Frank Case* (New York: Columbia University Press, 1968); Joel Williamson, *The Crucible of Race: Black-White Relations in the American South since Emancipation* (New York: Oxford University Press, 1984), 468–72; Nancy MacLean, "The Leo Frank Case Reconsidered: Gender and Sexual Politics in the Making of Reactionary Populism," *Journal of American History* 78 (December 1991): 917–48; C. Vann Woodward, *Tom Watson: Agrarian Rebel* (New York: Oxford University Press, 1963 [1938]), 431–50; and Steve Oney, *And the Dead Shall Rise: The Murder of Mary Phagan and the Lynching of Leo Frank* (New York: Pantheon Books 2003).

22. Wiggins, *Fiddlin' Georgia Crazy*, 26–33. On Carson's ballads about the case, see Saundra Keyes, "'Little Mary Phagan': A Native American Ballad in Context," *Journal of Country Music* 3 (Spring 1972): 1–16; D. K. Wilgus and Nathan Hurvitz, "'Little Mary Phagan': Further Notes on a Native American Ballad in Context," *Journal of Country Music* 4 (Spring 1973): 17–30; and Wiggins, *Fiddlin' Georgia Crazy*, 26–29, 31, 33–38. Besides "Little Mary Phagan," Carson composed two additional ballads about the case, "The Grave of Little Mary Phagan," which he later waxed for OKeh in December 1925, and "Dear Old Oak in Georgia," which glorifies the vigilantes who avenged Phagan's murder. Though neither Carson nor his daughter ever recorded "Dear Old Oak in Georgia," a paean to the tree from which Frank was lynched, Carson did sell copies of it on broadsides. In the ballad, he praises Phagan's avengers and employs explicitly anti-Semitic language. One of the stanzas goes: "Little Mary is in Heaven, where the streets are paved with Gold, / While Frank is in the pits of H—— kicking with the coals. Two years we have waited and tails [*sic*] we have listened to, / But the boys of old Georgia had to get that brutal Jew." See ibid., 42–43.

23. Woodward, *Tom Watson*, 436, 438, 440; Wiggins, *Fiddlin' Georgia Crazy*, 31–32.

24. *Atlanta Constitution*, August 18, 1915; Wayne W. Daniel, *Pickin' on Peachtree: A History of Country Music in Atlanta, Georgia* (Urbana: University of Illinois Press, 1990), 90–91. On the spread of "Little Mary Phagan," see, for example, Franklyn Bliss Snyder, "Leo Frank and Mary Phagan," *Journal of American Folk-Lore* 31 (April–June 1918): 264–66; Patrick Huber, "'Battle Songs of the Southern Class Struggle': Songs of the Gastonia Textile Strike of 1929," *Southern Cultures* 4 (Summer 1998): 121; and Wiggins, *Fiddlin' Georgia Crazy*, 38–43. In June 1925, fifteen-year-old Rosa Lee Carson recorded her father's murder ballad, "Little Mary Phagan," at her debut session for OKeh in a New York studio. Less than two months later, in August, Charlie Oaks waxed a version for Vocalion under the title "Mary Phagan." And the prolific freelance recording artist, Vernon Dalhart, recorded Carson's murder ballad three times: for Columbia in May 1925, for Cameo in October 1925, and for OKeh in February 1926. See Russell, *Country Music Records*, 175, 247, 251, 255, 664.

25. Johnson interview; Carson, *Time and Changes in a City Called Atlanta*, 7–8,

9; Grable, "The Other Side of the Tracks," 52, 55–57; Clifford M. Kuhn, Harlon E. Joye, and E. Bernard West, *Living Atlanta: An Oral History of the City, 1914–1948* (Atlanta and Athens: Atlanta Historical Society/University of Georgia Press, 1990), 36; Wiggins, *Fiddlin' Georgia Crazy*, 22.

26. Kuhn, *Contesting the New South Order*, 6, 34–36; Bayor, *Race and the Shaping of Twentieth-Century Atlanta*, 54, 148; Ray Stannard Baker, "Following the Color Line," *American Magazine* 63 (April 1907): 569; Wiggins, *Fiddlin' Georgia Crazy*, 21. For studies of the Atlanta Race Riot of 1906, on which this account is based, see Charles Crowe, "Racial Massacre in Atlanta, September 22, 1906," *Journal of Negro History* 54 (April 1969): 150–73; John Dittmer, *Black Georgia in the Progressive Era, 1900–1920* (Urbana: University of Illinois Press, 1977), 123–31; Williamson, *The Crucible of Race*, 209–23; Mark Bauerlein, *Negrophobia: A Race Riot in Atlanta, 1906* (San Francisco: Encounter Books, 2001); David Fort Godshalk, *Veiled Visions: The 1906 Atlanta Race Riot and the Reshaping of American Race Relations* (Chapel Hill: University of North Carolina Press, 2005); and Gregory Mixon, *The Atlanta Riot: Race, Class, and Violence in a New South City* (Gainesville: University of Florida Press, 2005).

27. On southern fiddling in the late nineteenth and early twentieth centuries, see, for example, Charles K. Wolfe, *Tennessee Strings: The Story of Country Music in Tennessee* (Knoxville: University of Tennessee Press, 1977), 19–22; Daniel, *Pickin' on Peachtree*, 15–44; Charles K. Wolfe, *The Devil's Box: Masters of Southern Fiddling* (Nashville: Country Music Foundation Press/Vanderbilt University Press, 1997); and Joyce H. Cauthen, *With Fiddle and Well-Rosined Bow: Old-Time Fiddling in Alabama* (Tuscaloosa: University of Alabama Press, 1989). On the modern urban origins of large-scale southern fiddlers' conventions, see, for example, Wolfe, *Tennessee Strings*, 22; Cauthen, *With Fiddle and Well-Rosined Bow*, 164–66, 184–96; and Gavin James Campbell, *Music and the Making of a New South* (Chapel Hill: University of North Carolina Press, 2004), 135, 173n182.

28. *Atlanta Constitution*, April 1, 1913. The following account of the Georgia Old-Time Fiddlers' Conventions draws heavily on Wayne W. Daniel, "The Georgia Old-Time Fiddlers' Convention: 1920 Edition," *John Edwards Memorial Foundation Quarterly* 16 (Summer 1980): 67–73; Wayne W. Daniel, "Old Time Georgians Recall the Georgia Old Time Fiddlers' Conventions," *Devil's Box* 15 (March 1981): 7–16; Daniel, *Pickin' on Peachtree*, 15–44; Wiggins, *Fiddlin' Georgia Crazy*, 46–60; Charles K. Wolfe, "The Atlanta Fiddling Contests, 1913–1916," *Devil's Box* 14 (June 1980): 12–29; Charles K. Wolfe, "The Atlanta Contests, 1921–1934," *Devil's Box* 15 (March 1981): 17–25; and Campbell, *Music and the Making of a New South*, 100–142.

29. *Atlanta Journal*, April 2, 1913; *Atlanta Constitution*, April 4, 1913; Daniel, *Pickin' on Peachtree*, 22, 36; Wiggins, *Fiddlin' Georgia Crazy*, 48–49; Cohen, "'Fiddlin' John Carson," 139; Linton K. Starr, "Georgia's Unwritten Airs Played by Old 'Fiddlers' for Atlanta Prizes," *Musical America* (March 21, 1914), reprinted in Guthrie Meade, "From the Archives: 1914 Atlanta Fiddle Convention," *John Edwards Memorial Foundation Quarterly* 5 (Spring 1969): 29. See also *Atlanta Constitution*, February 15, 1914.

30. Cohen, "'Fiddlin' John Carson," 139; Wiggins, *Fiddlin' Georgia Crazy*, 52; Daniel, *Pickin' on Peachtree*, 89; *Atlanta Journal*, November 18, 1919.

31. Wiggins, *Fiddlin' Georgia Crazy*, 49; Campbell, *Music and the Making of a New South*, 101; Daniel, *Pickin' on Peachtree*, 33; *Atlanta Constitution*, February 18, 1914.

32. *Atlanta Constitution*, March 1, 1918; Charles K. Wolfe, "The Birth of an Industry," in *The Illustrated History of Country Music*, ed. Patrick Carr (New York: Random House/Time Books, 1995 [1980]), 44; *Atlanta Journal*, February 1, 1915; "Fiddling to Henry Ford," *Literary Digest* 88 (January 2, 1926): 33–34, 36, 38; David L. Lewis, "The Square Dancing Master," *American Heritage* 23 (February 1972): 49–51; Bill C. Malone, *Don't Get Above Your Raisin': Country Music and the Southern Working Class* (Urbana: University of Illinois Press, 2002), 24–25; unidentified Tennessee newspaper, ca. 1926, clipping in Guthrie T. Meade Papers, SFC.

33. William Goodell Frost, "Our Contemporary Ancestors in the Southern Mountains," *Atlantic Monthly* 83 (March 1899): 311–19; William Goodell Frost, "The Southern Mountaineer: Our Kindred of the Boone and Lincoln Types," *American Review of Reviews* 21 (March 1900): 303–11; C. Brenden Martin, "To Keep the Spirit of Mountain Culture Alive: Tourism and Historical Memory in the Southern Highlands," in *Where These Memories Grow: History, Memory, and Southern Identity*, ed. W. Fitzhugh Brundage (Chapel Hill: University of North Carolina Press, 2000), 251–52. My discussion of the invention of Southern Appalachia draws chiefly on Martin, "To Keep the Spirit of Mountain Culture Alive"; Henry D. Shapiro, *Appalachia on Our Mind: The Southern Mountains and Mountaineers in the American Consciousness, 1870–1920* (Chapel Hill: University of North Carolina Press, 1978); David E. Whisnant, *All That Is Native and Fine: The Politics of Culture in an American Region* (Chapel Hill: University of North Carolina Press, 1983); and Allen W. Batteau, *The Invention of Appalachia* (Tucson: University of Arizona Press, 1990).

34. Green, "Hillbilly Music," 204. On the emergence and development of the hillbilly stereotype, see J. W. Williamson, *Hillbillyland: What the Movies Did to the Mountains and What the Mountains Did to the Movies* (Chapel Hill: University of North Carolina Press, 1995), especially 1–4; Batteau, *The Invention of Appalachia*, 127–32; and Anthony Harkins, *Hillbilly: A Cultural History of an American Icon* (New York: Oxford University Press, 2004), especially 47–69, 103–40.

35. Malone, *Singing Cowboys and Musical Mountaineers*, 76; Wiggins, *Fiddlin' Georgia Crazy*, 31; *Atlanta Journal Magazine*, June 21, 1914.

36. John A. Burrison, "Fiddlers in the Alley: Atlanta as an Early Country Music Center," *Atlanta Historical Society Bulletin* 21 (Summer 1977): 59; Goodson, *Highbrows, Hillbillies, and Hellfire*, 162; Wayne W. Daniel, "Bill Gatins and His Jug Band," *Old Time Music* 37 (Autumn 1981–Spring 1982): 9–10; Kuhn et al., *Living Atlanta*, 306–10; Wiggins, *Fiddlin' Georgia Crazy*, 66–67, 109, 116–17.

37. *Atlanta Constitution*, October 26, 1923; Burrison, "Fiddlers in the Alley," 73–84; Daniel, *Pickin' on Peachtree*, 32, 87–108. For other newspaper accounts of the musical exchanges that occurred at these fiddlers' contests, see *Atlanta Journal*, February 28, 1918; and *Atlanta Journal Magazine*, March 18, 1934.

38. Fourteenth Census of the United States, 1920: Fulton County, Georgia,

Population Schedule, 28B (microfilm); Donald Lee Nelson, "Earl Johnson—Professional Musician," *John Edwards Memorial Foundation Quarterly* 10 (Winter 1974): 169–75; Wiggins, *Fiddlin' Georgia Crazy*, 66–67, 72; poster reproduced in Gene Wiggins, "John Carson: Early Road, Radio and Records," *Journal of Country Music* 8 (May 1979): 34; Wilson, liner notes to Carson, *The Old Hen Cackled and the Rooster's Going to Crow*, 1. Among the regulars who toured with Carson, fiddler Earl Johnson could reportedly perform classical pieces and popular hits on his fiddle just as well as he could saw off old-time reels and breakdowns, supposedly due to a Chicago musical correspondence course he took. Guitarist T. M. "Bully" Brewer, a Tennessee native who was one-quarter Cherokee, anchored the Carson accompanists. Born in 1885, Brewer had worked as a brakeman on the Southern Railway, first in Knoxville and then, after 1917, in Atlanta, until he lost one of his legs in a train derailment a few years later. After he had squandered the compensation settlement he received from the railroad, Brewer turned to music making and bootlegging to earn a living. See Nelson, "Earl Johnson," 169–75; and Wiggins, *Fiddlin' Georgia Crazy*, 66–67.

39. Wiggins, *Fiddlin' Georgia Crazy*, 64, 66–68, 97 (for a photograph of Carson and his daughter Rosa Lee seated on the bumper of his Model A Ford, see the section of illustrations between pages 140 and 141). Of course, Progressive-era Georgia's "Good Roads" programs and the extension of hard-surfaced roads throughout the South made Carson and the Virginia Reelers' tours possible. By 1920, seven state highways connected Atlanta to the major cities of Georgia and the southeastern United States. See Daniel, *Pickin' on Peachtree*, 3–4.

40. *Charleston (W.Va.) Gazette*, June 28, 1924; Wiggins, *Fiddlin' Georgia Crazy*, 65, 97.

41. "Radio Made 'Fiddlin' John Carson' Famous," *Radio Digest* (November 7, 1925), reprinted in Wilson, liner notes to Carson, *The Old Hen Cackled and the Rooster's Going to Crow*, 8; *Atlanta Journal*, June 10, 1923; *Welcome South, Brother: Fifty Years of Broadcasting at WSB, Atlanta, Georgia* (Atlanta: Cox Broadcasting Corporation, 1974), 7–16; Daniel, *Pickin' on Peachtree*, 47–49, 56–57.

42. *Atlanta Journal*, September 10, 1922; Wiggins, *Fiddlin' Georgia Crazy*, 70–71, 73; Daniel, *Pickin' on Peachtree*, 50, 92–93.

43. *Atlanta Journal*, November 30, 1922; Wiggins, *Fiddlin' Georgia Crazy*, 72; Daniel, *Pickin' on Peachtree*, 51–53, 55–62; Coltman, "Look Out! Here He Comes . . . Fiddlin' John Carson," 21. For accounts of old-time fiddling and barn dances on early 1920s radio, see, for example, Norm Cohen, comp., "Materials toward a Study of Early Country Music on Radio I: Nashville," *John Edwards Memorial Foundation Newsletter* 4 (September 1968): 109–13; Guthrie T. Meade, comp., "Materials toward a Study of Early Country Music on Radio II: Dallas, Texas," *John Edwards Memorial Foundation Newsletter* 4 (December 1968): 131–33; Guthrie T. Meade, comp., "Materials toward a Study of Early Country Music on Radio IV: Dallas, Texas," *John Edwards Memorial Foundation Quarterly* 5 (Summer 1969): 131–33; George C. Biggar, "The WLS National Barn Dance: The Early Years," *John Edwards Memorial Foundation Quarterly* 7 (Autumn 1971): 105–12; and Charles K. Wolfe,

A *Good-Natured Riot: The Birth of the Grand Ole Opry* (Nashville, Tenn.: Country Music Foundation Press/Vanderbilt University Press, 1999).

44. On the history of the General Phonograph Corporation and its OKeh label, see Ross Laird and Brian Rust, *Discography of OKeh Records, 1918–1934* (Westport, Conn.: Praeger, 2004), 2–6; Allan Sutton and Kurt Nauck, *American Record Labels and Companies: An Encyclopedia (1891–1943)* (Denver, Colo.: Mainspring Press, 2000), 145–49, 283–85; and Russell, *Country Music Records*, 21–22.

45. The following account of Carson's debut recording session and OKeh's marketing of his first record relies chiefly on Green, "Hillbilly Music," 207–11. One form of modern commercial entertainment, silent films, apparently had inspired the cultural production of another, phonograph records. As Robert Cantwell reminds us, "The documentary powers of one medium, apparently, had alerted [Brockman] to the documentary powers of the other, and, interestingly, both were in about the same stage of technical development." See Robert Cantwell, *Bluegrass Breakdown: The Making of the Old Southern Sound* (New York: Da Capo Press, 1992 [1984]), 190.

46. *Atlanta Constitution*, July 10, 1923; Green, "Hillbilly Music," 208–10.

47. Green, "Hillbilly Music," 210; "Fiddlin' John Carson's Records Widely Popular," *Talking Machine World* 21 (August 15, 1925): 81. Originally, Fiddlin' John Carson's first record was promoted in an *Atlanta Journal* advertisement, "not with a mountain or rural symbol," as Archie Green has noted, "but, rather under portraits of Byron Warner's Seven Aces, an Atlanta hotel jazz band." See Archie Green, "Graphics #68: Winding Down," *John Edwards Memorial Foundation Quarterly* 21 (Fall/Winter 1985): 99.

48. On this point, see, for example, Thomas A. Ekkens, "Earliest?? Folkers on Disc," *Record Research* 92 (September 1968): 4, 10; Green, "Hillbilly Music," 207; Simon J. Bronner, "Old-Time Tunes on Edison Records, 1899–1923," *Journal of Country Music* 8 (May 1979): 95–100; and Cohen, liner notes to various artists, *Minstrels and Tunesmiths*, 30. As early as 1892, for example, a New Orleans black Creole and semiprofessional minstrel banjoist named Louis "Bebe" Vasnier made a cylinder recording of "Turkey in the Straw" for the Louisiana Phonograph Company. See Tim Brooks, "Early Black Vaudeville on Record: Louis 'Bebe' Vasnier and the Louisiana Phonograph Company," *ARSC Journal* 28 (Fall 1997): 143, 146, 152.

49. OKeh Records, *OKeh Records Catalog* (New York: General Phonograph Corporation, 1924); Green, "Hillbilly Music," 210; Cantwell, *Bluegrass Breakdown*, 191–92; "Fiddlin' John Carson Joins OKeh," *Talking Machine World* 19 (September 15, 1923): 30.

50. OKeh Records ad, *Talking Machine World* 20 (June 15, 1924): between pages 66 and 67; Archie Green, "Commercial Music Graphics: Two," *John Edwards Memorial Foundation Newsletter* 3 (September 1967): 15, 17.

51. Green, "Commercial Music Graphics: Two," 16.

52. Wiggins, *Fiddlin' Georgia Crazy*, 77; "OKeh Artist Visits New York," *Talking Machine World* 19 (December 15, 1923): 52.

53. "OKeh 45000 Series," *Old Time Music* 1 (Summer 1971): 25; Green, "Hillbilly

Music," 211, 215. Competing record companies clearly tried to emulate Carson's successful OKeh hits by, in several cases, actually recording cover versions of those selections. At their first Columbia recording session in March 1924, for example, Riley Puckett sang "Little Old Log Cabin in the Lane," accompanied by his own guitar and Gid Tanner's fiddle. In July, Uncle Dave Macon cut a banjo version of the song, accompanied by fiddler Sid Harkreader, for the Vocalion label. The following month, Fiddlin' Cowan Powers and Family, one of Victor's newly signed old-time artists, waxed the number under its original sheet music title, "The Little Old Cabin in the Lane." See Russell, *Country Music Records*, 574, 703, 715.

54. *Middlesboro (Ky.) Daily News*, June 11, 1924; *Portsmouth (Ohio) Daily Times*, June 23, 1924; *Charleston (W.Va.) Gazette*, June 26 and 27, 1924; Wiggins, *Fiddlin' Georgia Crazy*, 80-81. During the late nineteenth and early twentieth centuries, the growth of cities, textile towns, and coal camps across the Southern Piedmont and Southern Appalachia, as well as the development of hard-surfaced highways and roads there during the 1920s, created regional markets of working-class consumers who avidly listened to Carson's radio broadcasts and purchased his phonograph records, song folios, and concert tickets.

55. Johnson interview; Wiggins, *Fiddlin' Georgia Crazy*, 84-85.

56. Johnson interview; Mary A. Bufwack and Robert K. Oermann, *Finding Her Voice: The Saga of Women in Country Music* (New York: Crown Publishers, 1993), 66-68, 72-73; Wilson, liner notes to Carson, *The Old Hen Cackled and the Rooster's Going to Crow*, 1; Wiggins, *Fiddlin' Georgia Crazy*, 68-69, 97, 99-100.

57. Cohen, "'Fiddlin' John Carson," 141; Tony Russell, review of Carson, *The Old Hen Cackled and the Rooster's Going to Crow*, *Old Time Music* 12 (Spring 1974): 33; *Atlanta Journal*, November 21, 1919; Wiggins, *Fiddlin' Georgia Crazy*, 152-61, 183-203, 204-19, 256-72. For a discography of Carson's OKeh and Bluebird recordings, see Russell, *Country Music Records*, 175-79, 667-68; and for those of his daughter, Rosa Lee Carson, see 179-80. Carson belonged to Atlanta's East Side Baptist Church (where Rosa Lee sang in the choir) and saw to it that one of his grandsons was baptized—repeatedly—at religious revivals. As biographer Gene Wiggins points out, "Recording religious songs conflicted with the image of Carson presented to the public—that of a rambunctious old rascal who made 'good licker.'" See Wiggins, *Fiddlin' Georgia Crazy*, 162.

58. Wiggins, *Fiddlin' Georgia Crazy*, 101-5. On Gid Tanner and the the Skillet Lickers, see Norm Cohen, "The Skillet Lickers: A Study of a Hillbilly String Band and Its Repertoire," *Journal of American Folklore* 78 (July-September 1965): 242; all fourteen sides of "A Corn Licker Still in Georgia" can be heard on Gid Tanner and His Skillet Lickers, *A Corn Licker Still in Georgia* (Voyager VRCD303).

59. Kuhn, *Contesting the New South Order*, 47-49; Goodson, *Highbrows, Hillbillies, and Hellfire*, 167-69; OKeh "'Old Time' Tunes" monthly supplement, April 1925, Archie Green Papers, SFC; Wiggins, *Fiddlin' Georgia Crazy*, 63, 152, 154, 156, 158-59, 242-44, 245-55.

60. Scott Reynolds Nelson, *Steel Drivin' Man: John Henry, the Untold Story of an American Legend* (New York: Oxford University Press, 2006), 139; Frank Walker interview by Mike Seeger, probably in New York, New York, June 19, 1962, SFC;

"Who Chose These Records?: A Look into the Life, Tastes, and Procedures of Frank Walker," in *Anthology of American Folk Music*, ed. Josh Dunson and Ethel Raim (New York: Oak Publications, 1973), 15–16; Cohen, *Long Steel Rail*, 61–89, 304–15; Wiggins, *Fiddlin' Georgia Crazy*, 112–13, 156, 159, 190–92, 210–12; Wilson, liner notes to Carson, *The Old Hen Cackled and the Rooster's Going to Crow*, 3; *Atlanta Journal Magazine*, June 21, 1914.

61. On the extensive black-white musical exchange that characterized hillbilly music, especially in regard to the musicians listed above, see, for example, John Cohen, "The Folk Music Interchange: Negro and White," *Sing Out!* 14 (January 1965): 42–49; Tony Russell, *Blacks, Whites and Blues* (New York: Stein and Day, 1970); John S. Otto and Augustus M. Burns, "Black and White Cultural Interaction in the Early Twentieth Century South: Race and Hillbilly Music," *Phylon* 35 (4th Quarter, 1974): 407–17; Charles Wolfe, "A Lighter Shade of Blue: White Country Blues," in *Nothing but the Blues: The Music and the Musicians*, ed. Lawrence Cohn (New York: Abbeville Press, 1993), 233–63; and George Lipsitz, *Rainbow at Midnight: Labor and Culture in the 1940s* (Urbana: University of Illinois Press, 1994), 312–13.

62. Wiggins, *Fiddlin' Georgia Crazy*, 33–38, 112, 114, 118, 231–39; MacLean, "The Leo Frank Case Reconsidered," 920.

63. *Atlanta Journal Magazine*, March 18, 1934; Wiggins, *Fiddlin' Georgia Crazy*, 67, 78, 194, 199.

64. Wiggins, *Fiddlin' Georgia Crazy*, 94–96, 101–6, 160, 233–34, 239.

65. Ibid., 231–39

66. Lee Glazer and Susan Key, "Carry Me Back: Nostalgia for the Old South in Nineteenth-Century Popular Culture," *Journal of American Studies* 30 (April 1996): 1–24; Bill C. Malone, "Will Hays," in *Encyclopedia of Southern Culture*, ed. Charles Reagan Wilson and William Ferris (Chapel Hill: University of North Carolina Press, 1989), 1061–62; Bronner, "Old-Time Tunes on Edison Records," 95; Cohen, liner notes to various artists, *Minstrels and Tunesmiths*, 30.

67. Wiggins, *Fiddlin' Georgia Crazy*, 221–25.

68. Ibid., 221; Wilson, liner notes to Carson, *The Old Hen Cackled and the Rooster's Going to Crow*, 3; Malone, *Singing Cowboys and Musical Mountaineers*, 64.

69. On the Ku Klux Klan in Atlanta, see Kenneth T. Jackson, *The Ku Klux Klan in the City, 1915–1930* (New York: Oxford University Press, 1967), 3–4, 9–12, 29–44, 262n17; Kuhn et al., *Living Atlanta*, 14, 313; Green, "Hillbilly Music," 214; Joe Wilson, liner notes to various artists, *A Fiddlers' Convention in Mountain City, Tennessee: 1924–1930 Recordings* (County 525); Wiggins, *Fiddlin' Georgia Crazy*, 114.

70. *Daily Worker* (New York, N.Y.), May 13, 1933; Wiggins, *Fiddlin' Georgia Crazy*, 241. On the Herndon case, see Charles H. Martin, *The Angelo Herndon Case and Southern Justice* (Baton Rouge: Louisiana State University Press, 1976); Angelo Herndon, *Let Me Live* (New York: Arno Press, 1969 [1937]); John Hammond Moore, "The Angelo Herndon Case, 1932–1937," *Phylon* 32 (First Quarter 1971): 60–71; and Charles H. Martin, "Communists and Blacks: The ILD and the Angelo Herndon Case," *Journal of Negro History* 64 (Spring 1979): 131–41.

71. MacLean, "The Leo Frank Case Reconsidered," 920.

72. Kuhn et al., *Living Atlanta*, 306; Daniel, *Pickin' on Peachtree*, 65–66, 95; Robert Coltman, "Across the Chasm: How the Depression Changed Country Music," *Old Time Music* 23 (Winter 1976–77): 6–12.

73. Roland Gelatt, *The Fabulous Phonograph, 1877–1977*, 2nd rev. ed. (New York: Collier Books, 1977 [1955]), 255; Sutton and Nauck, *American Record Labels and Companies*, xviii; "OKeh 45000 Series," 25; Russell, *Country Music Records*, 21–22, 179; Wiggins, *Fiddlin' Georgia Crazy*, 123–25; Cohen, "'Fiddlin' John Carson," 140.

74. Wiggins, *Fiddlin' Georgia Crazy*, 12–14, 76, 108–10, 112, 134. Although the stories may be apocryphal, Carson claimed that he had fiddled at political rallies and barbecues for Bob Taylor in 1886 when he ran for governor of Tennessee against his brother Alf Taylor, and Carson may have entertained for Thomas E. Watson when he ran for U.S. Congress on the Populist ticket in the elections of 1892 and 1894. But it is certain that Carson worked as a campaign fiddler for Watson during his successful 1920 bid for the U.S. Senate. In fact, during the contest, Carson composed a campaign song for his political hero and patron, titled "Tom Watson Special," which he set to the unlikely melody of the popular 1915 hit, "The Hesitating Blues," by the renowned black composer W. C. Handy. In November 1923, less than fourteen months after Watson died in office, Carson recorded the song for OKeh at a New York session. See Woodward, *Tom Watson*, 416–30; Judith McCulloh, "Notes on Thomas E. Watson," *John Edwards Memorial Foundation Quarterly* 7 (Summer 1971): 65–67; and Wiggins, *Fiddlin' Georgia Crazy*, 112–13.

75. William Anderson, *The Wild Man from Sugar Creek: The Political Career of Eugene Talmadge* (Baton Rouge: Louisiana State University Press, 1975), especially 76, 78, 156; Wiggins, *Fiddlin' Georgia Crazy*, 115–17, 231; *Atlanta Journal*, June 5, 1949. An image of Talmadge's 1926 campaign poster can be accessed under the title "A Real Dirt Farmer, Eugene Talmadge, Candidate for State Commissioner of Agriculture," at the Georgia Archives' Vanishing Georgia digital photograph collection, <http://dlg.galileo.usg.edu/vanga/html/vanga_homeframe_default .html?link=vang> (July 28, 2007).

76. Bufwack and Oermann, *Finding Her Voice*, 66; Tammy Harden Galloway, "'Tribune of the Masses and a Champion of the People': Eugene Talmadge and the Three-Dollar Tag," *Georgia Historical Quarterly* 79 (Fall 1995): 673–84; *Atlanta Constitution*, February 13, 1947; Wiggins, *Fiddlin' Georgia Crazy*, 117–20, 121–22, 126–28, 132–37, 139–40, 141–45. Carson contributed at least two additional songs to the campaign, "Talmadge Special" and "Talmadge Highball." See ibid., 118.

77. *Lima (Ohio) News*, July 25, 1939; Wiggins, *Fiddlin' Georgia Crazy*, 122, 132, 135–36, 194–96.

78. *Atlanta Journal*, June 5, 1949; Wiggins, *Fiddlin' Georgia Crazy*, 132, 144–46; funeral notice, undated newspaper clipping, ca. December 12, 1949, in "Artists Files," SFC; Wilson, liner notes to Carson, *The Old Hen Cackled and the Rooster's Going to Crow*, 2.

79. Daniel, *Pickin' on Peachtree*, 232; *Atlanta Journal*, June 5, 1949; Johnson interview; Wiggins, *Fiddlin' Georgia Crazy*, xv, 120. For additional examples of Carson's disparaging comments about the state of contemporary music, see *Atlanta Journal Magazine*, March 18, 1934, April 16, 1939.

80. Kuhn, *Contesting the New South Order*, 6, 215–16; Russell, review of Carson, *The Old Hen Cackled and the Rooster's Going to Crow*, 33.

81. Wiggins, *Fiddlin' Georgia Crazy*, xiii.

82. Ibid., 65, 95, 112–21, 123, 132; Wilson, liner notes to Carson, *The Old Hen Cackled and the Rooster's Going to Crow*, 3; Russell, review of Carson, *The Old Hen Cackled and the Rooster's Going to Crow*, 33; Cohen, "'Fiddlin' John Carson," 141.

Chapter Two

1. *Greensboro (N.C.) Daily News*, July 29, 1976; Kinney Rorrer, liner notes to Charlie Poole and the North Carolina Ramblers, *Charlie Poole and the North Carolina Ramblers: Old Time Songs Recorded from 1925 to 1930, Vol. 2* (County CO-3508). For a similar account of a stringband broadcasting music over telephone party lines, see Kinney Rorrer, "Red Patterson and the Piedmont Log Rollers," *Old Time Music* 34 (Summer/Autumn 1980): 6.

2. Kinney Rorrer, "Charlie Poole and the North Carolina Ramblers," in *The Encyclopedia of Country Music: The Ultimate Guide to the Music*, ed. Paul Kingsbury (New York: Oxford University Press, 1998), 418; Rorrer, liner notes to Poole and the North Carolina Ramblers, *Charlie Poole and the North Carolina Ramblers, Vol. 2*; Kinney Rorrer, *Rambling Blues: The Life and Songs of Charlie Poole* (Danville, Va.: McCain Printing Company, 1992 [1982]), 9, 34, 53. Besides being related to Poole by marriage, Kinney Rorrer is also related to Poole's bandmate and brother-in-law, Posey Rorer, the uncle and legal guardian of Kinney Rorrer's father. The different spellings of the family's surname are attributed to the fact that, during the 1950s, Kinney's family began to spell the name as "Rorrer."

3. Rorrer, "Charlie Poole and the North Carolina Ramblers," in *The Encyclopedia of Country Music*, 418; Ivan M. Tribe, "Charlie Poole," in *Definitive Country: The Ultimate Encyclopedia of Country Music and Its Performers*, ed. Barry McCloud (New York: Perigree Books, 1995), 640–41; Patrick Huber, "Charlie Poole," in *The North Carolina Century: Tar Heels Who Made a Difference, 1900–2000*, ed. Howard E. Covington and Marion A. Ellis (Charlotte, N.C.: Levine Museum of the New South, 2002), 443–46; Charles K. Wolfe, "Columbia Records and Old-Time Music," *John Edwards Memorial Foundation Quarterly* 14 (Autumn 1978): 125; Rorrer, *Rambling Blues*, 31; *Burlington (N.C.) Daily Times*, February 11, 1927; Frank Walker interview by Mike Seeger, probably New York, New York, June 19, 1962, SFC; "Who Chose These Records? A Look into the Life, Tastes, and Procedures of Frank Walker," in *Anthology of American Folk Music*, ed. Josh Dunson and Ethel Raim (New York: Oak Publications, 1973), 15. The figure of eighty-three sides given here does not include the more than forty additional recordings that Posey Rorer and Roy Harvey made together without Charlie Poole between May 1927 and February 1928. Despite the absence of Poole on these recordings, approximately half of them were released under the artist billings of "North Carolina Ramblers," "North Carolina Ramblers and Roy Harvey," or "Roy Harvey and the North Carolina Ramblers." For a discography of Poole and the North Carolina Ramblers and the other combinations of the band, see Tony Russell, *Country Music Records: A Discography, 1921–1942*, with editorial research by Bob Pinson, assisted by the staff of the Country

Music Hall of Fame and Museum (New York: Oxford University Press, 2004), 409–10, 698–700.

4. Rorrer, liner notes to Poole and the North Carolina Ramblers, *Charlie Poole and the North Carolina Ramblers, Vol. 2*; Kinney Rorrer, liner notes to Charlie Poole and the North Carolina Ramblers, *Charlie Poole and the North Carolina Ramblers: Old Time Songs Recorded from 1925 to 1930* (County CO-3501); Norm Cohen, "Early Pioneers," in *Stars of Country Music: Uncle Dave Macon to Johnny Rodriguez*, ed. Bill C. Malone and Judith McCulloh (Urbana: University of Illinois Press, 1975), 26; Bill C. Malone, *Country Music, U.S.A.*, rev. ed. (Austin: University of Texas Press, 1985 [1968]), 51; Robert Cantwell, *Bluegrass Breakdown: The Making of the Old Southern Sound* (New York: Da Capo Press, 1992 [1984]), 53, 191; Rorrer, *Rambling Blues*, 44.

5. Columbia Records, *Old Familiar Tunes* (New York: Columbia Phonograph Company, 1929); Rorrer, *Rambling Blues*, 38, 43, 54.

6. Rorrer, liner notes to Poole and the North Carolina Ramblers, *Charlie Poole and the North Carolina Ramblers, Vol. 2*; Rorrer, liner notes to Poole and the North Carolina Ramblers, *Charlie Poole and the North Carolina Ramblers*; Clifford Kinney Rorrer, "Charlie Poole and the North Carolina Ramblers," in *Country Music Who's Who: 1972*, ed. Chuck Neese (New York: Record World Publications, 1971), H-3; Clifford Kinney Rorrer, *Charlie Poole and the North Carolina Ramblers* (Eden, N.C.: privately published, 1968), 6–7; Cohen, "Early Pioneers," 25–26; Rorrer, *Rambling Blues*, 13; Henry "Hank" Sapoznik, liner notes to Charlie Poole, *"You Ain't Talkin' to Me": Charlie Poole and the Roots of Country Music*, 3-CD boxed set (Columbia/Legacy C3K-92781–83), 2, 11–12.

7. Twelfth Census of the United States, 1900: Randolph County, N.C., Population Schedule, 120B (microfilm); Rorrer, *Rambling Blues*, 13. According to Kinney Rorrer, "Charlie Poole's mother died while he was a small child and his father remarried, with his wife's sister Betsy Anne Johnson." Neither the 1900 nor the 1910 census substantiates this claim, however. On April 29, 1910, John and Bettie Poole told the census official that they had been married for thirty-eight years. See ibid.; Twelfth Census of the United States, 1900: Randolph County, N.C., Population Schedule, 120B (microfilm); and Thirteenth Census of the United States, 1910: Alamance County, N.C., Population Schedule, 80A (microfilm). It should also be noted that Charlie Poole's World War I draft registration card, filled out on June 5, 1917, lists his place of birth as Statesville, in Iredell County—not Millboro, in Randolph County—North Carolina. A 1931 Rockingham County, North Carolina, newspaper obituary also lists his birthplace as Iredell County, North Carolina. See Charles Cleveland Pool [*sic*], World War I draft registration card, Guilford County, N.C., no. 86, June 5, 1917, accessed on Ancestry.com (May 24, 2006); and Rorrer, *Rambling Blues*, 13.

8. Randolph County Historical Society and the Randolph Arts Guild, *Randolph County, 1779–1979* (Winston-Salem, N.C.: Hunter Publishing Company, 1980), 249, 94–106; Twelfth Census of the United States, 1900: Randolph County, N.C., Population Schedule, 120B (microfilm); Rorrer, *Rambling Blues*, 13, 16.

9. Rorrer, *Rambling Blues*, 13; Walter Whitaker, *Centennial History of Alamance County, 1849–1949* (Burlington, N.C.: Burlington Chamber of Commerce, ca. 1950), 140, 164–65; Gail Knauff and Bob Knauff, *Fabric of a Community: The Story of Haw River, North Carolina* (Haw River, N.C.: Haw River Historical Association, 1996), 10–30; *Alamance Gleaner* (Graham, N.C.), November 1, 8, 15, 22, 1900. The most comprehensive account of the Haw River Strike of 1900 can be found in Bess Beatty, *Alamance: The Holt Family and Industrialization in a North Carolina County, 1837–1900* (Baton Rouge: Louisiana State University Press, 1999), 204–12; but see also Paul D. Escott, *Many Excellent People: Power and Privilege in North Carolina, 1850–1900* (Chapel Hill: University of North Carolina Press, 1985), 261–62; and Jacquelyn Dowd Hall, James Leloudis, Robert Korstad, Mary Murphy, Lu Ann Jones, and Christopher B. Daly, *Like a Family: The Making of a Southern Cotton Mill World*, with a new afterword by the authors (Chapel Hill: University of North Carolina Press, 2000 [1987]), 103–5.

10. Thirteenth Census of the United States, 1910: Alamance County, N.C., Population Schedule, 80A (microfilm); Rorrer, *Rambling Blues*, 13, 17.

11. Rorrer, *Charlie Poole and the North Carolina Ramblers*, 1–2; Clifford Kinney Rorrer, "Charlie Clay Poole," in *Dictionary of North Carolina Biography*, ed. William S. Powell, 6 vols. (Chapel Hill: University of North Carolina Press, 1994), 5:122; Sapoznik, liner notes to Poole, *"You Ain't Talkin' to Me,"* 2; Rorrer, *Rambling Blues*, 18; Charlie Poole Jr. interview by Eugene W. Earle and Archie Green, Mountain Home, Tennessee, August 13, 1962, SFC. For a transcript of this interview, see Norm Cohen and Ed Kahn, "Tapescripts: Interview with Charlie Poole, Jr.," *John Edwards Memorial Foundation Newsletter* 1 (June 1966): 31–35.

12. On the early history of the banjo as an African American folk instrument and its adoption by white entertainers on the antebellum minstrel stage, see Dena Epstein, "The Folk Banjo: A Documentary History," *Ethnomusicology* 19 (September 1975): 347–71; Gene Bluestein, "America's Folk Instrument: Notes on the Five-String Banjo," *Western Folklore* 23 (October 1964): 241–45; Jay Bailey, "Historical Origins and Stylistic Developments of the Five-String Banjo," *Journal of American Folklore* 85 (January–March 1972): 58–62; Robert B. Winans, "The Folk, the Stage, and the Five-String Banjo in the Nineteenth Century," *Journal of American Folklore* 89 (October–December 1976): 407–37; and Robert B. Winans and Elias J. Kaufman, "Minstrel and Classic Banjo: American and English Connections," *American Music* 12 (Spring 1994): 1–8. On Manly Reece, see Andy Cahan, "Manly Reece and the Dawn of North Carolina Banjo," essay in liner notes to various artists, *The North Carolina Banjo Collection*, 2-CD set (Rounder CD 0439/0440); and Andy Cahan, "Adam Manly Reece: An Early Banjo Player of Grayson County, Virginia," in *American Musical Traditions, Vol. 3, British Isles Music*, ed. Jeff Todd Titon and Bob Carlin (New York: Schirmer Reference, 2002), 87–93.

13. Winans, "The Folk, the Stage, and the Five-String Banjo," 415n17, 429; Karen Linn, *That Half-Barbaric Twang: The Banjo in American Popular Culture* (Urbana: University of Illinois Press, 1991), 17; Lowell H. Schreyer, "The Banjo in Phonograph Recording History," in *The Banjo on Record: A Bio-Discography*, ed. Uli

Heier and Rainer E. Lotz (Westport, Conn.: Greenwood Press, 1993), 1–3; Wayne Shrubsall, "Banjo as Icon," *Journal of Popular Culture* 20 (Spring 1987): 51n5. The literature on the cultural history of the banjo in the nineteenth and early twentieth centuries is extensive, but on the development of the "clawhammer" and "classic" banjo styles, see, for example, Winans, "The Folk, the Stage, and the Five-String Banjo," 407–37; Lowell H. Schreyer, "The Banjo in Ragtime," in *Ragtime: Its History, Composers, and Music*, ed. John Edward Hasse (New York: Schirmer Books, 1985), 54–69; Shrubsall, "Banjo as Icon," 31–54; Linn, *That Half-Barbaric Twang*, especially 5–39, 116–59; Winans and Kaufman, "Minstrel and Classic Banjo," 1–30; Cecilia Conway, *African Banjo Echoes in Appalachia: A Study of Folk Traditions* (Knoxville: University of Tennessee Press, 1995), especially 199–221; and Sapoznik, liner notes to Poole, *"You Ain't Talkin' to Me,"* 9–12. On the emergence of mass-produced, modern five-string banjos and the technological innovations that industrial production introduced, see Robert Lloyd Webb, "Confidence and Admiration: The Enduring Ringing of the Banjo," in *The Banjo on Record*, 14–16; and Philip F. Gura and James F. Bollman, *America's Instrument: The Banjo in the Nineteenth Century* (Chapel Hill: University of North Carolina Press, 1999).

14. Webb, "Confidence and Admiration," 13–18; Linn, *That Half-Barbaric Twang*, 5–39; Schreyer, "The Banjo in Ragtime," 59; Winans and Kaufman, "Minstrel and Classic Banjo," 19–22; Sapoznik, liner notes to Poole, *"You Ain't Talkin' to Me,"* 11.

15. Webb, "Confidence and Admiration," 13–18; Schreyer, "The Banjo in Ragtime," 59; Winans and Kaufman, "Minstrel and Classic Banjo," 19–22; Schreyer, "The Banjo in Phonograph Recording History," 1–3; Schreyer, "The Banjo in Ragtime," 54–69; Shrubsall, "Banjo as Icon," 38–40; Linn, *That Half-Barbaric Twang*, 5–39, 116–40; Winans, "The Folk, the Stage, and the Five-String Banjo," 407, 419–36.

16. Rorrer, *Rambling Blues*, 17–18. The best, though still sketchy, account of Johnson's life can be found in Bob Carlin, *String Bands in the North Carolina Piedmont* (Jefferson, N.C.: McFarland, 2004), 147–48. On the various banjo traditions of North Carolina and the South generally, see Winans, "The Folk, the Stage, and the Five-String Banjo," 424–27, 432–35; and Conway, *African Banjo Echoes in Appalachia*, especially 199–221.

17. Rorrer, *Rambling Blues*, 14, 15, 29–30.

18. Ibid., 9, 17; Charlie Poole and Maude Gibson, marriage certificate, issued February 24, 1912, Alamance County Marriage Records, 1911–17, NCDAH (microfilm); Hall et al., *Like a Family*, 260; Poole interview. Poole's World War I draft registration card lists him in 1917 as still being married, with one child, perhaps in the hope of attaining a preferable draft status. See Pool [*sic*], World War I draft registration card, accessed on Ancestry.com.

19. Rorrer, *Rambling Blues*, 18, 25. Poole's World War I draft registration card, completed on June 5, 1917, lists his occupation as "Cotton Mill Laborer" and his place of employment as the Oak Dale Cotton Mills, in Jamestown, Guilford County, North Carolina. See Pool [*sic*], World War I draft registration card, accessed on Ancestry.com.

20. Kinney Rorrer, "Posey Rorer of Franklin County, Virginia," *Old-Time Herald* 11 (December 2007–January 2008): 31–32; Rorrer, *Rambling Blues*, 25–26.

21. Sapoznik, liner notes to Poole, *"You Ain't Talkin' to Me,"* 14; Rorrer, "Posey Rorer of Franklin County, Virginia," 31, 32; Rorrer, *Rambling Blues*, 27, 29, 38.

22. Charlie Poole and Lou Emma Rorer, marriage certificate, issued December 11, 1920, Rockingham County Marriage Register, 1896–1945, NCDAH (microfilm); Rorrer, "Posey Rorer of Franklin County, Virginia," 32–33; Rorrer, *Rambling Blues*, 18, 19, 27.

23. Rorrer, *Rambling Blues*, 19; *Danville (Va.) Bee*, August 23, 1924; *Mill News* (Charlotte, N.C.), October 14, 1920, 68–69; Charles Dyson Rodenbough, ed., *The Heritage of Rockingham County, North Carolina* (Winston-Salem, N.C.: Rockingham Historical Society, 1983), 128–30; Lindley S. Butler, *Rockingham County: A Brief History* (Raleigh: North Carolina Department of Cultural Resources, 1982), 72–74, 78–81.

24. Rorrer, *Rambling Blues*, 19, 20; Harriet L. Herring, *Welfare Work in Mill Villages: The Story of Extra-Mill Activities in North Carolina* (Chapel Hill: University of North Carolina Press, 1929), 143; Kinney Rorrer, liner notes to various artists, *Cotton Mills and Fiddles* (Flying Cloud FC-014); Otto August Kircheis, World War I draft registration card, Lafayette County, Mo., no. 1082, September 12, 1918, accessed on Ancestry.com (July 20, 2007); *Danville (Va.) Bee*, May 14, 1928; Fifteenth Census of the United States, 1930: Rockingham County, N.C., Population Schedule, 144A (microfilm); *Mill News* (Charlotte, N.C.), October 14, 1920, 68–69. For more on the Carolina Cotton and Woolen Mills Company's music programs, see the 1921 *Leaksville (N.C.) Arrow* article, reprinted in Rorrer, *Rambling Blues*, 20.

25. Sapoznik, liner notes to Poole, *"You Ain't Talkin' to Me,"* 8; Rorrer, *Rambling Blues*, 18.

26. Rorrer, *Rambling Blues*, 19, 24, 34–35.

27. Ibid., 19, 22.

28. *Danville (Va.) Bee*, June 15, 1929, June 27, 1930; Kinney Rorrer, liner notes to Blue Ridge Highballers, *The Blue Ridge Highballers: Original Recordings of 1926* (County CY 407); Tony Russell, liner notes to Walter "Kid" Smith, *Walter Smith and Friends, Vol. 1 (1929–March 1930)* (Document DOCD-8062); Kinney Rorrer, "The Four Virginians," *Old Time Music* 14 (Autumn 1974): 18; Kip Lornell, *Virginia's Blues, Country, and Gospel Records, 1902–1943: An Annotated Discography* (Lexington: University Press of Kentucky, 1989), 28–31, 65–67; Rorrer, liner notes to various artists, *Cotton Mills and Fiddles*.

29. Russell, liner notes to Smith, *Walter Smith and Friends, Vol. 1*; Tony Russell, "Kelly Harrell and the Virginia Ramblers: An OTM Report," *Old Time Music* 2 (Autumn 1971): 8–11; Lornell, *Virginia's Blues, Country, and Gospel Records*, 83–84; Rorrer, *Rambling Blues*, 23–24, 63; Rorrer, liner notes to various artists, *Cotton Mills and Fiddles*.

30. Lornell, *Virginia's Blues, Country, and Gospel Records*, 136–38; Rorrer, "Red Patterson and the Piedmont Log Rollers," 5–6; Rorrer, *Rambling Blues*, 23–24, 27. "Don't Let Your Deal Go Down Blues," which was to become both Charlie Poole's

first and best-selling hit, represents one good example of the extensive musical exchange that occurred in Carolina Piedmont textile towns. Sometime after moving to Spray in 1919, Poole learned the lyrics to the song from a white guitarist named Tyler Meeks, originally from Henry County, Virginia, who led a popular Leaksville stringband. Around 1911, at the age of seventeen, Meeks had learned to play the guitar from black guitarists who hung around a country store in the nearby African American community of Blue Creek. One of them was a thirty-year-old professional guitarist named Charlie Blackstock, who had moved to New York City but sometimes returned to Rockingham County to visit relatives in the summer. Blackstock taught Meeks to play the tune of "Don't Let Your Deal Go Down," and one of Meeks's cousins later taught him the words to the song. Meeks claimed that he, in turn, taught "Don't Let Your Deal Go Down" to Poole. See ibid., 22–23, 70.

31. Rorrer, *Rambling Blues*, 23, 27; Janet Kerr, "Lonnie Austin/Norman Woodlieff," *Old Time Music* 17 (Summer 1975): 7; Harold Titus, "Norman Woodlieff Folk Discography," *Journal of Country Music* 2 (Winter 1971): 18–19.

32. Rorrer, *Rambling Blues*, 27–29.

33. *Kingsport (Tenn.) Times*, March 1 and 5, 1925. See also Rorrer, "Posey Rorer of Franklin County, Virginia," 33–34.

34. Ivan M. Tribe, *The Stonemans: An Appalachian Family and the Music That Shaped Their Lives* (Urbana: University of Illinois Press, 1993), 46; Rorrer, *Rambling Blues*, 29.

35. Rorrer, *Rambling Blues*, 29, 30; Lornell, *Virginia's Blues, Country, and Gospel Records*, 83–84; Russell, "Kelly Harrell and the Virginia Ramblers," 8–11.

36. Rorrer, *Rambling Blues*, 30–31; Russell, *Country Music Records*, 14–15; Wolfe, "Columbia Records and Old-Time Music," 118–25, 144. For examples of Columbia's aggressive marketing campaign of its old-time records, see Columbia Records ad, *Talking Machine World* 20 (May 15, 1924): 153; "Columbia Signs Artists from Hills of Georgia," *Talking Machine World* 20 (May 15, 1924): 26; Columbia Records ad, *Talking Machine World* 20 (June 15, 1924): 17, reprinted in Archie Green, "Commercial Music Graphics: Three," *John Edwards Memorial Foundation Newsletter* 3 (December 1967): 45; "Two New Columbia Artists from Carolina," *Talking Machine World* 20 (June 15, 1924): 26; and "Columbia Co. Issues Booklet on the Old Familiar Tunes," *Talking Machine World* 20 (November 15, 1924): 51.

37. "Columbia Co. Issues Booklet on the Old Familiar Tunes," 51; "Columbia Issues New 'Familiar Tunes' Catalog," *Talking Machine World* 22 (August 15, 1926): 122; Patrick Huber, "Inventing Hillbilly Music: Record Catalog and Advertising Imagery, 1922–1929," International Country Music Conference, Nashville, Tennessee, May 27, 2005 (in author's possession).

38. Wolfe, "Columbia Records and Old-Time Music," 125; Russell, *Country Music Records*, 698–99; Titus, "Norman Woodlieff Folk Discography," 18; Rorrer, *Rambling Blues*, 30–31.

39. Titus, "Norman Woodlieff Folk Discography," 18, 19–20; Rorrer, *Rambling Blues*, 31, 34. Even after he left the North Carolina Ramblers, Woodlieff maintained his interest in music and still sat in with his former bandmates when they

performed in Spray and other nearby towns. Although he never again toured or recorded with the North Carolina Ramblers, Woodlieff did go on to record as a backup guitarist with several other local stringbands between 1929 and 1939, including Walter "Kid" Smith's family band, the Carolina Buddies, the Virginia Dandies, and the Four Pickled Peppers. He also, according to his biographer Janet Kerr, "took a correspondence course in cartooning" and later, in the late 1930s, worked as a sign painter. See Russell, *Country Music Records*, 170, 356, 846, 932; and Kerr, "Lonnie Austin/Norman Woodlieff," 7, 8. Two examples of Woodlieff's cartoons about his former band, titled "Comic-Ade: North Carolina Ramblers," can be found in *Old Time Music* 14 (Autumn 1974): 4, 31.

40. Rorrer, *Rambling Blues*, 34, 49; Archie Green, liner notes to Mike Seeger, *Tipple, Loom and Rail: Songs of the Industrialization of the South* (Folkways FH 5273), 11; Norm Cohen, *Long Steel Rail: The Railroad in American Folksong* (Urbana: University of Illinois Press, 1981), 591–95; *Beckley (W.Va.) Post-Herald and Register*, July 13, 1958; Mrs. Roy Harvey interview by Eugene W. Earle and Archie Green, Beckley, West Virginia, August 13, 1962, SFC. For a transcript of this interview, see Norm Cohen, "Tapescripts: Interview with Mrs. Roy Harvey," *John Edwards Memorial Foundation Newsletter* 4 (June 1968): 74–77.

41. Rorrer, *Rambling Blues*, 34, 37.

42. Ibid., 35–36, 64; Russell, *Country Music Records*, 409, 699; Cohen, *Long Steel Rail*, 592.

43. Rorrer, *Rambling Blues*, 36. The exact terms of Poole's original 1926 Columbia contract remain uncertain, but on June 27, 1927, he signed a one-year contract with the firm to make twelve recordings, for which he was to receive a half-cent royalty per record on 90 percent of the copies sold, plus a seventy-five-dollar flat payment per side. The contract further stipulated that he was guaranteed at least nine hundred dollars and that Columbia was to pay for his railroad fare and traveling expenses. See Charlie Poole contract, June 27, 1927, among the Columbia ledger sheets, in the Guthrie T. Meade Papers, SFC.

44. Russell, "Kelly Harrell and the Virginia Ramblers," 8–11; Rorrer, "Red Patterson and the Piedmont Log Rollers," 5–6; Rorrer, "The Four Virginians," 18; *Greensboro (N.C.) Daily News*, December 22, 1974, under "Charlie Poole" in Clipping File, 1976–89, NCC; Russell, *Country Music Records*, 109–10, 170, 180–81, 214, 318–19, 356, 357, 403–4, 409–10, 412, 424, 538–39, 682, 826, 835, 846–47, 932, 972–73; Rorrer, liner notes to various artists, *Cotton Mills and Fiddles*; Rorrer, *Rambling Blues*, 39–41, 63; Tony Russell, "Good Old Times Makin' Music: The Preston Young Story," *Old Time Music* 7 (Winter 1972/1973): 4; Marshall Wyatt, "'I Ain't Never Heared Such a Rattlin' Bunch!': The Story of Frank Blevins and His Tar Heel Rattlers," *Old-Time Herald* 2 (February–April 1991): 14–15.

45. Sapoznik, liner notes to Poole, *"You Ain't Talkin' to Me,"* 26; Rorrer, *Rambling Blues*, 37–38, 48, 65; Poole interview; Josh Guthman, "From the Mills to Manhattan: Charlie Poole's Machine-Age Music," unpublished seminar paper, Department of History, University of North Carolina at Chapel Hill, 1985 (copy in the author's possession), 14. A 1935 sociological study of Leaksville, Spray, and Draper revealed the significant degree to which millworkers embraced the new forms of

national mass culture. Of 122 textile workers surveyed, Frances Hampton found that eighty-seven owned radios and fifty-two owned phonographs. Forty of these owned both a radio and a phonograph. Seventy-three millhands attended the "movie shows," more than half of them at least once a week. See Frances Hampton, "New Leisure: How Is It Spent? A Study of What One Hundred Twenty-Two Textile Workers of Leaksville, Spray, and Draper Are Doing with the New Leisure Created by the N.R.A., as Applied to Certain Types of Activities" (master's thesis, University of North Carolina, 1935), 61–63, 75–77.

46. Cantwell, *Bluegrass Breakdown*, 53; Sapoznik, liner notes to Poole, *"You Ain't Talkin' to Me,"* 3, 24; Rorrer, *Rambling Blues*, 38, 47, 54, 63, 99.

47. Poole interview; Rorrer, *Rambling Blues*, 37, 47. See also the Fifteenth Census of the United States, 1930: Rockingham County, N.C., Population Schedule, 93A (microfilm), in which Poole (spelled "Charlie Pool")—or his wife Lou Emma—listed his occupation as "Record Artist" and his employer as "Victrola Co."

48. Rorrer, *Rambling Blues*, 53.

49. Ibid., 29–30, 37, 46; Poole interview.

50. Rorrer, *Rambling Blues*, 48.

51. Ibid., 48; Poole interview.

52. Russell, *Country Music Records*, 410, 699; Rorrer, *Rambling Blues*, 37–38; Linn, *That Half-Barbaric Twang*, 87–88, 91–94.

53. Guthman, "From the Mills to Manhattan," 12; Poole interview; Rorrer, *Rambling Blues*, 36, 38; Columbia Records, *Old Familiar Tunes* (New York: Columbia Phonograph Company, 1927), 11.

54. Rorrer, *Rambling Blues*, 41.

55. Ibid., 41, 45–46, 50–52, 57–58; Rorrer, liner notes to various artists, *Cotton Mills and Fiddles*; Russell, *Country Music Records*, 170, 180–81, 318–19, 813, 846, 972–73.

56. Kerr, "Lonnie Austin/Norman Woodlieff," 7–10; Tony Russell, "H. M. Barnes' Blue Ridge Ramblers," *Old Time Music* 17 (Summer 1975): 11; Bob L. Cox, *Fiddlin' Charlie Bowman: An East Tennessee Old-Time Music Pioneer and His Musical Family* (Knoxville: University of Tennessee Press, 2007), 87–103; *Charleston (W.Va.) Gazette*, January 24, 1931; Russell, *Country Music Records*, 699–700; Rorrer, *Rambling Blues*, 21–22, 41. In January 1929, Austin played piano on eleven of the fourteen sides that H. M. Barnes and His Blue Ridge Ramblers recorded for Brunswick in New York City. See Russell, *Country Music Records*, 94–95.

57. Rorrer, *Rambling Blues*, 42–43.

58. Ibid., 43–44; Richard Nevins, liner notes to Charlie Poole and the North Carolina Ramblers, *The North Carolina Ramblers, 1928–1930* (Biograph BLP-RC-6005); Norm Cohen, "The Skillet Lickers: A Study of a Hillbilly String Band and Its Repertoire," *Journal of American Folklore* 78 (July–September 1965): 240–41; Russell, *Country Music Records*, 700.

59. Russell, *Country Music Records*, 410, 700; Rorrer, *Rambling Blues*, 44.

60. Rorrer, "Charlie Poole and the North Carolina Ramblers," in *Country Music Who's Who: 1972*, H-4; Sapoznik, liner notes to Poole, *"You Ain't Talkin' to Me,"* 12–13; Rorrer, *Rambling Blues*, 48–49, 64.

61. Rorrer, "Charlie Poole and the North Carolina Ramblers," in *Country Music Who's Who: 1972*, H-4; John Cohen, "Introduction," in Rorrer, *Rambling Blues*, 8; Cohen, "Early Pioneers," 25–26; Cantwell, *Bluegrass Breakdown*, 191; Malone, *Country Music, U.S.A.*, 51–52.

62. Rorrer, liner notes to Poole and the North Carolina Ramblers, *Charlie Poole and the North Carolina Ramblers, Vol. 2*; Rorrer, liner notes to Poole and the North Carolina Ramblers, *Charlie Poole and the North Carolina Ramblers*; Sapoznik, liner notes to Poole, *"You Ain't Talkin' to Me,"* 2–3, 7; Rorrer, *Rambling Blues*, 26, 37, 65. According to the 1910 census, Charlie Poole, then eighteen years old and working as an oiler in an Alamance County textile mill, could neither read nor write. See Thirteenth Census of the United States, 1910: Alamance County, N.C., Population Schedule, 80A (microfilm).

63. Rorrer, liner notes to Poole and the North Carolina Ramblers, *Charlie Poole and the North Carolina Ramblers, Vol. 2*; Rorrer, *Rambling Blues*, 26, 30–31, 35, 36, 37, 43, 48, 65, 70.

64. Cohen, "Early Pioneers," 26; Rorrer, *Rambling Blues*, 65, 69, 88. Although the North Carolina Ramblers featured a few religious hymns in their stage shows, none of them found their way onto the band's commercial records, perhaps an appropriate omission given the facts of Poole's dissolute life.

65. The North Carolina Ramblers recorded a relatively large percentage of African American–derived numbers, including gritty blues ballads ("Don't Let Your Deal Go Down Blues" and "Take a Drink on Me"), popular blues compositions ("If the River Was Whiskey" and "Ramblin' Blues"), and black-influenced minstrel numbers and "coon songs" ("Sweet Sunny South" and "Good-Bye Sweet Liza Jane"). See Cohen, "Early Pioneers," 26; and Rorrer, *Rambling Blues*, 65, 76.

66. Sigmund Spaeth, *A History of Popular Music in America* (New York: Random House, 1948), 317, 422–23; Rorrer, *Rambling Blues*, 88.

67. Spaeth, *A History of Popular Music in America*, 390; W. C. Handy, ed., *Blues: An Anthology* (New York: Macmillan, 1972 [1926]), 116–19; Rorrer, *Rambling Blues*, 81. On Memphis, particularly the Beale Street music scene during the early decades of the twentieth century, see William Barlow, *Looking Up at Down: The Emergence of Blues Culture* (Philadelphia: Temple University Press, 1989), 205, 228–29.

68. Rorrer, liner notes to Poole and the North Carolina Ramblers, *Charlie Poole and the North Carolina Ramblers*; Sapoznik, liner notes to Poole, *"You Ain't Talkin' to Me,"* 2, 3; Rorrer, *Ramblin' Blues*, 37, 65.

69. Russell, *Country Music Records*, 700; Rorrer, *Rambling Blues*, 48–49.

70. Russell, *Country Music Records*, 700; Rorrer, *Rambling Blues*, 49, 53–54; Walker interview; "Who Chose These Records?" 16. Old-time music historian Charles K. Wolfe estimates that Columbia hillbilly records released in 1930 averaged sales of only 2,480 copies. The following year this figure fell to only 886. See Wolfe, "Columbia Records and Old-Time Music," 125.

71. Poole interview; Rorrer, *Rambling Blues*, 49–50, 54.

72. Rorrer, *Rambling Blues*, 54–55; Charlie C. Poole, death certificate, May 21, 1931, Book 1479, p. 92, North Carolina Death Certificates, NCDAH (microfilm).

73. Norm Cohen, "Walter 'Kid' Smith," *John Edwards Memorial Foundation Quarterly* 9 (Autumn 1973): 130; Rorer, *Rambling Blues*, 57, 98. For biographies of Jimmie Rodgers and Hank Williams, see, for example, Nolan Porterfield, *Jimmie Rodgers: The Life and Times of America's Blue Yodeler* (Urbana: University of Illinois Press, 1992 [1979]); Roger Williams, *Sing a Sad Song: The Life of Hank Williams* (Urbana: University of Illinois Press, 1981 [1970]); and Colin Escott, with George Merritt and William MacEwen, *Hank Williams: The Biography* (Boston: Little, Brown, 1994).

74. Russell, *Country Music Records*, 180–81; Rorer, *Rambling Blues*, 57–58. Incidentally, in 1966, Rodney McElrea, a hillbilly music enthusiast and longtime fan of the North Carolina Ramblers from Northern Ireland, launched a fund-raising campaign in the pages of *Country News and Views* magazine and, with the donations he had collected from its readers, erected large granite monuments, complete with images of a banjo and fiddle, over both Poole's and Rorer's graves, respectively. See *Greensboro (N.C.) Daily News*, July 29, 1976.

75. Russell, *Country Music Records*, 125–26, 356, 409–12, 831–32; Green, liner notes to Seeger, *Tipple, Loom and Rail*, 11; Harvey interview; Rorer, *Rambling Blues*, 50, 57, 60; *Beckley (W.Va.) Post-Herald and Register*, July 13, 1958.

76. Russell, *Country Music Records*, 885; Poole interview; Carlin, *String Bands in the North Carolina Piedmont*, 183–84; Rorer, *Rambling Blues*, 60–62.

77. Various artists, *Anthology of American Folk Music*, ed. Harry Smith, 3-LP set (Folkways FP 251 to FP 253); Greil Marcus, *The Old, Weird America: The World of Bob Dylan's Basement Tapes* (New York: Henry Holt, 2001 [1997]), 87; Neil Rosenberg, "Biblio-Discographies: The 'White House Blues'–'McKinley'–'Cannonball Blues' Complex," *John Edwards Memorial Foundation Newsletter* 4 (June 1968): 50–53; Rorer, *Rambling Blues*, 13; Sapoznik, liner notes to Poole, *"You Ain't Talkin' to Me,"* 2. Of the forty-four other hillbilly tracks reissued on Smith's *Anthology of American Folk Music*, seven of them are by southern textile worker singers, musicians, or stringbands, providing another indication of the high regard for, and far-reaching influence of, southern millhands' prewar recordings in postwar America.

78. Sapoznik, liner notes to Poole, *"You Ain't Talkin' to Me,"* 2; *Spectator* (Raleigh, N.C.), May 23, 1985, and *High Point (N.C.) Enterprise*, March 11, 1986, both clippings under "Charlie Poole" in Clipping File, 1976–89, NCC; Jack Bernhardt, "Legends — No. 2: Charlie Poole," *Old-Time Herald* 3 (August–October 1991): 9, 51. For album reissues devoted to Charlie Poole and the North Carolina Ramblers, see *Charlie Poole and the North Carolina Ramblers* (County 505); *Charlie Poole and the North Carolina Ramblers, Vol. 2* (County 509); *The Legend of Charlie Poole* (County 516); *Charlie Poole and the North Carolina Ramblers, Vol. 4* (County 540); *The North Carolina Ramblers, 1928–1930* (Biograph BLP-6005); *Charlie Poole and the Highlanders* (Arbor 201), reissued on Puritan 3002; and *Charlie Poole, 1926–1930: A Young Boy Left His Home One Day* (Historical HLP 8005). For CD reissues of Charlie Poole and the North Carolina Ramblers' vintage recordings, see Appendix B. A photograph of the Poole historical marker can be viewed on the North Carolina Department of Cultural Resources website, <http://www.ncdcr.gov/> (July 17, 2007). For infor-

mation about Eden's annual Charlie Poole Music Festival, visit its official website at Charlie-Poole.com, <http://www.charlie-poole.com/> (May 24, 2007).

Chapter Three

1. The following account of McCarn's debut recording session is based upon David McCarn interview by Archie Green and Ed Kahn, Stanley, North Carolina, August 19, 1961, SFC.

2. "Well, we made two copies of each song," McCarn recalled, "but I was a little nervous. 'Course, the first time, naturally, you would be, in front of a microphone. I sang one 'Cotton Mill Colic' pretty good, I thought. But the next one I sang, about the last of it I got a little nervous. And instead of following through with 'I'm a-gonna starve, ever'body will,' I said right on the last verse, 'I'm a-gonna starve, *nobody* will' [quoting the lyrics], but when they got it to Camden, New Jersey, they didn't seem to notice my mistake, so they published that one." Nearly every recorded and published version of "Cotton Mill Colic" that has followed duplicates McCarn's flubbed line in the final chorus, a clue that allows scholars to trace their provenance to McCarn's 1930 Victor record, and one that also, interestingly, reveals the exacting attention that southern musicians paid when learning new songs directly from phonograph records. Ibid.

3. Ibid.

4. Bill C. Malone, *Country Music, U.S.A.*, rev. ed. (Austin: University of Texas Press, 1985 [1968]), 134; Mike Paris, liner notes to Dave McCarn and Gwin S. Foster, *Singers of the Piedmont* (Folk Variety FV 12505), 2; Patrick Huber, "'Cain't Make a Living at a Cotton Mill': The Life and Hillbilly Songs of Dave McCarn," *North Carolina Historical Review* 80 (July 2003): 297–333. In his brief account of McCarn's career, Malone mistakenly claims that "six of [McCarn's recordings] deal directly with cotton mill conditions." Actually, only three do—the aforementioned trio of "Cotton Mill Colics." See Malone, *Country Music, U.S.A.*, 134.

5. McCarn and Foster, *Singers of the Piedmont*, also features five selections by Gwin S. Foster, a fellow Gaston County millhand and harmonica virtuoso with whom McCarn once worked and who served as one of McCarn's major musical influences on the harmonica. Other album and CD anthologies on which McCarn's recordings have appeared include various artists, *Black and White Hillbilly Music: Early Harmonica Recordings from the 1920s and 30s* (Trikont US-0226); various artists, *Drunk and Nutty Blues: Hillbillies Foolin' with the Blues* (Indigo IGODCD 2520); various artists, *Hard Times Come Again No More: Early American Rural Songs of Hard Times and Hardships, Vols. 1 and 2* (Yazoo 2036 and 2037); various artists, *Hard Times in the Country: Down and Out in the Rural South: Songs and Tunes from 1927–1938* (County CO CD-3527); various artists, *Harmonica Masters: Classic Recordings from the 1920's and 30's* (Yazoo 2019); various artists, *Hillbilly Honeymoon: Manhaters, Misogynists, and Marital Mayhem* (Acrobat 4015); various artists, *Jake Leg Blues* (Jass J-CD-642); various artists, *Poor Man, Rich Man: American Country Songs of Protest* (Rounder 1026); various artists, *The Road to Nashville: A History of Country Music, 1926–1953* (Indigo IGOTCD 2559); and various artists, *Songs of Complaint*

and Protest, Folk Music in America, vol. 7 (Library of Congress, Music Division, Recording Laboratory LBC 7). One of McCarn's songs also appears on the CD companion to William L. Andrews, Minrose C. Gwin, Trudier Harris, and Fred Hobson, eds., *The Literature of the American South* (New York: W. W. Norton, 1998).

6. Charles K. Wolfe, "Dave McCarn," in *Definitive Country: The Ultimate Encyclopedia of Country Music and Its Performers*, ed. Barry McCloud (New York: Perigree Books, 1995), 521. For a sampling of cover versions of McCarn's songs, see, for example, Pete Seeger, "Cotton Mill Colic," *American Industrial Ballads* (Folkways FH 5251); New Lost City Ramblers, "Serves Them Fine," *Songs from the Depression* (Folkways FH 5264); New Lost City Ramblers, "Everyday Dirt," *New Lost City Ramblers, Vol. 2* (Folkways FA2397); Pete Seeger, "Cotton Mill Colic," *American History in Ballad and Song* (Folkways FH 5801); Alice Stuart, "Every Day Dirt," *All the Good Times* (Arhoolie F-4002); Blue Sky Boys, "Cotton Mill Colic," *Presenting the Blue Sky Boys* (Capitol ST 2483); Mike Seeger, "Cotton Mill Colic," *Tipple, Loom and Rail* (Folkways FH 5273); Doc Watson, "Every Day Dirt," *The Doc Watson Family* (Folkways FA2366); New Lost City Ramblers, "Take Them for A Ride," *Modern Times* (Folkways FTS 31027); J. E. Mainer, "Cotton Mill Colic," *Volume 6: Fiddling with His Girl Susan* (Rounder RR 222); New Lost City Ramblers, "Serves Them Fine," *Sing Songs of the New Lost City Ramblers* (Aravel AB 1005); Joe Glazer, "Cotton Mill Colic," *Textile Voices* (Collector 1922); Mountain Musicians' Cooperative, "Cotton Mill Colic"/"Serves 'Em Fine," *Brown Lung Cotton Mill Blues* (June Appal 006); Riley Shepard, "Cotton Mill Colic," *Old-Time Comedy Favorites* (Rounder RR 1166); West Orrtana String Band, "Cotton Mill Colic," *West Orrtana String Band* (Revonah RS-924); Southern Eagle String Band, "Cotton Mill Colic," *That Nasty Swing* (Bear Family BF15010); Roy Berkeley, with Tim Woodbridge, "Cotton Mill Colic," *Folk and Country Songs of the FDR Years* (Longview L241); and Jumpin' Bill Carlisle, "John Came Home" ("Everyday Dirt"), *Gonna Shake This Shack Tonight: Busy Body Boogie* (Bear Family BCD 15980).

7. Of the more than three hundred hillbilly acts that appeared in Columbia's 15000-D "Familiar Tunes—Old and New" series between 1925 and 1932, Charles K. Wolfe estimates that "well over half" of these made "only one record" (two selections). Most of the hopeful musicians who auditioned for him, recalled Columbia's A & R man Frank B. Walker, had repertoires "of eight or ten things that they did well, and that was all they knew. So, when you picked out the three or four that were best in a man's so-called repertoire, you were through with that man as an artist. It was all. He was finished. It was a culling job, taking the best that they had. You might come out with two selections or you might come out with six or eight, but you did it at that time. You said good-bye. They went back home. They had made a phonograph record, and that was the next thing to being President of the United States in their mind." On the short-lived recording careers of most hillbilly musicians and stringbands, see Charles K. Wolfe, "Columbia Records and Old-Time Music," *John Edwards Memorial Foundation Quarterly* 14 (Autumn 1978): 120; Frank Walker interview by Mike Seeger, probably New York, New York, June 19, 1962, SFC; and "Who Chose These Records? A Look into the Life, Tastes, and

Procedures of Frank Walker," in *Anthology of American Folk Music*, ed. Josh Dunson and Ethel Raim (New York: Oak Publications, 1973), 12.

8. Wolfe, "Dave McCarn," 521; Alan Lomax, Woody Guthrie, and Pete Seeger, comps. and eds., *Hard Hitting Songs for Hard-Hit People* (New York: Oak Publications, 1967), 120.

9. William Henry Koon, "Dave McCarn," *John Edwards Memorial Foundation Quarterly* 11 (Winter 1975): 169.

10. David McCarn interview. Of Scots-Irish ancestry, the McCarn family had lived in Rowan County, North Carolina, at least since 1794. Born on May 13, 1822, in the eastern half of Rowan County (in what later that year became part of Davidson County), McCarn's paternal grandfather, John McCarn, started working as a common laborer at a local gold-mining operation while still in his teens. Over the next two decades he worked at several mines in the central Piedmont counties of Davidson, Rowan, and Stanly, the center of the North Carolina gold-mining industry before the Civil War, and, after gaining extensive experience, he eventually became a full-fledged miner, at the time a highly skilled and well-paid position. By 1860, McCarn and his wife, Fanny (Crayton), and their two daughters were living near China Grove, in Rowan County, and John was working as a gold miner at a nearby operation. At the time, the family owned land valued at three hundred dollars. See Rowan County, N.C., Deed Book, vol. 13, NCDAH; Rowan County, N.C., *Rowan County, North Carolina, Tax Lists, 1757–1800*, comp. by Jo White Linn (Salisbury, N.C.: privately published, 1995), 343; Rowan County, *1815 Rowan County, North Carolina, Tax List*, comp. by Jo White Linn (Salisbury, N.C.: privately published, 1987), 56; Davidson County, N.C., *Davidson County, North Carolina, Will Summaries, Vol. 1, 1823–1846*, comp. by Henry Reeves and Mary Jo Davis Shoaf (Lexington, N.C.: privately published, 1979), 3; Sixth Census of the United States, 1840: Davidson County, N.C., Population Schedule, 273B (microfilm); Eighth Census of the United States, 1860: Rowan County, N.C., Population Schedule, 455A (microfilm).

At the turn of the century, John and Fanny McCarn, both of them by now quite elderly, were living in McAdenville's mill village, supported by several of their children and grandchildren who worked at McAden Mills. When John McCarn died in 1902 at the age of eighty, the local newspaper editor observed in his obituary, "The children of the deceased have been untiring in their efforts to relieve the suffering of their parents and did all in their power for them. We would, in a special manner, mention one of the sons, Levi, who has been very kind and worked hard to alleviate their sufferings. He sets a noble example for all the young men of the present generation to follow." Such editorial praise not only suggested something of the public esteem with which middle-class community members regarded Levi McCarn; it also reflected mounting concerns that southern industrialism had begun to disrupt traditional patterns of family support, even in small communities like McAdenville. In 1926, for example, one survey reported that two-thirds of the sixty inmates at the Gaston County Poor Home came from textile worker families. "The superintendent of the county home made the statement that a large number of inmates of the county home in this county were not there because of poverty-stricken conditions of their children, but because of the refusal of the younger people to support their parents," noted sociologist Jennings J. Rhyne: "He gave as a reason for this statement his observation that the children of these aged inmates from the mill sections usually come to visit their parents in their own automobiles." See Twelfth Census of the United States, 1900: Gaston County, N.C., Population Schedule, 236B (microfilm); *Gastonia (N.C.) Gazette*, August 22, 1902; and Jennings J. Rhyne, *Some Southern Cotton Mill Workers and Their Villages* (Chapel Hill: University of North Carolina Press, 1930), 191.

11. On the development of McAdenville and McAden Mills, see *Gastonia (N.C.) Gazette*, September 30, 1902, July 2, 1919; Ila Poole, "Town of McAdenville," in *Souvenir Program, Gaston Centennial* (Gastonia, N.C.: Gaston County Centennial Committee, 1946), 123–24; Billy Robert Miller, *McAdenville: Spun from the Wilderness* (Shelby, N.C.: Riviere Printing Company, 1987 [1982]), especially 31–32, 34, 36, 38–45, 76; and Robert Allison Ragan, "The Pioneer Cotton Mills of Gaston County, North Carolina: 'The First Thirty' (1848–1904) and Gaston County Textile Pioneers," unpublished manuscript, NCC, ca. 1973, 1–5.

12. Miller, *McAdenville*, especially 31–32, 38–45, 76; Ragan, "The Pioneer Cotton Mills of Gaston County," 4–5; David McCarn interview; *Charlotte Observer*, August 10, 1969. Dave's father, Levi McCarn, married late for a man of his generation, just as his discontented son would later do. The elder McCarn was a few weeks past his thirty-ninth birthday when, in 1904, he wed Sallie Cousins, a woman eighteen years his junior. See Levi L. McCarn and Sallie Cozzens, January 28, 1904, Gaston County Register of Deeds, Original Marriage Licenses, 1904–10, NCDAH (microfilm); Levi L. McCarn and Sallie Cozzens, marriage license, issued January 29, 1904, Gaston County Marriage Register, 1883–1905, NCDAH; Twelfth Census of the United States, 1900: Gaston County, N.C., Population Schedule, 269A (microfilm); and *Gastonia (N.C.) Gazette*, February 5, 1904, June 25, 1919.

13. Thirteenth Census of the United States, 1910: Gaston County, N.C., Population Schedule, 59B (microfilm); *Gastonia (N.C.) Gazette*, June 11, 1919; Mrs. Paul Neal, "City of Belmont," in *Souvenir Program, Gaston Centennial*, 94–95; R. L. Stowe Sr., *Early History of Belmont and Gaston County, North Carolina* (n.p.: privately published, 1951); Ragan, "The Pioneer Cotton Mills of Gaston County," 1–4; miscellaneous newspaper clippings under "Belmont, North Carolina," in Clipping File, 1976–89, NCC; David McCarn interview.

14. *Charlotte Observer*, August 10, 1969; Thirteenth Census of the United States, 1910: Gaston County, N.C., Population Schedule, 60A, 60B, 61B–62A (microfilm); David McCarn interview. On the expansion of the southern textile industry during World War I, see Jacquelyn Dowd Hall, James Leloudis, Robert Korstad, Mary Murphy, Lu Ann Jones, and Christopher B. Daly, *Like a Family: The Making of a Southern Cotton Mill World*, with a new afterword by the authors (Chapel Hill: University of North Carolina Press, 2000 [1987]), 183–85.

15. Ollie Louisa McCarn, death certificate, February 27, 1917, Book D222, p. 339; Raymond L. McCarn, death certificate, October 15, 1918, Book D357, p. 240; James Pinckney McCarn, death certificate, October 30, 1918, Book D357, p. 239; Levi Mc-

Carn, death certificate, June 7, 1919, Book D470, p. 211, all of which can be found in North Carolina Death Certificates, 1909–January 1930, NCDAH; *Charlotte Observer*, August 10, 1969. On the 1918 influenza epidemic in Gaston County, see assorted articles in the *Gastonia (N.C.) Gazette*, October 7–October 30, 1918, especially the "Belmont Budget" columns of October 7 and 25.

16. Fourteenth Census of the United States, 1920: Gaston County, N.C., Population Schedule, 139B and 246A (microfilm); email messages from Martha Moore to Patrick Huber, June 27 and July 9, 2007 (copies in the author's possession); Sallie E. Harrison, death certificate, July 31, 1920, Gaston County, N.C., Death Certificates, Register of Deeds, Gaston County Courthouse, Gastonia, N.C.; *Charlotte Observer*, August 10, 1969.

17. Archie Green, "Second Visit of Archie Green and Ed Kahn to David McCarn, Stanley, North Carolina, August 18, 1963," 5, Archie Green Papers, SFC; Martha (Sansing) Sipe telephone conversation with Patrick Huber, October 26, 1997 (notes in the author's possession).

18. John A. Salmond, *Gastonia 1929: The Story of the Loray Mill Strike* (Chapel Hill: University of North Carolina Press, 1995), 10–13; David L. Carlton, *Mill and Town in South Carolina, 1880–1920* (Baton Rouge: Louisiana State University Press, 1982), 78; Liston Pope, *Millhands and Preachers: A Study of Gastonia* (New Haven: Yale University Press, 1970 [1942]), 16. On this brand of mill boosterism in Gaston County, see Mildred Gwin Barnwell, *Faces We See* (Gastonia, N.C.: Southern Combed Yarn Spinners Association, 1939), 17–18.

19. On Gastonia's urban and industrial development, see S. H. Hobbs Jr., *Gaston County: Economic and Social* (Raleigh, N.C.: Edwards and Broughton Printing Company, 1920), 6, 18–19; Robert L. Williams, *Gaston County: A Pictorial History* (Norfolk, Va.: Donning Company, 1981), especially 81–84; Gastonia Chamber of Commerce, *Gastonia, North Carolina: Combed Yarn Manufacturing Center of the South* (Gastonia, N.C.: Chamber of Commerce, 1924), 1–3; *Gastonia (N.C.) Daily Gazette*, September 10, 1926; Rhyne, *Some Southern Cotton Mill Workers and Their Villages*, 9; Pope, *Millhands and Preachers*, 3–20; Salmond, *Gastonia 1929*, 10–13; and Pamela Grundy, "'We Always Tried to Be Good People': Respectability, Crazy Water Crystals, and Hillbilly Music on the Air, 1933–1935," *Journal of American History* 81 (March 1995): 1592.

20. Pope, *Millhands and Preachers*, 29, 31, 151–61; Grundy, "'We Always Tried to Be Good People,'" especially 1606–17; Salmond, *Gastonia 1929*, 3–5; Hall et al., *Like a Family*, 116–17, 121–39.

21. Rhyne, *Some Southern Cotton Mill Workers and Their Villages*, 11; *Charlotte Observer*, August 10, 1969; David McCarn interview. Throughout the 1920s and 1930s, McCarn was employed at a series of Gastonia and Gaston County textile-manufacturing firms, including the Gray Manufacturing Company, the Clara Manufacturing Company, the Dunn Manufacturing Company, the Armstrong Cotton Mills Company, the Winget Yarn Mills Company, the Victory Yarn Mills Company, the Ranlo Manufacturing Company, and the Priscilla Spinning Company. See David McCarn interview; *Gastonia (N.C.) Daily Gazette*, November 26, 1937, February 11, 1939; and *Charlotte Observer*, August 10, 1969.

22. *Gastonia (N.C.) Daily Gazette*, August 11, 1928; John Salmond, "Aspects of Modernization in the Loray Mill Strike of 1929," in *Varieties of Southern History: New Essays on a Region and Its People*, ed. Bruce Clayton and John Salmond (Westport, Conn.: Greenwood Press, 1996), 169–76; Jacquelyn Dowd Hall, "Disorderly Women: Gender and Labor Militancy in the Appalachian South," *Journal of American History* 73 (September 1986): 354–82; Hall et al., *Like a Family*, 183, 185, 196, 252–55. A 1930 sociological study of one Gaston County textile town revealed similar patterns of working-class consumerism. "There is to be found throughout the village" of Smyre, Bertha Carl Hipp wrote, "the usual luxuries now common with mill workers [such] as victrolas, pianos, radios, and automobiles." Of the 160 families interviewed, Hipp noted that 100 owned phonographs, 31 owned radios, and approximately one-third to one-half owned automobiles. "Picture shows take more people from the village than any other attraction," she observed. "Shows in Gastonia are frequented regularly by Smyre people while many go to Charlotte for shows. In addition to cars owned by the people, these towns can be reached easily by the Charlotte-Asheville and Charlotte-Greenville busses which pass the village hourly." Bertha Carl Hipp, "A Gaston County Cotton Mill and Its Community" (master's thesis, University of North Carolina, 1930), 45–47.

Since the mid-1970s, as a dimension of the new social history, the number of studies of working-class leisure in late nineteenth- and early twentieth-century America has multiplied rapidly. For some of the best examples of these studies, see John F. Kasson, *Amusing the Million: Coney Island at the Turn of the Century* (New York: Hill and Wang, 1978); John T. Cumbler, *Working-Class Communities in Industrial America: Work, Leisure, and Struggle in Two Industrial Cities, 1880–1930* (Westport, Conn.: Greenwood Press, 1979); Roy Rosenzweig, *Eight Hours for What We Will: Workers and Leisure in an Industrial City, 1870–1920* (Cambridge: Cambridge University Press, 1983); Kathy Peiss, *Cheap Amusements: Working Women and Leisure in Turn-of-the-Century New York* (Philadelphia: Temple University Press, 1986); Tera W. Hunter, *To 'Joy My Freedom: Southern Black Women's Lives and Labors after the Civil War* (Cambridge, Mass.: Harvard University Press, 1997), especially 145–86; Randy D. McBee, *Dance Hall Days: Intimacy and Leisure among Working-Class Immigrants in the United States* (New York: New York University Press, 2001); and Steve Goodson, *Highbrows, Hillbillies, and Hellfire: Public Entertainment in Atlanta, 1880–1930* (Athens: University of Georgia Press, 2002).

23. Rhyne, *Some Southern Cotton Mill Workers and Their Villages*, 17–18, 54–55, 173–76. See, for example, the advertisements for films, radios, clothing, and beauty products in *Gastonia (N.C.) Daily Gazette*, October 9, 11, 12, 16, 1928. On the number of Gastonia retail stores and shops, see *Gastonia (N.C.) Daily Gazette*, May 4 and September 10, 1926.

24. *Charlotte Observer*, April 5 and July 30, 1929; Hall et al., *Like a Family*, 237, 257–62. Indispensable on this topic are Hall, "Disorderly Women," 372–80; Salmond, "Aspects of Modernization in the Loray Mill Strike of 1929," 169–76; and Paula S. Fass, *The Damned and the Beautiful: American Youth in the 1920s* (New York: Oxford University Press, 1977).

25. Robin Hood, "The Loray Mill Strike" (master's thesis, University of North

Carolina, 1932), 21; Pope, *Millhands and Preachers*, 137, 323; *Charlotte News* article, reprinted in *Gastonia (N.C.) Daily Gazette*, April 6, 1929; *Gastonia (N.C.) Daily Gazette*, April 25, 1929; Salmond, "Aspects of Modernization in the Loray Mill Strike of 1929," 170; Ellen Grigsby, "The Politics of Protest: Theoretical, Historical, and Literary Perspectives on Labor Conflict in Gaston County, North Carolina" (Ph.D. diss., University of North Carolina at Chapel Hill, 1986), 223–26. "Older persons whose formative years had been spent in a rural environment were found to be almost universally opposed to the more modern forms of recreation," sociologist Jennings J. Rhyne reported in his 1926 study of Gaston County textile villages. "The motion picture theatre is [an] institution that receives a considerable amount of censure from parents, while the young people regard it as a very popular means of amusement." See Rhyne, *Some Southern Cotton Mill Workers and Their Villages*, 199.

26. On the increasing ownership of automobiles and the popularity of "motoring" among Gaston County millhands, see Rhyne, *Some Southern Cotton Mill Workers and Their Villages*, 175.

27. Koon, "Dave McCarn," 169; J. E. Lighter, ed., *Random House Historical Dictionary of American Slang* (New York: Random House, 1994), 1:227; Tony Russell, review of McCarn and Foster, *Singers of the Piedmont*, in *Old Time Music* 11 (Winter 1973–74): 26. On the black spiritual upon which McCarn based his parody, see Carl Sandburg, *The American Songbag* (New York: Harcourt, Brace, and World, 1927), 470–71; John A. Lomax and Alan Lomax, *American Ballads and Folk Songs* (New York: Macmillan, 1934), 597–600; and Alan Lomax, *The Folk Songs of North America* (London: Cassell, 1960), 476.

28. Johnnie E. McCarn interview by Patrick Huber, Florence, South Carolina, October 17, 1996; David McCarn interview. On the Prohibition-era usage of Jamaican ginger and other intoxicants in Carolina Piedmont towns, see *Burlington (N.C.) Daily Times*, September 23, 1929, April 1, June 19, 1930.

29. Johnnie E. McCarn interview; *Burlington (N.C.) Daily Times*, September 23, 1929, June 19, 1930; Archie Green, "Rough Notes on and Information from Dave McCarn," April 20, 1961, 1, Archie Green Papers, SFC.

30. Sipe conversation; [no first name given] Sprinkles, November 26, 1931, Johnnie Elwood McCarn, October 26, 1933, and Helen Elizabeth McCarn, September 18, 1935, all in Gaston County, N.C., Index to Birth Records, L–Z, 1930–47, NCDAH; Johnnie E. McCarn telephone conversation with Patrick Huber, October 9, 1996 (notes in the author's possession); Johnnie E. McCarn interview. It remains unclear if Dave McCarn ever legally married Johnnie's mother, Maefry Dell Sprinkles. The couple's first child, a daughter named Opal, born in 1931, is listed in the Gaston County Index to Birth Records as "Illegitimate," and no father's name is provided. Both of the index's entries for the other two children, born in 1933 and 1935, list Dave McCarn as the father, however. When I spoke with him in 1996, Johnnie McCarn was unsure if his parents ever married; he had heard once that they had and another time that they had not.

31. *Gastonia (N.C.) Daily Gazette*, November 25, 26, 29, 1937, September 21, October 1, 1938, January 7, February 11, 1939; Superior Court Criminal Docket of

Gaston County, Book 8, 1934–47, Superior Court Clerk's Office, Gaston County Courthouse, Gastonia, N.C. At the time of his arrest, McCarn also became a suspect in the shooting of a South Gastonia Boy Scout master and the related interstate robbery of a Gastonia taxi driver and three of his passengers, both of which had occurred five days earlier. However, the cabdriver, after viewing the suspect in his jail cell, indicated that McCarn was not one of the two bandits who had held him up, and the Gaston County sheriff's department became convinced that McCarn was not involved in either of the other two crimes. See *Gastonia (N.C.) Daily Gazette*, November 20, 25, 26, 29, 1937.

32. David McCarn interview; Green, "Second Visit," 3.

33. David McCarn interview; Archie Green and Eugene Earle, liner notes to Carolina Tar Heels, *The Carolina Tar Heels* (Folk Legacy FSA-24), 2–4; Charles K. Wolfe, "The Carolina Tar Heels," in *Definitive Country*, 134; Paris, liner notes to McCarn and Foster, *Singers of the Piedmont*, 1; Tony Russell, *Country Music Records: A Discography, 1921–1942*, with editorial research by Bob Pinson, assisted by the staff of the Country Music Hall of Fame and Museum (New York: Oxford University Press, 2004), 68, 110–11, 173, 174, 349–50, 353; *Gastonia (N.C.) Daily Gazette*, May 27 and 28, 1927. Although often spelled "Gwen," the correct spelling of Foster's Christian name is, according to his obituary and tombstone, "Gwin." See *Gastonia (N.C.) Gazette*, November 26, 1954; and Terry James Waldrop, comp., *Old Gravesites Revisited in Gaston and Lincoln Counties, Vol. 2* (Stanley, N.C., privately published, 1989), 122.

34. Malcolm V. Blackard, "Wilmer Watts and the Lonely Eagles," *John Edwards Memorial Foundation Quarterly* 5 (Winter 1969): 126–40; Donald Lee Nelson, "'Walk Right in Belmont': The Wilmer Watts Story," *John Edwards Memorial Foundation Quarterly* 9 (Autumn 1973): 91–96; Tony Russell, "Step Stones," *Old Time Music* 40 (Winter 1984): 11, 14; Russell, *Country Music Records*, 941.

35. See the advertisements for these vaudeville shows in *Gastonia (N.C.) Daily Gazette*, January 10, 1929, December 10, 1930. For announcements for upcoming radio shows, see, for example, *Gastonia (N.C.) Daily Gazette*, January 2, 1928, April 13, 1929.

36. Paris, liner notes to McCarn and Foster, *Singers of the Piedmont*, 1; Green, "Rough Notes," 1; Archie Green, "Visit to Mr. And Mrs. McCarn, Sunday afternoon, August 18, 1963, Stanley, N.C.," 1, Archie Green Papers, SFC; Archie Green, notes on "Gwen Foster," Archie Green Papers, SFC.

37. David McCarn interview. On Puckett, see Bill Malone and Charles K. Wolfe, "Riley Puckett," in *Definitive Country*, 651–52; Norm Cohen, "Riley Puckett," in *The Encyclopedia of Country Music: The Ultimate Guide to the Music*, ed. Paul Kingsbury (New York: Oxford University Press, 1998), 425; and Norm Cohen, "Riley Puckett: 'King of the Hillbillies,'" *John Edwards Memorial Foundation Quarterly* 12 (Winter 1976): 175–84.

38. David McCarn interview; Paris, liner notes to McCarn and Foster, *Singers of the Piedmont*, 1. On Rodgers, see Nolan Porterfield, *Jimmie Rodgers: The Life and Times of America's Blue Yodeler* (Urbana: University of Illinois Press, 1992); and on the Carter Family, see Charles Wolfe, "Carter Family," in *The Encyclopedia of Coun-*

try Music, 84–85; and Mark Zwonitzer, with Charles Hirschberg, *Will You Miss Me When I'm Gone? The Carter Family and Their Legacy in American Music* (New York: Simon and Schuster, 2002).

39. Carol J. Oja, "The USA, 1918–45," in *Modern Times: From World War I to the Present*, ed. Robert P. Morgan (Englewood Cliffs, N.J.: Prentice Hall, 1993), 208; George Lipsitz, *Rainbow at Midnight: Labor and Culture in the 1940s* (Urbana: University of Illinois Press, 1994), 310.

40. Archie Green, "Will the Weaver's Hillbilly Kinfolk," *Caravan* 18 (August–September 1959): 14–23; David McCarn interview; Archie Green, "Visit by Archie Green and Ed Kahn to Howard Long and Charles Mcgaha Families, Saturday and Sunday, August 19, 20, 1961, Lowell and Belmont, North Carolina," 2, Archie Green Papers, SFC.

41. Green, "Will the Weaver's Hillbilly Kinfolk," 14–23; David McCarn interview.

42. David McCarn interview.

43. Ibid.; *Gastonia (N.C.) Daily Gazette*, May 2, 1940; Green, "Visit by Archie Green and Ed Kahn to Howard Long and Charles Mcgaha Families," 5–6; *Charlotte Observer*, August 10, 1969.

44. Green, "Rough Notes," 1; Green, "Visit by Archie Green and Ed Kahn to Howard Long and Charles Mcgaha Families," 3.

45. Green, "Second Visit," 2; David McCarn interview. One hundred and fifty miles northeast of Gastonia, in Danville, Virginia, McCarn's "Cotton Mill Colic" was also enthusiastically received, as evidenced by an L. B. Clarke Music Company advertisement that appeared in the October 3, 1930, edition of the *Danville (Va.) Bee*. Record sales of "Cotton Mill Colic," the ad noted, are "going strong."

46. For a discography of McCarn's recordings, see Russell, *Country Music Records*, 527.

47. The commercial recording of all four of these textile songs occurred shortly after the implementation of the "stretch-out" system in southern mills, and the recording of three of them coincided with the wave of 1929 Piedmont textile strikes. The earliest of these songs to be recorded was "Cotton Mill Girl," by Lester Smallwood, a former sweeper who had begun work at the New Holland Mills near Gainesville, Georgia, at the age of fourteen. In October 1928, Smallwood waxed his song (which he had cobbled together from circulating versions of the lyric lament "Hard Times in the Mill") at a Victor field-recording session in Atlanta, under the supervision of Ralph S. Peer. Accompanied by his finger-picked banjo and wheezing harmonica, Smallwood complains about overbearing second hands and harsh shop-floor rules: "Slipped out one day to get a drink of water, / Around came the boss and he docked me a quarter. / Hard times in this old mill, / Hard times everywhere." One year later, in October 1929, Frank Welling and John McGhee, two prolific Huntington, West Virginia, musicians who collaborated on nearly two hundred recorded sides between 1927 and 1932 (but neither of whom, apparently, ever worked in a textile mill), commemorated the recent Carolina Piedmont strikes in a pair of turgid bass duets on the Paramount label. Their record, "The Marion Massacre"/"North Carolina Textile Strike," appeared under the billing of

the "Martin Brothers." Later that month, Wilmer Watts and the Lonely Eagles, a Belmont, North Carolina, mill village stringband, recorded "Cotton Mill Blues" for Paramount in New York City. In the song, the band forcefully confronts the social stigma attached to millworkers, complaining that "Uptown people call us trash, / Say we never have no cash. / That is why the people fret, / Call us [the] ignorant factory set." On these cotton mill songs, see Charles Wolfe, "Lester Smallwood and His Cotton Mill Song," *Old Time Music* 25 (Summer 1977): 23; Ivan M. Tribe, "John McGhee and Frank Welling: West Virginia's Most-Recorded Old-Time Artists," *John Edwards Memorial Foundation Quarterly* 17 (Summer 1981): 61; Ivan M. Tribe, "Frank Welling and John McGhee," in *Definitive Country*, 853-54; Blackard, "Wilmer Watts and the Lonely Eagles," 138-39; Nelson, "'Walk Right in Belmont,'" 96; Archie Green, "A Southern Cotton Mill Rhyme," in *Wobblies, Pile Butts, and Other Heroes: Laborlore Explorations* (Urbana: University of Illinois Press, 1993), 297-99, 312-14; and Doug DeNatale and Glenn Hinson, "The Southern Textile Song Tradition Reconsidered," in *Songs about Work: Essays in Occupational Culture for Richard A. Reuss*, ed. Archie Green, Special Publications of the Folklore Institute no. 3 (Bloomington: Indiana University Press, 1993), 80-81, 82, 85. An earlier version of DeNatale and Hinson's essay appeared under the same title in *Journal of Folklore Research* 28 (May–December 1991): 103-33.

48. Mark Wilson, liner notes to various artists, *Poor Man, Rich Man*, 1; Phil Hardy and Dave Laing, "Bob Miller," in *The Da Capo Companion to 20th-Century Popular Music* (New York: Da Capo Press, 1995), 641; Russell, *Country Music Records*, 616, 800. Compare, for example, one of the stanzas of the two-part "Eleven Cent Cotton Forty Cent Meat" to "Cotton Mill Colic": "Eleven cent cotton, forty cent meat / How in the world can a poor man eat? / Pray for the sunshine, 'cause it will rain / Things getting worse, driving all insane / Built a nice barn, painted it brown / Lightning came along and burnt it down / No use talking, any man's beat / With eleven cent cotton and forty cent meat."

49. Hall et al., *Like a Family*, 195-212; David McCarn interview.

50. "Southern Stirrings," *Time* 13 (April 15, 1929): 13; Tom Tippett, *When Southern Labor Stirs* (New York: Jonathan Cape and Harrison Smith, 1931); Bryant Simon, *A Fabric of Defeat: The Politics of South Carolina Millhands, 1910–1948* (Chapel Hill: University of North Carolina Press, 1998), 50-56; Hall et al., *Like a Family*, 212-21, 226-35; Salmond, *Gastonia 1929*, 9-10.

51. Pope, *Millhands and Preachers*, 229-30; Salmond, *Gastonia 1929*, 13-16; Bertha Hendrix, "I Was in the Gastonia Strike," in *Working Lives: The Southern Exposure History of Labor in the South*, ed. Marc S. Miller (New York: Pantheon Books, 1980), 169.

52. Robert Weldon Whalen, *"Like Fire in Broom Straw": Southern Journalism and the Textile Strikes of 1929–1931* (Westport, Conn.: Greenwood Press, 2001), especially 1-2, 28-29; Christina L. Baker and William J. Baker, "Shaking All the Corners of the Sky: The Global Response to the Gastonia Strike of 1929," *Canadian Review of American Studies* 21 (Winter 1990): 321-31; W. J. Cash, "The War in the South," *American Mercury* 19 (February 1930): 163-69; *New York Times*, June 15, 1930. The literature on the Gastonia Textile Strike of 1929 is extensive, but for two

of the most comprehensive accounts, from which much of the following account of the conflict is drawn, see Pope, *Millhands and Preachers*; and Salmond, *Gastonia 1929*.

53. Hall et al., *Like a Family*, 214–15; Salmond, *Gastonia 1929*, 23–28.

54. Pope, *Millhands and Preachers*, 254; Hall et al., *Like a Family*, 215; Salmond, *Gastonia 1929*, 24, 26, 38, 41–44, 56–57; Hendrix, "I Was in the Gastonia Strike," 170.

55. Salmond, *Gastonia 1929*, 70–76, 122–25, 128–29; Margaret Larkin, "The Story of Ella May," *New Masses* 5 (November 1929): 3–4; Hall et al., *Like a Family*, 215.

56. Fred E. Beal, *Proletarian Journey: New England, Gastonia, Moscow* (New York: Hillman-Curl, 1937), 132; folder "Textiles—Gastonia Strike Songs," Mary Heaton Vorse Papers, ALUA; Vera Buch Weisbord, *A Radical Life* (Bloomington: Indiana University Press, 1977), 225.

57. John Greenway, *American Folksongs of Protest* (Philadelphia: University of Pennsylvania Press, 1953), 135–36; "Textiles—Gastonia Strike Songs," Mary Heaton Vorse Papers, ALUA; Hall et al., *Like a Family*, 220; *Daily Worker* (New York, N.Y.), April 15 and July 30, 1929. On the Gastonia strike songs, see Margaret Larkin, "Ella May's Songs," *Nation* 129 (October 9, 1929): 382–83; Greenway, *American Folksongs of Protest*, 133–39, 244–52; Stephen R. Wiley, "Songs of the Gastonia Textile Strike of 1929: Models of and for Southern Working-Class Women's Militancy," *North Carolina Folklore Journal* 30 (Fall–Winter 1982): 87–98; Patrick Huber, "'Battle Songs of the Southern Class Struggle': Songs of the Gastonia Textile Strike of 1929," *Southern Cultures* 4 (Summer 1998): 109–22; and Timothy P. Lynch, *Strike Songs of the Depression* (Jackson: University Press of Mississippi, 2001), 12–48.

58. Greenway, *American Folksongs of Protest*, 136–37; "Textiles—Gastonia Strike Songs," Mary Heaton Vorse Papers, ALUA.

59. *Daily Worker* (New York, N.Y.), September 18, 1929; Mary E. Frederickson, "Ella May Wiggins," in *Dictionary of North Carolina Biography*, ed. William S. Powell, 6 vols. (Chapel Hill: University of North Carolina Press, 1996), 6:193–95; Larkin, "The Story of Ella May," 3; Larkin, "Ella May's Songs," 382–83; Margaret Larkin, "Revolutionary Music," *New Masses* 8 (February 1933): 27; Greenway, *American Folksongs of Protest*, 244–52; Salmond, "Aspects of Modernization in the Loray Mill Strike of 1929," 169–76; Huber, "'Battle Songs of the Southern Class Struggle,'" 121. The best account of Wiggins's life, though unpublished, is Lynn Haessly's superb "'Mill Mother's Lament': Ella May, Working Women's Militancy, and the 1929 Gaston County Strikes" (master's thesis, University of North Carolina at Chapel Hill, 1987).

60. Weisbord, *A Radical Life*, 185; Beal, *Proletarian Journey*, 159.

61. Larkin, "The Story of Ella May," 3–4.

62. *Daily Worker* (New York, N.Y.), September 14, 1938; Haessly, "'Mill Mother's Lament,'" 19; *Labor Defender*, October 1929, n.p. For the shorter, better-known version of this song titled "Mill Mother's Lament," see Greenway, *American Folksongs of Protest*, 251–52; and Seeger, *American Industrial Ballads*.

63. *Daily Worker* (New York, N.Y.), July 26, 1929; Greenway, *American Folksongs*

of Protest, 135–39; folder "Textiles—Gastonia Strike Songs," Mary Heaton Vorse Papers, ALUA; Huber, "'Battle Songs of the Southern Class Struggle,'" 121–22; Haessly, "'Mill Mother's Lament,'" 153–57, 163–66.

64. David McCarn interview. The word "colic," as used by McCarn to mean "complain" or "complaint," does not appear in Norman E. Eliason, *Tarheel Talk: An Historical Study of the English Language in North Carolina to 1860* (Chapel Hill: University of North Carolina Press, 1956), nor is it included in J. A. Simpson and E. S. C. Weiner, eds., *The Oxford English Dictionary*, 2nd ed., 20 vols. (Oxford: Clarendon Press, 1989).

65. McCarn was a contemporary of Allen Tate, Donald Davidson, Robert Penn Warren, and the other privileged, Vanderbilt-based Agrarians who invoked tradition as a means of preserving the American South from the onslaught of encroaching industrial capitalism and materialism. McCarn's critique in "Cotton Mill Colic," in contrast, is a grassroots one, the dissenting voice of a working-class insider. Moreover, his critique is far more concrete than the arguments posited by these upper- and middle-class intellectuals in their manifesto, Twelve Southerners, *I'll Take My Stand: The South and the Agrarian Tradition, by Twelve Southerners* (New York: Harper, 1930), published the same year that McCarn's song was recorded. Unlike the Agrarians, McCarn condemns southern industrial development chiefly on economic grounds. He criticizes industrialism not because it threatened to destroy some organic, idealized southern culture, but because the textile mills failed to pay him enough to be able to participate in the very modern consumerism and mass culture that the Agrarians decried. McCarn's three cotton mill songs indicate that a variety of anti-industrial ideologies circulated during the late 1920s and early 1930s, and that they did so on many different class levels within southern society. See James C. Cobb, "From Rocky Top to Detroit City: Country Music and the Economic Transformation of the South," in *You Wrote My Life: Lyrical Themes in Country Music*, ed. Melton A. McLaurin and Richard A. Peterson, Cultural Perspectives on the American South, Vol. 6 (Philadelphia: Gordon and Breach, 1992), 63–64.

66. Green, "Second Visit," 2; David McCarn interview.

67. Larkin, "Ella May's Songs," 382; Hall et al., *Like a Family*, 227.

68. Andrews et al., *The Literature of the American South*, 1109; Green, liner notes to Seeger, *Tipple, Loom and Rail*, 10; David McCarn interview.

69. David McCarn interview; Andrews et al., *The Literature of the American South*, 1115–16; DeNatale and Hinson, "The Southern Textile Song Tradition Reconsidered," 83.

70. DeNatale and Hinson, "The Southern Textile Song Tradition Reconsidered," 89; Tippett, *When Southern Labor Stirs*, 250, 251n14. A perceptive social observer and an avid collector of hillbilly records, Tippett pointed out in a footnote that "the song can be purchased on a Victor phonograph record, No. V40274 A." See ibid., 251n14. In September 1930, only a month after its release, "Cotton Mill Colic" sparked a controversy during the 1930–31 strike at the Riverside and Dan River Cotton Mills Company in Danville, Virginia. Doug DeNatale and Glenn Hinson's research not only reveals how the song circulated among strikers during that pro-

tracted labor struggle but also illuminates the conflicting political connotations that textile manufacturers and their employees ascribed to McCarn's song. "Seeing the commercial possibilities of the song during the strike," they write, "Luther B. Clarke, a Danville record store owner who had previously arranged recording sessions for several mill worker musicians, promoted the record through his store and arranged to have it played on a local radio station. . . . In response, H. R. Fitzgerald, the president of [Riverside and] Dan River Mills, pressured the local media to suppress the song on the grounds that 'it was degrading to cotton mill work.'" In deference to Fitzgerald, a powerful city businessman and civic leader, the local radio station (probably WBTM) stopped broadcasting McCarn's record. By then, however, "Cotton Mill Colic" had already apparently become wildly popular among Danville strikers. See DeNatale and Hinson, "The Southern Textile Song Tradition Reconsidered," 89. The phrase "serious social statement" is cultural historian George Lipsitz's. See Lipsitz, *Rainbow at Midnight*, 305, where he makes a similar comment about Louis Jordan's "Ain't Nobody Here but Us Chickens."

71. Ed Kahn, liner notes to Blue Sky Boys, *Presenting the Blue Sky Boys*; DeNatale and Hinson, "The Southern Textile Song Tradition Reconsidered," 84.

72. Joe Sharp, "Cotton Mill Colic," recorded by Alan Lomax, Washington, D.C., ca. May 12, 1938, for Archive of Folk Culture, Library of Congress (AFS 1629 B2), in AFC; Alan Lomax, "Archive of American Folk-Song," Library of Congress, *Annual Report of the Librarian of Congress for the Fiscal Year Ended June 30, 1938* (Washington, D.C.: Government Printing Office, 1939), 188. Sharp had traveled to the nation's capital that May as one of the members of the Skyline Farms band and dance team to entertain First Lady Eleanor Roosevelt and her guests at a White House afternoon garden party. On Skyline Farms and its band's 1938 White House performance, see David Campbell and David Coombs, "Skyline Farms: A Case Study of Community Development and Rural Rehabilitation," *Appalachian Journal* 10 (Spring 1983): 244–54; Wayne Flynt, *Poor but Proud: Alabama's Poor Whites* (Tuscaloosa: University of Alabama Press, 1989), 306–18; Joyce H. Cauthen, *With Fiddle and Well-Rosined Bow: Old-Time Fiddling in Alabama* (Tuscaloosa: University of Alabama Press, 1989), 159; and "Music Program by Skyline Group, Executive Garden Party, May 12, 1938," in White House Office of Social Entertainments, Box 61, in Franklin D. Roosevelt Library, Hyde Park, New York.

73. John A. Lomax and Alan Lomax, comps., *Our Singing Country: A Second Volume of American Ballads and Folk Songs* (New York: Macmillan, 1941), 291–92; Lomax, *The Folk Songs of North America*, 279, 287; Lomax, Guthrie, and Seeger, *Hard Hitting Songs for Hard-Hit People*, 120; B. A. Botkin, ed., *A Treasury of Southern Folklore: Stories, Ballads, Traditions, and Folkways of the People of the South* (New York: Crown Publishers, 1950 [1949]), 731–32; Andrews et al., *The Literature of the American South*, 1115–16.

74. For a sampling of these postwar cover versions, see note 6 for this chapter.

75. See New Lost City Ramblers, "Serves Them Fine," *Songs from the Depression*; and "Everyday Dirt," *New Lost City Ramblers, Vol. 2*. Later, the band also covered McCarn's "Take Them for a Ride," on its 1968 Folkways album, *Modern Times*;

Archie Green interview by Patrick Huber, Chapel Hill, North Carolina, October 3, 1994; Mike Seeger telephone conversation with Patrick Huber, September 12, 1996 (notes in the author's possession).

76. Green, "Visit by Archie Green and Ed Kahn to Howard Long and Charles Mcgaha Families," 1; Johnnie E. McCarn interview; David McCarn interview.

77. David McCarn interview; Green, "Second Visit," 3–4; Ed Kahn, "Further Notes on Second McCarn Visit," December 1, 1965, 6, Archie Green Papers, SFC.

78. Wilson, liner notes to various artists, *Poor Man, Rich Man*, 1; David McCarn interview; Kahn, "Further Notes," 6.

79. Arthur Palmer Hudson to Archie Green, September 24, 1961, Archie Green Papers, SFC.

80. Johnnie E. McCarn interview; Green, "Second Visit," 5; *Gastonia (N.C.) Gazette*, November 9, 1964; North Carolina Department of Vital Records, John David McCarn death certificate, November 7, 1964, Raleigh.

81. This and the following paragraph are based upon Johnnie E. McCarn interview; a copy of Johnnie E. McCarn's obituary can be found in the *Gaston Gazette* (Gastonia, N.C.), January 13, 2004.

Chapter Four

1. Dorsey Dixon, "Early Life of Dorsey M. Dixon, Song Writer and Composer and Author of the Famous Wreck on the Highway and Many Others," May 30, 1948, 2, Archie Green Papers, SFC. Three of the Dixons' seven children succumbed to deadly diseases before turning sixteen, and Dorsey himself had another close brush with death as a child. In 1903, at the age of five, he contracted double pneumonia, and in treating him, an inexperienced doctor "salivated" his patient, administering an overdose of calomel (mercurous chloride) to Dixon. As a result, Dixon later wrote, "my upper teeth came loose and came out by the roots. after which my upper jaw bone tore loose and dropped down in my mouth. and we were not able to get it out. and there I was no way to take food and I quickly started back the other way." Dixon's father took his starving son to a dentist to perform the dangerous procedure of removing the bone. If he removed the bone and the main artery refused to close, the dentist warned, Dixon would bleed to death in ten minutes. "That put dear old dad on the spot," Dorsey continued. "But my pleading with him to let the doctor pull it out. encouraged him some what and he findly told the doctor to go a head and pull it out for it was death both ways. The doctor told him that he was right about that to. The doctor brought it out on the secound try. and the blood shot out. in a terrible gush. The doctor stood with his back to me But dear old dad stood by me with his arms around me. And I don't know just how many times the doctor asked him was the blood slaking. But it was more then one. It findly started letting up and father was able to tell him that it was. and I never saw a doctor move so fast from that day till this. My mother had put a cloth around my neck before we left home and it was the bloodest peice of cloth that I have ever seen before or after. I again started back up the ladder. and made it o.k. from then on with the exception of a few hard falls one of which busted the drum of my right ear." Dixon's ordeal left him with a slight, almost undetectable lisp

that can be discerned on his Bluebird recordings. It also reinforced his steadfast belief that the Lord had charged him with a special purpose in life. See ibid.

2. *Rockingham (N.C.) Post-Dispatch*, April 14, 1932; Dixon, "Early Life of Dorsey M. Dixon," 2. On the deadly Alabama tornadoes, see, for example, *New York Times*, March 23, 26, 28, 1932.

3. Archie Green, liner notes to Dorsey Dixon, Howard Dixon, and Nancy Dixon, *Babies in the Mill: Carolina Traditional, Industrial, Sacred Songs* (Testament T-3301), reissued on CD under the same title (HMG 2502), on back of album cover; other citations below with page numbers refer to the accompanying booklet of song notes; Dorsey M. Dixon, "The Angel Guided Child," unfinished manuscript in "Songs Composed by Dorsey M. Dixon, 1918 E. Pratt St., Baltimore, MD," ca. 1953, Dorsey M. Dixon Notebooks (copy in the author's possession). Album and CD reissues of the Dixon Brothers' music include *Beyond Black Smoke* (Country Turtle 6000); *Rambling and Gambling* (Country Turtle 6002); *The Dixon Brothers, Vol. 1* (Old Homestead OHCS-151); *The Dixon Brothers, Vol. 2* (Old Homestead OHCS-164); *The Dixon Brothers, Vol. 3* (Old Homestead OHCS-178); *The Dixon Brothers, Vol. 4* (Old Homestead OHCS-179); *Babies in the Mill*; and *The Dixon Brothers: How Can a Broke Man Be Happy?* (Acrobat 4022). Between 2000 and 2001, Austria-based Document Records label released the complete recordings of the Dixon Brothers on four compact discs. See Dixon Brothers, *The Dixon Brothers: Complete Recorded Works in Chronological Order, Vols. 1–4 (1936–1938)* (Document DOCD-8046–DOCD-8049). The Dixon Brothers' recordings have also been widely reissued on old-time music anthologies, including, for example, various artists, *Are You from Dixie? Great Country Brother Teams of the 1930's* (RCA 8417-2-R); various artists, *Ballads and Songs* (Old Timey 102); various artists, *Classic Country Duets* (Old Timey OT126); various artists, *The Cold-Water Pledge: Songs of Moonshine and Temperance Recorded in the Golden Age, Vol. 2* (Marimac 9105); various artists, *Country Slide* (Acrobat ACRCD 242); various artists, *Down in the Basement: Joe Bussard's Treasure Trove* (Old Hat 1004); various artists, *Drunk and Nutty Blues: Hillbillies Foolin' with the Blues* (Indigo IGODCD 2520); various artists, *Hard Times in the Country: Down and Out in the Rural South: Songs and Tunes from 1927–1938* (County CO-CD-3527); various artists, *High Rollers: Vintage Gambling Songs, 1920–1952* (Buzzola 006); various artists, *A Joyful Noise, Vol. 2* (Marimac 9101); various artists, *O Brothers!* (ASV CDAJA 5467); various artists, *Poor Man, Rich Man: American Country Songs of Protest* (Rounder Records 1026); various artists, *Prayers from Hell: White Gospel and Sinners Blues, 1927–1940* (Trikont US 267); various artists, *Rare and Red Hot Gospel* (Catfish KATCD 171); various artists, *The Road to Nashville: A History of Country Music* (Indigo IGOTCD 2559); various artists, *Roll and Tumble Blues: A History of Slide Guitar* (Indigo IGOTCD 2548); various artists, *Songs of Death and Tragedy*, Folk Music in America, vol. 9 (Library of Congress, Music Division, Recording Laboratory LBC 9); various artists, *Times Ain't Like They Used to Be: Early American Rural Music, Vol. 4* (Yazoo 2048); and various artists, *Titanic Songs* (Unsinkable Music TSCD 22798).

4. Green, liner notes to Dixon et al., *Babies in the Mill*, on back of album cover. For recorded cover versions of "Weave Room Blues" or "Weaver's Life," see, for

example, Pete Seeger, *Folksongs for Young People* (Folkways FC 7532); New Lost City Ramblers, *New Lost City Ramblers, Vol. 3* (Folkways FA 2398); Joe Glazer, *Textile Voices* (Collector 1922); Mike Seeger, *Tipple, Loom and Rail: Songs of the Industrialization of the South* (Folkways FH 5273); and Mountain Musicians' Cooperative, *Brown Lung Cotton Mill Blues* (June Appal 006). For published transcriptions of these songs, see, for example, John Greenway, *American Folksongs of Protest* (Philadelphia: University of Pennsylvania Press, 1953), 128–29; and Alan Lomax, Woody Guthrie, and Pete Seeger, comps., *Hard Hitting Songs for Hard-Hit People* (New York: Oak Publications 1967), 130–31, 132–33.

5. Pat Conte, liner notes to Dixon Brothers, *Rambling and Gambling*; Green, liner notes to Dixon et al., *Babies in the Mill*, on back of album cover.

6. Dixon, "Early Life of Dorsey M. Dixon," 1; O. L. Warr, C. W. Flowers, and Valerie Schaible, *Darlington County: Economic and Social*, Bulletin of the University of South Carolina no. 196 (February 1, 1927), 14–15; Horace Fraser Rudisill, *Darlington County: A Pictorial History* (Norfolk, Va.: Donning Company, 1986), 41, 95–98; Dorsey M. Dixon interview by Eugene Earle and Archie Green, East Rockingham, North Carolina, August 8, 1962, SFC.

7. Dixon, "Early Life of Dorsey M. Dixon," 1; Nancy A. Dixon interview by Dorsey M. Dixon, East Rockingham, North Carolina, ca. December 1961, SFC; Twelfth Census of the United States, 1900: Kershaw County, S.C., Population Schedule, 14B (microfilm); Thirteenth Census of the United States, 1910: Darlington County, S.C., Population Schedule, 40A (microfilm); Dorsey M. Dixon interview, August 8, 1962.

8. Dorsey M. Dixon interview by Eugene Earle and Archie Green, East Rockingham, North Carolina, August 7, 1962, SFC; Dorsey M. Dixon interview, August 8, 1962; Dorsey M. Dixon interview by Archie Green and Ed Kahn, East Rockingham, North Carolina, August 20, 1961, SFC.

9. Dorsey M. Dixon interviews, August 20, 1961, August 8, 1962. On Gainey, see Eliza Cowan Ervin and Horace Fraser Rudisill, eds., *Darlingtoniana: A History of People, Places and Events in Darlington County, South Carolina* (Columbia, S.C.: R. L. Bryan, 1964), 212–13.

10. Green, liner notes to Dixon et al., *Babies in the Mill*, 5; Dorsey M. Dixon interview, August 20, 1961.

11. Dorsey Dixon, "Dixon Bros—Howard-Dorsey," ca. 1962, 1, Archie Green Papers, SFC; Dorsey M. Dixon interviews, August 20, 1961, August 8, 1962.

12. Warr et al., *Darlington County*, 14–15; Rudisill, *Darlington County*, 41, 95–98; *Darlington (S.C.) News and Press*, August 12, 1915.

13. Green, liner notes to Dixon et al., *Babies in the Mill*, 3, 6–7, 8–9; Dorsey M. Dixon interviews, August 20, 1961, August 8, 1962.

14. Dorsey M. Dixon interview, August 8, 1962. On "The Wreck of the Old 97," see Norm Cohen, "Robert W. Gordon and the Second Wreck of the 'Old 97,'" *Journal of American Folklore* 87 (January 1974): 12–38; Norm Cohen, *Long Steel Rail: The Railroad in American Folksong* (Urbana: University of Illinois Press, 1981), 197–226; and Kate Letcher Lyle, *Scalded to Death by the Steam: Authentic Stories of Railroad*

Disasters and the Ballads That Were Written about Them (Chapel Hill, N.C.: Algonquin Books, 1991), 14–33.

15. Fourteenth Census of the United States, 1920: Darlington County, S.C., Population Schedule, 12B (microfilm); Dorsey M. Dixon interview, August 8, 1962.

16. Nancy A. Dixon interview by Dorsey M. Dixon.

17. *Rockingham (N.C.) Post-Dispatch*, June 13, 1929; James E. Huneycutt and Ida C. Huneycutt, *A History of Richmond County* (Raleigh, N.C.: Edwards and Broughton Company, 1976), 354–74; Fifteenth Census of the United States, 1930: Richmond County, N.C., Population Schedule, 235A and 270A (microfilm); Dorsey M. Dixon interview, August 8, 1962.

18. Dorsey Dixon, "Dixon Bros—Howard-Dorsey," ca. 1962, 2, Archie Green Papers, SFC; Fifteenth Census of the United States, 1930: Richmond County, N.C., Population Schedule, 270A (microfilm); Dorsey M. Dixon interview, August 8, 1962.

19. Mack McCormick, liner notes to various artists, *Songs of Death and Tragedy*; Thomas J. Kirkland and Robert M. Kennedy, *Historic Camden, Part Two: Nineteenth Century* (Columbia, S.C.: State Printing Company, 1926 [1905]), 329–30; John Oliver Moseley, *The Terrible Cleveland Fire: Its Victims and Survivors* (Charleston, S.C.: Southern Printing and Publishing, 1923); Dorsey M. Dixon interview, August 20, 1961. Originally, Dixon composed the elegy as a poem, but when his brother Howard noticed that the poem fit the melody of the late nineteenth-century popular hymn "Life's Railway to Heaven," the Dixons began performing the composition as a song for small audiences in East Rockingham's mill villages. The song soon became a local favorite in their community. See Dorsey M. Dixon interview, August 20, 1961.

20. *Rockingham (N.C.) Post-Dispatch*, March 31, April 14, April 28, May 26, October 27, 1932, July 6, 1933. Even in these topical songs, it is important to note, Dixon often attached moral taglines, and thus transformed what were songs about newsworthy events into religious, homiletic numbers. In "The Shooting of Otto Wood," for example, Dixon concludes his account of the 1930 death of this North Carolina escaped convict with the following stanza: "Watch your step as you travel this life, / Don't make that great mistake, / And then cry out for mercy / And help for it may be too late. / Otto Wood is now peacefully sleeping / Beneath the cold, cold clay, / But, oh, the stand that he must take / In that Resurrection Day!" See ibid., April 28, 1932.

21. Ibid., June 9, 1932, July 20, 1933.

22. Ibid., July 28, 1932, February 27, 1936.

23. Ibid., June 23, 1932, August 4, 1932, July 20, 1933.

24. Dixon, "Early Life of Dorsey M. Dixon," 3; Dorsey M. Dixon to Eugene Earle, September 25, 1961, Archie Green Papers, SFC; Jacquelyn Dowd Hall, James Leloudis, Robert Korstad, Mary Murphy, Lu Ann Jones, and Christopher B. Daly, *Like a Family: The Making of a Southern Cotton Mill World*, with a new afterword by the authors (Chapel Hill: University of North Carolina Press, 2000 [1987]), 178–79; Liston

Pope, *Millhands and Preachers: A Study of Gastonia* (New Haven: Yale University Press, 1970 [1942]), 117–40. I am indebted to Harry L. Watson for clarifying several of the religious concepts in this paragraph.

25. Nancy A. Dixon interview by Dorsey M. Dixon (this is Dixon's paraphrase of Job 14:1); "Book One, Musical Compositions Composed and Written by Dorsey M. Dixon," ca. 1954, n.p., Dorsey M. Dixon Notebooks (copy in the author's possession).

26. Jack Palmer, *Vernon Dalhart: First Star of Country Music* (Denver, Colo.: Mainspring Press, 2005), 126–29; Cohen, "Robert W. Gordon and the Second Wreck of the 'Old 97,'" 20–21; Charles K. Wolfe, "Event Songs," in *Readin' Country Music: Steel Guitars, Opry Stars, and Honky Tonk Bars*, ed. Cecelia Tichi, a special issue of *South Atlantic Quarterly* 94 (Winter 1995): 217–30; "Mournful Melodies on Edison Records Popular," *Talking Machine World* 21 (October 15, 1925): 199.

27. Palmer, *Vernon Dalhart*; Hugh Leamy, "Now Come All You Good People," *Collier's* 84 (November 2, 1929): 20; Wolfe, "Event Songs," 217–30.

28. Norm Cohen, *Traditional Anglo-American Folk Music: An Annotated Discography of Published Sound Recordings* (New York: Garland, 1994), 35; Norm Cohen, "The Urge to Write Songs: The Case of Dorsey Dixon," *John Edwards Memorial Foundation Quarterly* 10 (Summer 1974): 83–84; Dixon, "Early Life of Dorsey M. Dixon," 3.

29. Dorsey M. Dixon interview, August 20, 1961; Dorsey M. Dixon to Gerald F. Mills, August 2, 1966, Archie Green Papers, SFC. It was not until 1966, however, when he used an $895 royalty check from "Wreck on the Highway" for a down payment on a brand-new Chevrolet Impala, that Dixon was able to purchase his first automobile.

30. Steven Biel, *Down with the Old Canoe: A Cultural History of the Titanic Disaster* (New York: W. W. Norton, 1996), 66–69; Dorsey M. Dixon interview, August 8, 1962.

31. *Rockingham (N.C.) Post-Dispatch*, March 24, 1938. Because of the three-minute limit for 78-rpm recordings, the Dixon Brothers omitted the final stanza of the original song, as published in the *Rockingham (N.C.) Post-Dispatch*, on their 1938 Bluebird record. The final stanza goes: "Now, dear sinners, hear my plea, / You may wreck out on life's sea, / In a slanting dive you may go down out there. / So why don't you heed the call / Jesus sends out to you all, / So you can smile and face that chilly air?" See ibid.

32. Dorsey M. Dixon interview, August 20, 1961; Charlie Bowman interview by Dorsey Dixon, Union City, Georgia, ca. November 1961, SFC. For a differing account of the accident that provided the song's inspiration, see the comments of Dixon's son, Rev. Dorsey M. Dixon Jr., in Dorothy Horstman, *Sing Your Heart Out, Country Boy* (New York: E. P. Dutton, 1975), 88–89.

33. *Rockingham (N.C.) Post-Dispatch*, March 10, 1938. The original song that Dorsey published in his hometown newspaper is essentially the same as the one the Dixon Brothers recorded for RCA-Victor in 1938. Dixon probably based his song upon an old African American spiritual, "I Couldn't Hear Nobody Pray,"

which had been collected in Texas as early as the 1920s. See Alan Lomax, *The Folk-songs of North America* (London: Cassell, 1960), 473–74.

34. Billy Altman, liner notes to various artists, *Something Got a Hold of Me: A Treasury of Sacred Music* (RCA 2100-2-R). For an analysis of the song, see the superb essay by Tony Hilfer, "'Wreck on the Highway': Rhetoric and Religion in a Country Song," *John Edwards Memorial Foundation Quarterly* 21 (Fall/Winter 1985): 116–19.

35. Dorsey M. Dixon interview, August 20, 1961.

36. Green, liner notes to Dixon et al., *Babies in the Mill*, 3; Dorsey M. Dixon interview, August 8, 1962; *Rockingham (N.C.) Post-Dispatch*, February 25, 1932. Except for the chorus and the omission of the final stanza, the Dixon Brothers' 1936 recorded version of "Weave Room Blues" remains essentially the same as the original song that Dixon published in the *Rockingham (N.C.) Post-Dispatch*.

37. *Rockingham (N.C.) Post-Dispatch*, February 25, 1932; Dorsey M. Dixon interview, August 8, 1962.

38. On the strike, see *Rockingham (N.C.) Post-Dispatch*, August 25, September 1, October 6, 20, 27, 1932.

39. Douglas DeNatale, "Dorsey Murdock Dixon," in *Dictionary of North Carolina Biography*, ed. William S. Powell, 6 vols. (Chapel Hill: University of North Carolina Press, 1986), 2:74; Dorsey M. Dixon interview, August 8, 1962. Dixon at various times belonged to the Order of Railroad Telegraphers (AFL), the Textile Workers Union of America (CIO), and an unknown AFL-affiliated union when he worked at a munitions plant in Baltimore, Maryland.

40. *Richmond County Daily Journal* (Rockingham, N.C.), April 24, 1980.

41. Dorsey M. Dixon interview, August 8, 1962.

42. Ed Kahn, liner notes to Tom Darby and Jimmie Tarlton, *Darby and Tarlton: Complete Recordings*, 3-CD boxed set (Bear Family BCD-15764), 6–7, 10; Charles K. Wolfe, "Darby and Tarlton," in *Definitive Country: The Ultimate Encyclopedia of Country Music and Its Performers*, ed. Barry McCloud (New York: Perigree Books, 1995), 214–15; Norm Cohen and Anne Cohen, "The Legendary Jimmie Tarlton," *Sing Out!* 16 (September 1966): 16–19; Graham Wickham, "Darby and Tarlton," special edition of *Blue Yodeler*, 3–19, Archie Green Papers, SFC.

43. Dorsey M. Dixon interview, August 8, 1962; Columbia Records, *Old Familiar Tunes* (New York: Columbia Phonograph Company, 1929); Kahn, liner notes to Darby and Tarlton, *Darby and Tarlton*, 4, 11, 16; Wolfe, "Darby and Tarlton," 214–15.

44. Dorsey M. Dixon interview, August 8, 1962.

45. Ibid., August 20, 1961, August 8, 1962.

46. Cohen, "The Urge to Write Songs," 84; Dorsey M. Dixon interviews, August 20, 1961, August 8, 1962.

47. Dorsey M. Dixon interviews, August 20, 1961, August 8, 1962.

48. Ibid., August 20, 1961, August 8, 1962; Kahn, liner notes to Darby and Tarlton, *Darby and Tarlton*, 40; Dorsey M. Dixon to Dick Spotswood, August 5, 1963, AFC.

49. Dorsey M. Dixon interview, August 8, 1962.

50. Crazy Water Crystals Company of the Carolinas and Georgia, *Souvenir of the Crazy Barn Dance and the Crazy Bands*, 2nd ed. (Charlotte, N.C.: Crazy Water Crystals Company, ca. 1934), n.p; Pat Ahrens, "The Role of the Crazy Water Crystals Company in Promoting Hillbilly Music," *John Edwards Memorial Foundation Quarterly* 6 (Autumn 1970): 108. See the photograph on the cover of the Old Homestead LP, Dixon Brothers, *The Dixon Brothers, Vol. 1*. My discussion of the *Crazy Barn Dance* draws heavily upon Ahrens, "The Role of the Crazy Water Crystals Company in Promoting Hillbilly Music," 107–9; Pamela Grundy, "'We Always Tried to Be Good People': Respectability, Crazy Water Crystals, and Hillbilly Music on the Air, 1933–1935," *Journal of American History* 81 (March 1995): 1591–1620; and Bob Carlin, *String Bands in the North Carolina Piedmont* (Jefferson, N.C.: McFarland, 2004), 175–77.

51. Dorsey M. Dixon interview, August 8, 1962; Ivan M. Tribe, "The Dixon Brothers," in *Definitive Country*, 239; Crazy Water Crystals Company of the Carolinas and Georgia, *Souvenir of the Crazy Barn Dance and the Crazy Bands*, n.p.

52. Ahrens, "The Role of the Crazy Water Crystals Company," 108; Della Coulter, "The Piedmont Tradition," in *The Charlotte Country Music Story*, ed. George Holt (Charlotte: North Carolina Arts Council, 1985), 11.

53. Ahrens, "The Role of the Crazy Water Crystals Company," 108; *Rockingham (N.C.) Post-Dispatch*, August 16, 1934.

54. *Burlington (N.C.) Daily Times-News*, October 9, 1935; Dorsey M. Dixon interview, August 8, 1962.

55. Tom Hanchett, "Recording in Charlotte, 1927–1945," in *The Charlotte Country Music Story*, 13–14; Conte, liner notes to Dixon Brothers, *Rambling and Gambling*; Ivan M. Tribe, liner notes to Dixon Brothers, *Dixon Brothers, Vol. 2*; *Rockingham (N.C.) Post-Dispatch*, February 20, July 2, 1936. For a complete discography of the Dixon Brothers and related groups, see Tony Russell, *Country Music Records: A Discography, 1921–1942*, with editorial research by Bob Pinson, assisted by the staff of the Country Music Hall of Fame and Museum (New York: Oxford University Press, 2004), 321–22, 367–68.

56. Dorsey M. Dixon interviews, August 20, 1961, August 8, 1962; Tribe, liner notes to Dixon Brothers, *Dixon Brothers, Vol. 2*; Bill C. Malone, "The Dixon Brothers," in *The Encyclopedia of Country Music: The Ultimate Guide to the Music*, ed. Paul Kingsbury (New York: Oxford University Press, 1998), 149.

57. Dorsey M. Dixon interview, August 8, 1962. On Oberstein, see David Diehl, "'Call It Bootlegging but It's Legal': Eli Oberstein and the Coarse Art of Indie Record Production," *ARSC Journal* 31 (Fall 2000): 283–93.

58. Tribe, liner notes to Dixon Brothers, *Dixon Brothers, Vol. 2*; Ivan M. Tribe and John W. Morris, "J. E. and Wade Mainer," *Bluegrass Unlimited* 10 (November 1975): 12–21; "Artists," in *The Charlotte Country Music Story*, 25; Dorsey M. Dixon interview, August 8, 1962; Dorsey Dixon, "Dixon Bros—Howard-Dorsey," ca. 1962, 5, Archie Green Papers, SFC.

59. "A List of Recordings Dealing with Wade Mainer in the Archive of Folk Song," in "Field Notes" file, AFC; Archie Green, field notes of a visit with Lloyd

Harris, East Rockingham, North Carolina, August 7, 1962, Archie Green Papers, SFC. In 1941, Wade Mainer and the Sons of the Mountaineers recorded nine traditional songs for Alan Lomax, the director of the Library of Congress's Archive of American Folk Song, including Howard's haunting solo performance of the traditional British ballad, "Barbara Allen." See "A List of Recordings Dealing with Wade Mainer in the Archive of Folk Song."

60. *Richmond County Daily Journal* (Rockingham, N.C.), April 24, 1980; Dorsey M. Dixon to Archie Green, August 31, 1961, Archie Green Papers, SFC; Maurice Zolotow, "Hillbilly Boom," *Saturday Evening Post* 216 (February 12, 1944), reprinted in Linnell Gentry, *A History and Encyclopedia of Country, Western, and Gospel Music* (Nashville, Tenn.: McQuiddy Press, 1961), 58; Elizabeth Schlappi, *Roy Acuff: The Smoky Mountain Boy* (Gretna, La.: Pelican, 1978), 122–24.

61. Schlappi, *Roy Acuff*, 122–24; *Richmond County Daily Journal* (Rockingham, N.C.), April 24, 1980; Dorsey M. Dixon to Archie Green, August 31, 1961, Archie Green Papers, SFC.

62. *Richmond County Daily Journal* (Rockingham, N.C.), April 24, 1980.

63. Dorsey M. Dixon interview, August 20, 1961; Dorsey Dixon, "Dixon Bros—Howard-Dorsey," ca. 1962, 7–8, Archie Green Papers, SFC.

64. Dorsey M. Dixon interview, August 8, 1962; Dorsey Dixon, "Dixon Bros—Howard-Dorsey," ca. 1962, 9, Archie Green Papers, SFC; *Richmond County Journal* (Rockingham, N.C.), July 25, 1963.

65. Green, field notes, Lloyd Harris visit; Dorsey Dixon, "Dixon Bros—Howard-Dorsey," ca. 1962, 9, Archie Green Papers, SFC.

66. Dorsey M. Dixon interview, August 20, 1961; Dorsey Dixon, "Dixon Bros—Howard-Dorsey," ca. 1962, 11, Archie Green Papers, SFC.

67. Bowman interview; Green, liner notes to Dixon et al., *Babies in the Mill*, 10; Conte, liner notes to Dixon Brothers, *Rambling and Gambling*; Dorsey M. Dixon interview, August 20, 1961.

68. Dorsey Dixon, "Dixon Bros—Howard-Dorsey," ca. 1962, 9, Archie Green Papers, SFC; Dorsey M. Dixon interview, August 20, 1961.

69. Dorsey M. Dixon interview, August 20, 1961.

70. Ibid.

71. Recording of 24 Songs from Dorsey Dixon to Wesley Rose, East Rockingham, North Carolina, ca. May 1961, SFC; Dorsey M. Dixon interview, August 20, 1961; *Richmond County Journal* (Rockingham, N.C.), August 3, 8, 1962; Dixon et al., *Babies in the Mill*.

72. Tristam Potter Coffin and Hennig Cohen, eds., *Folklore from the Working Folk of America* (Garden City, N.Y.: Anchor Press/Doubleday, 1973), 128, 431n63; Dorsey Dixon, "Dixon Bros—Howard-Dorsey," ca. 1962, 10, Archie Green Papers, SFC; Nancy A. Dixon interview by Eugene Earle and Archie Green, East Rockingham, North Carolina, August 7, 1962, SFC.

73. Coffin and Cohen, *Folklore from the Working Folk of America*, 128; Nancy A. Dixon interview by Eugene Earle and Archie Green; Green, liner notes to Dixon et al., *Babies in the Mill*, 2.

74. Douglas DeNatale, "Nancy Alena Dixon," in *Dictionary of North Carolina*

Biography, 2:78; Archie Green to Irving Kahan, October 5, 1964, Archie Green Papers, SFC; "Dorsey Dixon: A Place in the Sun for a Real Textile Troubadour," *Textile Labor* 25 (November 1964): 4. For a case study of "The Lowell Factory Girl," see Francis Tamburro, "A Tale of a Song: 'The Lowell Factory Girl,'" *Southern Exposure* 2 (Spring/Summer 1974): 42–51.

75. For reviews of the album, see Irwin Silber, "Folk Music on Records: Topical Singers," *Sing Out!* (September 15, 1965): 87; Joseph Haas, "Folk Records in Brief," *Chicago News*, January 15, 1965; Nat Hentoff, "Folk: Recordings of Special Merit," *HiFi/Stereo Review* 15 (August 1965): 98; Dorsey M. Dixon to Archie Green, October 29, 1964, Archie Green Papers, SFC; *Richmond County Journal* (Rockingham, N.C.), July 25, 1963; various artists, *Old Time Music at Newport* (Vanguard VRS 9147); Dorsey M. Dixon to Joseph Hickerson, December 3, 1963, AFC; "Dorsey Dixon Recording Project," in "Collector's Files," AFC.

76. Dorsey M. Dixon to Gene Earle, September 25, 1961, Archie Green Papers, SFC; Dorsey M. Dixon interview, August 8, 1962.

77. Dorsey M. Dixon to Gerald F. Mills, August 2, 1966, Archie Green Papers, SFC; Dorsey M. Dixon to Archie Green, October 29, 1964, Archie Green Papers, SFC; Dorsey M. Dixon to Joseph Hickerson, August 2, 1965, AFC.

78. Dorsey M. Dixon to Joseph Hickerson, August 2, 1965, AFC; Dorsey M. Dixon to Gerald F. Mills, July 8, 1966, Archie Green Papers, SFC.

79. Dorsey M. Dixon interview, August 20, 1961.

80. *Hamlet (N.C.) News-Messenger*, April 19, 1968; *Richmond County Daily Journal* (Rockingham, N.C.), April 19, 1968.

81. Dorsey M. Dixon interview, August 20, 1961; *Richmond County Journal* (Rockingham, N.C.), July 25, 1963.

82. Nancy A. Dixon interview by Dorsey M. Dixon; Dixon, "Early Life of Dorsey M. Dixon," 1–4; Dorsey Dixon, "Dixon Bros—Howard-Dorsey," ca. 1962, 1–12, Archie Green Papers, SFC; Dorsey M. Dixon to Gerald F. Mills, February 10, 1966, Archie Green Papers, SFC.

83. Dixon, "Early Life of Dorsey M. Dixon," 4.

Epilogue

1. For a fuller discussion of these points, see, for example, Jacquelyn Dowd Hall, James Leloudis, Robert Korstad, Mary Murphy, Lu Ann Jones, and Christopher B. Daly, *Like a Family: The Making of a Southern Cotton Mill World*, with a new afterword by the authors (Chapel Hill: University of North Carolina Press, 2000 [1987]); I. A. Newby, *Plain Folk in the New South: Social Change and Cultural Persistence, 1880–1915* (Baton Rogue: Louisiana State University Press, 1989); and Allen Tullos, *Habits of Industry: White Culture and the Transformation of the Carolina Piedmont* (Chapel Hill: University of North Carolina Press, 1989).

2. On this point, see Anthony Harkins, *Hillbilly: A Cultural History of an American Icon* (Oxford: Oxford University Press, 2004).

3. Ronnie Pugh, "Country Music Is Here to Stay?" *Journal of Country Music* 19 (1997): 32–38; Harkins, *Hillbilly*, 99–101, 246n50; Bill C. Malone, *Country Music, U.S.A.*, rev. ed. (Austin: University of Texas Press, 1985 [1968]), 177–97; Jeffrey J.

Lange, *Smile When You Call Me a Hillbilly: Country Music's Struggle for Respectability, 1939–1954* (Athens: University of Georgia Press, 2004), 67–88; "Bull Market in Corn," *Time* 42 (October 4, 1943): 33–34, reprinted in Linnell Gentry, *A History and Encyclopedia of Country, Western, and Gospel Music* (Nashville, Tenn.: McQuiddy Press, 1961), 52. On these various musical innovators and the distinctive regional musical styles they helped to create and popularize, see, for example, Charles R. Townsend, *San Antonio Rose: The Life and Music of Bob Wills* (Urbana: University of Illinois Press, 1976); Ronnie Pugh, *Ernest Tubb: The Texas Troubadour* (Durham: Duke University Press, 1996); Robert Cantwell, *Bluegrass Breakdown: The Making of the Old Southern Sound* (New York: Da Capo Press, 1992 [1984]); and Richard D. Smith, *Can't You Hear Me Callin': The Life of Bill Monroe, Father of Bluegrass* (Boston: Little, Brown, 2000).

4. On the expansion of the country music industry and the rise of Nashville in the immediate postwar period, see Malone, *Country Music, U.S.A.*, especially 199–200; Ronnie Pugh, "Country across the Country," in *Country: The Music and the Musicians*, ed. Paul Kingsbury, rev. and updated ed. (New York: Abbeville Press, 1994 [1988]), 112–15, 118–22; Martin Hawkins, *A Shot in the Dark: Making Records in Nashville, 1945–1955* (Nashville: Vanderbilt University Press/Country Music Foundation Press, 2006), especially 221–44; and Michael Kosser, *How Nashville Became Music City, U.S.A.: 50 Years of Music Row* (Milwaukee, Wis.: Hal Leonard Corporation, 2006), especially 1–31.

5. Harriet L. Herring, *Welfare Work in Mill Villages: The Story of Extra-Mill Activities in North Carolina* (Chapel Hill: University of North Carolina Press, 1929), 25, 31; Harriet L. Herring, *Passing of the Mill Village: Revolution in a Southern Institution* (Chapel Hill: University of North Carolina Press, 1949), 6, 9–12. Herring's *Passing of the Mill Village* remains the definitive account of the dismantling of the southern mill village system.

6. Alan Lomax, "Bluegrass Background: Folk Music with Overdrive," *Esquire* 52 (October 1959): 108; Neil V. Rosenberg, *Bluegrass: A History* (Urbana: University of Illinois Press, 2005 [1985]), especially 68–71, 78–80, 250, 259–66; Neil V. Rosenberg, liner notes to Lester Flatt and Earl Scruggs, *Flatt and Scruggs: Country and Western Classics*, 3-LP boxed set (Time Life Records TLCW-04).

7. John W. Rumble, "Country Music and the Rural South: Reminiscing with Whitey and Hogan," *Journal of Country Music* 10 (1985): 41–53; "Artists," in *The Charlotte Country Music Story*, ed. George Holt (Charlotte: North Carolina Arts Council, 1985), 17–18, 20, 28–29; Donna Campbell and Susan Campbell, "Arthur Smith," in *1998 North Carolina Folk Heritage Award* program (Raleigh: Folklife Program, North Carolina Arts Council, 1998), n.p.; Barry McCloud, "Jerry Reed," in *Definitive Country: The Ultimate Encyclopedia of Country Music and Its Performers*, ed. Barry McCloud (New York: Perigree Books, 1995), 663–64; Peter Cooper, *Hub City Music Makers: One Southern Town's Popular Music Legacy* (Spartanburg, S.C.: Holocene Publishing, 1997), 105–7. Other country artists—such as R. D. Norred, onetime steel guitarist for Hank Williams and the Drifting Cowboys; Glen Neaves, the fiddler and leader of the Grayson County Boys, and guitarist Cecil Kinzer, one of his band members; Roy Lear, the guitarist for various stringbands, includ-

ing the Tennessee Ramblers and the Carolina Crackerjacks; and, most recently, singer and songwriter Jimmy Wayne—also emerged out of southern textile mills but have remained less well known. See Steve A. Maze, *Hank Williams and His Drifting Cowboys* (Arab, Ala.: privately published, 2004), 100; Doug DeNatale and Glenn Hinson, "The Southern Textile Song Tradition Reconsidered," in *Songs about Work: Essays in Occupational Culture for Richard A. Reuss*, ed. Archie Green, Special Publications of the Folklore Institute no. 3 (Bloomington: Indiana University Press, 1993), 105, 106; "The Patton Brothers with Raymond Swinney and Glen Neeves," SwinneyPlace.com. <http://www.swinneyplace.com/Raymond Swinney.htm> (February 24, 2008); "Artists," 24; and Biography, Jimmy Wayne website, <http://www.jimmy wayne.com/index.php?content=biography> (August 29, 2006).

8. See Biography, Jimmy Wayne website.

9. *Charlotte Observer*, September 17, 2001. On the post-1970 decline of the Piedmont textile industry and the economic crisis it now faces, see Timothy J. Minchin, *Fighting against the Odds: A History of Southern Labor since World War II* (Gainesville: University Press of Florida, 2005), 144–46, 158–64; John Gaventa and Barbara Ellen Smith, "The Deindustrialization of the Textile South: A Case Study," in *Hanging by a Thread: Social Change in Southern Textiles*, ed. Jeffrey Leiter, Michael D. Schulman, and Rhonda Zingraff (Ithaca, N.Y.: ILR Press, 1991), especially 181–88; Rhonda Zingraff, "Facing Extinction?" in *Hanging by a Thread*, 199–216; and the miscellaneous newspaper articles under "Textile Industry," in Clipping File, 1990–, NCC.

Appendix A

1. Doug DeNatale and Glenn Hinson, "The Southern Textile Song Tradition Reconsidered," in *Songs about Work: Essays in Occupational Culture for Richard A. Reuss*, edited by Archie Green, Special Publications of the Folklore Institute, No. 3 (Bloomington: Indiana University Press, 1993), 104. This directory is based in part on DeNatale and Hinson, "Appendix B: Early Southeastern Textile Recording Artists," which accompanies their essay in *Songs about Work* (104–7). Their appendix contains entries for fifty prewar hillbilly artists, and I have augmented their list with the addition of a roughly equal number of names. I have also compiled a section of entries in this directory for hillbilly recording artists who were married or closely related to southern textile workers but who themselves are not known to have worked in the mills. The biographical information found in the artists' entries comes from DeNatale and Hinson's appendix, the U.S. census and other government documents, and various books and articles listed in the bibliography. The discographical information is drawn chiefly from Tony Russell, *Country Music Records: A Discography, 1921–1942*, with editorial research by Bob Pinson, assisted by the staff of the Country Music Hall of Fame and Museum (New York: Oxford University Press, 2004).

BIBLIOGRAPHY

Manuscript Collections
Chapel Hill, North Carolina
    Louis Round Wilson Library, University of North Carolina
        North Carolina Collection
            Clipping File, 1976–89
            Clipping File, 1990–
        Southern Folklife Collection
            Artists Files
            Discographical Files
            John Edwards Papers
            Archie Green Papers
            Guthrie T. Meade Papers
            Mike Seeger Papers
Detroit, Michigan
    Archives of Labor and Urban Affairs, Walter P. Reuther Library,
            Wayne State University
        Mary Heaton Vorse Papers
Hyde Park, New York
    Franklin D. Roosevelt Library
        Franklin D. Roosevelt Papers
            Social Entertainments, White House Office Collection
Nashville, Tennessee
    Frist Library and Archive, Country Music Hall of Fame and Museum
        WBT Charlotte File
Raleigh, North Carolina
    North Carolina Department of Archives and History
        Alamance County Marriage Records, 1911–17
        Gaston County Index to Birth Records, L–Z, 1930–47
        Gaston County Marriage Register, 1883–1905
        Gaston County Register of Deeds, Original Marriage Licenses, 1904–10
        North Carolina Death Certificates
        Rockingham County Marriage Register, 1896–1945
        Rowan County Deed Book, vol. 13
Rolla, Missouri
    Author's Private Collection
        Dorsey M. Dixon Notebooks
Washington, D.C.
    Archive of Folk Culture, American Folklife Center, Library of Congress
            Collector's Files
        Dorsey Dixon Papers

Field Notes
Field Recordings Collection

Interviews

Unless otherwise indicated, all interview tapes are located in the Southern Folklife Collection, Louis Round Wilson Library, University of North Carolina at Chapel Hill. Transcripts of these interviews, completed by the author, remain in his possession.

Bowman, Charlie. Interview by Dorsey M. Dixon, Union City, Georgia, ca. November 1961.

Dixon, Dorsey M. Interview by Archie Green and Ed Kahn, East Rockingham, North Carolina, August 20, 1961.

———. Interview by Eugene Earle and Archie Green, East Rockingham, North Carolina, August 7, 1962.

———. Interview by Eugene Earle and Archie Green, East Rockingham, North Carolina, August 8, 1962.

Dixon, Nancy A. Interview by Dorsey M. Dixon, East Rockingham, North Carolina, ca. December 1961.

———. Interview by Eugene Earle and Archie Green, East Rockingham, North Carolina, August 7, 1962.

Green, Archie. Interview by Patrick Huber, Chapel Hill, North Carolina, October 3, 1994. Tape recording in author's possession.

Harvey, Mrs. Roy. Interview by Eugene W. Earle and Archie Green, Beckley, West Virginia, August 13, 1962.

Johnson, Rosa Lee (Carson). Interview by Archie Green and Ed Kahn, Decatur, Georgia, August 27, 1963.

McCarn, David. Interview by Archie Green and Ed Kahn, Stanley, North Carolina, August 19, 1961.

McCarn, Johnnie E. Interview by Patrick Huber, Florence, South Carolina, October 17, 1996. Tape recording in author's possession.

———. Telephone conversation with Patrick Huber, October 9, 1996. Notes in author's possession.

Poole, Charlie, Jr. Interview by Eugene W. Earle and Archie Green, Mountain Home, Tennessee, August 13, 1962.

Seeger, Mike. Telephone conversation with Patrick Huber, September 12, 1996. Notes in author's possession.

Sipe, Martha (Sansing). Telephone conversation with Patrick Huber, October 26, 1997. Notes in author's possession.

Walker, Frank. Interview by Mike Seeger, probably New York, New York, June 19, 1962.

Government Documents

Davidson County, N.C. *Davidson County, North Carolina, Will Summaries, Vol. 1: 1823–1846*, compiled by Henry Reeves and Mary Jo Davis Shoaf. Lexington, N.C.: privately published, 1979.

Gaston County, N.C. Death Certificates. Register of Deeds, Gaston County
Courthouse, Gastonia, N.C.

———. Superior Court Criminal Docket of Gaston County, 1934–47. Superior
Court Clerk's Office, Gaston County Courthouse, Gastonia, N.C.

Library of Congress. *Annual Report of the Librarian of Congress for the Fiscal Year
Ended June 30, 1938.* Washington, D.C.: Government Printing Office, 1939.

North Carolina Department of Vital Records. John David McCarn death
certificate, November 7, 1964, Raleigh.

Rowan County, N.C. *Rowan County, North Carolina, Tax Lists, 1757–1800*,
compiled by Jo White Linn. Salisbury, N.C.: privately published, 1995.

———. *1815 Rowan County, North Carolina, Tax List*, compiled by Jo White Linn.
Salisbury, N.C.: privately published, 1987.

U.S. Bureau of the Census. Sixth Census of the United States, 1840: Davidson
County, North Carolina, Population Schedule (microfilm).

———. Eighth Census of the United States, 1860: Rowan County, North
Carolina, Population Schedule (microfilm).

———. Tenth Census of the United States, 1880: Cabarrus County, North
Carolina, Population Schedule (microfilm).

———. Tenth Census of the United States, 1880: Cobb County, Georgia,
Population Schedule (microfilm).

———. *Twelfth Census of the United States, 1900.* Vol. 1, *Population.* Washington,
D.C.: U.S. Census Office, 1901.

———. Twelfth Census of the United States, 1900: Fulton County, Georgia,
Population Schedule (microfilm).

———. Twelfth Census of the United States, 1900: Gaston County, North
Carolina, Population Schedule (microfilm).

———. Twelfth Census of the United States, 1900: Kershaw County, South
Carolina, Population Schedule (microfilm).

———. Twelfth Census of the United States, 1900: Randolph County, North
Carolina, Population Schedule (microfilm).

———. Thirteenth Census of the United States, 1910: Alamance County, North
Carolina, Population Schedule (microfilm).

———. Thirteenth Census of the United States, 1910: Darlington County, South
Carolina, Population Schedule (microfilm).

———. Thirteenth Census of the United States, 1910: Gaston County, North
Carolina, Population Schedule (microfilm).

———. *Fourteenth Census of the United States, 1920.* Vol. 1, *Population.*
Washington, D.C.: Government Printing Office, 1921.

———. Fourteenth Census of the United States, 1920: Darlington County, South
Carolina, Population Schedule (microfilm).

———. Fourteenth Census of the United States, 1920: Fulton County, Georgia,
Population Schedule (microfilm).

———. Fourteenth Census of the United States, 1920: Gaston County, North
Carolina, Population Schedule (microfilm).

———. *Fifteenth Census of the United States, 1930.* Vol. 1, *Population.* Washington, D.C.: Government Printing Office, 1931.

———. Fifteenth Census of the United States, 1930: Richmond County, North Carolina, Population Schedule (microfilm).

———. Fifteenth Census of the United States, 1930: Rockingham County, North Carolina, Population Schedule (microfilm).

U.S. Selective Service. Draft Registration Cards, World War I. Accessed on Ancestry.com. <http://www.ancestry.com/>.

Newspapers and Periodicals

Alamance Gleaner (Graham, N.C.)

American Magazine

American Mercury

American Review of Reviews

Atlanta Constitution

Atlanta Journal

Atlantic Monthly

Beckley (W.Va.) Post-Herald and Register

Burlington (N.C.) Daily Times

Burlington (N.C.) Daily Times-News

Carolina Watchman (Salisbury, N.C.)

Charleston (W.Va.) Gazette

Charlotte News

Charlotte Observer

Chicago News

Collier's

Colored American Magazine

Daily Worker (New York, N.Y.)

Danville (Va.) Bee

Darlington (S.C.) News and Press

Esquire

Gaston Gazette (Gastonia, N.C.)

Gastonia (N.C.) Daily Gazette

Greensboro (N.C.) Daily News

Hamlet (N.C.) News-Messenger

HiFi/Stereo Review

High Point (N.C.) Enterprise

Jeffersonian (Atlanta)

Kingsport (Tenn.) Times

Labor Defender

Leaksville (N.C.) Arrow

Leaksville (N.C.) News

Lima (Ohio) News

Literary Digest

Middlesboro (Ky.) Daily News

Mill News (Charlotte, N.C.)

Musical America

Nation

New Masses

New Republic

New York Journal

New York Times

Portsmouth (Ohio) Daily Times

Radio Digest

Richmond County Daily Journal (Rockingham, N.C.)

Roanoke (Va.) Times & World-News

Rockingham (N.C.) Post-Dispatch

Saturday Evening Post

Sing Out!

Spectator (Raleigh, N.C.)

S.S. Stewart's Banjo and Guitar Journal

Talking Machine World

Textile Labor

Time

Uniontown (Pa.) Daily News Standard

Uniontown (Pa.) Morning Herald

University of North Carolina News Letter

Washington Post

Books, Souvenir Programs, and Record Catalogs

Anderson, William. *The Wild Man from Sugar Creek: The Political Career of Eugene Talmadge*. Baton Rouge: Louisiana State University Press, 1975.

Andrews, William L., Minrose C. Gwin, Trudier Harris, and Fred Hobson, eds. *The Literature of the American South*. New York: W. W. Norton, 1998.

Ayers, Edward L. *The Promise of the New South: Life after Reconstruction*. New York: Oxford University Press, 1992.

Barlow, William. *Looking Up at Down: The Emergence of Blues Culture*. Philadelphia: Temple University Press, 1989.

Barnwell, Mildred Gwin. *Faces We See*. Gastonia, N.C.: Southern Combed Yarn Spinners Association, 1939.

Bastin, Bruce. *Red River Blues: The Blues Tradition in the Southeast*. Urbana: University of Illinois Press, 1995.

Batteau, Allen W. *The Invention of Appalachia*. Tucson: University of Arizona Press, 1990.

Bauerlein, Mark. *Negrophobia: A Race Riot in Atlanta, 1906*. San Francisco: Encounter Books, 2001.

Bayor, Ronald H. *Race and the Shaping of Twentieth-Century Atlanta*. Chapel Hill: University of North Carolina Press, 1996.

Beal, Fred E. *Proletarian Journey: New England, Gastonia, Moscow*. New York: Hillman-Curl, 1937.

Beatty, Bess. *Alamance: The Holt Family and Industrialization in a North Carolina County, 1837–1900*. Baton Rouge: Louisiana State University Press, 1999.

Biel, Steven. *Down with the Old Canoe: A Cultural History of the Titanic Disaster*. New York: W. W. Norton, 1996.

Blanshard, Paul. *Labor in Southern Cotton Mills*. New York: New Republic, 1927.

Botkin, B. A., ed. *A Treasury of Southern Folklore: Stories, Ballads, Traditions, and Folkways of the People of the South*. New York: Crown Publishers, 1950 (1949).

Bufwack, Mary A., and Robert K. Oermann. *Finding Her Voice: The Saga of Women in Country Music*. New York: Crown Publishers, 1993.

Butler, Lindley S. *Rockingham County: A Brief History*. Raleigh: North Carolina Department of Cultural Resources, 1982.

Campbell, Gavin James. *Music and the Making of a New South*. Chapel Hill: University of North Carolina Press, 2004.

Cantwell, Robert. *Bluegrass Breakdown: The Making of the Old Southern Sound*. New York: Da Capo Press, 1992 (1984).

Carlin, Bob. *String Bands in the North Carolina Piedmont*. Jefferson, N.C.: McFarland, 2004.

Carlton, David L. *Mill and Town in South Carolina, 1880–1920*. Baton Rouge: Louisiana State University Press, 1982.

Carson, Horace. *Time and Changes in a City Called Atlanta: The Story of a Man, His Family and a City*. Atlanta: privately published, 1979.

Cauthen, Joyce H. *With Fiddle and Well-Rosined Bow: Old-Time Fiddling in Alabama*. Tuscaloosa: University of Alabama Press, 1989.

Coffin, Tristam Potter, and Hennig Cohen, eds. *Folklore from the Working Folk of America*. Garden City, N.Y.: Anchor Press/Doubleday, 1973.

Cohen, Norm. *Long Steel Rail: The Railroad in American Folksong*. Urbana: University of Illinois Press, 1981.

———. *Traditional Anglo-American Folk Music: An Annotated Discography of Published Sound Recordings*. New York: Garland, 1994.

Columbia Records. *Old Familiar Tunes*. New York: Columbia Phonograph Company, 1927.

———. *Old Familiar Tunes*. New York: Columbia Phonograph Company, 1929.

Conway, Cecilia. *African Banjo Echoes in Appalachia: A Study of Folk Traditions*. Knoxville: University of Tennessee Press, 1995.

Cooper, Peter. *Hub City Music Makers: One Southern Town's Popular Music Legacy*. Spartanburg, S.C.: Holocene Publishing, 1997.

Cox, Bob L. *Fiddlin' Charlie Bowman: An East Tennessee Old-Time Music Pioneer and His Musical Family*. Knoxville: University of Tennessee Press, 2007.

Crazy Water Crystals Company of the Carolinas and Georgia. *Souvenir of the Crazy Barn Dance and the Crazy Bands*. 2nd ed. Charlotte, N.C.: Crazy Water Crystals Company, ca. 1934.

Cumbler, John T. *Working-Class Communities in Industrial America: Work, Leisure, and Struggle in Two Industrial Cities, 1880–1930*. Westport, Conn.: Greenwood Press, 1979.

Daniel, Wayne W. *Pickin' on Peachtree: A History of Country Music in Atlanta, Georgia*. Urbana: University of Illinois Press, 1990.

Dinnerstein, Leonard. *The Leo Frank Case*. New York: Columbia University Press, 1968.

Dittmer, John. *Black Georgia in the Progressive Era, 1900–1920*. Urbana: University of Illinois Press, 1977.

Eliason, Norman E. *Tarheel Talk: An Historical Study of the English Language in North Carolina to 1860*. Chapel Hill: University of North Carolina Press, 1956.

Ervin, Eliza Cowan, and Horace Fraser Rudisill, eds. *Darlingtoniana: A History of People, Places and Events in Darlington County, South Carolina*. Columbia, S.C.: R. L. Bryan, 1964.

Escott, Colin, with George Merritt and William MacEwen. *Hank Williams: The Biography*. Boston: Little, Brown, 1994.

Escott, Paul D. *Many Excellent People: Power and Privilege in North Carolina, 1850–1900*. Chapel Hill: University of North Carolina Press, 1985.

Fass, Paula S. *The Damned and the Beautiful: American Youth in the 1920s*. New York: Oxford University Press, 1977.

Fink, Gary M. *The Fulton Bag and Cotton Mills Strike of 1914–1915: Espionage, Labor Conflict, and New South Industrial Relations*. Ithaca, N.Y.: ILR Press, 1993.

Flamming, Douglas. *Creating the Modern South: Millhands and Managers in Dalton, Georgia, 1884–1984*. Chapel Hill: University of North Carolina Press, 1992.

Flynt, Wayne. *Poor but Proud: Alabama's Poor Whites*. Tuscaloosa: University of Alabama Press, 1989.

Gastonia Chamber of Commerce. *Gastonia, North Carolina: Combed Yarn Manufacturing Center of the South*. Gastonia, N.C.: Chamber of Commerce, 1924.

Gelatt, Roland. *The Fabulous Phonograph, 1877 1977*. 2nd rev. ed. New York: Collier Books, 1977 (1955).

Gentry, Linnell. *A History and Encyclopedia of Country, Western, and Gospel Music*. Nashville, Tenn.: McQuiddy Press, 1961.

Ginell, Cary, with special assistance from Roy Lee Brown. *Milton Brown and the Founding of Western Swing*. Urbana: University of Illinois Press, 1994.

Godshalk, David Fort. *Veiled Visions: The 1906 Atlanta Race Riot and the Reshaping of American Race Relations*. Chapel Hill: University of North Carolina Press, 2005.

Goodson, Steve. *Highbrows, Hillbillies, and Hellfire: Public Entertainment in Atlanta, 1880–1930*. Athens: University of Georgia Press, 2002.

Greenway, John. *American Folksongs of Protest*. Philadelphia: University of Pennsylvania Press, 1953.

Gura, Philip F., and James F. Bollman. *America's Instrument: The Banjo in the Nineteenth Century*. Chapel Hill: University of North Carolina Press, 1999.

Hall, Jacquelyn Dowd, James Leloudis, Robert Korstad, Mary Murphy, Lu Ann Jones, and Christopher B. Daly. *Like a Family: The Making of a Southern Cotton*

Mill World. With a new afterword by the authors. Chapel Hill: University of North Carolina Press, 2000 (1987).

Hanchett, Thomas W. *Sorting Out the New South City: Race, Class, and Urban Development in Charlotte, 1875–1975.* Chapel Hill: University of North Carolina Press, 1998.

Handy, W. C., ed. *Blues: An Anthology.* New York: Macmillan, 1972 (1926).

Hardy, Phil, and Dave Laing. *The Da Capo Companion to 20th-Century Popular Music.* New York: Da Capo Press, 1995.

Harkins, Anthony. *Hillbilly: A Cultural History of an American Icon.* New York: Oxford University Press, 2004.

Hawkins, Martin. *A Shot in the Dark: Making Records in Nashville, 1945–1955.* Nashville, Tenn.: Vanderbilt University Press/Country Music Foundation Press, 2006.

Herndon, Angelo. *Let Me Live.* New York: Arno Press, 1969 (1937).

Herring, Harriet L. *Passing of the Mill Village: Revolution in a Southern Institution.* Chapel Hill: University of North Carolina Press, 1949.

———. *Welfare Work in Mill Villages: The Story of Extra-Mill Activities in North Carolina.* Chapel Hill: University of North Carolina Press, 1929.

Hobbs, S. H., Jr. *Gaston County: Economic and Social.* Raleigh, N.C.: Edwards and Broughton Printing Company, 1920.

Holt, George, ed. *The Charlotte Country Music Story.* Charlotte: North Carolina Arts Council, 1985.

Horstman, Dorothy. *Sing Your Heart Out, Country Boy.* New York: E. P. Dutton, 1975.

Huneycutt, James E., and Ida C. Huneycutt. *A History of Richmond County.* Raleigh, N.C.: Edwards and Broughton Company, 1976.

Hunter, Tera W. *To 'Joy My Freedom: Southern Black Women's Lives and Labor after the Civil War.* Cambridge, Mass.: Harvard University Press, 1997.

Irons, Janet. *Testing the New Deal: The General Strike of 1934 in the American South.* Urbana: University of Illinois Press, 2000.

Jackson, Kenneth T. *The Ku Klux Klan in the City, 1915–1930.* New York: Oxford University Press, 1967.

Kasson, John F. *Amusing the Million: Coney Island at the Turn of the Century.* New York: Hill and Wang, 1978.

Kenney, William Howland. *Recorded Music in American Life: The Phonograph and Popular Memory, 1890–1945.* Oxford: Oxford University Press, 1999.

Kingsbury, Paul, ed. *The Encyclopedia of Country Music: The Ultimate Guide to the Music.* New York: Oxford University Press, 1998.

Kirkland, Thomas J., and Robert M. Kennedy. *Historic Camden, Part Two: Nineteenth Century.* Columbia, S.C.: State Printing Company, 1926 (1905).

Knauff, Gail, and Bob Knauff. *Fabric of a Community: The Story of Haw River, North Carolina.* Haw River, N.C.: Haw River Historical Association, 1996.

Kosser, Michael. *How Nashville Became Music City, U.S.A.: 50 Years of Music Row.* Milwaukee, Wis.: Hal Leonard Corporation, 2006.

Kuhn, Clifford M. *Contesting the New South Order: The 1914–1915 Strike at Atlanta's Fulton Mills*. Chapel Hill: University of North Carolina Press, 2001.

Kuhn, Clifford M., Harlon E. Joye, and E. Bernard West. *Living Atlanta: An Oral History of the City, 1914–1948*. Atlanta and Athens: Atlanta Historical Society/University of Georgia Press, 1990.

Kyriakoudes, Louis M. *The Social Origins of the Urban South: Race, Gender, and Migration in Nashville and Middle Tennessee, 1890–1930*. Chapel Hill: University of North Carolina Press, 2003.

Lahne, Herbert J. *The Cotton Mill Worker*. New York: Farrar and Rinehart, 1944.

Laird, Ross, and Brian Rust. *Discography of OKeh Records, 1918–1934*. Westport, Conn.: Praeger, 2004.

Lange, Jeffrey J. *Smile When You Call Me a Hillbilly: Country Music's Struggle for Respectability, 1939–1954*. Athens: University of Georgia Press, 2004.

Lemert, Ben F. *The Cotton Textile Industry of the Southern Appalachian Piedmont*. Chapel Hill: University of North Carolina Press, 1933.

Lighter, J. E., ed. *Random House Historical Dictionary of American Slang*. 2 vols. New York: Random House, 1994.

Linn, Karen. *That Half-Barbaric Twang: The Banjo in American Popular Culture*. Urbana: University of Illinois Press, 1991.

Lipsitz, George. *Rainbow at Midnight: Labor and Culture in the 1940s*. Urbana: University of Illinois Press, 1994.

Lornell, Kip. *Virginia's Blues, Country, and Gospel Records, 1902–1943: An Annotated Discography*. Lexington: University Press of Kentucky, 1989.

Lomax, Alan. *The Folk Songs of North America*. London: Cassell, 1960.

Lomax, Alan, Woody Guthrie, and Pete Seeger, comps. and eds. *Hard Hitting Songs for Hard-Hit People*. New York: Oak Publications, 1967.

Lomax, John A., and Alan Lomax. *American Ballads and Folk Songs*. New York: Macmillan, 1934.

———, comps. *Our Singing Country: A Second Volume of American Ballads and Folk Songs*. New York: Macmillan, 1941.

Lyle, Kate Letcher. *Scalded to Death by the Steam: Authentic Stories of Railroad Disasters and the Ballads That Were Written about Them*. Chapel Hill, N.C.: Algonquin Books, 1991.

Lynch, Timothy P. *Strike Songs of the Depression*. Jackson: University Press of Mississippi, 2001.

MacDonald, Lois. *Southern Mill Hills: A Study of Social and Economic Forces in Certain Textile Mill Villages*. New York: Alex L. Hillman, 1928.

Malone, Bill C. *Country Music, U.S.A.* Rev. ed. Austin: University of Texas Press, 1985 (1968).

———. *Country Music, U.S.A.: A Fifty-Year History*. Austin: University of Texas Press, 1968.

———. *Don't Get Above Your Raisin': Country Music and the Southern Working Class*. Urbana: University of Illinois Press, 2002.

———. *Singing Cowboys and Musical Mountaineers: Southern Culture and the Roots of Country Music*. Athens: University of Georgia Press, 1993.

BIBLIOGRAPHY

————. *Southern Music, American Music*. Lexington: University of Kentucky Press, 1979.

Marcus, Greil. *The Old, Weird America: The World of Bob Dylan's Basement Tapes*. New York: Henry Holt, 2001 (1997).

Martin, Charles H. *The Angelo Herndon Case and Southern Justice*. Baton Rouge: Louisiana State University Press, 1976.

Maze, Steve A. *Hank Williams and His Drifting Cowboys*. Arab, Ala.: privately published, 2004.

McBee, Randy D. *Dance Hall Days: Intimacy and Leisure among Working-Class Immigrants in the United States*. New York: New York University Press, 2001.

McCloud, Barry, ed. *Definitive Country: The Ultimate Encyclopedia of Country Music and Its Performers*. New York: Perigree Books, 1995.

Meade, Guthrie T., Jr., with Dick Spottswood and Douglas S. Meade. *Country Music Sources: A Biblio-Discography of Commercially Recorded Traditional Music*. Chapel Hill, N.C.: Southern Folklife Collection, University of North Carolina at Chapel Hill Libraries in Association with the John Edwards Memorial Forum, 2002.

Millard, Andre. *America on Record: A History of Recorded Sound*. Cambridge: Cambridge University Press, 1995.

Miller, Billy Robert. *McAdenville: Spun from the Wilderness*. Shelby, N.C.: Riviere Printing Company, 1987 (1982).

Minchin, Timothy J. *Fighting against the Odds: A History of Southern Labor since World War II*. Gainesville: University Press of Florida, 2005.

Mitchell, Broadus, and George Sinclair Mitchell. *The Industrial Revolution in the South*. Baltimore: Johns Hopkins University Press, 1930.

Mixon, Gregory. *The Atlanta Riot: Race, Class, and Violence in a New South City*. Gainesville: University of Florida Press, 2005.

Moseley, John Oliver. *The Terrible Cleveland Fire: Its Victims and Survivors*. Charleston, S.C.: Southern Printing and Publishing, 1923.

Nelson, Scott Reynolds. *Steel Drivin' Man: John Henry, the Untold Story of an American Legend*. New York: Oxford University Press, 2006.

Newby, I. A. *Plain Folk in the New South: Social Change and Cultural Persistence, 1880–1915*. Baton Rogue: Louisiana State University Press, 1989.

OKeh Records. *OKeh Records Catalog*. New York: General Phonograph Corporation, 1924.

Oney, Steve. *And the Dead Shall Rise: The Murder of Mary Phagan and the Lynching of Leo Frank*. New York: Pantheon Books, 2003.

Palmer, Jack. *Vernon Dalhart: First Star of Country Music*. Denver, Colo.: Mainspring Press, 2005.

Peiss, Kathy. *Cheap Amusements: Working Women and Leisure in Turn-of-the-Century New York*. Philadelphia: Temple University Press, 1986.

Peterson, Richard A. *Creating Country Music: Fabricating Authenticity*. Chicago: University of Chicago Press, 1997.

Pope, Liston. *Millhands and Preachers: A Study of Gastonia*. New Haven: Yale University Press, 1970 (1942).

Porterfield, Nolan. *Jimmie Rodgers: The Life and Times of America's Blue Yodeler.* Urbana: University of Illinois Press, 1992 (1979).

Potwin, Marjorie. *Cotton Mill People of the Piedmont: A Study in Social Change.* New York: Columbia University Press, 1927.

Pugh, Ronnie. *Ernest Tubb: The Texas Troubadour.* Durham: Duke University Press, 1996.

Randolph County Historical Society and the Randolph Arts Guild. *Randolph County, 1779–1979.* Winston-Salem, N.C.: Hunter Publishing Company, 1980.

Rhyne, Jennings J. *Some Mill Workers and Their Villages.* Chapel Hill: University of North Carolina Press, 1930.

Rodenbough, Charles Dyson, ed. *The Heritage of Rockingham County, North Carolina.* Winston-Salem, N.C.: Rockingham Historical Society, 1983.

Rorrer, Clifford Kinney. *Charlie Poole and the North Carolina Ramblers.* Eden, N.C.: privately published, 1968.

Rorrer, Kinney. *Rambling Blues: The Life and Songs of Charlie Poole.* Danville, Va.: McCain Printing Company, 1992 (1982).

Roscigno, Vincent J., and William F. Danaher. *The Voice of Southern Labor: Radio, Music, and Textile Strikes, 1929–1934.* Social Movements, Protest, and Contention, vol. 19. Minneapolis: University of Minnesota Press, 2004.

Rosenberg, Neil V. *Bluegrass: A History.* Urbana: University of Illinois Press, 2005 (1985).

Rosenzweig, Roy. *Eight Hours for What We Will: Workers and Leisure in an Industrial City, 1870–1920.* Cambridge: Cambridge University Press, 1983.

Rudisill, Horace Fraser. *Darlington County: A Pictorial History.* Norfolk, Va.: Donning Company, 1986.

Russell, Tony. *Blacks, Whites and Blues.* New York: Stein and Day, 1970.

———. *Country Music Originals: The Legends and the Lost.* New York: Oxford University Press, 2007.

———. *Country Music Records: A Discography, 1921–1942.* With editorial research by Bob Pinson, assisted by the staff of the Country Music Hall of Fame and Museum. New York: Oxford University Press, 2004.

Rust, Brian, comp. *The Victor Master Book, Vol. 2 (1925–1936).* Pinner, Middlesex, England: privately published, 1969.

Salmond, John A. *Gastonia 1929: The Story of the Loray Mill Strike.* Chapel Hill: University of North Carolina Press, 1995.

Sandburg, Carl. *The American Songbag.* New York: Harcourt, Brace, and World, 1927.

Schlappi, Elizabeth. *Roy Acuff: The Smoky Mountain Boy.* Gretna, La.: Pelican, 1978.

Shapiro, Henry D. *Appalachia on Our Mind: The Southern Mountains and Mountaineers in the American Consciousness, 1870–1920.* Chapel Hill: University of North Carolina Press, 1978.

Simon, Bryant. *A Fabric of Defeat: The Politics of South Carolina Millhands, 1910–1948.* Chapel Hill: University of North Carolina Press, 1998.

Simpson, J. A., and E. S. C. Weiner, eds. *The Oxford English Dictionary*. 2nd ed. 20 vols. Oxford: Clarendon Press, 1989.

Singal, Daniel J. *The War Within: From Victorian to Modernist Thought in the South, 1919–1945*. Chapel Hill: University of North Carolina Press, 1982.

Smith, Richard D. *Can't You Hear Me Callin': The Life of Bill Monroe, Father of Bluegrass*. Boston: Little, Brown, 2000.

Souvenir Program, Gaston Centennial. Gastonia, N.C.: Gaston County Centennial Committee, 1946.

Spaeth, Sigmund. *A History of Popular Music in America*. New York: Random House, 1948.

Stowe, R. L., Sr. *Early History of Belmont and Gaston County, North Carolina*. N.p.: privately published, 1951.

Sutton, Allan, and Kurt Nauck. *American Record Labels and Companies: An Encyclopedia (1891–1943)*. Denver, Colo.: Mainspring Press, 2000.

Thompson, Holland. *From the Cotton Field to the Cotton Mill: A Study of the Industrial Transition in North Carolina*. New York: Macmillan, 1906.

Tippett, Tom. *When Southern Labor Stirs*. New York: Jonathan Cape and Harrison Smith, 1931.

Townsend, Charles R. *San Antonio Rose: The Life and Music of Bob Wills*. Urbana: University of Illinois Press, 1976.

Tribe, Ivan M. *The Stonemans: An Appalachian Family and the Music That Shaped Their Lives*. Urbana: University of Illinois Press, 1993.

Tullos, Allen. *Habits of Industry: White Culture and the Transformation of the Carolina Piedmont*. Chapel Hill: University of North Carolina Press, 1989.

Twelve Southerners. *I'll Take My Stand: The South and the Agrarian Tradition, by Twelve Southerners*. New York: Harper, 1930.

Vance, Rupert B. *All These People: The Nation's Human Resources in the South*. Chapel Hill: University of North Carolina Press, 1945.

———. *Human Geography of the South: A Study in Regional Resources and Human Adequacy*. Chapel Hill: University of North Carolina Press, 1932.

Victor Talking Machine Company. *Olde Time Fiddlin' Tunes*. New York: Victor Talking Machine Company, 1924.

Waldrep, G. C., III. *Southern Workers and the Search for Community: Spartanburg County, South Carolina*. Urbana: University of Illinois Press, 2000.

Waldrop, Terry James, comp. *Old Gravesites Revisited in Gaston and Lincoln Counties, Vol. 2*. Stanley, N.C.: privately published, 1989.

Ward, George Gordon. *The Annals of Upper Georgia Centered in Gilmer County*. Carrollton, Ga.: Thomasson Print and Office Equipment Company, 1965.

Warlick, Tom, and Lucy Warlick. *The WBT Briarhoppers: Eight Decades of a Bluegrass Band Made for Radio*. Jefferson, N.C.: McFarland, 2007.

Warr, O. L., C. W. Flowers, and Valerie Schaible. *Darlington County: Economic and Social*, Bulletin of the University of South Carolina no. 196 (February 1, 1927).

Weisbord, Vera Buch. *A Radical Life*. Bloomington: Indiana University Press, 1977.

Welcome South, Brother: Fifty Years of Broadcasting at WSB, Atlanta, Georgia.
Atlanta: Cox Broadcasting Corporation, 1974.

Whalen, Robert Weldon. *"Like Fire in Broom Straw": Southern Journalism and the Textile Strikes of 1929–1931.* Westport, Conn.: Greenwood Press, 2001.

Whisnant, David E. *All That Is Native and Fine: The Politics of Culture in an American Region.* Chapel Hill: University of North Carolina Press, 1983.

Whitaker, Walter. *Centennial History of Alamance County, 1849–1949.* Burlington, N.C.: Burlington Chamber of Commerce, ca. 1950.

Wiggins, Gene. *Fiddlin' Georgia Crazy: Fiddlin' John Carson, His Real World, and the World of His Songs.* Urbana: University of Illinois Press, 1987.

Williams, Robert L. *Gaston County: A Pictorial History.* Norfolk, Va.: Donning Company, 1981.

Williams, Roger. *Sing a Sad Song: The Life of Hank Williams.* Urbana: University of Illinois Press, 1981 (1970).

Williamson, J. W. *Hillbillyland: What the Movies Did to the Mountains and What the Mountains Did to the Movies.* Chapel Hill: University of North Carolina Press, 1995.

Williamson, Joel. *The Crucible of Race: Black-White Relations in the American South since Emancipation.* New York: Oxford University Press, 1984.

Wolfe, Charles K. *The Devil's Box: Masters of Southern Fiddling.* Nashville, Tenn.: Country Music Foundation Press/Vanderbilt University Press, 1997.

———. *A Good-Natured Riot: The Birth of the Grand Ole Opry.* Nashville, Tenn.: Country Music Foundation Press/Vanderbilt University Press, 1999.

———. *Tennessee Strings: The Story of Country Music in Tennessee.* Knoxville: University of Tennessee Press, 1977.

Wolfe, Charles K., and Ted Olson, eds. *The Bristol Sessions: Writings about the Big Bang of Country Music.* Contributions to Southern Appalachian Studies no. 12. Jefferson, N.C.: McFarland, 2005.

Woodward, C. Vann. *Tom Watson: Agrarian Rebel.* New York: Oxford University Press, 1963 (1938).

Zwonitzer, Mark, with Charles Hirschberg. *Will You Miss Me When I'm Gone? The Carter Family and Their Legacy in American Music.* New York: Simon and Schuster, 2002.

Articles

Ahrens, Pat. "The Role of the Crazy Water Crystals Company in Promoting Hillbilly Music." *John Edwards Memorial Foundation Quarterly* 6 (Autumn 1970): 107–9.

"Artists." In *The Charlotte Country Music Story*, edited by George Holt, 17–30. Charlotte: North Carolina Arts Council, 1985.

Bailey, Jay. "Historical Origins and Stylistic Developments of the Five-String Banjo." *Journal of American Folklore* 85 (January–March 1972): 58–65.

Baker, Christina L., and William J. Baker. "Shaking All the Corners of the Sky: The Global Response to the Gastonia Strike of 1929." *Canadian Review of American Studies* 21 (Winter 1990): 321–31.

Baker, Ray Stannard. "Following the Color Line." *American Magazine* 63 (April 1907): 563–79.

Bernhardt, Jack. "Legends—No. 2: Charlie Poole." *Old-Time Herald* 3 (August–October 1991): 8–9, 51.

Biggar, George C. "The WLS National Barn Dance: The Early Years." *John Edwards Memorial Foundation Quarterly* 7 (Autumn 1971): 105–12.

Blackard, Malcolm V. "Wilmer Watts and the Lonely Eagles." *John Edwards Memorial Foundation Quarterly* 5 (Winter 1969): 126–40.

Bluestein, Gene. "America's Folk Instrument: Notes on the Five-String Banjo." *Western Folklore* 23 (October 1964): 241–48.

Bronner, Simon J. "Old-Time Tunes on Edison Records, 1899–1923." *Journal of Country Music* 8 (May 1979): 95–100.

Brooks, Tim. "Early Black Vaudeville on Record: Louis 'Bebe' Vasnier and the Louisiana Phonograph Company." *ARSC Journal* 28 (Fall 1997): 143–54.

Brownell, Blaine A. "A Symbol of Modernity: Attitudes toward the Automobile in Southern Cities in the 1920s." *American Quarterly* 24 (March 1972): 20–44.

"Bull Market in Corn." *Time* 42 (October 4, 1943): 33–34.

Burrison, John A. "Fiddlers in the Alley: Atlanta as an Early Country Music Center." *Atlanta Historical Society Bulletin* 21 (Summer 1977): 59–87.

Cahan, Andy. "Adam Manly Reece: An Early Banjo Player of Grayson County, Virginia." In *American Musical Traditions, Vol. 3, British Isles Music*, edited by Jeff Todd Titon and Bob Carlin, 87–93. New York: Schirmer Reference, 2002.

Campbell, David, and David Coombs. "Skyline Farms: A Case Study of Community Development and Rural Rehabilitation." *Appalachian Journal* 10 (Spring 1983): 244–54.

Campbell, Donna, and Susan Campbell. "Arthur Smith." In *1998 North Carolina Folk Heritage Award* program, n.p. Raleigh: Folklife Program, North Carolina Arts Council, 1998.

Carter, Tom. "The Blackard-Shelor Story: Biography of a Hillbilly Stringband." *Old Time Music* 24 (Spring 1977): 4–7, 31.

Cash, W. J. "The War in the South." *American Mercury* 19 (February 1930): 163–69.

Cobb, James C. "From Rocky Top to Detroit City: Country Music and the Economic Transformation of the South." In *You Wrote My Life: Lyrical Themes in Country Music*, edited by Melton A. McLaurin and Richard A. Peterson, 63–79. Cultural Perspectives on the American South, vol. 6. Philadelphia: Gordon and Breach, 1992.

Cohen, John. "The Folk Music Interchange: Negro and White." *Sing Out!* 14 (January 1965): 42–49.

———. "Introduction." In Kinney Rorrer, *Rambling Blues: The Life and Songs of Charlie Poole*, 8. Danville, Va.: McCain Printing Company, 1992 (1982).

Cohen, Norm. "Clayton McMichen: His Life and Music." *John Edwards Memorial Foundation Quarterly* 11 (Autumn 1975): 117–24.

———. "Early Pioneers." In *Stars of Country Music: Uncle Dave Macon to Johnnie Rodriguez*, edited by Bill C. Malone and Judith McCulloh, 3–39. Urbana: University of Illinois Press, 1975.

———. "Fiddlin' John Carson: An Appreciation and a Discography." *John Edwards Memorial Foundation Quarterly* 10 (Winter 1974): 138–56.

———. "Folk Music Discography." *Western Folklore* 30 (July 1971): 235–46.

———. "Henry Whitter: His Life and Music." *John Edwards Memorial Foundation Quarterly* 11 (Summer 1975): 57–66.

———, comp. "Materials toward a Study of Early Country Music on Radio I: Nashville." *John Edwards Memorial Foundation Newsletter* 4 (September 1968): 109–13.

———. "Riley Puckett." In *The Encyclopedia of Country Music: The Ultimate Guide to the Music*, edited by Paul Kingsbury, 425. New York: Oxford University Press, 1998.

———. "Riley Puckett: 'King of the Hillbillies.'" *John Edwards Memorial Foundation Quarterly* 12 (Winter 1976): 175–84.

———. "Robert W. Gordon and the Second Wreck of the 'Old 97.'" *Journal of American Folklore* 87 (January 1974): 12–38.

———. "The Skillet Lickers: A Study of a Hillbilly String Band and Its Repertoire." *Journal of American Folklore* 78 (July–September 1965): 229 44.

———. "Tapescripts: Interview with Bill Helms." *John Edwards Memorial Foundation Newsletter* 3 (December 1967): 54–58.

———. "Tapescripts: Interview with Mrs. Roy Harvey." *John Edwards Memorial Foundation Newsletter* 4 (June 1968): 74–77.

———. "The Urge to Write Songs: The Case of Dorsey Dixon." *John Edwards Memorial Foundation Quarterly* 10 (Summer 1974): 83 84.

———. "Walter 'Kid' Smith." *John Edwards Memorial Foundation Quarterly* 9 (Autumn 1973): 128–32.

Cohen, Norm, and Anne Cohen. "The Legendary Jimmie Tarlton." *Sing Out!* 16 (September 1966): 16–19.

Cohen, Norm, and Ed Kahn. "Tapescripts: Interview with Charlie Poole, Jr." *John Edwards Memorial Foundation Newsletter* 1 (June 1966): 31–35.

Coltman, Robert. "Across the Chasm: How the Depression Changed Country Music." *Old Time Music* 23 (Winter 1976–77): 6–12.

———. "Look Out! Here He Comes . . . Fiddlin' John Carson, One of a Kind and Twice as Feisty." *Old Time Music* 9 (Summer 1973): 16–21.

"Columbia Co. Issues Booklet on the Old Familiar Tunes." *Talking Machine World* 20 (November 15, 1924): 51.

"Columbia Issues New 'Familiar Tunes' Catalog." *Talking Machine World* 22 (August 15, 1926): 122.

Columbia Records ad. *Talking Machine World* 20 (May 15, 1924): 153.

———. *Talking Machine World* 20 (June 15, 1924): 17.

"Columbia Signs Artists from Hills of Georgia." *Talking Machine World* 20 (May 15, 1924): 26.

Coulter, Della. "The Piedmont Tradition." In *The Charlotte Country Music Story*, edited by George Holt, 7–11. Charlotte: North Carolina Arts Council, 1985.

Crawford, Bruce. "Folk Music at White Top." *New Republic* 76 (August 30, 1933): 74–75.

Crichton, Kyle. "Thar's Gold in Them Hillbillies." *Collier's* 101 (April 30, 1938): 24, 27.

Crowe, Charles. "Racial Massacre in Atlanta, September 22, 1906." *Journal of Negro History* 54 (April 1969): 150–73.

Daniel, Wayne W. "Bill Gatins and His Jug Band." *Old Time Music* 37 (Autumn 1981–Spring 1982): 9–13.

———. "Fiddlin' John Carson: The World's First Commercial Country Artist." *Bluegrass Unlimited* (July 1985): 40–43.

———. "The Georgia Old-Time Fiddlers' Convention: 1920 Edition." *John Edwards Memorial Foundation Quarterly* 16 (Summer 1980): 67–73.

———. "Old Time Georgians Recall the Georgia Old Time Fiddlers' Conventions." *Devil's Box* 15 (March 1981): 7–16.

DeNatale, Douglas. "Dorsey Murdock Dixon." In *Dictionary of North Carolina Biography*, edited by William S. Powell, 2:74–75. 6 vols. Chapel Hill: University of North Carolina Press, 1986.

———. "Howard Briten Dixon." In *Dictionary of North Carolina Biography*, edited by William S. Powell, 2:76. 6 vols. Chapel Hill: University of North Carolina Press, 1986.

———. "Nancy Alena Dixon." In *Dictionary of North Carolina Biography*, edited by William S. Powell, 2:77–78. 6 vols. Chapel Hill: University of North Carolina Press, 1986.

DeNatale, Douglas, and Glenn Hinson. "The Southern Textile Song Tradition Reconsidered." *Journal of Folklore Research* 28 (May–December 1991): 103–33. Reprinted in *Songs about Work: Essays in Occupational Culture for Richard A. Reuss*, edited by Archie Green, 77–107. Special Publications of the Folklore Institute no. 3. Bloomington: Indiana University Press, 1993.

Diehl, David. "'Call It Bootlegging but It's Legal': Eli Oberstein and the Coarse Art of Indie Record Production." *ARSC Journal* 31 (Fall 2000): 283–93.

"Dorsey Dixon: A Place in the Sun for a Real Textile Troubadour." *Textile Labor* 25 (November 1964): 4–5.

Ekkens, Thomas A. "Earliest?? Folkers on Disc." *Record Research* 92 (September 1968): 4, 10.

Epstein, Dena. "The Folk Banjo: A Documentary History." *Ethnomusicology* 19 (September 1975): 347–71.

"Fiddlin' John Carson: The Last Interview?" *Old Time Music* 1 (Summer 1971): 20.

"Fiddlin' John Carson Joins OKeh." *Talking Machine World* 19 (September 15, 1923): 30.

"Fiddlin' John Carson OKeh Records Popular in Trade." *Talking Machine World* 21 (April 15, 1925): 56.

"Fiddlin' John Carson's Records Widely Popular." *Talking Machine World* 21 (August 15, 1925): 81.

"Fiddling to Henry Ford." *Literary Digest* 88 (January 2, 1926): 33–34, 36, 38.

Frederickson, Mary E. "Ella May Wiggins." In *Dictionary of North Carolina Biography*, edited by William S. Powell, 6:193–95. 6 vols. Chapel Hill: University of North Carolina Press, 1996.

Frost, William Goodell. "Our Contemporary Ancestors in the Southern Mountains." *Atlantic Monthly* 83 (March 1899): 311–19.

———. "The Southern Mountaineer: Our Kindred of the Boone and Lincoln Types." *American Review of Reviews* 21 (March 1900): 303–11.

Galloway, Tammy Harden. "'Tribune of the Masses and a Champion of the People': Eugene Talmadge and the Three-Dollar Tag." *Georgia Historical Quarterly* 79 (Fall 1995): 673–84.

Gaventa, John, and Barbara Ellen Smith. "The Deindustrialization of the Textile South: A Case Study." In *Hanging by a Thread: Social Change in Southern Textiles*, edited by Jeffrey Leiter, Michael D. Schulman, and Rhonda Zingraff, 181–96. Ithaca, N.Y.: ILR Press, 1991.

Glazer, Lee, and Susan Key. "Carry Me Back: Nostalgia for the Old South in Nineteenth-Century Popular Culture." *Journal of American Studies* 30 (April 1996): 1–24.

Grable, Stephen W. "The Other Side of the Tracks: Cabbagetown—A Working-Class Neighborhood in Transition during the Early Twentieth Century." *Atlanta Historical Journal* 26 (Summer–Fall 1982): 51–66.

Green, Archie. "Commercial Music Graphics: Two." *John Edwards Memorial Foundation Newsletter* 3 (September 1967): 15–17.

———. "Commercial Music Graphics: Three." *John Edwards Memorial Foundation Newsletter* 3 (December 1967): 43–45.

———. "Commercial Music Graphics: Four." *John Edwards Memorial Foundation Newsletter* 4 (March 1968): 8–13.

———. "Dorsey Dixon: Minstrel of the Mills." *Sing Out!* 16 (July 1966): 10–12.

———. "Graphics #68: Winding Down." *John Edwards Memorial Foundation Quarterly* 21 (Fall/Winter 1985): 99–115.

———. "Hillbilly Music: Source and Symbol." *Journal of American Folklore* 78 (July–September 1965): 204–28.

———. "A Southern Cotton Mill Rhyme." In *Wobblies, Pile Butts, and Other Heroes: Laborlore Explorations*, 275–319. Urbana: University of Illinois Press, 1993.

———. "Will the Weaver's Hillbilly Kinfolk." *Caravan* 18 (August–September 1959): 14–23.

Greenway, John. "Jimmie Rodgers: A Folksong Catalyst." *Journal of American Folklore* 70 (July–September 1957): 231–35.

Grundy, Pamela. "From *Il Trovatore* to the Crazy Mountaineers: The Rise and Fall of Elevated Culture on WBT-Charlotte, 1922–1930." *Southern Cultures* 1 (Fall 1994): 51–73.

———. "'We Always Tried to Be Good People': Respectability, Crazy Water Crystals, and Hillbilly Music on the Air, 1933–1935." *Journal of American History* 81 (March 1995): 1591–1620.

Haden, Walter Darrell. "Vernon Dalhart." In *Stars of Country Music: Uncle Dave Macon to Johnnie Rodriguez*, edited by Bill C. Malone and Judith McCulloh, 64–85. Urbana: University of Illinois Press, 1975.

Hall, Jacquelyn Dowd. "Disorderly Women: Gender and Labor Militancy in the Appalachian South." *Journal of American History* 73 (September 1986): 354–82.

———. "Private Eyes, Public Women: Images of Class and Sex in the Urban South, Atlanta, Georgia, 1913–1915." In *Work Engendered: Toward a New History of American Labor*, edited by Ava Baron, 243–72. Ithaca, N.Y.: Cornell University Press, 1991.

Hanchett, Tom. "Recording in Charlotte, 1927–1945." In *The Charlotte Country Music Story*, edited by George Holt, 12–16. Charlotte: North Carolina Arts Council, 1985.

———. Review of various artists, *Cotton Mills and Fiddles* (Flyin' Cloud FC-014). *Old-Time Herald* 3 (Winter 1991/1992): 51.

Hardy, Phil, and Dave Laing. "Bob Miller." In *The Da Capo Companion to 20th-Century Popular Music*, 641. New York: Da Capo Press, 1995.

———. "Fiddlin' John Carson." In *The Da Capo Companion to 20th-Century Popular Music*, 151. New York: Da Capo Press, 1995.

Hendrix, Bertha. "I Was in the Gastonia Strike." In *Working Lives: The* Southern Exposure *History of Labor in the South*, edited by Marc S. Miller, 169–71. New York: Pantheon Books, 1980.

Hentoff, Nat. "Folk: Recordings of Special Merit." *HiFi/Stereo Review* 15 (August 1965): 98.

Herring, Harriet L. "The Industrial Worker." In *Culture in the South*, edited by W. T. Couch, 344–60. Chapel Hill: University of North Carolina Press, 1934.

Hilfer, Tony. "'Wreck on the Highway': Rhetoric and Religion in a Country Song." *John Edwards Memorial Foundation Quarterly* 21 (Fall/Winter 1985): 116–19.

Hoeptner, Fred, and Bob Pinson. "Clayton McMichen Talking." *Old Time Music* 1 (Summer 1971): 8–10.

Huber, Patrick. "'Battle Songs of the Southern Class Struggle': Songs of the Gastonia Textile Strike of 1929." *Southern Cultures* 4 (Summer 1998): 109–22.

———. "'A Blessing to People': Dorsey Dixon and His Sacred Mission of Song." Music Issue. *Southern Cultures* 12 (Winter 2006): 111–31.

———. "'Cain't Make a Living at a Cotton Mill': The Life and Hillbilly Songs of Dave McCarn." *North Carolina Historical Review* 80 (July 2003): 297–333.

———. "Charlie Poole." In *The North Carolina Century: Tar Heels Who Made a Difference, 1900–2000*, edited by Howard E. Covington and Marion A. Ellis, 443–46. Charlotte, N.C.: Levine Museum of the New South, 2002.

———. "The Dixon Brothers." In *The North Carolina Century: Tar Heels Who Made a Difference, 1900–2000*, edited by Howard E. Covington and Marion A. Ellis, 425–28. Charlotte, N.C.: Levine Museum of the New South, 2002.

———. "A Hillbilly Barnum: Fiddlin' John Carson and the Modern Origins of His Old-Time Music in Atlanta." *Atlanta History* 46 (2004): 24–53.

Huber, Patrick, and Kathleen Drowne. "'I Don't Want Nothin' 'Bout My Life Wrote Out, Because I Had It Too Rough in Life': Dorsey Dixon's Autobiographical Writings." *Southern Cultures* 6 (Summer 2000): 94–100.

Ingalls, Gerald L. "Urbanization." In *The North Carolina Atlas: Portrait of a New*

Century, edited by Douglas M. Orr Jr. and Alfred W. Stuart, 103–21. Chapel Hill: University of North Carolina Press, 2000.

Johnson, Thomas S. "Charles Nabell (1887–1970)." In *The New Georgia Encyclopedia*. Forthcoming from University of Georgia Press.

Kahn, Ed. "Hillbilly Music: Source and Resource." *Journal of American Folklore* 78 (July–September 1965): 257–66.

Kerr, Janet. "Lonnie Austin/Norman Woodlieff." *Old Time Music* 17 (Summer 1975): 7–8.

Keyes, Saundra. "'Little Mary Phagan': A Native American Ballad in Context." *Journal of Country Music* 3 (Spring 1972): 1–16.

Kimball, Gregg D., and Ron T. Curry. "On the Beach of Waikiki: Hopewell's Tubize Royal Hawaiian Orchestra." *Virginia Cavalcade* 51 (Summer 2002): 112–23.

Koon, William Henry. "Dave McCarn." *John Edwards Memorial Foundation Quarterly* 11 (Winter 1975): 167–76.

Larkin, Margaret. "Ella May's Songs." *Nation* 129 (October 9, 1929): 382–83.

———. "The Story of Ella May." *New Masses* 5 (November 1929): 3–4.

LaRose, Joe. "An Interview with Lowe Stokes." *Old Time Music* 39 (Spring 1984): 6–9.

Leamy, Hugh. "Now Come All You Good People." *Collier's* 84 (November 2, 1929): 20, 58–59.

Lewis, David L. "The Square Dancing Master." *American Heritage* 23 (February 1972): 49–51.

Lomax, Alan. "Bluegrass Background: Folk Music with Overdrive." *Esquire* 52 (October 1959): 108.

Lornell, Kip. "'The Jug Didn't Mean a Thing': The Roanoke Jug Band." *Old Time Music* 41 (Spring 1985): 15–16.

———. "Spatial Perspectives on the Field Recording of Traditional American Music: A Case Study from Tennessee in 1928." *Tennessee Folklore Society Bulletin* 47 (1981): 153–59. Reprinted in *The Sounds of People and Places: A Geography of American Folk and Popular Music*, edited by George O. Carney, 77–84. Lanham, Md.: Rowman and Littlefield, 1994.

Lornell, Kip, and Ted Mealor. "A & R Men and the Geography of Piedmont Blues Recordings from 1924–1941." *ARSC Journal* 26 (Spring 1995): 1–22.

MacLean, Nancy. "The Leo Frank Case Reconsidered: Gender and Sexual Politics in the Making of Reactionary Populism." *Journal of American History* 78 (December 1991): 917–48.

Mainer, J. E. "J. E. Mainer of Concord, North Carolina." *Sing Out!* 18 (March/April 1968): 22–26.

Malone, Bill C. "The Dixon Brothers." In *The Encyclopedia of Country Music: The Ultimate Guide to the Music*, edited by Paul Kingsbury, 149. New York: Oxford University Press, 1998.

———. "Will Hays." In *Encyclopedia of Southern Culture*, edited by Charles Reagan Wilson and William Ferris, 1061–62. Chapel Hill: University of North Carolina Press, 1989.

Malone, Bill C., and Ronnie Pugh. "Hillbilly Music." In *The New Grove Dictionary of American Music*, edited by H. Wiley Hitchcock and Stanley Sadie, 1:387. 4 vols. London: Macmillan, 1986.

Malone, Bill C., and Charles K. Wolfe. "Riley Puckett." In *Definitive Country: The Ultimate Encyclopedia of Country Music and Its Performers*, edited by Barry McCloud, 651–52. New York: Perigree Books, 1995.

Mancini, J. M. "'Messin' with the Furniture Man': Early Country Music, Regional Culture, and the Search for an Anthological Modernism." *American Literary History* 16 (Summer 2004): 208–37.

Martin, C. Brenden. "To Keep the Spirit of Mountain Culture Alive: Tourism and Historical Memory in the Southern Highlands." In *Where These Memories Grow: History, Memory, and Southern Identity*, edited by W. Fitzhugh Brundage, 249–69. Chapel Hill: University of North Carolina Press, 2000.

Martin, Charles H. "Communists and Blacks: The ILD and the Angelo Herndon Case." *Journal of Negro History* 64 (Spring 1979): 131–41.

McCloud, Barry. "Jerry Reed." In *Definitive Country: The Ultimate Encyclopedia of Country Music and Its Performers*, edited by Barry McCloud, 663–64. New York: Perigree Books, 1995.

McCulloh, Judith. "Notes on Thomas E. Watson." *John Edwards Memorial Foundation Quarterly* 7 (Summer 1971): 65–67.

McElrea, Rodney. "A Portrait of the Life and Phonograph Recordings of the Dixon Brothers—Howard and Dorsey." *Country News and Views* 1 (July 1963): 6–12.

Meade, Guthrie T. "From the Archives: 1914 Atlanta Fiddle Convention." *John Edwards Memorial Foundation Quarterly* 5 (Spring 1969): 27–30.

———, comp. "Materials toward a Study of Early Country Music on Radio II: Dallas, Texas." *John Edwards Memorial Foundation Newsletter* 4 (December 1968): 131–33.

———, comp. "Materials toward a Study of Early Country Music on Radio IV: Dallas, Texas." *John Edwards Memorial Foundation Quarterly* 5 (Summer 1969): 131–33.

Moore, John Hammond. "The Angelo Herndon Case, 1932–1937." *Phylon* 32 (First Quarter 1971): 60–71.

"Mournful Melodies on Edison Records Popular." *Talking Machine World* 21 (October 15, 1925): 199.

Neal, Mrs. Paul. "City of Belmont." In *Souvenir Program, Gaston Centennial*, 94–95. Gastonia, N.C.: Gaston County Centennial Committee, 1946.

Nelson, Donald Lee. "Earl Johnson—Professional Musician." *John Edwards Memorial Foundation Quarterly* 10 (Winter 1974): 169–75.

———. "Ridgel's Fountain Citians." *John Edwards Memorial Foundation Quarterly* 9 (Spring 1973): 9.

———. "'Walk Right in Belmont': The Wilmer Watts Story." *John Edwards Memorial Foundation Quarterly* 9 (Autumn 1973): 91–96.

Newman, Harvey K. "Decatur Street: Atlanta's African American Paradise Lost." *Atlanta History* 44 (Summer 2000): 5–20.

Nobley, Robert E. "Dewey and Gassie Bassett." *Old Time Music* 7 (Winter 1972/1973): 18.

Oja, Carol J. "The USA, 1918–45." In *Modern Times: From World War I to the Present*, edited by Robert P. Morgan, 206–30. Englewood Cliffs, N.J.: Prentice Hall, 1993.

"OKeh Artist Visits New York." *Talking Machine World* 19 (December 15, 1923): 52.

"OKeh 45000 Series." *Old Time Music* 1 (Summer 1971): 25–26.

OKeh Records ad. *Talking Machine World* 20 (June 15, 1924): between pp. 66 and 67.

———. *Talking Machine World* 20 (September 15, 1924): between pp. 58 and 59.

Otto, John S., and Augustus M. Burns. "Black and White Cultural Interaction in the Early Twentieth Century South: Race and Hillbilly Music." *Phylon* 35 (4th Quarter, 1974): 407–17.

Paris, Mike. "The Dixons of South Carolina." *Old Time Music* 10 (Autumn 1973): 13–16.

Park, Robert E. "The National Negro Business League." *Colored American Magazine* 11 (October 1906): 222.

Poole, Ila. "Town of McAdenville." In *Souvenir Program, Gaston Centennial*, 123–24. Gastonia, N.C.: Gaston County Centennial Committee, 1946.

Pugh, Ronnie. "Country across the Country." In *Country: The Music and the Musicians*, edited by Paul Kingsbury, rev. and updated ed., 105–23. New York: Abbeville Press, 1994.

———. "Country Music Is Here to Stay." *Journal of Country Music* 19 (1997): 32–38.

Rattray, Bill. "Scottdale Boys." *Old Time Music* 1 (Summer 1971): 22.

"Real Country Orchestra Is Making Okeh Records." *Talking Machine World* 20 (May 15, 1924): 99.

"Recording and Radio: WRVA and the 1929 Richmond OKeh Sessions." *Virginia Cavalcade* 51 (Summer 2002): 136–42.

Rorrer, Clifford Kinney. "Charlie Clay Poole." In *Dictionary of North Carolina Biography*, edited by William S. Powell, 5:122. 6 vols. Chapel Hill: University of North Carolina Press, 1994.

———. "Charlie Poole and the North Carolina Ramblers." In *Country Music Who's Who: 1972*, edited by Chuck Neese, H-3–H-5. New York: Record World Publications, 1971.

Rorrer, Kinney. "The Bunch of Nuts from Hickory." *Old Time Music* 2 (Autumn 1971): 19.

———. "Charlie Poole and the North Carolina Ramblers." In *The Encyclopedia of Country Music: The Ultimate Guide to the Music*, edited by Paul Kingsbury, 418. New York: Oxford University Press, 1998.

———. "The Four Virginians." *Old Time Music* 14 (Autumn 1974): 18.

———. "Posey Rorer of Franklin County, Virginia." *Old-Time Herald* 11 (December 2007–January 2008): 31–35.

———. "Red Patterson and the Piedmont Log Rollers." *Old Time Music* 34 (Summer/Autumn 1980): 5–6.

Roscigno, Vincent J., and William F. Danaher. "Media and Mobilization: The Case of Radio and Southern Textile Insurgency, 1929 to 1934." *American Sociological Review* 66 (February 2001): 21–48.

Rosenberg, Neil. "Biblio-Discographies: The 'White House Blues'–'McKinley'–'Cannonball Blues' Complex." *John Edwards Memorial Foundation Newsletter* 4 (June 1968): 45–58.

Rumble, John W. "Charlotte Country: A Sixty Year Tradition." In *The Charlotte Country Music Story*, edited by George Holt, 4–6. Charlotte: North Carolina Arts Council, 1985.

———. "Country Music and the Rural South: Reminiscing with Whitey and Hogan." *Journal of Country Music* 10 (1985): 41–53.

Russell, Tony. "Alias Walter Smith." *Old Time Music* 17 (Summer 1975): 12–17.

———. "Country Music on Location: 'Field Recording' before Bristol." *Popular Music* 26 (January 2007): 23–31.

———. "Good Old Times Makin' Music: The Preston Young Story." *Old Time Music* 7 (Winter 1972/1973): 4–7.

———. "H. M. Barnes' Blue Ridge Ramblers." *Old Time Music* 17 (Summer 1975): 11.

———. "Kelly Harrell and the Virginia Ramblers: An OTM Report." *Old Time Music* 2 (Autumn 1971): 8–11.

———. Review of Dave McCarn and Gwin S. Foster, *Singers of the Piedmont. Old Time Music* 11 (Winter 1973–74): 26.

———. Review of Fiddlin' John Carson, *The Old Hen Cackled and the Rooster's Going to Crow. Old Time Music* 12 (Spring 1974): 33.

———. "Step Stones." *Old Time Music* 40 (Winter 1984): 11, 14.

Salmond, John. "Aspects of Modernization in the Loray Mill Strike of 1929." In *Varieties of Southern History: New Essays on a Region and Its People*, edited by Bruce Clayton and John Salmond, 169–76. Westport, Conn.: Greenwood Press, 1996.

Samuelson, Dave. "Arthur 'Guitar Boogie' Smith." In *The Encyclopedia of Country Music: The Ultimate Guide to the Music*, edited by Paul Kingsbury, 489. New York: Oxford University Press, 1998.

Schreyer, Lowell H. "The Banjo in Phonograph Recording History." In *The Banjo on Record: A Bio-Discography*, edited by Uli Heier and Rainer E. Lotz, 1–5. Westport, Conn.: Greenwood Press, 1993.

———. "The Banjo in Ragtime." In *Ragtime: Its History, Composers, and Music*, edited by John Edward Hasse, 54–69. New York: Schirmer Books, 1985.

Shrubsall, Wayne. "Banjo as Icon." *Journal of Popular Culture* 20 (Spring 1987): 31–54.

Silber, Irwin. "Folk Music on Records: Topical Singers." *Sing Out!* 15 (September 1965): 87.

Snyder, Franklyn Bliss. "Leo Frank and Mary Phagan." *Journal of American Folk-Lore* 31 (April–June 1918): 264–66.

"Southern Stirrings." *Time* 13 (April 15, 1929): 13.

Stambler, Irwin, and Grelun Landon. "Dorsey Dixon." In *The Encyclopedia of Folk, Country and Western Music*, 191–92. 2nd ed. New York: St. Martin's, 1983 (1969).

Strachwitz, Chris A. "Mainer's Mountaineers." *American Folk Music Occasional* 1 (1964): 49–55.

Tamburro, Francis. "A Tale of a Song: 'The Lowell Factory Girl.'" *Southern Exposure* 2 (Spring/Summer 1974): 42–51.

Titus, Harold. "Norman Woodlieff Folk Discography." *Journal of Country Music* 2 (Winter 1971): 18–21.

Tribe, Ivan M. "Charlie Poole." In *Definitive Country: The Ultimate Encyclopedia of Country Music and Its Performers*, edited by Barry McCloud, 640–41. New York: Perigree Books, 1995.

———. "The Dixon Brothers." In *Definitive Country: The Ultimate Encyclopedia of Country Music and Its Performers*, edited by Barry McCloud, 238–39. New York: Perigree Books, 1995.

———. "Frank Welling and John McGhee." In *Definitive Country: The Ultimate Encyclopedia of Country Music and Its Performers*, edited by Barry McCloud, 853–54. New York: Perigree Books, 1995.

———. "John McGhee and Frank Welling: West Virginia's Most-Recorded Old-Time Artists." *John Edwards Memorial Foundation Quarterly* 17 (Summer 1981): 57–74.

———. "Roy Hall." In *Definitive Country: The Ultimate Encyclopedia of Country Music and Its Performers*, edited by Barry McCloud, 361–62. New York: Perigree Books, 1995.

Tribe, Ivan M., and John W. Morris. "J. E. and Wade Mainer." *Bluegrass Unlimited* 10 (November 1975): 12–21.

Trotti, Michael Ayers. "When Coney Island Arrived in Richmond: Leisure in the Capital at the Turn of the Century." *Virginia Cavalcade* 51 (Autumn 2002): 168–79.

"Two New Columbia Artists from Carolina." *Talking Machine World* 20 (June 15, 1924): 26.

Webb, Robert Lloyd. "Confidence and Admiration: The Enduring Ringing of the Banjo." In *The Banjo on Record: A Bio-Discography*, edited by Uli Heier and Rainer E. Lotz, 7–26. Westport, Conn.: Greenwood Press, 1993.

"Who Chose These Records? A Look into the Life, Tastes, and Procedures of Frank Walker." In *Anthology of American Folk Music*, edited by Josh Dunson and Ethel Raim, 8–17. New York: Oak Publications, 1973.

Wiggins, Gene. "Fiddlin' John Carson." In *The Encyclopedia of Country Music: The Ultimate Guide to the Music*, edited by Paul Kingsbury, 81. New York: Oxford University Press, 1998.

———. "John Carson: Early Road, Radio and Records." *Journal of Country Music* 8 (May 1979): 20–38.

Wiggins, Gene, with Tony Russell. "Hell Broke Loose in Gordon County, Georgia." *Old Time Music* 25 (Summer 1977): 9–16.

Wiley, Stephen R. "Songs of the Gastonia Textile Strike of 1929: Models of and for Southern Working-Class Women's Militancy." *North Carolina Folklore Journal* 30 (Fall–Winter 1982): 87–98.

Wilgus, D. K. "The Hillbilly Movement." In *Our Living Traditions: An Introduction to American Folklore*, edited by Tristram Potter Coffin, 263–71. New York: Basic Books, 1968.

———. "An Introduction to the Study of Hillbilly Music." *Journal of American Folklore* 78 (July–September 1965): 195–203.

Wilgus, D. K., and Nathan Hurvitz. "'Little Mary Phagan': Further Notes on a Native American Ballad in Context." *Journal of Country Music* 4 (Spring 1973): 17–30.

Winans, Robert B. "The Folk, the Stage, and the Five-String Banjo in the Nineteenth Century." *Journal of American Folklore* 89 (October–December 1976): 407–37.

Winans, Robert B., and Elias J. Kaufman. "Minstrel and Classic Banjo: American and English Connections." *American Music* 12 (Spring 1994): 1–30.

Wolfe, Charles K. "The Atlanta Contests, 1921–1934." *Devil's Box* 15 (March 1981): 17–25.

———. "The Atlanta Fiddling Contests, 1913–1916." *Devil's Box* 14 (June 1980): 12–29.

———. "Bill Helms on the Old-Time Fiddling Conventions." *Devil's Box* 24 (March 1, 1974): 14–18.

———. "The Birth of an Industry." In *The Illustrated History of Country Music*, edited by Patrick Carr, 33–75. New York: Random House/Time Books, 1995 (1980).

———. "The Bristol Syndrome: Field Recordings of Early Country Music." In *Country Music Annual 2002*, edited by Charles K. Wolfe and James E. Akenson, 202–21. Lexington: University Press of Kentucky, 2002.

———. "The Carolina Tar Heels." In *Definitive Country: The Ultimate Encyclopedia of Country Music and Its Performers*, edited by Barry McCloud, 134–35. New York: Perigree Books, 1995.

———. "Carter Family." In *The Encyclopedia of Country Music: The Ultimate Guide to the Music*, edited by Paul Kingsbury, 84–85. New York: Oxford University Press, 1998.

———. "Clayton McMichen." In *Definitive Country: The Ultimate Encyclopedia of Country Music and Its Performers*, edited by Barry McCloud, 537–38. New York: Perigree Books, 1995.

———. "Columbia Records and Old-Time Music." *John Edwards Memorial Foundation Quarterly* 14 (Autumn 1978): 118–25, 144.

———. "Darby and Tarlton." In *Definitive Country: The Ultimate Encyclopedia of Country Music and Its Performers*, edited by Barry McCloud, 214–15. New York: Perigree Books, 1995.

———. "Dave McCarn." In *Definitive Country: The Ultimate Encyclopedia of Country Music and Its Performers*, edited by Barry McCloud, 521. New York: Perigree Books, 1995.

———. "Dixon Brothers." In *American National Biography*, edited by John A. Garraty and Mark C. Carnes, 6:651–52. 24 vols. New York: Oxford University Press, 1999.

———. "Early Country Music in Knoxville: The Brunswick Sessions and the End of an Era." *Old Time Music* 12 (Spring 1974): 19–31.

———. "Event Songs." In *Readin' Country Music: Steel Guitars, Opry Stars, and Honky Tonk Bars*, edited by Cecelia Tichi. Special issue of *South Atlantic Quarterly* 94 (Winter 1995): 217–30.

———. "Fiddling John Carson." In *Definitive Country: The Ultimate Encyclopedia of Country Music and Its Performers*, edited by Barry McCloud, 135–36. New York: Perigree Books, 1995.

———. "Five Years with the Best: Bill Shores and North Georgia Fiddling." *Old Time Music* 25 (Summer 1977): 4–8.

———. "Joe Lee: A Further Note." *Old Time Music* 26 (Autumn 1977): 4.

———. "The Legend That Peer Built: Reappraising the Bristol Sessions." In *The Bristol Sessions: Writings about the Big Bang of Country Music*, edited by Charles K. Wolfe and Ted Olson, 17–39. Jefferson, N.C.: McFarland, 2005.

———. "Lester Smallwood and His Cotton Mill Song." *Old Time Music* 25 (Summer 1977): 22–23.

———. "A Lighter Shade of Blue: White Country Blues." In *Nothing but the Blues: The Music and the Musicians*, edited by Lawrence Cohn, 233–63. New York: Abbeville Press, 1993.

———. "Ralph Peer at Work: The Victor 1927 Bristol Sessions. *Old Time Music* 5 (Summer 1972): 10–15.

———. "The Rest of the Story: Other Early Recordings Sessions in the Tri-Cities Area." In *The Bristol Sessions: Writings about the Big Bang of Country Music*, edited by Charles K. Wolfe and Ted Olson, 235–56. Jefferson, N.C.: McFarland, 2005.

Wolfe, Charles K., and Tony Russell. "The Asheville Session." *Old Time Music* 31 (Winter 1978/1979): 5–12.

Woodlieff, Norman. "Comic-Ade: North Carolina Ramblers" (cartoons). *Old Time Music* 14 (Autumn 1974): 4, 31.

Wyatt, Marshall. "'I Ain't Never Heared Such a Rattlin' Bunch!': The Story of Frank Blevins and His Tar Heel Rattlers." *Old-Time Herald* 2 (February–April 1991): 14–17, 20, 51.

Zieger, Robert H. "Textile Workers and Historians." In *Organized Labor in the Twentieth-Century South*, edited by Robert H. Zieger, 35–59. Knoxville: University of Tennessee Press, 1991.

Zingraff, Rhonda. "Facing Extinction?" In *Hanging by a Thread: Social Change in Southern Textiles*, edited by Jeffrey Leiter, Michael D. Schulman, and Rhonda Zingraff, 199–216. Ithaca, N.Y.: ILR Press, 1991.

Zolotow, Maurice. "Hillbilly Boom." *Saturday Evening Post* 216 (February 12, 1944): 22–23, 36, 38.

Dissertations, Theses, and Unpublished Papers

Grigsby, Ellen. "The Politics of Protest: Theoretical, Historical, and Literary Perspectives on Labor Conflict in Gaston County, North Carolina." Ph.D. diss., University of North Carolina at Chapel Hill, 1986.

Guthman, Josh. "From the Mills to Manhattan: Charlie Poole's Machine-Age Music." Unpublished seminar paper, Department of History, University of North Carolina at Chapel Hill, 1985. Copy in author's possession.

Hacssly, Lynn. "'Mill Mother's Lament': Ella May, Working Women's Militancy, and the 1929 Gaston County Strikes." Master's thesis, University of North Carolina at Chapel Hill, 1987.

Hampton, Frances. "New Leisure: How Is It Spent? A Study of What One Hundred Twenty-Two Textile Workers of Leaksville, Spray, and Draper Are Doing with the New Leisure Created by the N.R.A., as Applied to Certain Types of Activities." Master's thesis, University of North Carolina, 1935.

Hipp, Bertha Carl. "A Gaston County Cotton Mill and Its Community." Master's thesis, University of North Carolina, 1930.

Hood, Robin. "The Loray Mill Strike." Master's thesis, University of North Carolina, 1932.

Huber, Patrick J. "Inventing Hillbilly Music: Record Catalog and Advertising Imagery, 1922–1929." Unpublished conference paper, International Country Music Conference, Nashville, Tenn., May 27, 2005.

———. "The Modern Origins of an Old-Time Sound: Southern Millhands and Their Hillbilly Music, 1923–1942." Ph.D. diss., University of North Carolina at Chapel Hill, 2000.

———, comp. "Southern Field-Recording Sessions of Hillbilly Music, 1923–1932." Unpublished list, compiled in 2006. Copy in author's possession.

———, comp. "Southern Textile Workers on Hillbilly Records, 1923–1942." Unpublished list, compiled in 2006. Copy in author's possession.

Ragan, Robert Allison. "The Pioneer Cotton Mills of Gaston County, North Carolina: 'The First Thirty' (1848–1904) and Gaston County Textile Pioneers." Unpublished manuscript, North Carolina Collection, Wilson Library, University of North Carolina at Chapel Hill, ca. 1973.

Websites

Biography. Jimmy Wayne website. <http://www.jimmywayne.com/index.php?content=biography>. August 29, 2006.

Chadbourne, Eugene. "Phebel Wright." *All Music Guide*. MusicMatch Guide. <http://www.mmguide.musicmatch.com/artist/artist.cgi?ARTISTID=1225343&TMPL=LONG#bio>. September 2, 2006.

Charlie-Poole.com: The Official Web Site of the Charlie Poole Music Festival. <http://www.charlie-poole.com/>. May 24, 2007.

Daniel, Wayne W. "The Rice Brothers: Hillbillies with Uptown Ambitions." HillbillyMusic.com. <http://www.hillbilly-music.com/groups/story/printgroup.php?groupid=11764>. July 16, 2006.

Lewey-Payne, Shirley. "Daughters in Search of Their Father." ezFolk.com.

<http://www.ezfolk.com/bgbanjo/bgb-tabs/wreck97/wreckbio/wreckbio
.html>. June 18, 2006.

North Carolina Department of Cultural Resources website. <http://www.ncdcr
.gov/>. July 17, 2007.

"The Patton Brothers with Raymond Swinney and Glen Neeves." SwinneyPlace
.com. <http://www.swinneyplace.com/RaymondSwinney.htm>. February 24,
2008.

"A Real Dirt Farmer, Eugene Talmadge, Candidate for State Commissioner
of Agriculture." Georgia Archives' Vanishing Georgia digital photograph
collection. <http://dlg.galileo.usg.edu/vanga/html/vanga_homeframe_
default.html?link=vang>. July 28, 2007.

Liner Notes to Albums and Compact Discs

Altman, Billy. Liner notes to various artists, *Something Got a Hold of Me: A
Treasury of Sacred Music*. RCA 2100-2-R.

Cahan, Andy. "Manly Reece and the Dawn of North Carolina Banjo." Essay in
liner notes to various artists, *The North Carolina Banjo Collection*. 2-CD set.
Rounder 0439, 0440.

Cohen, Norm. Liner notes to various artists, *Minstrels and Tunesmiths: The
Commercial Roots of Early Country Music*. JEMF LP-109.

Conte, Pat. Liner notes to Dixon Brothers, *Rambling and Gambling*. Country
Turtle 6002.

Fulcher, Bob. Liner notes to Roane County Ramblers, *Roane County Ramblers:
Complete Recordings, 1928–1929*. County CO-CD-3530.

Green, Archie. Liner notes to Dorsey Dixon, Howard Dixon, and Nancy Dixon,
Babies in the Mill: Carolina Traditional, Industrial, Sacred Songs. Testament
T-3301.

———. Liner notes to Mike Seeger, *Tipple, Loom and Rail: Songs of the
Industrialization of the South*. Folkways FH 5273.

Green, Archie, and Eugene Earle. Liner notes to Carolina Tar Heels, *The Carolina
Tar Heels*. Folk Legacy FSA-24.

Kahn, Ed. Liner notes to Blue Sky Boys, *Presenting the Blue Sky Boys*. Capitol ST
2483.

———. Liner notes to Tom Darby and Jimmie Tarlton, *Darby and Tarlton:
Complete Recordings*. 3-CD boxed set. Bear Family BCD-15764.

McCormick, Mack. Liner notes to various artists, *Songs of Death and Tragedy*.
Folk Music in America, Vol. 9. Library of Congress, Music Division, Recording
Laboratory LBC 9.

Nevins, Richard. Liner notes to Charlie Poole and the North Carolina Ramblers,
The North Carolina Ramblers, 1928–1930. Biograph BLP-6005.

Paris, Mike. Liner notes to Dave McCarn and Gwin S. Foster, *Singers of the
Piedmont*. Folk Variety FV 12505.

Rorrer, Kinney. Liner notes to Blue Ridge Highballers, *The Blue Ridge Highballers:
Original Recordings of 1926*. County CY 407.

———. Liner notes to Charlie Poole and the North Carolina Ramblers, *Charlie*

Poole and the North Carolina Ramblers: Old Time Songs Recorded from 1925 to 1930. County CO-3501.

———. Liner notes to Charlie Poole and the North Carolina Ramblers, *Charlie Poole and the North Carolina Ramblers: Old Time Songs Recorded from 1925 to 1930, Vol. 2.* County CO-3508.

———. Liner notes to various artists, *Cotton Mills and Fiddles.* Flyin' Cloud FC-014.

Rosenberg, Neil V. Liner notes to Lester Flatt and Earl Scruggs, *Flatt and Scruggs: Country and Western Classics.* 3-LP boxed set. Time Life Records TLCW-04.

Russell, Tony. Liner notes to Walter "Kid" Smith, *Walter Smith and Friends: Complete Recorded Works in Chronological Order, Vols. 1–3 (1929–1936).* Document DOCD-8062—DOCD-8064.

Sapoznik, Henry "Hank." Liner notes to Charlie Poole, *"You Ain't Talkin' to Me": Charlie Poole and the Roots of Country Music.* 3-CD boxed set. Columbia/ Legacy C3K-92780.

Smith, Harry. Liner notes to various artists, *Anthology of American Folk Music.* 3-LP boxed set. Folkways FP 251—FP 253.

Tribe, Ivan. Liner notes to Dixon Brothers, *The Dixon Brothers: Vol. 2.* Old Homestead OHCS-164.

———. Liner notes to Tobacco Tags, *Songs of the Tobacco Tags, Vol. 1.* Old Homestead OHCS 156.

Wilson, Joe. Liner notes to various artists, *A Fiddlers' Convention in Mountain City, Tennessee: 1924–1930 Recordings.* County 525.

Wilson, Mark. Liner notes to Fiddlin' John Carson, *The Old Hen Cackled and the Rooster's Going to Crow.* Rounder 1003.

———. Liner notes to various artists, *Poor Man, Rich Man: American Country Songs of Protest.* Rounder Records 1026.

DISCOGRAPHY

Berkeley, Roy, with Tim Woodbridge. *Folk and Country Songs of the FDR Years.* Longview L241.

Blue Ridge Highballers, The. *The Blue Ridge Highballers: Original Recordings of 1926.* County CY 407.

Blue Sky Boys, The. *Presenting the Blue Sky Boys.* Capitol ST 2483.

Carlisle, Jumpin' Bill. *Gonna Shake This Shack Tonight: Busy Body Boogie.* Bear Family BCD 15980.

Carolina Tar Heels, The. *The Carolina Tar Heels.* Folk Legacy FSA-24.

———. *The Carolina Tar Heels.* Old Homestead OHCD-4113.

Carson, Fiddlin' John. *Fiddlin' John Carson: Complete Recorded Works in Chronological Order, Vols. 1–7 (1923–1934).* Document DOCD-8014–DOCD-8020.

———. *The Old Hen Cackled and the Rooster's Going to Crow.* Rounder 1003.

———. Unnumbered cassette tape accompanying *Fiddlin' Georgia Crazy: Fiddlin' John Carson, His Real World, and the World of His Songs,* by Gene Wiggins. Urbana: University of Illinois Press, 1987.

Darby, Tom, and Jimmie Tarlton. *Darby and Tarlton: Complete Recordings.* 3-CD boxed set. Bear Family BCD-15764.

———. *Darby and Tarlton: On the Banks of a Lonely River.* County CO-3503.

———. *Darby and Tarlton: Ooze It Up to Me.* Acrobat ACMCD 4016.

Dixon, Dorsey, Howard Dixon, and Nancy Dixon. *Babies in the Mill: Carolina Traditional, Industrial, Sacred Songs.* Testament T-3301. Reissued under the same title on HMG/HighTone. HMG 2502.

Dixon Brothers. *Beyond Black Smoke.* Country Turtle 6000.

———. *The Dixon Brothers, Vols. 1–4.* Old Homestead OHCS-151, 164, 178–79.

———. *The Dixon Brothers: Complete Recorded Works in Chronological Order, Vols. 1–4 (1936–1938).* Document DOCD-8046–DOCD-8049.

———. *The Dixon Brothers: How Can a Broke Man Be Happy?* Acrobat 4022.

———. *The Dixon Brothers: Spinning Room Blues.* Old Homestead OHCD-4164.

———. *The Dixon Brothers: Weave Room Blues.* Old Homestead OHCD-4151.

———. *Rambling and Gambling.* Country Turtle 6002.

Flatt, Lester, and Earl Scruggs. *Flatt and Scruggs: Country and Western Classics.* 3-LP boxed set. Time Life Records TLCW-04.

Georgia Yellow Hammers, The. *Georgia Yellow Hammers: Johnson's Old Grey Mule.* British Archive of Country Music BACM CD D 073.

Glazer, Joe. *Textile Voices.* Collector 1922.

Grayson, G. B., and Henry Whitter. *G. B. Grayson and Henry Whitter: Early Classics, Vols. 1–2.* Old Homestead OHCD-157/165.

———. *Grayson and Whitter: Complete Recorded Works in Chronological*

Order, Vols. 1–2 (1927–1929). Document DOCD-8054–DOCD-8055.

———. *Grayson and Whitter: Recordings, 1928–1930*. County CO-3517.

Harrell, Kelly. *Kelly Harrell: Complete Recorded Works in Chronological Order, Vols. 1–2 (1925–1929)*. Document DOCD-8026/DOCD-8027.

Mainer, J. E. *Volume 6: Fiddling with His Girl Susan*. Rounder RR 222.

J. E. Mainer's Mountaineers. *The Golden Age of J. E. Mainer's Mountaineers*. Cattle CCD 238.

———. *J. E. Mainer's Mountaineers, 1935–1939*. British Archive of Country Music BACM CD D 122.

Wade Mainer and the Sons of the Mountaineers. *Wade Mainer's Mountaineers, Vol. 1, 1935–1936*. Old Homestead OHCD-4043.

McCarn, Dave, and Gwin S. Foster. *Singers of the Piedmont*. Folk Variety FV 12505.

Mountain Musicians' Cooperative. *Brown Lung Cotton Mill Blues*. June Appal 006.

New Lost City Ramblers, The. *Modern Times*. Folkways FTS 31027.

———. *New Lost City Ramblers, Vols. 2–3*. Folkways FA 2397/2398.

———. *Sing Songs of the New Lost City Ramblers*. Aravel AB 1005.

———. *Songs from the Depression*. Folkways FH 5264.

Poole, Charlie, and the North Carolina Ramblers. *Charlie Poole, 1926–1930: A Young Boy Left His Home One Day*. Historical HLP 8005.

———. *Charlie Poole and the Highlanders*. Arbor 201. Reissued under the same title on Puritan 3002.

———. *Charlie Poole and the North Carolina Ramblers*. County 505.

———. *Charlie Poole and the North Carolina Ramblers, Vols. 2, 4*. County 509, 540.

———. *Charlie Poole and the North Carolina Ramblers: Old Time Songs Recorded from 1925 to 1930*. County CO-3501.

———. *Charlie Poole and the North Carolina Ramblers: Old Time Songs Recorded from 1925 to 1930, Vol. 2*. County CO-3508.

———. *Charlie Poole with the North Carolina Ramblers and the Highlanders*. 4-CD boxed set. JSP JSP7734.

———. *The Legend of Charlie Poole*. County 516.

———. *The Legend of Charlie Poole: Original Recordings, 1925–1930, Vol. 3*. County CO-3516.

———. *The North Carolina Ramblers, 1928–1930*. Biograph BLP-6005.

———. *"You Ain't Talkin' to Me": Charlie Poole and the Roots of Country Music*. 3-CD boxed set. Columbia/Legacy C3K-92780.

Rice Brothers' Gang, The. *King Cotton Stomp*. British Archive of Country Music BACM CD C 117.

Roane County Ramblers. *Roane County Ramblers: Complete Recordings, 1928–1929*. County CO-CD-3530.

Seeger, Mike. *Tipple, Loom and Rail: Songs of the Industrialization of the South*. Folkways FH 5273.

Seeger, Pete. *American History in Ballad and Song*. Folkways FH 5801.

———. *American Industrial Ballads*. Folkways FH 5251.

———. *Folksongs for Young People*. Folkways FC 7532.

Sharp, Joe. "Cotton Mill Colic." Field recording by Alan Lomax,

Washington, D.C., ca. May 12, 1938. Archive of Folk Culture, American Folklife Center, Library of Congress, Washington, D.C. AFS 1629 B2.

Shepard, Riley. *Old-Time Comedy Favorites*. Rounder RR 1166.

Smith, Walter "Kid." *Walter Smith and Friends: Complete Recorded Works in Chronological Order, Vols. 1–3 (1929–1936)*. Document DOCD-8062–DOCD-8064.

Southern Eagle String Band, The. *That Nasty Swing*. Bear Family BF15010.

Stoneman, Ernest V. *Ernest V. Stoneman: Edison Recordings, 1928*. County CO-CD-3510.

———. *Ernest V. Stoneman: With Family and Friends, Vols. 1–2*. Old Homestead OHCD-4172/4173.

Stuart, Alice. *All the Good Times*. Arhoolie F-4002.

Tanner, Gid, and His Skillet Lickers. *A Corn Licker Still in Georgia*. Voyager VRCD303.

Tobacco Tags, The. *Songs of the Tobacco Tags, Vol. 1*. Old Homestead OHCS 156.

———. *The Tobacco Tags: Get Your Head in Here*. British Archive of Country Music BACM CD D 131.

Various artists. *Anthology of American Folk Music*. 3-LP set. Folkways FP 251–FP 253.

———. *Are You from Dixie? Great Country Brother Teams of the 1930's*. RCA 8417-2-R.

———. *Ballads and Songs*. Old Timey 102.

———. *Black and White Hillbilly Music: Early Harmonica Recordings from the 1920s and 30s*. Trikont US-0226.

———. *The Bristol Sessions: Historic Recordings from Bristol Tennessee*. 2-CD set. Country Music Foundation CMF-011-D.

———. *Can't You Hear Me Callin'— Bluegrass: 80 Years of American Music*. 4-CD boxed set. Columbia/ Legacy C4K 90628.

———. *Classic Country Duets*. Old Timey OT126.

———. *The Cold-Water Pledge: Songs of Moonshine and Temperance Recorded in the Golden Age, Vol. 2*. Marimac 9105.

———. *The Cornshucker's Frolic: Downhome Music and Entertainment from the American Countryside, Vol. 2*. Yazoo 2046.

———. *Cotton Mills and Fiddles*. Flyin' Cloud FC-014.

———. *Country Slide*. Acrobat ACRCD 242.

———. *The Decca 5000 Series: Classic Old Time Music*. British Archive of Country Music BACM CD C 077.

———. *Down in the Basement: Joe Bussard's Treasure Trove*. Old Hat 1004.

———. *Drunk and Nutty Blues: Hillbillies Foolin' with the Blues*. Indigo IGODCD 2520.

———. *A Fiddlers' Convention in Mountain City, Tennessee: 1924–1930 Recordings*. County 525.

———. *Goodbye, Babylon*. 6-CD boxed set. Dust-to-Digital DTD-01.

———. *Good for What Ails You: Music of the Medicine Shows, 1926–1937*. 2-CD set. Old Hat CD-1005.

———. *Hard Times Come Again No More: Early American Rural Songs of Hard Times and Hardships, Vols. 1–2*. Yazoo 2036/2037.

———. *Hard Times in the Country: Down and Out in the Rural South: Songs and Tunes from 1927–1938*. County CO-CD-3527.

————. *Harmonica Masters: Classic Recordings from the 1920's and 30's.* Yazoo 2019.

————. *Hawaiian Steel Guitar Classics, 1927–1938.* Arhoolie 7027.

————. *High Rollers: Vintage Gambling Songs, 1920–1952.* Buzzola 006.

————. *Hillbilly Blues: 25 Country Classics, 1929–1947.* Living Era CD AJA 5361.

————. *Hillbilly Honeymoon: Manhaters, Misogynists, and Marital Mayhem.* Acrobat 4015.

————. *The Iron Horse: Vintage Railroad Songs, 1926–1952.* Buzzola 008.

————. *It's Hotter in Hawaii: Early Hits from a Unique Musical Style.* 4-CD boxed set. JSP JSP7738.

————. *Jake Leg Blues.* Jass J-CD-642.

————. *A Joyful Noise, Vol. 2.* Marimac 9101.

————. *Man of Constant Sorrow and Other Timeless Mountain Ballads: Classic Recordings of the 1920's and 30's.* Yazoo 3001.

————. *Minstrels and Tunesmiths: The Commercial Roots of Early Country Music.* JEMF LP-109.

————. *Mountain Blues: Blues, Ballads, and String Bands, 1927–1938.* 4-CD boxed set. JSP JSP7740.

————. *Mountain Gospel: The Sacred Roots of Country Music.* 4-CD boxed set. JSP JSP7755.

————. *My Rough and Rowdy Ways: Badman Ballads and Hellraising Songs, Vols. 1–2.* Yazoo 2039/2040.

————. *The North Carolina Banjo Collection.* 2-CD set. Rounder 0439/0440.

————. *O Brothers!* ASV CDAJA 5467.

————. *The OKeh Label: Classic Old Time Music.* British Archive of Country Music BACM CD C 050.

————. *Old Time Mountain Ballads.* County CO-CD-3504.

————. *Old-Time Mountain Blues: Rural Classics, 1927–1939.* County CO-CD-3528.

————. *Old-Time Mountain Guitar: Vintage Recordings, 1926–1931.* County CO-CD-3512.

————. *Old Time Music at Newport.* Vanguard VRS 9147.

————. *Outside the Law: Gangsters, Racketeers, and the Feds: Vintage Songs, 1922–1947.* Buzzola 012.

————. *Paramount Old Time Recordings.* 4-CD boxed set. JSP JSP7774.

————. *Poor Man, Rich Man: American Country Songs of Protest.* Rounder Records 1026.

————. *Prayers from Hell: White Gospel and Sinners Blues, 1927–1940.* Trikont US 267.

————. *Rags, Breakdowns, Stomps and Blues: Vintage Mandolin Music, 1927–1946.* Document DOCD-32-20-3.

————. *Rare and Red Hot Gospel.* Catfish KATCD 171.

————. *The Road to Nashville: A History of Country Music, 1926–1953.* Indigo IGOTCD 2559.

————. *Roll and Tumble Blues: A History of Slide Guitar.* Indigo IGOTCD 2548.

————. *Rural String Bands of Tennessee.* County CO-CD-3511.

————. *Rural String Bands of Virginia.* County CO-CD-3502.

————. *Something Got a Hold of Me: A Treasury of Sacred Music.* RCA 2100-2-R.

————. *Songs of Complaint and Protest.* Folk Music in America, Vol. 7. Library of Congress, Music

Division, Recording Laboratory LBC 7.

———. *Songs of Death and Tragedy.* Folk Music in America, Vol. 9. Library of Congress, Music Division, Recording Laboratory LBC 9.

———. *Sounds Like Jimmie Rodgers: Stars That Followed the Master.* 4-CD boxed set. JSP JSP7751.

———. *The Story That the Crow Told Me: Early American Rural Children's Songs, Vol. 1.* Yazoo 2051.

———. *The Stuff That Dreams Are Made Of: Super Rarities and Gems of the 1920s and '30s.* 2-CD set. Yazoo 2202.

———. *Times Ain't Like They Used to Be: Early American Rural Music: Classic Recordings of the 1920s and 30s, Vols. 1–5, 8.* Yazoo 2028, 2029, 2047, 2048, 2063, 2068.

———. *Titanic Songs.* Unsinkable Music TSCD 22798.

———. Unnumbered CD companion to *The Literature of the American South,* edited by William L. Andrews, Minrose C. Gwin, Trudier Harris, and Fred Hobson. New York: W. W. Norton, 1998.

———. *The Victor Label: Classic Old Time Music.* British Archive of Country Music BACM CD C 129.

———. *Virginia Roots: The 1929 Richmond Sessions.* 2-CD set. Outhouse Records 1001.

———. *The Vocalion Label: Classic Old Time Music.* British Archive of Country Music BACM CD D 140.

———. *Worried Blues: The Complete Commercial Output of Frank Hutchison and Kelly Harrell.* 4-CD boxed set. JSP JSP7743.

Watson, Doc. *The Doc Watson Family.* Folkways FA2366.

West Orrtana String Band. *West Orrtana String Band.* Revonah RS-924.

ACKNOWLEDGMENTS

"If the river was whiskey and I was a duck," Charlie Poole sings on one of his best-known 1930 Columbia recordings, "I'd dive to the bottom and I'd never come up." While writing this book, I sometimes had days when I felt the same way. Conducting the research for it, however, was a sheer joy. Being able to listen to music and justifiably call it historical research, I have long maintained, is a splendid thing, and listening to the wonderful old 78-rpm records of Charlie Poole and the North Carolina Ramblers and of the other textile mill artists profiled in this book was a tremendous pleasure. Since this book's conception, I have had the great fortune to work with a large group of scholars who share my appreciation for the extraordinary old-time music that ordinary working-class southerners created during the 1920s and 1930s. One of the most gratifying aspects of completing this book is the chance to thank them and the many other scholars, librarians, archivists, family members, and friends who assisted and supported me in this endeavor.

At the University of North Carolina at Chapel Hill, I enjoyed the rare opportunity to work with some of the nation's preeminent historians and folklorists. First and foremost, I wish to thank Jacquelyn Dowd Hall, my mentor and former adviser, whose own scholarship and commitment to studying southern textile workers served as an inspiring model for this project. She provided constant encouragement, generously shared her own research materials, and offered helpful criticism on more drafts of this work than she probably cares to remember. At the University of North Carolina at Chapel Hill, I also benefited immensely from the wisdom and support of Leon Fink, Glenn Hinson, James Leloudis, David Whisnant, and particularly Robert Cantwell. My conversations with Bob always seemed to energize me, in both mind and spirit, at precisely those moments when I most needed it, and for that I am deeply thankful.

Several other scholars and colleagues also played significant roles in the conceptualization, researching, and writing of this study. In 1992, Archie Green first suggested to me the idea that became this book. Although he may not recognize his idea in its present, highly modified form, I hope that he will realize how much he has inspired this work and how much I have learned from him. David M. Anderson shared dozens of insights with me that sharpened and strengthened the focus of this book. Other friends and colleagues shared their ideas, their responses to chapters, and even their own research materials as this project took shape. I am particularly grateful to James E. Akenson, Bruce Baker, Gavin James Campbell, Norm Cohen, Jefferson Cowie, George Goehl, Pamela Grundy, Josh Guthman, Tom Hanchett, Anne Goodwyn Jones, Lu Ann Jones, Robert Korstad, Cliff Kuhn, Bill Mansfield, Harriet Ottenheimer, Daniel Patterson, Steve Pfaff, the late Anne Romaine, David Roediger, Tony Russell, Robert Taylor, George C. Waldrep III, Harry L. Watson, Joel Williamson, the late Charles K. Wolfe, and Lisa Yarger. Several others, including Archie Green, the late Ed Kahn, the late Johnnie

ACKNOWLEDGMENTS

E. McCarn, Mike Seeger, and Martha Sipe, agreed to be interviewed, and the book benefited greatly from their insights and memories. I am also indebted to Helen McCarn Wertz, the daughter of Dave McCarn, who graciously supplied the family photograph of her father (one of only two known to me) that appears in Chapter 3. Norm Cohen, Tom Hanchett, and Kinney Rorrer also generously provided me with rare photographs and images from their own private collections. It has been a privilege to work with the talented staff at the University of North Carolina Press, and I am particularly grateful for the support and assistance of David Perry, Paula Wald, and Vicky Wells.

This book is based in large part on the remarkable holdings of 78-rpm phonograph records, artist files, record catalogs and advertisements, photographs, manuscripts, and oral histories housed in the Southern Folklife Collection, in Louis Round Wilson Library, at the University of North Carolina at Chapel Hill. My research there benefited from the expertise and courteous assistance of several archivists and reference librarians, especially Steve Green, Steve Weiss, Amy Davis, Sally Council, and Kelly Kress. Thanks are also due to Tim West, Richard Schrader, John White, and the staff of the Southern Historical Collection at the University of North Carolina at Chapel Hill; Joseph Hickerson and the staff of the Archive of Folk Culture, in the American Folklife Center, at the Library of Congress in Washington, D.C.; Ronnie Pugh, Dawn Oberg, and the late Bob Pinson of the Frist Library and Archive at the Country Music Hall of Fame and Museum in Nashville; and the staffs of the following libraries and archives: the North Carolina Collection, Louis Round Wilson Library, at the University of North Carolina at Chapel Hill, particularly Nicholas Graham and Jessica Sedgwick for tracking down several last-minute research requests; the Rare Book, Manuscript, and Special Collections Library, Duke University, Durham, North Carolina; the North Carolina Department of Archives and History in Raleigh; the Levine Museum of the New South, Charlotte, North Carolina; the Public Library of Charlotte and Mecklenburg County, Charlotte, North Carolina; the Thomas H. Leath Memorial Library, Rockingham, North Carolina; the South Caroliniana Library at the University of South Carolina, Columbia; the South Carolina Department of Archives and History in Columbia; Appomattox Regional Library, Hopewell, Virginia, particularly Jeanie Langford; Special Collections and Archives, Georgia State University Library, Atlanta; the Archives of Labor and Urban Affairs, Walter P. Reuther Library, at Wayne State University in Detroit; and the Franklin D. Roosevelt Library, Hyde Park, New York. The librarians at Curtis Laws Wilson Library on the campus of Missouri University of Science and Technology in Rolla, especially Jane Driber, Marsha Fuller, Jim Morisaki, Scott Peterson, and Virginia Schnabel, cheerfully helped me to secure dozens of interlibrary loan books and articles.

Several sections of this book have previously been published, in abbreviated form, as articles, research notes, and biographical essays, and I am grateful to the editors, particularly Dave Shaw, Lisa Eveleigh, Karen Leathem, and Anne Miller, for the comments I received and to the publishers of the following reference work and journals for allowing me to use these materials here: "The Dixon Brothers" and "Charlie Poole," in *The North Carolina Century: Tar Heels Who Made a Differ-*

ence, 1900–2000, edited by Howard E. Covington and Marion A. Ellis (Charlotte, N.C.: Levine Museum of the New South, 2002), 425–28 and 443–46, respectively; "A Hillbilly Barnum: Fiddlin' John Carson and the Modern Origins of His Old-Time Music in Atlanta," *Atlanta History* 46 (2004): 24–53; "'Cain't Make a Living at a Cotton Mill': The Life and Hillbilly Songs of Dave McCarn," *North Carolina Historical Review* 80 (July 2003): 297–333; "'Battle Songs of the Southern Class Struggle': Songs of the Gastonia Textile Strike of 1929," *Southern Cultures* 4 (Summer 1998): 109–22; "'I Don't Want Nothin' 'Bout My Life Wrote Out, Because I Had It Too Rough in Life': Dorsey Dixon's Autobiographical Writings" (co-authored with Kathleen Drowne), *Southern Cultures* 6 (Summer 2000): 94–100; and "'A Blessing to People': Dorsey Dixon and His Sacred Mission of Song," *Southern Cultures* 12 (Winter 2006): 111–31.

Much of the research for this book was conducted between 1994 and 1998 at the University of North Carolina at Chapel Hill, and the generous support of several grants and fellowships helped to accelerate the completion of this study. An Archie Green Occupational Folklife Graduate Fellowship from the University of North Carolina at Chapel Hill's Folklore Curriculum and an Archie K. Davis Fellowship from the North Caroliniana Society helped to fund several stages of the research for this project. In addition, a series of grants from the Department of History allowed me to make summer research trips to various libraries and archives in North Carolina, South Carolina, and Tennessee. I am also thankful for a 2003–4 Visiting Scholar Fellowship from the university's Center for the Study of the American South that allowed me to return to Chapel Hill to complete the final stages of research for this book. An On-Campus Dissertation Fellowship from the Graduate School of the University of North Carolina at Chapel Hill and, later, a Summer Stipend Award from the National Endowment for the Humanities enabled me to complete much of the writing and revision.

Many family members and friends sustained me during the long slog of researching and writing this book. In Chapel Hill, David M. Anderson, Jefferson Cowie, Richard Frankel, Gary Frost, Trent Jernigan, Lu Ann Jones, Steven Niven, Steve Pemberton, Steve Pfaff, Scott Sherman, Michael Trotti, and Lisa Yarger proved themselves to be true and dear friends throughout this project. Even though I managed to visit my hometown of Ste. Genevieve, Missouri, only once or twice a year while I was living in North Carolina, Carl Roth, Stupe Papin, Flick Samples, Piss Schweiss, Art Schwent, Hummer Spraul, Brian Dunlap, Pup Schwent, Bob Oberle, and Johnny Myers never let me forget where it was that I came from. Merk Bleckler, Humper Wipfler, Pat Meyer, Posi Basler, and the late Larry Basler—who left us far too soon—did their part to help me escape my writing struggles and enjoy summer camping trips, fish fries, frog-gigging excursions, squirrel hunts, and, at Christmas, headcheese-making parties. My colleagues at Missouri University of Science and Technology have made the campus a congenial environment in which to teach and write, and I am especially grateful for the friendship and collegiality of Wayne Bledsoe, Russell Buhite, Lawrence O. Christensen, Liz Cummins, Shannon Fogg, Larry Gragg, John McManus, Jack B. Ridley, Kris Swenson, and the late Larry Vonalt. My immediate family, Paul "Bucky" and

Helen Huber, Rick and Nan Morein, Ned and Susan Huber, and Mark "Boots" and Lisa Huber, also lent significant support, each in his or her own way. In particular, I wish to thank my oldest brother, Bucky, himself an accomplished mandolin player, who presented me with a circa 1940 Sears Silvertone mandolin on my thirtieth birthday. Struggling to learn to play that inexpensive but prized instrument made me appreciate more fully the extraordinary creativity and talent of the hillbilly musicians about whom I was writing.

I owe my greatest debt to my parents, Mary Jean "Midge" Huber and the late Paul A. Huber, for their unconditional love and support and for teaching me the importance of education and hard work. My father, a mechanical engineer turned local historian and genealogist, regaled me with colorful stories of our French and German ancestors, his childhood on a Missouri farm during the 1920s and Great Depression, and his later naval service aboard the USS *LCS(L) 102* in the Pacific during World War II. These stories filled me with a deep and abiding fascination with the historical past and inspired me to pursue a career as a historian. My mother, in turn, taught me Christian compassion, tolerance, and patient perseverance in the face of difficult circumstances. Although they must have often wondered when I would ever finish this project, my parents never for a moment questioned the value of what I was doing. Now all of my mother's prayers to St. Jude, the patron saint of hopeless causes, have been answered. I deeply regret, though, that my father did not live long enough to see this book published.

Finally, I could not have completed this book without the unwavering support and assistance of Katie Drowne, my wife, best friend, and editor, all rolled into one. She has been both the most enthusiastic cheerleader and the keenest critic of this study, and I remain eternally grateful for her love, friendship, and support. She and our two children, Genevieve and Will, both of whom were born while I was working on this book, have lived under the long shadow of this project and accepted, with few complaints, the many sacrifices it required on their part. Katie took time away from her own hectic academic schedule and research projects to edit and comment on dozens of chapter drafts with great patience, cheer, and understanding. Only she knows how much I truly owe her. And only I know how much she and the children have truly blessed my life. This book is dedicated to them.

INDEX